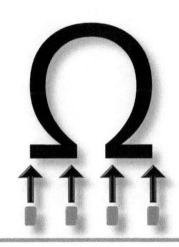

Book 2

Chapter 5-9

9781716745515

Contents

Authors' Profiles

Steven Halim, PhD[1]

stevenhalim@gmail.com

Steven Halim is a senior lecturer in School of Computing, National University of Singapore (SoC, NUS). He teaches several programming courses in NUS, ranging from basic programming methodology, intermediate to hard data structures and algorithms, web programming, and also the 'Competitive Programming' module that uses this book. He is the coach of both the NUS ICPC teams and the Singapore IOI team. He participated in several ICPC Regionals as a student (Singapore 2001, Aizu 2003, Shanghai 2004). So far, he and other trainers @ NUS have successfully groomed various ICPC teams that won ten different ICPC Regionals (see below), advanced to ICPC World Finals eleven times (2009-2010; 2012-2020) with current best result of Joint-14th in ICPC World Finals Phuket 2016 (see below), as well as seven gold, nineteen silver, and fifteen bronze IOI medalists (2009-2019). He is also the Regional Contest Director of ICPC Asia Singapore 2015+2018 and is the Deputy Director+International Committee member for the IOI 2020+2021 in Singapore. He has been invited to give international workshops about ICPC/IOI at various countries, e.g., Bolivia ICPC/IOI camp in 2014, Saudi Arabia IOI camp in 2019, Cambodia NOI camp in 2020.

Steven is happily married to Grace Suryani Tioso and has two daughters and one son: Jane Angelina Halim, Joshua Ben Halim, and Jemimah Charissa Halim.

ICPC Regionals	#	Year(s)
Asia Jakarta	5	2013 (ThanQ), 2014 (ThanQ+), 2015 (RRwatameda), 2017 (DomiNUS), 2019 (Send Bobs to Alice)
Asia Manila	2	2017 (Pandamiao), 2019 (7 Halim)
Asia Nakhon Pathom	1	2018 (Pandamiao)
Asia Yangon	1	2018 (3body2)
Asia Kuala Lumpur	1	2019 (3body3)

Table 1: NUS ICPC Regionals Wins in 2010s

ICPC World Finals	Team Name	Rank	Year
Phuket, Thailand	RRwatameda	Joint-14/128	2016
Ekaterinburg, Russia	ThanQ+	Joint-19/122	2014
Rapid City, USA	TeamTam	Joint-20/133	2017

Table 2: NUS ICPC World Finals Top 3 Results in 2010s

[1]PhD Thesis: "An Integrated White+Black Box Approach for Designing and Tuning Stochastic Local Search Algorithms", 2009.

Felix Halim, PhD[2]

felix.halim@gmail.com

Felix Halim is a senior software engineer at Google. While in Google, he worked on distributed system problems, data analysis, indexing, internal tools, and database related stuff. Felix has a passion for web development. He created uHunt to help UVa online judge users find the next problems to solve. He also developed a crowdsourcing website, `https://kawalpemilu.org`, to let the Indonesian public to oversee and actively keep track of the Indonesia general election in 2014 and 2019.

As a contestant, Felix participated in IOI 2002 Korea (representing Indonesia), ICPC Manila 2003-2005, Kaohsiung 2006, and World Finals Tokyo 2007 (representing Bina Nusantara University). He was also one of Google India Code Jam 2005 and 2006 finalists. As a problem setter, Felix set problems for ICPC Jakarta 2010, 2012, 2013, ICPC Kuala Lumpur 2014, and several Indonesian national contests.

Felix is happily married to Siska Gozali. The picture on the right is one of their Europe honeymoon travel photos (in Switzerland) after ICPC World Finals @ Porto 2019. For more information about Felix, visit his website at `https://felix-halim.net`.

Suhendry Effendy, PhD[3]

suhendry.effendy@gmail.com

Suhendry Effendy is a research fellow in the School of Computing of the National University of Singapore (SoC, NUS). He obtained his bachelor degree in Computer Science from Bina Nusantara University (BINUS), Jakarta, Indonesia, and his PhD degree in Computer Science from National University of Singapore, Singapore. Before completing his PhD, he was a lecturer in BINUS specializing in algorithm analysis and served as the coach for BINUS competitive programming team (nicknamed as "Jollybee").

Suhendry is a recurring problem setter for the ICPC Asia Jakarta since the very first in 2008. From 2010 to 2016, he served as the chief judge for the ICPC Asia Jakarta collaborating with many other problem setters. He also set problems in many other contests, such as the ICPC Asia Kuala Lumpur, the ICPC Asia Singapore, and *Olimpiade Sains Nasional bidang Komputer* (Indonesia National Science Olympiad in Informatic) to name but a few.

---

[2]PhD Thesis: "Solving Big Data Problems: from Sequences to Tables and Graphs", 2012.

[3]PhD Thesis: "Graph Properties and Algorithms in Social Networks: Privacy, Sybil Attacks, and the Computer Science Community", 2017.

Chapter 5

Mathematics

We all use math every day; to predict weather, to tell time, to handle money.
Math is more than formulas or equations; it's logic, it's rationality,
it's using your mind to solve the biggest mysteries we know.
— **TV show NUMB3RS**

5.1 Overview and Motivation

The appearance of mathematics-related problems in programming contests is not surprising since Computer Science is deeply rooted in Mathematics. Many interesting real life problems can be modeled as mathematical problems as you will frequently see in this chapter.

Recent ICPC problem sets (based on our experience in Asian Regionals) usually contain one or two mathematical problems. Recent IOIs usually do not contain *pure* mathematics tasks, but many tasks do require mathematical insights. This chapter aims to prepare contestants in dealing with many of these mathematical problems.

We are aware that different countries place different emphases in mathematics training in pre-University education. Thus, some contestants are familiar with the mathematical terms listed in Table 5.1. But for others, these mathematical terms do not ring a bell, perhaps because the contestant has not learnt it before, or perhaps the term is different in the contestant's native language. In this chapter, we want to make a more level-playing field for the readers by listing as many common mathematical terminologies, definitions, problems, and algorithms that frequently appear in programming contests as possible.

Arithmetic Progression	Geometric Progression	Polynomial
Algebra	Logarithm/Power	Big Integer
Number Theory	Prime Number	Sieve of Eratosthenes
Miller-Rabin	Greatest Common Divisor	Lowest Common Multiple
Factorial	Euler Phi	Modified Sieve
Extended Euclidean	Linear Diophantine	Modular Inverse
Combinatorics	Fibonacci	Golden Ratio
Binet's Formula	Zeckendorf's Theorem	Pisano Period
Binomial Coefficients	Fermat's little theorem	Lucas' Theorem
Catalan Numbers	Inclusion-Exclusion	Probability Theory
Cycle-Finding	Game Theory	Zero-Sum Game
Decision Tree	Perfect Play	Minimax
Nim Game	Sprague-Grundy Theorem	Matrix Power

Table 5.1: List of *some* mathematical terms discussed in this chapter

5.2 Ad Hoc Mathematical Problems

We start this chapter with something light: the Ad Hoc mathematical problems. These are programming contest problems that require no more than basic programming skills and some fundamental mathematics. As there are still too many problems in this category, we further divide them into sub-categories, as shown below. These problems are not placed in Book 1 as they are Ad Hoc problems with (heavier) mathematical flavor. But remember that many of these Ad Hoc mathematical problems are the easier ones. To do well in the actual programming contests, contestants must also master *the other sections* of this chapter.

- Finding (Simple) Formula or Pattern
  These problems require the problem solver to read the problem description carefully to get a simplified formula or to spot the pattern. Attacking them directly will usually result in a TLE verdict. The actual solutions are usually short and do not require loops or recursions. Example: Let set S be an infinite set of *square integers*: $\{1, 4, 9, 16, 25, \ldots\}$. Given an integer X ($1 \leq X \leq 10^{18}$), count how many integers in S are less than X. The answer is simply: $\lfloor\sqrt{X-1}\rfloor$. This is an $O(1)$ solution.

  Note that in Section 5.4, we will discuss Combinatorics problems that will also end up with some (not necessarily simple) formula. We also have Section 9.15 where we discuss a few known but very rare mathematical formulas.

- Base Number Conversion or Variants
  These are the mathematical problems involving base numbers. The most frequent type involves the *standard* conversion problems that can be easily solved manually or with C/C++/Python/OCaml (limited) or Java Integer/BigInteger (most generic) library.

  For example, to convert 132 in base 8 (octal) into base 2 (binary), we can use base 10 (decimal) as the intermediate step: $(132)_8$ is $1\times8^2+3\times8^1+2\times8^0 = 64+24+2 = (90)_{10}$ and $(90)_{10}$ is $90 \rightarrow 45(0) \rightarrow 22(1) \rightarrow 11(0) \rightarrow 5(1) \rightarrow 2(1) \rightarrow 1(0) \rightarrow 0(1) = (1011010)_2$ (that is, divide by 2 until 0, then read the remainders from backwards).

  However, we can also use built-in libraries:

  - C/C++:

    ```
    int v; scanf("%o", &v);                    // read v in octal
    bitset<32> bin(v);                         // use bitset
    printf("%s\n", bin.to_string().c_str());   // print in binary
    ```

  - Python:

    ```
    print("{0:b}".format(int(str(input()), 8)))    # octal to binary
    ```

  - OCaml:

    ```
    Printf.sprintf "%X" (int_of_string "0o374");;   # octal to hexa
    ```

  - Java:
    If we know Java Integer/BigInteger class, we can actually construct an instance of Integer/BigInteger class in any base (radix) and use its `toString(int radix)` method to print the value of that instance in any base (radix). This is a much more flexible library solution than C/C++ or Python solutions earlier that are limited to popular bases = 2/8/10/16. See an example below for Kattis - basicremains (also available at UVa 10551 - Basic Remains). Given a base b and two non-negative integers p and m—both in base b, compute p % m and print the result as a base b integer. The solution is as follows:

```
class Main {
  public static void main(String[] args) {
    Scanner sc = new Scanner(System.in);          // a few test cases
    while (true) {
      int b = sc.nextInt(); if (b == 0) break;
      BigInteger p = new BigInteger(sc.next(), b); // 2nd parameter
      BigInteger m = new BigInteger(sc.next(), b); // is the base
      System.out.println((p.mod(m)).toString(b)); // print in base b
    }
  }
}
```

Source code: `ch5/basicremains_UVa10551.java`

- Number Systems or Sequences
  Some Ad Hoc mathematical problems involve definitions of existing (or made-up) Number Systems or Sequences, and our task is to produce either the number (sequence) within some range or just the n-th number, verify if the given number (sequence) is valid according to the definition, etc. Usually, following the problem description carefully is the key to solving the problem. But some harder problems require us to simplify the formula first. Some well-known examples are:

  1. Fibonacci numbers (Section 5.4.1): 0, 1, 1, 2, 3, 5, 8, 13, 21, 34, 55, ...
  2. Factorial (Section 5.3.7): 1, 1, 2, 6, 24, 120, 720, 5 040, 40 320, 362 880, ...
  3. Derangement (Section 5.5 and 9.15): 1, 0, 1, 2, 9, 44, 265, 1 854, 14 833, ...
  4. Catalan numbers (Section 5.4.3): 1, 1, 2, 5, 14, 42, 132, 429, 1 430, 4 862, ...
  5. Bell numbers (Section 9.15): 1, 1, 2, 5, 15, 52, 203, 877, 4 140, ...
  6. Arithmetic progression sequence: a, $(a+d)$, $(a+2\times d)$, $(a+3\times d)$, ..., e.g., 1, 2, 3, 4, 5, 6, 7, 8, 9, 10, ... that starts with $a = 1$ and with difference of $d = 1$ between consecutive terms. The sum of the first n terms of this arithmetic progression series is $S_n = \frac{n}{2} \times (2 \times a + (n-1) \times d)$.
  7. Geometric progression sequence: a, $a \times r$, $a \times r^2$, $a \times r^3$, ..., e.g., 1, 2, 4, 8, 16, 32, 64, 128, 256, 512, ... that starts with $a = 1$ and with common ratio $r = 2$ between consecutive terms. The sum of the first n terms of this geometric progression series is $S_n = \text{a} \times \frac{1-r^n}{1-r}$. Note that $r > 1$.

- Logarithm, Exponentiation, or Power
  These problems involve the (clever) usage of `log()`, `exp()`, and/or `pow()` functions. Some of the important techniques are shown below:

  These are library solutions to compute logarithm of a decimal a in any base $b \geq 2$:

  - `<cmath>` library in C/C++ has functions: `log(a)` (base e), `log2(a)` (base 2), and `log10(a)` (base 10);
  - `Java.lang.Math` has `log(a)` (base e) and `log10(a)`.
  - Python has `log(a, Base)` (any base, default is e), `log2(a)`, and `log10(a)`.
  - OCaml has `log(a)` (base e) and `log10(a)`.

Note that if a certain programming language only has `log` function in a specific base, we can get `log`$_b$`(a)` (base b) by using the fact that `log`$_b$`(a) = log(a)/log(b)`.

A nice feature of the logarithmic function is that it can be used to count the number of digits of a given decimal a. This formula `(int)floor(1 + log10((double)a))` returns the number of digits in decimal number `a`. To count the number of digits in other base `b`, we can use: `(int)floor(1 + log10((double)a) / log10((double)b))`.

We are probably aware of the square root function, e.g., `sqrt(a)`, but some of us stumble when asked to compute $\sqrt[n]{a}$ (the n-th root of a). Fortunately, $\sqrt[n]{a}$ can be rewritten as $a^{1/n}$. We can then use built in formula like `pow((double)a, 1.0 / (double)n)` or `exp(log((double)a) * 1.0 / (double)n)`.

- Grid
  These problems involve grid manipulation. The grid can be complex, but the grid follows some primitive rules. The 'trivial' 1D/2D grid are not classified here (review 1D/2D array section in Book 1). The solution usually depends on the problem solver's creativity in finding the patterns to manipulate/navigate the grid or in converting the given one into a simpler one.

  See an example for Kattis - beehouseperimeter. You are given a honeycomb structure described by R, the number of cells of the side of honeycomb. The cells are numbered from 1 to $R^3 - (R-1)^3$ in row major order. For example for $R = 3$, the honeycomb looks like Figure 5.1.

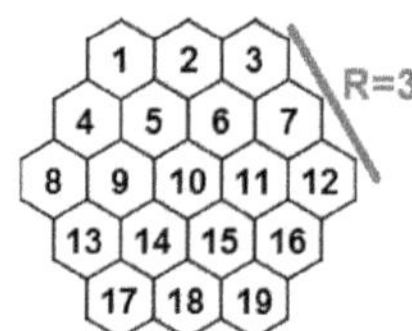

Figure 5.1: A Honeycomb Grid

  Working on this honeycomb structure directly is hard, but we will get a familiar 2D array after we do this transformation: let $N = 2 * R$-1. We fill the transformed $N \times N$ 2D array row by row, initially R cells, grows to $2 * R$-1 cells, and then shrinks again to R (with prefix offset). For $R = 3$ in Figure 5.1 above, $N = 5$ and here is the transformed 5×5 2D array (-1 to indicate unused cell).

```
      0  1  2  3  4
    ----------------
0 |   1  2  3 -1 -1
1 |   4  5  6  7 -1
2 |   8  9 10 11 12
3 |  -1 13 14 15 16
4 |  -1 -1 17 18 19
```

  Now, we can easily navigate from any cell in this transformed 2D array to its 6 directions: E/SE/S/W/NW/N (no SW nor NE directions).

- Polynomial
  These problems involve polynomial evaluation, multiplication, division, differentiation,

etc. We can represent a polynomial by storing the coefficients of the polynomial's terms sorted by (descending order of) their powers. The (basic) operations on polynomials usually require some careful usage of loops. Some polynomials are special:

Degree-2, e.g., $g(x) = ax^2 + bx + c$ (with classic roots $r = (-b \pm \sqrt{b^2 - 4ac})/2a$), and

Degree-3, e.g., $h(x) = ax^3 + bx^2 + cx + d$ that on some applications can be derived back into a Degree-2 polynomial of $h'(x) = 3ax^2 + 2bx + c$.

Later in Section 9.11, we discuss $O(n^2)$ straightforward polynomial multiplication and the faster $O(n \log n)$ one using Fast Fourier Transform.

- Fraction
  These problems involve representing number as fraction: $\frac{numerator}{denominator}$. Most frequent operation is to simplify the given fraction to its simplest form. We can do this by dividing both numerator n and denominator d with their greatest common divisor ($gcd(n, d)$, also see Section 5.3.6). Another frequent operations are to add, subtract, multiply two (or more) fractions. Python has a built-in `Fraction` class that are well equipped to deal with all these basic fraction operations.

  See an example below for UVa 10814 - Simplifying Fractions where we are asked to reduce a large fraction to its simplest form.

```
class Main {
  public static void main(String[] args) {
    Scanner sc = new Scanner(System.in);
    int N = sc.nextInt();
    while (N-- > 0) {                                // we have to use > 0
      BigInteger p = sc.nextBigInteger();
      String ch = sc.next();                         // ignore this char
      BigInteger q = sc.nextBigInteger();
      BigInteger gcd_pq = p.gcd(q);                  // wow :)
      System.out.println(p.divide(gcd_pq) + " / " + q.divide(gcd_pq));
    }
  }
}
```

```
from fractions import Fraction                       # Python's built in
N = int(input())
for _ in range(N):
    frac = Fraction("".join(input().split(" "))) # simplified form
    print(str(frac.numerator) + " / " + str(frac.denominator))
```

Source code: `ch5/UVa10814.java|py`

- Really Ad Hoc
  These are other mathematics-related problems outside the sub-categories above.

We suggest that the readers—especially those who are new to mathematical problems—kick-start their training programme on mathematical problems by solving at least 2 or 3 problems *from each sub-category*, especially the ones that we highlighted as **must try ***.

Exercise 5.2.1*: All these sequence of numbers below have *at least one* formula(s)/pattern(s). Please give your best guess of what are the next three numbers in each sequence!

1. 1, 2, 4, 8, 16, ...

2*. 1, 2, 4, 8, 16, 31, ...

3. 2, 3, 5, 7, 11, 13, ...

4*. 2, 3, 5, 7, 11, 13, 19, ...

Exercise 5.2.2*: Study (Ruffini-)Horner's method for finding the roots of a polynomial equation $f(x) = 0$.

Exercise 5.2.3*: Given $1 < a < 10, 1 \leq n \leq 10^9$, show how to compute the value of $(1 \times a + 2 \times a^2 + 3 \times a^3 + \ldots + n \times a^n)$ modulo $10^9 + 7$ efficiently, i.e., in $O(\log n)$. Both a and n are integers. Note that the naïve $O(n)$ solution is not acceptable. You may need to read Section 5.3.9 (modular arithmetic) and Section 5.8 (fast (modular) exponentiation).

Programming Exercises related to Ad Hoc Mathematical problems:

a. Finding (Simple) Formula (or Pattern), Easier

1. Entry Level: **Kattis - twostones** * (just check odd or even)
2. **UVa 10751 - Chessboard** * (trivial for $N = 1$ and $N = 2$; derive the formula first for $N > 2$; hint: use diagonal as much as possible)
3. **UVa 12004 - Bubble Sort** * (try small n; get the pattern; use long long)
4. **UVa 12918 - Lucky Thief** * (sum of arithmetic progression; long long)
5. *Kattis - averageshard* * (find $O(n)$ formula; also see Kattis - averageseasy)
6. *Kattis - bishops* * (chess pattern involving bishops; from IPSC 2004)
7. *Kattis - crne* * (simulate cutting process on small numbers; get formula)

Extra UVa: *01315, 10014, 10110, 10170, 10499, 10696, 10773, 10940, 11202, 11393, 12027, 12502. 12725, 12992, 13049, 13071, 13216.*

Extra Kattis: *alloys, averageseasy, chanukah, limbo1, pauleigon, sequential-manufacturing, soylent, sumkindofproblem.*

b. Finding (Simple) Formula (or Pattern), Harder

1. Entry Level: **UVa 10161 - Ant on a Chessboard** * (`sqrt` and `ceil`)
2. **UVa 11038 - How Many O's** * (define a function f that counts the number of 0s from 1 to n; also available at *Kattis - howmanyzeros* *)
3. **UVa 11231 - Black and White Painting** * (there is an $O(1)$ formula)
4. **UVa 11718 - Fantasy of a Summation** * (convert loops to a closed form formula; use `modPow` to compute the results)
5. *Kattis - mortgage* * (geometric progression; divergent but finite; special case when r = 1.0 (no interest))
6. *Kattis - neighborhoodwatch* * (sum of AP; inclusion-exclusion)
7. *Kattis - nine* * (find the required formula)

Extra UVa: *00651, 00913, 10493, 10509, 10666, 10693, 10710, 10882, 10970, 10994, 11170, 11246, 11296, 11298, 11387, 12909, 13096, 13140.*

Extra Kattis: *appallingarchitecture, beautifulprimes, dickandjane, doorman, eatingout, limbo2, loorolls, otherside, rectangularspiral, sequence.*

c. Base Number Conversion

1. Entry Level: *Kattis - basicremains* * (also involving BigInteger mod; also available at UVa 10551 - Basic Remains)
2. **UVa 00343 - What Base Is This? *** (try all possible pair of bases)
3. **UVa 00389 - Basically Speaking *** (use Java `Integer`[1] class)
4. **UVa 11952 - Arithmetic *** (check base 2 to 18; special case for base 1)
5. *Kattis - arithmetic* * (conversion of octal (per 4 bits) to hexa (per 3 bits); be careful with leading zeroes)
6. *Kattis - allaboutthatbase* * (check base 1 to 36; base 1 is special; BigInteger)
7. *Kattis - oktalni* * (convert each 3-bits of binary strings to octal; BigInteger)

Extra UVa: *00290, 00355, 00446, 10473, 11185.*

Extra Kattis: *whichbase.*

d. Base Number Variants

1. Entry Level: **UVa 00575 - Skew Binary** * (base modification)
2. **UVa 00377 - Cowculations *** (base 4 operations)
3. **UVa 10931 - Parity *** (convert decimal to binary; count number of 1s)
4. **UVa 11121 - Base -2 *** (search for the term 'negabinary')
5. *Kattis - aliennumbers* * (source base to decimal; decimal to target base)
6. *Kattis - ignore* * (actually a base 7 conversion problem as only 7 digits are meaningful when rotated)
7. *Kattis - mixedbasearithmetic* * (mix of base 10 and two versions of base 26)

Extra UVa: *00636, 10093, 10677, 11005, 11398, 12602.*

Extra Kattis: *babylonian, basic, crypto, parsinghex, sumsquareddigits.*

Others: IOI 2011 - Alphabets (practice task; use space-efficient base 26).

e. Number Systems or Sequences

1. Entry Level: *Kattis - collatz* *[2] (similar to UVa 00694; just do as asked)
2. **UVa 00443 - Humble Numbers *** (try all $2^i \times 3^j \times 5^k \times 7^l$; sort)
3. **UVa 10408 - Farey Sequences *** (first, generate `(i, j)` pairs such that `gcd(i, j) = 1`; then sort)
4. **UVa 11970 - Lucky Numbers *** (square numbers; divisibility; brute force)
5. *Kattis - candlebox* * (sum of arithmetic series $[1..N]$; -6 for Rita or -3 for Theo; brute force Rita's age; also available at UVa 13161 - Candle Box)
6. *Kattis - permutedarithmeticsequence* * (sort differences of adjacent items)
7. *Kattis - rationalsequence* * (pattern finding; tree traversal on a special tree)

Extra UVa: *00136, 00138, 00413, 00640, 00694, 00927, 00962, 00974, 10006, 10042, 10049, 10101, 10930, 11028, 11063, 11461, 11660, 12149, 12751.*

Extra Kattis: *hailstone, sheldon.*

[1] Using Java `BigInteger` class gets TLE verdict for this problem. For base number conversion of 32-bit (i.e., not big) integers, we can just use `parseInt(String s, int radix)` and `toString(int i, int radix)` in the faster Java **Integer** class. Additionally, you can also use `BufferedReader` and `BufferedWriter` for faster I/O.

[2] The (Lothar) Collatz's Conjecture is an open problem in Mathematics.

f. Logarithm, Exponentiation, Power

1. Entry Level: **UVa 12416 - Excessive Space Remover** * (the answer is $\log_2$ of the max consecutive spaces in a line)
2. **UVa 00701 - Archaelogist's Dilemma** * (use log to count # of digits)
3. **UVa 11384 - Help is needed for Dexter** * (find the smallest power of two greater than n; can be solved easily using $ceil(eps + \log_2(n))$)
4. **UVa 11847 - Cut the Silver Bar** * ($O(1)$ math formula exists: $\lfloor \log_2(n) \rfloor$)
5. *Kattis - cokolada* * (the answers involve powers of two and a simulation)
6. *Kattis - factstone* * (use logarithm; power; also available at UVa 10916 - Factstone Benchmark)
7. *Kattis - thebackslashproblem* * (actually power of two)

Extra UVa: *00107, 00113, 00474, 00545, 11636, 11666, 11714, 11986.*

Extra Kattis: *3dprinter, bestcompression, bus, differentdistances, lemonadetrade, pot, schoolspirit, slatkisi, stirlingsapproximation, tetration, triangle.*

g. Grid

1. Entry Level: **UVa 00264 - Count on Cantor** * (grid; pattern)
2. **UVa 10022 - Delta-wave** * (this is not an SSSP problem; find the pattern in this grid (triangle)-like system)
3. **UVa 10182 - Bee Maja** * (grid)
4. **UVa 10233 - Dermuba Triangle** * (the number of items in row forms arithmetic progression series; use hypot)
5. *Kattis - beehouseperimeter* * (transform the hexagonal grid like Kattis - honeyheist; flood fill from outside Alice's house; count #walls touched)
6. *Kattis - honeyheist* * (transform the hexagonal grid input into 2D grid first; then run SSSP on unweighted graph; BFS)
7. *Kattis - maptiles2* * (simple conversion between two grid indexing systems)

Extra UVa: *00121, 00808, 00880, 10642, 10964, 12705.*

Extra Kattis: *fleaonachessboard, settlers2.*

h. Polynomial

1. Entry Level: **UVa 10302 - Summation of ...** * (use long double)
2. **UVa 00930 - Polynomial Roots** * (Ruffini's rule; roots of quadratic eq)
3. **UVa 10268 - 498'** * (polynomial derivation; Horner's rule)
4. **UVa 10586 - Polynomial Remains** * (division; manipulate coefficients)
5. *Kattis - ada* * (polynomial problem; apply the given procedure recursively)
6. *Kattis - curvyblocks* * (differentiate degree 3 to degree 2 polynomial; get roots of quadratic equation; the two blocks will touch at either roots)
7. *Kattis - plot* * (analyze the given pseudocode; the required pattern involves Binomial Coefficients)

Extra UVa: *00126, 00392, 00498, 10215, 10326, 10719.*

Extra Kattis: *polymul1.*

Also see Section 9.11 about Fast Fourier Transform algorithm.

i. Fraction

1. Entry Level: *Kattis - mixedfractions* * (convert fraction to mixed fraction)
2. **UVa 00332 - Rational Numbers ... *** (use GCD)
3. **UVa 00834 - Continued Fractions *** (do as asked)
4. **UVa 12068 - Harmonic Mean *** (involving fraction; use LCM and GCD)
5. *Kattis - deadfraction* * (try every single possible repeating decimals; also available at UVa 10555 - Dead Fraction)
6. *Kattis - fraction* * (continued fraction to normal fraction and vice versa)
7. *Kattis - thermostat* * (convert one temperature to another; use fraction; use Java BigInteger; gcd)

Extra UVa: *10814*, *10976*. *12848*, *12970*.

Extra Kattis: *fractionallotion*, *jointattack*, *rationalarithmetic*, *rationalratio*, *temperatureconfusion*.

j. Really Ad Hoc

1. Entry Level: **UVa 00496 - Simply Subsets** * (set manipulation)
2. **UVa 11241 - Humidex *** (the hardest case is computing Dew point given temperature and Humidex; derive it with Algebra)
3. **UVa 11526 - H(n) *** (brute force up to $\sqrt{n}$; find the pattern; avoid TLE)
4. **UVa 12036 - Stable Grid *** (use pigeon hole principle)
5. *Kattis - matrix* * (use simple linear algebra; one special case when $c = 0$)
6. *Kattis - trip* * (be careful with precision error; also available at UVa 10137 - The Trip)
7. *Kattis - yoda* * (ad hoc; 9 digits comparison)

Extra UVa: *00276*, *00613*, *10023*, *10190*, *11042*, *11055*, *11715*, *11816*.

Profile of Algorithm Inventors

Eratosthenes of Cyrene ($\approx$ 300-200 years BC) was a Greek mathematician. He invented geography, did measurements of the circumference of Earth, and invented a simple algorithm to generate prime numbers which we discussed in this book.

Marin Mersenne (1588-1648) was a French mathematicians best known for Mersenne primes, prime number that can be written as 2^n-1 for some integer n.

Gary Lee Miller is a professor of Computer Science at Carnegie Mellon University. He is the initial inventor of Miller-Rabin primality test algorithm.

Michael Oser Rabin (born 1931) is an Israeli computer scientist. He improved Miller's idea and invented the Miller-Rabin primality test algorithm. Together with Richard Manning Karp, he also invented Rabin-Karp's string matching algorithm.

Leonhard Euler (1707-1783) was a Swiss mathematician and one of the greatest mathematician from the 18th century. Some of his inventions mentioned in this book include the frequently used $f(x)/\Sigma/e/\pi$ mathematical notations, the Euler totient (Phi) function, the Euler tour/path (Graph), and Handshaking lemma.

5.3 Number Theory

Number Theory is the study of the *integers* and *integer-valued* functions. Mastering as many topics as possible in the field of *number theory* is important as some mathematical problems become easy (or easier) if you know the theory behind the problems. Otherwise, either a plain brute force attack leads to a TLE response, or you simply cannot work with the given input as it is too large without some pre-processing.

5.3.1 Prime Numbers

A natural number starting from 2: $\{2, 3, 4, 5, 6, 7, \ldots\}$ is considered a **prime** if it is only divisible by 1 and itself. The first and only even prime is 2. The next prime numbers are: 3, 5, 7, 11, 13, 17, 19, 23, 29, ..., and infinitely many more primes (proof in [33]). There are 25 primes in range `[0..100]`, 168 primes in `[0..1000]`, 1000 primes in `[0..7919]`, 1229 primes in `[0..10 000]`, etc. Some large prime numbers are[3] $104\,729, 1\,299\,709, 1e9+7$ (easy to remember[4]), 2 147 483 647 (8th Mersenne[5] prime, or 2^{31}-1), 112 272 535 095 293, etc.

Prime number is an important topic in number theory and the source for many programming problems. In this section, we will discuss algorithms involving prime numbers.

Optimized Prime Testing Function

The first algorithm presented in this section is for testing whether a given natural number N is prime, i.e., `bool isPrime(N)`. The most naïve version is to test by definition, i.e., test if N is divisible by *divisor* $\in$ `[2..`N`-1]`. This works, but runs in $O(N)$—in terms of number of divisions. This is not the best way and there are several possible improvements.

The first improvement is to test if N is divisible by a *divisor* $\in$ `[2..`$\lfloor\sqrt{N}\rfloor$`]`, i.e., we stop when the *divisor* is greater than $\sqrt{N}$. We claim that if $a \times b = N$, then $a \leq \sqrt{N}$ or $b \leq \sqrt{N}$. Quick proof by contradiction: Let's suppose that it is not the case, i.e., $a > \sqrt{N}$ and $b > \sqrt{N}$. This implies that $a \times b > \sqrt{N} \times \sqrt{N}$ or $a \times b > N$. Contradiction. Thus $a = d$ and $b = \frac{N}{d}$ cannot *both* be greater than $\sqrt{N}$. This improvement is $O(\sqrt{N})$ which is already much faster than the previous version, but can still be improved to be twice as fast.

The second improvement is to test if N is divisible by *divisor* $\in$ `[3, 5, .., `$\sqrt{N}$`]`, i.e., we only test odd numbers up to $\sqrt{N}$. This is because there is only one even prime number, i.e., number 2, which can be tested separately. This is $O(\sqrt{N}/2)$, which is also $O(\sqrt{N})$.

The third improvement[6] which is already good enough for contest problems is to test if N is divisible by *prime divisors* $\leq \sqrt{N}$ (but see below for probabilistic prime testing). This is because if a prime number X cannot divide N, then there is no point testing whether multiples of X divide N or not. This is faster than $O(\sqrt{N})$ and is about $O(\#primes \leq \sqrt{N})$. For example, there are 500 odd numbers in `[1..`$\sqrt{10^6}$`]`, but there are only 168 primes in the same range. Prime number theorem [33] says that the number of primes less than or equal to M—denoted by $\pi(M)$—is bounded by $O(M/(\ln(M)$-1$))$. Therefore, the complexity of this prime testing function is about $O(\sqrt{N}/\ln(\sqrt{N}))$. The code is shown below.

[3]Having a list of large prime numbers is good for testing as these are the numbers that are hard for algorithms like the prime testing/factoring algorithms. At least, remember $1e9+7$ and 2^{31}-1 are primes.

[4]But 1e6+7 is *not* a prime.

[5]A Mersenne prime is a prime number that is one less than a power of two.

[6]This is a bit recursive—testing whether a number is a prime by using another (smaller) prime number. But the reason should be obvious after reading the next section.

Sieve of Eratosthenes: Generating List of Prime Numbers

If we want to generate a list of prime numbers within the range `[0..N]`, there is a better algorithm than testing each number in the range for primality. The algorithm is called 'Sieve of *Eratosthenes*' invented by Eratosthenes of Cyrene.

First, this Sieve algorithm sets all integers in the range to be 'probably prime' but sets 0 and 1 to be not prime. Then, it takes 2 as prime and crosses out all multiples[7] of 2 starting from $2 \times 2 = 4, 6, 8, 10, \ldots$ until the multiple is greater than N. Then it takes the next non-crossed 3 as a prime and crosses out all multiples of 3 starting from $3 \times 3 = 9, 12, 15, \ldots$. Then it takes 5 and crosses out all multiples of 5 starting from $5 \times 5 = 25, 30, 35, \ldots$. And so on .... After that, integers that remain uncrossed within the range `[0..N]` are primes. This algorithm does approximately ($N\times$ (1/2 + 1/3 + 1/5 + 1/7 + ... + 1/last prime in range $\leq N$)) operations. Using 'sum of reciprocals[8] of primes up to N', we end up with the time complexity of *roughly* $O(N \log \log N)$.

Since generating a list of primes $\leq 10K$ using the sieve is fast (our code below can go up to 10^7 in $\approx$ 1s), we opt to use the sieve for smaller primes and reserve the optimized prime testing function for larger primes—see previous discussion.

```
typedef long long ll;

ll _sieve_size;
bitset<10000010> bs;                           // 10^7 is the rough limit
vll p;                                         // compact list of primes

void sieve(ll upperbound) {                    // range = [0..upperbound]
  _sieve_size = upperbound+1;                  // to include upperbound
  bs.set();                                    // all 1s
  bs[0] = bs[1] = 0;                           // except index 0+1
  for (ll i = 2; i < _sieve_size; ++i) if (bs[i]) {
    // cross out multiples of i starting from i*i
    for (ll j = i*i; j < _sieve_size; j += i) bs[j] = 0;
    p.push_back(i);                            // add prime i to the list
  }
}

bool isPrime(ll N) {                           // good enough prime test
  if (N < _sieve_size) return bs[N];           // O(1) for small primes
  for (int i = 0; i < (int)p.size() && p[i]*p[i] <= N; ++i)
    if (N%p[i] == 0)
      return false;
  return true;                                 // slow if N = large prime
} // note: only guaranteed to work for N <= (last prime in vll p)^2

// inside int main()
  sieve(10000000);                             // up to 10^7 (<1s)
  printf("%d\n", isPrime((1LL<<31)-1));        // 8th Mersenne prime
  printf("%d\n", isPrime(136117223861LL));     // 104729*1299709
```

[7]Slower implementation is to start from 2 × i instead of i × i, but the difference is not that much.
[8]Reciprocal is also known as multiplicative inverse. A number multiplied by its reciprocal yield 1.

5.3.2 Probabilistic Prime Testing (Java Only)

We have just discussed the Sieve of Eratosthenes algorithm and a deterministic prime testing algorithm that is good enough for many contest problems. However, you have to type in a few lines of C++/Java/Python code to do that. If you just need to check whether a single (or at most, a few[9]) and usually (very) large integer (beyond the limit of 64-bit integer) is a prime, e.g., UVa 10235 below to decide if the given N is not a prime, an 'emirp' (the reverse of its digits is also a prime), or just a normal prime, then there is an alternative and shorter approach with the function `isProbablePrime` in Java[10] BigInteger[11]—a probabilistic prime testing function based on Miller-Rabin algorithm [26, 32]. There is an important parameter of this function: `certainty`. If this function returns true, then the probability that the tested BigInteger is a prime exceeds $1 - \frac{1}{2}^{certainty}$. Usually, `certainty = 10` should be enough[12] as $1 - (\frac{1}{2})^{10} = 0.9990234375$ is ≈ 1.0. Note that using larger value of `certainty` obviously decreases the probability of WA but doing so slows down your program and thus increases the risk of TLE[13].

```
class Main {
  public static void main(String[] args) {
    Scanner sc = new Scanner(System.in);
    while (sc.hasNext()) {
      int N = sc.nextInt(); System.out.printf("%d is ", N);
      BigInteger BN = BigInteger.valueOf(N);
      String R = new StringBuffer(BN.toString()).reverse().toString();
      int RN = Integer.parseInt(R);
      BigInteger BRN = BigInteger.valueOf(RN);
      if (!BN.isProbablePrime(10))                    // certainty 10 is enough
        System.out.println("not prime.");
      else if ((N != RN) && BRN.isProbablePrime(10))
        System.out.println("emirp.");
      else
        System.out.println("prime.");
    }
  }
}
```

Source code: `ch5/UVa10235.java`

5.3.3 Finding Prime Factors with Optimized Trial Divisions

In number theory, we know that a prime number N only has 1 and itself as factors but a **composite** number N, i.e., the non-primes, can be written uniquely as a product of its prime factors. That is, prime numbers are multiplicative building blocks of integers (the fundamental theorem of arithmetic). For example, $N = 1200 = 2 \times 2 \times 2 \times 2 \times 3 \times 5 \times 5 = 2^4 \times 3 \times 5^2$ (the latter form is called as **prime-power factorization**).

[9]Note that if your aim is to generate a list of the first few million prime numbers, the Sieve of Eratosthenes algorithm should run faster than a few million calls of this `isProbablePrime` function.

[10]A note for pure C/C++/Python/OCaml programmers: It is good to be a *multi*-lingual programmer by switching to Java whenever it is more beneficial to do so, like in this instance.

[11]As of year 2020, there is no equivalent C++/Python/OCaml library for to do this, yet.

[12]This rule of thumb setting is a result of our empirical testings over the years.

[13]This randomized algorithm is a 'Monte Carlo Algorithm' that can give a WA with a (small) probability.

A naïve algorithm generates a list of primes (e.g., with sieve) and checks which prime(s) can actually divide the integer N—without changing N. This can be improved!

A better algorithm utilizes a kind of Divide and Conquer spirit. An integer N can be expressed as: $N = p \times N'$, where p is a prime factor and N' is another number which is N/p—i.e., we can reduce the size of N by taking out its prime factor p. We can keep doing this until eventually $N' = 1$. To speed up the process even further, we utilize the divisibility property that there is no more than one prime divisor greater than $\sqrt{N}$, so we only repeat the process of finding prime factors until $p > \sqrt{N}$. Stopping at $\sqrt{N}$ entails a special case: if (current $p)^2 > N$ and N is still not 1, then N is the *last* prime factor. The code below takes in an integer N and returns the list of prime factors.

In the worst case, when N is prime, this prime factoring algorithm with trial division requires testing all smaller primes up to $\sqrt{N}$, mathematically denoted as $O(\pi(\sqrt{N})) = O(\sqrt{N}/ln\sqrt{N})$ can be very slow[14]—see the example of factoring a large composite number 136 117 223 861 into two large prime factors: 104 729 × 1 299 709 in the code below. However, if given composite numbers with lots of small prime factors, this algorithm is reasonably fast[15]—see 142 391 208 960 which is $2^{10} \times 3^4 \times 5 \times 7^4 \times 11 \times 13$.

```
vll primeFactors(ll N) {                             // pre-condition, N >= 1
  vll factors;
  for (int i = 0; (i < (int)p.size()) && (p[i]*p[i] <= N); ++i)
    while (N%p[i] == 0) {                            // found a prime for N
      N /= p[i];                                     // remove it from N
      factors.push_back(p[i]);
    }
  if (N != 1) factors.push_back(N);                  // remaining N is a prime
  return factors;
}

// inside int main()
  sieve(10000000);
  vll r;

  r = primeFactors((1LL<<31)-1);                     // Mersenne prime
  for (auto &pf : r) printf("> %lld\n", pf);

  r = primeFactors(136117223861LL);                  // large prime factors
  for (auto &pf : r) printf("> %lld\n", pf);        // 104729*1299709

  r = primeFactors(5000000035LL);                    // large prime factors
  for (auto &pf : r) printf("> %lld\n", pf);        // 5*1000000007

  r = primeFactors(142391208960LL);                  // large composite
  for (auto &pf : r) printf("> %lld\n", pf);        // 2^10*3^4*5*7^4*11*13

  r = primeFactors(100000380000361LL);               // 10000019^2
  for (auto &pf : r) printf("> %lld\n", pf);        // fail to factor! (why?)
```

[14]In real life applications, very large primes are commonly used in cryptography and encryption (e.g., RSA algorithm) because it is computationally challenging to factor a very large number into its prime factors, i.e., $x = p_1 p_2$ where both p_1 and p_2 are very large primes.

[15]Also see Section 9.12 for a faster (but rare) integer factoring algorithm.

5.3.4 Functions Involving Prime Factors

There are other well-known number theoretic functions involving prime factors shown below. All variants have similar $O(\sqrt{N}/ln\sqrt{N})$ time complexity with the basic prime factoring via trial division. Interested readers can read Chapter 7: "Multiplicative Functions" of [33].

1. `numPF(N)`: Count the number of *prime factors* of integer `N`.

   For example: $N = 60$ has 4 prime factors: $\{2, 2, 3, 5\}$. The solution is a simple tweak of the trial division algorithm to find prime factors shown earlier.

```
int numPF(ll N) {
  int ans = 0;
  for (int i = 0; (i < (int)p.size()) && (p[i]*p[i] <= N); ++i)
    while (N%p[i] == 0) { N /= p[i]; ++ans; }
  return ans + (N != 1);
}
```

2. `numDiv(N)`: Count the number of *divisors* of integer `N`.

   A divisor of N is defined as an integer that divides N without leaving a remainder. If a number $N = a^i \times b^j \times \ldots \times c^k$, then N has $(i+1) \times (j+1) \times \ldots \times (k+1)$ divisors. This is because there are $i+1$ ways to choose prime factor a $(0, 1, \ldots, i-1, i$ times), $j+1$ ways to choose prime factor b, ..., and $k+1$ ways to choose prime factor c. The total number of ways is the multiplication of these numbers.

   Example: $N = 60 = 2^2 \times 3^1 \times 5^1$ has $(2+1) \times (1+1) \times (1+1) = 3 \times 2 \times 2 = 12$ divisors. The 12 divisors are: $\{1, \underline{\mathbf{2}}, \underline{\mathbf{3}}, 4, \underline{\mathbf{5}}, 6, 10, 12, 15, 20, 30, 60\}$. The prime factors of 60 are **highlighted**. See that N has more divisors than prime factors.

```
int numDiv(ll N) {
  int ans = 1;                                        // start from ans = 1
  for (int i = 0; (i < (int)p.size()) && (p[i]*p[i] <= N); ++i) {
    int power = 0;                                    // count the power
    while (N%p[i] == 0) { N /= p[i]; ++power; }
    ans *= power+1;                                   // follow the formula
  }
  return (N != 1) ? 2*ans : ans;                      // last factor = N^1
}
```

3. `sumDiv(N)`: *Sum* the divisors of integer `N`.

   In the previous example, $N = 60$ has 12 divisors. The sum of these divisors is 168. This can be computed via prime factors too. If a number $N = a^i \times b^j \times \ldots \times c^k$, then the sum of divisors of N is $\frac{a^{i+1}-1}{a-1} \times \frac{b^{j+1}-1}{b-1} \times \ldots \times \frac{c^{k+1}-1}{c-1}$. This closed form is derived from summation of geometric progression series. $\frac{a^{i+1}-1}{a-1}$ is the summation of $a^0, a^1, \ldots, a^{i-1}, a^i$. The total sum of divisors is the multiplication of these summation of geometric progression series of each prime factor.

   Example: $N = 60 = 2^2 \times 3^1 \times 5^1$, `sumDiv(60)` $= \frac{2^{2+1}-1}{2-1} \times \frac{3^{1+1}-1}{3-1} \times \frac{5^{1+1}-1}{5-1} = \frac{7 \times 8 \times 24}{1 \times 2 \times 4} = 168$.

   We can avoid raising a prime factor p_i to a certain power k using $O(\log k)$ exponentiation (see Section 5.8) by writing this `sumDiv(N)` function iteratively:

```
ll sumDiv(ll N) {
  ll ans = 1;                                  // start from ans = 1
  for (int i = 0; (i < (int)p.size()) && (p[i]*p[i] <= N); ++i) {
    ll multiplier = p[i], total = 1;
    while (N%p[i] == 0) {
      N /= p[i];
      total += multiplier;
      multiplier *= p[i];
    }                                          // total for
    ans *= total;                              // this prime factor
  }
  if (N != 1) ans *= (N+1);                    // N^2-1/N-1 = N+1
  return ans;
}
```

4. `EulerPhi(N)`: Count the number of positive integers $< N$ that are relatively prime to N. Recall: Two integers a and b are said to be relatively prime (or coprime) if $gcd(a, b) = 1$, e.g., 25 and 42. A naïve algorithm to count the number of positive integers $< N$ that are relatively prime to N starts with `counter = 0`, iterates through $i \in$ `[1..`N`-1]`, and increases the `counter` if $gcd(i, N) = 1$. This is slow for large N.

   A better algorithm is the Euler's Phi (Totient) function $\varphi(N) = N \times \prod_{p_i} (1 - \frac{1}{p_i})$, where p_i is prime factor of N.

   Example: $N = 36 = 2^2 \times 3^2$. $\varphi(36) = 36 \times (1 - \frac{1}{2}) \times (1 - \frac{1}{3}) = 12$. Those 12 positive integers that are relatively prime to 36 are $\{1, 5, 7, 11, 13, 17, 19, 23, 25, 29, 31, 35\}$.

```
ll EulerPhi(ll N) {
  ll ans = N;                                  // start from ans = N
  for (int i = 0; (i < (int)p.size()) && (p[i]*p[i] <= N); ++i) {
    if (N%p[i] == 0) ans -= ans/p[i];          // count unique
    while (N%p[i] == 0) N /= p[i];             // prime factor
  }
  if (N != 1) ans -= ans/N;                    // last factor
  return ans;
}
```

Source code: `ch5/primes.cpp|java|py|ml`

Exercise 5.3.4.1: Implement `numDiffPF(N)` and `sumPF(N)` that are similar to `numPF(N)`!
`numDiffPF(N)`: Count the number of *different* prime factors of `N`.
`sumPF(N)`: *Sum* the prime factors of `N`.

Exercise 5.3.4.2: What are the answers for `numPF(N)`, `numDiffPF(N)`, `sumPF(N)`, `numDiv(N)`, `sumDiv(N)`, and `EulerPhi(N)` when N is a prime?

5.3.5 Modified Sieve

If the number of different prime factors has to be determined for *many* (or a *range* of) integers, then there is a better solution than calling `numDiffPF(N)` as shown in Section 5.3.4 *many times*. The better solution is the modified sieve algorithm. Instead of finding the prime factors and then calculating the required values, we start from the prime numbers and modify the values of their multiples. The short modified sieve code is shown below:

```
int numDiffPFarr[MAX_N+10] = {0};                    // e.g., MAX_N = 10^7
for (int i = 2; i <= MAX_N; ++i)
  if (numDiffPFarr[i] == 0)                          // i is a prime number
    for (int j = i; j <= MAX_N; j += i)
      ++numDiffPFarr[j];                             // j is a multiple of i
```

Similarly, this is the modified sieve code to compute the Euler Totient function:

```
int EulerPhi[MAX_N+10];
for (int i = 1; i <= MAX_N; ++i) EulerPhi[i] = i;
for (int i = 2; i <= MAX_N; ++i)
  if (EulerPhi[i] == i)                              // i is a prime number
    for (int j = i; j <= MAX_N; j += i)
      EulerPhi[j] = (EulerPhi[j]/i) * (i-1);
```

These $O(N \log \log N)$ modified sieve algorithms should be preferred over (up to) N individual calls to $O(\sqrt{N}/ln\sqrt{N})$ `numDiffPF(N)` or `EulerPhi(N)` if there are many queries over a large range, e.g., $[1..n]$, but `MAX_N` is at most 10^7 (note that we need to prepare a rather big array in a sieve method). However, if we just need to compute the number of different prime factors or Euler Phi for a single (or a few) but (very) large integer N, it may be faster to just use individual calls of `numDiffPF(N)` or `EulerPhi(N)`.

Exercise 5.3.5.1*: Can we write the modified sieve code for the other functions listed in Section 5.3.4 (i.e., other than `numDiffPF(N)` and `EulerPhi(N)`) without increasing the time complexity of sieve? If we can, write the required code! If we cannot, explain why!

5.3.6 Greatest Common Divisor & Least Common Multiple

The Greatest Common Divisor (GCD) of two integers: a, b denoted by $gcd(a, b)$, is the largest positive integer d such that $d \mid a$ and $d \mid b$ where $x \mid y$ means that x divides y. Example of GCD: $gcd(4, 8) = 4$, $gcd(6, 9) = 3$, $gcd(20, 12) = 4$. One practical usage of GCD is to simplify fractions (see UVa 10814 in Section 5.2), e.g., $\frac{6}{9} = \frac{6/gcd(6,9)}{9/gcd(6,9)} = \frac{6/3}{9/3} = \frac{2}{3}$.

Finding the GCD of two integers is an easy task with an effective Divide and Conquer *Euclid* algorithm [33, 7] which can be implemented as a one liner code (see below). Thus finding the GCD of two integers is usually not the main issue in a Mathematics-related contest problem, but just part of a bigger solution.

The GCD is closely related to Least (or Lowest) Common Multiple (LCM). The LCM of two integers (a, b) denoted by $lcm(a, b)$, is defined as the smallest positive integer l such that $a \mid l$ and $b \mid l$. Example of LCM: $lcm(4, 8) = 8$, $lcm(6, 9) = 18$, $lcm(20, 12) = 60$.

It has been shown (see [33]) that: $lcm(a, b) = a \times b / gcd(a, b) = a / gcd(a, b) \times b$. This can also be implemented as a one liner code (see below). Both GCD and LCM algorithms run in $O(\log_{10} n) = O(\log n)$, where $n = min(a, b)$.

```
int gcd(int a, int b) { return b == 0 ? a : gcd(b, a%b); }
int lcm(int a, int b) { return a / gcd(a, b) * b; }
```

Note[16] that since C++17, both gcd and lcm functions are already built-in `<numeric>` library. In Java, we can use method `gcd(a, b)` in BigInteger class. In Python, we can use `gcd(a, b)` in math module.

The GCD of more than 2 numbers can be found via multiple calls of gcd of 2 numbers, e.g., $gcd(a, b, c) = gcd(a, gcd(b, c))$. The strategy to find the LCM of more than 2 numbers is similar.

Exercise 5.3.6.1: The LCM formula is `lcm(a, b) = a×b / gcd(a, b)` but why do we use `a / gcd(a, b) × b` instead? Try $a = 2 \times 10^9$ and $b = 8$ using 32-bit signed integers.

Exercise 5.3.6.2: Please write the `gcd(a, b)` routine in iterative fashion!

Exercise 5.3.6.3*: Study alternative 'binary gcd' computation that replaces division (inside modulo operation) with bit shift operations, subtractions, and comparisons. This version is known as Stein's algorithm.

5.3.7 Factorial

Factorial[17] of n, i.e., $n!$ or $fac(n)$ is defined as 1 if $n = 0$ and $n \times fac(n\text{-}1)$ if $n > 0$. However, it is usually more convenient to work with the iterative version, i.e., $fac(n) = 2 \times 3 \times 4 \times \ldots \times (n\text{-}1) \times n$ (loop from 2 to n, skipping 1). The value of $fac(n)$ grows very fast. We are only able to use C/C++ `long long`/Java `long`/OCaml `Int64` for up to $fac(20)$. Beyond that, we may need to work with the prime factors of a factorial (see Section 5.3.8), get the intermediate and final results modulo a smaller (usually a prime) number (see Section 5.3.9), or to use either Python or Java BigInteger for precise but slow computation (see Book 1).

5.3.8 Working with Prime Factors

Other than using the Big Integer technique (see Book 1) which is 'slow', we can work with the *intermediate computations* of large integers *accurately* by working with the *prime factors* of the integers instead of the actual integers themselves. Therefore, for some non-trivial number theoretic problems, we have to work with the prime factors of the input integers even if the main problem is not really about prime numbers. After all, prime factors are the building blocks of integers. Let's see the next case study.

[16]There is no built-in gcd function in OCaml.

[17]We can also have multifactorial. The most common form of multifactorial is the double factorial, denoted as $n!!$, e.g., $14!! = 14 \times 12 \times 10 \times \ldots \times 2 = 645\,120$. This is used in Section 8.2.1.

Kattis - factovisors/UVa 10139 - Factovisors

Abridged problem description: "Does m divide $n!$ ($0 \leq n, m \leq 2^{31}$-1)?". Recall that in Section 5.3.7, we note that $n!$, i.e., $fac(n)$, grows very fast. We mention that with *built-in data types*, the largest factorial that we can still compute precisely is only 20!. In Book 1, we show that we can compute large integers with Big Integer technique. However, it is *very slow* to precisely compute the exact value of $n!$ for large n.

The solution for this problem is to work with the prime factors of m and check if each of those prime factors has 'support' in $n!$. This check is called the Legendre's formula. Let $v_p(n!)$ be the highest power of p that divides n. We can compute $v_p(n!)$ via $\sum_{i=1}^{\infty} \lfloor \frac{n}{p^i} \rfloor$.

For example, when $n = 6$, we have $6! = 2 \times 3 \times 4 \times 5 \times 6 = 2 \times 3 \times (2^2) \times 5 \times (2 \times 3) = 2^4 \times 3^2 \times 5$ when expressed as its prime power factorization (we do not actually need to do this). Now if $m_1 = 9 = 3^2$, then this prime factor 3^2 has support in 6! because $v_3(6!) = 2$ and $3^2 \leq 3^2$. Thus, $m_1 = 9$ divide 6!. However, $m_2 = 54 = 2^1 \times 3^3$ has *no* support because although $v_2(6!) = 4$ and $2^1 \leq 2^4$, we have $v_3(6!) = 2$ and $3^3 > 3^2$. Thus $m_2 = 54$ does *not* divide 6!.

Source code: `ch5/factovisors_UVa10139.cpp|java|py`

Exercise 5.3.8.1: Determine what is the GCD and LCM of $(2^6 \times 3^3 \times 97^1, 2^5 \times 5^2 \times 11^2)$?

Exercise 5.3.8.2: Count the number of trailing zeroes of $n!$ (assume $1 \leq n \leq 200\,000$).

5.3.9 Modular Arithmetic

Some (mathematical) computations in programming problems can end up having very large positive (or very small negative) intermediate/final integer results that are beyond the range of the largest built-in integer data type (currently the 64-bit `long long` in C++ or `long` in Java). In Book 1, we have shown a way to compute Big Integers precisely. In Section 5.3.8, we have shown another way to work with Big Integers via its prime factors. For some other problems[18], we are only interested in the result *modulo* a number (usually a prime, to minimize collision) so that the intermediate/final results always fit inside built-in integer data type. In this subsection, we discuss these types of problems.

In UVa 10176 - Ocean Deep! Make it shallow!!, we are asked to convert a long binary number (up to 100 digits) to decimal. A quick calculation shows that the largest possible number is 2^{100}-1 which is beyond the range of a 64-bit integer. But the problem only asks if the result is divisible by 131 071 (a prime number). So what we need to do is to convert binary to decimal digit by digit, while performing % 131 071 operation to the intermediate result (note that '%' is a symbol of modulo operation). If the final result is 0, then the *actual number in binary* (which we never compute in its entirety), is divisible by 131 071.

Important: The modulo of a negative integer can be surprising to some who are not aware of their programming language specific behavior, e.g., $-10 \% 7 = 4$ (in Python) but C++/Java % operator and OCaml `mod` operator produces -3 instead. To be safer if we need to find a non-negative integer $a \pmod{m}$, we use $((a \% m) + m) \% m$. For the given example, we have $((-10 \% 7) + 7) \% 7 = (-3 + 7) \% 7 = 4 \% 7 = 4$.

[18]As of year 2020, we observe that the number of problems that require Big Integer technique is *decreasing* whereas the number of problems that require modular arithmetic technique is *increasing*.

The following are true involving modular arithmetic:

1. $(a + b) \% m = ((a \% m) + (b \% m)) \% m$
   Example: `(15 + 29) % 8`
   `= ((15 % 8) + (29 % 8)) % 8 = (7 + 5) % 8 = 4`

2. $(a - b) \% m = ((a \% m) - (b \% m)) \% m$
   Example: `(37 - 15) % 6`
   `= ((37 % 6) - (15 % 6)) % 6 = (1 - 3) % 6 = -2` or `4`

3. $(a \times b) \% m = ((a \% m) \times (b \% m)) \% m$
   Example: `(23 × 12) % 5`
   `= ((23 % 5) × (12 % 5)) % 5 = (3 × 2) % 5 = 1`

Modular Multiplicative Inverse

Now, $(a \ / \ b) \% m$ is harder to compute assuming a is very large, otherwise, simply divide a by b and modulo the result by b. Note that a might appear in the form of $a = a_1 \times a_2 \times \cdots \times a_n$ where each a_i is small enough to fit in a built-in integer data type. Thus, it might be tempting to modulo a and b to m independently, perform the division, and modulo the result again. However, this approach is wrong! $(((a_1 \times a_2 \times \cdots \times a_n) \% m) \ / \ (b \% m)) \% m$ does not necessarily equal to $(a \ / \ b) \% m$, i.e., the previous modular arithmetic does not work for division. For example, $(30 \ / \ 5) \% 10 = 6$ is not equal to $((30 \% 10) \ / \ (5 \% 10)) \% 10 = 0$. Another example, $(27 \ / \ 3) \% 13 = 9$ is not equal to $((27 \% 13) \ / \ (3 \% 13)) \% 13 = \frac{1}{3}$.

Fortunately, we can rewrite $(a \ / \ b) \% m$ as $(a \times b^{-1}) \% m$ where b^{-1} is the modular multiplicative inverse of b with respect to modulus m. In other words, b^{-1} is an integer such that $(b \times b^{-1}) \% m = 1$. Then, all we have to do is solving $(a \times b^{-1}) \% m$ using the previous modular arithmetic (for multiplication). So, how do we find $b^{-1} \% m$?

If m is a prime number, then we can use Fermat's little theorem for b and m where $gcd(b, m) = 1$, i.e., $b^{m-1} \equiv 1 \pmod{m}$. If we multiply both sides with b^{-1}, then we will obtain $b^{m-1} \cdot b^{-1} \equiv 1 \cdot b^{-1} \pmod{m}$ or simply $b^{m-2} \equiv b^{-1} \pmod{m}$. Then, to find the modular multiplicative inverse of b (i.e., $b^{-1} \% m$), simply compute $b^{m-2} \% m$, e.g., using efficient modular exponentiation discussed in Section 5.8.2 combined with the previous modular arithmetic for multiplication. Therefore, $(a \times b^{-1}) \% m$ when m is a prime number equals to $((a \% m) \times (b^{m-2} \% m)) \% m$.

If m is not necessarily a prime number but $gcd(b, m) = 1$, then we can use Euler's Theorem, i.e., $b^{\varphi(m)} \equiv 1 \pmod{m}$ where $\varphi(m)$ is the Euler's Phi (Totient) of m, the number of positive integers $< m$ which are relative prime to m. Observe that when m is a prime number, Euler's Theorem reduces to Fermat's little theorem, i.e., $\varphi(m) = m - 1$. Similar to the previous, we simply need to compute $b^{\varphi(m)-1} \% m$ to get the modular multiplicative inverse of b. Therefore, $(a \times b^{-1}) \% m$ equals to $((a \% m) \times (b^{\varphi(m)-1} \% m)) \% m$.
Example 1: $a = 27$, $b = 3$, $m = 13$. $(27 \ / \ 3) \% 13 = ((27 \% 13) \times (3^{-1} \% 13)) \% 13 = ((27 \% 13) \times (3^{11} \% 13)) \% 13 = (1 \times 9) \% 13 = 9$.
Example 2: $a = 27$, $b = 3$, $m = 10$. $(27 \ / \ 3) \% 10 = ((27 \% 10) \times (3^{-1} \% 10)) \% 10 = ((27 \% 10) \times (3^{3} \% 10)) \% 10 = (1 \times 9) \% 10 = 9$.

Alternatively, we can also use the Extended Euclid algorithm to compute the modular multiplicative inverse of b (while still assuming $gcd(b, m) = 1$). We discuss this version in the next Section 5.3.10. Note that if $gcd(b, m) \neq 1$, then b does not have a modular multiplicative inverse with respect to modulus m.

5.3.10 Extended Euclidean Algorithm

In Section 5.3.6, we have seen that `gcd(a, 0) = a` and `gcd(a, b) = gcd(b, a%b)` but this Euclid's algorithm can be extended. On top of computing the `gcd(a, b) = d`, the Extended Euclidean algorithm can also computes the coefficients of Bézout identity (lemma), i.e., integers `x` and `y` such that `ax + by = gcd(a, b)`. The implementation is as follows:

```
int extEuclid(int a, int b, int &x, int &y) {       // pass x and y by ref
  int xx = y = 0;
  int yy = x = 1;
  while (b) {                                        // repeats until b == 0
    int q = a/b;
    int t = b; b = a%b; a = t;
    t = xx; xx = x-q*xx; x = t;
    t = yy; yy = y-q*yy; y = t;
  }
  return a;                                          // returns gcd(a, b)
}
```

For example: $a = 25, b = 18$
`extendedEuclid(25, 18, x, y)` updates $x = -5, y = 7$, and returns $d = 1$.
This means $25 \times -5 + 18 \times 7 =$ `gcd(25, 18) = 1`.

Solving Linear Diophantine Equation

Problem: Suppose a housewife buys apples and oranges with cost of 8.39 dollars.
An apple costs 25 cents. An orange costs 18 cents. How many of each fruit does she buy?

This problem can be modeled as a linear equation with two variables: $25x + 18y = 839$. Since we know that both x and y must be integers, this linear equation is called the Linear Diophantine Equation. We can solve Linear Diophantine Equation with two variables even if we only have one equation! The solution is as follows:

Let a and b be integers with $d = gcd(a, b)$. The equation $ax + by = c$ has no integral solutions if $d \mid c$ is not true. But if $d \mid c$, then there are infinitely many integral solutions. The first solution (x_0, y_0) can be found using the Extended Euclidean algorithm and the rest can be derived from $x = x_0 + (b/d)n$, $y = y_0 - (a/d)n$, where n is an integer. Programming contest problems may have additional constraints to make the output finite (and unique).

Using `extendedEuclid`, we can solve the motivating problem shown earlier above:
The Linear Diophantine Equation with two variables $25x + 18y = 839$.
Recall that `extendedEuclid(25, 18)` helps us get:
$25 \times -5 + 18 \times 7 = gcd(25, 18) = 1$.

We multiply the left and right hand side of the equation above by $839/gcd(25, 18) = 839$:
$25 \times -4195 + 18 \times 5873 = 839$.
Thus $x = -4195 + (18/1)n$ and $y = 5873 - (25/1)n$.

Since we need to have non-negative x and y (non-negative number of apples and oranges), we have two more additional constraints:
$-4195 + 18n \geq 0$ and $5873 - 25n \geq 0$, or
$4195/18 \leq n \leq 5873/25$, or
$233.05 \leq n \leq 234.92$.

The only possible integer n is 234. Thus the unique solution is $x = -4195 + 18 \times 234 = 17$ and $y = 5873 - 25 \times 234 = 23$, i.e., 17 apples (of 25 cents each) and 23 oranges (of 18 cents each) for a total of 8.39 dollars.

Modular Multiplicative Inverse with Extended Euclidean Algorithm

Now let's compute x such that $b \times x = 1 \pmod{m}$. This $b \times x = 1 \pmod{m}$ is equivalent to $b \times x = 1 + m \times y$ where y can be any integer. We rearrange the formula into $b \times x - m \times y = 1$ or $b \times x + m \times y = 1$ as y is a variable that can absorb the negative sign. This is a Linear Diophantine Equation that can be solved with the Extended Euclidean algorithm to obtain the value of x (and y—ignored). This $x = b^{-1} \pmod{m}$.

Note that the result $b^{-1} \pmod{m}$ can only be found if `b` and `m` are relatively prime, i.e., `gcd(b, m) = 1`. It can be implemented as follows (notice our safeguard mod sub-routine to deal with the case when $a \% m$ is negative):

```
int mod(int a, int m) {                          // returns a (mod m)
  return ((a%m) + m) % m;                        // ensure positive answer
}

int modInverse(int b, int m) {                   // returns b^(-1) (mod m)
  int x, y;
  int d = extEuclid(b, m, x, y);                 // to get b*x + m*y == d
  if (d != 1) return -1;                         // to indicate failure
  // b*x + m*y == 1, now apply (mod m) to get b*x == 1 (mod m)
  return mod(x, m);
}
```

Now we can compute `(a` × `b`$^{-1}$`) % m` even if `m` is not a prime but `gcd(b, m) == 1` via `((a % m)` × `modInverse(b, m)) % m`.

Example 1: `((27 * 3`$^{-1}$`) % 7`
`= ((27 % 7)` × `modInverse(3, 7)) % 7 = (6` × `5) % 7 = 30 % 7 = 2.`

Example 2: `((27 * 4`$^{-1}$`) % 7`
`= ((27 % 7)` × `modInverse(4, 7)) % 7 = (6` × `2) % 7 = 12 % 7 = 2.`

Example 3 (m is not a prime but `gcd(b, m) == 1`: `((520 * 25`$^{-1}$`) % 18`
`= ((520 % 18)` × `modInverse(25, 18) % 18 = (16` × `13) % 18 = 208 % 18 = 10.`
This is because `extendedEuclid(25, 18, x, y)` updates $x = -5, y = 7$, and returns $d = 1$, so we have `x = ((-5%18) + 18) % 18 = (-5 + 18) % 18 = 13 % 18 = 13.`

Source code: `ch5/modInverse.cpp|java|py`

5.3.11 Number Theory in Programming Contests

We will discuss Pollard's rho (a faster integer factoring algorithm than the one shown in Section 5.3.3) in Section 9.12. We will also discuss Chinese Remainder Theorem (CRT) (that uses the Extended Euclidean algorithm in Section 5.3.10) in Section 9.13.

However, there are many other number theoretic problems that cannot be discussed one by one in this book (e.g., the various divisibility properties). Based on our experience, number theory problems frequently appear in ICPCs especially in Asia. It is a good idea for one team member to specifically study number theory listed in this book and beyond.

Programming Exercises related to Number Theory:

a. Prime Numbers

1. Entry Level: **UVa 00543 - Goldbach's Conjecture** * (sieve; complete search; Goldbach's conjecture[19]; similar to UVa 00686, 10311, and 10948)
2. **UVa 01644 - Prime Gap *** (LA 3883 - Tokyo07; sieve; prime check, upper bound - lower bound)
3. **UVa 10650 - Determinate Prime *** (3 uni-distance consecutive primes)
4. **UVa 11752 - The Super ... *** (try base 2 to 2^{16}; composite power; sort)
5. *Kattis - enlarginghashtables* * (use sieve up to 40 000; prime test numbers greater than 2n; check primality of n itself)
6. *Kattis - primesieve* * (use sieve up to 10^8; it is fast enough)
7. *Kattis - reseto* * (sieve of Eratosthenes until the k-th crossing)

   Extra UVa: *00406, 00686, 00897, 00914, 10140, 10168, 10311, 10394, 10490, 10852, 10948.*

b. (Probabilistic) Prime Testing

1. Entry Level: *Kattis - pseudoprime* * (yes if `!isPrime(p) && a.modPow(p, p) = a`; Big Integer; also available at UVa 11287 - Pseudoprime Numbers)
2. **UVa 01180 - Perfect Numbers *** (LA 2350 - Dhaka01; small prime check)
3. **UVa 01210 - Sum of Consecutive ... *** (LA 3399 - Tokyo05; simple)
4. **UVa 10235 - Simply Emirp *** (case analysis: prime/emirp/not prime; emirp is prime number that if reversed is still a prime number)
5. *Kattis - flowergarden* * (Euclidean `dist`; small prime check; use isProbablePrime; simulation; faster solutions exist)
6. *Kattis - goldbach2* * (simple brute force problem; use isProbablePrime; faster solutions exist)
7. *Kattis - primes2* * (convert input to either base 2/8/10/16; skip those that cause NumberFormatException error; use isProbablePrime test and gcd)

   Extra UVa: *00960, 10924, 12542.*

c. Finding Prime Factors

1. Entry Level: **UVa 00583 - Prime Factors** * (basic factorization problem)
2. **UVa 11466 - Largest Prime Divisor *** (use efficient sieve implementation to get the largest prime factors)
3. **UVa 12703 - Little Rakin *** (uses small Fibonacci numbers up to 40 and simple prime factorization as a and b can be non primes)
4. **UVa 12805 - Raiders of the Lost Sign *** (prime check; primes of format $4m-1$ and $4m+1$; simple prime factorization)
5. *Kattis - pascal* * (find lowest prime factor of N; special case: $N = 1$)
6. *Kattis - primalrepresentation* * (factorization problem; use sieve to avoid TLE; use long long; $2^{31}-1$ is a prime)
7. *Kattis - primereduction* * (factorization problem)

   Extra UVa: *00516, 10392.*

   Also see Section 9.12 for a faster (but rare) integer factoring algorithm.

[19]Christian Goldbach's conjecture (updated by Leonhard Euler) is as follows: Every even number ≥ 4 can be expressed as the sum of two prime numbers

d. Functions Involving Prime Factors

1. Entry Level: **UVa 00294 - Divisors** * (`numDiv(N)`)
2. **UVa 10179 - Irreducible Basic ...** * (`EulerPhi(N)`)
3. **UVa 11353 - A Different kind of ...** * (`numPF(N)`; sort variant)
4. **UVa 11728 - Alternate Task** * (`sumDiv(N)`)
5. *Kattis - almostperfect* * (`sumDiv(N)-N`; minor variation)
6. *Kattis - divisors* * (return `numDiv(nCk)`; but do not compute nCk directly; work with its prime factors)
7. *Kattis - relatives* * (`EulerPhi(N)`; also available at UVa 10299 - Relatives)

   Extra UVa: *00884*, *01246*, *10290*, *10820*, *10958*, *11064*, *11086*, *11226*, *12005*, *13185*, *13194*.

   Extra Kattis: *listgame*.

e. Modified Sieve

1. Entry Level: **UVa 10699 - Count the ...** * (`numDiffPF(N)` for a range)
2. **UVa 10990 - Another New Function** * (compute a range of Euler Phi values; DP to compute depth Phi values; finally Max 1D Range Sum DP)
3. **UVa 11426 - GCD - Extreme (II)** * (pre-calculate `EulerPhi(N)`, the answer involves EulerPhi)
4. **UVa 12043 - Divisors** * (`sumDiv(N)` and `numDiv(N)`; brute force)
5. *Kattis - data* * (`numDiffPF(V)` for V up to $N \times 1000$; Brute force combination/all subsets; DP Subset)
6. *Kattis - farey* * (pre-calculate `EulerPhi(N)`; do prefix sum (1D RSQ) of `EulerPhi(N)` from 1 to each N; the answer is related to this value)
7. *Kattis - nonprimefactors* * (`numDiv(i) - numDiffPF(i)` $\forall i$ in the range; the I/O files are large so Buffered I/O speed is needed)

   Extra UVa: *10738*, *11327*.

f. GCD and/or LCM[20]

1. Entry Level: **UVa 11417 - GCD** * (just use brute force as input is small)
2. **UVa 10407 - Simple Division** * (subtract the set s with s[0]; find gcd)
3. **UVa 10892 - LCM Cardinality** * (number of divisor pairs of N: (m, n) such that $lcm(m, n) = N$)
4. **UVa 11388 - GCD LCM** * (use GCD-LCM relationship)
5. *Kattis - prsteni* * (GCD of first circle radius with subsequent circle radiuses)
6. *Kattis - jackpot* * (similar to Kattis - smallestmultiple; use Java BigInteger or other faster solutions)
7. *Kattis - smallestmultiple* * (simple LCMs of all numbers; use Java BigInteger to be safe)

   Extra UVa: *00106*, *00412*, *10193*, *11774*, *11827*, *12708*, *12852*.

   Extra Kattis: *doodling*, *dasblinkenlights*.

[20]GCD and/or LCM problems that requires factorization are in 'Working with Prime Factors' category.

g. Factorial[21]

1. Entry Level: *Kattis - tutorial* * (factorial is just part of the problem; pruning)
2. **UVa 11076 - Add Again *** (do not use `next_permutation` for 12!, TLE; observe the digits in all permutations; hint: the solution involves factorial)
3. **UVa 12335 - Lexicographic Order *** (given the k-th permutation, recover the 1st permutation; use factorial; use Java BigInteger)
4. **UVa 12869 - Zeroes *** (LA 6847 - Bangkok 2014; every zero in factorial(n) is due to product of factor 2 and 5; factor 2 grows faster than factor 5)
5. *Kattis - inversefactorial* * (good problem; number of digits in factorial)
6. *Kattis - loworderzeros* * (last non zero digit of factorial; classic)
7. *Kattis - namethatpermutation* * (permutation number; involving factorial)

Extra UVa: *00324, 00568, 00623, 10220, 10323, 10338, 12934.*

Extra Kattis *eulersnumber, howmanydigits.*

h. Working with Prime Factors

1. Entry Level: *Kattis - factovisors* * (factorize m; see if it has support in $n!$; Legendre's formula; also available at UVa 10139 - Factovisors)
2. **UVa 10680 - LCM *** (use primefactors(`[1..N]`) to get LCM(1, 2, ..., N))
3. **UVa 11347 - Multifactorials *** (prime-power factorization; `numDiv(N)`)
4. **UVa 11395 - Sigma Function *** (key hint: a square number multiplied by powers of two, i.e., $2^k \times i^2$ for $k \geq 0, i \geq 1$ has *odd* sum of divisors)
5. *Kattis - consecutivesums* * (work with factor; sum of AP series)
6. *Kattis - fundamentalneighbors* * (reverse prime power notation)
7. *Kattis - iks* * (sieve of Eratosthenes; prime factorize each number; spread the factors around to maximize final GCD/minimize total operations)

Extra UVa: *00160, 00993, 10061, 10484, 10780, 10791, 11889, 13067.*

Extra Kattis: *olderbrother, parket, perfectpowers, persistent.*

i. Modular Arithmetic

1. Entry Level: **UVa 10176 - Ocean Deep; Make it ... *** (convert binary to decimal digit by digit; do modulo 131071 to the intermediate result)
2. **UVa 10174 - Couple-Bachelor- ... *** (no Spinster number)
3. **UVa 10212 - The Last Non-zero ... *** (multiply numbers from N down to N-M+1; use /10 to discard the trailing zero(es); use %1 Billion)
4. **UVa 10489 - Boxes of Chocolates *** (keep values small with modulo)
5. *Kattis - anothercandies* * (simple modular arithmetic)
6. *Kattis - ones* * (no factor of 2 and 5 implies that there is no trailing zero; also available at UVa 10127 - Ones)
7. *Kattis - threedigits* * (simulate factorial computation; remove trailing zeroes; keep many last few non-zero digits using modulo)

Extra UVa: *00128.*

Extra Kattis: *modulo, vauvau.*

[21]Factorial problems that requires factorization are categorized in 'Working with Prime Factors' category.

j. Extended Euclidean

1. Entry Level: **UVa 10104 - Euclid Problem** * (pure Ext Euclid problem)
2. **UVa 10090 - Marbles *** (use solution for Linear Diophantine Equation)
3. **UVa 10633 - Rare Easy Problem *** (let C = N-M, N = 10a+b, and $M = a$; Linear Diophantine Equation: 9a+b = C)
4. **UVa 10673 - Play with Floor and Ceil *** (uses Extended Euclidean)
5. *Kattis - candydistribution* * (the problem boils down to finding C^{-1} (mod K); be careful when the answer is "IMPOSSIBLE" or $\leq K$)
6. *Kattis - modulararithmetic* * (the division operation requires modular inverse; use Extended Euclidean algorithm)
7. *Kattis - soyoulikeyourfoodhot* * (Linear Diophantine Equation; still solvable with brute force)

Extra Kattis: *jughard*, *wipeyourwhiteboards*.

k. Divisibility Test

1. Entry Level: **UVa 10929 - You can say 11** * (test divisibility by 11)
2. **UVa 10922 - 2 the 9s *** (test divisibility by 9)
3. **UVa 11344 - The Huge One *** (use divisibility theory of `[1..12]`)
4. **UVa 11371 - Number Theory for ... *** (the solving strategy is given)
5. *Kattis - divisible* * (divisibility; linear pass algorithm)
6. *Kattis - meowfactor* * (divisibility test of 9^{ans}; small range of ans)
7. *Kattis - thinkingofanumber* * (simple range; use min/max properly; then small divisibility tests)

Extra Kattis: *cocoacoalition*, *magical3*.

Profile of Algorithm Inventors

Christian Goldbach (1690-1764) was a German mathematician. He is remembered today for Goldbach's conjecture that he discussed extensively with Leonhard Euler.

Diophantus of Alexandria ($\approx$ 200-300 AD) was an Alexandrian Greek mathematician. He did a lot of study in algebra. One of his works is the Linear Diophantine Equations.

Leonardo Fibonacci (or **Leonardo Pisano**) (1170-1250) was an Italian mathematician. He published a book titled 'Liber Abaci' (Book of Abacus/Calculation) in which he discussed a problem involving the growth of a population of *rabbits* based on idealized assumptions. The solution was a sequence of numbers now known as the Fibonacci numbers.

Edouard Zeckendorf (1901-1983) was a Belgian mathematician. He is best known for his work on Fibonacci numbers and in particular for proving Zeckendorf's theorem.

Jacques Philippe Marie Binet (1786-1856) was a French mathematician. He made significant contributions to number theory. Binet's formula expressing Fibonacci numbers in closed form is named in his honor, although the same result was known earlier.

Blaise Pascal (1623-1662) was a French mathematician. One of his famous inventions discussed in this book is the Pascal's triangle of binomial coefficients.

Eugène Charles Catalan (1814-1894) was a French and Belgian mathematician. He is the one who introduced the Catalan numbers to solve a combinatorial problem.

5.4 Combinatorics

Combinatorics is a branch of *discrete mathematics*[22] concerning the study of **countable** discrete structures. In programming contests, problems involving combinatorics are usually titled 'How Many [Object]', 'Count [Object]', etc, though some problem authors choose to hide this fact from their problem titles. Enumerating the objects one by one in order to count them usually leads to TLE. The solution code is usually *short*, but finding the (potentially recursive) formula takes some mathematical brilliance and also patience.

It is also a good idea to study/memorize the common ones like the Fibonacci-related formulas (see Section 5.4.1), Binomial Coefficients (see Section 5.4.2), and Catalan Numbers (see Section 5.4.3) to quickly recognize them. In a team-based competition like ICPC, if such a problem exists in the given problem set, ask one team member who is strong in mathematics to derive the formula (a quick revision on more general combinatorics techniques is in Section 5.4.4) whereas the other two concentrate on *other* problems. Quickly code the usually short formula once it is obtained—interrupting whoever is currently using the computer.

Some of these combinatorics formulas may yield overlapping subproblems that entail the need to use DP (review Book 1). Some computation values can also be large and entail the need to use Big Integer (see Book 1) or modular arithmetic (see Section 5.3.9).

5.4.1 Fibonacci Numbers

Leonardo *Fibonacci*'s numbers are defined as $fib(0) = 0$, $fib(1) = 1$, and for $n \geq 2$, $fib(n) = fib(n\text{-}1) + fib(n\text{-}2)$. This generates the following familiar pattern: 0, 1, 1, 2, 3, 5, 8, 13, 21, 34, 55, 89, 144, 233, 377, 610, and so on. This pattern sometimes appears in contest problems which do not mention the term 'Fibonacci' at all, like in some problems in the list of programming exercises in this section (e.g., UVa 10334, Kattis - anti11, etc).

We usually derive the Fibonacci numbers with a 'trivial' $O(n)$ (usually bottom-up) DP technique and not implement the given recurrence directly (as it is very slow). However, the $O(n)$ DP solution is *not* the fastest for all cases. Later in Section 5.8, we will show how to compute the n-th Fibonacci number (where n is large) in $O(\log n)$ time using the efficient matrix power. As a note, there is an $O(\log n)$ closed-form formula to get the n-th Fibonacci number: We compute the value of $(\phi^n\text{-}(\text{-}\phi)^{-n})/\sqrt{5}$ (Binet's formula) where ϕ (golden ratio) is $((1+\sqrt{5})/2) \approx 1.618$. This value is theoretically exact, however this is not so accurate for large Fibonacci numbers due to imprecision in floating point computations.

Fibonacci numbers have many interesting properties. One of them is Zeckendorf's theorem: every positive integer can be written in a unique way as a sum of one or more distinct Fibonacci numbers such that the sum does not include any two consecutive Fibonacci numbers. For any given positive integer, a representation that satisfies Zeckendorf's theorem can be found by using a *Greedy* algorithm: choose the largest possible Fibonacci number at each step. For example: $100 = 89 + 8 + 3$; $77 = 55 + 21 + 1$, $18 = 13 + 5$, etc.

Another property is the Pisano Period where the last one/last two/last three/last four digit(s) of a Fibonacci number repeats with a period of 60/300/1 500/15 000, respectively.

Exercise 5.4.1.1: Try $fib(n) = (\phi^n - (-\phi)^{-n})/\sqrt{5}$ on small n and see if this Binet's formula really produces $fib(7) = 13$, $fib(9) = 34$, $fib(11) = 89$. Now, write a simple program to find out the first value of n such that the actual value of $fib(n)$ differs from this formula?

---

[22] Discrete mathematics is a study of structures that are discrete (e.g., integers $\{0, 1, 2, \ldots\}$, graphs/trees (vertices and edges), logic (true/false)) rather than continuous (e.g., real numbers).

5.4.2 Binomial Coefficients

Another classical combinatorics problem is in finding the *coefficients* of the algebraic expansion of powers of a binomial[23]. These coefficients are also the numbers of ways that n items can be taken k at a time, usually written as $C(n,k)$ or ${}^nC_k$. For example, $(x+y)^3 = \mathbf{1}x^3 + \mathbf{3}x^2y + \mathbf{3}xy^2 + \mathbf{1}y^3$. The **{1, 3, 3, 1}** are the binomial coefficients of $n = 3$ with $k = \{0,1,2,3\}$ respectively. Or in other words, the numbers of ways that $n = 3$ items can be taken $k = \{0,1,2,3\}$ item(s) at a time are $\{1,3,3,1\}$, respectively.

We can compute a single (exact) value of $C(n,k)$ with this formula: $C(n,k) = \frac{n!}{(n-k)! \times k!}$ implemented iteratively. However, computing $C(n,k)$ can be a challenge when n and/or k are large. There are several techniques like: making k smaller (if $k > n\text{-}k$, then we set $k = n\text{-}k$) because ${}^nC_k = {}^nC_{(n-k)}$; during intermediate computations, we divide the numbers first before multiplying it with the next number; or use Big Integer technique discussed in Book 1 (this should be used only as the last resort as Big Integer operations are slow).

We can also compute the value of $C(n,k)$ using top-down DP recurrences as shown below and then use a 2D memo table to avoid re-computations.

$C(n,0) = C(n,n) = 1$ // base cases.
$C(n,k) = C(n\text{-}1,k\text{-}1) + C(n\text{-}1,k)$ // take or ignore an item, $n > k > 0$.

Alternatively, we can also compute the values of $C(n,k)$ from $n = 0$ up to a certain value of n by constructing the *Pascal's Triangle*, a triangular array of binomial coefficients. The leftmost and rightmost entries at each row are always 1. The inner values are the sum of two values diagonally above it, as shown for row $n = 4$ below. This is essentially the bottom-up version of the DP solution above. Notice that the sum of each row is always 2^n.

```
n = 0             1                              row sum = 1  = 2^0
n = 1           1   1                            row sum = 2  = 2^1
n = 2         1   2   1                          row sum = 4  = 2^2
n = 3       1   3   3   1  <- as shown above,    row sum = 8  = 2^3
             \ / \ / \ /
n = 4     1   4   6   4   1                      row sum = 16 = 2^4, and so on
```

As the values of $C(n,k)$ grows very fast, modern programming problems often ask for the value of $C(n,k)\%p$ instead where p is a prime number. If time limit is not strict, we can modify the DP formula above to compute the correct values of $C(n,k)\%p$. For a faster solution, we can apply Fermat's little theorem on the standard $C(n,k)$ formula (if p is a sufficiently large prime number greater than `MAX_N`) – see the implementation below with $O(n)$ pre-calculation of the values of $n!\%p$ – or Lucas' Theorem (if p is just a prime number but without the greater than `MAX_N` guarantee) – see Section 9.14.

```
typedef long long ll;
const int MAX_N = 100010;
const int p = 1e9+7;                              // p is a prime > MAX_N

ll inv(ll a) {                                    // Fermat's little theorem
  return modPow(a, p-2, p);                       // modPow in Section 5.8
}                                                 // that runs in O(log p)

ll fact[MAX_N];
```

[23]Binomial is a special case of polynomial that only has two terms.

```
ll C(int n, int k) {                                   // O(log p)
  if (n < k) return 0;                                 // clearly
  return (((fact[n] * inv(fact[k])) % p) * inv(fact[n-k])) % p;
}

// inside int main()
  fact[0] = 1;
  for (int i = 1; i < MAX_N; ++i)                      // O(MAX_N) pre-processing
    fact[i] = (fact[i-1]*i) % p;                       // fact[i] in [0..p-1]
  cout << C(100000, 50000) << "\n";                    // the answer is 149033233
```

Exercise 5.4.2.1: A frequently used k for $C(n,k)$ is $k = 2$. Show that $C(n,2) = O(n^2)$.

Exercise 5.4.2.2: Why the code above only works when $p >$ MAX_N? Try $p = 997$ (also a prime) and compute $C(100000, 50000)\%p$ again! What should we use to address this issue? Is it helpful if we use Extended Euclidean algorithm instead of Fermat's little theorem?

Exercise 5.4.2.3: In the given code above, we pre-calculate the values of $n!\%p$ $\forall n \in [0..n]$ in $O(n)$. Actually, we can also pre-calculate the values of inv[$n!\%p$] $\forall n \in [0..n]$ in $O(n)$. Then, each computation of $C(n,k)$ can be $O(1)$. Show how to do it!

5.4.3 Catalan Numbers

First, let's define the n-th Catalan number — written using binomial coefficients notation ${}^nC_k$ above — as: $Cat(n) = ({}^{(2\times n)}C_n)/(n+1)$; $Cat(0) = 1$. We will see its purposes below.

If we are asked to compute the values of $Cat(n)$ for *several* values of n, it may be better to compute the values using (bottom-up) DP. If we know $Cat(n)$, we can compute $Cat(n+1)$ by manipulating the formula like shown below.

$Cat(n) = \frac{(2n)!}{n!\times n!\times(n+1)}$

$Cat(n+1) = \frac{(2\times(n+1))!}{(n+1)!\times(n+1)!\times((n+1)+1)} = \frac{(2n+2)\times(2n+1)\times(2n)!}{(n+1)\times n!\times(n+1)\times n!\times(n+2)} = \frac{(2\times(n+1))\times(2n+1)\times[(2n)!]}{(n+2)\times(n+1)\times[n!\times n!\times(n+1)]}$.

Therefore, $Cat(n+1) = \frac{(4n+2)}{(n+2)} \times Cat(n)$.

The values of $Cat(n)$ also grows very fast so sometimes the value of $Cat(n)\%p$ is the one asked. If p is prime (and p is a sufficiently large prime number greater than MAX_N), we can use the following Fermat's little theorem implementation.

```
ll Cat[MAX_N];

// inside int main()
  Cat[0] = 1;
  for (int n = 0; n < MAX_N-1; ++n)                    // O(MAX_N log p)
    Cat[n+1] = ((4*n+2)%p * Cat[n]%p * inv(n+2)) % p;
  cout << Cat[100000] << "\n";                         // the answer is 945729344
```

We provide our modular arithmetic-style implementations in the source code below:

Source code: ch5/combinatorics.cpp|java|py

Catalan numbers are (surprisingly) found in various combinatorial problems. Here, we list down some of the more interesting ones (there are several others). All examples below use $n = 3$ and $Cat(3) = ({}^{(2\times3)}C_3)/(3+1) = ({}^{6}C_3)/4 = 20/4 = 5$.

1. $Cat(n)$ counts the number of distinct binary trees with n vertices, e.g., for $n = 3$:

2. $Cat(n)$ counts the number of expressions containing n pairs of parentheses which are correctly matched, e.g., for $n = 3$, we have: ()()(), ()(()), (())(), ((())), and (()()). For more details about this problem, see Book 1.
3. $Cat(n)$ counts the number of different ways $n + 1$ factors can be completely parenthesized, e.g., for $n = 3$ and $3 + 1 = 4$ factors: {a, b, c, d}, we have: (ab)(cd), a(b(cd)), ((ab)c)d, (a(bc))d, and a((bc)d).
4. $Cat(n)$ counts the number of ways a convex polygon (see Section 7.3) of $n + 2$ sides can be triangulated. See Figure 5.2—left.
5. $Cat(n)$ counts the number of monotonic paths along the edges of an $n \times n$ grid, which do not pass above the diagonal. A monotonic path is one which starts in the lower left corner, finishes in the upper right corner, and consists entirely of edges pointing rightwards or upwards. See Figure 5.2—right.

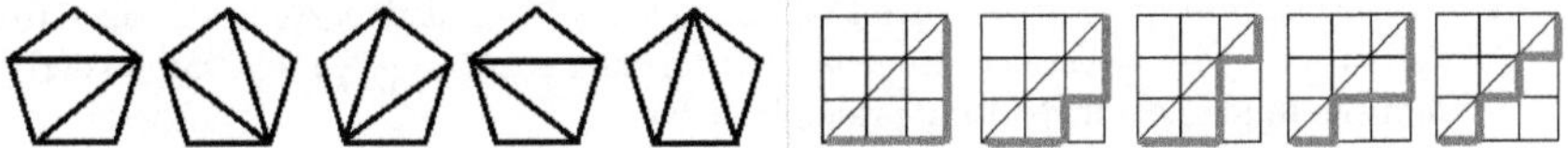

Figure 5.2: Left: Triangulation of a Convex Polygon, Right: Monotonic Paths

---

Exercise 5.4.3.1*: Which one is the hardest to factorize (see Section 5.3.3) assuming that n is an arbitrary large integer: $fib(n)$, $C(n, k)$ (assume that $k = n/2$), or $Cat(n)$? Why?

Exercise 5.4.3.2*: Catalan numbers $Cat(n)$ appear in some other interesting problems other than the ones shown in this section. Investigate!

5.4.4 Combinatorics in Programming Contests

The classic combinatorics-related problems involving (pure) Fibonacci and Catalan numbers are getting rare as of year 2020. However, there are still many other combinatorics problems involving permutations (Section 5.3.7) and combinations (that is, Binomial Coefficients, Section 5.4.2). Some of the basic ones are listed in the programming exercises below and the more interesting ones (but (very) rare) are listed in Section 9.15. Note that a *pure* and/or *classic* combinatorics problem is rarely used in modern IOI/ICPC but combinatorics is usually a subproblem of a bigger problem (Section 8.7).

In *online* programming contests where contestant can access the Internet, there is one more technique that may be useful. First, generate the output for small instances and then search for that sequence at OEIS (The On-Line Encyclopedia of Integer Sequences) hosted at `https://oeis.org/`. If you are lucky, OEIS can tell you the name of the sequence and/or the required general formula for the larger instances. Moreover, you can also use `https://wolframalpha.com/` to help you process/simplify mathematical formulas.

There are still many other counting principles and formulas, too many to be discussed in this book. As this is not a pure (discrete) mathematics book, we close this section by giving a quick revision on some combinatorics techniques and give a few written exercises to test/further improve your combinatorics skills.

- Fundamental counting principle (rule of sum): If there are n ways to do one action, m ways to do another action, and these two actions cannot be done at the same time, then there are $n + m$ ways to choose one of these combined actions. We can classify Counting Paths on DAG (review Book 1 and also see Section 8.3) as this.
- Fundamental counting principle (rule of product): If there are n ways to do one action and m ways to do another action afterwards, then there are $n \times m$ ways to do both.
- A *permutation* is an arrangement of objects without repetition and the order is important. There are $n!$ permutations of a set of size n distinct elements.
- If the set is actually a multiset (with duplicates), then there are fewer than $n!$ permutations. Suppose that there are k distinct elements, then the actual number of permutations is : $\frac{n!}{(n_1)! \times (n_2)! \times \ldots \times (n_k)!}$ where n_i is the frequency of each distinct element i and $n_1 + n_2 + \ldots + n_k = n$. This formula is also called as the *multinomial* coefficients, the generalization of the binomial coefficients discussed in Section 5.4.2.
- A *k-permutation* is an arrangement of a fixed length k of distinct elements taken from a given set of size n distinct elements. The formula is ${}_nP_k = \frac{n!}{(n-k)!}$ and can be derived from the fundamental counting principle above.
- Principle of inclusion-exclusion: $|A \bigcup B| = |A| + |B| - |A \bigcap B|$
- There 2^n subsets (or combinations) of n distinct elements.
- There are $C(n, k)$ number of ways to take k items out of a set of n distinct elements.

Exercise 5.4.4.1: Count the number of different possible outcomes if you roll two 6-sided dices and flip three 2-sided coins? Will the answer be different if we do this (rolling and flipping) one by one in some order versus if we do this in one go?

Exercise 5.4.4.2: How many ways to form a three digits number from {0, 1, 2, ..., 9}, each digit can only be used once, 0 cannot be used as the leading digit, and one of the digit must be 7?

Exercise 5.4.4.3: How many possible passwords are there if the length of the password is between 1 to 10 characters and each character can either be alphabet letters ['a'..'z'] or ['A'..'Z'] or digits [0..9]? Please output the answer modulo 1e9+7.

Exercise 5.4.4.4: Suppose you have a 6-letter word 'FACTOR'. If we take 3 letters from this word 'FACTOR', we may have another word, like 'ACT', 'CAT', 'ROT', etc. What is the number of different 3-letter words that can be formed with the letters from 'FACTOR'?

Exercise 5.4.4.5: Given the 5-letter word 'BOBBY', rearrange the letters to get another word, e.g., 'BBBOY', 'YOBBB', etc. How many *different* permutations are possible?

Exercise 5.4.4.6: Using the principle of inclusion-exclusion, count this: how many integers in [1..1M] that are multiples of 5 and 7?

Exercise 5.4.4.7: Solve UVa 11401 - Triangle Counting! "Given n rods of length 1, 2, $\ldots$, n, pick any 3 of them and build a triangle. How many distinct triangles can you make (consider triangle inequality, see Section 7.2)? ($3 \leq n \leq 1M$) ".

Exercise 5.4.4.8*: There are A boys and B girls. Count the number of ways to select a group of people such that the number of boys is equal to the number of girls in the chosen group, e.g., $A = 3$ and $B = 2$, then there are 1/6/3 way(s) to select a group with 0/2/4 people, respectively, with a total of 1+6+3 = 10 ways.

Programming Exercises related to Combinatorics:

a. Fibonacci Numbers

1. Entry Level: **UVa 00495 - Fibonacci Freeze** * ($O(n)$ DP; Big Integer)
2. **UVa 00763 - Fibinary Numbers** * (Zeckendorf representation; greedy; Big Integer)
3. **UVa 10334 - Ray Through Glasses** * (combinatorics; Big Integer)
4. **UVa 10689 - Yet Another Number ...** * (easy; Pisano period)
5. *Kattis - anti11* * (this problem is a modified Fibonacci numbers)
6. *Kattis - batmanacci* * (Fibonacci; observation on N; Divide and Conquer)
7. *Kattis - rijeci* * (simple simulation with a single loop; Fibonacci)

   Extra UVa: *00580, 00900, 00948, 01258, 10183, 10450, 10497, 10579, 10862, 11000, 11089, 11161, 11780, 12281, 12620.*

   Extra Kattis: *interestingintegers.*

b. Binomial Coefficients:

1. Entry Level: **UVa 00369 - Combinations** * (be careful with overflow issue)
2. **UVa 10541 - Stripe** * (a good combinatorics problem)
3. **UVa 11955 - Binomial Theorem** * (pure application; DP)
4. **UVa 12712 - Pattern Locker** * (the answer is $\sum_{i=M}^{N} C(L*L, i) * i!$, but simplify the computation of this formula instead of running it directly)
5. *Kattis - election* * (compute the answers with help of binomial coefficients)
6. *Kattis - lockedtreasure* * (the answer is ${}^nC_{m-1}$)
7. *Kattis - oddbinom* * (OEIS A006046)

   Extra UVa: *00326, 00485, 00530, 00911, 10105, 10375, 10532.*

   Extra Kattis: *insert, perica.*

Profile of Algorithm Inventor

Pierre de Fermat (1607-1665) was a French Lawyer and a mathematician. In context of Competitive Programming, he is best known for his Fermat's *little* theorem as used in Section 5.3.9, 5.4.2, and 5.4.3.

c. Catalan Numbers

1. Entry Level: **UVa 10223 - How Many Nodes?** * (you can precalculate the answers as there are only 19 Catalan Numbers < 2^{32}-1)
2. **UVa 00991 - Safe Salutations** * (Catalan Numbers)
3. **UVa 10007 - Count the Trees** * (answer is $Cat(n) \times n!$; Big Integer)
4. **UVa 10312 - Expression Bracketing** * (number of binary bracketing = $Cat(n)$; number of bracketing = *Super-Catalan* numbers)
5. *Kattis - catalan* * (basic Catalan Numbers)
6. *Kattis - catalansquare* * (Catalan Numbers++; follow the description)
7. *Kattis - fiat* * (N-th Catalan Number; use Fermat's little theorem)

Extra UVa: *10303*, *10643*.

c. Others, Easier

1. Entry Level: **UVa 11401 - Triangle Counting** * (spot the pattern)
2. **UVa 11310 - Delivery Debacle** * (requires DP: let `dp[i]` be the number of ways the cakes can be packed for a box 2× `i`)
3. **UVa 11597 - Spanning Subtree** * (graph theory; trivial)
4. **UVa 12463 - Little Nephew** * (double the socks and the shoes first)
5. *Kattis - character* * (OEIS A000295)
6. *Kattis - honey* * (OEIS A002898)
7. *Kattis - integerdivision* * (count frequencies of each remainder of [0..d-1]; add C(freq, 2) per such remainder)

Extra UVa: *10079*, *11115*, *11480*, *11609*.

c. Others, Harder

1. Entry Level: **UVa 10784 - Diagonal** * (the number of diagonals in n-gon $= n * (n-3)/2$; use it to derive the solution)
2. **UVa 01224 - Tile Code** * (LA 3904 - Seoul07; derive formula from observing the small instances first)
3. **UVa 11069 - A Graph Problem** * (use Dynamic Programming)
4. **UVa 11538 - Chess Queen** * (count along rows/columns/diagonals)
5. *Kattis - anagramcounting* * (use Java BigInteger)
6. *Kattis - incognito* * (count frequencies; combinatorics; minus one)
7. *Kattis - tritiling* * (there are two related recurrences here; also available at UVa 10918 - Tri Tiling)

Extra UVa: *00153*, *00941*, *10359*, *10733*, *10790*, *11204*, *11270*, *11554*, *12001*, *12022*.

Extra Kattis: *kitchencombinatorics*.

c. Also see Section 9.15 for a few *rare* (combinatorics) formulas and theorems.

Profile of Algorithm Inventor

François Édouard Anatole Lucas (1842-1891) was a French mathematician. Lucas is known for his study of the Fibonacci and Lucas sequence. In this book, we discuss Lucas' Theorem to compute the remainder of division of the binomial coefficient $C(n, k)$ by a prime number p in terms of the base p expansions of the integers m and n. This solution that is discussed in Section 9.14 is stronger than the one presented in Section 5.4.2.

5.5 Probability Theory

Probability Theory is a branch of mathematics dealing with the analysis of random phenomena. Although an event like an individual (fair) coin toss is random, the sequence of random events will exhibit certain statistical patterns if the event is repeated many times. This can be studied and predicted. For example, the probability of a head appearing is 1/2 (similarly with a tail). Therefore, if we flip a (fair) coin n times, we *expect* that we see heads $n/2$ times.

In programming contests, problems involving probability are either solvable with:

- Closed-form formula. For these problems, one has to derive the required (usually $O(1)$) formula. For example, let's discuss how to derive the solution for UVa 10491 - Cows and Cars[24], which is a generalized version of a TV show: 'The Monty Hall problem'[25].

  You are given N_{COWS} number of doors with cows, N_{CARS} number of doors with cars, and N_{SHOW} number of doors (with cows) that are opened for you by the presenter. Now, you need to count the probability of winning a car (by opening a door that has a car behind it) assuming that you will always switch to another unopened door.

  The first step is to realize that there are two ways to get a car. Either you pick a cow first and then switch to a car, or you pick a car first, and then switch to another car. The probability of each case can be computed as shown below.

  In the first case, the chance of picking a cow first is $(N_{COWS}/(N_{COWS} + N_{CARS}))$. Then, the chance of switching to a car is $(N_{CARS}/(N_{CARS} + N_{COWS} - N_{SHOW} - 1))$. Multiply these two values together to get the probability of the first case. The -1 is to account for the door that you have already chosen, as you cannot switch to it.

  The probability of the second case can be computed in a similar manner. The chance of picking a car first is $(N_{CARS}/(N_{CARS} + N_{COWS}))$. Then, the chance of switching to a car is $((N_{CARS} - 1)/(N_{CARS} + N_{COWS} - N_{SHOW} - 1))$. Both -1 accounts for the car that you have already chosen.

  Sum the probability values of these two cases together to get the final answer.

- Exploration of the search (sample) space to count number of events (usually harder to count; may deal with combinatorics—see Section 5.4, Complete Search—see Book 1, or Dynamic Programming–see Book 1) over the countable sample space (usually much simpler to count). Examples:
  - 'UVa 12024 - Hats' is a problem of n people who store their n hats in a cloakroom for an event. When the event is over, these n people take their hats back. Some take a wrong hat. Compute how likely is that *everyone* takes a wrong hat.

    This problem can be solved via brute-force and pre-calculation by trying all $n!$ permutations and see how many times the required events appear over $n!$ because $n \leq 12$ in this problem and such $O(n! \times n)$ naïve solution will only take about a minute to run. However, a more math-savvy contestant can use this Derangement (DP) formula instead: $A_n = (n\text{-}1) \times (A_{n-1} + A_{n-2})$ that will be fast enough for much higher n, possibly combined with modular arithmetic.

[24]You may be interested to attempt an interactive problem : Kattis - askmarilyn too.

[25]This is an interesting probability puzzle. Readers who have not heard this problem before are encouraged to do some Internet search and read the history of this problem. In the original problem, $N_{COWS} = 2$, $N_{CARS} = 1$, and $N_{SHOW} = 1$. The probability of staying with your original choice is $\frac{1}{3}$ and the probability of switching to another unopened door is $\frac{2}{3}$ and therefore it is always beneficial to switch.

- Abridged problem description of UVa 10759 - Dice Throwing: n common cubic dice are thrown. What is the probability that the sum of all thrown dices is at least x? (constraints: $1 \leq n \leq 24$, $0 \leq x < 150$).

  The sample space (the denominator of the probability value) is very simple to compute. It is 6^n.

  The number of events is slightly harder to compute. We need a (simple) DP because there are lots of overlapping subproblems. The state is $(dice\_left, score)$ where $dice\_left$ keeps track of the remaining dice that we can still throw (starting from n) and $score$ counts the accumulated score so far (starting from 0). DP can be used as there are only $n \times (n \times 6) = 6n^2$ distinct states for this problem.

  When $dice\_left = 0$, we return 1 (event) if $score \geq x$, or return 0 otherwise; When $dice\_left > 0$, we try throwing one more dice. The outcome v for this dice can be one of six values and we move to state $(dice\_left\text{-}1, score{+}v)$. We sum all the events. The time complexity is $O(6n^2 \times 6) = O(36n^2)$ which is very small as $n \leq 24$ in this problem.

  One final requirement is that we have to use gcd (see Section 5.3.6) to simplify the probability fraction (see Section 5.2). In some other problems, we may be asked to output the probability value correct to a certain digit after decimal point (either between [0.0..1.0] or as percentages [0.0..100.0]).

- Abridged problem description of Kattis - bobby: Betty has an S-sided fair dice (having values 1 through S). Betty challenges Bobby to obtain a total value $\geq R$ on at least X out of Y rolls. If Bobby is successful, Betty will give Bobby W times of his initial bet. Should Bobby take the bet? Or in another word, is his expected return greater than his original bet?

  To simplify, let's assume that Bobby bets 1 unit of currency, is his expected return strictly greater than 1 unit?

  For a single roll of an S-sided fair dice, Bobby's chance to hit R or higher (a success) is $p_{success} = \frac{S-R+1}{S}$ and consequently Bobby's chance to hit R-1 or lower (a failure) is $\frac{R-1}{S}$ (or $1 - p_{success}$).

  We can then write a recursive function $exp\_val(num\_roll, num\_success)$. We simulate the roll one by one. The base case is when $num\_roll == Y$ where we return W if $num\_success \geq X$ or 0 otherwise. In general case, we do one more throw that can be either a success with probability $p_{success}$ or a failure with probability $(1 - p_{success})$ and add both expected values due to linearity of expectation. The time complexity is $O(Y^2)$ which is very small as $Y \leq 10$.

Exercise 5.5.1: Instead of memorizing the formula, show how to derive the Derangement DP formula $A_n = (n\text{-}1) \times (A_{n-1} + A_{n-2})$.

Exercise 5.5.2: There are 15 students in a class. 8 of them are boys and the other 7 are girls. The teacher wants to form a group of 5 students in random fashion. What is the probability that the formed group consists of all girls?

Programming Exercises about Probability Theory:

a. Probability Theory, Easier

1. Entry Level: **UVa 10491 - Cows and Cars** * (2 ways: either pick a cow first, then switch to a car; or pick a car first, and then switch to another car)
2. **UVa 01636 - Headshot** * (LA 4596 - NorthEasternEurope09; ad hoc probability question, one tricky special case involving all zeroes)
3. **UVa 10238 - Throw the Dice** * (DP; s: (dice_left, score); try F values; Big Integer; no need to simplify the fraction; see UVa 10759)
4. **UVa 11181 - Probability (bar) Given** * (iterative brute force; try all possibilities)
5. *Kattis - bobby* * (computation of expected value)
6. *Kattis - dicebetting* * (s: (dice_left, distinct_numbers_so_far); each throw can increase distinct_numbers_so_far or not)
7. *Kattis - odds* * (complete search; simple probability)

   Extra UVa: *10328, 10759, 12024, 12114, 12230, 12457, 12461.*

   Extra Kattis: *dicegame, orchard, password, secretsanta.*

b. Probability Theory, Harder

1. Entry Level: **UVa 11628 - Another lottery** * (p[i] = ticket bought by i at the last round/total tickets bought at the last round by all n; gcd)
2. **UVa 10056 - What is the Probability?** * (get the closed form formula)
3. **UVa 10648 - Chocolate Box** * (DP; s: (rem_boxes, num_empty))
4. **UVa 11176 - Winning Streak** * (DP, s: (rem_games, streak); t: lose this game, or win the next W = [1..n] games and lose the (W+1)-th game)
5. *Kattis - anthony* * (DP probability; need to drop one parameter (N or M) and recover it from the other one)
6. *Kattis - goodcoalition* * (DP probability; like KNAPSACK)
7. *Kattis - lostinthewoods* * (simulate random walks of various lengths and distribute the probabilities per iteration; the answer will converge eventually)

   Extra UVa: *00542, 00557, 10218, 10777, 11021, 11346, 11500, 11762.*

   Extra Kattis: *2naire, anotherdice, bond, bribe, explosion, genius, gnollhypothesis, pollygone, raffle, redsocks.*

Profile of Algorithm Inventors

John M. Pollard (born 1941) is a British mathematician who has invented algorithms for the factorization of large numbers (the Pollard's rho algorithm, see Section 9.12) and for the calculation of discrete logarithms (not discussed in this book).

Richard Peirce Brent (born 1946) is an Australian mathematician and computer scientist. His research interests include number theory (in particular factorization), random number generators, computer architecture, and analysis of algorithms. He has invented or co-invented various mathematics algorithms.

5.6 Cycle-Finding

5.6.1 Problem Description

Given a function $f : S \rightarrow S$ (that maps a natural number from a *finite set* S to another natural number in the same finite set S) and an initial value $x_0 \in N$, the sequence of **iterated function values**: $\{x_0, x_1 = f(x_0), x_2 = f(x_1), \ldots, x_i = f(x_{i-1}), \ldots\}$ must eventually use the same value twice, i.e., $\exists i < j$ such that $x_i = x_j$. Once this happens, the sequence must then repeat the cycle of values from x_i to x_{j-1}. Let μ (the start of cycle) be the smallest index i and λ (the cycle length) be the smallest positive integer such that $x_\mu = x_{\mu+\lambda}$. The **cycle-finding** problem[26] is defined as the problem of finding μ and λ given $f(x)$ and x_0.

For example, in UVa 00350 - Pseudo-Random Numbers, we are given a pseudo-random number generator $f(x) = (Z \times x + I)\%M$ with $x_0 = L$ and we want to find out the sequence length before any number is repeated (i.e., the λ). A good pseudo-random number generator should have a large λ. Otherwise, the numbers generated will not look 'random'.

Let's try this process with the sample test case $Z = 7, I = 5, M = 12, L = 4$, so we have $f(x) = (7 \times x + 5)\%12$ and $x_0 = 4$. The sequence of iterated function values is $\{\underline{4, 9, 8, 1, 0, 5}, 4, \ldots\}$. We have $\mu = 0$ and $\lambda = 6$ as $x_0 = x_{\mu+\lambda} = x_{0+6} = x_6 = 4$. The sequence of iterated function values cycles from index 6 onwards.

On another test case $Z = 26, I = 11, M = 80, L = 7$, we have $f(x) = (26 \times x + 11)\%80$ and $x_0 = 7$. The sequence of iterated function values is $\{7, 33, 69, \underline{45, 61, 77, 13, 29}, 45, \ldots\}$. This time, we have $\mu = 3$ and $\lambda = 5$.

5.6.2 Solutions using Efficient Data Structures

A simple algorithm that will work for *many cases* and/or *variants* of this cycle-finding problem uses an efficient data structure to store key to value information: a number x_i (the key) has been *first* encountered at iteration i (the value) in the sequence of iterated function values. Then for x_j that is encountered later ($j > i$), we test if x_j is already stored in the data structure. If it is, it implies that $x_j = x_i$, $\mu = i$, $\lambda = j - i$. This algorithm runs in $O((\mu + \lambda) \times DS\_cost)$ where DS_cost is the cost per one data structure operation (insert/search). This algorithm requires at least $O(\mu + \lambda)$ space to store past values.

For many cycle-finding problems with rather large S (and likely large $\mu + \lambda$), we can use $O(\mu + \lambda + buffer)$ space C++ STL `unordered_map`/Java `HashMap`/Python `dict`/OCaml `Hashtbl` to store/check the iteration indices of past values in $O(1)$ time. But if we just need to stop the algorithm upon encountering the *first* repeated number, we can use C++ STL `unordered_set`/Java `HashSet`/Python `set` (curly braces {}) instead.

For other cycle-finding problems with relatively small S (and likely small $\mu + \lambda$), we may even use the $O(|S|)$ space Direct Addressing Table (DAT) to store/check the iteration indices of past values also in $O(1)$ time.

Note that by trading-off (large, up to $O(\mu + \lambda)$) memory space, we can actually solve this cycle-finding problem in efficient $O(\mu + \lambda)$ runtime.

Exercise 5.6.2.1: Notice that on many random test cases of UVa 00350, the values of μ and λ are close to 0. However, generate a simple test case (choose Z, I, M, and L) for UVa 00350 so that even an $O(\mu+\lambda)$ algorithm really runs in $O(M)$, i.e., almost, if not all possible integers $\in [0..M\text{-}1]$ are used before a cycle is detected.

---

[26]We can also view this problem as a graph problem, i.e., finding the start and length of a cycle in a functional graph/pseudo tree.

5.6.3 Floyd's Cycle-Finding Algorithm

However, there is an even better algorithm called Floyd's cycle-finding algorithm that also runs in $O(\mu + \lambda)$ time complexity but *only* uses $O(1)$ memory[27] space—much smaller than the solutions using efficient data structures above. This algorithm is also called 'the tortoise and hare (rabbit)' algorithm. It has three components that we describe below using the function $f(x) = (Z \times x + I)\%M$ and $Z = 26, I = 11, M = 80, L = 7$.

1. Efficient Way to Detect a Cycle: Finding $k\lambda$

Observe that for any $i \geq \mu$, $x_i = x_{i+k\lambda}$, where $k > 0$, e.g., in Table 5.2, $x_3 = x_{3+1\times5} = x_8 = x_{3+2\times5} = x_{13} = 45$, and so on. If we set $k\lambda = i$, we get $x_i = x_{i+i} = x_{2i}$. Floyd's cycle-finding algorithm exploits this technique.

i	x_0 7	x_1 33	x_2 69	x_3 45	x_4 61	x_5 77	x_6 13	x_7 29	x_8 45	x_9 61	x_{10} 77	x_{11} 13	x_{12} 29	x_{13} 45
0	TH													
1		T	H											
2			T		H									
3				T			H							
4					T				H					
5						<u>T</u>					<u>H</u>			

Table 5.2: Part 1: Finding $k\lambda$, $f(x) = (26 \times x + 11)\%80$, $x_0 = 7$

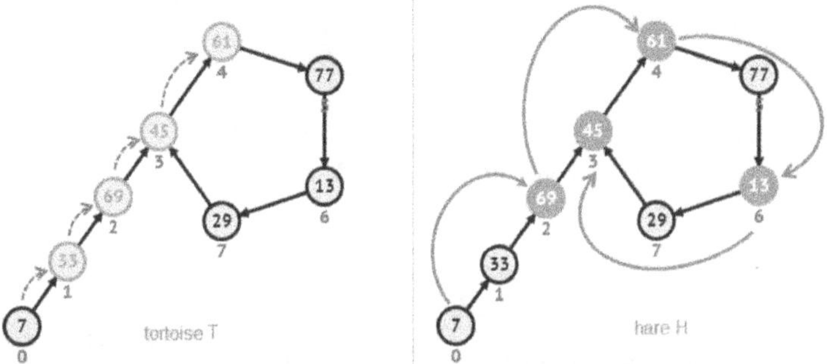

Figure 5.3: An Example of Finding $k\lambda = 5$ (one step before t and h point at $x_5 = x_{10} = 77$)

The Floyd's cycle-finding algorithm maintains two pointers called the 'tortoise' (the slower one) at x_i and the 'hare' (the faster one) at x_{2i}. Initially, both are at x_0. At each step of the algorithm, tortoise is moved *one step* to the right and the hare is moved *two steps* to the right[28] in the sequence. Then, the algorithm compares the sequence values at these two pointers. The smallest value of $i > 0$ for which both tortoise and hare point to equal values is the value of $k\lambda$ (multiple of λ). We will determine the actual λ from $k\lambda$ using the next two steps. In Table 5.2 and Figure 5.3, when $i = 5$, we have $x_5 = x_{10} = x_{5+\underline{5}} = x_{5+k\lambda} = 77$. So, $k\lambda = 5$. In this example, we will see below that k is eventually 1, so $\lambda = 5$ too.

[27]But this advantage is hard to test in an online judge setup though, thus the efficient data structure solutions shown earlier are probably enough to solve most cycle-finding problems.

[28]To move right one step from x_i, we use $x_i = f(x_i)$. To move right two steps from x_i, we use $x_i = f(f(x_i))$.

2. Finding μ

Next, we reset hare back to x_0 and keep tortoise at its current position. Now, we advance *both* pointers to the right one step at a time, thus maintaining the $k\lambda$ gap between the two pointers. When tortoise and hare points to the same value, we have just found the *first* repetition of length $k\lambda$. Since $k\lambda$ is a multiple of λ, it must be true that $x_\mu = x_{\mu+k\lambda}$. The first time we encounter the first repetition of length $k\lambda$ is the value of the μ. In Table 5.3 and Figure 5.4—left, we find that $\mu = 3$.

μ	x_0	x_1	x_2	x_3	x_4	x_5	x_6	x_7	x_8	x_9	x_{10}	x_{11}	x_{12}	x_{13}
	7	33	69	45	61	77	13	29	45	61	77	13	29	45
0	H					T								
1		H					T							
2			H					T						
3				$\underline{\text{H}}$					$\underline{\text{T}}$					

Table 5.3: Part 2: Finding μ

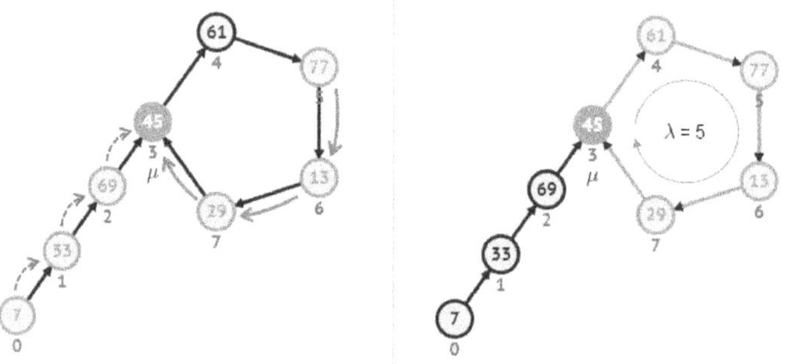

Figure 5.4: Left: Finding $\mu = 3$; Right: Finding $\lambda = 5$

3. Finding λ

λ	x_0	x_1	x_2	x_3	x_4	x_5	x_6	x_7	x_8	x_9	x_{10}	x_{11}	x_{12}	x_{13}
	7	33	69	45	61	77	13	29	45	61	77	13	29	45
1									T	H				
2									T		H			
3									T			H		
4									T				H	
5									$\underline{\text{T}}$					$\underline{\text{H}}$

Table 5.4: Part 3: Finding λ

Once we get μ, we let the tortoise stay in its current position and set hare next to it. Now, we move the hare iteratively to the right one by one. The hare will point to a value that is the same as the tortoise for the *first* time after λ steps. In Table 5.4 and Figure 5.4—right, we see that after the hare moves five times, $x_8 = x_{8+5} = x_{13} = 45$. So, $\lambda = 5$. Therefore, we report $\mu = 3$ and $\lambda = 5$ for $f(x) = (26 \times x + 11)\%80$ and $x_0 = 7$. Overall, this algorithm runs in $O(\mu + \lambda)$ with *only* $O(1)$ memory space.

4. The Implementation of Floyd's Cycle-Finding Algorithm

The working C/C++ implementation of this algorithm (with comments) is shown below:

```
ii floydCycleFinding(int x0) {                         // f(x) is defined above
  // 1st part: finding k*mu, hare h's speed is 2x tortoise t's
  int t = f(x0), h = f(f(x0));                         // f(x0) is after x0
  while (t != h) { t = f(t); h = f(f(h)); }
  // 2nd part: finding mu, hare h and tortoise t move at the same speed
  int mu = 0; h = x0;
  while (t != h) { t = f(t); h = f(h); ++mu; }
  // 3rd part: finding lambda, hare h moves, tortoise t stays
  int lambda = 1; h = f(t);
  while (t != h) { h = f(h); ++lambda; }
  return {mu, lambda};
}
```

For more examples, visit the VisuAlgo, cycle-finding visualization and define your own[29] $f(x) = (a \times x^2 + b \times x + c)\%M$ and your own x_0 to see this algorithm in action.

Visualization: `https://visualgo.net/en/cyclefinding`

Source code: `ch5/UVa00350.cpp|java|py|ml`

Exercise 5.6.3.1*: Richard Peirce Brent invented an improved version of Floyd's cycle-finding algorithm shown above. Study and implement Brent's algorithm [4].

Programming Exercises related to Cycle-Finding:

1. Entry Level: **UVa 00350 - Pseudo-Random Numbers** * (very basic cycle-finding problem; simply run Floyd's cycle-finding algorithm)
2. **UVa 11036 - Eventually periodic ...** * (cycle-finding; evaluate Reverse Polish `f` with a `stack`)
3. **UVa 11053 - Flavius Josephus ...** * (cycle-finding; the answer is N-λ)
4. **UVa 11511 - Frieze Patterns** * (cycle-finding on vectors; notice that the pattern will cycle fast)
5. *Kattis - dragondropped* * (interactive cycle finding problem; tight constraints)
6. *Kattis - fibonaccicycles* * (detect cycle of $fib(n)\%k$ using fast data structure)
7. *Kattis - rats* * (string processing plus cycle-finding; `unordered_set`)

   Extra UVa: *00202*, *00275*, *00408*, *00547*, *00942*, *00944*, *10162*, *10515*, *10591*, *11549*, *11634*, *12464*, *13217*.

   Extra Kattis: *cool1*, *happyprime*, *partygame*.

---

[29] This is slightly more generic than the $f(x) = (Z \times x + I)\%M$ shown in this section.

5.7 Game Theory (Basic)

Problem Description

Game Theory is a mathematical model of strategic situations (not necessarily *games* as in the common meaning of 'games') in which a player's success in making choices depends on the choices of *others*. Many programming problems involving game theory are classified as **Zero-Sum Games**—a mathematical way of saying that if one player wins, then the other player loses. For example, a game of Tic-Tac-Toe (e.g., UVa 10111), Chess, various number/integer games (e.g., UVa 10368, 10578, 10891, 11489, Kattis - amultiplicationgame), and others (Kattis - bachetsgame) are games with two players playing alternately (usually perfectly) and (usually) there can only be one winner.

The common question asked in programming contest problems related to game theory is whether the starting player of a two player competitive game has a winning move assuming that both players are doing **Perfect Play**. That is, each player always chooses the most optimal choice available to him.

Decision Tree

One way is to write a recursive code to explore the **Decision Tree** of the game (a.k.a. the Game Tree). If there is no overlapping subproblem, pure recursive backtracking is suitable. Otherwise, Dynamic Programming is needed. Each vertex describes the current player and the current state of the game. Each vertex is connected to all other vertices legally reachable from that vertex according to the game rules. The root vertex describes the starting player and the initial game state. If the game state at a leaf vertex is a winning state, it is a win for the current player (and a lose for the other player). At an internal vertex, the current player chooses a vertex that guarantees a win with the largest margin (or if a win is not possible, chooses a vertex with the least loss). This is called the **Minimax** strategy.

For example, in UVa 10368 - Euclid's Game, there are two players: Stan (player 0) and Ollie (player 1). The state of the game is a triple of integers (id, a, b). The current player id can subtracts any positive multiple of the lesser of the two numbers, integer b, from the greater of the two numbers, integer a, provided that the resulting number must be nonnegative. We always maintain that $a \geq b$. Stan and Ollie plays alternately, until one player is able to subtract a multiple of the lesser number from the greater to reach 0, and thereby wins. The first player is Stan. The decision tree for a game with initial state $id = 0$, $a = 34$, and $b = 12$ is shown in Figure 5.5.

Let's trace what happens in Figure 5.5. At the root (initial state), we have triple $(0, 34, 12)$. At this point, player 0 (Stan) has two choices: either to subtract $a-b = 34-12 = 22$ and move to vertex $(1, 22, 12)$ (the left branch) or to subtract $a - 2 \times b = 34 - 2 \times 12 = 10$ and move to vertex $(1, 12, 10)$ (the right branch). We try both choices recursively.

Let's start with the left branch. At vertex $(1, 22, 12)$—(Figure 5.5—B), the current player 1 (Ollie) has no choice but to subtract $a-b = 22-12 = 10$. We are now at vertex $(0, 12, 10)$—(Figure 5.5—C). Again, Stan only has one choice which is to subtract $a - b = 12 - 10 = 2$. We are now at leaf vertex $(1, 10, 2)$—(Figure 5.5—D). Ollie has several choices but Ollie can definitely win as $a - 5 \times b = 10 - 5 \times 2 = 0$ and it implies that vertex $(0, 12, 10)$ is a losing state for Stan and vertex $(1, 22, 12)$ is a winning state for Ollie.

Now we explore the right branch. At vertex $(1, 12, 10)$—(Figure 5.5—E), the current player 1 (Ollie) has no choice but to subtract $a - b = 12 - 10 = 2$. We are now at leaf vertex $(0, 10, 2)$—(Figure 5.5—F). Stan has several choices but Stan can definitely win as $a - 5 \times b = 10 - 5 \times 2 = 0$ and it implies that vertex $(1, 12, 10)$ is a losing state for Ollie.

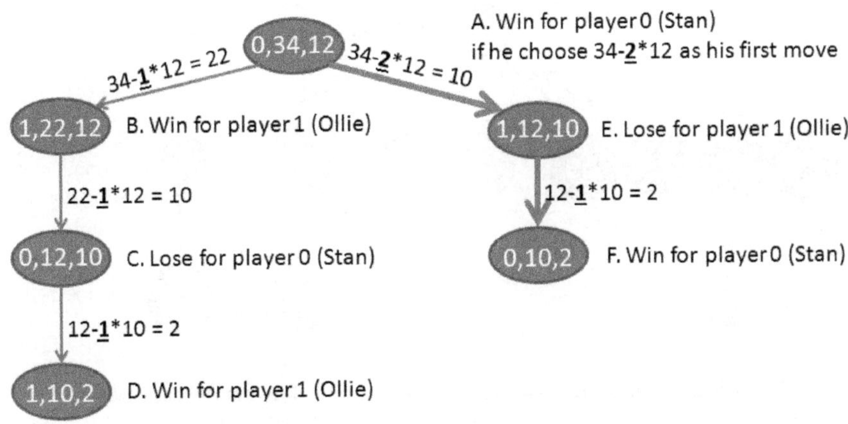

Figure 5.5: Decision Tree for an instance of 'Euclid's Game'

Therefore, for player 0 (Stan) to win this game, Stan should choose $a - 2 \times b = 34 - 2 \times 12$ first, as this is a winning move for Stan—(Figure 5.5—A).

Implementation wise, the first integer *id* in the triple can be dropped as we know that depth 0 (root), 2, 4, ... are always Stan's turns and depth 1, 3, 5, ... are always Ollie's turns. This integer *id* is used in Figure 5.5 to simplify the explanation.

Mathematical Insights to Speed-up the Solution

Not all game theory problems can be solved by exploring the *entire* decision tree of the game, especially if the size of the tree is large. If the problem involves numbers, we may need to come up with some mathematical insights to speed up the computation.

For example, in UVa 00847 - A multiplication game, there are two players: Stan (player 0) and Ollie (player 1) again. The state of the game[30] is an integer p. The current player can multiply p with any number between 2 to 9. Stan and Ollie again play alternately, until one player is able to multiply p with a number between 2 to 9 such that $p \geq n$ (n is the target number), and thereby win. The first player is Stan with $p = 1$.

Figure 5.6 shows an instance of this multiplication game with $n = 17$. Initially, player 0 (Stan) has up to 8 choices (to multiply $p = 1$ by [2..9]). However, all of these 8 states are winning states of player 1 as player 1 can always multiply the current p by [2..9] to make $p \geq 17$—(Figure 5.6—B). Therefore player 0 (Stan) will surely lose—(Figure 5.6—A).

As $1 < n < 4\,294\,967\,295$, the resulting decision tree on the largest test case can be extremely huge. This is because each vertex in this decision tree has a *huge* branching factor of 8 (as there are 8 possible numbers to choose from between 2 to 9). It is not feasible to actually explore the decision tree.

It turns out that the optimal strategy for Stan to win is to *always* multiply p with 9 (the largest possible) while Ollie will *always* multiply p with 2 (the smallest possible). Such optimization insights can be obtained by observing the pattern found in the output of smaller instances of this problem. Note that math-savvy contestant may want to prove this observation first before coding the solution.

[30]This time we omit the player *id*. However, this parameter *id* is still shown in Figure 5.6 for clarity.

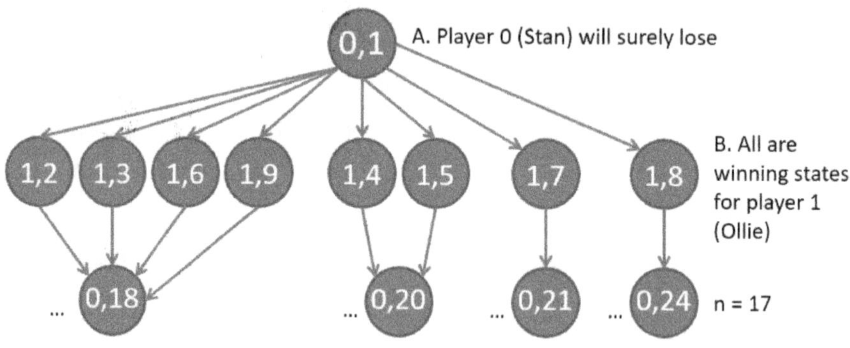

Figure 5.6: Partial Decision Tree for an instance of 'A multiplication game'

Game Theory in Programming Contests

Game Theory problems that are discussed in this section are the basic ones that can still be solved with basic problem solving paradigms/algorithms discussed earlier. However, there are more challenging forms of Game Theory-related problems that is discussed later in Section 9.16.

Programming Exercises related to Game Theory (Basic):

1. Entry Level: *Kattis - euclidsgame* * (minimax; backtracking; also available at UVa 10368 - Euclid's Game)
2. **UVa 10111 - Find the Winning ... *** (Tic-Tac-Toe; minimax; backtracking)
3. **UVa 10536 - Game of Euler *** (model the 4×4 board and 48 possible pins as bitmask; then this is a simple two player game)
4. **UVa 11489 - Integer Game *** (game theory; reducible to simple math)
5. *Kattis - bachetsgame* * (2 players game; Dynamic Programming; also available at UVa 10404 - Bachet's Game)
6. *Kattis - blockgame2* * (observe the pattern; 2 winnable cases if $N == M$ and $N\%M == 0$; only 1 move if $M < N < 2M$; we can always win if $N > 2M$)
7. *Kattis - linije* * (game theory; check conditions on how Mirko can win and when Slavko can win; involves MCBM)

   Extra UVa: *10578*, *12293*, *12469*.

   Extra Kattis: *amultiplicationgame*, *cuttingbrownies*, *irrationaldivision*, *ivana*, *joylessgame*, *peggamefortwo*.

5.8 Matrix Power

5.8.1 Some Definitions and Sample Usages

In this section, we discuss a special case of matrix[31]: the *square matrix*, a matrix with the same number of rows and columns, i.e., it has size $n \times n$. To be precise, we discuss a special operation of square matrix: the *powers of a square matrix*. Mathematically, $M^0 = I$ and $M^p = \prod_{i=1}^{p} M$. I is the *Identity* matrix[32] and p is the given power of square matrix M. If we can do this operation in $O(n^3 \log p)$—which is the main topic of this subsection, we can solve some more interesting problems in programming contests, e.g.,:

- Compute a *single*[33] Fibonacci number $fib(p)$ in $O(\log p)$ time instead of $O(p)$. If $p = 2^{30}$, $O(p)$ solution will get TLE[34] but $O(\log_2(p))$ solution just needs 30 steps. This is achievable by using the following equality[35]:

$$\begin{bmatrix} 1 & 1 \\ 1 & 0 \end{bmatrix}^p = \begin{bmatrix} fib(p+1) & \underline{\mathbf{fib(p)}} \\ \underline{\mathbf{fib(p)}} & fib(p-1) \end{bmatrix}$$

  For example, to compute $fib(11)$, we simply multiply the Fibonacci matrix 11 times, i.e., raise it to the power of 11. The answer is in the secondary diagonal of the matrix.

$$\begin{bmatrix} 1 & 1 \\ 1 & 0 \end{bmatrix}^{11} = \begin{bmatrix} 144 & \underline{\mathbf{89}} \\ \underline{\mathbf{89}} & 55 \end{bmatrix} = \begin{bmatrix} fib(12) & \underline{\mathbf{fib(11)}} \\ \underline{\mathbf{fib(11)}} & fib(10) \end{bmatrix}$$

- Compute the number of paths of length L of a graph stored in an Adjacency Matrix—which is a square matrix—in $O(n^3 \log L)$. Example: See the small graph of size $n = 4$ stored in an Adjacency Matrix M below. The various paths from vertex 0 to vertex 1 with different lengths are shown in entry $M[0][1]$ after M is raised to power L.

```
The graph:   0->1 with length 1: 0->1 (only 1 path)
             0->1 with length 2: impossible
 0--1        0->1 with length 3: 0->1->2->1 (and 0->1->0->1)
    |        0->1 with length 4: impossible
    2--3     0->1 with length 5: 0->1->2->3->2->1 (and 4 others)
```

$$M = \begin{bmatrix} 0 & 1 & 0 & 0 \\ 1 & 0 & 1 & 0 \\ 0 & 1 & 0 & 1 \\ 0 & 0 & 1 & 0 \end{bmatrix} M^2 = \begin{bmatrix} 1 & 0 & 1 & 0 \\ 0 & 2 & 0 & 1 \\ 1 & 0 & 2 & 0 \\ 0 & 1 & 0 & 1 \end{bmatrix} M^3 = \begin{bmatrix} 0 & 2 & 0 & 1 \\ 2 & 0 & 3 & 0 \\ 0 & 3 & 0 & 2 \\ 1 & 0 & 2 & 0 \end{bmatrix} M^5 = \begin{bmatrix} 0 & 5 & 0 & 3 \\ 5 & 0 & 8 & 0 \\ 0 & 8 & 0 & 5 \\ 3 & 0 & 5 & 0 \end{bmatrix}$$

- Speed-up *some* DP problems as shown later in this section.

[31]A matrix is a rectangular (2D) array of numbers. Matrix of size $m \times n$ has m rows and n columns. The elements of the matrix is usually denoted by the matrix name with two subscripts.

[32]Identity matrix is a square matrix with all zeroes except that cells along the main diagonal are all ones.

[33]If we need $fib(n)$ **for all** $n \in$ `[0..n]`, use $O(n)$ DP solution mentioned in Section 5.4.1 instead.

[34]If you encounter input size of 'gigantic' value in programming contest problems, like 1B, the problem author is *usually* looking for a logarithmic solution. Notice that $\log_2(1B) \approx \log_2(2^{30})$ is still just 30!

[35]The derivation of this Fibonacci matrix is shown in Section 5.8.4.

5.8.2 Efficient Modular Power (Exponentiation)

For this subsection, let's assume that we are using C++/OCaml that does not have built-in library function *yet* for raising an integer[36] b to a certain integer power p (mod m) efficiently. This modular exponentiation function `modPow(b, p, m)` gets more important in modern programming contests because the value of b^p can easily go beyond the limit of 64-bit integer data type and using Big Integer technique is slow (review Book 1).

For the discussion below, let's use UVa 01230 (LA 4104) - MODEX that simply asks us to compute $x^y (\text{mod } n)$. Now, if we do modular exponentiation 'by definition' as shown below, we will have an inefficient $O(p)$ solution, especially if p is large.

```
int mod(int a, int m) { return ((a%m)+m) % m; }  // ensure positive answer

int slow_modPow(int b, int p, int m) {           // assume 0 <= b < m
  int ans = 1;
  for (int i = 0; i < p; ++i)                    // this is O(p)
    ans = mod(ans*b, m);                         // ans always in [0..m-1]
  return ans;
}
```

There is a better solution that uses Divide & Conquer principle. We can express $b^p \% m$ as:

$b^0 = 1$ (base case).
$b^p = (b^{p/2} \times b^{p/2}) \% m$ if p is even.
$b^p = (b^{p-1} \times b) \% m$ if p is odd.
As this approach keeps halving the value of p by two, it runs in $O(\log p)$.

Let's assume that m is (very) large and $0 \le b < m$.
If we compute by definition: $2^9 = 2 \times 2 \times 2 \times 2 \times 2 \times 2 \times 2 \times 2 \times 2 \approx O(p)$ multiplications.
But with Divide & Conquer: $2^9 = 2^8 \times 2 = (2^4)^2 \times 2 = ((2^2)^2)^2 \times 2 \approx O(\log p)$ multiplications.

A typical recursive implementation of this efficient Divide & Conquer modular exponentiation that solves UVa 01230 (LA 4104) is shown below (runtime: 0.000s):

```
int modPow(int b, int p, int m) {                // assume 0 <= b < m
  if (p == 0) return 1;
  int ans = modPow(b, p/2, m);                   // this is O(log p)
  ans = mod(ans*ans, m);                         // double it first
  if (p&1) ans = mod(ans*b, m);                  // *b if p is odd
  return ans;                                    // ans always in [0..m-1]
}

int main() {
  ios::sync_with_stdio(false); cin.tie(NULL);
  int c; cin >> c;
  while (c--) {
    int x, y, n; cin >> x >> y >> n;
    cout << modPow(x, y, n) << "\n";
  }
  return 0;
}
```

[36]Technically, an integer is a 1×1 square matrix.

Java and Python Versions

Fortunately, Java and Python have built-in library functions to compute modular exponentiation efficiently in $O(\log p)$ time. The Java code uses function `modPow(BigInteger exponent, BigInteger m)` of Java BigInteger class to compute ($this^{exponent}$ mod m) (however, the runtime: 0.080s is slower than the manual C++/Python versions).

```
class Main {                                          // UVa 01230 (LA 4104)
  public static void main(String[] args) {
    Scanner sc = new Scanner(System.in);
    int c = sc.nextInt();
    while (c-- > 0) {
      BigInteger x, y, n;
      x = BigInteger.valueOf(sc.nextInt());           // valueOf converts
      y = BigInteger.valueOf(sc.nextInt());           // simple integer
      n = BigInteger.valueOf(sc.nextInt());           // into BigInteger
      System.out.println(x.modPow(y, n));             // it's in the library!
    }
  }
}
```

Next, the Python code uses function `pow(x, y[, z])` to compute (x^y mod z). The resulting code is even shorter and fast (runtime: 0.000s).

```
c = int(input())
while c > 0:
    c -= 1
    [x, y, n] = map(int, input().split())             # Big Integer by default
    print(pow(x, y, n))                               # it's in the library!
```

Source code: `ch5/UVa01230.cpp|java|py`

5.8.3 Efficient Matrix Modular Power (Exponentiation)

We can use the same $O(\log p)$ efficient exponentiation technique shown above to perform square matrix exponentiation (matrix power) in $O(n^3 \log p)$, because each matrix multiplication[37] is $O(n^3)$. The *iterative* implementation (for comparison with the recursive implementation shown earlier) is shown below:

```
ll MOD;

const int MAX_N = 2;                                  // 2x2 for Fib matrix

struct Matrix { ll mat[MAX_N][MAX_N]; };              // we return a 2D array

ll mod(ll a, ll m) { return ((a%m)+m) % m; }          // ensure positive answer
```

[37]There exists a faster but more complex algorithm for matrix multiplication: The $O(n^{2.8074})$ Strassen's algorithm. Usually we do not use this algorithm for programming contests. Multiplying two Fibonacci matrices shown in this section only requires $2^3 = 8$ multiplications as $n = 2$. This can be treated as $O(1)$. Thus, we can compute $fib(p)$ in $O(\log p)$.

```
Matrix matMul(Matrix a, Matrix b) {                    // normally O(n^3)
  Matrix ans;                                          // but O(1) as n = 2
  for (int i = 0; i < MAX_N; ++i)
    for (int j = 0; j < MAX_N; ++j)
      ans.mat[i][j] = 0;
  for (int i = 0; i < MAX_N; ++i)
    for (int k = 0; k < MAX_N; ++k) {
      if (a.mat[i][k] == 0) continue;                  // optimization
      for (int j = 0; j < MAX_N; ++j) {
        ans.mat[i][j] += mod(a.mat[i][k], MOD) * mod(b.mat[k][j], MOD);
        ans.mat[i][j] = mod(ans.mat[i][j], MOD); // modular arithmetic
      }
    }
  return ans;
}

Matrix matPow(Matrix base, int p) {                    // normally O(n^3 log p)
  Matrix ans;                                          // but O(log p) as n = 2
  for (int i = 0; i < MAX_N; ++i)
    for (int j = 0; j < MAX_N; ++j)
      ans.mat[i][j] = (i == j);                        // prepare identity matrix
  while (p) {                                          // iterative D&C version
    if (p&1)                                           // check if p is odd
      ans = matMul(ans, base);                         // update ans
    base = matMul(base, base);                         // square the base
    p >>= 1;                                           // divide p by 2
  }
  return ans;
}
```

5.8.4 DP Speed-up with Matrix Power

In this section, we discuss how to derive the required square matrices for three DP problems and show that raising these three square matrices to the required powers can speed-up the computation of the original DP problems.

The Derivation of the 2×2 Fibonacci Matrix

We know that $fib(0) = 0$, $fib(1) = 1$, and for $n \geq 2$, we have $fib(n) = fib(n-1) + fib(n-2)$. In Section 5.4.1, we have shown that we can compute $fib(n)$ in $O(n)$ by using Dynamic Programming by computing $fib(n)$ *one by one* progressively from $[2..n]$. However, these DP transitions *can be made faster* by re-writing the Fibonacci recurrence into matrix form as shown below:

First, we write two versions of Fibonacci recurrence as there are two terms in the recurrence:

$$fib(n+1) + fib(n) = fib(n+2)$$
$$fib(n) + fib(n-1) = fib(n+1)$$

Then, we re-write the recurrence into matrix form:

$$\begin{bmatrix} a & b \\ c & d \end{bmatrix} \times \begin{bmatrix} fib(n+1) \\ fib(n) \end{bmatrix} = \begin{bmatrix} fib(n+2) \\ fib(n+1) \end{bmatrix}$$

Now we have $a \times fib(n+1) + b \times fib(n) = fib(n+2)$ and $c \times fib(n+1) + d \times fib(n) = fib(n+1)$. Notice that by writing the DP recurrence as shown above, we now have a 2×2 *square matrix*. The appropriate values for a, b, c, and d must be 1, 1, 1, 0 and this is the 2×2 Fibonacci matrix shown earlier in Section 5.8.1. One matrix multiplication advances DP computation of Fibonacci number one step forward. If we multiply this 2×2 Fibonacci matrix p times, we advance DP computation of Fibonacci number p steps forward. We now have:

$$\underbrace{\begin{bmatrix} 1 & 1 \\ 1 & 0 \end{bmatrix} \times \begin{bmatrix} 1 & 1 \\ 1 & 0 \end{bmatrix} \times \ldots \times \begin{bmatrix} 1 & 1 \\ 1 & 0 \end{bmatrix}}_{p} \times \begin{bmatrix} fib(n+1) \\ fib(n) \end{bmatrix} = \begin{bmatrix} fib(n+1+p) \\ fib(n+p) \end{bmatrix}$$

For example, if we set $n = 0$ and $p = 11$, and then use $O(\log p)$ matrix power instead of actually multiplying the matrix p times, we have the following calculations:

$$\begin{bmatrix} 1 & 1 \\ 1 & 0 \end{bmatrix}^{11} \times \begin{bmatrix} fib(1) \\ fib(0) \end{bmatrix} = \begin{bmatrix} 144 & 89 \\ 89 & 55 \end{bmatrix} \times \begin{bmatrix} 1 \\ 0 \end{bmatrix} = \begin{bmatrix} 144 \\ \underline{\mathbf{89}} \end{bmatrix} = \begin{bmatrix} fib(12) \\ \underline{\mathbf{fib(11)}} \end{bmatrix}$$

This Fibonacci matrix can also be written as shown earlier in Section 5.8.1, i.e.,

$$\begin{bmatrix} 1 & 1 \\ 1 & 0 \end{bmatrix}^{p} = \begin{bmatrix} fib(p+1) & fib(p) \\ fib(p) & fib(p-1) \end{bmatrix}$$

The given sample source code implements this $O(\log p)$ algorithm to solve UVa 10229 - Modular Fibonacci that simply asks for $Fib(n)\%2^m$.

Source code: `ch5/UVa10229.cpp|java|py|ml`

UVa 10655 - Contemplation, Algebra

Next, we discuss another example on how to derive the required square matrix for another DP problem: UVa 10655 - Contemplation, Algebra. Abridged problem description: Given the value of $p = a + b$, $q = a \times b$, and n, find the value of $a^n + b^n$.

First, we tinker with the formula so that we can use $p = a + b$ and $q = a \times b$:

$$a^n + b^n = (a+b) \times (a^{n-1} + b^{n-1}) - (a \times b) \times (a^{n-2} + b^{n-2})$$

Next, we set $X_n = a^n + b^n$ to have $X_n = p \times X_{n-1} - q \times X_{n-2}$.
Then, we write this recurrence twice in the following form:

$$p \times X_{n+1} - q \times X_n = X_{n+2}$$
$$p \times X_n - q \times X_{n-1} = X_{n+1}$$

Then, we re-write the recurrence into matrix form:

$$\begin{bmatrix} p & -q \\ 1 & 0 \end{bmatrix} \times \begin{bmatrix} X_{n+1} \\ X_n \end{bmatrix} = \begin{bmatrix} X_{n+2} \\ X_{n+1} \end{bmatrix}$$

If we raise the 2×2 square matrix to the power of n (in $O(\log n)$ time) and then multiply the resulting square matrix with $X_1 = a^1 + b^1 = a + b = p$ and $X_0 = a^0 + b^0 = 1 + 1 = 2$, we have X_{n+1} and X_n. The required answer is X_n. This is faster than $O(n)$ standard DP computation for the same recurrence.

$$\begin{bmatrix} p & -q \\ 1 & 0 \end{bmatrix}^{n} \times \begin{bmatrix} X_1 \\ X_0 \end{bmatrix} = \begin{bmatrix} X_{n+1} \\ X_n \end{bmatrix}$$

Kattis - linearrecurrence

We close this section by discussing yet another example on how to derive the required square matrix for another DP problem: Kattis - linearrecurrence. This is the more general form compared to the previous two examples. Abridged problem description: Given a linear recurrence with degree N as $N+1$ integers $a_0, a_1, \ldots, a_N$ that describes linear recurrence $x_t = a_0 + \sum_{i=1}^{N} a_i \times x_{t-i}$ as well as N integers $x_0, x_1, \ldots, x_{N-1}$ giving the initial values, compute the value of $x_T \% M$. Constraints: $0 \leq T \leq 10^{18}; 1 \leq M \leq 10^9$.

Notice that T is very big and thus we are expecting a $O(\log T)$ solution. A general degree N linear recurrence has $N+1$ terms, so M will be an $(N+1) \times (N+1)$ square matrix. We can write $N+1$ versions of consecutive x_t(s) and rewrite it into matrix form.

Example 1 (Fibonacci, 1st sample test case): $N = 2$, $a = \{0, 1, 1\}$, and $x = \{0, 1\}$, we have $x_t = 0 + 1 \times x_{t-1} + 1 \times x_{t-2}$ that can be written in matrix form as:

$$\begin{bmatrix} 1 & 0 & 0 \\ 0 & 1 & 1 \\ 0 & 1 & 0 \end{bmatrix} \times \begin{bmatrix} 1 \\ X_i \\ X_{i-1} \end{bmatrix} = \begin{bmatrix} a_0 = 1 \\ X_{i+1} \text{ (what we want)} \\ X_i \end{bmatrix}$$

Example 2 (2nd sample test case): $N = 2$, $a = \{5, 7, 9\}$, and $x = \{36\,713, 5\,637\,282\}$, we have $x_t = 5 + 7 \times x_{t-1} + 9 \times x_{t-2}$ that can be written in matrix form as:

$$\begin{bmatrix} 1 & 0 & 0 \\ 5 & 7 & 9 \\ 0 & 1 & 0 \end{bmatrix} \times \begin{bmatrix} 1 \\ X_1 = 5\,637\,282 \\ X_0 = 36\,713 \end{bmatrix} = \begin{bmatrix} a_0 = 1 \\ X_2 \text{ (what we want)} \\ X_1 = 5\,637\,282 \end{bmatrix}$$

Note: the first row and column in M are needed as there is a_0 in the given linear recurrence.

Exercise 5.8.4.1: Derive Tribonacci matrix using the format of Kattis - linearrecurrence: $N = 3$, $a = \{0, 1, 1, 1\}$, and $x = \{0, 0, 1\}$. The first 9 terms are $\{0, 0, 1, 1, 2, 4, 7, 13, 24, \ldots\}$.

Exercise 5.8.4.2*: Show how to compute $C(n, k)$ for a very large n but small k (e.g., $0 \leq n \leq 10^{18}; 1 \leq k \leq 1000$) in $O(k^2 \log n)$ time using Matrix Power instead of $O(n \times k)$ or in $O(1)$ after $O(n)$ pre-processing as shown in Section 5.4.

Programming Exercises related to Matrix Power:

1. Entry Level: **UVa 10229 - Modular Fibonacci** * (Fibonacci; modPow)
2. **UVa 10655 - Contemplation, Algebra** * (derive the square matrix)
3. **UVa 11582 - Colossal Fibonacci ...** * (Pisano period: The sequence $f(i)\%n$ is periodic; use modPow)
4. **UVa 12796 - Teletransport** * (count the number of paths of length L in an undirected graph where L can be up to 2^{30})
5. *Kattis - checkingforcorrectness* * (Java Big Integer; one subtask uses `modPow`)
6. *Kattis - porpoises* * (Fibonacci; matrix power; modulo)
7. *Kattis - squawk* * (count the number of paths of length L in an undirected graph after t steps that are reachable from source s)

Extra UVa: *00374, 01230, 10518, 10870, 11029, 11486, 12470.*

Extra Kattis: *linearrecurrence, powers.*

5.9 Solution to Non-Starred Exercises

Exercise 5.2.1*: Ability to spot patterns in data can be very crucial in Competitive Programming. These are many *possible* interpretations for sequence no 1 and 3 (we show the most probable ones). Sequence no 2 and 4 are more interesting. There are a few plausible interpretations and we challenge you to suggest at least one.

1. 1, 2, 4, 8, 16, ...
   This is probably a sequence of powers of two.
   So the next three terms are 32, 64, 12.

2*. 1, 2, 4, 8, 16, 31, ...
   Hint: the last shown term is not 32; maybe *not* a sequence of powers of two.

3. 2, 3, 5, 7, 11, 13, ...
   This is probably a sequence of the first few primes.
   So the next three terms are 17, 19, 23.

4*. 2, 3, 5, 7, 11, 13, 19, ...
   Hint: the last shown term is not 17, maybe *not* a sequence of the first few primes.

Exercise 5.3.4.1:

```
int numDiffPF(ll N) {
  int ans = 0;
  for (int i = 0; i < p.size() && p[i]*p[i] <= N; ++i) {
    if (N%p[i] == 0) ++ans;                     // count this prime factor
    while (N%p[i] == 0) N /= p[i];              // only once
  }
  if (N != 1) ++ans;
  return ans;
}
```

```
ll sumPF(ll N) {
  ll ans = 0;
  for (int i = 0; i < p.size() && p[i]*p[i] <= N; ++i)
    while (N%p[i] == 0) { N /= p[i]; ans += p[i]; }
  if (N != 1) ans += N;
  return ans;
}
```

Exercise 5.3.4.2: When N is a prime, then `numPF(N) = 1`, `numDiffPF(N) = 1`, `sumPF(N) = N`, `numDiv(N) = 2`, `sumDiv(N) = N+1`, and `EulerPhi(N) = N-1`.

Exercise 5.3.6.1: Multiplying $a \times b$ first before dividing the result by $gcd(a, b)$ has a higher chance of overflow in programming contest than $a/gcd(a, b) \times b$. In the example given, we have $a = 2\,000\,000\,000$ and $b = 8$. The LCM is $2\,000\,000\,000$—which should fit in 32-bit signed integers—can only be properly computed with $a/gcd(a, b) \times b$.

Exercise 5.3.6.2: An implementation of iterative gcd:

```
int gcd(int a, int b) {
  while (b){
    a %= b;
    swap(a, b);
  }
  return a;
}
```

Exercise 5.3.8.1: GCD(A, B) can be obtained by taking the lower power of the common prime factors of A and B. LCM(A, B) can be obtained by taking the greater power of all the prime factors of A and B. So, GCD($2^6 \times 3^3 \times 97^1$, $2^5 \times 5^2 \times 11^2$) $= 2^5 = 32$ and LCM($2^6 \times 3^3 \times 97^1$, $2^5 \times 5^2 \times 11^2$) $= 2^6 \times 3^3 \times 5^2 \times 11^2 \times 97^1 = 507\,038\,400$.

Exercise 5.3.8.2: We obviously cannot compute 200 000! using Big Integer technique in 1s and see how many trailing zeroes that it has. Instead, we have to notice that a trailing zero is produced every time a prime factor 2 is multiplied with a prime factor 5 of $n!$ and the number of prime factor 2 is always greater than or equal to the number of prime factor 5. Hence, it is sufficient to just compute Legendre's formula $v_5(n!)$ as the answer.

Exercise 5.4.1.1: Binet's closed-form formula for Fibonacci: $fib(n) = (\phi^n - (-\phi)^{-n})/\sqrt{5}$ should be correct for larger n. But since double precision data type is limited, we have discrepancies for larger n. This closed form formula is correct up to $fib(75)$ if implemented using typical double data type in a computer program. This is unfortunately too small to be useful in typical programming contest problems involving Fibonacci numbers.

Exercise 5.4.2.1: $C(n,2) = \frac{n!}{(n-2)! \times 2!} = \frac{n \times (n-1) \times (n-2)!}{(n-2)! \times 2} = \frac{n \times (n-1)}{2} = 0.5n^2 - 0.5n = O(n^2)$.

Exercise 5.4.2.2: The value of $n!\%p = 0$ when $n \geq p$ as $p|n!$ in that case. Then, the output of $C(n,k)\%p$ when $n \geq p$ will always be 0, i.e., $C(100000, 50000)\%997 = 0$. To address this 'always 0' issue (which is not about whether we use Extended Euclidean algorithm or Fermat's little theorem to compute the modular multiplicative inverse), we need to use Lucas' theorem that is discussed in Section 9.14.

Exercise 5.4.2.3: This alternative solution is commented inside `ch5/combinatorics.cpp`.

Exercise 5.4.4.1: $6 \times 6 \times 2 \times 2 \times 2 = 6^2 \times 2^3 = 36 \times 8 = 288$ different possible outcomes. Each (of the two) dice has 6 possible outcomes and each (of the three) coin has 2 possible outcomes. There is no difference whether we do this process one by one or in one go.

Exercise 5.4.4.2: 9×8 (if 7 is the first digit) $+ 2 \times 8 \times 8$ (if 7 is the second or third digit, recall that the first digit cannot be 0) $= 200$ different possible ways.

Exercise 5.4.4.3: $(62 + 62^2 + \ldots + 62^{10})\%1e9 + 7 = 894\,773\,311$ possible passwords with the given criteria.

Exercise 5.4.4.4: $\frac{6!}{(6-3)!} = 6 \times 5 \times 4 = 120$ 3-letters words.

Exercise 5.4.4.5: $\frac{5!}{3! \times 1! \times 1!} = \frac{120}{6} = 20$ because there are 3 'B's, 1 'O', and 1 'Y'.

Exercise 5.4.4.6: Let A be the set of integers in [1..1M] that are multiples of 5, then $|A| = 1M/5 = 200\,000$.
Let A be the set of integers in [1..1M] that are multiples of 7, then $|A| = 1M/7 = 142\,857$.
Let $A \bigcap B$ be the set of integers in [1..1M] that are multiples of both 5 and 7 (multiples of $5 \times 7 = 35$), then $|A| = 1M/35 = 28\,571$.
So, $|A \bigcup B| = 200\,000 + 142\,857 - 28\,571 = 314\,286$.

Exercise 5.4.4.7: The answers for few smallest $n = \{4, 5, 6, 7, 8, 9, 10, 11, 12, 13, \ldots\}$ are $\{1, 3, 7, 13, 22, 34, 50, 70, 95, 125\}$. You can generate these numbers using brute force solution first. Then find the pattern and use it. Notice that the 9 differences between these 10 numbers are $\{+2, +4, +6, +9, +12, +16, +20, +25, +30, \ldots\}$. The 8 differences of these 9 differences are $\{+2, +2, +3, +3, +4, +4, +5, +5, \ldots\}$, which can be exploited.

Exercise 5.5.1: Let's label the people with $p_1, p_2, \ldots, p_n$ and the hats with $h_1, h_2, \ldots, h_n$. Now consider the first person p_1. This person has n-1 choices of taking someone else's hat (h_i not h_1). Now consider the follow up action of the original owner of h_i, which is p_i. There are two possibilities for p_i:

- p_i does not take h_1, then this problem reduces to derangement problem with n-1 people and n-1 hats because each of the other n-1 people has 1 forbidden choice from among the remaining n-1 hats (p_i is forbidden to take h_1).
- p_i somehow takes h_1, then this problem reduces to derangement problem with n-2 people and n-2 hats.

Hence, $A_n = (n\text{-}1) \times (A_{n-1} + A_{n-2})$.

Exercise 5.5.2: We need to use Combinatorics. $C(7,5)/C(15,5) = \frac{7 \times 6}{15 \times 14} = \frac{42}{210} = 0.2$.

Exercise 5.6.2.1: Simply set $Z = 1$, $I = 1$, M as large as possible, e.g., $M = 10^8$, and $L = 0$. Then the sequence of iterated function values is $\{0, 1, 2, \ldots, M\text{-}2, M\text{-}1, 0, \ldots\}$.

Exercise 5.8.4.1: For Tribonacci with $N = 3$, $a = \{0, 1, 1, 1\}$ and $x = \{0, 0, 1\}$,
we have $x_t = 0 + 1 \times x_{t-1} + 1 \times x_{t-2} + 1 \times x_{t-3}$ that can be written in matrix form as:

$$\begin{bmatrix} 1 & 0 & 0 & 0 \\ 0 & 1 & 1 & 1 \\ 0 & 1 & 0 & 0 \\ 0 & 0 & 1 & 0 \end{bmatrix} \times \begin{bmatrix} 1 \\ X_i \\ X_{i-1} \\ X_{i-2} \end{bmatrix} = \begin{bmatrix} a_0 = 1 \\ X_{i+1} \\ X_i \\ X_{i-1} \end{bmatrix}$$

5.10 Chapter Notes

This chapter has grown significantly since the first edition of this book. However, even after we reach the fourth edition, we are aware that there are still many more mathematical problems and algorithms that have not been discussed in this chapter, e.g.,

- There are many more rare **combinatorics** problems and formulas,
- There are other theorems, hypotheses, and conjectures,
- (Computational) Geometry is also part of Mathematics, but since we have a special chapter for that, we reserve the discussions about geometry problems in Chapter 7.
- Later in Chapter 9, we discuss more rare mathematics algorithms/problems, e.g.,
  - Fast Fourier Transform for fast polynomial multiplication (Section 9.11),
  - Pollard's rho algorithm for fast integer factorization (Section 9.12),
  - Chinese Remainder Theorem to solve system of congruences (Section 9.13),
  - Lucas' Theorem to compute $C(n, k)\%p$ (Section 9.14),
  - Rare Formulas or Theorems (Section 9.15),
  - Sprague-Grundy Theorem in Combinatorial Game Theory (Section 9.16),
  - Gaussian Elimination for solving systems of linear equations (Section 9.17).

There are really *many* topics about mathematics. This is not surprising since various mathematical problems have been investigated by people since hundreds of years ago. Some of them are discussed in this chapter and in Chapter 7-9, many others are not, and yet only 1 or 2 will actually appear in a problem set. To do well in ICPC, it is a good idea to have at least *one strong mathematician* in your ICPC team in order to have those 1 or 2 mathematical problems solved. Mathematical prowess is also important for IOI contestants. Although the amount of problem-specific topics to be mastered is smaller, many IOI tasks require some form of 'mathematical insights'.

We end this chapter by listing some pointers that may be of interest: read number theory books, e.g., [33], investigate mathematical topics in `https://www.wolframalpha.com` or Wikipedia, and attempt programming exercises related to mathematical problems like the ones in `https://projecteuler.net` [14] and `https://brilliant.org` [5].

Statistics	1st	2nd	3rd	4th
Number of Pages	17	29	41	52 (+27%)
Written Exercises	-	19	30	21+10*=31 (+3%)
Programming Exercises	175	296	369	533 (+44%)

The breakdown of the number of programming exercises from each section is shown below:

Section	Title	Appearance	% in Chapter	% in Book
5.2	**Ad Hoc Mathematics ...**	212	≈ 40%	≈ 6.1%
5.3	**Number Theory**	147	≈ 28%	≈ 4.3%
5.4	Combinatorics	77	≈ 14%	≈ 2.2%
5.5	Probability Theory	43	≈ 8%	≈ 1.2%
5.6	Cycle-Finding	22	≈ 4%	≈ 0.6%
5.7	Game Theory (Basic)	16	≈ 3%	≈ 0.5%
5.8	Matrix Power	16	≈ 3%	≈ 0.5%
	Total	533		≈ 15.4%

Chapter 6

String Processing

The Human Genome has approximately 3.2 Giga base pairs
— **Human Genome Project**

6.1 Overview and Motivation

In this chapter, we present one more topic that appears in ICPC—although not as frequently[1] as graph and mathematics problems—string processing. String processing is common in the research field of *bioinformatics*. As the strings (e.g., DNA strings) that the researchers deal with are usually (very) long, efficient string-specific data structures and algorithms are necessary. Some of these problems are presented as contest problems in ICPCs. By mastering the content of this chapter, ICPC contestants will have a better chance at tackling those string processing problems.

String processing tasks also appear in IOI, but usually they do not require advanced string data structures or algorithms due to syllabus [15] restrictions. Additionally, the input and output format of IOI tasks are usually simple[2]. This eliminates the need to code tedious input parsing or output formatting commonly found in the ICPC problems. IOI tasks that require string processing are usually still solvable using basic problem solving paradigms (Complete Search, D&C, Greedy, or DP). It is sufficient for IOI contestants to skim through all sections in this chapter except Section 6.3 which is about string processing with DP. However, we believe that it may be advantageous for some IOI contestants to learn some of the more advanced materials outside of their syllabus ahead of time.

This chapter is structured as follows: it starts with a list of medium to hard/tedious Ad Hoc string problems solvable with just basic string processing skills (but harder than the ones discussed in Book 1). Solving many of them will definitely improve your programming skills, but we have to make a remark that recent contest problems in ICPC (and also IOI) usually do not ask for basic string processing solutions *except* for the 'giveaway' problem that most teams (contestants) should be able to solve. The more important sections are the string processing problems solvable with Dynamic Programming (DP) (Section 6.3), string matching problems (Section 6.4), an extensive discussion on string processing problems where we have to deal with reasonably **long** strings using **Trie**/Suffix **Trie**/**Tree**/**Array** (Section 6.5), an alternative string matching algorithm using hashing (Section 6.6), and finally a discussion of medium Ad Hoc string problems that uses various string techniques: Anagram and Palindrome (Section 6.7).

---

[1]One potential reason: String input is harder to parse correctly (due to issues like whitespaces, newlines, etc) and string output is harder to format correctly, making such string-based I/O less preferred over the more precise integer-based I/O.

[2]IOI 2010-2019 require contestants to implement functions instead of coding I/O routines.

6.2 Ad Hoc String (Harder)

Earlier in Book 1, we discussed Ad Hoc string processing problems. In this section, we list the harder forms that are left here instead of placed in Chapter 1.

- Cipher/Encode/Encrypt/Decode/Decrypt (Harder)
  This is the harder form of this big category.

- Input Parsing (Recursive)
  This is the harder form involving grammars that require recursive (descent) parsers.

- Regular Expression (C++ 11 onwards/Java/Python/OCaml)

  Some (but rare) string processing problems are solvable with one liner code that uses `regex_match` in `<regex>`; `replaceAll(String regex, String replacement)`, `matches(String regex)`, useful functions of Java `String/Pattern` class, Python `re`, or OCaml `Str` module. To be able to do this, one has to master the concept of **Regular Expression** (Regex). We will not discuss Regex in detail but we will show two usage examples:

  1. In UVa 00325 - Identifying Legal Pascal Real Constants, we are asked to decide if the given line of input is a legal Pascal Real constant. Suppose the line is stored in `String s`, then the following one-liner Java code is the required solution:

     ```
     s.matches("[-+]?\\d+(\\.\\d+([eE][-+]?\\d+)?|[eE][-+]?\\d+)")
     ```

  2. In UVa 00494 - Kindergarten Counting Game, we are asked to count how many words are there in a given line. Here, a word is defined as a consecutive sequence of letters (upper and/or lower case). Suppose the line is stored in `String s`, then the following one-liner Java code is the required solution:

     ```
     s.replaceAll("[^a-zA-Z]+", " ").trim().split(" ").length
     ```

- Output Formatting
  This is the harder form of this big category.

- String Comparison
  In this group of problems, the contestants are asked to compare strings with various criteria. This sub-category is similar to the string matching problems in Section 6.4, but these problems mostly use `strcmp`-related functions.

- Really Ad Hoc
  These are other Ad Hoc string related problems that cannot be classified into one of the other sub categories above.

Profile of Algorithm Inventor

Donald Ervin Knuth (born 1938) is a computer scientist and Professor Emeritus at Stanford University. He is the author of the popular Computer Science book: *"The Art of Computer Programming"*. Knuth has been called the 'father' of the analysis of algorithms. Knuth is also the creator of the TEX, the computer typesetting system used in this book.

Programming Exercises related to Ad Hoc String Processing (Harder):

a. Cipher/Encode/Encrypt/Decode/Decrypt, Harder
   1. Entry Level: *Kattis - itsasecret* * (playfair cipher; 2D array; quite tedious)
   2. **UVa 00213 - Message ... *** (LA 5152 - WorldFinals SanAntonio91)
   3. **UVa 00554 - Caesar Cypher *** (try all shifts; output formatting)
   4. **UVa 11385 - Da Vinci Code *** (string manipulation and Fibonacci)
   5. *Kattis - crackingthecode* * (one corner case involving the 25th to 26th character determination)
   6. *Kattis - playfair* * (follow the description; a bit tedious; also available at UVa 11697 - Playfair Cipher)
   7. *Kattis - textencryption* * (convert input alphabets to UPPERCASEs; loop)

   Extra UVa: *00179, 00306, 00385, 00468, 00726, 00741, 00850, 00856.*

   Extra Kattis: *goodmessages, grille, monumentmaker, kleptography, permutationencryption, progressivescramble, ummcode.*

b. Input Parsing (Recursive)
   1. Entry Level: *Kattis - polish* * (recursive parser)
   2. **UVa 10854 - Number of Paths *** (recursive parsing plus counting)
   3. **UVa 11070 - The Good Old Times *** (recursive grammar evaluation)
   4. **UVa 11291 - Smeech *** (recursive grammar check)
   5. *Kattis - calculator* * (recursive parser and evaluator)
   6. *Kattis - otpor* * (parallel vs series evaluation; write a recursive parser; or use linear pass with stack)
   7. *Kattis - subexpression* * (recursive parsing; use DP; similar to `https://visualgo.net/en/recursion` tree versus DAG)

   Extra UVa: *00134, 00171, 00172, 00384, 00464, 00533, 00586, 00620, 00622, 00743.*

   Extra Kattis: *selectgroup.*

c. Regular Expression[3]
   1. Entry Level: **UVa 00494 - Kindergarten ... *** (trivial with regex)
   2. **UVa 00325 - Identifying Legal ... *** (trivial with regex)
   3. **UVa 00576 - Haiku Review *** (solvable with regex)
   4. **UVa 10058 - Jimmi's Riddles *** (solvable with regex)
   5. *Kattis - apaxiaaans* * (solvable with regex)
   6. *Kattis - hidden* * (just 1D array manipulation; we can also use regex)
   7. *Kattis - lindenmayorsystem* * (DAT; map char to string; simulation; max answer $\leq 30 \times 5^5$; we can also use regex)

[3]There are a few other string processing problems that are solvable with regex too. However, since almost every string processing problems that can be solved with regex can also be solved with standard ways, it is not crucial to use regex in competitive programming.

d. Output Formatting, Harder

1. Entry Level: *Kattis - imagedecoding* * (simple Run-Length Encoding)
2. **UVa 00918 - ASCII Mandelbrot *** (tedious; follow the steps)
3. **UVa 11403 - Binary Multiplication *** (similar with UVa 00338; tedious)
4. **UVa 12155 - ASCII Diamondi *** (LA 4403 - KualaLumpur08; use proper index manipulation)
5. *Kattis - asciifigurerotation* * (rotate the input 90 degrees clockwise; remove trailing whitespaces; tedious)
6. *Kattis - juryjeopardy* * (tedious problem)
7. *Kattis - nizovi* * (formatting with indentation; not that trivial but sample input/output helps)

Extra UVa: *00159, 00330, 00338, 00373, 00426, 00570, 00645, 00848, 00890, 01219, 10333, 10562, 10761, 10800, 10875.*

Extra Kattis: *mathworksheet, pathtracing, rot, wordsfornumbers.*

e. String Comparison

1. Entry Level: **UVa 11734 - Big Number of ...** * (custom comparison)
2. **UVa 00644 - Immediate Decodability *** (use brute force)
3. **UVa 11048 - Automatic Correction ... *** (flexible string comparison with respect to a dictionary)
4. **UVa 11056 - Formula 1 *** (sorting; case-insensitive string comparison)
5. *Kattis - phonelist* * (sort the numbers; see if num i is a prefix of num $i + 1$)
6. *Kattis - rhyming* * (compare suffix of a common word with the list of other given words)
7. *Kattis - smartphone* * (compare prefix so far with the target string and the 3 suggestions; output 1 of 4 options with shortest number of keypresses)

Extra UVa: *00409, 00671, 00912, 11233, 11713.*

Extra Kattis: *aaah, detaileddifferences, softpasswords.*

f. Really Ad Hoc

1. Entry Level: *Kattis - raggedright* * (just simulate the requirement)
2. **UVa 10393 - The One-Handed Typist *** (follow problem description)
3. **UVa 11483 - Code Creator *** (straightforward; use 'escape character')
4. **UVa 12916 - Perfect Cyclic String *** (factorize n; string period; also see UVa 11452)
5. *Kattis - irepeatmyself* * (string period; complete search)
6. *Kattis - periodicstrings* * (brute force; skip non divisor)
7. *Kattis - zipfslaw* * (sort the words to simplify this problem; also available at UVa 10126 - Zipf's Law)

Extra UVa: *00263, 00892, 00943, 01215, 10045, 10115, 10197, 10361, 10391, 10508, 10679, 11452, 11839, 11962, 12243, 12414.*

Extra Kattis: *apaxianparent, help2, kolone, nimionese, orderlyclass, quickestimate, rotatecut, textureanalysis, thore, tolower.*

6.3 String Processing with DP

In this section, we discuss several string processing problems that are solvable with DP technique discussed in Book 1. We discuss two *classical* problems: String Alignment and Longest Common Subsequence that should be known by all competitive programmers (quite rare nowadays) and one *non classical* technique: Digit DP (more popular nowadays). Additionally, we have added a collection of some known twists of these problems.

Note that for DP problems on string, we usually manipulate the *integer indices* of the strings and not the actual strings (or substrings) themselves. Passing substrings as parameters of recursive functions is strongly discouraged as it is very slow and hard to memoize.

6.3.1 String Alignment (Edit Distance)

The String Alignment (or Edit Distance[4]) problem is defined as follows: Align[5] two strings `A` with `B` with the maximum alignment score (or minimum number of edit operations):

After aligning `A` with `B`, there are a few possibilities between character `A[i]` and `B[i]`:
1. Character `A[i]` and `B[i]` **match** and we do nothing (assume this worth '+2' score),
2. Character `A[i]` and `B[i]` **mismatch** and we replace `A[i]` with `B[i]` (assume '-1' score),
3. We insert a space in `A[i]` (also '-1' score),
4. We delete a letter from `A[i]` (also '-1' score).

For example: (note that we use a special symbol '_' to denote a space)

```
A = 'ACAATCC' -> 'A_CAATCC'
B = 'AGCATGC' -> 'AGCATGC_'                      // A non optimal alignment
                  2-22--2-                       // Score = 4*2 + 4*-1 = 4
```

A brute force solution that tries all possible alignments will get TLE even for medium-length strings `A` and/or `B`. The solution for this problem is the Needleman-Wunsch (bottom-up) DP algorithm [34]. Consider two strings `A[1..n]` and `B[1..m]`. We define $V(i, j)$ to be the score of the optimal alignment between prefix `A[1..i]` and `B[1..j]`, and $score(C1, C2)$ is a function that returns the score if character $C1$ is aligned with character $C2$.

Base cases:
$V(0,0) = 0$ // no score for matching two empty strings
$V(i,0) = i \times score(A[i], \_)$ // delete substring `A[1..i]` to make the alignment, $i > 0$
$V(0,j) = j \times score(\_, B[j])$ // insert substring `B[1..j]` to make the alignment, $j > 0$

Recurrences: For $i > 0$ and $j > 0$:
$V(i,j) = max(option1, option2, option3)$, where
$option1 = V(i-1, j-1) + score(A[i], B[j])$ // score of match or mismatch
$option2 = V(i-1, j) + score(A[i], \_)$ // delete A_i
$option3 = V(i, j-1) + score(\_, B[j])$ // insert B_j

In short, this DP algorithm concentrates on the three possibilities for the last pair of characters, which must be either a match/mismatch, a deletion, or an insertion. Although we do not know which one is the best, we can try all possibilities while avoiding the re-computation of overlapping subproblems (i.e., basically a DP technique).

[4]Another name for 'edit distance' is 'Levenshtein Distance'. One notable application of this algorithm is the spelling checker feature commonly found in popular text editors. If a user misspells a word, like 'probelm', then a clever text editor that realizes that this word has a very close edit distance to the correct word 'problem' can do the correction automatically.

[5]Aligning is a process of inserting spaces to strings A or B such that they have the same number of characters. You can view 'inserting spaces to B' as 'deleting the corresponding aligned characters of A'.

```
A = 'xxx...xx'      A = 'xxx...xx'      A = 'xxx...x_'
           |                   |                   |
B = 'yyy...yy'      B = 'yyy...y_'      B = 'yyy...yy'
match/mismatch      delete              insert
```

	_	A	G	C	A	T	G	C
_	0	-1	-2	-3	-4	-5	-6	-7
A	-1							
C	-2		Base Cases					
A	-3							
A	-4							
T	-5							
C	-6							
C	-7							

	_	A	G	C	A	T	G	C
_	0	-1	-2	-3	-4	-5	-6	-7
A	-1	2	1	0	-1	-2	-3	-4
C	-2	1	1	3				
A	-3							
A	-4							
T	-5							
C	-6							
C	-7							

	_	A	G	C	A	T	G	C
_	0	-1	-2	-3	-4	-5	-6	-7
A	-1	2	1	0	-1	-2	-3	-4
C	-2	1	1	3	2	1	0	-1
A	-3	0	0	2	5	4	3	2
A	-4	-1	-1	1	4	4	3	2
T	-5	-2	-2	0	3	6	5	4
C	-6	-3	-3	0	2	5	5	7
C	-7	-4	-4	-1	1	4	4	7

Figure 6.1: Example: A = "ACAATCC" and B = "AGCATGC" (alignment score = 7)

With a simple scoring function where a match gets +2 points and mismatch, insert, and delete all get -1 point, the details of the string alignment score of A = "ACAATCC" and B = "AGCATGC" are shown in Figure 6.1. Initially, only the base cases are known. Then, we can fill the values row by row, left to right. To fill in $V(i,j)$ for $i,j > 0$, we need three other values: $V(i-1,j-1)$, $V(i-1,j)$, and $V(i,j-1)$—see the highlighted cell at Figure 6.1, middle, row 2, column 3. The best alignment score is stored at the bottom right cell (7).

To reconstruct the solution, we follow the back arrows (see the darker cells) from the bottom right cell. The solution for the given strings A and B is shown below. Diagonal arrow means a match or a mismatch (e.g., the last character ..C). Vertical arrow means a deletion (e.g., ..CAA.. to ..C_A..). Horizontal arrow means an insertion (e.g., A_C.. to AGC..).

```
A = 'A_CAAT[C]C'                          // Optimal alignment
B = 'AGC_AT[G]C'                          // Score = 5*2 + 3*-1 = 7
```

The space complexity of this (bottom-up) DP algorithm is $O(nm)$—the size of the DP table. We need to fill in all cells in the table in $O(1)$ per cell. Thus, the time complexity is $O(nm)$.

Source code: ch6/string_alignment.cpp|java|py|ml

Exercise 6.3.1.1: Why is the cost of a match +2 and the costs of replace, insert, delete are all -1? Are they magic numbers? Will +1 for match work? Can the costs for replace, insert, delete be different? Restudy the algorithm and discover the answer.

Exercise 6.3.1.2: The example source code given in this section only shows the optimal alignment *score*. Modify the given code to actually show the *actual alignment*!

Exercise 6.3.1.3: Show how to use the 'space saving technique' shown in Book 1 to improve this Needleman-Wunsch (bottom-up) DP algorithm! What will be the new space and time complexity of your solution? What is the drawback of using such a formulation?

Exercise 6.3.1.4: The String Alignment problem in this section is called the **global** alignment problem and runs in $O(nm)$. If the given contest problem is limited to d insertions or deletions only, we can have a faster algorithm. Find a simple tweak to the Needleman-Wunsch algorithm so that it performs at most d insertions or deletions and runs faster!

Exercise 6.3.1.5: Investigate the improvement of Needleman-Wunsch algorithm (**Smith-Waterman** algorithm [34]) to solve the **local** alignment problem!

6.3.2 Longest Common Subsequence

The Longest Common Subsequence (LCS) problem is defined as follows: Given two strings A and B, what is the longest common subsequence between them? For example, `A` = "`ACAATCC`" and `B` = "`AGCATGC`" have LCS of length 5, i.e., "`ACATC`".

This LCS problem can be reduced to the String Alignment problem presented earlier, so we can use the same DP algorithm. We set the score for mismatch as negative infinity (e.g., -1 Billion), score for insertion and deletion as 0, and the score for match as 1. This makes the Needleman-Wunsch algorithm for String Alignment never consider mismatches.

Exercise 6.3.2.1: What is the LCS of `A` = "`apple`" and `B` = "`people`"?

Exercise 6.3.2.2: The Hamming distance problem, i.e., finding the number of different characters between two equal-length strings can be easily done in $O(n)$. But it can also be reduced to a String Alignment problem. For theoretical interest, assign appropriate scores to match, mismatch, insert, and delete so that we can compute the answer using Needleman-Wunsch algorithm instead!

Exercise 6.3.2.3: The LCS problem can be solved in $O(n \log k)$ when all characters are distinct, e.g., if you are given two permutations of length n as in UVa 10635. k is the length of the answer. Solve this variant!

6.3.3 Non Classical String Processing with DP

In this section, we discuss Kattis - hillnumbers. A hill number is a positive integer, the digits of which possibly rise and then possibly fall, but never fall and then rise, like 12321, 12223, and 33322111. However, 1232321 is not a hill number. Verifying if a given number is a hill number or not is trivial. The hard part of the problem is this: Given a single integer n (assume it is already vetted as a hill number), count the number of positive hill numbers less than or equal to n. The main issue is $1 \leq n \leq 10^{18}$.

Initially, it may seem impossible to try all numbers $\leq n$ (TLE) or create a DP table up to 10^{18} cells (MLE). However, if we realize that there are only up to 19 digits in 10^{18}, then we can actually treat the numbers as strings of at most 20 digits and process the digits one by one. This is called 'Digit DP' in the competitive programming community and not considered as a classic solution *yet*. Basically, there are some big numbers and the problem is asking for some property of the number that is decomposable to its individual digits.

Realizing this, we can then quickly come up with the initial state `s: (pos)` and the initial transition of trying all possible next digit [0..9] one by one. However, we will quickly realize that we need to remember what was the previous used digit so we update our state to `s: (pos, prev_digit)`. Now we can check if `prev_digit` and `next_digit` is rising, plateau, or falling as per requirement. However, we will quickly realize that we also need to remember if we have reached the peak before and are now concentrating on the falling part, so we update our state to `s: (pos, prev_digit, is_rising)`. We start with `is_rising = true` and can only set `is_rising` at most once in a valid hill number.

Up to here, this state is almost complete but after some initial testing, we will then realize that we count the answer wrongly. It turns out that we still need one more parameter `is_lower` to have this complete state `s: (pos, prev_digit, is_rising, is_lower)` where `is_lower = false` initially and we set `is_lower = true` once we use `next_digit` that is strictly lower than the actual digit of n at that `pos`. With this state, we can correctly compute the required answer and the details are left behind for the readers.

Programming Exercises related to String Processing with DP:

a. Classic

1. Entry Level: **UVa 10405 - Longest Common ...** * (classic LCS problem)
2. **UVa 01192 - Searching Sequence ...** * (LA2460 - Singapore01; classic String Alignment DP problem with a bit of (unclear) output formatting)
3. **UVa 12747 - Back to Edit ...** * (similar to UVa 10635)
4. **UVa 13146 - Edid Tistance** * (classic Edit Distance problem)
5. *Kattis - inflagrantedelicto* * (k_p is always 2 (read the problem description); k_r is the LCS of the two permutations plus one; $O(n \log k)$ solution)
6. *Kattis - pandachess* * (LCS of 2 permutations → LIS; $O(n \log k)$ solution; also see UVa 10635)
7. *Kattis - princeandprincess* * (find LCS of two permutations; also available at UVa 10635 - Prince and Princess)

Extra UVa: *00164*, *00526*, *00531*, *01207*, *01244*, *10066*, *10100*, *10192*.

Extra Kattis: *declaration*, *ls*, *signals*.

b. Non Classic

1. Entry Level: *Kattis - stringfactoring* * (s: the min weight of substring [i..j]; also available at UVa 11022 - String Factoring)
2. **UVa 11258 - String Partition** * (dp(i) = int from substring [i..k] + dp(k))
3. **UVa 11361 - Investigating Div-Sum ...** * (counting paths in DAG; need insights for efficient implementation; $K > 90$ is useless; digit DP)
4. **UVa 11552 - Fewest Flops** * (dp(i, c) = minimum number of chunks after considering the first i segments ending with character c)
5. *Kattis - exam* * (s: (pos, correct_left); t: either your friend is wrong or your friend is right, process accordingly; easier solution exists)
6. *Kattis - heritage* * (s: (cur_pos); t: try all N words in dictionary; output final answer modulo a prime)
7. *Kattis - hillnumbers* * (digit DP; s: (pos, prev_digit, is_rising, is_lower); try digit by digit; see the discussion in this section)

Extra UVa: *11081*, *11084*, *12855*,

Extra Kattis: *chemistsvows*, *cudak*, *digitsum*, *haiku*, *zapis*.

Also see Section 6.7.2 for a classic string problem: Palindrome that has a few interesting variants that require DP solutions.

Profile of Algorithm Inventors

James Hiram Morris (born 1941) is a Professor of Computer Science. He is a co-discoverer of the Knuth-Morris-Pratt algorithm for string search.

Vaughan Ronald Pratt (born 1944) is a Professor Emeritus at Stanford University. He was one of the earliest pioneers in the field of computer science. He has made several contributions to foundational areas such as search algorithms, sorting algorithms, and primality testing. He is also a co-discoverer of the Knuth-Morris-Pratt algorithm for string-search.

6.4 String Matching

String *Matching* (a.k.a String *Searching*[6]) is a problem of finding the starting index (or indices) of a (sub)string (called *pattern* P) in a longer string (called *text* T). Example: Let's assume that we have T = "STEVEN EVENT". If P = "EVE", then the answers are index 2 and 7 (0-based indexing). If P = "EVENT", then the answer is index 7 only. If P = "EVENING", then there is no answer (no matching found and usually we return either -1 or NULL).

6.4.1 Library Solutions

For most *pure* String Matching problems on reasonably short strings, we can just use the string library in our programming language. It is **strstr** in C **<string.h>**, **find** in C++ **<string>**, **indexOf** in Java **String** class, **find** in Python string, and **search_forward** in OCaml **Str** module. Please revisit Chapter 1 for a mini task that discusses these string library solutions.

6.4.2 Knuth-Morris-Pratt (KMP) Algorithm

In Book 1, we have an exercise of finding all the occurrences of a substring P (of length m) in a (long) string T (of length n), if any. The code snippet, reproduced below with comments, is actually the *naïve* implementation of a String Matching algorithm.

```
void naiveMatching() {
  for (int i = 0; i < n-m; ++i) {                  // try all starting index
    bool found = true;
    for (int j = 0; (j < m) && found; ++j)
      if ((i+j >= n) || (P[j] != T[i+j]))          // if mismatch found
        found = false;                             // abort this, try i+1
    if (found)                                     // T[i..i+m-1] = P[0..m-1]
      printf("P is found at index %d in T\n", i);
  }
}
```

This naïve algorithm can run in $O(n)$ *on average* if applied to natural text like the paragraphs of this book, but it can run in $O(nm)$ with the worst case programming contest input like this: T = "AAAAAAAAAAB" ('A' ten times and then one 'B') and P = "AAAAB". The naïve algorithm will keep failing at the last character of pattern P and then try the next starting index which is just one further than the previous attempt. This is not efficient. Unfortunately, a good problem author will include such test cases in their secret test data.

In 1977, Knuth, Morris, and Pratt—thus the name of KMP—invented a better String Matching algorithm that makes use of the information gained by previous character comparisons, especially those that match. KMP algorithm *never* re-compares a character in T that has matched a character in P. However, it works similarly to the naïve algorithm if the *first* character of pattern P and the current character in T is a mismatch. In the following example[7], comparing P[j] and T[i] and from i = 0 to 13 with j = 0 (the first character of P) is no different from the naïve algorithm.

[6]We deal with this String Matching problem almost every time we read/edit text using a computer. How many times have you pressed the well-known 'CTRL + F' shortcut (standard Windows shortcut for the 'find feature') in typical word processing softwares, web browsers, etc?

[7]The sentence in string T below is just for illustration. It is not grammatically correct.

```
              1         2         3         4         5
    012345678901234567890123456789012345678901234567890
T = I DO NOT LIKE SEVENTY SEV BUT SEVENTY SEVENTY SEVEN
P = SEVENTY SEVEN
    0123456789012
              1
    ^ the first character of P mismatches with T[i] from index i = 0 to 13
    KMP has to shift the starting index i by +1, as with naive matching.
... at i = 14 and j = 0 ...
              1         2         3         4         5
    012345678901234567890123456789012345678901234567890
T = I DO NOT LIKE SEVENTY SEV BUT SEVENTY SEVENTY SEVEN
P =               SEVENTY SEVEN
                  0123456789012
                            1
                             ^ then mismatches at index i = 25 and j = 11
```

There are 11 matches from index i = 14 to 24, but one mismatch at i = 25 (j = 11). The naïve matching algorithm will inefficiently restart from index i = 15 but KMP can resume from i = 25. This is because the matched characters before the mismatch are "SEVENTY SEV". "SEV" (of length 3) appears as BOTH proper suffix and prefix of "SEVENTY SEV". This "SEV" is also called the **border** of "SEVENTY SEV". We can safely skip index i = 14 to 21: "SEVENTY " in "SEVENTY SEV" as it will not match again, but we cannot rule out the possibility that the next match starts from the second "SEV". So, KMP resets j back to 3, skipping 11-3 = 8 characters of "SEVENTY " (notice the trailing space), while i remains at index 25. This is the major difference between KMP and the naïve matching algorithm.

```
... at i = 25 and j = 3 (This makes KMP efficient) ...
              1         2         3         4         5
    012345678901234567890123456789012345678901234567890
T = I DO NOT LIKE SEVENTY SEV BUT SEVENTY SEVENTY SEVEN
P =                       SEVENTY SEVEN
                          0123456789012
                                    1
                             ^ immediate mismatches at index i = 25, j = 3
```

This time the prefix of P before mismatch is "SEV", but it does not have a border, so KMP resets j back to 0 (or in other words, restart matching pattern P from the front again).

```
... mismatches from i = 25 to i = 29... then matches from i = 30 to i = 42
              1         2         3         4         5
    012345678901234567890123456789012345678901234567890
T = I DO NOT LIKE SEVENTY SEV BUT SEVENTY SEVENTY SEVEN
P =                               SEVENTY SEVEN
                                  0123456789012
                                            1
```

This is a match, so P = 'SEVENTY SEVEN' is found at index i = 30. After this, KMP knows that "SEVENTY SEVEN" has "SEVEN" (of length 5) as border, so KMP resets j back to 5, effectively skipping 13-5 = 8 characters of "SEVENTY " (notice the trailing space), immediately resumes the search from i = 43, and gets another match. This is efficient.

```
... at i = 43 and j = 5, we have matches from i = 43 to i = 50 ...
So P = 'SEVENTY SEVEN' is found again at index i = 38.
              1         2         3         4         5
    012345678901234567890123456789012345678901234567890
T = I DO NOT LIKE SEVENTY SEV BUT SEVENTY SEVENTY SEVEN
P =                                       SEVENTY SEVEN
                                          0123456789012
                                                    1
```

To get such speed up, KMP has to preprocess the pattern string and get the 'reset table' `b` (back). If given pattern string P = "`SEVENTY SEVEN`", then table `b` will look like this:

```
                        1
     0 1 2 3 4 5 6 7 8 9 0 1 2 3
P =  S E V E N T Y   S E V E N
b = -1 0 0 0 0 0 0 0 0 1 2 3 4 5
```

This means, if mismatch happens in `j = 11` (see the example above), i.e., after finding a match for "`SEVENTY SEV`", then we know that we have to retry matching `P` from index `j = b[11] = 3`, i.e., KMP now assumes that it has matched only the first three characters of "SEVENTY SEV", which is "SEV", because the next match can start with that prefix "SEV". The relatively short implementation of the KMP algorithm with comments is shown below. This implementation has a time complexity of $O(n + m)$, or usually just $O(n)$ as $n > m$.

```
const int MAX_N = 200010;

char T[MAX_N], P[MAX_N];                            // T = text, P = pattern
int n, m;                                           // n = |T|, m = |P|
int b[MAX_N], n, m;                                 // b = back table

void kmpPreprocess() {                              // call this first
  int i = 0, j = -1; b[0] = -1;                     // starting values
  while (i < m) {                                   // pre-process P
    while ((j >= 0) && (P[i] != P[j])) j = b[j]; // different, reset j
    ++i; ++j;                                       // same, advance both
    b[i] = j;
  }
}

void kmpSearch() {                                  // similar as above
  int i = 0, j = 0;                                 // starting values
  while (i < n) {                                   // search through T
    while ((j >= 0) && (T[i] != P[j])) j = b[j]; // if different, reset j
    ++i; ++j;                                       // if same, advance both
    if (j == m) {                                   // a match is found
      printf("P is found at index %d in T\n", i-j);
      j = b[j];                                     // prepare j for the next
    }
  }
}
```

We provide our source code that compares the library solution, naïve matching, and one other string matching algorithm: Rabin-Karp that will be discussed in Section 6.6 with the KMP algorithm discussed in this section.

Source code: `ch6/string_matching.cpp|java|py|ml`

Exercise 6.4.1*: Run `kmpPreprocess()` on P = "ABABA" and show the reset table `b`!

Exercise 6.4.2*: Run `kmpSearch()` with P = "ABABA" and T = "ACABAABABDABABA". Explain how the KMP search looks like?

6.4.3 String Matching in a 2D Grid

The string matching problem can also be posed in 2D. Given a 2D grid/array of characters (instead of the well-known 1D array of characters), find the occurrence(s) of pattern P in the grid. Depending on the problem requirement, the search direction can be up to 4 or 8 cardinal directions, and either the pattern must be in a straight line or it can bend.

For the example from Kattis - boggle below, the pattern can bend. The solution for such 'bendable' string matching in a 2D grid is usually *recursive backtracking* (see Book 1). This is because unlike the 1D counterpart where we always go to the right, at every coordinate (row, col) of the 2D grid, we have *more than one choice* to explore. The time complexity is exponential thus this can only work for a small grid.

To speed up the backtracking process, usually we employ this simple pruning strategy: once the recursion depth exceeds the length of pattern P, we can immediately prune that recursive branch. This is also called as *depth-limited search* (see Section 9.20).

```
ACMA             // From Kattis - boggle
APcA             // We can go to 8 directions and the pattern can bend
toGI             // 'contest' is highlighted as lowercase in the grid
nest             // can you find 'CONTEST', 'ICPC', 'ACM', and 'GCPC'?
```

For the example from UVa 10010, the pattern can must be in a straight line. If the grid is small we can still use the easier to code recursive backtracking mentioned earlier. However if the grid is large, we probably need to do multiple $O(n+m)$ string matchings, one for each row/column/diagonal and their reverse directions.

```
abcdefghigg      // From UVa 10010 - Where's Waldorf?
hebkWaldork      // We can go to 8 directions, but must be straight
ftyawAldorm      // 'WALDORF' is highlighted as UPPERCASE in the grid
ftsimrLqsrc
byoarbeDeyv      // Can you find 'BAMBI' and 'BETTY'?
klcbqwikOmk
strebgadhRb      // Can you find 'DAGBERT' in this row?
yuiqlxcnbjF
```

Note that the topic of String Matching will be revisited two more times. In Section 6.5, we will discuss how to solve this problem using string-specific data structures. In Section 6.6, we will discuss how to solve this problem using a probabilistic algorithm.

Programming Exercises related to String Matching:

a. Standard

1. Entry Level: *Kattis - quiteaproblem* * (trivial string matching per line)
2. **UVa 00455 - Periodic String *** (find s in s+s; similar with UVa 10298)
3. **UVa 01449 - Dominating Patterns *** (LA 4670 - Hefei09; just use strstr, Suffix Array will get TLE as there are too many long strings to be processed)
4. **UVa 11837 - Musical Plagiarism *** (transform the input of X notes into $X - 1$ distances; then apply KMP)
5. *Kattis - geneticsearch* * (multiple string matchings)
6. *Kattis - powerstrings* * (find s in s+s[8]; similar with UVa 00455; also available at UVa 10298 - Power Strings)
7. *Kattis - scrollingsign* * (modified string matching; complete search; also available at UVa 11576 - Scrolling Sign)

   Extra UVa: *00886*, *11362*.

   Extra Kattis: *avion*, *cargame*, *deathknight*, *fiftyshades*, *hangman*, *ostgotska*, *redrover*, *simon*, *simonsays*.

b. In 2D Grid

1. Entry Level: **UVa 10010 - Where's Waldorf?** * (2D grid; backtracking)
2. **UVa 00422 - Word Search Wonder *** (2D grid; backtracking)
3. **UVa 00736 - Lost in Space *** (2D grid; a bit modified)
4. **UVa 11283 - Playing Boggle *** (2D grid; backtracking)
5. *Kattis - boggle* * (2D grid; backtracking)
6. *Kattis - kinarow* * (brute the top left point of each possible x or o row, then straight-line (horizontal, vertical) or two diagonals 2D string matching)
7. *Kattis - knightsearch* * (2D grid; backtracking or DP)

   Extra UVa: *00604*.

   Extra Kattis: *hiddenwords*.

Profile of Algorithm Inventors

Saul B. Needleman and **Christian D. Wunsch** jointly published the string alignment Dynamic Programming algorithm in 1970. Their DP algorithm is discussed in this book.

Temple F. Smith is a Professor in biomedical engineering who helped to develop the Smith-Waterman algorithm developed with Michael Waterman in 1981. The Smith-Waterman algorithm serves as the basis for multi sequence comparisons, identifying the segment with the maximum *local* sequence similarity for identifying similar DNA, RNA, and protein segments.

Michael S. Waterman is a Professor at the University of Southern California. Waterman is one of the founders and current leaders in the area of computational biology. His work has contributed to some of the most widely-used tools in the field. In particular, the Smith-Waterman algorithm is the basis for many sequence comparison programs.

[8]Transforming s into s+s is a classic technique in string processing to simplify 'wrap around' cases.

6.5 Suffix Trie/Tree/Array

Suffix Trie, Suffix Tree, and Suffix Array are efficient and related data structures for strings. We did not discuss this topic in Book 1 as these data structures are unique to strings.

6.5.1 Suffix Trie and Applications

The **suffix** i (or the i-th suffix) of a string is a 'special case' of substring that goes from the i-th character of the string up to the *last* character of the string. For example, the 2-nd suffix of 'STEVEN' is 'EVEN', the 4-th suffix of 'STEVEN' is 'EN' (0-based indexing).

A **Suffix Trie**[9] of a set of strings S is a tree of all possible suffixes of strings in S. Each edge label represents a character. Each vertex represents a suffix indicated by its path label: a sequence of edge labels from root to that vertex. Each vertex is connected to (some of) the other 26 vertices (assuming that we only use uppercase Latin letters) according to the suffixes of strings in S. The common prefix of two suffixes is shared. Each vertex has two boolean flags. The first/second one is to indicate that there exists a suffix/word in S *terminating* in that vertex, respectively. Example: If we have S = {'CAR', 'CAT', 'RAT'}, we have the following suffixes {'CAR', 'AR', 'R', 'CAT', 'AT', 'T', 'RAT', 'AT', 'T'}. After sorting and removing duplicates, we have: {'AR', 'AT', 'CAR', 'CAT', 'R', 'RAT', 'T'}. Figure 6.2 shows the Suffix Trie with 7 suffix terminating vertices (filled circles) and 3 word terminating vertices (filled circles indicated with label 'In Dictionary').

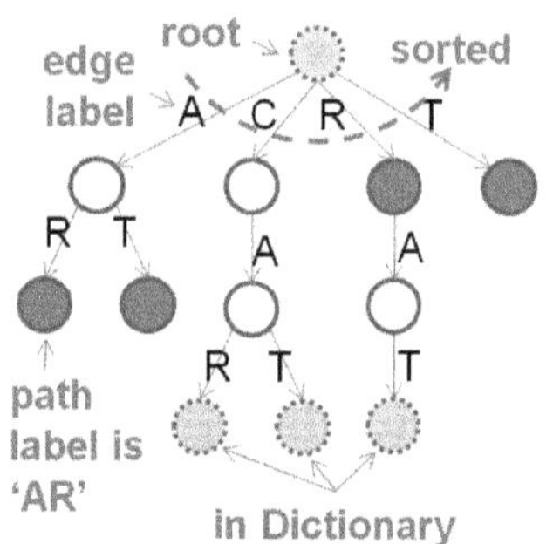

Figure 6.2: Suffix Trie

Suffix Trie is typically used as an efficient data structure for a *dictionary*. Assuming that the Suffix Trie of a set of strings in the dictionary has been built, we can determine if a query/pattern string P exists in this dictionary (Suffix Trie) in $O(m)$ where m is the length of string P—this is efficient[10]. We do this by traversing the Suffix Trie from the root. For example, if we want to find whether the word P = 'CAT' exists in the Suffix Trie shown in Figure 6.2, we can start from the root node, follow the edge with label 'C', then 'A', then 'T'. Since the vertex at this point has the word-terminating flag set to true, then we know that there is a word 'CAT' in the dictionary. Whereas, if we search for P = 'CAD', we go through this path: root → 'C' → 'A' but then we do not have an edge with edge label 'D', so we conclude that 'CAD' is not in the dictionary.

Below, we provide a basic implementation of a **Trie** (not the full Suffix Trie). Assuming that we deal with only UPPERCASE alphabets ['A'..'Z'], we set each vertex to have up to 26 ordered edges that represent 'A' to 'Z' and word terminating flags. We insertion of each (full) word/string (not the suffixes) of length up to m in S into the Trie one by one. This runs in $O(m)$ per insertion and there are up to n words to be inserted so the construction can go up to $O(nm)$. Then, given any pattern string P, we can start from the root and follow the corresponding edge labels to decide if P is inside S or not in $O(m)$.

[9]This is not a typo. The word 'TRIE' comes from the word 'information reTRIEval'.

[10]Another data structure for dictionary is balanced BST. It has $O(\log n \times m)$ performance for each dictionary query where n is the number of words in the dictionary. This is because one string comparison already costs $O(m)$. Hash Table may not be suitable as we need to order the words in the dictionary.

```
struct vertex {
  char alphabet;
  bool exist;
  vector<vertex*> child;
  vertex(char a): alphabet(a), exist(false) { child.assign(26, NULL); }
};

class Trie {                                       // this is TRIE
private:                                           // NOT Suffix Trie
  vertex* root;
public:
  Trie() { root = new vertex('!'); }

  void insert(string word) {                       // insert a word into trie
    vertex* cur = root;
    for (int i = 0; i < (int)word.size(); ++i) { // O(n)
      int alphaNum = word[i]-'A';
      if (cur->child[alphaNum] == NULL)            // add new branch if NULL
        cur->child[alphaNum] = new vertex(word[i]);
      cur = cur->child[alphaNum];
    }
    cur->exist = true;
  }

  bool search(string word) {                       // true if word in trie
    vertex* cur = root;
    for (int i = 0; i < (int)word.size(); ++i) { // O(m)
      int alphaNum = word[i]-'A';
      if (cur->child[alphaNum] == NULL)            // not found
        return false;
      cur = cur->child[alphaNum];
    }
    return cur->exist;                             // check exist flag
  }

  bool startsWith(string prefix) {                 // true if match prefix
    vertex* cur = root;
    for (int i = 0; i < (int)prefix.size(); ++i) {
      int alphaNum = prefix[i]-'A';
      if (cur->child[alphaNum] == NULL)            // not found
        return false;
      cur = cur->child[alphaNum];
    }
    return true;                                   // reach here, return true
  }
};
```

Source code: ch6/Trie.cpp|py

6.5.2 Suffix Tree

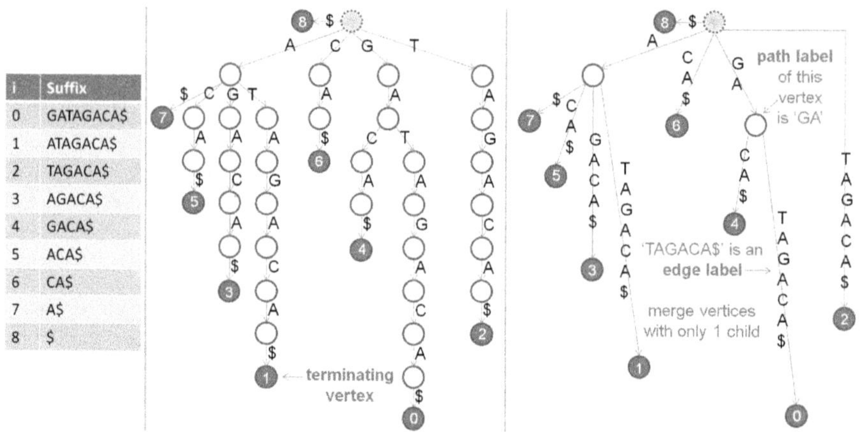

i	Suffix
0	GATAGACA$
1	ATAGACA$
2	TAGACA$
3	AGACA$
4	GACA$
5	ACA$
6	CA$
7	A$
8	$

Figure 6.3: Suffixes, Suffix Trie, and Suffix Tree of T = "GATAGACA$"

Now, instead of working with several short strings, we work with one *long(er)* string. Consider a string T = "GATAGACA$". The last character '$' is a special terminating character appended to the original string "GATAGACA". It has an ASCII value smaller[11] than the characters in T. This terminating character ensures that all suffixes terminate in leaf vertices.

The Suffix **Trie** of T is shown in Figure 6.3—middle. This time, the **terminating vertex** stores the *index* of the suffix that terminates in that vertex. Observe that the longer the string T is, there will be more duplicated vertices in the Suffix Trie. This can be inefficient. Suffix **Tree** of T is a Suffix Trie where we *merge* vertices with only one child (essentially a path compression). Compare Figure 6.3—middle and right to see this path compression process. Notice the **edge label** and **path label** in the figure. This time, the edge label can have more than one character. Suffix **Tree** is much more *compact* than Suffix **Trie** with at most $O(n)$ vertices only[12] (and thus at most $O(n)$ edges). Thus, rather than using Suffix Trie for a long string T, we will use Suffix Tree in the subsequent sections.

Suffix Tree can be a new data structure for most readers of this book. Therefore we have built a Suffix Tree visualization in VisuAlgo to show the structure of the Suffix Tree of any (but relatively short) input string T specified by the readers themselves. Several Suffix Tree applications shown in the next Section 6.5.3 are also included in the visualization.

Visualization: `https://visualgo.net/en/suffixtree`

Exercise 6.5.2.1: Given two vertices that represent two different suffixes, e.g., suffix 1 and suffix 5 in Figure 6.3—right, determine what is their Longest Common Prefix (LCP)! Consequently, what does this LCP between two suffixes mean?

Exercise 6.5.2.2*: Draw the Suffix Trie and the Suffix Tree of T = "BANANA$"!
Hint: Use the Suffix Tree visualization tool in VisuAlgo.

---

[11] Hence, we cannot use ' ' (a space, ASCII value 32) in T as '$' has ASCII value 36.

[12] There are up to n leaves for n suffixes. All internal vertices are always branching thus there can be up to n-1 such vertices (e.g., a complete binary tree). Total: n (leaves) + (n-1) (internal vertices) = $2n$-1 vertices.

6.5.3 Applications of Suffix Tree

Assuming that the Suffix Tree of a string T is *already built*, we can use it for these applications (this list is not exhaustive):

String Matching in $O(m + occ)$

With Suffix Tree, we can find all (exact) occurrences of a pattern string P in T in $O(m+occ)$ where m is the length of the pattern string P itself and occ is the total number of occurrences of P in T—*no matter how long* the string T (of length n) is[13]. When the Suffix Tree is *already built*, this approach is *much faster* than the string matching algorithms discussed earlier in Section 6.4.

Given the Suffix Tree of T, our task is to search for the vertex x in the Suffix Tree whose path label represents the pattern string P. Note that a matching is simply a *common prefix* between the pattern string P and some suffixes of string T. This is done by just one root to (at worst) leaf traversal of the Suffix Tree of T following the edge labels. The vertex closest to the root with path label that starts with P is the desired vertex x. Then, the suffix indices stored in the terminating vertices (leaves) of the subtree rooted at x are the occurrences of P in T.

Example: In the Suffix Tree of T = "GATAGACA$" shown in Figure 6.4 and P = "A", we can simply traverse from root, go along the edge with edge label 'A' to find vertex x with the path label 'A'. There are 4 occurrences[14] of 'A' in the subtree rooted at x. They are suffix 7: "A$", suffix 5: "ACA$", suffix 3: "AGACA$", and suffix 1: "ATAGACA$". If P = "Z", then the Suffix Tree traversal will not be able to find a suitable vertex x and reports that "P is not found". To deepen your understanding of this application, visit VisuAlgo, Suffix Tree visualization, to create your own Suffix Tree (on a small string T) and test this `String Matching` application using a pattern string P of your choice.

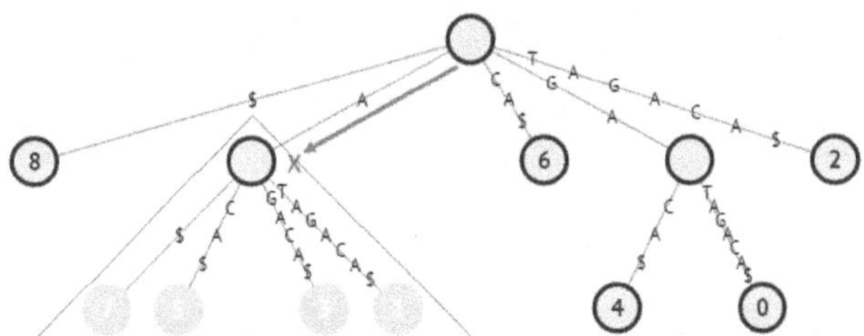

Figure 6.4: String Matching of T = "GATAGACA$" with Pattern String P = "A"

Finding the Longest Repeated Substring in $O(n)$

Given the Suffix Tree of T, we can also find the Longest Repeated Substring[15] (LRS) in T efficiently. The LRS problem is the problem of finding the longest substring of a string that occurs *at least twice*. The path label of the *deepest internal* vertex x in the Suffix Tree of T is the answer. Vertex x can be found with an $O(n)$ tree traversal (DFS/BFS). The fact that x is an internal vertex implies that it represents more than one suffix of T (there will

[13]Usually, m is much smaller than n.

[14]To be precise, occ is the *size* of subtree rooted at x, which can be larger—but not more than double—than the actual number (occ) of terminating vertices (leaves) in the subtree rooted at x.

[15]This problem has several interesting applications: finding the chorus section of a song (that is repeated several times); finding the (longest) repeated sentences in a (long) political speech, etc. Note that there is another version of this problem, see **Exercise 6.5.3.4***.

be > 1 terminating vertices in the subtree rooted at x) and these suffixes share a common prefix (which implies a repeated substring). The fact that x is the *deepest* internal vertex (from root) implies that its path label is the *longest* repeated substring.

Example: In the Suffix Tree of T = "GATAGACA$" in Figure 6.5, the LRS is "GA" as it is the path label of the deepest internal vertex x—"GA" is repeated twice in "GATAGACA$". The answer can be found with $O(n)$ pass through the Suffix Tree. To deepen your understanding of this application, visit VisuAlgo, Suffix Tree visualization, to create your own Suffix Tree (on small string T with unique longest repeat substring or several equally-longest repeat substrings) and test this **`Longest Repeated Substring`** application.

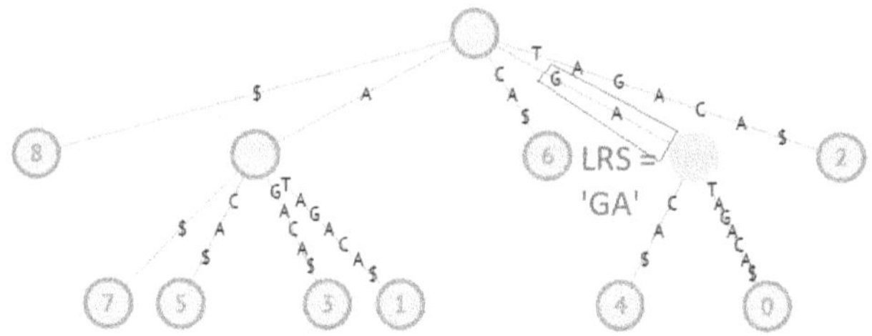

Figure 6.5: Longest Repeated Substring of T = "GATAGACA$"

Finding the Longest Common Substring in $O(n)$

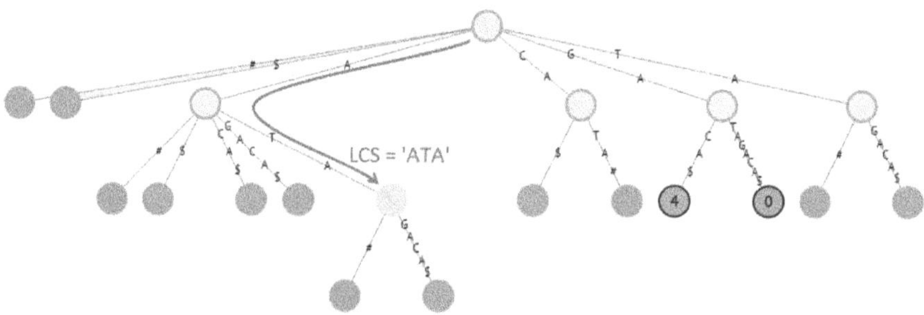

Figure 6.6: Generalized ST of T_1 = "GATAGACA$" and T_2 = "CATA#" and their LCS

The problem of finding the Longest Common **Substring** (LCS[16]) of two **or more** strings can be solved in linear time[17] with Suffix Tree. Without loss of generality, let's consider the case with *two* strings only: T_1 and T_2. We can build a **generalized Suffix Tree** that combines the Suffix Tree of T_1 and T_2. To differentiate the source of each suffix, we use two different terminating vertex symbols, one for each string. Then, we mark *internal vertices* which have vertices in their subtrees with *different* terminating symbols in $O(n)$. The suffixes represented by these marked internal vertices share a common prefix and come from *both* T_1 and T_2. That is, these marked internal vertices represent the common substrings between T_1 and T_2. As we are interested in the *longest* common substring, we report the path label of the *deepest* marked vertex as the answer also in $O(n)$.

[16]Note that 'Substring' is different from 'Subsequence'. For example, "BCE" is a subsequence but not a substring of "ABCDEF" whereas "BCD" (contiguous) is both a subsequence and a substring of "ABCDEF".

[17]Only if we use the linear time Suffix Tree construction algorithm (not discussed in this book, see [35]).

For example, with T_1 = "GATAGACA$" and T_2 = "CATA#", The Longest Common Substring is "ATA" of length 3. In Figure 6.6, we see the vertices with path labels "A", "ATA", "CA", and "TA" have two different terminating symbols (notice that vertex with path label "GA" is *not* considered as both suffix "GACA$" and "GATAGACA$" come from T_1). These are the common substrings between T_1 and T_2. The deepest marked vertex is "ATA" and this is the longest common substring between T_1 and T_2. To deepen your understanding of this application, visit VisuAlgo, Suffix Tree visualization, to create your own Suffix Tree (on *two* small strings: T_1 and T_2) and test this **Longest Common Substring** application.

Exercise 6.5.3.1: Use the Suffix Tree in Figure 6.4; Find P_1 = "C" and P_2 = "CAT"!

Exercise 6.5.3.2: Find the LRS in T = "CGACATTACATTA$"! Build the Suffix Tree first.

Exercise 6.5.3.3: Find the LCS of T_1 = "STEVEN$" and T_2 = "SEVEN#"!

Exercise 6.5.3.4*: Instead of finding the LRS, we now want to find the repeated substring *that occurs the most*. Among several possible candidates, pick the longest one. For example, if T = "DEFG1ABC2DEFG3ABC4ABC$", the answer is "ABC" of length 3 that occurs three times (not "BC" of length 2 or "C" of length 1 which also occur three times) instead of "DEFG" of length 4 that occurs only two times. Outline the strategy to find the solution!

Exercise 6.5.3.5*: The Longest Repeated Substring (LRS) problem presented in this section allows overlap. For example, the LRS of T = "AAAAAAAA$" is "AAAAAAA" of length 7. What should we do if we do not allow the LRS to overlap? For example, the LRS without overlap of T = "AAAAAAAA$" should be "AAAA" of length 4.

Exercise 6.5.3.6*: Think of how to generalize this approach to find the LCS of *more than two strings*. For example, given three strings T_1 = "STEVEN$", T_2 = "SEVEN#", and T_3 = "EVE@", how to determine that their LCS is "EVE"?

Exercise 6.5.3.7*: Customize the solution further so that we find the LCS of *k out of n strings*, where $k \leq n$. For example, given the same three strings T_1, T_2, and T_3 as above, how to determine that the LCS of 2 out of 3 strings is "EVEN"?

Exercise 6.5.3.8*: The Longest Common Extension (LCE) problem is as follows: Given a string T and two indices i and j, compute the longest substring of T that starts at both i and j. Examples assuming T = "CGACATTACATTA$". If i = 4, and j = 9, the answer is "ATTA". If i = 7, and j = 9, the answer is "A". How to solve this with Suffix Tree?

6.5.4 Suffix Array

In the previous subsection, we have shown several string processing problems that can be solved *if the Suffix Tree is already built*. However, the efficient implementation of linear time Suffix Tree construction (see [35]) is complex and thus risky under a programming contest setting. Fortunately, the next data structure that we are going to describe—the **Suffix Array** invented by Udi Manber and Gene Myers [25]—has similar functionalities as the Suffix Tree but is (much) simpler to construct and use, especially in a programming contest setting. Thus, we will skip the discussion on $O(n)$ Suffix Tree construction (see [35]) and instead focus on the $O(n \log n)$ Suffix Array construction (see [37]) which is easier to use[18]. Then, in the next subsection, we will show that we can apply Suffix Array to solve problems that have been shown to be solvable with Suffix Tree.

[18]The difference between $O(n)$ and $O(n \log n)$ algorithms in programming contest setup is not much.

i	Suffix
0	GATAGACA$
1	ATAGACA$
2	TAGACA$
3	AGACA$
4	GACA$
5	ACA$
6	CA$
7	A$
8	$

Sort →

i	SA[i]	Suffix
0	8	$
1	7	A$
2	5	ACA$
3	3	AGACA$
4	1	ATAGACA$
5	6	CA$
6	4	GACA$
7	0	GATAGACA$
8	2	TAGACA$

Figure 6.7: Sorting the Suffixes of T = "**GATAGACA$**"

Basically, Suffix Array is an integer array that stores a permutation of n indices of *sorted* suffixes. For example, consider the same[19] T = "**GATAGACA$**" with $n = 9$. The Suffix Array of T is a permutation of integers `[0..n-1] = {8, 7, 5, 3, 1, 6, 4, 0, 2}` as shown in Figure 6.7. That is, the suffixes in sorted order are suffix `SA[0]` = suffix 8 = "**$**", suffix `SA[1]` = suffix 7 = "**A$**", suffix `SA[2]` = suffix 5 = "**ACA$**", ..., and finally suffix `SA[8]` = suffix 2 = "**TAGACA$**".

Suffix Tree versus Suffix Array

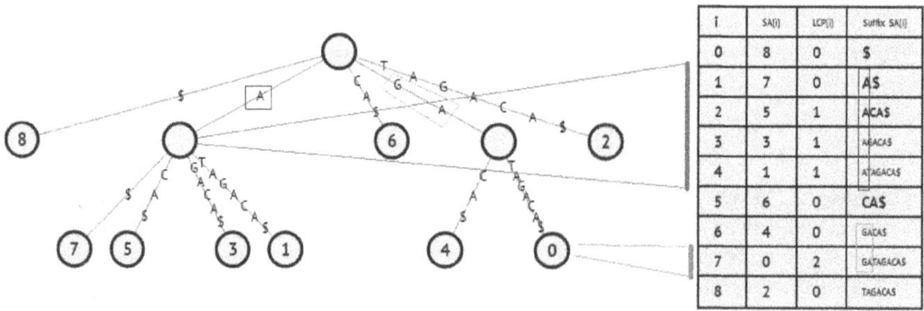

i	SA[i]	LCP[i]	Suffix SA[i]
0	8	0	$
1	7	0	A$
2	5	1	ACA$
3	3	1	AGACA$
4	1	1	ATAGACA$
5	6	0	CA$
6	4	0	GACA$
7	0	2	GATAGACA$
8	2	0	TAGACA$

Figure 6.8: Suffix Tree (Left) and Suffix Array (Right) of T = "**GATAGACA$**"

Suffix Tree and Suffix Array are closely related[20]. As we can see in Figure 6.8, the DFS tree traversal (neighbors are ordered based on sorted edge labels) of the Suffix Tree visits the terminating vertices (the leaves) in Suffix Array order. An **internal vertex** in the Suffix Tree corresponds to a **range** in the Suffix Array (a collection of sorted suffixes that share a Longest Common Prefix (LCP)—to be computed below). A **terminating vertex** (always at leaf due to the usage of a terminating character) in the Suffix Tree corresponds to an **individual index** in the Suffix Array (a single suffix). Keep these similarities in mind. They will be useful in the next subsection when we discuss applications of Suffix Array.

[19]Notice that we also use the terminating symbol '$' to simplify Suffix Array discussion.

[20]Memory usage: Suffix Tree has $n|\Sigma|$ pointers where $|\Sigma|$ is the number of different characters in T thus it requires $O(n|\Sigma| \log n)$ bits to store its data. On the other hand, Suffix Array is just an array of n indices thus it only needs $O(n \log n)$ bits to store its data, slightly more memory efficient.

Naïve Suffix Array Construction

It is very easy to construct a Suffix Array given a string `T[0..n-1]` if we are not given a very long string `T`, as shown below:

```
// in int main()
  scanf("%s", &T);                                     // read T
  int n = (int)strlen(T);                              // count n
  T[n++] = '$';                                        // add terminating symbol
  vi SA(n);
  iota(SA.begin(), SA.end(), 0);                       // the initial SA
  // analysis of this sort below: O(n log n) * cmp: O(n) = O(n^2 log n)
  sort(SA.begin(), SA.end(), [](int a, int b) {  // O(n^2 log n)
    return strcmp(T+a, T+b) < 0;
  });                                                  // continued below
```

When applied to string T = "GATAGACA$", the naïve SA construction code above that sorts all suffixes with built-in sorting and string comparison *library* really produces the correct Suffix Array = {8, 7, 5, 3, 1, 6, 4, 0, 2}. However, this is barely useful except for contest problems with $n \leq 2500$. The overall runtime of this algorithm is $O(n^2 \log n)$ because the `strcmp` operation that is used to determine the order of two (possibly long) suffixes is too costly, up to $O(n)$ per pair of suffix comparison.

Computing Longest Common Prefix Between Consecutive Sorted Suffixes

Given the Suffix Array of `T`, we can compute the Longest Common Prefix (LCP) between *consecutive* sorted suffixes in Suffix Array order. By definition, `LCP[0] = 0` as suffix `SA[0]` is the first suffix in Suffix Array order without any other suffix preceding it. For `i > 0`, `LCP[i]` = the length of LCP between suffix `SA[i]` and suffix `SA[i-1]`. For example, in Figure 6.8—right, we see that suffix `SA[7]` = suffix 0 = "<u>GA</u>CAGATA$" has an LCP "<u>GA</u>" of length 2 with its previous sorted suffix `SA[6]` = suffix 4 = "<u>GA</u>CA$". We can compute LCP directly by definition by using the code below. However, this approach is slow as it can increase the value of L up to $O(n^2)$ times, e.g., try T = "AAAAAAA$".

```
  // continuation from above
  vi LCP(n);
  LCP[0] = 0;                                          // default value
  for (int i = 1; i < n; ++i) {                        // compute by def, O(n^2)
    int L = 0;                                         // always reset L to 0
    while ((SA[i]+L < n) && (SA[i-1]+L < n) &&
           (T[SA[i]+L] == T[SA[i-1]+L])) ++L;          // same L-th char, ++L
    LCP[i] = L;
  }
  printf("T = '%s'\n", T);
  printf(" i SA[i] LCP[i]   Suffix SA[i]\n");
  for (int i = 0; i < n; ++i)
    printf("%2d    %2d    %2d    %s\n", i, SA[i], LCP[i], T+SA[i]);
```

The source code of this slow algorithm is given below using the fastest language (C++), but it is probably not that useful to be used in a modern programming contest.

Source code: `ch6/sa_lcp_slow.cpp`

Efficient Suffix Array Construction

A *better way* to construct Suffix Array is to sort the *ranking pairs* (small integers) of suffixes in $O(\log_2 n)$ iterations from $k = 1, 2, 4, \ldots$, the last **power of 2** that is less than n. At each iteration, this construction algorithm sorts the suffixes based on the ranking pair `(RA[SA[i]], RA[SA[i]+k])` of suffix `SA[i]`. This algorithm is called the Prefix Doubling (Karp-Miller-Rosenberg) algorithm [21, 37]. An example execution is shown below for `T` = "`GATAGACA$`" and $n = 9$.

- First, `SA[i] = i` and `RA[i] = ASCII value of T[i]` $\forall$`i` $\in$ `[0..n-1]` (Table 6.1—left). At iteration $k = 1$, the ranking pair of suffix `SA[i]` is `(RA[SA[i]], RA[SA[i]+1])`.

i	SA[i]	Suffix	RA[SA[i]]	RA[SA[i]+k]
0	0	GATAGACA$	71	65
1	1	ATAGACA$	65	84
2	2	TAGACA$	84	65
3	3	AGACA$	65	71
4	4	GACA$	71	65
5	5	ACA$	65	67
6	6	CA$	67	65
7	7	A$	65	36
8	8	$	36	0

i	SA[i]	Suffix	RA[SA[i]]	RA[SA[i]+k]
0	8	$	36	0
1	7	A$	65	36
2	5	ACA$	65	67
3	3	AGACA$	65	71
4	1	ATAGACA$	65	84
5	6	CA$	67	65
6	0	GATAGACA$	71	65
7	4	GACA$	71	65
8	2	TAGACA$	84	65

Table 6.1: L/R: Before/After Sorting; k = 1; the initial sorted order appears

Example 1: The rank of suffix 5 "`ACA$`" is ('`A`', '`C`') = (65, 67).

Example 2: The rank of suffix 3 "`AGACA$`" is ('`A`', '`G`') = (65, 71).

After we sort these ranking pairs, the order of suffixes is now like Table 6.1—right, where suffix 5 "`ACA$`" comes before suffix 3 "`AGACA$`", etc.

- At iteration $k = 2$, the ranking pair of suffix `SA[i]` is `(RA[SA[i]], RA[SA[i]+2])`. This ranking pair is now obtained by looking at the first pair and the second pair of characters only. To get the new ranking pairs, we do not have to recompute many things. We set the first one, i.e., Suffix 8 "`$`" to have new rank $r = 0$. Then, we iterate from `i = [1..n-1]`. If the ranking pair of suffix `SA[i]` is different from the ranking pair of the previous suffix `SA[i-1]` in sorted order, we increase the rank $r = r + 1$. Otherwise, the rank stays at r (see Table 6.2—left).

i	SA[i]	Suffix	RA[SA[i]]	RA[SA[i]+k]
0	8	$	0	0
1	7	A$	1	0
2	5	ACA$	2	1
3	3	AGACA$	3	2
4	1	ATAGACA$	4	3
5	6	CA$	5	0
6	0	GATAGACA$	6	7
7	4	GACA$	6	5
8	2	TAGACA$	7	6

i	SA[i]	Suffix	RA[SA[i]]	RA[SA[i]+k]
0	8	$	0	0
1	7	A$	1	0
2	5	ACA$	2	1
3	3	AGACA$	3	2
4	1	ATAGACA$	4	3
5	6	CA$	5	0
6	4	GACA$	6	5
7	0	GATAGACA$	6	7
8	2	TAGACA$	7	6

Table 6.2: L/R: Before/After Sorting; k = 2; "`GATAGACA`" and "`GACA`" are swapped

Example 1: In Table 6.1—right, the ranking pair of suffix 7 "<u>`A$`</u>" is (65, 36) which is different with the ranking pair of previous suffix 8 "<u>`$-`</u>" which is (36, 0). Therefore in Table 6.2—left, suffix 7 has a new rank 1.

Example 2: In Table 6.1—right, the ranking pair of suffix 4 "<u>`GA`</u>`CA$`" is (71, 65) which is similar with the ranking pair of previous suffix 0 "<u>`GA`</u>`TAGACA$`" which is also (71, 65).

Therefore in Table 6.2—left, since suffix 0 is given a new rank 6, then suffix 4 is also given the same new rank 6.

Once we have updated `RA[SA[i]]` $\forall$`i` $\in$ `[0..n-1]`, the value of `RA[SA[i]+k]` can be easily determined too. In our explanation, if `SA[i]+k` $\geq$ `n`, we give a default rank 0. See **Exercise 6.5.4.1** for more details on the implementation aspect of this step.

At this stage, the ranking pair of suffix 0 "**GATAGACA$**" is (6, 7) and suffix 4 "**GACA$**" is (6, 5). These two suffixes are still not in sorted order whereas all the other suffixes are already in their correct order. After another round of sorting, the order of suffixes is now like Table 6.2—right.

- At iteration $k = 4$—notice that we *double* $k = 2$ to $k = 4$, skipping $k = 3$—, the ranking pair of suffix `SA[i]` is `(RA[SA[i]], RA[SA[i]+4])`. This ranking pair is now obtained by looking at the first quadruple and the second quadruple of characters only. At this point, notice that the previous ranking pairs of Suffix 4 (6, 5) and Suffix 0 (6, 7) in Table 6.2—right are now different. Therefore, after re-ranking, all n suffixes in Table 6.3 now have different rankings. This can be easily verified by checking if `RA[SA[n-1]] == n-1`. When this happens, we have successfully obtained the Suffix Array. Notice that the major sorting work is done in the first few iterations only and we usually do not need many iterations when T is a random string (also see **Exercise 6.5.4.3**).

i	SA[i]	Suffix	RA[SA[i]]	RA[SA[i]+k]
0	8	$	0	0
1	7	A$	1	0
2	5	ACA$	2	0
3	3	AGACA$	3	1
4	1	ATAGACA$	4	2
5	6	CA$	5	0
6	4	GACA$	6	0
7	0	GATAGACA$	7	6
8	2	TAGACA$	8	5

Table 6.3: Before/After sorting; k = 4; no change

Suffix Array construction algorithm can be new for most readers of this book. Thus, we have built a Suffix Array visualization tool in VisuAlgo to show the steps of this construction algorithm for any (but short) input string `T` specified by the reader themselves. Several Suffix Array applications shown in the next Section 6.5.5 are also included in the visualization.

Visualization: `https://visualgo.net/en/suffixarray`

We can implement the sorting of ranking pairs above using (built-in) $O(n \log n)$ sorting library. As we repeat the sorting process up to $\log n$ times, the overall time complexity is $O(\log n \times n \log n) = O(n \log^2 n)$. With this time complexity, we can now work with strings of length up to $\approx 30K$. However, since the sorting process only sorts *pair of small integers*, we can use a *linear time* two-pass Radix Sort (that internally calls Counting Sort—see the details in Book 1) to reduce the sorting time to $O(n)$. As we repeat the sorting process up to $\log n$ times, the overall time complexity is $O(\log n \times n) = O(n \log n)$. Now, we can work with strings of length up to $\approx 450K$—typical programming contest range.

Efficient Computation of LCP Between Two Consecutive Sorted Suffixes

A better way to compute Longest Common Prefix (LCP) between two *consecutive* sorted suffixes in Suffix Array order is by using the Permuted Longest-Common-Prefix (PLCP) theorem [20]. The idea is simple: it is *easier* to compute the LCP in the original position order of the suffixes instead of the lexicographic order of the suffixes. In Table 6.4—right, we have the original position order of the suffixes of `T = 'GATAGACA$'`. Observe that column `PLCP[i]` forms a pattern: decrease-by-1 block ($2 \rightarrow 1 \rightarrow 0$); increase to 1; decrease-by-1 block again ($1 \rightarrow 0$); increase to 1 again; decrease-by-1 block again ($1 \rightarrow 0$), etc.

i	SA[i]	LCP[i]	Suffix	i	Phi[i]	PLCP[i]	Suffix
0	8	0	$	0	4	2	GATAGACA$
1	7	0	A$	1	3	1	ATAGACA$
2	5	1	ACA$	2	0	0	TAGACA$
3	3	1	AGACA$	3	5	1	AGACA$
4	1	1	ATAGACA$	4	6	0	GACA$
5	6	0	CA$	5	7	1	ACA$
6	4	0	GACA$	6	1	0	CA$
7	0	2	GATAGACA$	7	8	0	A$
8	2	0	TAGACA$	8	-1	0	$

LCP[7] = PLCP[SA[7]] = PLCP[0] = 2

Phi[SA[3]] = SA[3-1]
Phi[3] = SA[2]
Phi[3] = 5

Table 6.4: Computing the LCP given the SA of T = "GATAGACA$"

The PLCP theorem says that the total number of increase (and decrease) operations is at most $O(n)$. This pattern and this $O(n)$ guarantee are exploited in the code below.

First, we compute `Phi[SA[i]]`, i.e., we store the suffix index of the previous suffix of suffix `SA[i]` in Suffix Array order. By definition, `Phi[SA[0]] = -1`, i.e., there is no previous suffix that precedes suffix `SA[0]`. Take some time to verify the correctness of column `Phi[i]` in Table 6.4—right. For example, `Phi[SA[3]] = SA[3-1]`, so `Phi[3] = SA[2] = 5`.

Now, with `Phi[i]`, we can compute the permuted LCP. The first few steps of this algorithm is elaborated below. When `i = 0`, we have `Phi[0] = 4`. This means suffix 0 "GATAGACA$" has suffix 4 "GACA$" before it in Suffix Array order. The first two characters (`L = 2`) of these two suffixes match, so `PLCP[0] = 2`.

When `i = 1`, we know that *at least* `L-1 = 1` characters can match as the next suffix in position order will have one less starting character than the current suffix. We have `Phi[1] = 3`. This means suffix 1 "ATAGACA$" has suffix 3 "AGACA$" before it in Suffix Array order. Observe that these two suffixes indeed have at least 1 character match (that is, we do not start from `L = 0` as in `computeLCP_slow()` function shown earlier and therefore this is more efficient). As we cannot extend this further, we have `PLCP[1] = 1`.

We continue this process until `i = n-1`, bypassing the case when `Phi[i] = -1`. As the PLCP theorem says that L will be increased/decreased at most n times, this part runs in amortized $O(n)$. Finally, once we have the PLCP array, we can put the permuted LCP back to the correct position. The code is relatively short, as shown below.

The Efficient Implementation

We provide our efficient $O(n \log n)$ SA construction code combined with efficient $O(n)$ computation of LCP between consecutive[21] sorted suffixes below. Now this SA construction and LCP computation code is good enough for many challenging string problems involving *long strings* in programming contests. Please scrutinize the code to understand how it works.

For ICPC contestants: as you can bring hard copy materials to the contest, it is a good idea to put this code in your team's library.

[21] Also see **Exercise 6.5.4.5*** that asks for the LCP between a *range* of sorted suffixes.

```
typedef pair<int, int> ii;
typedef vector<int> vi;

class SuffixArray {
private:
  vi RA;                                          // rank array

  void countingSort(int k) {                      // O(n)
    int maxi = max(300, n);                       // up to 255 ASCII chars
    vi c(maxi, 0);                                // clear frequency table
    for (int i = 0; i < n; ++i)                   // count the frequency
      ++c[i+k < n ? RA[i+k] : 0];                 // of each integer rank
    for (int i = 0, sum = 0; i < maxi; ++i) {
      int t = c[i]; c[i] = sum; sum += t;
    }
    vi tempSA(n);
    for (int i = 0; i < n; ++i)                   // sort SA
      tempSA[c[SA[i]+k < n ? RA[SA[i]+k] : 0]++] = SA[i];
    swap(SA, tempSA);                             // update SA
  }

  void constructSA() {                            // can go up to 400K chars
    SA.resize(n);
    iota(SA.begin(), SA.end(), 0);                // the initial SA
    RA.resize(n);
    for (int i = 0; i < n; ++i) RA[i] = T[i];     // initial rankings
    for (int k = 1; k < n; k <<= 1) {             // repeat log_2 n times
      // this is actually radix sort
      countingSort(k);                            // sort by 2nd item
      countingSort(0);                            // stable-sort by 1st item
      vi tempRA(n);
      int r = 0;
      tempRA[SA[0]] = r;                          // re-ranking process
      for (int i = 1; i < n; ++i)                 // compare adj suffixes
        tempRA[SA[i]] = // same pair => same rank r; otherwise, increase r
          ((RA[SA[i]] == RA[SA[i-1]]) && (RA[SA[i]+k] == RA[SA[i-1]+k])) ?
            r : ++r;
      swap(RA, tempRA);                           // update RA
      if (RA[SA[n-1]] == n-1) break;              // nice optimization
    }
  }

  void computeLCP() {
    vi Phi(n);
    vi PLCP(n);
    PLCP.resize(n);
    Phi[SA[0]] = -1;                              // default value
    for (int i = 1; i < n; ++i)                   // compute Phi in O(n)
      Phi[SA[i]] = SA[i-1];                       // remember prev suffix
```

```
    for (int i = 0, L = 0; i < n; ++i) {           // compute PLCP in O(n)
      if (Phi[i] == -1) { PLCP[i] = 0; continue; } // special case
      while ((i+L < n) && (Phi[i]+L < n) && (T[i+L] == T[Phi[i]+L]))
        ++L;                                       // L incr max n times
      PLCP[i] = L;
      L = max(L-1, 0);                             // L dec max n times
    }
    LCP.resize(n);
    for (int i = 0; i < n; ++i)                    // compute LCP in O(n)
      LCP[i] = PLCP[SA[i]];                        // restore PLCP
  }

public:
  const char* T;                                   // the input string
  const int n;                                     // the length of T
  vi SA;                                           // Suffix Array
  vi LCP;                                          // of adj sorted suffixes

  SuffixArray(const char* initialT, const int _n) : T(initialT), n(_n) {
    constructSA();                                 // O(n log n)
    computeLCP();                                  // O(n)
  }
};

int main() {
  scanf("%s", &T);                                 // read T
  int n = (int)strlen(T);                          // count n
  T[n++] = '$';                                    // add terminating symbol
  SuffixArray S(T, n);                             // construct SA+LCP
  printf("T = '%s'\n", T);
  printf(" i SA[i] LCP[i]   Suffix SA[i]\n");
  for (int i = 0; i < n; ++i)
    printf("%2d    %2d    %2d    %s\n", i, S.SA[i], S.LCP[i], T+S.SA[i]);
} // return 0;
```

Exercise 6.5.4.1: In the SA construction code shown above, will the following line:

```
((RA[SA[i]] == RA[SA[i-1]]) && (RA[SA[i]+k] == RA[SA[i-1]+k])) ?
```

causes index out of bound in some cases?
That is, will `SA[i]+k` or `SA[i-1]+k` ever be $\geq$ `n` and crash the program? Explain!

Exercise 6.5.4.2: Will the SA construction code shown above works if the input string `T` contains a space (ASCII value = 32) inside? If it doesn't work, what is the required solution? Hint: The default terminating character used—i.e., '$'—has ASCII value = 36.

Exercise 6.5.4.3: Give an input string `T` of length 16 so that the given $O(n \log n)$ SA construction code use up all $\log_2 16 = 4$ iterations!

Exercise 6.5.4.4*: Show the steps to compute the Suffix Array of `T` = "`BANANA$`" with $n = 7$. How many sorting iterations do you need to get the Suffix Array?
Hint: Use the Suffix Array visualization tool in VisuAlgo.

Exercise 6.5.4.5*: Show how to extend the computation of LCP between two consecutive sorted suffixes into computation of LCP between a range of sorted suffixes, i.e., answer `LCP(i, j)`. For example in Figure 6.8, `LCP(1, 4) = 1` ("A"), `LCP(6, 7) = 2` ("GA"), and `LCP(0, 8) = 0` (nothing in common).

Exercise 6.5.4.6*: Show how to use LCP information to compute the number of distinct substrings in `T` in $O(n \log n)$ time.

6.5.5 Applications of Suffix Array

We have mentioned earlier that Suffix Array is closely related to Suffix Tree. In this subsection, we show that with Suffix Array (which is easier to construct), we can solve the string processing problems shown in Section 6.5.3 that are solvable using Suffix Tree.

String Matching in $O(m \log n)$

After we obtain the Suffix Array of `T`, we can search for a pattern string `P` (of length m) in `T` (of length n) in $O(m \log n)$. This is a factor of $\log n$ times slower than the Suffix Tree version but in practice it is quite acceptable. The $O(m \log n)$ complexity comes from the fact that we can do two $O(\log n)$ binary searches on sorted suffixes and do up to $O(m)$ suffix comparisons[22]. The first/second binary search is to find the lower/upper bound respectively. This lower/upper bound is the smallest/largest `i` such that the prefix of suffix `SA[i]` matches the pattern string `P`, respectively. All the suffixes between the lower and upper bound are the occurrences of pattern string `P` in `T`. Our implementation is shown below:

```
// extension of class Suffix Array above
  ii stringMatching(const char *P) {                  // in O(m log n)
    int m = (int)strlen(P);                           // usually, m < n
    int lo = 0, hi = n-1;                             // range = [0..n-1]
    while (lo < hi) {                                 // find lower bound
      int mid = (lo+hi) / 2;                          // this is round down
      int res = strncmp(T+SA[mid], P, m);             // P in suffix SA[mid]?
      (res >= 0) ? hi = mid : lo = mid+1;             // notice the >= sign
    }
    if (strncmp(T+SA[lo], P, m) != 0) return {-1, -1}; // if not found
    ii ans; ans.first = lo;
    hi = n-1;                                         // range = [lo..n-1]
    while (lo < hi) {                                 // now find upper bound
      int mid = (lo+hi) / 2;
      int res = strncmp(T+SA[mid], P, m);
      (res > 0) ? hi = mid : lo = mid+1;              // notice the > sign
    }
    if (strncmp(T+SA[hi], P, m) != 0) --hi;           // special case
    ans.second = hi;
    return ans;                                       // returns (lb, ub)
  }                                                   // where P is found
```

A sample execution of this string matching algorithm on the Suffix Array of `T` = "GATAGACA$" with `P` = "GA" is shown in Table 6.5.

[22]This is achievable by using the `strncmp` function to compare only the first m characters of both suffixes.

We start by finding the lower bound. The current range is `i = [0..8]` and thus the middle one is `i = 4`. We compare the first two characters of suffix `SA[4]`, which is "`ATAGACA$`", with `P = 'GA'`. As `P = 'GA'` is larger, we continue exploring `i = [5..8]`. Next, we compare the first two characters of suffix `SA[6]`, which is "`GACA$`", with `P = 'GA'`. It is a match. As we are currently looking for the *lower* bound, we do not stop here but continue exploring `i = [5..6]`. `P = 'GA'` is larger than suffix `SA[5]`, which is "`CA$`". We stop after checking that `SA[8]` doesn't start with prefix `P = 'GA'`. Index `i = 6` is the lower bound, i.e., suffix `SA[6]`, which is "`GACA$`", is the *first* time pattern `P = 'GA'` appears as a prefix of a suffix in the list of sorted suffixes.

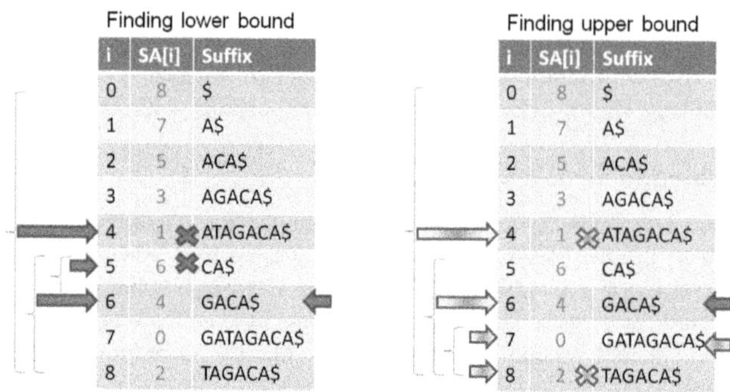

Finding lower bound

i	SA[i]	Suffix
0	8	$
1	7	A$
2	5	ACA$
3	3	AGACA$
4	1	ATAGACA$
5	6	CA$
6	4	GACA$
7	0	GATAGACA$
8	2	TAGACA$

Finding upper bound

i	SA[i]	Suffix
0	8	$
1	7	A$
2	5	ACA$
3	3	AGACA$
4	1	ATAGACA$
5	6	CA$
6	4	GACA$
7	0	GATAGACA$
8	2	TAGACA$

Table 6.5: String Matching using Suffix Array

Next, we search for the upper bound. The first step is the same as above. But at the second step, we have a match between suffix `SA[6]`, which is "`GACA$`", with `P = 'GA'`. Since now we are looking for the *upper* bound, we continue exploring `i = [7..8]`. We find another match when comparing suffix `SA[7]`, which is "`GATAGACA$`", with `P = 'GA'`. We stop here. This `i = 7` is the upper bound in this example, i.e., suffix `SA[7]`, which is "`GATAGACA$`", is the *last* time pattern `P = 'GA'` appears as a prefix of a suffix in the list of sorted suffixes.

Finding the Longest Repeated Substring in $O(n)$

If we have computed the Suffix Array in $O(n \log n)$ and the LCP between consecutive suffixes in Suffix Array order in $O(n)$, then we can determine the length of the Longest Repeated Substring (LRS) of `T` in $O(n)$.

The length of the LRS is just the highest number in the LCP array. In Table 6.4—left that corresponds to the Suffix Array and the LCP of `T` = "`GATAGACA$`", the highest number is 2 at index `i = 7`. The first 2 characters of the corresponding suffix `SA[7]` (suffix `0`) is "`GA`". This is the LRS in `T`.

Finding the Longest Common Substring in $O(n)$

Without loss of generality, let's consider the case with only *two* strings. We use the same example as in the Suffix Tree section earlier: T_1 = "`GATAGACA$`" and T_2 = "`CATA#`". To solve the Longest Common Substring (LCS) problem using Suffix Array, first we have to concatenate both strings (note that the terminating characters of both strings *must be different*) to produce `T` = "`GATAGACA$CATA#`". Then, we compute the Suffix and LCP array of `T` as shown in Table 6.6.

i	SA[i]	LCP[i]	Owner	Suffix
0	13	0	2	#
1	8	0	1	$CATA#
2	12	0	2	A#
3	7	1	1	A$CATA#
4	5	1	1	ACA$CATA#
5	3	1	1	AGACA$CATA#
6	10	1	2	ATA#
7	1	3	1	ATAGACA$CATA#
8	6	0	1	CA$CATA#
9	9	2	2	CATA#
10	4	0	1	GACA$CATA#
11	0	2	1	GATAGACA$CATA#
12	11	0	2	TA#
13	2	2	1	TAGACA$CATA#

Table 6.6: The Suffix Array, LCP, and owner of T = "GATAGACA$CATA#"

Then, we go through consecutive suffixes in $O(n)$. If two consecutive suffixes belong to different owners (can be easily checked[23], for example we can test if suffix `SA[i]` belongs to T_1 by testing if `SA[i]` < the length of T_1), we look at the LCP array and see if the maximum LCP found so far can be increased. After one $O(n)$ pass, we will be able to determine the LCS. In Figure 6.6, this happens when `i = 7`, as suffix `SA[7]` = suffix `1` = "ATAGACA$CATA#" (owned by T_1) and its previous suffix `SA[6]` = suffix `10` = "ATA#" (owned by T_2) have a common prefix of length 3 which is "ATA". This is the LCS.

Finally, we close this section and this chapter by highlighting the availability of our source code. Please spend some time understanding the source code which may not be trivial for those who are new with Suffix Array.

Source code: `ch6/sa_lcp.cpp|java|py|ml`

Exercise 6.5.5.1*: Suggest some possible improvements to the `stringMatching()` function shown in this section so that the time complexity improves to $O(m + \log n)$!

Exercise 6.5.5.2*: Compare the KMP algorithm shown in Section 6.4 and Rabin-Karp algorithm in Section 6.6 with the string matching feature of Suffix Array, then decide a rule of thumb on when it is better to use Suffix Array to deal with string matching and when it is better to use KMP, Rabin-Karp, or just standard string libraries.

Exercise 6.5.5.3*: Solve the exercises on Suffix Tree applications using Suffix Array instead:

- **Exercise 6.5.3.4*** (repeated substrings that occurs the most, and if ties, the longest),
- **Exercise 6.5.3.5*** (LRS with no overlap),
- **Exercise 6.5.3.6*** (LCS of $n \geq 2$ strings),
- **Exercise 6.5.3.7*** (LCS of k out of n strings where $k \leq n$), and
- **Exercise 6.5.3.8*** (LCE of `T` given `i` and `j`).

---

[23] With three or more strings, this check will have more 'if statements'.

Programming Exercises related to Suffix Array[24]:

1. Entry Level: *Kattis - suffixsorting* * (basic Suffix Array construction problem; be careful with terminating symbol)
2. **UVa 01254 - Top 10 *** (LA 4657 - Jakarta09; Suffix Array with Segment Tree or Sparse Table; LCP range)
3. **UVa 01584 - Circular Sequence *** (LA 3225 - Seoul04; min lexicographic rotation[25]; similar with UVa 00719; other solutions exist)
4. **UVa 11512 - GATTACA *** (Longest Repeated Substring)
5. *Kattis - automatictrading* * (Suffix Array; LCP of a range; use Sparse Table)
6. *Kattis - buzzwords* * (Longest Repeated Substring that appears X times ($2 \leq X < N$); also available at UVa 11855 - Buzzwords)
7. *Kattis - suffixarrayreconstruction* * (clever creative problem involving Suffix Array concept; be careful that '*' can be more than one character)

Extra UVa: *00719, 00760, 01223, 12506.*

Extra Kattis: *aliens, burrowswheeler, dvaput, lifeforms, repeatedsubstrings, stringmultimatching, substrings.*

Others: SPOJ SARRAY - Suffix Array (problem author: Felix Halim), IOI 2008 - Type Printer (DFS traversal of Suffix Trie).

Also see Section 8.7 for some harder problems that uses (Suffix) Trie data structure as sub-routine.

Profile of Data Structure Inventors

Udi Manber is an Israeli computer scientist. He works in Google as one of their vice presidents of engineering. Along with Gene Myers, Manber invented Suffix Array data structure in 1991.

Eugene "Gene" Wimberly Myers, Jr. is an American computer scientist and bioinformatician, who is best known for his development of the BLAST (Basic Local Alignment Search Tool) tool for sequence analysis. His 1990 paper that describes BLAST has received over 24 000 citations making it among the most highly cited paper ever. He also invented Suffix Array with Udi Manber.

[24]You can try solving these problems with Suffix Tree, but you have to learn how to code the Suffix Tree construction algorithm by yourself. The programming problems listed here are solvable with Suffix Array.

[25]Min Lexicographic Rotation is a problem of finding the rotation of a string with the lowest lexicographical order of all possible rotations. For example, the lexicographically minimal rotation of "CGAGTC][AGCT" (emphasis of '][' added) is "AGCTCGAGTC".

6.6 String Matching with Hashing

Given two strings `A` and `B`, compare a substring of `A` with a substring of `B`, e.g., determine whether `A[i..j]` = `B[k..l]`. The brute force way to solve this problem is by comparing the characters in both substrings one by one, which leads to an $O(m)$ solution where m is the (sub)string length. If this comparison is repeated many times (with different substrings), then such solution might get Time Limit Exceeded (TLE) unless n is small enough or repeated only a few times. For example, consider the following String Matching problem: Given two strings: text `T` of length n and pattern `P` of length m ($m \leq n$), count how many tuples $\langle$`i, j`$\rangle$ are there such that `T[i..j]` = `P`. As there are $O(n\text{-}m)$ substrings of a fixed length m from a string `T` of length n, then the brute force solution has an $O(nm)$ complexity. In Section 6.4, we have learned about the Knuth-Morris-Pratt's (KMP) algorithm that can solve this String Matching problem in $O(n+m)$ complexity. In Section 6.5, we have learned about Suffix Array data structure that can solve this String Matching problem in $O(m \log n)$ complexity (after the Suffix Array is built in $O(n \log n)$ time). In this Section, we will learn another technique to solve this problem with **hashing**.

The idea of string hashing is to convert its substrings into integers so that we can do string comparison in $O(1)$ by comparing their (integers) hash values. We can find the hash value of each substring in $O(1)$ and one time preparation of $O(n)$ with **rolling hash**.

6.6.1 Hashing a String

A hash of a string `T` of length n (0-based indexing) is usually defined as follows:

$$h(\mathtt{T}_{0,n-1}) = \sum_{i=0}^{n-1} \mathtt{T}_i \cdot \mathtt{p}^i \mod \mathtt{M}$$

Where the *base* `p` and the *modulo* `M` are integers and chosen with these recommendations:

- `p` is at least the size of alphabets (number of distinct characters, denoted as $|\Sigma|$),
- `M` is large (otherwise, our hash function will suffer from Birthday Paradox[26]),
- `p` and `M` are relatively prime (otherwise, there will be too many collisions; we also need this requirement for the multiplicative inverse component later).

For example, consider `p` = 131 and `M` = $10^9 + 7$ where `p` and `M` are relatively prime. Then, h(‘`ABCBC`’) = (‘`A`’$\cdot 131^0+$‘`B`’$\cdot 131^1+$‘`C`’$\cdot 131^2+$‘`B`’$\cdot 131^3+$‘`C`’$\cdot 131^4$) mod 1 000 000 007. If we replace (‘`A`’, ‘`B`’, ‘`C`’) with $(0, 1, 2)$, then we will get h(‘`ABCBC`’) = 591 282 386. Most of the time, we do not need to map the alphabets into $(0, 1, .., |\Sigma|\text{-}1)$ like what we just did. Using the ASCII value of each alphabet is already sufficient. In this case, h(‘`ABCBC`’) = 881 027 078.

6.6.2 Rolling Hash

The beauty of rolling hash lies in its ability to compute the hash value of a substring in $O(1)$, given we already have the hash value of all its prefix substrings. Let $\mathtt{T}_{i,j}$ where $\mathtt{i} \leq \mathtt{j}$ be the substring of `T` from index `i` to `j`, inclusive.

First, observe that the hash value of all prefixes of a string (where `i` = `0`) can be computed altogether in $O(n)$, or $O(1)$ per prefix. See the derivation and the rolling hash code that computes the hash values of all prefixes of `T` in $O(n)$.

[26]What is the probability that 2 out of 23 random people are having the same birthday? *Hint*: It is more than 50% chance, which is far higher than what most untrained people thought, hence the ‘paradox’.

$$h(\texttt{T}_{0,0}) = (\texttt{S}_0 \cdot \texttt{p}^0) \mod \texttt{M}$$
$$h(\texttt{T}_{0,1}) = (\texttt{S}_0 \cdot \texttt{p}^0 + \texttt{S}_1 \cdot \texttt{p}^1) \mod \texttt{M}$$
$$h(\texttt{T}_{0,2}) = (\texttt{S}_0 \cdot \texttt{p}^0 + \texttt{S}_1 \cdot \texttt{p}^1 + \texttt{S}_2 \cdot \texttt{p}^2) \mod \texttt{M}$$
$$\vdots$$
$$h(\texttt{T}_{0,R}) = (h(\texttt{S}_{0,R-1}) + \texttt{S}_R \cdot \texttt{p}^R) \mod \texttt{M}$$

```
typedef vector<int> vi;
typedef long long ll;
const int p = 131;                                // p and M are
const int M = 1e9+7;                              // relatively prime

vi P;                                             // to store p^i % M

vi prepareP(int n) {                              // compute p^i % M
  P.assign(n, 0);
  P[0] = 1;
  for (int i = 1; i < n; ++i)                     // O(n)
    P[i] = ((ll)P[i-1]*p) % M;
  return P;
}

vi computeRollingHash(string T) {                 // Overall: O(n)
  vi P = prepareP((int)T.length());               // O(n)
  vi h(T.size(), 0);
  for (int i = 0; i < (int)T.length(); ++i) {     // O(n)
    if (i != 0) h[i] = h[i-1];                    // rolling hash
    h[i] = (h[i] + ((ll)T[i]*P[i]) % M) % M;
  }
  return h;
}
```

Now, if we want to compute the hash value of a substring $\texttt{T}_{L,R}$ (notice that $L > 0$ now), then, the rolling hash equation becomes (note: we can treat substring $\texttt{T}_{L,R}$ as a new string T'):

$$h(\texttt{T}_{L,R}) = \sum_{i=L}^{R} \texttt{T}_i \cdot \texttt{p}^{i-L} \mod \texttt{M}$$

Similar to computing the sum of a subarray in $O(1)$ using its prefix sum (see Book 1), the value of $h(\texttt{T}_{L,R})$ can be computed in $O(1)$ with the hash value of its prefix (see Figure 6.9). Note that we have take out p^L from the result (mod M). The derivation is as follows:

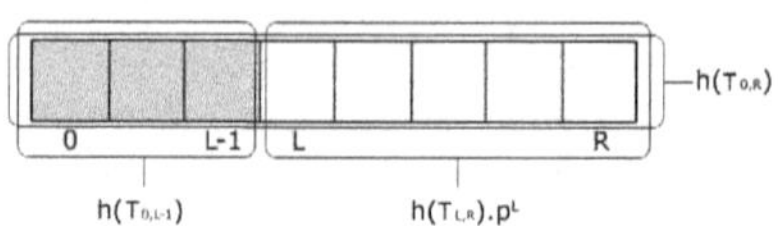

Figure 6.9: Rolling Hash

$$\begin{aligned} h(\mathtt{T}_{\mathtt{L,R}}) &= \frac{h(\mathtt{T}_{\mathtt{0,R}}) - h(\mathtt{T}_{\mathtt{0,L-1}})}{\mathtt{p}^{\mathtt{L}}} \mod \mathtt{M} \\ &= \frac{\sum_{i=0}^{\mathtt{R}} \mathtt{T_i} \cdot \mathtt{p}^i - \sum_{i=0}^{L-1} \mathtt{T_i} \cdot p^i}{\mathtt{p}^{\mathtt{L}}} \mod \mathtt{M} \\ &= \frac{\sum_{i=\mathtt{L}}^{\mathtt{R}} \mathtt{T_i} \cdot \mathtt{p}^i}{\mathtt{p}^{\mathtt{L}}} \mod \mathtt{M} \\ &= \sum_{i=\mathtt{L}}^{\mathtt{R}} \mathtt{T_i} \cdot \mathtt{p}^{i-\mathtt{L}} \mod \mathtt{M} \end{aligned}$$

Now, to compute the division part $(1/\mathtt{p}^{\mathtt{L}})$, we need to convert it into its multiplicative inverse $(\mathtt{p}^{-\mathtt{L}})$ such that the equation becomes:

$$h(\mathtt{T}_{\mathtt{L,R}}) = (h(\mathtt{T}_{\mathtt{0,R}}) - h(\mathtt{T}_{\mathtt{0,L-1}})) \cdot \mathtt{p}^{-\mathtt{L}} \mod \mathtt{M}$$

That can be implemented[27] as shown below:

```
int hash_fast(int L, int R) {                         // O(1) hash of any substr
  if (L == 0) return h[R];                            // h is the prefix hashes
  int ans = 0;
  ans = ((h[R] - h[L-1]) % M + M) % M;                // compute differences
  ans = ((ll)ans * modInverse(P[L], M)) % M;          // remove P[L]^-1 (mod M)
  return ans;
}
```

6.6.3 Rabin-Karp String Matching Algorithm

Let us consider the String Matching problem described earlier. The well-known KMP algorithm can solve this problem in $O(n+m)$ where n is the length of string T and m is the length of string P. Alternatively, we can also solve this problem with rolling hash computation.

In the brute force approach, we compare each substring of length m in T. However, instead of comparing the (sub)strings directly in $O(m)$, we can compare their hash values in $O(1)$. First, do a rolling hash computation on string T and also compute the hash value of string P (one time). Next, for each substring of T of length m, get its hash value and compare it with $h(\mathtt{P}_{\mathtt{0,m-1}})$. Therefore, the overall algorithm has an $O(n+m)$ complexity. This algorithm is known as **Rabin-Karp** algorithm. We have implemented this algorithm as a working code below (this code is an extension from the code shown in Section 6.4.2).

Source code: `ch6/string_matching.cpp|java|py|ml`

One advantage of learning string hashing is that we can solve various variants of String Matching problems in which it may not be easy to use or modify the KMP algorithm. For example, counting the number of palindromic substring or counting the number of tuples $\langle \mathtt{i,j,k,l} \rangle$ such that $\mathtt{T}_{\mathtt{i,j}} = \mathtt{P}_{\mathtt{k,l}}$.

[27]Please review the inclusion-exclusion principle like the one shown in Book 1 and Section 5.3.10 on extended Euclidean algorithm/modular multiplicative inverse.

6.6.4 Collisions Probability

You might notice that there may be a case where two different strings have the same hash value; in other words, a *collision* happens. Such a collision is inevitable as the number of possible string is "infinite" (often much larger[28] than M). What we want with hashing are: $h(\texttt{T}) = h(\texttt{P})$ if $\texttt{T} = \texttt{P}$, and $h(\texttt{T}) \neq h(\texttt{P})$ if $\texttt{T} \neq \texttt{P}$. The first one is obvious from the hash function, but the second one is not guaranteed. So, we want $h(\texttt{T}) \neq h(\texttt{P})$ to be very likely when $\texttt{T} \neq \texttt{P}$. Now let us analyze the collisions probability on these scenarios:

- Comparing 2 random strings.
  The collision probability is $\frac{1}{\texttt{M}}$ and with $\texttt{M} = 10^9 + 7$ shown in this section, the collisions probability is quite small.
- Comparing 1 string with k other strings,
  i.e., whether there exists a particular string in a set of k strings.
  In this case, the collisions probability is $\frac{k}{\texttt{M}}$.
- Comparing k strings to each other, e.g., determine whether these k strings are unique.
  In this case, it is easier for us to first compute the non-collision probability, which is $\frac{\texttt{M}}{\texttt{M}} \cdot \frac{\texttt{M}-1}{\texttt{M}} \cdots \frac{\texttt{M}-k+1}{\texttt{M}} = \frac{P(\texttt{M},k)}{\texttt{M}^k}$, where $P(\texttt{M}, k)$ is k-permutation of M.
  Then, the collisions probability is $1 - \frac{P(\texttt{M},k)}{\texttt{M}^k}$.
  Let $\texttt{M} = 10^9 + 7$, with $k = 10^4$, the collisions probability is $\approx 5\%$.
  With $k = 10^5$, the collisions probability becomes $\approx 99\%$.
  With $k = 10^6$, it is pretty much guaranteed there is a collision[29].

The collisions probability on the third scenario is extremely bad with a large number of strings, so how can we handle this? One option is to use a larger M, e.g., $10^{18} + 9$ (need to use 64-bit[30] integer data type). However, using M larger than 32-bit integer may cause an overflow when computing the hash value[31]. Another better alternative is using **multiple hashes**. Thus, a string T has multiple hash values (usually 2 suffices) with different p and M, i.e., $\langle h_1(\texttt{T}_{0,n-1}), h_2(\texttt{T}_{0,n-1}), ...\rangle$, and so on. Then, two strings are considered the same only when all their hash values are the same.

Programming exercises related to String Hashing (most have alternative solutions):

1. Entry Level: *Kattis - stringmatching* * (try Rabin-Karp or KMP)
2. **UVa 11475 - Extend to Palindromes *** (similar with UVa 12467)
3. **UVa 12467 - Secret word *** (hashing/'border' of KMP; see UVa 11475)
4. **UVa 12604 - Caesar Cipher *** (try Rabin-Karp/KMP up to 62 times)
5. *Kattis - animal* * (Singapore15 preliminary; hash the subtrees and compare them)
6. *Kattis - hashing* * (the problem description is very clear; good hashing practice; or use Suffix Array+Sparse Table)
7. *Kattis - typo* * (rolling hash; update hash value when character $s[i]$ is deleted from string s; use 2 large prime modulo to be safe)

   Also see String Matching programming exercises at Section 6.4.

---

[28]Consider the Pigeonhole Principle.

[29]Try $k = 23$ and $\texttt{M} = 355$ to understand the Birthday Paradox mentioned earlier.

[30]Or 128-bit prime if the contest supports 128-bit integer, which may not always be the case.

[31]Observe that in `prepareP()`, `computeRollingHash(T)`, and `hash_fast(L, R)`, we cast `int` to `ll` when multiplying to avoid overflow.

6.7 Anagram and Palindrome

In this section, we will discuss two not-so-rare string processing problems that may require more advanced (string) data structure(s) and/or algorithm(s) compared to the ones discussed in Section 6.2. They are anagram and palindrome.

6.7.1 Anagram

An anagram is a word (or phrase/string) whose letters (characters) can be rearranged to obtain another word, e.g., '`elevenplustwo`' is an anagram of '`twelveplusone`'. Two words/strings that have different lengths are obviously not anagram.

Sorting Solution

The common strategy to check if two equal-length words/strings of n characters are anagram is to sort the letters of the words/strings and compare the results. For example, take `wordA = 'cab'`, `wordB = 'bca'`. After sorting, `wordA = 'abc'` and `wordB = 'abc'` too, so they are anagram. Review Book 1 for various sorting techniques. This runs in $O(n \log n)$.

Direct Addressing Table Solution

Another potential strategy to check if two words are anagram is to check if the character frequencies of both words are the same. We do not have to use a full fledged Hash Table but we can use a simpler Direct Addressing Table (DAT) (review Hash Table section in Book 1) to map characters of the first word to their frequencies in $O(n)$. We do the same with the characters of the second word. Then we compare those frequencies in $O(k)$ where k is the number of size of alphabets, e.g., 255 for ASCII characters, 26 for lowercase alphabet characters, 52 for both lowercase and uppercase alphabet characters, etc.

6.7.2 Palindrome

A palindrome is a word (or a sequence/string) that can be read the same way in either direction. For example, '**AB<u>C</u>D<u>C</u>BA**' is a palindrome.

Simple $O(n)$ Palindrome Check

Given a string s with length n characters, we can check whether s is a palindrome via definition, i.e. by reversing[32] the string s and then comparing s with its reverse. However, we can be slightly more clever by just comparing the characters in string s up to its middle character. It does not matter if the palindrome is of even length or odd length. This one is $O(n/2) = O(n)$.

```
// we assume that s is a global variable
bool isPal(int l, int r) {                    // is s[l..r] a palindrome
  int n = (r-l)+1;
  for (int i = 0; i < n/2; ++i)
    if (s[l+i] != s[r-i])
      return false;
  return true;
}
```

[32]In C++, we can use reverse(s.begin(), s.end()) to reverse a C++ string s.

$O(n^2)$ Palindrome Substrings Checks

A common variant of palindrome problems involves counting the number of substrings (l, r) of a string s with length n characters that are palindromes. We can obviously do a naive Complete Search check in $O(n^3)$ like this:

```
int countPal() {
  int n = (int)strlen(s), ans = 0;
  for (int i = 0; i < n; ++i)                  // this is O(n^2)
    for (int j = i+1; j < n; ++j)
      if (isPal(i, j))                         // x O(n), so O(n^3) total
        ++ans;
  return ans;
}
```

But if we realize that many subproblems (substrings) are clearly overlapping, we can define a memo table to describe that substring so that each substring is only computed once. This way, we have an $O(n^2)$ Dynamic Programming solution.

```
int isPalDP(int l, int r) {                    // is s[l..r] a palindrome
  if (l == r) return 1;                        // one character
  if (l+1 == r) return s[l] == s[r];           // two characters
  int &ans = memo[l][r];
  if (ans != -1) return ans;                   // has been computed
  ans = 0;
  if (s[l] == s[r]) ans = isPalDP(l+1, r-1);   // if true, recurse inside
  return ans;
}

int countPalDP() {
  int n = (int)strlen(s), ans = 0;
  memset(memo, -1, sizeof memo);
  for (int i = 0; i < n; ++i)                  // this is O(n^2)
    for (int j = i+1; j < n; ++j)
      if (isPalDP(i, j))                       // x O(1), so O(n^2) total
        ++ans;
  return ans;
}
```

Generating Palindrome from a Non-Palindrome String with $O(n^2)$ DP

If the original string s is not a palindrome, we can edit it to make it a palindrome, by either adding a new character to s, deleting existing characters from s, or replacing a character in s with another character. This is like the edit distance problem, but customized to this palindrome problem. Typical state is: s(l, r) and the typical transition is: if str[l] == str[r], then recurse to (l+1, r-1), otherwise find min of (l+1, r) or (l, r-1), as illustrated below.

UVa 11151 - Longest Palindrome

Abridged problem description: Given a string of up to $n = 1000$ characters, determine the length of the longest palindrome that you can make from it by deleting zero or more characters. Examples:

'ADAM' → 'ADA' (of length 3, delete 'M')
'MADAM' → 'MADAM' (of length 5, delete nothing)
'NEVERODDOREVENING' → 'NEVERODDOREVEN' (of length 14, delete 'ING')
'RACEF1CARFAST' → 'RACECAR' (of length 7, delete 'F1' and 'FAST')

The DP solution: let $len(l, r)$ be the length of the longest palindrome from string `A[l..r]`.

Base cases:
If $(l = r)$, then $len(l, r) = 1$. // odd-length palindrome
If $(l + 1 = r)$, then $len(l, r) = 2$ if $(A[l] = A[r])$, or 1 otherwise. // even-length palindrome

Recurrences:
If $(A[l] = A[r])$, then $len(l, r) = 2 + len(l + 1, r - 1)$. // corner characters are the same
else $len(l, r) = max(len(l, r - 1), len(l + 1, r))$. // increase/decrease left/right side

This DP solution has time complexity of $O(n^2)$.

Anadrome and Palinagram

We can combine the concept of Anagram and Palindrome into Anadrome or Palinagram. Anadrome is a word that reads that have proper meaning when read forwards or backwards (like the palindrome), but also a different word for the different order of letters (like the anagram). For example, 'BATS' = 'STAB'. Palinagram is a palindrome that is an anagram with another word. For example, 'DAAMM' (not a proper English word) is an anagram of 'MADAM', which is also a palindrome. This version is asked in UVa 12770 - Palinagram.

Exercise 6.7.2.1*: Suppose that we are now interested to find the length of the longest substring that is also a palindrome in a given string s with length up to $n = 200\,000$ characters. For example, the Longest Palindromic Substring of "BANANA" is "ANANA" (of length 5) and the Longest Palindromic Substring of "STEVEN" is "EVE" (of length 3). Note that while the Longest Palindromic Substring(s) of a given string s is not necessarily unique, the (longest) length is unique. Show how to solve this problem using either:

- $O(n \log n)$ Suffix Tree/Array as discussed in Section 6.5.
  Hint: use the solution for **Exercise 6.5.3.8*** (LCE),
- $O(n \log n)$ String Hashing as discussed in Section 6.6,
- $O(n)$ using Manacher's algorithm [24].

Programming exercises related to Anagram and Palindrome:

- Anagram
  1. Entry Level: **UVa 00195 - Anagram** * (use `algorithm::next_permutation`)
  2. **UVa 00156 - Ananagram** * (easier with `algorithm::sort`)
  3. **UVa 00642 - Word Amalgamation** * (go through the given small dictionary for the list of possible anagrams)
  4. **UVa 12641 - Reodrnreig Lteetrs ...** * (anagram problem variation)
  5. **UVa 12770 - Palinagram** * (count frequencies; print odd frequency characters with except the last one – put it in the middle of a palindrome)
  6. *Kattis - multigram* * (brute force lengths that is divisor of the original length of the string; test)
  7. *Kattis - substringswitcheroo* * (anagram; generate all signature frequencies of all substrings of B; compare with all substrings of A; 9s TL)

  Extra UVa: *00148, 00454, 00630, 10098.*
- Palindrome (Checking)
  1. Entry Level: **UVa 00401 - Palindromes** * (simple palindrome check)
  2. **UVa 10848 - Make Palindrome Checker** * (related to UVa 10453; palindrome check, character frequency check, and a few others)
  3. **UVa 11584 - Partitioning by ...** * (use two $O(n^2)$ DP string; one for palindrome check and the other for partitioning)
  4. **UVa 11888 - Abnormal 89's** * (let ss = s+s; find reverse(s) in ss, but it cannot match the first n chars or the last n chars of ss)
  5. *Kattis - kaleidoscopicpalindromes* * (test all; when you try enlarging k, the answers are actually 'small')
  6. *Kattis - palindromesubstring* * (try all pairs of $O(n^2)$ substrings with at least 2 characters; keep the ones that are palindrome (use DP) in a sorted `set`)
  7. *Kattis - peragrams* * (only one odd frequency character can be in the center of palindrome once; the rest need to have even frequency)

  Extra UVa: *00257, 00353, 10945, 11221, 11309, 12960.*
- Palindrome (Generating)
  1. Entry Level: **UVa 10018 - Reverse and Add** * (generating palindrome with specific math simulation; very easy)
  2. **UVa 01239 - Greatest K-Palindrome ...** * (LA 4144 - Jakarta08; as $S \leq 1000$, brute-force is enough; consider odd and even length palindromes)
  3. **UVa 11404 - Palindromic Subsequence** * (similar to UVa 10453, 10739, and 11151; print the solution in lexicographically smallest manner)
  4. **UVa 12718 - Dromicpalin Substrings** * (LA 6659 - Dhaka13; try all substrings; count character frequencies in them and analyze)
  5. *Kattis - evilstraw* * (greedily match leftmost char s[0]/rightmost char s[n-1] with rightmost/leftmost matching s[i], respectively)
  6. *Kattis - makingpalindromes* * (s: (l, r, k); t: a bit challenging)
  7. *Kattis - names* * (add a letter or change a letter; complete search)

  Extra UVa: *10453, 10617, 10739, 11151.*

6.8 Solution to Non-Starred Exercises

Exercise 6.3.1.1: Different scoring schemes will yield different (global) alignments. If given a string alignment problem, read the problem statement and see what is the required cost for match, mismatch, insert, and delete. Adapt the algorithm accordingly.

Exercise 6.3.1.2: You have to save the predecessor information (the arrows) during the DP computation. Then follow the arrows using recursive backtracking.

Exercise 6.3.1.3: The DP solution only needs to refer to the previous row so it can utilize the 'space saving technique' by just using two rows, the current row and the previous row. The new space complexity is just $O(min(n, m))$, that is, put the shorter string as string 2 so that each row has fewer columns (less memory). The time complexity of this solution is still $O(nm)$. The only drawback of this approach, as with any other space saving technique is that we will not be able to reconstruct the optimal solution. So if the actual optimal solution is needed, we cannot use this space saving technique.

Exercise 6.3.1.4: Simply concentrate along the main diagonal with width d. We can speed up Needleman-Wunsch algorithm to $O(dn)$ by doing this.

Exercise 6.3.1.5: It involves Kadane's algorithm again (see maximum sum problem discussed in Book 1).

Exercise 6.3.2.1: "`pple`".

Exercise 6.3.2.2: Set score for match = 0, mismatch = 1, insert and delete = negative infinity and run the $O(nm)$ Needleman-Wunsch DP algorithm. However, this solution is not efficient and not natural, as we can simply use an $O(n)$ algorithm to scan both string 1 and string 2 and count how many characters are different.

Exercise 6.3.2.3: Reduced to LIS, $O(n \log k)$ solution. The reduction to LIS is not shown. Draw it and see how to reduce this problem into LIS.

Exercise 6.5.2.1: The LCP of suffix 1 and suffix 5 in Figure 6.3—right is '`A`'. The LCP of any 2 suffixes (that ends in a leaf vertex due to the usage of terminating symbol '$') is the Lowest Common Ancestor (LCA) between these 2 suffixes. It means that the path label of this LCA is shared between these 2 suffixes and the longest. It has several applications in Section 6.5.3.

Exercise 6.5.3.1: "`C`" is found (at index 6), "`CAT`" is not.

Exercise 6.5.3.2: "`ACATTA`". PS: The no overlap version (see **Exercise 6.5.3.5***) is "`ACATT`" or "`CATTA`".

Exercise 6.5.3.3: "`EVEN`".

Exercise 6.5.4.1: Index out of bound will never happen because when the first equality check holds, we always guarantee the first k characters of those two suffixes cannot contain the terminating character '$' thus checking $+k$ more characters would still not exceed the string length of `T`. Otherwise, the first equality check doesn't hold and the second equality check will be skipped.

Exercise 6.5.4.2: The given SA construction code uses terminating symbol '$' (ASCII 36). Therefore, it will think that a space: ' ' (ASCII 32) is another terminating symbol and confuses the sorting process. One way to deal with this is to replace all spaces with something higher than ASCII 36 (but still below 'A') or do not use space at all in `T`.

Exercise 6.5.4.3: "`AAAAAAAAAAAAAAA$`".

6.9 Chapter Notes

The material about String Alignment (Edit Distance), Longest Common Subsequence, and Trie/Suffix Trie/Tree/Array are originally from **A/P Sung Wing Kin, Ken** [34], School of Computing, National University of Singapore. The material has since evolved from a more theoretical style into the current competitive programming style.

The section about the harder Ad Hoc string processing problems (Section 6.2) was born from our experience with string-related problems and techniques. The number of programming exercises mentioned there is about half of all other string processing problems discussed in this chapter (the easier ones are in Book 1). These are not the typical ICPC problems/IOI tasks, but they are still good exercises to improve your programming skills.

We have expanded the discussion of *non classical* DP problems involving string in Section 6.3. We feel that the classical ones will be rarely asked in modern programming contests.

In Section 6.4, we discuss the library solutions and one fast algorithm (Knuth-Morris-Pratt (KMP) algorithm) for the String Matching problem. The KMP implementation will be useful if you have to modify basic string matching requirement yet you still need fast performance. We believe KMP is fast enough for finding pattern string in a long string for typical contest problems. Through experimentation, we conclude that the KMP implementation shown in this book is slightly faster than the built-in C `strstr`, C++ `string.find`, Java `String.indexOf`, Python `string.find`, and OCaml `search_forward`. If an even faster string matching algorithm is needed during contest time for one longer string and much more queries, we suggest using Suffix Array discussed in Section 6.5.4. In Section 6.6, we discuss string hashing techniques inside Rabin-Karp algorithm for solving some string processing problems including the String Matching algorithm. There are several other string matching algorithms that are not discussed yet like **Boyer-Moore**, **Z** algorithm, **Aho-Corasick**, **Finite State Automata**, etc. Interested readers are welcome to explore them.

The applications of Prefix Doubling algorithm of [21] for Suffix Array construction are inspired from the article "Suffix arrays - a programming contest approach" by [37]. We have integrated and synchronized many examples given there in this section. It is a good idea to solve *all* the programming exercises listed in Section 6.5 although they are only a few.

Compared to the first three editions of this book, this chapter has grown even more—similar case as with Chapter 5. However, there are more string topics that we have not touched yet: the **Shortest Common Superstring** problem, **Burrows-Wheeler transformation** algorithm, **Suffix Automaton**, **Radix Tree**, **Manacher's** algorithm, etc.

Statistics	1st	2nd	3rd	4th
Number of Pages	10	24	35	40 (+14%)
Written Exercises	4	24	33	15+16* = 30 (-9%)
Programming Exercises	54	129	164	245 (+49%)

The breakdown of the number of programming exercises from each section is shown below:

Section	Title	Appearance	% in Chapter	% in Book
6.2	**Ad Hoc Strings (Harder)**	123	≈ 50%	≈ 3.6%
6.3	String Processing with DP	33	≈ 13%	≈ 1.0%
6.4	String Matching	27	≈ 11%	≈ 0.8%
6.5	Suffix Trie/Tree/Array	20	≈ 8%	≈ 0.6%
6.6	String Hashing	7	≈ 3%	≈ 0.2%
6.7	**Anagram and Palindrome**	35	≈ 14%	≈ 1.0%
	Total	245		≈ 7.1%

Chapter 7

(Computational) Geometry

Let no man ignorant of geometry enter here.
— **Plato's Academy in Athens**

7.1 Overview and Motivation

(Computational[1]) Geometry is yet another topic that frequently appears in programming contests. Almost all ICPC problem sets have *at least one* geometry problem. If you are lucky, it will ask you for some geometry solution that you have learned before. Usually you draw the geometrical object(s), and then derive the solution from some basic geometric formulas. However, many geometry problems are the *computational* ones that require some complex algorithm(s).

In IOI, the existence of geometry-specific problems depends on the tasks chosen by the Scientific Committee that year. In recent years (2009-2019), IOI tasks have not feature a *pure* geometry-specific problems. However, in the earlier years [36], every IOI contained one or two geometry-related problems.

We have observed that geometry-related problems are usually not attempted during the early parts of the contest for *strategic reasons*[2] because the solutions for geometry-related problems have *lower* probability of getting Accepted (AC) during contest time compared to the solutions for other problem types in the problem set, e.g., Complete Search or Dynamic Programming problems. The typical issues with geometry problems are as follows:

- Many geometry problems have one and usually several tricky 'corner test cases', e.g., What if the lines are vertical (infinite gradient)?, What if the points are collinear?, What if the polygon is concave?, What if the polygon has too few points and it degenerates to a point or a line? What if the convex hull of a set of points is the set of points itself?, etc. Therefore, it is usually a very good idea to test your team's geometry solution with lots of corner test cases before you submit it for judging.

- There is a possibility of having floating point precision errors that cause even a 'correct' algorithm to get a Wrong Answer (WA) response.

- The solutions for geometry problems usually involve *tedious* coding.

[1]We differentiate between *pure* geometry problems and the *computational* geometry ones. Pure geometry problems can normally be solved by hand (pen and paper method). Computational geometry problems typically require running an algorithm using computer to obtain the solution.

[2]In programming contests that use a penalty-time policy like ICPC, the first hour is crucial for teams who aim to win as they have to quickly clear as many easier problems as fast as they can using as minimal contest time as possible. Unfortunately, typical geometry problems tend to be long and tricky.

These reasons cause many contestants to view spending precious (early) minutes attempting *other* problem types in the problem set to be more worthwhile than attempting a geometry problem that has a lower probability of acceptance.

However, another not-so-good reason for the noticeably fewer attempts for geometry problems in programming contests is because the contestants are not well prepared.

- The contestants forget some important basic formulas or are unable to derive the required (more complex) formulas from the basic ones.
- The contestants do not prepare well-written library functions *before* contests, and their attempts to code such functions during the stressful contest environment end up with not just one, but usually several[3], bug(s). In ICPC, the top teams usually fill a sizeable part of their hard copy material (which they can bring into the contest room) with lots of geometry formulas and library functions.

The main aim of this chapter is therefore to increase the number of attempts (and also AC[4] solutions) for geometry-related problems in programming contests. Study this chapter for some ideas on tackling (computational) geometry problems in ICPCs and IOIs. There are only two sections in this chapter.

In Section 7.2, we present many (it is impossible to enumerate all) English geometric terminologies[5] and various basic formulas for 0D, 1D, and 2D **geometry objects**[6] commonly found in programming contests. This section can be used as a quick reference when contestants are given geometry problems and are not sure of certain terminologies or forget some basic formulas.

In Section 7.3, we discuss several algorithms on 2D **polygons**. There are several nice pre-written library routines which can differentiate good from average teams (contestants) like the algorithms for deciding if a polygon is convex or concave, deciding if a point is inside or outside a polygon, cutting a polygon with a straight line, finding the convex hull of a set of points, etc.

In Section 7.4, we close the chapter by discussing a few topics involving the rare 3D geometry related problems.

The implementations of the formulas and computational geometry algorithms shown in this chapter use the following techniques to increase the probability of acceptance:

1. We highlight the special cases that can potentially arise and/or choose the implementation that reduces the number of such special cases.
2. We try to avoid floating point operations (i.e., divisions, square roots, and any other operations that can produce numerical errors) and work with precise integers whenever possible (i.e., integer additions, subtractions, multiplications).

[3]As a reference, the library code on points, lines, circles, triangles, and polygons shown in this chapter required several iterations of bug fixes since the first edition of this book to ensure that as many (usually subtle) bugs and special cases are handled properly.

[4]Attempting any problem, including a (computational) geometry problem, consumes contest time that can backfire if the solution is eventually not AC.

[5]IOI and ICPC contestants come from various nationalities and backgrounds. Therefore, we would like to get many contestants to be familiar with the English geometric terminologies.

[6]3D objects are very rare in programming contests due to their additional complexity. This is called the 'curse of dimensionality'. We defer the discussion of 3D geometry until Section 7.4.

3. However, if we really need to work with floating points, we will:

   (a) Do floating point equality test this way: `fabs(a-b) < EPS` where `EPS` is a small number[7] like `1e-9` (i.e., 10^{-9} or 0.000000001) instead of testing if `a == b`.

   (b) Check if a floating point number $x \geq 0.0$ by using `x > -EPS` (similarly to check if $x \leq 0.0$, we use `x < EPS`).

   (c) Use double-precision data type by default instead of single-precision data type.

   (d) Defer the floating point operation(s) as late as possible to reduce the effect of compounding errors.

   (e) Reduce the number of such floating point operation(s) as much as we can, e.g., instead of computing $a/b/c$ (two floating point divisions), we compute $a/(b * c)$ instead (only one floating point division).

Profile of Algorithm Inventors

Pythagoras of Samos ($\approx$ 500 BC) was a Greek mathematician and philosopher born on the island of Samos. He is best known for the Pythagorean theorem involving right triangles.

Euclid of Alexandria ($\approx$ 300 BC) was a Greek mathematician, the 'Father of Geometry'. He was from the city of Alexandria. His most influential work in mathematics (especially geometry) is the 'Elements'. In the 'Elements', Euclid deduced the principles of what is now called Euclidean geometry from a small set of axioms.

Heron of Alexandria ($\approx$ 10-70 AD) was an ancient Greek mathematician from the city of Alexandria, Roman Egypt—the same city as Euclid. His name is closely associated with his formula for finding the area of a triangle from its side lengths.

Ronald Lewis Graham (1935-2020) was an American mathematician. In 1972, he invented the Graham's scan algorithm for finding the convex hull of a finite set of points in the plane. There are now many other algorithm variants and improvements for finding the convex hull.

A.M. Andrew is a relatively unknown figure other than the fact that he published yet another convex hull algorithm in 1979 [1]. We use Andrew's Monotone Chain algorithm as the default algorithm for finding the convex hull in this book.

[7] Unless otherwise stated, this `1e-9` is the default value of EPS(ilon) that we use in this chapter.

7.2 Basic Geometry Objects with Libraries

7.2.1 0D Objects: Points

1. A **point** is the basic building block of higher dimensional geometry objects. In 2D Euclidean[8] space, points are usually represented with a struct in C/C++ (or Class in Java/Python/OCaml) with two[9] members: the **x** and **y** coordinates w.r.t. origin, i.e., coordinate (0, 0).

   If the problem description uses integer coordinates, use `ints`; otherwise, use `doubles`. In order to be generic, we use the floating-point version of `struct point` in this book. Default and user-defined constructors can be used to simplify coding later.

```
// struct point_i { int x, y; };                      // minimalist form
struct point_i {
  int x, y;                                           // default
  point_i() { x = y = 0; }                            // default
  point_i(int _x, int _y) : x(_x), y(_y) {}           // user-defined
};

struct point {
  double x, y;                                        // higher precision
  point() { x = y = 0.0; }                            // default
  point(double _x, double _y) : x(_x), y(_y) {}       // user-defined
};
```

2. Sometimes we need to sort the points based on some criteria. One frequently used sort criteria is to sort the points based on increasing x-coordinates and if tie, by increasing y-coordinates. This has application in Andrew's Monotone Chain algorithm in Section 7.3.7. We can easily do that by overloading the less than operator inside `struct point` and using a sorting library.

```
struct point {
  double x, y;                                        // higher precision
  point() { x = y = 0.0; }                            // default
  point(double _x, double _y) : x(_x), y(_y) {}       // user-defined
  bool operator < (point other) const {               // override <
    if (fabs(x-other.x) > EPS)                        // useful for sorting
      return x < other.x;                             // first, by x
    return y < other.y;                               // if tie, by y
  }
};

// in int main(), assuming we already have a populated vector<point> P
  sort(P.begin(), P.end());                           // P is now sorted
```

[8]For simplicity, the 2D and 3D Euclidean spaces are the 2D and 3D world that we encounter in real life.

[9]Add one more member, **z**, if you are working in 3D Euclidean space. As 3D-related problems are very rare, we omit **z** from the default implementation. See Section 7.4 for some 3D geometry discussions.

Note that the implementation of sorting a set of n points uses our default `EPS = 1e-9`. While this value is small enough, it is still not fully precise. Here is a rare counter example where the given implementation (that uses `EPS = 1e-9`) does not work.

```
// in int main()
  vector<point> P;
  P.emplace_back(2e-9, 0);                        // largest
  P.push_back({0, 2});                            // smallest
  P.push_back({1e-9, 1});                         // second smallest
  sort(P.begin(), P.end());
  for (auto &pt : P)                              // the result is
    printf("%.9lf, %.9lf\n", pt.x, pt.y);         // unexpected
```

To counter this issue, we need to make `EPS` even smaller. Rule of Thumb: when solving a geometry problem, check the required precision and set `EPS` appropriately.

3. Sometimes we need to test if two points are equal. We can easily do that by overloading the equal operator inside `struct point`. Note that this test is easier in the integer version (`struct point_i`).

```
struct point {
  double x, y;                                    // higher precision
  .. // same as above
  bool operator == (const point &other) const {  // use EPS
    return (fabs(x-other.x) < EPS) && (fabs(y-other.y) < EPS);
  }
};

// in int main()
  point P1 = {0, 0}, P2(0, 0), P3(0, 1);          // two init methods
  printf("%d\n", P1 == P2);                       // true
  printf("%d\n", P1 == P3);                       // false
```

4. We can measure the Euclidean distance[10] between two points by using this function:

```
double dist(const point &p1, const point &p2) {  // Euclidean distance
  // hypot(dx, dy) returns sqrt(dx*dx + dy*dy)
  return hypot(p1.x-p2.x, p1.y-p2.y);             // returns double
}
```

[10] The Euclidean distance between two points is simply the distance that can be measured with a ruler. Algorithmically, it can be found with the Pythagorean formula that we will see again in the subsection about triangles later. Here, we simply use a library function.

5. We can rotate a point by an angle[11] θ counterclockwise around the origin (0, 0) by using a rotation matrix:

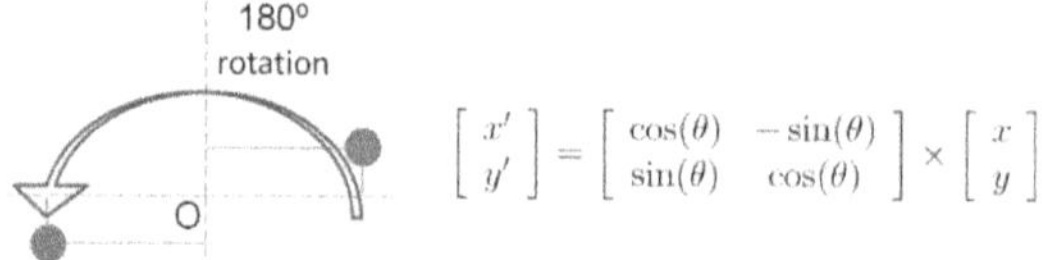

Figure 7.1: Rotating the point (10, 3) by 180° counterclockwise around the origin (0, 0)

```
// M_PI is in <cmath>, but if your compiler does not have it, use
// const double PI = acos(-1.0)                    // or 2.0 * acos(0.0)

double DEG_to_RAD(double d) { return d*M_PI / 180.0; }
double RAD_to_DEG(double r) { return r*180.0 / M_PI; }

// rotate p by theta degrees CCW w.r.t. origin (0, 0)
point rotate(const point &p, double theta) {      // theta in degrees
  double rad = DEG_to_RAD(theta);                 // convert to radians
  return point(p.x*cos(rad) - p.y*sin(rad),
               p.x*sin(rad) + p.y*cos(rad));
}
```

Exercise 7.2.1.1: In this section, you have seen a simple way to sort a set of n points based on increasing x-coordinates and if tie, by increasing y-coordinates. Show a way to sort n-1 points with respect to a pivot point p that has the lowest y-coordinate and if tie, rightmost x-coordinate!

Exercise 7.2.1.2: Compute the Euclidean distance between the points (2, 2) and (6, 5)!

Exercise 7.2.1.3: Rotate the point (10, 3) by 90 degrees *counterclockwise* around the origin. What is the new coordinate of the rotated point? The answer is easy to compute by hand. Notice that *counterclockwise* rotation is different than *clockwise* rotation (especially when the rotation angle is not 0 or 180 degree(s)).

Exercise 7.2.1.4: Rotate the same point (10, 3) by 77 degrees counterclockwise around the origin. What is the new coordinate of the rotated point? (This time you need to use a calculator and the rotation matrix).

---

[11]Humans usually work with degrees, but many mathematical functions in most programming languages (e.g., C/C++/Java/Python/OCaml) work with radians. To convert an angle from degrees to radians, multiply the angle by $\frac{\pi}{180.0}$. To convert an angle from radians to degrees, multiply the angle with $\frac{180.0}{\pi}$.

7.2.2 1D Objects: Lines

1. A **line** in 2D Euclidean space is the set of points whose coordinates satisfy a given linear equation $ax + by + c = 0$. Subsequent functions in this subsection assume that this linear equation has $b = 1$ for non-vertical lines and $b = 0$ for vertical lines unless otherwise stated. Lines are usually represented with a struct in C/C++ (or Class in Java/Python/OCaml) with three members: the three coefficients a, b, and c of that line equation.

```
struct line { double a, b, c; };                          // most versatile
```

2. We can compute the line equation if we are given *at least* two points on that line via the following function.

```
// the answer is stored in the third parameter (pass by reference)
void pointsToLine(const point &p1, const point &p2, line &l) {
  if (fabs(p1.x-p2.x) < EPS)                              // vertical line
    l = {1.0, 0.0, -p1.x};                                // default values
  else
    l = {-(double)(p1.y-p2.y) / (p1.x-p2.x),
         1.0,                                             // IMPORTANT: b = 1.0
         -(double)(l.a*p1.x) - p1.y};
}
```

3. We can compute the line equation if we are given *one* point and the gradient of that non-vertical line (see the other line equation in **Exercise 7.2.2.1** and its limitation).

```
// convert point and gradient/slope to line, not for vertical line
void pointSlopeToLine(point p, double m, line &l) { // m < Inf
  l.a = -m;                                               // always -m
  l.b = 1.0;                                              // always 1.0
  l.c = -((l.a * p.x) + (l.b * p.y));                     // compute this
}
```

4. We can test whether two lines are *parallel* by checking if their coefficients a and b are the same. We can further test whether two lines are *the same* by checking if they are parallel and their coefficients c are the same (i.e., all three coefficients a, b, c are the same). Recall that in our implementation, we have fixed the value of coefficient b to 0.0 for all vertical lines and to 1.0 for all *non* vertical lines.

```
bool areParallel(line l1, line l2) {                      // check a & b
  return (fabs(l1.a-l2.a) < EPS) && (fabs(l1.b-l2.b) < EPS);
}

bool areSame(line l1, line l2) {                          // also check c
  return areParallel(l1, l2) && (fabs(l1.c-l2.c) < EPS);
}
```

5. If two lines[12] are not parallel (and also not the same), they will intersect at a point. That intersection point (x, y) can be found by solving the system of two linear algebraic equations[13] with two unknowns: $a_1x + b_1y + c_1 = 0$ and $a_2x + b_2y + c_2 = 0$.

```
// returns true (+ intersection point p) if two lines are intersect
bool areIntersect(line l1, line l2, point &p) {
  if (areParallel(l1, l2)) return false;            // no intersection
  // solve system of 2 linear algebraic equations with 2 unknowns
  p.x = (l2.b*l1.c - l1.b*l2.c) / (l2.a*l1.b - l1.a*l2.b);
  // special case: test for vertical line to avoid division by zero
  if (fabs(l1.b) > EPS) p.y = -(l1.a*p.x + l1.c);
  else                  p.y = -(l2.a*p.x + l2.c);
  return true;
}
```

6. **Line Segment** is a line with two end points with *finite length.*

7. **Vector**[14] is a line segment (thus it has two end points and length/magnitude) with a *direction.* Usually[15], vectors are represented with a struct in C/C++ (or Class in Java/Python/OCaml) with two members: the **x** and **y** magnitude of the vector. The magnitude of the vector can be scaled if needed.

8. We can translate (move) a point with respect to a vector as a vector describes the displacement magnitude in the x- and y-axes.

```
struct vec { double x, y; // name: 'vec' is different from STL vector
  vec(double _x, double _y) : x(_x), y(_y) {}
};

vec toVec(const point &a, const point &b) {       // convert 2 points
  return vec(b.x-a.x, b.y-a.y);                   // to vector a->b
}

vec scale(const vec &v, double s) {               // s = [<1..1..>1]
  return vec(v.x*s, v.y*s);                       // shorter/eq/longer
}                                                 // return a new vec

point translate(const point &p, const vec &v) {  // translate p
  return point(p.x+v.x, p.y+v.y);                 // according to v
}                                                 // return a new point
```

[12]To avoid confusion, please differentiate between the line (infinite) and the line *segment* (finite) that will be discussed later.

[13]See Section 9.17 for the general solution of a system of linear equations.

[14]Do not confuse this with C++ STL `vector` or Java `Vector`.

[15]Another potential design strategy is to merge `struct point` with `struct vec` as they are similar.

9. We can compute the angle aob given three *distinct* points: a, o, and b, using dot product of vector oa and ob. Since $oa \cdot ob = |oa| \times |ob| \times \cos(\theta)$, we have[16] $\theta = \arccos(oa \cdot ob/(|oa| \times |ob|))$.

```
double angle(const point &a, const point &o, const point &b) {
  vec oa = toVec(o, a), ob = toVec(o, b);          // a != o != b
  return acos(dot(oa, ob) / sqrt(norm_sq(oa) * norm_sq(ob)));
}                                                  // angle aob in rad
```

10. Given three points p, q, and r, we can determine whether point p, q, and then r, in that order, makes a left (counterclockwise) or a right (clockwise turn); or whether the three points p, q, and r are collinear. This can be determined with *cross product*. Let pq and pr be the two vectors obtained from these three points. The cross product $pq \times pr$ results in another vector that is perpendicular to both pq and pr. The magnitude of this vector is equal to the area of the *parallelogram* that the vectors span[17]. If the magnitude is positive/zero/negative, then we know that $p \rightarrow q \rightarrow r$ is a left turn/collinear/right turn, respectively (see Figure 7.2—right). The left turn test is more famously known as the **CCW (Counter Clockwise) Test**.

```
double cross(vec a, vec b) { return a.x*b.y - a.y*b.x; }
// returns true if point r is on the left side of line pq
bool ccw(point p, point q, point r) {
  return cross(toVec(p, q), toVec(p, r)) > EPS;
}
// returns true if point r is on the same line as the line pq
bool collinear(point p, point q, point r) {
  return fabs(cross(toVec(p, q), toVec(p, r))) < EPS;
}
```

11. Given a point p and a line l (described by two points a and b), we can compute the minimum distance from p to l by first computing the location of point c in l that is closest to point p (see Figure 7.2—left) and then obtaining the Euclidean distance between p and c. We can view point c as point a translated by a scaled magnitude u of vector ab, or $c = a + u \times ab$. To get u, we do a scalar projection of vector ap onto vector ab by using dot product (see the dotted vector $ac = u \times ab$ in Figure 7.2—left).

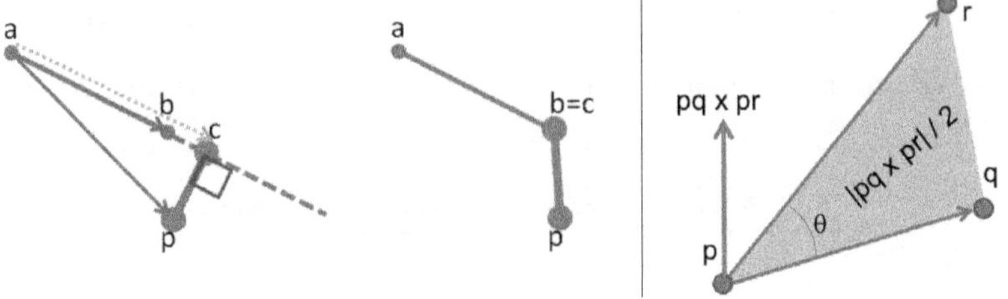

Figure 7.2: Distance to Line (left) and to Line Segment (middle); Cross Product (right)

[16] `acos` is the C/C++ function name for mathematical function `arccos`.

[17] The area of triangle pqr is therefore *half* of the area of this parallelogram.

The short implementation of this solution is shown below.

```
double dot(vec a, vec b) { return (a.x*b.x + a.y*b.y); }

double norm_sq(vec v) { return v.x*v.x + v.y*v.y; }

// returns the distance from p to the line defined by
// two points a and b (a and b must be different)
// the closest point is stored in the 4th parameter (byref)
double distToLine(point p, point a, point b, point &c) {
  vec ap = toVec(a, p), ab = toVec(a, b);
  double u = dot(ap, ab) / norm_sq(ab);
  // formula: c = a + u*ab
  c = translate(a, scale(ab, u));                 // translate a to c
  return dist(p, c);                              // Euclidean distance
}
```

Note that this is not the only way to get the required answer.
Check the written exercise in this section for the alternative way.

12. If we are given a line *segment* instead (defined by two *end* points a and b), then the minimum distance from point p to line segment ab must also consider two special cases, the end points a and b of that line segment (see Figure 7.2—middle). The implementation is very similar to `distToLine` function above.

```
// returns the distance from p to the line segment ab defined by
// two points a and b (technically, a has to be different than b)
// the closest point is stored in the 4th parameter (byref)
double distToLineSegment(point p, point a, point b, point &c) {
  vec ap = toVec(a, p), ab = toVec(a, b);
  double u = dot(ap, ab) / norm_sq(ab);
  if (u < 0.0) {                                  // closer to a
    c = point(a.x, a.y);
    return dist(p, a);                            // dist p to a
  }
  if (u > 1.0) {                                  // closer to b
    c = point(b.x, b.y);
    return dist(p, b);                            // dist p to b
  }
  return distToLine(p, a, b, c);                  // use distToLine
}
```

Source code: `ch7/points_lines.cpp|java|py|ml`

Exercise 7.2.2.1: A line can also be described with this mathematical equation: $y = mx+c$ where m is the 'gradient'/'slope' of the line and c is the 'y-intercept' constant.
Which form is better ($ax + by + c = 0$ or the slope-intercept form $y = mx + c$)? Why?

Exercise 7.2.2.2: Find the equation of the line that passes through these two points:

a. (2, 2) and (4, 3).
b. (2, 2) and (2, 4).

Exercise 7.2.2.3: Suppose we insist to use the other line equation: $y = mx + c$. Show how to compute the required line equation given two points the line passes through! Try on two points (2, 2) and (2, 4) as in **Exercise 7.2.2.2** (b). Do you encounter any problem?

Exercise 7.2.2.4: Translate a point *c* (3, 2) according to a vector *ab* (defined below). What is the new coordinate of the point?

a. Vector *ab* is defined by two points: *a* (2, 2) and *b* (4, 3).
b. Same as (a) above, but the magnitude of vector *ab* is reduced by *half*.
c. Same as (a) above (without halving the magnitude of vector *ab* in (b) above), but then we rotate the resulting point by 90 degrees counterclockwise around the origin.

Exercise 7.2.2.5: Rotate a point *c* (3, 2) by 90 degrees counterclockwise around the origin, then translate the resulting point according to a vector *ab* (same as in **Exercise 7.2.2.5** (a)). What is the new coordinate of the point? Is the result similar with the previous **Exercise 7.2.2.5** (a)? What can we learn from this phenomenon?

Exercise 7.2.2.6: Rotate a point *c* (3, 2) by 90 degrees counterclockwise but around the point *p* (2, 1) (note that point *p* is *not* the origin). Hint: You need to translate the point.

Exercise 7.2.2.7: Compute the angle *aob* in degrees:

a. *a* (2, 2), *o* (2, 6), and *b* (6, 6)
b. *a* (2, 2), *o* (2, 4), and *b* (4, 3)

Exercise 7.2.2.8: Determine if point *r* (35, 30) is on the left side of, collinear with, or is on the right side of a line that passes through two points *p* (3, 7) and *q* (11, 13).

Exercise 7.2.2.9: We can compute the location of point *c* in line *l* that is closest to point *p* by finding the other line l' that is perpendicular with line *l* and passes through point *p*. The closest point *c* is the intersection point between line *l* and l'. Now, how do we obtain a line perpendicular to *l*? Are there special cases that we have to be careful with?

Exercise 7.2.2.10: Given a point *p* and a line *l* (described by two points *a* and *b*), compute the location of a reflection point *r* of point *p* when mirrored against line *l*.

Exercise 7.2.2.11*: Given two line *segments* (each line segment is given by two endpoints), determine whether they intersect. For example, line segment 1 between (0, 0) to (10, 0) does *not* intersect line segment 2 between (7, 1) to (7, 0.1) whereas that line segment 1 intersects line segment 3 between (7, 1) to (7, -1).

7.2.3 2D Objects: Circles

1. A **circle** centered at coordinate (a, b) in a 2D Euclidean space with **radius** r is the set of all points (x, y) such that $(x - a)^2 + (y - b)^2 = r^2$.

2. To check if a point is inside, outside, or exactly on the border of a circle, we can use the following function. Modify this function a bit for the floating point version.

```
int insideCircle(const point_i &p, const point_i &c, int r) {
  int dx = p.x-c.x, dy = p.y-c.y;
  int Euc = dx*dx + dy*dy, rSq = r*r;              // all integer
  return Euc < rSq ? 1 : (Euc == rSq ? 0 : -1);  // in/border/out
}
```

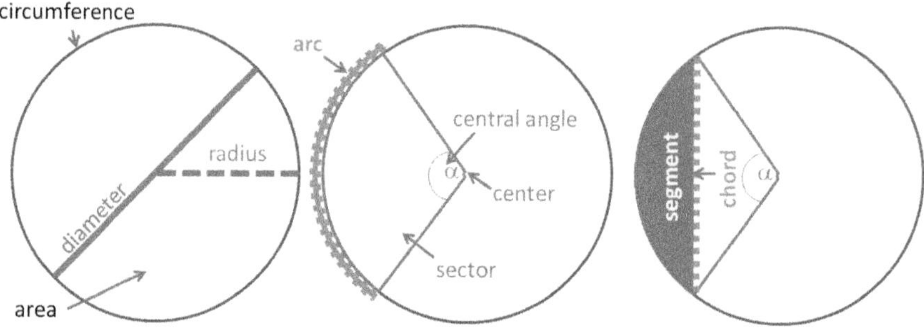

Figure 7.3: Circles

3. The constant **Pi** (π) is the ratio of *any* circle's circumference to its diameter. For some programming language, this constant is already defined, e.g., `M_PI` in C++ <cmath> library. Otherwise, the safest value to be used in programming contest is `PI` $= \arccos(-1.0)$ or `PI` $= 2 * \arccos(0.0)$.

4. A circle with radius r has **diameter** $d = 2 \times r$ and **circumference** (or **perimeter**) $c = 2 \times \pi \times r$.

5. A circle with radius r has **area** $A = \pi \times r^2$

6. **Arc** of a circle is defined as a connected section of the circumference c of the circle. Given the central angle α (angle with vertex at the circle's center, see Figure 7.3—middle) in degrees, we can compute the length of the corresponding arc as $\frac{\alpha}{360.0} \times c$.

7. **Chord** of a circle is defined as a line segment whose endpoints lie on the circle[18]. A circle with radius r and a central angle α in degrees (see Figure 7.3—right) has the corresponding chord with length $\sqrt{2 \times r^2 \times (1 - \cos(\alpha))}$. This can be derived from the **Law of Cosines**—see the explanation of this law in the discussion about Triangles later. Another way to compute the length of chord given r and α is to use Trigonometry: $2 \times r \times \sin(\alpha/2)$. Trigonometry is also discussed below.

[18]Diameter is the longest chord in a circle.

8. **Sector** of a circle is defined as a region of the circle enclosed by two radii and an arc lying between the two radii. A circle with area A and a central angle α (in degrees)—see Figure 7.3, middle—has the corresponding sector area $\frac{\alpha}{360.0} \times A$.

9. **Segment** of a circle is defined as a region of the circle enclosed by a chord and an arc lying between the chord's endpoints (see Figure 7.3—right). The area of a segment can be found by subtracting the area of the corresponding sector with the area of an isosceles triangle with sides: r, r, and chord-length.

10. Given 2 points on the circle ($p1$ and $p2$) and radius r of the corresponding circle, we can determine the location of the centers ($c1$ and $c2$) of the two possible circles (see Figure 7.4). The code is shown below.

```
bool circle2PtsRad(point p1, point p2, double r, point &c) {
  double d2 = (p1.x-p2.x) * (p1.x-p2.x) + (p1.y-p2.y) * (p1.y-p2.y);
  double det = r*r/d2 - 0.25;
  if (det < EPS) return false;
  double h = sqrt(det);
  // to get the other center, reverse p1 and p2
  c.x = (p1.x+p2.x) * 0.5 + (p1.y-p2.y) * h;
  c.y = (p1.y+p2.y) * 0.5 + (p2.x-p1.x) * h;
  return true;
}
```

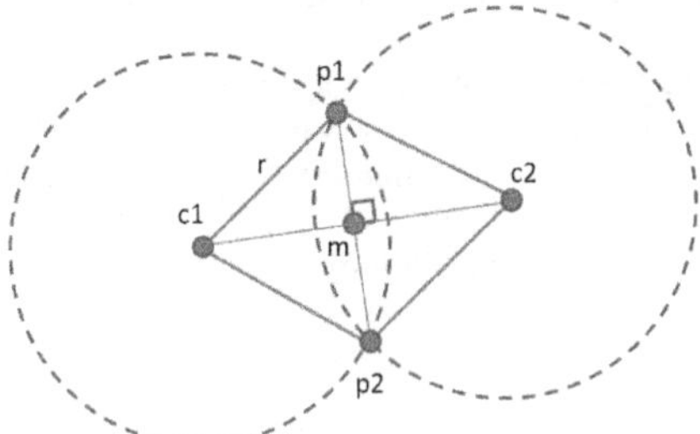

Figure 7.4: Explanation for Circle Through 2 Points and Radius

Explanation: Let $c1$ and $c2$ be the centers of the 2 possible circles that go through 2 given points $p1$ and $p2$ and have radius r. The quadrilateral $p1 - c2 - p2 - c1$ is a rhombus (see Section 7.2.5), since its four sides (or length r) are equal.

Let m be the intersection of the 2 diagonals of the rhombus $p1 - c2 - p2 - c1$. According to the property of a rhombus, m bisects the 2 diagonals, and the 2 diagonals are perpendicular to each other. We realize that $c1$ and $c2$ can be calculated by scaling the vectors $mp1$ and $mp2$ by an appropriate ratio ($mc1/mp1$) to get the same magnitude as $mc1$, then rotating the points $p1$ and $p2$ around m by 90 degrees.

In the code above, variable h is *half* the ratio $mc1/mp1$ (work out on paper why h can be calculated as such). In the 2 lines calculating the coordinates of one of the centers, the first operands of the additions are the coordinates of m, while the second operands of the additions are the result of scaling and rotating the vector $mp2$ around m.

Source code: `ch7/circles.cpp|java|py|ml`

7.2.4 2D Objects: Triangles

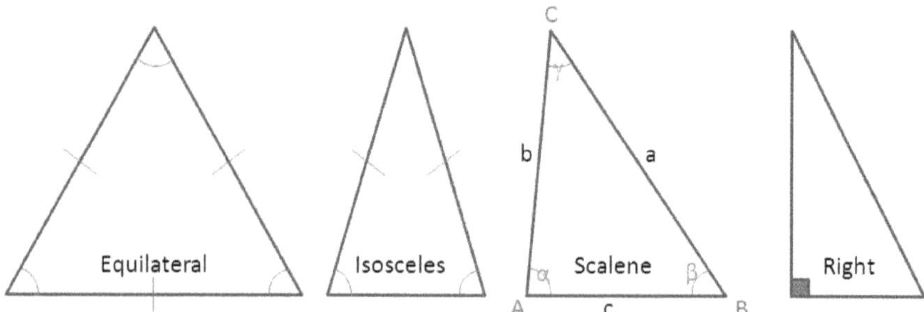

Figure 7.5: Triangles

1. **Triangle** (three angles) is a polygon with three vertices and three edges.
   There are several types of triangles:
   a. **Equilateral**: Three equal-length edges and all inside (interior) angles are 60 degrees,
   b. **Isosceles**: Two edges have the same length and two interior angles are the same,
   c. **Scalene**: All edges have different lengths,
   d. **Right**: *One* of its interior angle is 90 degrees (or a **right angle**).

2. To check if three line segments of length a, b and c can form a triangle, we can simply check these *triangle inequalities*: $(a + b > c)$ && $(a + c > b)$ && $(b + c > a)$.
   If the result is false, then the three line segments cannot form a triangle.
   If the three lengths are sorted, with a being the smallest and c the largest, then we can simplify the check to just $(a + b > c)$.

3. A triangle with base b and height h has **area** $A = 0.5 \times b \times h$.

4. A triangle with three sides: a, b, c has **perimeter** $p = a + b + c$ and **semi-perimeter** $s = 0.5 \times p$.

5. A triangle with 3 sides: a, b, c and semi-perimeter s has area
   $A = \sqrt{(s \times (s - a) \times (s - b) \times (s - c))}$.
   This formula is called the **Heron's Formula**.

6. A triangle with area A and semi-perimeter s has an **inscribed circle (incircle)** with radius $r = A/s$.

```
double rInCircle(double ab, double bc, double ca) {
  return area(ab, bc, ca) / (0.5 * perimeter(ab, bc, ca));
}

double rInCircle(point a, point b, point c) {
  return rInCircle(dist(a, b), dist(b, c), dist(c, a));
}
```

7. The center of incircle is the meeting point between the triangle's *angle bisectors* (see Figure 7.6—left). We can get the center if we have two angle bisectors and find their intersection point. The implementation is shown below:

```
// assumption: the required points/lines functions have been written
// returns true if there is an inCircle center, or false otherwise
// if this function returns true, ctr will be the inCircle center
// and r is the same as rInCircle
bool inCircle(point p1, point p2, point p3, point &ctr, double &r) {
  r = rInCircle(p1, p2, p3);
  if (fabs(r) < EPS) return false;                   // no inCircle center

  line l1, l2;                                       // 2 angle bisectors
  double ratio = dist(p1, p2) / dist(p1, p3);
  point p = translate(p2, scale(toVec(p2, p3), ratio / (1+ratio)));
  pointsToLine(p1, p, l1);

  ratio = dist(p2, p1) / dist(p2, p3);
  p = translate(p1, scale(toVec(p1, p3), ratio / (1+ratio)));
  pointsToLine(p2, p, l2);

  areIntersect(l1, l2, ctr);                         // intersection point
  return true;
}
```

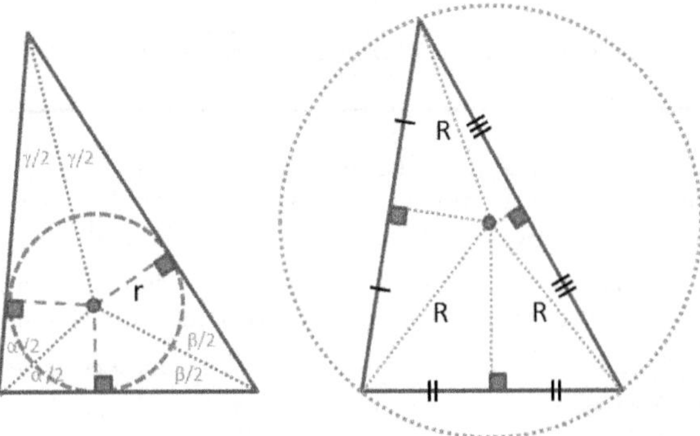

Figure 7.6: Incircle and Circumcircle of a Triangle

8. A triangle with 3 sides: a, b, c and area A has a **circumscribed circle (circumcircle)** with radius $R = a \times b \times c/(4 \times A)$.

```
double rCircumCircle(double ab, double bc, double ca) {
  return ab * bc * ca / (4.0 * area(ab, bc, ca));
}

double rCircumCircle(point a, point b, point c) {
  return rCircumCircle(dist(a, b), dist(b, c), dist(c, a));
}
```

9. The center of circumcircle is the meeting point between the triangle's *perpendicular bisectors* (see Figure 7.6—right).

10. When we study triangles, we should not forget **Trigonometry**—the study of the relationships between triangle sides and the angles between sides.

    In Trigonometry, the **Law of Cosines** (a.k.a. the **Cosine Formula** or the **Cosine Rule**) is a statement about a general triangle that relates the lengths of its sides to the cosine of one of its angles. See the scalene triangle in Figure 7.5. With the notations described there, we have: $c^2 = a^2 + b^2 - 2 \times a \times b \times \cos(\gamma)$, or $\gamma = \arccos(\frac{a^2+b^2-c^2}{2 \times a \times b})$. The formulas for the other two angles α and β are similarly defined.

11. In Trigonometry, the **Law of Sines** (a.k.a. the **Sine Formula** or the **Sine Rule**) is an equation relating the lengths of the sides of an arbitrary triangle to the sines of its angles. See the scalene (middle) triangle in Figure 7.5. With the notations described there and R is the radius of its circumcircle, we have: $\frac{a}{\sin(\alpha)} = \frac{b}{\sin(\beta)} = \frac{c}{\sin(\gamma)} = 2R$.

12. The **Pythagorean Theorem** specializes the Law of Cosines. This theorem only applies to right triangles. If the angle γ is a right angle (of measure 90° or $\pi/2$ radians), then $\cos(\gamma) = 0$, and thus the Law of Cosines reduces to: $c^2 = a^2 + b^2$. Pythagorean theorem is used in finding the Euclidean distance between two points, as shown earlier.

13. The **Pythagorean Triple** is a triple with three positive integers a, b, and c—commonly written as (a, b, c)—such that $a^2 + b^2 = c^2$. A well-known example is $(3, 4, 5)$. If (a, b, c) is a Pythagorean triple, then so is (ka, kb, kc) for any positive integer k. A Pythagorean Triple describes the integer lengths of the three sides of a Right Triangle.

Source code: `ch7/triangles.cpp|java|py|ml`

Exercise 7.2.4.1: Let a, b, and c of a triangle be 2^{18}, 2^{18}, and 2^{18}. Can we compute the area of this triangle with Heron's formula as shown in point 4 above without experiencing overflow (assuming that we use 64-bit integers)? What should we do to avoid this issue?

Exercise 7.2.4.2*: Implement the code to find the center of the circumCircle of three points a, b, and c. The function structure is similar as function `inCircle` shown in this section.

Exercise 7.2.4.3*: Implement another code to check if a point d is inside the circumCircle of three points a, b, and c.

Exercise 7.2.4.4*: Fermat-Torricelli point is a point inside a triangle such that the total distance from the three triangle vertices to that Fermat-Torricelli point is the minimum possible. For example, if the triangle vertices are $\{(0, 0), (0, 1), (1, 0)\}$, then the Fermat-Torricelli point is at $(0.211, 0.211)$. Study the geometric solution and the algorithmic solution for this problem. It is also the solution (Steiner point) for the (Euclidean) STEINER-TREE problem with 3 (terminal) points (see Section 8.6.10 and try Kattis - europeantrip).

7.2.5 2D Objects: Quadrilaterals

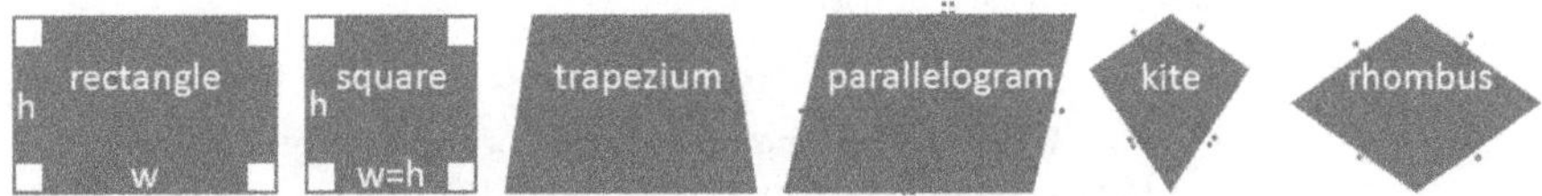

Figure 7.7: Quadrilaterals

1. **Quadrilateral** or **Quadrangle** is a polygon with four edges (and four vertices). The term 'polygon' itself is described in more detail later (Section 7.3). Figure 7.7 shows a few examples of Quadrilateral objects.

2. **Rectangle** is a polygon with four edges, four vertices, and four right angles.

3. A rectangle with width w and height h has **area** $A = w \times h$ and **perimeter** $p = 2 \times (w + h)$.

4. Given a rectangle described with its bottom left corner (x, y) plus its width w and height h, we can use the following checks to determine if another point (a, b) is inside, at the border, or outside this rectangle:

```
int insideRectangle(int x, int y, int w, int h, int a, int b) {
  if ((x < a) && (a < x+w) && (y < b) && (b < y+h))
    return 1;                                        // strictly inside
  else if ((x <= a) && (a <= x+w) && (y <= b) && (b <= y+h))
    return 0;                                        // at border
  else
    return -1;                                       // outside
}
```

5. **Square** is a special case of a rectangle where $w = h$.

6. **Trapezium** is a polygon with four vertices, four edges, and one pair of parallel edges among these four edges. If the two non-parallel sides have the same length, we have an **Isosceles Trapezium**.

7. A trapezium with a pair of parallel edges of lengths $w1$ and $w2$; and a height h between both parallel edges has area $A = 0.5 \times (w1 + w2) \times h$.

8. **Parallelogram** is a polygon with four edges and four vertices. Moreover, the opposite sides must be parallel.

9. **Kite** is a quadrilateral which has two pairs of sides of the same length which are adjacent to each other. The area of a kite is $diagonal_1 \times diagonal_2/2$.

10. **Rhombus** is a special parallelogram where every side has equal length. It is also a special case of kite where every side has equal length.

Programming Exercises related to Basic Geometry:

a. Points

1. Entry Level: **UVa 00587 - There's treasure ...** * (Euclidean `dist`)
2. **UVa 01595 - Symmetry** * (use `set` to record the positions of all sorted points; check half of the points if the symmetries are in the set too?)
3. **UVa 10927 - Bright Lights** * (sort points by gradient; Euclidean `dist`)
4. **UVa 11894 - Genius MJ** * (about rotating and translating points)
5. *Kattis - browniepoints* * (points and quadrants; simple; also available at UVa 10865 - Brownie Points)
6. *Kattis - cursethedarkness* * (Euclidean `dist`)
7. *Kattis - imperfectgps* * (Euclidean `dist`; simulation)

   Extra UVa: *00152, 00920, 10357, 10466, 10585, 10832, 11012, 12704.*

   Extra Kattis: *logo, mandelbrot, sibice.*

b. Lines

1. Entry Level: *Kattis - unlockpattern* * (complete search; Euclidean `dist`)
2. **UVa 10263 - Railway** * (use `distToLineSegment`)
3. **UVa 11783 - Nails** * ($O(N^2)$ brute force line segment intersection tests)
4. **UVa 13117 - ACIS, A Contagious ...** * (`dist` + `distToLineSegment`)
5. *Kattis - hurricanedanger* * (distance from point to line (not vector); be careful of precision error; work with integers)
6. *Kattis - logo2* * (n vectors that sum to 0; given n-1 vectors, find the unknown vector; also available at UVa 11519 - Logo 2)
7. *Kattis - platforme* * (line segment intersection tests; $N \leq 100$; so we can use complete search)

   Extra UVa: *00191, 00378, 00833, 00837, 00866, 01249, 10242, 10250, 10902, 11068, 11343.*

   Extra Kattis: *completingthesquare, countingtriangles, goatrope, rafting, segmentdistance, svm, triangleornaments, trojke.*

c. Circles (only)

1. Entry Level: *Kattis - estimatingtheareaofacircle* * (PI estimation experiment)
2. **UVa 01388 - Graveyard** * (LA 3708 - NortheasternEurope06; divide the circle into n sectors first and then into $(n + m)$ sectors)
3. **UVa 10005 - Packing polygons** * (complete search; use `circle2PtsRad`)
4. **UVa 10678 - The Grazing Cows** * (area of an *ellipse*; generalization of the formula for area of a circle)
5. *Kattis - amsterdamdistance* * (arcs of circles; no need to model this as an SSSP problem/Dijkstra's)
6. *Kattis - biggest* * (find biggest area of sector using simulation; use array (not that large) to avoid precision error)
7. *Kattis - ornaments* * (arc length plus two times tangent lengths)

   Extra UVa: *10136, 10180, 10209, 10221, 10283, 10287, 10432, 10451, 10573, 10589, 12578, 12748.*

   Extra Kattis: *anthonyanddiablo, ballbearings, dartscores, fractalarea, halfacookie, herman, pizza2, racingalphabet, sanic, tracksmoothing, watchdog.*

d. Triangles (Trigonometry)

1. Entry Level: *Kattis - egypt* * (Pythagorean theorem/triple; also available at UVa 11854 - Egypt)
2. **UVa 00427 - FlatLand Piano Movers *** (for each 2 consecutive corridors, try rotating the piano by a angle $\alpha \in [0.1..89.9]$ degrees; trigonometry)
3. **UVa 11326 - Laser Pointer *** (trigonometry; tangent; reflection)
4. **UVa 11909 - Soya Milk *** (Law of Sines (or tangent); two possible cases)
5. *Kattis - alldifferentdirections* * (trigonometry; compute x/y displacement)
6. *Kattis - billiard* * (enlarge the billiard table; then this is solvable with `atan2`)
7. *Kattis - mountainbiking* * (up to 4 line segments; simple trigonometry; simple Physics/Kinematic equation)

   Extra UVa: *00313, 10210, 10286, 10387, 10792, 12901.*

   Extra Kattis: *bazen, humancannonball2, ladder, santaklas, vacuumba.*

e. Triangles (plus Circles)

1. Entry Level: **UVa 00438 - The Circumference of ... *** (compute triangle's circumcircle)
2. **UVa 10577 - Bounding box *** (get center+radius of outer circle from 3 points; get all vertices; get the min-x/max-x/min-y/max-y of the polygon)
3. **UVa 11281 - Triangular Pegs in ... *** (circumcircle for a non obtuse triangle; largest side of the triangle for an obtuse triangle)
4. **UVa 13215 - Polygonal Park *** (area of rectangle minus area of squares and equilateral triangles)
5. *Kattis - cropeasy* * (try all 3 points/tree; see if the center is integer)
6. *Kattis - stickysituation* * (see if 3 sides form a triangle; see UVa 11579)
7. *Kattis - trilemma* * (triangle properties; sort the 3 sides first)

   Extra UVa: *00143, 00190, 00375, 10195, 10347, 10522, 10991, 11152, 11164, 11437, 11479, 11579, 11936.*

   Extra Kattis: *greedypolygons, queenspatio.*

f. Quadrilaterals

1. Entry Level: *Kattis - cetvrta* * (sort the x and y points, then you will know the 4th point)
2. **UVa 00209 - Triangular Vertices *** (LA 5148 - WorldFinals SanAntonio91; brute force check; answer is either triangle, parallelogram, or hexagon)
3. **UVa 11800 - Determine the Shape *** (use `next_permutation` to try all possible $4! = 24$ permutations of 4 points; check the requirements)
4. **UVa 12256 - Making Quadrilaterals *** (LA 5001 - KualaLumpur10; first 3 sides are 1, 1, 1; the 4th side onwards are sum of previous threes)
5. *Kattis - officespace* * (rectangles; small numbers; 2D Boolean arrays)
6. *Kattis - rectanglesurrounding* * (rectangles; small; 2D Boolean arrays)
7. *Kattis - roundedbuttons* * (in-rectangle/in-square test; in-4-circles tests)

   Extra UVa: *00155, 00460, 00476, 00477, 11207, 11314, 11345, 11455, 11639, 11648, 11834, 12611, 12894.*

   Extra Kattis: *areal, flowlayout, frosting, grassseed, hittingtargets, kornislav, pieceofcake2, taisformula.*

7.3 Algorithms on Polygon with Libraries

Polygon is a plane figure that is bounded by a closed path (path that starts and ends at the same vertex) composed of a finite sequence of straight line segments. These segments are called edges or sides. The point where two edges meet is the polygon's vertex or corner. The polygon is the source of many (computational) geometry problems as it allows the problem author to present more realistic 2D shapes than the ones discussed in Section 7.2.

7.3.1 Polygon Representation

The standard way to represent a polygon is to simply enumerate the vertices of the polygon in either clockwise/cw/right turn or counterclockwise/ccw/left turn order, with the first vertex being equal to the last vertex (some of the functions mentioned later in this section require this arrangement to simplify the implementation). In this book, our default vertex ordering is counterclockwise. We also assume that the input polygon is a **Simple** polygon with at least 3 edges (not a point or a line) and without edge crossing that may complicate or render certain functions below meaningless. The resulting polygon after executing the code below is shown in Figure 7.8—left. See that this example polygon is not **Convex**, i.e., it is **Concave** (see Section 7.3.4 for details).

```
// 6(+1) points, entered in counter clockwise order, 0-based indexing
vector<point> P;
P.emplace_back(1, 1);                              // P0
P.emplace_back(3, 3);                              // P1
P.emplace_back(9, 1);                              // P2
P.emplace_back(12, 4);                             // P3
P.emplace_back(9, 7);                              // P4
P.emplace_back(1, 7);                              // P5
P.push_back(P[0]);                                 // loop back, P6 = P0
```

7.3.2 Perimeter of a Polygon

The perimeter of a (convex or concave) polygon with n vertices given in some order (either clockwise or counter-clockwise) can be computed via a simple function below.

Figure 7.8—right shows the snapshot of the near completion of this function with only the final length of the last edge (P[5], P[0]) not computed yet. This last edge is (P[5], P[6]) in our implementation as P[6] = P[0]. Visit VisuAlgo, Polygon visualization, to draw your own simple polygon and test this `perimeter` function.

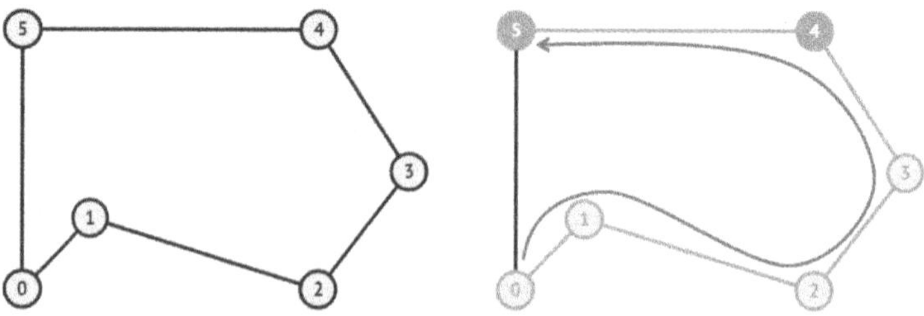

Figure 7.8: Left: (Concave) Polygon Example, Right: (Partial) Execution of `perimeter`

```
// returns the perimeter of polygon P, which is the sum of
// Euclidian distances of consecutive line segments (polygon edges)
double perimeter(const vector<point> &P) {       // by ref for efficiency
  double ans = 0.0;
  for (int i = 0; i < (int)P.size()-1; ++i)      // note: P[n-1] = P[0]
    ans += dist(P[i], P[i+1]);                   // as we duplicate P[0]
  return ans;
}
```

7.3.3 Area of a Polygon

The signed[19] area A of a (convex or concave) polygon with n vertices given in some order (either clockwise or counter-clockwise) can be found by computing the cross multiplication of coordinates in the matrix as shown below. This formula, which is called the *Shoelace formula*, can be easily written into the library code.

$$A = \frac{1}{2} \times \begin{bmatrix} x_0 & y_0 \\ x_1 & y_1 \\ x_2 & y_2 \\ \ldots & \ldots \\ x_{n-1} & y_{n-1} \end{bmatrix} = \frac{1}{2} \times (x_0 \times y_1 + x_1 \times y_2 + \ldots + x_{n-1} \times y_0 - x_1 \times y_0 - x_2 \times y_1 - \ldots - x_0 \times y_{n-1})$$

```
// returns the area of polygon P
double area(const vector<point> &P) {
  double ans = 0.0;
  for (int i = 0; i < (int)P.size()-1; ++i)      // Shoelace formula
    ans += (P[i].x*P[i+1].y - P[i+1].x*P[i].y);
  return fabs(ans)/2.0;                          // only do / 2.0 here
}
```

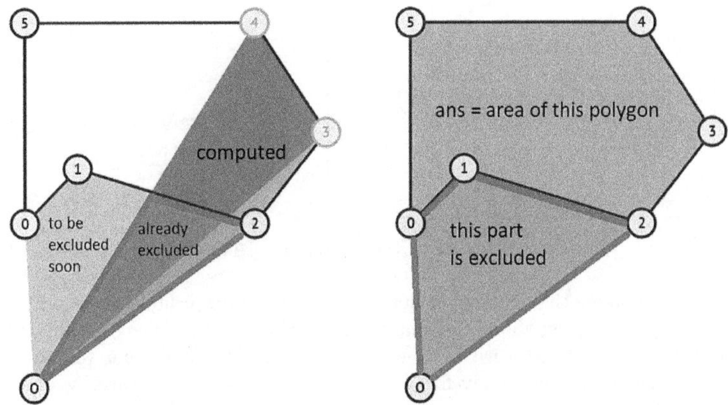

Figure 7.9: Left: Partial Execution of **area**, Right: The End Result

[19]Area is positive/negative when the vertices of the polygon are given in CCW/CW order, respectively.

The Shoelace formula above is derived from successive sums of signed areas of triangles defined by Origin point (0, 0) and the edges of the polygon. If Origin, P[i], P[i+1] form a clockwise turn, the signed area of the triangle will be negative, otherwise it will be positive. When all signed areas of triangles have been computed, we have the final answer = sum of all absolute triangle areas minus the sum of areas outside the polygon. The similar code[20] that produces the same answer but written in vector operations, can be found below.

```
// returns the area of polygon P, which is half the cross products
// of vectors defined by edge endpoints
double area_alternative(const vector<point> &P) {
  double ans = 0.0; point O(0.0, 0.0);           // O = the Origin
  for (int i = 0; i < (int)P.size()-1; ++i)      // sum of signed areas
    ans += cross(toVec(O, P[i]), toVec(O, P[i+1]));
  return fabs(ans)/2.0;
}
```

Figure 7.9—left shows the snapshot of the partial execution this **area** function while Figure 7.9—right shows the final result for this example. Visit VisuAlgo, Polygon visualization, to draw your own simple polygon and test this **area** function.

7.3.4 Checking if a Polygon is Convex

A polygon is said to be **Convex** if any line segment drawn inside the polygon does not intersect any edge of the polygon. Otherwise, the polygon is called **Concave**. However, to test whether a polygon is convex, there is an easier computational approach than "trying to check if all line segments can be drawn inside the polygon". We can simply check whether all three consecutive vertices of the polygon form the same turns (all left turns/ccw if the vertices are listed in counterclockwise order—the default setting in this book—or all right turns/cw if the vertices are listed in clockwise order). If we can find at least one triple where this is false, then the polygon is concave.

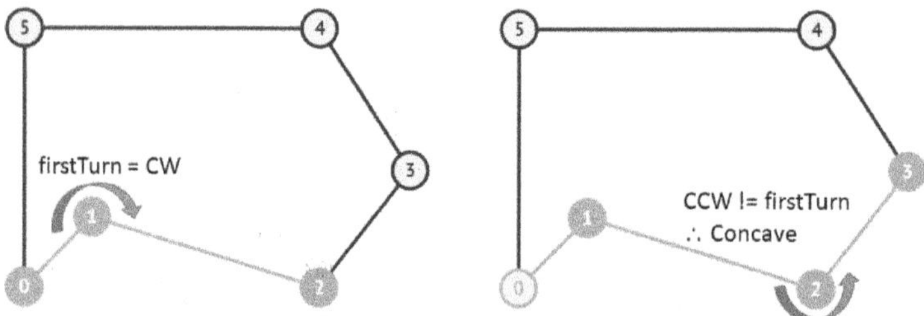

Figure 7.10: Left: First turn: Clockwise, Right: Found a Counterclockwise Turn → Concave

Figure 7.10—left shows the first step of this **isConvex** function (it finds a clockwise turn 0-1-2) while Figure 7.10—right shows the final result for this example where **isConvex** function discovers a counterclockwise turn 1-2-3 which is different than the first (clockwise) turn. Therefore it concludes that the given polygon is not convex, i.e., concave. Visit VisuAlgo, Polygon visualization, to draw your own simple polygon and test this **isConvex** function.

[20]However, we do not recommend using this version as it uses a few more lines of code (to define **toVec** and **cross** functions) than the direct Shoelace formula implementation shown earlier.

```
// returns true if we always make the same turn
// while examining all the edges of the polygon one by one
bool isConvex(const vector<point> &P) {
  int n = (int)P.size();
  // a point/sz=2 or a line/sz=3 is not convex
  if (n <= 3) return false;
  bool firstTurn = ccw(P[0], P[1], P[2]);        // remember one result,
  for (int i = 1; i < n-1; ++i)                  // compare with the others
    if (ccw(P[i], P[i+1], P[(i+2) == n ? 1 : i+2]) != firstTurn)
      return false;                              // different -> concave
  return true;                                   // otherwise -> convex
}
```

Exercise 7.3.4.1*: Which part of the code above should you modify to accept collinear points? Example: Polygon {(0,0), (2,0), (4,0), (2,2), (0,0)} should be treated as convex.

7.3.5 Checking if a Point is Inside a Polygon

Another common test performed on a polygon P is to check if a point pt is inside or outside polygon P. The following function that implements 'winding number algorithm' allows such check for *either* convex or concave polygons. Similar with the Shoelace formula for computing area of polygon, this **inPolygon** function works by computing the signed sum of angles between three points: $\{P[i], pt, P[i+1]\}$ where $(P[i], P[i+1])$ are consecutive edges of polygon P, taking care of ccw/left turns (add the angle) and cw/right turns (subtract the angle) respectively. If the final sum is 2π (360 degrees), then pt is inside polygon P. Otherwise (if the final sum is 0π (0 degree)), pt is outside polygon P.

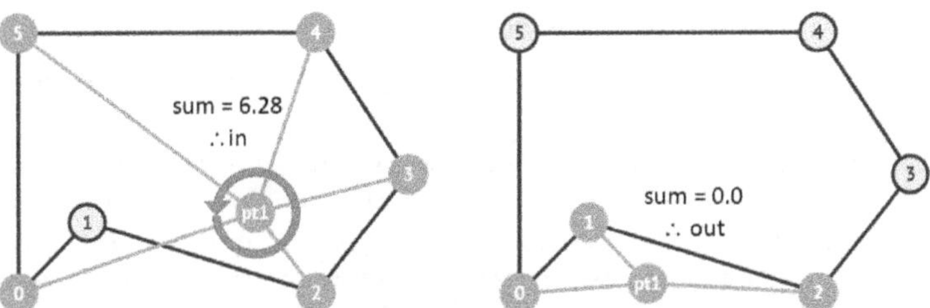

Figure 7.11: Left: Inside Polygon, Right: Outside Polygon

Figure 7.11—left shows an instance where this **inPolygon** function returns true. The 'mistake' of negative angle 0-pt1-1 is canceled by subsequent 1-pt1-2 as if we indirectly compute angle 0-pt1-2. Computing the next four angles 2-pt1-3, 3-pt1-4, 4-pt1-5, and 5-pt1-0 (or point 6) gives us the sum of 360 degrees and we conclude that the point is inside the polygon. On the other hand, Figure 7.11—right shows an instance where this **inPolygon** function returns false. 0-pt1-1 and 1-pt1-2 both form Clockwise turns and hence we have ≈ -187 degrees so far for angle 0-pt1-2. However, this will be canceled by the next four angles 2-pt1-3, 3-pt1-4,

4-pt1-5, and 5-pt1-0 (or point 6). As the sum of angles is not 360 degrees (it is 0 degree), we conclude that the point is outside the polygon. Visit VisuAlgo, Polygon visualization, to draw your own simple polygon, add your own reference point, and test whether that reference point is inside or outside the polygon using this **inPolygon** function.

Note that there is one potential corner case if the query point pt is one of the polygon vertex or along the polygon edge (collinear with any of the two successive points of the polygon). We have to declare that the query point pt is on polygon (vertex/edge). We have integrated that additional check in our library code below that can be tested directly at Kattis - pointinpolygon.

```
// returns 1/0/-1 if point p is inside/on (vertex/edge)/outside of
// either convex/concave polygon P
int insidePolygon(point pt, const vector<point> &P) {
  int n = (int)P.size();
  if (n <= 3) return -1;                          // avoid point or line
  bool on_polygon = false;
  for (int i = 0; i < n-1; ++i)                   // on vertex/edge?
    if (fabs(dist(P[i], pt) + dist(pt, P[i+1]) - dist(P[i], P[i+1])) < EPS)
      on_polygon = true;
  if (on_polygon) return 0;                       // pt is on polygon
  double sum = 0.0;                               // first = last point
  for (int i = 0; i < n-1; ++i) {
    if (ccw(pt, P[i], P[i+1]))
      sum += angle(P[i], pt, P[i+1]);             // left turn/ccw
    else
      sum -= angle(P[i], pt, P[i+1]);             // right turn/cw
  }
  return fabs(sum) > M_PI ? 1 : -1;               // 360d->in, 0d->out
}
```

Exercise 7.3.5.1: If the first vertex is not repeated as the last vertex, will the functions **perimeter**, **area**, **isConvex**, and **insidePolygon** presented above work correctly?

Exercise 7.3.5.2*: Discuss the pros and the cons of the following alternative methods for testing if a point is inside a polygon:

1. Triangulate/break a convex polygon into triangles and see if the sum of triangle areas is equal to the area of the convex polygon. Can we use this for concave polygon?
2. Ray casting algorithm: we draw a ray from the point to any fixed direction so that the ray intersects the edge(s) of the polygon. If there are odd/even number of intersections, the point is inside/outside, respectively.

7.3.6 Cutting Polygon with a Straight Line

Another interesting thing that we can do with a *convex* polygon (see **Exercise 7.3.6.2*** for concave polygon) is to cut it into two convex sub-polygons with a straight line defined with two points A and B (the order of A and B matters). There are a few interesting programming exercises in this section/book that use this function.

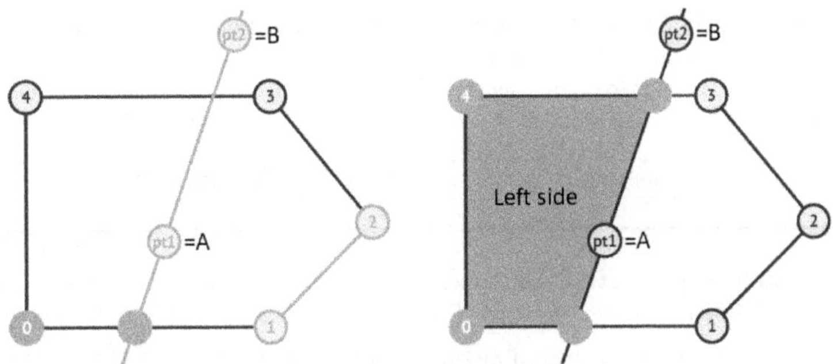

Figure 7.12: Left: Before Cut, Right: After Cut; pt1/pt2 = A/B, respectively

The basic idea of the following **cutPolygon** function is to iterate through the vertices of the original polygon Q one by one. If point A, point B, and polygon vertex v form a left turn (which implies that v is on the left side of the line AB (order matters)), we put v inside the new polygon P. Once we find a polygon edge that intersects with the line AB, we use that intersection point as part of the new polygon P (see Figure 7.12—left, the new vertex between edge (0-1)). We then skip the next few vertices of Q that are located on the right side of line AB (see Figure 7.12—left, vertices 1, 2, and later 3). Sooner or later, we will revisit another polygon edge that intersects with line AB again and we also use that intersection point as part of the new polygon P (see Figure 7.12—right, the new vertex between edge (3-4)). Then, we continue appending vertices of Q into P again because we are now on the left side of line AB again. We stop when we have returned to the starting vertex and return the resulting polygon P (see the shaded area in Figure 7.12—right).

```
// compute the intersection point between line segment p-q and line A-B
point lineIntersectSeg(point p, point q, point A, point B) {
  double a = B.y-A.y, b = A.x-B.x, c = B.x*A.y - A.x*B.y;
  double u = fabs(a*p.x + b*p.y + c);
  double v = fabs(a*q.x + b*q.y + c);
  return point((p.x*v + q.x*u) / (u+v), (p.y*v + q.y*u) / (u+v));
}

// cuts polygon Q along the line formed by point A->point B (order matters)
// (note: the last point must be the same as the first point)
vector<point> cutPolygon(point A, point B, const vector<point> &Q) {
  vector<point> P;
  for (int i = 0; i < (int)Q.size(); ++i) {
    double left1 = cross(toVec(A, B), toVec(A, Q[i])), left2 = 0;
    if (i != (int)Q.size()-1) left2 = cross(toVec(A, B), toVec(A, Q[i+1]));
    if (left1 > -EPS) P.push_back(Q[i]);          // Q[i] is on the left
    if (left1*left2 < -EPS)                       // crosses line AB
      P.push_back(lineIntersectSeg(Q[i], Q[i+1], A, B));
  }
  if (!P.empty() && !(P.back() == P.front()))
    P.push_back(P.front());                       // wrap around
  return P;
}
```

Visit VisuAlgo, Polygon visualization, to draw your own simple polygon (but only convex simple polygons are allowed). Add a line (defined by two reference points—order matters), and observe how this `cutPolygon` function works. The URL for the various computational geometry algorithms on polygons shown in Section 7.3.1 to Section 7.3.6 is shown below.

Visualization: `https://visualgo.net/en/polygon`

Exercise 7.3.6.1: This `cutPolygon` function returns the left side of the polygon Q after cutting it with line AB (order matters). What should we do to get the right side instead?

Exercise 7.3.6.2*: What happens if we run the `cutPolygon` function on a *concave* polygon?

7.3.7 Finding the Convex Hull of a Set of Points

The **Convex Hull** of a set of points Pts is the smallest convex polygon $CH(Pts)$ for which each point in Pts is either on the boundary of $CH(Pts)$ or in its interior. Imagine that the points are nails on a flat 2D plane and we have a long enough rubber band that can enclose all the nails. If this rubber band is released, it will try to enclose as small an area as possible. That area is the area of the convex hull of these set of points (see Figure 7.13). Finding convex hull of a set of points has natural applications in *packing* problems and can be used as pre-processing step for more complex computational geometry problems.

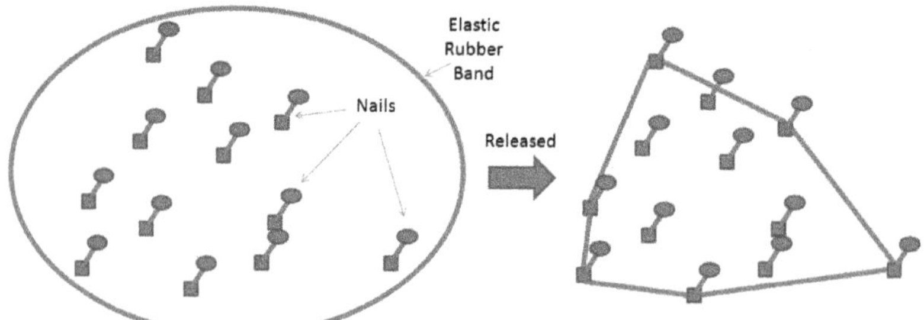

Figure 7.13: Rubber Band Analogy for Finding Convex Hull

As every vertex in $CH(Pts)$ is a vertex in the set of points Pts itself, the algorithm for finding convex hull is essentially an algorithm to decide[21] which points in Pts should be chosen as part of the convex hull. There are several efficient convex hull finding algorithms available. In this section, we present two of them: the $O(n \log n)$ Ronald *Graham's Scan* algorithm (for historical purpose) followed by the more efficient $O(n \log n)$ Andrew's Monotone Chain algorithm (our default).

Graham's Scan

Graham's scan algorithm first sorts all the n points of Pts (as Pts is a set of points and not a set of vertices of a polygon, the first point does not have to be replicated as the last point, see Figure 7.14—left) based on their angles around a point called pivot $P0$ and stores the

[21]Fortunately, this classic CS optimization problem is **not** NP-hard.

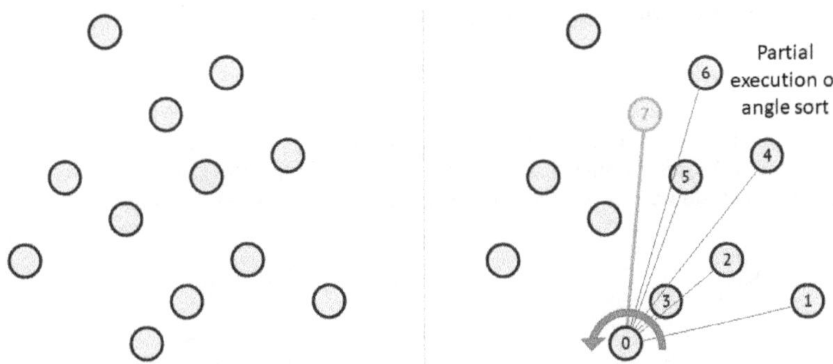

Figure 7.14: Sorting Set of 12 Points by Their Angles around a Pivot (Point 0)

sorted results in a 'temporary' set of points P. This algorithm uses the bottommost (and rightmost if tie) point in Pts as pivot $P0$. We sort the points based on angles around this pivot using CCW tests[22]. Consider 3 points: pivot, a, and b. Point a comes before b after sorting if and only if pivot, a, b makes a counter clockwise/left turn. Then, we can see that edge 0-1, 0-2, 0-3, ..., 0-6, and 0-7 are in counterclockwise order around pivot $P0$ in Figure 7.14—right. Note that this Figure 7.14—right snapshot shows *partial* execution of this angle sorting up to edge 0-7 and the order of the last 4 points are not determined yet.

Then, this algorithm maintains a stack S of candidate points. Each point of P is pushed *once* onto S and points that are not going to be part of convex hull will be eventually popped from S. Graham's Scan maintains this invariant: the top three items in stack S must always make a ccw/left turn (which is the basic property of a convex polygon).

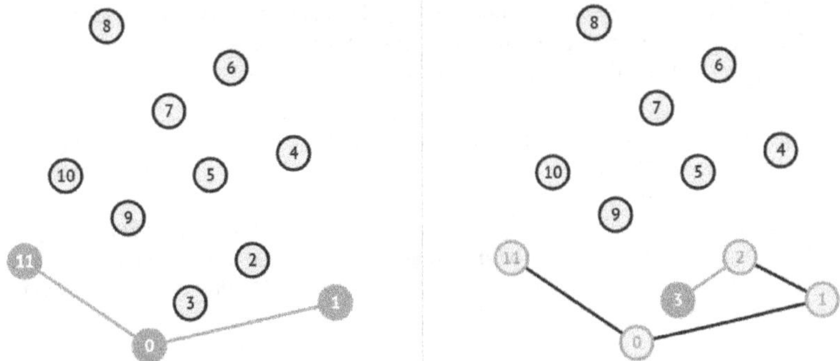

Figure 7.15: Left: Initial State of S, Right: After the Next 2 Steps

Initially we insert these three points, point N-1, 0, and 1. In our example, the stack initially contains (bottom) 11-0-1 (top). This always forms a left turn (see Figure 7.15—left). Next, 0-1-2 and 1-2-3 both make ccw/left turns, thus we currently accept both vertex 2 and vertex 3 and the stack now contains (bottom) 11-0-1-2-3 (top) (see Figure 7.15—right).

Next, when we examine 2-3-4, we encounter a cw/right turn, thus we know that vertex 3 should **not** be in the convex hull and pop it from S. However, 1-2-4 is also a cw/right

[22]Another way is to use `atan2` (arctangent) function with 2 arguments that can return the quadrant of the computed angle, but this is constant time slower

turn, so we also know that vertex 2 should also **not** be in the convex hull and pop it from S. Then, 0-1-4 is a ccw/left turn and we accept vertex 4 and the stack now contains (bottom) 11-0-1-4 (top) (see Figure 7.16—left).

We repeat this process until all vertices have been processed. When Graham's Scan terminates, whatever that is left in S are the points of $P = CH(Pts)$ (see Figure 7.16—right). Graham Scan's eliminates all the cw/right turns! As three consecutive vertices in S always make ccw/left turns, we have a convex polygon (as discussed in Section 7.3.4).

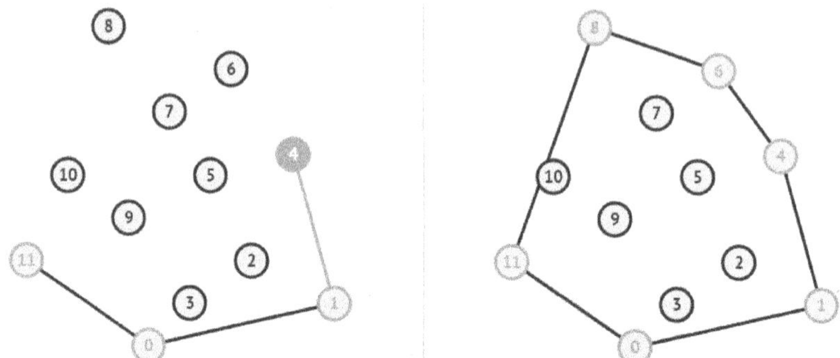

Figure 7.16: Left: Reject Vertex 2 & 3; Accept Vertex 4, Right: The Final Convex Hull

Our implementation of Graham's Scan is shown below. It uses a `vector<point> S` that behaves like a stack instead of using a real `stack<point> S` as we need access to not just the top of the stack but also the vertex below the top vertex of the stack. The first part of Graham's Scan (finding the pivot) is just $O(n)$. The third part (the ccw tests) is also $O(n)$ as each of the n vertices can only be pushed onto the stack once and popped from the stack once. The second part (sorts points by angle around a pivot `P[0]`) is the *bulkiest* part that requires $O(n \log n)$. Overall, Graham's scan runs in $O(n \log n)$.

```
vector<point> CH_Graham(vector<point> &Pts) {     // overall O(n log n)
  vector<point> P(Pts);                           // copy all points
  int n = (int)P.size();
  if (n <= 3) {                                   // point/line/triangle
    if (!(P[0] == P[n-1])) P.push_back(P[0]);    // corner case
    return P;                                     // the CH is P itself
  }

  // first, find P0 = point with lowest Y and if tie: rightmost X
  int P0 = min_element(P.begin(), P.end())-P.begin();
  swap(P[0], P[P0]);                              // swap P[P0] with P[0]

  // second, sort points by angle around P0, O(n log n) for this sort
  sort(++P.begin(), P.end(), [&](point a, point b) {
    return ccw(P[0], a, b);                       // use P[0] as the pivot
  });
```

```
  // third, the ccw tests, although complex, it is just O(n)
  vector<point> S({P[n-1], P[0], P[1]});          // initial S
  int i = 2;                                      // then, we check the rest
  while (i < n) {                                 // n > 3, O(n)
    int j = (int)S.size()-1;
    if (ccw(S[j-1], S[j], P[i]))                  // CCW turn
      S.push_back(P[i++]);                        // accept this point
    else                                          // CW turn
      S.pop_back();                               // pop until a CCW turn
  }
  return S;                                       // return the result
}
```

Andrew's Monotone Chain

Our Graham's Scan implementation above can be further simplified[23], especially the angle sorting part.

Actually, the same basic idea of the third part of Graham's Scan (ccw tests) also works if the input is sorted based on x-coordinate (and in case of a tie, by y-coordinate) instead of angle. But now the convex hull must now computed in two separate steps producing the *lower* and *upper* parts of the hull. This is because the third part of Graham's Scan (ccw tests) only going to get the lower hull when performed on a set of points that are sorted from left to right (see Figure 7.17—left). To complete the convex hull, we have to 'rotate' the entire set of points by 180 degrees and re-do the process, or simply perform the third part of Graham's Scan (ccw tests) but from right to left to get the upper hull (see Figure 7.17—right).

This modification was devised by A. M. Andrew and known as Andrew's Monotone Chain Algorithm. It has the same basic properties as Graham's Scan but avoids that costly comparisons between angles [10].

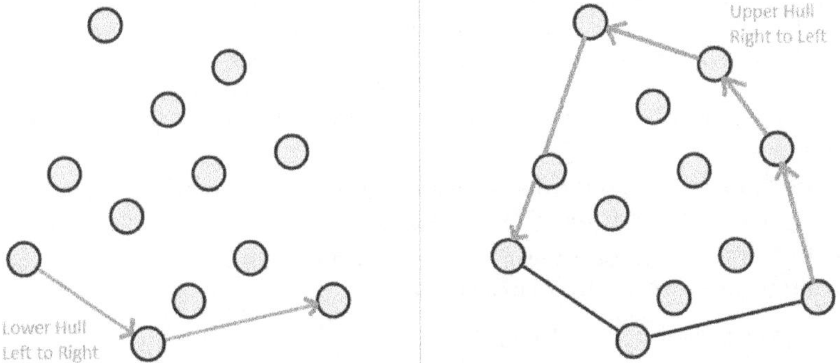

Figure 7.17: Left: Lower Hull (Left to Right), Right: Lower+Upper Hull (Right to Left)

Our much simpler implementation of the Monotone Chain algorithm is shown below. Due to its efficiency (still $O(n \log n)$ due to sorting based on coordinates, but a constant time factor faster than Graham's scan) and shorter code length, this is now our default.

[23] We already avoid using the expensive `atan2` operation in our Graham's Scan code.

```
vector<point> CH_Andrew(vector<point> &Pts) {      // overall O(n log n)
  int n = Pts.size(), k = 0;
  vector<point> H(2*n);
  sort(Pts.begin(), Pts.end());                    // sort the points by x/y
  for (int i = 0; i < n; ++i) {                    // build lower hull
    while ((k >= 2) && !ccw(H[k-2], H[k-1], Pts[i])) --k;
    H[k++] = Pts[i];
  }
  for (int i = n-2, t = k+1; i >= 0; --i) {         // build upper hull
    while ((k >= t) && !ccw(H[k-2], H[k-1], Pts[i])) --k;
    H[k++] = Pts[i];
  }
  H.resize(k);
  return H;
}
```

We end this section and this chapter by again pointing readers to visit VisuAlgo tool that we have built to enhance this book, as the static written explanations in this book cannot beat animated explanations of the visualizations. This time, enter a set of points *Pts* and execute your chosen convex hull algorithm. We also encourage readers to explore our source code and use it to solve various programming exercises listed in this section. The URL for the various convex hull algorithms on a set of points and the entire code used in this Section 7.3 are shown below.

Visualization: `https://visualgo.net/en/convexhull`

Source code: `ch7/polygon.cpp|java|py|ml`

Exercise 7.3.7.1: Suppose we have 5 points, $P = \{(0,0),(1,0),(2,0),(2,2),(0,2))\}$. The convex hull of these 5 points are these 5 points themselves (plus one, as we loop back to vertex (0, 0)). However, our Graham Scan's and Andrew's Monotone Chain implementations remove point (1, 0) as (0, 0)-(1, 0)-(2, 0) are collinear. Which part of the implementations do we have to modify to accept collinear points? (note that we usually prefer to remove collinear points though)

Exercise 7.3.7.2: What is the time complexity of Andrew's Monotone Chain algorithm if the input points are already sorted by increasing x-values and if ties, by increasing y-values?

Exercise 7.3.7.3*: Test the Graham's Scan and Andrew's Monotone Chain code above on these corner cases. What is the convex hull of:

1. A single point, e.g., $P_1 = \{(0,0)\}$?
2. Two points (a line), e.g., $P_2 = \{(0,0),(1,0)\}$?
3. Three points (a triangle), e.g., $P_3 = \{(0,0),(1,0),(1,1)\}$?
4. Three points (a collinear line), e.g., $P_4 = \{(0,0),(1,0),(2,0)\}$?
5. Four points (a collinear line), e.g., $P_5 = \{(0,0),(1,0),(2,0),(3,0)\}$?

Below, we provide a list of programming exercises related to polygon. Without pre-written library code discussed in this section, many of these problems look 'hard'. With the library code, many of these problems become manageable as they can now be decomposed into a few library routines. Spend some time to attempt them, especially the **must try *** ones.

Programming Exercises related to Polygon:

a. Polygon, Easier:

1. Entry Level: *Kattis - convexpolygonarea* * (even more basic problem about area of polygon than Kattis - polygonarea)
2. **UVa 00634 - Polygon *** (basic `inPolygon` routine; notice that the input polygon can be convex or concave)
3. **UVa 11447 - Reservoir Logs *** (`area` of polygon)
4. **UVa 11473 - Campus Roads *** (modified `perimeter` of polygon)
5. *Kattis - convexhull* * (basic convex hull problem; be careful with duplicate points and collinear points)
6. *Kattis - cuttingcorners* * (simulation of angle checks)
7. *Kattis - robotprotection* * (simply find the area of convex hull)

Extra UVa: *00478*, *00681*, *01206*, *10060*, *10112*, *11072*, *11096*, *11626*.

Extra Kattis: *convexhull2*, *cookiecutter*, *dartscoring*, *jabuke*, *polygonarea*, *simplepolygon*.

b. Polygon, Harder:

1. Entry Level: **UVa 11265 - The Sultan's Problem** * (seems to be a complex problem, but essentially just `cutPolygon`; `inPolygon`; `area`)
2. **UVa 00361 - Cops and Robbers *** (check if a point is inside `CH` of Cop/Robber; if *pt* is inside `CH`, *pt* satisfies the requirement)
3. **UVa 01111 - Trash Removal *** (LA 5138 - WorldFinals Orlando11; `CH`; output minimax distance of each CH side to the other vertices)
4. **UVa 10256 - The Great Divide *** (given 2 `CH`s, output 'No' if there is a point in 1st `CH` inside the 2nd one; 'Yes' otherwise)
5. *Kattis - convex* * (must understand the concept of convex polygon; a bit of mathematical insights: GCD; sort)
6. *Kattis - pointinpolygon* * (in/out and on polygon)
7. *Kattis - roberthood* * (the classic furthest pair problem; use convex hull and then rotating caliper)

Extra UVa: *00109*, *00132*, *00137*, *00218*, *00596*, *00858*, *10002*, *10065*, *10406*, *10445*.

Extra Kattis: *abstractart*, *largesttriangle*, *playingtheslots*, *skyline*, *wrapping*.

7.4 3D Geometry

Programming contest problems involving 3D objects are extremely rare. When such a problem does appear in a problem set, it can surprise some contestants who are not aware of its required 3D formulas/techniques. In this section, we discuss three 3D Geometry topics.

More Popular 3D Geometry Formulas

These formulas are rarely used compared to their 2D counterparts in Section 7.2.
But nevertheless, the ones listed at Table 7.1 are the slightly more popular ones.

Object	Volume	Surface Area	Remarks	Example
Cube	s^3	$6s^2$	s = side	UVa 00737
Cuboid	lwh	$2(lw+lh+wh)$	$l/w/h$ = length/width/height	Kattis - movingday
Sphere	$\frac{4}{3}\pi r^3$	$4\pi r^2$	r = radius	Kattis - pop

Table 7.1: Refresher on Some 3D Formulas

Volume of a Solid of Revolution

Abridged problem description of Kattis - flowers: function $f(x) = a \cdot e^{-x^2} + b \cdot \sqrt{x}$ describes an outline of a 3D flower pot with height h. If we rotate $f(x)$ along x-axis from $x = 0$ to $x = h$, we will get a solid of revolution (a 3D object). There are k flower pots as tuples (a, b, h) and our job is to identify which one has volume closest to the target volume V.

The difficult part of this problem is the computation of the volume of this solid. Let's look at an example flower pot below. In Figure 7.18—left, we are given a sample $f(x) = e^{-x^2} + 2 \cdot \sqrt{x}$. If we integrate this function from $x = 0$ to 2, we will compute the shaded 2D area under the curve. This idea can be extended to 3D to compute the volume. For each x, imagine that there is a circle around the x axis with radius $f(x)$, see Figure 7.18—right. The area of this circle is $\pi \times f(x)^2$. Now, if we integrate this area from $x = 0$ to 2, i.e., $\pi \times \int_0^2 (e^{-x^2} + 2 \cdot \sqrt{x})^2$ (we can take out π from the integral), we will get the volume of this solid (flower pot), which is 34.72 in this example.

We can use numerical techniques to compute this definite integral, e.g. Simpson's rule: $\int_a^b f(x)dx \approx \frac{\Delta x}{3}(f(x_0)+4f(x_1)+2f(x_2)+\ldots+4f(x_{n-1})+f(x_n))$, $\Delta x = \frac{b-a}{n}$, and $x_i = a+i\Delta x$. For more precision, we can set n to be high enough that does not TLE, e.g., $n = 1e6$.

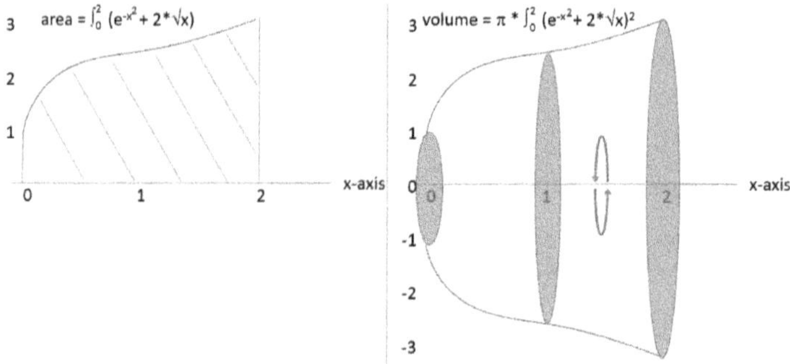

Figure 7.18: L: $f(x)$ and its Area; R: Solid of Revolution of $f(x)$ and its Volume

This rare 3D topic appears as a subproblem in recent ICPC World Finals (Kattis - bottles and Kattis - cheese).

Great-Circle Distance

The **Great-Circle Distance** between any two points A and B on sphere is the shortest distance along a path on the **surface of the sphere**. This path is an *arc* of the **Great-Circle** that passes through the two points A and B. We can imagine Great-Circle as the resulting circle that appears if we cut the sphere with a plane so that we have two *equal* hemispheres (see Figure 7.19—left and middle).

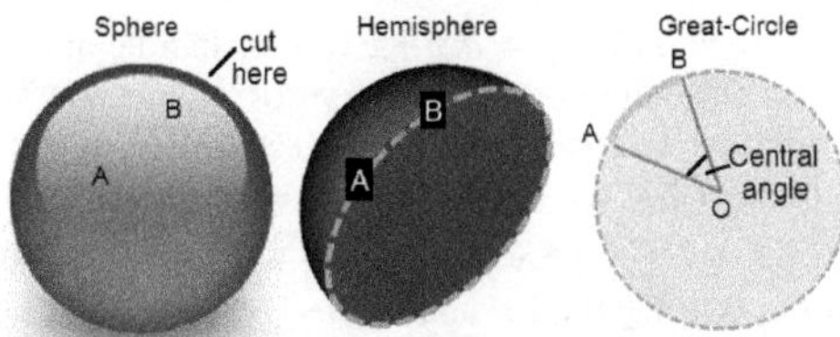

Figure 7.19: L: Sphere, M: Hemisphere and Great-Circle, R: gcDistance (Arc A-B)

To find the Great-Circle Distance, we have to find the central angle AOB (see Figure 7.19—right) of the Great-Circle where O is the center of the Great-Circle (which is also the center of the sphere). Given the radius of the sphere/Great-Circle, we can then determine the length of arc A-B, which is the required Great-Circle distance.

Although quite rare nowadays, some contest problems involving 'Earth', 'Airlines', etc. use this distance measurement. Usually, the two points on the surface of a sphere are given as the Earth coordinates, i.e., the (latitude, longitude) pair. The following library code will help us to obtain the Great-Circle distance given two points on the sphere and the radius of the sphere. We omit the derivation as it is not important for competitive programming.

```
double gcDist(double pLa, double pLo, double qLa, double qLo, double r) {
  pLa *= M_PI/180; pLo *= M_PI/180;              // degree to radian
  qLa *= M_PI/180; qLo *= M_PI/180;
  return r * acos(cos(pLa)*cos(pLo)*cos(qLa)*cos(qLo) +
         cos(pLa)*sin(pLo)*cos(qLa)*sin(qLo) + sin(pLa)*sin(qLa));
} // this formula has a name: Haversine formula
```

Source code: `ch7/UVa11817.cpp|java|py`

Programming exercises related to 3D geometry:

1. Entry Level: *Kattis - beavergnaw* * (volumes of cylinders and cones; inclusion-exclusion; also available at UVa 10297 - Beavergnaw)
2. **UVa 00737 - Gleaming the Cubes** * (cube and cube intersection)
3. **UVa 00815 - Flooded** * (LA 5215 - WorldFinals Eindhoven99; volume; greedy)
4. **UVa 11817 - Tunnelling The Earth** * (`gcDistance`; 3D Euclidean distance)
5. *Kattis - bottles* * (LA 6027 - WorldFinals Warsaw12; BSTA+geometric formula; also available at UVa 01280 - Curvy Little Bottles)
6. *Kattis - flowers* * (the key part of this problem is integration)
7. *Kattis - airlinehub* * (`gcDistance`; also available at UVa 10316 - Airline Hub)

   Extra UVa: *00535*, *10897*.

   Extra Kattis: *cheese*, *infiniteslides*, *movingday*, *pop*, *waronweather*.

7.5 Solution to Non-Starred Exercises

Exercise 7.2.1.1: See the first part of Graham's Scan algorithm in Section 7.3.7.

Exercise 7.2.1.2: 5.0.

Exercise 7.2.1.3: (-3.0, 10.0).

Exercise 7.2.1.4: (-0.674, 10.419).

Exercise 7.2.2.1: The line equation $y = mx + c$ cannot handle all cases: vertical lines has 'infinite' gradient/slope in this equation and 'near vertical' lines are also problematic. If we use this line equation, we have to treat vertical lines separately in our code which decreases the probability of acceptance. So, use the better line equation $ax + by + c = 0$.

Exercise 7.2.2.2: a). -0.5 * x + $\underline{1.0}$ * y - 1.0 = 0.0; b). 1.0 * x + $\underline{0.0}$ * y - 2.0 = 0.0. Notice that b (underlined) is $\underline{1.0}/\underline{0.0}$ for a non-vertical/vertical line, respectively.

Exercise 7.2.2.3: Given 2 points $(x1, y1)$ and $(x2, y2)$, the slope can be calculated with $m = (y2-y1)/(x2-x1)$. Subsequently the y-intercept c can be computed from the equation by substitution of the values of a point (either one) and the line gradient m. The code will looks like this. See that we have to deal with vertical line separately and awkwardly. When tried on **Exercise 7.2.2.2** (b), we will have $x = 2.0$ instead as we cannot represent a vertical line using this form $y = ?$.

```
struct line2 { double m, c; };                         // alternative way

int pointsToLine2(point p1, point p2, line2 &l) {
  if (p1.x == p2.x) {                                  // vertical line
    l.m = INF;                                         // this is to denote a
    l.c = p1.x;                                        // line x = x_value
    return 0;                                          // differentiate result
  }
  else {
    l.m = (double)(p1.y-p2.y) / (p1.x-p2.x);
    l.c = p1.y - l.m*p1.x;
    return 1;                                          // standard y = mx + c
  }
}
```

Exercise 7.2.2.4: a. (5.0, 3.0); b. (4.0, 2.5); c. (-3.0, 5.0).

Exercise 7.2.2.5: (0.0, 4.0). The result is different from **Exercise 7.2.2.4** (a). 'Translate then Rotate' is different from 'Rotate then Translate'. Be careful in sequencing them.

Exercise 7.2.2.6: (1.0, 2.0). If the rotation center is not the origin, we need to translate the input point c (3, 2) by a vector described by $-p$, i.e., (-2, -1) to point c' (1, 1). Then, we perform the 90 degrees counter clockwise rotation around origin to get c'' (-1, 1). Finally, we translate c'' to the final answer by a vector described by p to point (1, 2).

Exercise 7.2.2.7: a. 90.00 degrees; b. 63.43 degrees.

Exercise 7.2.2.8: Point p (3,7) $\rightarrow$ point q (11,13) $\rightarrow$ point r (35,30) form a right turn. Therefore, point r is on the right side of a line that passes through point p and point q. Note that if point r is at (35, 31), then p, q, r are collinear.

Exercise 7.2.2.9: The solution is shown below:

```
void closestPoint(line l, point p, point &ans) {
  // this line is perpendicular to l and pass through p
  line perpendicular;
  if (fabs(l.b) < EPS) {                          // vertical line
    ans.x = -(l.c);
    ans.y = p.y;
    return;
  }
  if (fabs(l.a) < EPS) {                          // horizontal line
    ans.x = p.x;
    ans.y = -(l.c);
    return;
  }
  pointSlopeToLine(p, 1/l.a, perpendicular);      // normal line
  // intersect line l with this perpendicular line
  // the intersection point is the closest point
  areIntersect(l, perpendicular, ans);
}
```

Exercise 7.2.2.10: The solution is shown below. Other solution exists:

```
// returns the reflection of point on a line
void reflectionPoint(line l, point p, point &ans) {
  point b;
  closestPoint(l, p, b);                          // similar to distToLine
  vec v = toVec(p, b);                            // create a vector
  ans = translate(translate(p, v), v);            // translate p twice
}
```

Exercise 7.2.4.1: We can use double data type that has larger range. However, to further reduce the chance of overflow, we can rewrite the Heron's formula into a safer $A = \sqrt{s} \times \sqrt{s-a} \times \sqrt{s-b} \times \sqrt{s-c}$. However, the result will be slightly less precise as we call *sqrt* 4 times instead of once.

Exercise 7.3.5.1: If the first vertex is not repeated as the last vertex, then:

- Functions `perimeter` and `area` will surely be wrong (they miss the last step) as we do this (duplicating first vertex as additional last vertex) to avoid using modular arithmetic to check 'wrap around' case throughout the loop,
- Function `isConvex` will only be incorrect if every other turns (except the last turn) are CCW turns but the last turn is actually a CW turn,
- Function `insidePolygon` will only be incorrect at extreme test case as `return fabs(sum) > M_PI ? 1 : -1;` is quite robust.

Exercise 7.3.6.1: Swap point a and b when calling `cutPolygon(a, b, Q)`.

Exercise 7.3.7.1: Edit the `ccw` function to accept collinear points.

Exercise 7.3.7.2: We can make Andrew's Monotone Chain algorithm to run in $O(n)$ if we are guaranteed that the input points are already sorted by increasing x-values and if ties, by increasing y-values by commenting the sort routine.

7.6 Chapter Notes

Some material in this chapter are derived from the material courtesy of **Dr Cheng Holun, Alan** from School of Computing, National University of Singapore. Some library functions were started from **Igor Navernioukk**'s library: `https://shygypsy.com/tools/` and has been expanded to include many other useful geometric library functions.

Compared to the earlier editions of this book, this chapter has, just like Chapter 5 and 6, gradually grown. However, the material mentioned here is still far from complete, especially for ICPC contestants. If you are preparing for ICPC, it is a good idea to dedicate one person in your team to study this topic in depth. This person should master basic geometry formulas and advanced computational geometry techniques, perhaps by reading relevant chapters in the following books: [30, 10, 7]. But not just the theory, this person must also train to code *robust* geometry solutions that are able to handle degenerate (special) cases and minimize precision errors.

We still have a few geometry related topics in this book. In Section 8.7, we will discuss (computational) geometry problems that are mixed with other data structure(s)/algorithm(s). In Chapter 9, we will discuss the **Art Gallery** problem, **The Closest Pair Problem**, and **line sweep** technique.

However, there are still more computational geometry techniques that have not been discussed yet, e.g., the intersection of **other geometric objects**, **The Furthest Pair Problem**, **Rotating Caliper** algorithm, etc.

Statistics	1st	2nd	3rd	4th
Number of Pages	13	22	29	36 (+24%)
Written Exercises	-	20	31	21+8*=29 (-6%)
Programming Exercises	96	103	96	199 (+107%)

The breakdown of the number of programming exercises from each section is shown below:

Section	Title	Appearance	% in Chapter	% in Book
7.2	**Basic Geometry Objects ...**	142	≈ 71%	4.1%
7.3	**Algorithm on Polygon ...**	43	≈ 22%	1.2%
7.4	3D Geometry	14	≈ 7%	0.2%
	Total	199		≈ 5.8%

Chapter 8

More Advanced Topics

Genius is one percent inspiration, ninety-nine percent perspiration.
— **Thomas Alva Edison**

8.1 Overview and Motivation

The main purpose of having this chapter is organizational. The next four sections of this chapter contain the harder material from Chapter 3 and 4: In Section 8.2 and Section 8.3, we discuss the more challenging variants and techniques involving the two most popular problem solving paradigms: Complete Search and Dynamic Programming. In Section 8.4 and Section 8.5, we discuss the more challenging Graph problems and their associated algorithms: Network Flow and Graph Matching. Putting these materials in the earlier chapters (the first half of this book) will probably scare off some *new* readers of this book.

In Section 8.6, we discuss a special class of computational problems that are classified as NP-hard (the optimization version with the key signature: maximize this or minimize that) or NP-complete (the decision version with the key signature: just output yes or no). In complexity theory, unless $P = NP$, nobody on earth currently (as of year 2020) knows how to solve them efficiently in polynomial time. Thus, the typical[1] solutions are either Complete Search on smaller instances, Dynamic Programming on instances with reasonably small parameters (if there are repeated computations), or we have to find and use the usually subtle but special constraints in the problem description that will turn the problems into polynomial problems again – a few involves Network Flow and/or Graph Matching. The theory of NP-completeness is usually only taught in final year undergraduate or in graduate level of typical CS curricula. Most (younger) competitive programmers are not aware of this topic. Thus, it is better to defer the discussion of NP-complete until this chapter.

In Section 8.7, we discuss complex problems that require *more than one* algorithm(s) and/or data structure(s). These discussions can be confusing for new programmers if they are listed in the earlier chapters, e.g., we repeat the discussion of Binary Search the Answer from Book 1 but this time we will also combine it with other algorithms in this book. It is more appropriate to discuss problem decomposition in this chapter, after various (easier) data structures and algorithms have been discussed. Thus, it is a very good idea to read the entire preceding chapters/sections first before starting to read this Section 8.7.

We also encourage readers to avoid rote memorization of the solutions but more importantly, please try to understand the key ideas that may be applicable to other problems.

[1]We avoid discussing approximation algorithms in Competitive Programming as the output of almost all programming contest problems must be exact.

8.2 More Advanced Search Techniques

In Book 1, we have discussed various (simpler) iterative and recursive (backtracking) Complete Search techniques. However, some harder problems require *more clever* Complete Search solutions to avoid the Time Limit Exceeded (TLE) verdict. In this section, we discuss some of these techniques with several examples.

8.2.1 Backtracking with Bitmask

In Book 1, we have seen that bitmasks can be used to model a small set of Booleans. Bitmask operations are very lightweight and therefore every time we need to use a small set of Booleans, we can consider using bitmask technique to speed up our (Complete Search) solution as illustrated in this subsection.

The N-Queens Problem, Revisited

In Book 1, we have discussed UVa 11195 - Another N-Queens Problem. But even after we have improved the left and right diagonal checks by storing the availability of each of the n rows and the $2 \times n - 1$ left/right diagonals in three **`bitsets`**, we still get TLE. Converting these three **`bitsets`** into three bitmasks helps a bit, but this is still TLE.

Fortunately, there is a better way to use these rows, left diagonals (from top left to bottom right), and right diagonals (from bottom left to top right) checks, as described below. This formulation[2] allows for efficient backtracking with bitmask. We will straightforwardly use three bitmasks for `rw`, `ld`, and `rd` to represent the state of the search. The on bits in bitmasks `rw`, `ld`, and `rd` describe which *rows* are attacked in the *next column*, due to *row*, *left diagonal*, or *right diagonal* attacks from previously placed queens, respectively. Since we consider one column at a time, there will only be n possible left/right diagonals, hence we can have three bitmasks of the same length of n bits (compared with $2 \times n - 1$ bits for the left/right diagonals in the earlier formulation in Book 1).

Notice that although both solutions (the one in Book 1 and the one above) use the same data structure: three bitmasks, the one described above is much more efficient. This highlights the need for problem solvers to think from various angles.

We first show the short code of this recursive backtracking with bitmask for the (general) N-Queens problem with $n = 5$ and then explain how it works.

```
#include <bits/stdc++.h>
using namespace std;

int ans = 0, OK = (1<<5) - 1;                    // test for n = 5-Queens

void backtrack(int rw, int ld, int rd) {
  if (rw == OK) { ans++; return; }               // all bits in rw are on
  int pos = OK & (~(rw | ld | rd));              // 1s in pos can be used
  while (pos) {                                  // faster than O(n)
    int p = pos & -pos;                          // LSOne---this is fast
    pos -= p;                                    // turn off that on bit
    backtrack(rw|p, (ld|p)<<1, (rd|p)>>1);       // clever
  }
}
```

[2]Although this solution is customized for this N-Queens problem, some techniques are still generic enough.

```
int main() {
  backtrack(0, 0, 0);                          // the starting point
  printf("%d\n", ans);                         // should be 10 for n = 5
} // return 0;
```

pos = 11111 & ~00000 = 11111 (p = 1)

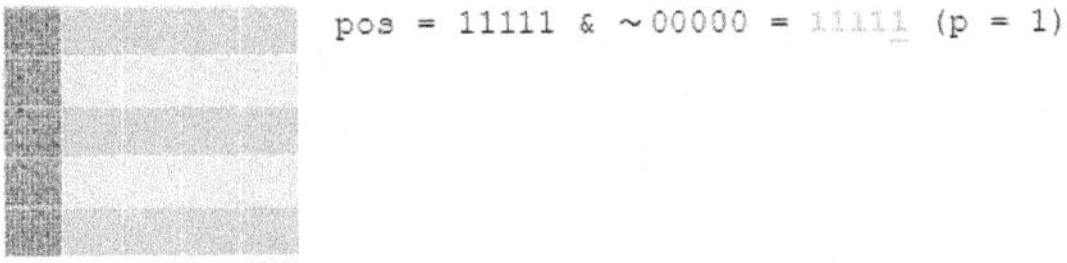

Figure 8.1: 5-Queens problem: The initial state

For $n = 5$, we start with the state `(rw, ld, rd) = (0, 0, 0) = (00000, 00000, 00000)`$_2$. This state is shown in Figure 8.1. The variable `OK = (1<<5)-1 = (11111)`$_2$ is used both as terminating condition check and to help decide which rows are available for a certain column. The operation `pos = OK & (~(rw|ld|rd))` *combines* the information of which rows in the next column are attacked by the previously placed queens (via row, left diagonal, or right diagonal attacks), *negates* the result, and *combines* it with variable `OK` to yield the rows that are *available* for the next column. Initially, all rows in column 0 are available.

Complete Search (the recursive backtracking) will try all possible rows (that is, all the *on bits* in variable `pos`) of a certain column one by one. Back in Book 1, we have discussed two ways to explore all the on bits of a bitmask. This $O(n)$ method below is slower.

```
for (int p = 0; p < n; ++p)                    // O(n)
  if (pos & (1<<p))                            // bit p is on in pos
    // process p
```

The other one below is faster. As the recursive backtracking goes deeper, fewer and fewer rows are available for selection. Instead of trying all n rows, we can speed up the loop above by just trying all the on bits in variable `pos`. The loop below runs in $O(k)$ where k is the number of bits that are on in variable `pos`:

```
while (pos) {                                  // O(k)
  int p = LSOne(pos);                          // LSOne(S) = (S) & (-S)
  int j = __builtin_ctz(p);                    // 2^j = p, get j
  // process p (or index j)
  pos -= p;                                    // turn off that on bit
}
```

Q0
rw = 00001 (1)
ld = 00001 << 1 = 00010 (2)
rd = 00001 >> 1 = 00000|1 (0, the LSB is removed)
----------------------- OR
00011 -> NEGATE -> 11100
pos = 11111 & 11100 = 11100 (p = 4)

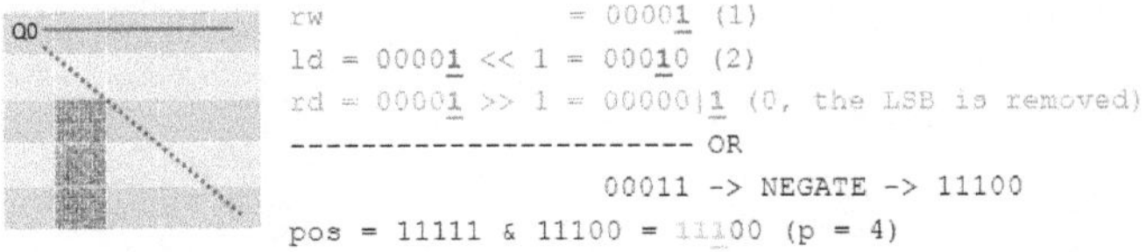

Figure 8.2: 5-Queens problem; After placing the first Queen

Back to our discussion, for `pos = (11111)`$_2$, we first start with `p = pos & -pos = 1`, or row 0. After placing the first Queen (Queen Q0) at row 0 of column 0, row 0 is no longer available for the next column 1 and this is quickly captured by bit operation `rw|p` (and also `ld|p` and `rd|p`). Now here is the beauty of this solution. A left/right diagonal increases/decreases the row number that it attacks by one as it changes to the next column, respectively. A shift left/right operation: `(ld|p) << 1` and `(rd|p) >> 1` can nicely capture these behaviours effectively. In Figure 8.2, we see that for the next column 1, row 1 is not available due to left diagonal attack by Queen Q0. Now only row 2, 3, and 4 are available for column 1. We will start with row 2.

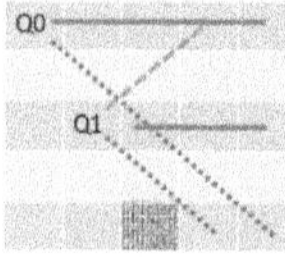

```
rw                 = 00101 (5)
ld = 00110 << 1 = 01100 (12)
rd = 00100 >> 1 = 00010 (2)
------------------------ OR
                   01111 -> NEGATE -> 10000
pos = 11111 & 10000 = 10000 (p = 16)
```

Figure 8.3: 5-Queens problem; After placing the second Queen

After placing the second Queen (Queen Q1) at row 2 of column 1, row 0 (due to Queen Q0) and now row 2 are no longer available for the next column 2. The shift left operation for the left diagonal constraint causes row 2 (due to Queen Q0) and now row 3 to be unavailable for the next column 2. The shift right operation for the right diagonal constraint causes row 1 to be unavailable for the next column 2. Therefore, only row 4 is available for the next column 2 and we have to choose it next (see Figure 8.3).

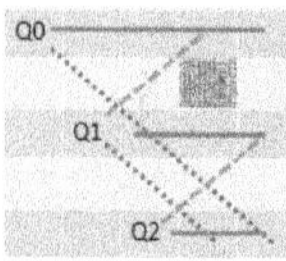

```
rw                 =  10101 (21)
ld = 11100 << 1 = 111000 (56, but the MSB is unused)
rd = 10010 >> 1 =  01001 (9)
------------------------ OR
                   111101 -> NEGATE -> 000010
pos = 11111 & 000010 = 00010 (p = 2)
```

Figure 8.4: 5-Queens problem; After placing the third Queen

After placing the third Queen (Queen Q2) at row 4 of column 2, row 0 (due to Queen Q0), row 2 (due to Queen Q1), and now row 4 are no longer available for the next column 3. The shift left operation for the left diagonal constraint causes row 3 (due to Queen Q0) and row 4 (due to Queen Q1) to be unavailable for the next column 3 (there is no row 5—the MSB in bitmask `ld` is unused). The shift right operation for the right diagonal constraint causes row 0 (due to Queen Q1) and now row 3 to be unavailable for the next column 3. Combining all these, only row 1 is available for the next column 3 and we have to choose it next (see Figure 8.4).

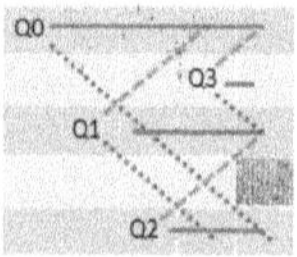

```
rw                  =   10111 (23)
ld = 111010 << 1 = 1110100 (116, two MSBs are unused)
rd =  01011 >> 1 =   00101 (5)
------------------------ OR
                   1110111 -> NEGATE -> 0001000
pos = 11111 & 0001000 = 01000 (p = 8)
```

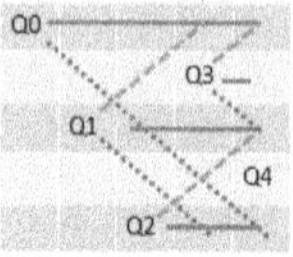

```
rw                  =   11111 (we get one solution)
```

Figure 8.5: 5-Queens problem; After placing the fourth and the fifth Queens

The same explanation is applicable for the fourth and the fifth Queen (Queen Q3 and Q4) to get the first solution $\{0, 2, 4, 1, 3\}$ as shown in Figure 8.5. We can continue this process to get the other 9 solutions for $n = 5$.

With this technique, we can solve UVa 11195. We just need to modify the given code[3] above to take the bad cells—which can also be modeled as bitmasks—into consideration. Let's roughly analyze the worst case for $n \times n$ board with no bad cell. Assuming that this recursive backtracking with bitmask has approximately two fewer rows available at each step, we have a time complexity of $O(n!!)$ where $n!!$ is a notation of multifactorial. For $n = 14$ with no bad cell, the recursive backtracking solution in Book 1 requires up to $14! \approx 87\,178\,M$ operations which is clearly TLE whereas the recursive backtracking with bitmask above *only* requires around $14!! = 14 \times 12 \times 10 \times \ldots \times 2 = 645\,120$ operations. In fact, $O(n!!)$ algorithm is probably good enough for up to $n \leq 17$ per test case.

Source code: `ch8/UVa11195.cpp|ml`

Exercise 8.2.1.1*: What to do if you just need to find and display *just one* solution of this N-Queens problem or state that there is no solution, but $1 \leq N \leq 200\,000$?

Exercise 8.2.1.2*: Another hard backtracking problem with bitmask is the cryptarithm puzzle where we are given an arithmetic equations, e.g., `SEND+MORE = MONEY` and we are supposed to replace each letter with a digit so that the equation is correct, e.g., `9567+1085 = 10652`. There can be 0-no solution, 1-unique (like the `SEND+MORE = MONEY` example), or multiple solutions for a given cryptarithm puzzle. Notice that there can only be 10 different characters used in the puzzle and this part can be converted into a bitmask. Challenge your backtracking skills by solving Kattis - greatswercporto and/or Kattis - sendmoremoney.

8.2.2 State-Space Search with BFS or Dijkstra's

In Chapter 4, we have discussed two standard graph algorithms for solving the Single-Source Shortest Paths (SSSP) problem. BFS can be used if the graph is unweighted while (appropriate version of) Dijkstra's algorithm should be used if the graph is weighted. The SSSP problems listed in Book 1 are easier in the sense that most of the time we can easily see 'the graph' in the problem description (sometimes they are given verbatim). This is no longer true for some harder graph searching problems listed in this section where the (implicit) graphs are no longer trivial to see and the state/vertex can be a complex object. In such case, we usually name the search as 'State-Space Search' instead of SSSP.

When the state is a complex object—e.g., a pair in UVa 00321 - The New Villa/Kattis - ecoins, a triple in UVa 01600 - Patrol Robot/Kattis - keyboard, a quad in UVa 10047 - The Monocycle/Kattis - robotmaze, etc—, we normally do not use the standard `vector<int> dist` to store the distance information as in the standard BFS/Dijkstra's implementation. This is because such state may not be easily converted into integer indices. In C++, we can use comparable C++ `pair<int, int>` (short form: `ii`) to store a pair of (integer) information. For anything more than pair, e.g., triple/quad, we can use comparable C++ `tuple<int, int, int>`/`tuple<int, int, int, int>`. Now, we can use C++ `pair` (or `tuple`) in conjunction with C++ `map<VERTEX-TYPE, int> dist` as our data structure to keep track of distance values of this complex `VERTEX-TYPE`. This technique adds a (small)

[3]For this runtime critical section, we prefer to use fast C++ code in order to pass the time limit.

$\log V$ factor to the time complexity of BFS/Dijkstra's. But for complex State-Space Search, this extra overhead is acceptable in order to bring down the overall coding complexity.

But what if `VERTEX-TYPE`[4] is a small array/vector (e.g., UVa 11212 - Editing a Book and Kattis - safe)? We will discuss an example of such complex State-Space Search below.

UVa 11212 - Editing a Book

Abridged problem description: Given n paragraphs numbered from 1 to n, arrange them in the order of $\{1, 2, ..., n\}$. With the help of a clipboard, you can press Ctrl-X (cut) and Ctrl-V (paste) several times. You cannot cut twice before pasting, but you can cut several contiguous paragraphs at the same time and these paragraphs will later be pasted in order. What is the minimum number of steps required?

Example 1: In order to make $\{2, 4, (1), 5, 3, 6\}$ sorted, we cut paragraph (1) and paste it before paragraph 2 to have $\{1, 2, 4, 5, (3), 6\}$. Then, we cut paragraph (3) and paste it before paragraph 4 to have $\{1, 2, 3, 4, 5, 6\}$. The answer is 2 steps.

Example 2: In order to make $\{(3, 4, 5), 1, 2\}$ sorted, we cut three paragraphs at the same time: (3, 4, 5) and paste them after paragraph 2 to have $\{1, 2, 3, 4, 5\}$. This is just 1 step. This solution is not unique as we can have the following answer: We cut two paragraphs at the same time: (1, 2) and paste them before paragraph 3 to get $\{1, 2, 3, 4, 5\}$.

The state of this problem is a *permutation* of paragraphs that is usually stored as an array/a vector. If we use C++ comparable `vector<int>` to represent the state, then we can use `map<vector<int>, int> dist` directly. However, we can use the slightly faster, more memory efficient, but slightly more complex route if we can create an encode and a decode functions that map a `VERTEX-TYPE` into a small integer and vice versa. For example, in this problem, the encode function can be as simple as turning a vector of n individual 1-digit integers into a single n-digits integer and the decode function is used to break a single n-digits integer back into a vector of n 1-digit integers, e.g., $\{1, 2, 3, 4, 5\}$ is encoded as an integer 12345 and an integer 12345 is decoded back to $\{1, 2, 3, 4, 5\}$.

Next, we need to analyze the size of the state-space. There are $n!$ permutations of paragraphs. With maximum $n = 9$ in the problem statement, this is 9! or 362 880. So, the size of the state-space is not that big actually. If we use the simple encode/decode functions shown above, we need `vector<int> dist(1e9, -1)` which is probably MLE. Fortunately, now we are dealing with integers so we can use `unordered_map<int, int> dist(2*363000)`. For a slightly faster and more memory efficient way, see **Exercise 8.2.2.2*** where we can use the much smaller `vector<int> dist(363000, -1)`. For the rest of this subsection, we will use the proposed simple encode/decode functions for clarity.

The loose upper bound of the number of steps required to rearrange these n paragraphs is $O(k)$, where k is the number of paragraphs that are initially in the wrong positions. This is because we can use the following 'trivial' algorithm (which is incorrect): cut a single paragraph that is in the wrong position and paste that paragraph in the correct position. After k such cut-paste operations, we will definitely have sorted paragraphs. But this may not be the shortest way.

For example, the 'trivial' algorithm above will process 54321 as follows:
$\underline{5}4321 \to \underline{4}3215 \to \underline{3}2145 \to \underline{2}1345 \to 12345$ of total 4 cut-paste steps.
This is not optimal, as we can solve this instance in only 3 steps:
$54\underline{32}1 \to 32\underline{5}41 \to 34\underline{12}5 \to 12345$.

[4]In Java, we do not have built-in `pair` (or `tuple`) like in C++ and thus we have to create a class that implements comparable. Now, we can use Java `TreeMap<VERTEX-TYPE, Integer> dist` to keep track of distances. In Python, tuples is common and can be used for this purpose. We can use Python set (curly braces `dist = {}`) to keep track of distances. In OCaml, we can use tuples too.

This problem has a *huge* search space that even for an instance with 'small' $n = 9$, it is nearly impossible for us to get the answer manually, e.g., We likely will not start drawing the recursion tree just to verify that we need at least 4 steps[5] to sort 549873216 and at least 5 steps[6] to sort 987654321.

The difficulty of this problem lies in the number of *edges* of the State-Space graph. Given a permutation of length n (a vertex), there are ${}^nC_2$ possible cutting points (index $i, j \in [1..n]$) and there are n possible pasting points (index $k \in [1..(n-(j-i+1))]$). Therefore, for each of the $n!$ vertex, there are about $O(n^3)$ edges connected to it.

The problem actually asks for the shortest path from the source vertex/state (the input permutation) to the destination vertex (a sorted permutation) on this unweighted but huge State-Space graph. The worst case behavior if we run a single $O(V+E)$ BFS on this State-Space graph is $O(n! + (n! * n^3)) = O(n! * n^3)$. For $n = 9$, this is $9! * 9^3 = 264\,539\,520 \approx 265M$ operations. This solution most likely will receive a TLE verdict.

We need a better solution, which we will see in the next Section 8.2.3.

Exercise 8.2.2.1: Is it possible that State-Space Search is cast as a maximization problem?

Exercise 8.2.2.2*: We have shown a simple way to encode a vector of n 1-digit integers into a single n-digits integer. When $n = 9$ (skipping integer 0 as in UVa 11212), we will use up to $10^9 = 1G$ memory space. However many of the cells will be empty. Note that these n integers form a permutation of n integers. Show a more efficient encoding and its corresponding decoding functions to map a vector of n integers to its permutation index, e.g., $\{1, 2, \ldots, n-1, n\}$ is index 0, $\{1, 2, \ldots, n, n-1\}$ is index 1, ..., and $\{n, n-1, \ldots, 2, 1\}$ is index $n! - 1$. This way, we only need $9! = 362K$ memory space.

8.2.3 Meet in the Middle

For certain SSSP (usually State-Space Search) problem on a huge graph and we know two vertices: the source vertex/state s and the destination vertex/state t, we may be able to *significantly* reduce the time complexity of the search by searching from *both directions* and hoping that the search will *meet in the middle*. We illustrate this technique by continuing our discussion of the hard UVa 11212 problem.

Note that the meet in the middle technique does not always refer to bidirectional search (BFS), e.g., see **Exercise 8.6.2.3***. It is a problem solving strategy of 'searching from two directions/parts' that may appear in another form in other difficult searching problems.

Bidirectional Search (BFS): UVa 11212 - Editing a Book (Revisited)

Although the worst case time complexity of the State-Space Search of this problem is bad, the largest possible answer for this problem is small. When we run BFS on the largest test case with $n = 9$ from the destination state t (the sorted permutation 123456789) to reach all other states, we find out that for this problem, the maximum depth of the BFS for $n = 9$ is just 5 (after running it for *a few minutes*—which is TLE in contest environment).

This important upperbound information allows us to perform bidirectional BFS by choosing only to go to depth 2 from each direction. While this information is not a necessary condition for us to run a bidirectional BFS, it can help to reduce the search space.

---

[5]In compressed form: 549873216 → 549816732 → 567349812 → 567812349 → 123456789.

[6]In compressed form: 987654321 → 985432761 → 943278561 → 327894561 → 345612789 → 123456789.

There are three possible cases which we discuss below.

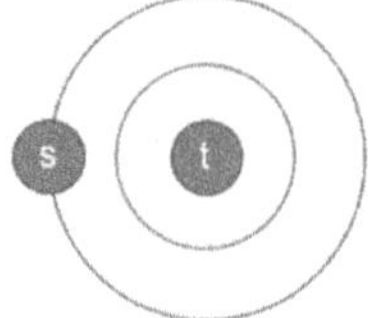

Figure 8.6: Case 1: Example when s is two steps away from t

Case 1: Vertex s is within two steps away from vertex t (see Figure 8.6).
We first run BFS (max depth of BFS = 2) from the target vertex t to populate distance information from t: `dist_t`. If the source vertex s is already found, i.e., `dist_t[s]` is not `INF`, then we return this value. The possible answers are: 0 (if $s = t$), 1, or 2 steps.

Case 2: Vertex s is within three to four steps away from vertex t (see Figure 8.7).

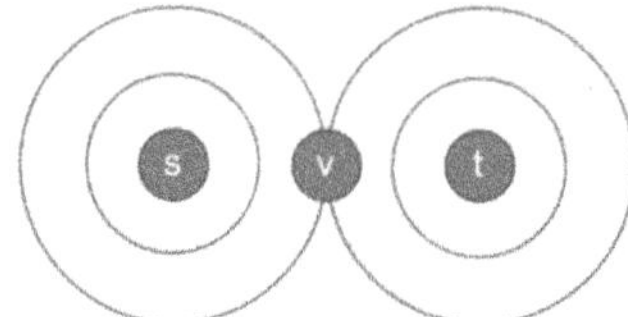

Figure 8.7: Case 2: Example when s is four steps away from t

If we do not manage to find the source vertex s after Case 1 above, i.e., `dist_t[s] = INF`, we know that s is located further away from vertex t. We now run BFS from the source vertex s (also with max depth of BFS = 2) to populate distance information from s: `dist_s`. If we encounter a common vertex v 'in the middle' during the execution of this second BFS, we know that vertex v is within two layers away from vertex t and s. The answer is therefore `dist_s[v]+dist_t[v]` steps. The possible answers are: 3 or 4 steps.

Case 3: Vertex s is exactly five steps away from vertex t (see Figure 8.8).

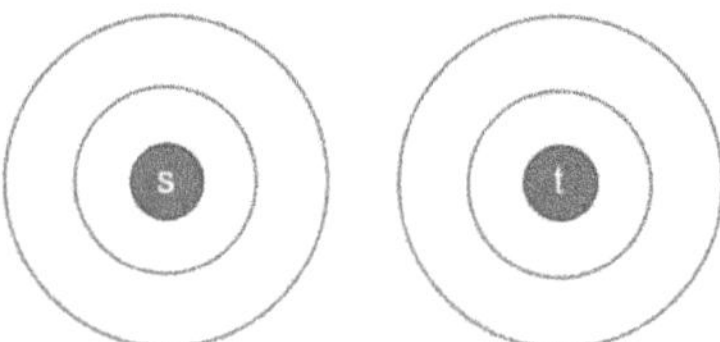

Figure 8.8: Case 3: Example when s is five steps away from t

If we do not manage to find any common vertex v after running the second BFS in Case 2 above, then the answer is clearly 5 steps that we know earlier as s and t must always be reachable. Stopping at depth 2 allows us to skip computing depth 3, which is *much more time consuming* than computing depth 2.

We have seen that given a permutation of length n (a vertex), there are about $O(n^3)$ branches in this huge State-Space graph. However, if we just run each BFS with at most depth 2, we only execute at most $O((n^3)^2) = O(n^6)$ operations per BFS. With $n = 9$, this is $9^6 = 531\,441$ operations (this value is greater than 9! as there are some overlaps). As the destination vertex t is unchanged throughout the State-Space search, we can compute the first BFS from destination vertex t just once. Then we compute the second BFS from source vertex s per query. Our BFS implementation will have an additional log factor due to the usage of table data structure (e.g., `map`) to store `dist_t` and `dist_s`. This is Accepted.

Source code: `ch8/UVa11212.cpp|ml`

In the event it is not possible to know the upperbound in advance, we can write a more general version of meet in the middle/bidirectional search (BFS) as follows: enqueue two sources: (s, from s) and (t, from t) initially and perform BFS as usual. We 'meet in the middle' if a vertex that has from s flag meets a vertex that has from t flag.

Programming Exercises solvable with More Advanced Search Techniques:

a. More Challenging Backtracking Problems

1. Entry Level: **UVa 00711 - Dividing up** * (backtracking with pruning)
2. **UVa 01052 - Bit Compression** * (LA 3565 - WorldFinals SanAntonio06; backtracking with some form of bitmask)
3. **UVa 11451 - Water Restrictions** * (the input constraints are small; backtracking with bitmask without memoization; or use DP)
4. **UVa 11699 - Rooks** * (try all the possible row combinations on which we put rooks and keep the best)
5. *Kattis - committeeassignment* * (backtracking; pruning; add a member to existing committee or create a new committee; TLE with DP bitmask)
6. *Kattis - holeynqueensbatman* * (similar with UVa 11195)
7. *Kattis - greatswercporto* * (use backtracking with pruning; testing up to 10! possible permutations possibly TLE)

   Extra UVa: *00131, 00211, 00387, 00710, 10202, 10309, 10318, 10890, 11090, 11127, 11195, 11464, 11471.*

   Extra Kattis: *bells, capsules, correspondence, knightsfen, minibattleship, pebblesolitaire, sendmoremoney.*

b. State-Space Search, BFS, Easier

1. Entry Level: **UVa 10047 - The Monocycle** * (s: (row, col, dir, color))
2. **UVa 01600 - Patrol Robot** * (LA 3670 - Hanoi06; s: (row, col, k_left); reset k_left to the original k as soon as the robot enters a non obstacle cell)
3. **UVa 11513 - 9 Puzzle** * (s: (vector of 9 integers); SDSP; BFS)
4. **UVa 12135 - Switch Bulbs** * (LA 4201 - Dhaka08; s: (bitmask); BFS; similar with UVa 11974)
5. *Kattis - ecoins* * (s: (conventional-value, infotechnological-value); BFS; also available at UVa 10306 - e-Coins)
6. *Kattis - flipfive* * (s: (bitmask); only $2^9 = 512$ grid configurations; BFS)
7. *Kattis - safe* * (s: (convert 3x3 grid into a base 4 integer); BFS)

   Extra UVa: *00298, 00928, 10097, 10682, 11974.*

   Extra Kattis: *hydrasheads, illiteracy.*

c. State-Space Search, BFS, Harder

1. Entry Level: **UVa 11212 - Editing a Book** * (meet in the middle)
2. **UVa 11198 - Dancing Digits *** (s: (permutation); tricky to code)
3. **UVa 11329 - Curious Fleas *** (s: (bitmask); 4 bits for die position; 16 bits for cells with fleas; 6 bits for side with a flea; use `map`; tedious)
4. **UVa 12445 - Happy 12 *** (meet in the middle; similar with UVa 11212)
5. *Kattis - keyboard* * (LA 7155 - WorldFinals Marrakech15; s: (row, col, char_typed); also available at UVa 01714 - Keyboarding)
6. *Kattis - robotmaze* * (s: (r, c, dir, steps); be careful of corner cases)
7. *Kattis - robotturtles* * (s: (r, c, dir, bitmask_ice_castles); print solution)

   Extra UVa: *00321, 00704, 00816, 00985, 01251, 01253, 10021, 10085, 11160, 12569.*

   Extra Kattis: *buggyrobot, distinctivecharacter, enteringthetime, jabuke2, jumpingmonkey, jumpingyoshi, ricochetrobots.*

d. State-Space Search, Dijkstra's

1. Entry Level: **UVa 00658 - It's not a Bug ...** * (s: (bitmask—whether a bug is present or not); the state-space graph is weighted)
2. **UVa 01048 - Low Cost Air Travel *** (LA 3561 - WorldFinals SanAntonio06; tedious state-space search problem, use Dijkstra's)
3. **UVa 01057 - Routing *** (LA 3570 - WorldFinals SanAntonio06; Floyd-Warshall; APSP; reduce to weighted SSSP problem; Dijkstra's)
4. **UVa 10269 - Adventure of Super Mario *** (use Floyd-Warshall to pre-compute APSP using only Villages; use Dijkstra's on s: (u, super_run_left))
5. *Kattis - bumped* * (s: (city, has_use_free_ticket); use Dijkstra's)
6. *Kattis - destinationunknown* * (use Dijkstra's twice; one normally; one with s: (point, has_edge_g_h_used); compare the results)
7. *Kattis - justpassingthrough* * (s: (r, c, n_left); Dijkstra's/SSSP on DAG)

   Extra UVa: *10923, 11374.*

   Extra Kattis: *bigtruck, kitchen, rainbowroadrace, treasure, xentopia.*

e. Also see additional (hard) search-related problems in Section 8.6, 8.7, and 9.20.

8.3 More Advanced DP Techniques

In various sections in Chapter 3+4+5+6, we have seen the introduction of Dynamic Programming (DP) technique, several classical DP problems and their solutions, plus a gentle introduction to the easier non classical DP problems. There are several more advanced DP techniques that we have not covered in those sections. Here, we present some of them.

In IOI, ICPC, and many other (online) programming contests, many of these more advanced techniques are actually used. Therefore if you want to do well in the real programming competitions, you need to also master this section.

8.3.1 DP with Bitmask

Some of the modern DP problems require a (small) set of Booleans as one of the parameters of the DP state. This is another situation where bitmask technique can be useful (also see Section 8.2.1). This technique is suitable for DP as the integer (that represents the bitmask) can be used as the index of the DP table. We have seen this technique once when we discussed DP TSP (see Book 1). Here, we give one more example.

UVa 10911 - Forming Quiz Teams

For the abridged problem statement and the solution code of this problem, please refer to the very first problem mentioned in the first page of Book 1. The grandiose name of this problem is "minimum weight perfect matching on a small complete (general) weighted graph" that will be formally discussed in Section 8.5. In the general case, this problem is hard. However, if the input size is small, up to $M \leq 20$, then DP with bitmask solution can be used.

The DP with bitmask solution for this problem is simple. The matching state is represented by a `bitmask`. We illustrate this with a small example when $M = 6$. We start with a state where nothing is matched yet, i.e., `bitmask=111111`. If item 0 and item 2 are matched, we can turn off two bits (bit 0 and bit 2) at the same time via this simple bit operation, i.e., `bitmask^(1<<0)^(1<<2)`, thus the state becomes `bitmask=111010`. Notice that index starts from 0 and is counted from the right. If from this state, item 1 and item 5 are matched next, the state will become `bitmask=011000`. The perfect matching is obtained when the state is all '0's, in this case: `bitmask=000000`.

Although there are many ways to arrive at a certain state, there are only $O(2^M)$ distinct states. For each state, we record the minimum weight of previous matchings that must be done in order to reach this state. We want a perfect matching. First, we find one 'on' bit i using $O(1)$ LSOne technique. Then, we find the best other 'on' bit j from `[`i`+1..`M`-1]` using another $O(k)$ loop of LSOne checks where k is the number of remaining 'on' bits in `bitmask` and recursively match i and j. This algorithm runs in $O(M \times 2^M)$. In problem UVa 10911, $M = 2N$ and $2 \leq N \leq 8$, so this DP with bitmask solution is feasible. For more details, please study the code.

Source code: `ch8/UVa10911.cpp|java|py|ml`

In this subsection, we have shown that DP with bitmask technique can be used to solve small instances ($M \leq 20$) of matching on general graph. In general, bitmask technique allows us to represent a small set of up to $\approx$ 20 items. The programming exercises in this section contain more examples when bitmask is used as *one of the parameters* of the DP state.

Exercise 8.3.1.1: Show the required DP with bitmask solution if we have to deal with "Maximum Cardinality Matching on a small general graph ($1 \leq V \leq 20$)". Note that the main difference compared to UVa 10911 is that this time the required matching does not need to be a perfect matching, but it has to be the one with maximum cardinality.

8.3.2 Compilation of Common (DP) Parameters

After solving lots of DP problems (including recursive backtracking without memoization), contestants will develop a sense of which parameters are commonly used to represent the states of the DP (or recursive backtracking) problems. Therefore, experienced contestants will try to get the correct set of required parameters from this list first when presented with a 'new' DP problem. Some of them are as follows (note that this list is not exhaustive and your own personal list will grow as you solve more DP problems):

1. Parameter: Index i in an array, e.g., [x_0, x_1, ..., x_i, ...].
   Transition: Extend subarray [0..i] (or [i..n-1]), process i, take item i or not, etc.
   Example: 1D Max Sum, LIS, part of 0-1 Knapsack, TSP, etc (Book 1).

2. Parameter: Indices (i, j) in two arrays, e.g., [x_0, x_1, ..., x_i] + [y_0, y_1, ..., y_j].
   Transition: Extend i, j, or both, etc.
   Example: String Alignment/Edit Distance, LCS, etc (Section 6.3).

3. Parameter: Subarray (i, j) of an array. [..., x_i, x_{i+1}, ..., x_j, ...].
   Transition: Split (i, j) into $(i, k) + (k + 1, j)$ or into $(i, i + k) + (i + k + 1, j)$, etc.
   Example: Matrix Chain Multiplication (Section 9.7), etc.

4. Parameter: A vertex (position) in a (usually implicit) DAG.
   Transition: Process the neighbors of this vertex, etc.
   Example: Shortest/Longest/Counting Paths in/on DAG, etc (Book 1).

5. Parameter: Knapsack-Style Parameter.
   Transition: Decrease (or increase) current value until zero (or until threshold), etc.
   Example: 0-1 Knapsack, Subset Sum, Coin Change variants, etc (Book 1).
   Note: This parameter is not DP friendly if its range is high (see the term 'pseudo-polynomial' in Section 8.6).
   Also see tips in Section 8.3.3 if the value of this parameter can go negative.

6. Parameter: Small set (usually using bitmask technique).
   Transition: Flag one (or more) item(s) in the set to on (or off), etc.
   Example: DP-TSP (Book 1), DP with bitmask (Section 8.3.1), etc.

Note that the harder DP problems usually combine two or more parameters to represent distinct states. Try to solve more DP problems listed in this section to build your DP skills.

8.3.3 Handling Negative Parameter Values with Offset

In rare cases, the possible range of a parameter used in a DP state can go negative. This causes issues for DP solutions as we map parameter values into indices of a DP table. The indices of a DP table must therefore be non negative. Fortunately, this issue can be dealt easily by using offset technique to make all the indices become non negative again. We illustrate this technique with another non trivial DP problem: Free Parentheses.

UVa 01238 - Free Parentheses (ICPC Jakarta08, LA 4143)

Abridged problem statement: You are given a simple arithmetic expression which consists of only *addition and subtraction* operators, i.e., `1 - 2 + 3 - 4 - 5`. You are free to put any *parentheses* to the expression anywhere and as many as you want as long as the expression is still *valid*. How many *different* numbers can you make? The answer for the simple expression above is 6:

```
1 - 2 + 3 - 4 - 5      = -7          1 - (2 + 3 - 4 - 5)   =  5
1 - (2 + 3) - 4 - 5    = -13         1 - 2 + 3 - (4 - 5)   =  3
1 - (2 + 3 - 4) - 5    = -5          1 - (2 + 3) - (4 - 5) = -3
```

The problem specifies the following constraints: the expression consists of only $2 \leq N \leq 30$ non-negative numbers less than 100, separated by addition or subtraction operators. There is no operator before the first and after the last number.

To solve this problem, we need to make three observations:

1. We only need to put an open bracket after a '-' (negative) sign as doing so will reverse the meaning of subsequent '+' and '-' operators;
2. We can only put X close brackets if we already use X open brackets—we need to store this information to process the subproblems correctly;
3. The maximum value is 100 + 100 + ... + 100 (100 repeated 30 times) = 3000 and the minimum value is 0 - 100 - ... - 100 (one 0 followed by 29 times of negative 100) = -2900—this information also need to be stored, as we will see below.

To solve this problem using DP, we need to determine which set of parameters of this problem represent distinct states. The DP parameters that are easier to identify are these two:

1. '`idx`'—the current position being processed, we need to know where we are now.
2. '`open`'—the number of open brackets so that we can produce a valid expression[7].

But these two parameters are not enough to uniquely identify the state yet. For example, this partial expression: '1-1+1-1...' has `idx = 3` (indices: 0, 1, 2, 3 have been processed), `open = 0` (cannot put close bracket anymore), which sums to 0. Then, '1-(1+1-1)...' also has the same `idx = 3`, `open = 0` and sums to 0. But '1-(1+1)-1...' has the same `idx = 3`, `open = 0`, *but* sums to -2. These two DP parameters do *not* identify a unique state yet. We need one more parameter to distinguish them, i.e., the value '`val`'. This skill of identifying the correct set of parameters to represent distinct states is something that one has to develop in order to do well with DP problems. The code and its explanation are shown below.

As we can see from the code, we can represent all possible states of this problem with a 3D array: `bool visited[idx][open][val]`. The purpose of this memo table `visited` is to flag if certain state has been visited or not. As '`val`' ranges from -2900 to 3000 (5901 distinct values), we have to offset this range to make the range non-negative. In this example, we use a safe constant +3000. The number of states (with extra buffer) is $35 \times 35 \times 6010 \approx 7.5M$ with $O(1)$ processing per state. This is fast enough.

[7]At `idx = N` (we have processed the last number), it is fine if we still have `open` > 0 as we can dump all the necessary closing brackets at the end of the expression, e.g.,: 1 - (2 + 3 - (4 - (5))).

```
void dp(int idx, int open, int val) {                   // OFFSET = 3000
  if (visited[idx][open][val+OFFSET])                   // has been reached before
    return;                                             // +3000 offset to make
                                                        // indices in [100..6000]
  visited[idx][open][val+OFFSET] = true;                // set this to true
  if (idx == N) {                                       // last number
    S.insert(val);                                      // val is one
    return;                                             // of expression result
  }
  int nval = val + num[idx] * sign[idx] * ((open%2 == 0) ? 1 : -1);
  if (sign[idx] == -1)                                  // 1: put open bracket
    dp(idx+1, open+1, nval);                            //    only if sign is -
  if (open > 0)                                         // 2: put close bracket
    dp(idx+1, open-1, nval);                            //    if we have >1 opens
  dp(idx+1, open, nval);                                // 3: do nothing
}

// Preprocessing: Set a Boolean array 'used' which is initially set to all
// false, then run this top-down DP by calling rec(0, 0, 0)
// The solution is the # of values in (or size of) unordered_set 'used'
```

Source code: ch8/UVa01238.cpp|java|py|ml

8.3.4 MLE/TLE? Use Better State Representation

Our 'correct' DP solution (which produces the correct answer but using more computing resources) may be given a Memory Limit Exceeded (MLE) or Time Limit Exceeded (TLE) verdict if the problem author used a better state representation and set larger input constraints that break our 'correct' DP solution. If that happens, we have no choice but to find a better DP state representation in order to reduce the DP table size (and subsequently speed up the overall time complexity). We illustrate this technique using an example:

UVa 01231 - ACORN (ICPC Singapore07, LA 4106)

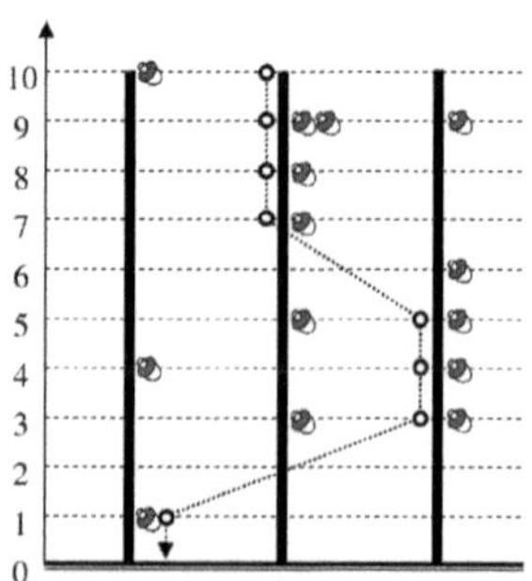

Figure 8.9: The Descent Path

Abridged problem statement: Given t oak trees, the height h of *all* trees, the height f that Jayjay the squirrel loses when it flies from one tree to another, $1 \leq t, h \leq 2000$,

$1 \leq f \leq 500$, and the positions of acorns on each of the oak trees: `acorn[tree][height]`, determine the max number of acorns that Jayjay can collect in *one single descent*. Example: if $t = 3, h = 10, f = 2$ and `acorn[tree][height]` as shown in Figure 8.9, the best descent path has a total of 8 acorns (see the dotted line).

Naïve DP Solution: use a table `total[tree][height]` that stores the best possible acorns collected when Jayjay is on a certain tree at certain height. Then Jayjay recursively tries to either go down (-1) unit on the *same* oak tree or flies ($-f$) unit(s) to t-1 *other* oak trees from this position. On the largest test case, this requires $2000 \times 2000 = 4M$ states and $4M \times 2000 = 8B$ operations. This approach is clearly TLE.

Better DP Solution: we can actually ignore the information: "On which tree Jayjay is currently at" as just memoizing the best among them is sufficient. This is because flying to any other t-1 other oak trees decreases Jayjay's height in the same manner. Set a table: `dp[height]` that stores the best possible acorns collected when Jayjay is at this `height`. The bottom-up DP code that requires only $2000 = 2K$ states and time complexity of $2000 \times 2000 = 4M$ is shown below:

```
for (int tree = 0; tree < t; ++tree)                    // initialization
  dp[h] = max(dp[h], acorn[tree][h]);

for (int height = h-1; height >= 0; --height)
  for (int tree = 0; tree < t; ++tree) {
    acorn[tree][height] +=
      max(acorn[tree][height+1],                        // from this tree +1 above
      ((height+f <= h) ? dp[height+f] : 0));            // from tree at height+f
    dp[height] = max(dp[height], acorn[tree][height]); // update this too
  }

printf("%d\n", dp[0]);                                  // the solution is here
```

Source code: `ch8/UVa01231.cpp|java|py|ml`

When the size of naïve DP states is too large that causes the overall DP time complexity to be infeasible, think of another more efficient (but usually not obvious) way to represent the possible states. Using a good state representation is a potential major speed up for a DP solution. Remember that no programming contest problem is unsolvable, the problem author must have known a technique.

8.3.5 MLE/TLE? Drop One Parameter, Recover It from Others

Another known technique to reduce the memory usage of a DP solution (and thereby speed up the solution) is to drop one important parameter which can actually be recovered by using the other parameter(s) or in another word, that parameter can be dropped to have a smaller DP state. We use one ICPC World Finals problem to illustrate this technique.

UVa 01099 - Sharing Chocolate (ICPC World Finals Harbin10)

Abridged problem description: Given a big chocolate bar of size $1 \leq w, h \leq 100$, $1 \leq n \leq 15$ friends, and the size request of each friend. Can we break the chocolate by using horizontal and vertical cuts that break the current chocolate into two parts so that each friend gets *one piece* of chocolate bar of his chosen size?

For example, see Figure 8.10—left. The size of the original chocolate bar is $w = 4$ and $h = 3$. If there are 4 friends, each requesting a chocolate piece of size $\{6, 3, 2, 1\}$, respectively, then we can break the chocolate into 4 parts using 3 cuts as shown in Figure 8.10—right.

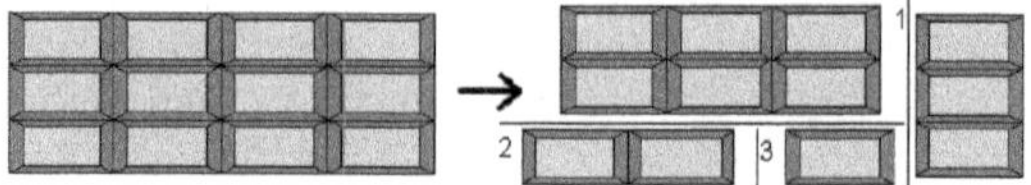

Figure 8.10: Illustration for ICPC WF2010 - J - Sharing Chocolate

For contestants who are already familiar with DP technique, then the following ideas should easily come to mind: first, if sum of all requests is not the same as $w \times h$, then there is no solution. Otherwise, we can represent a distinct state of this problem using three parameters: $(w, h, bitmask)$ where w and h are the dimensions of the chocolate that we are currently considering; and $bitmask$ is the subset of friends that already have chocolate piece of their chosen size. However, a quick analysis shows that this requires a DP table of size $100 \times 100 \times 2^{15} = 327M$. This is too much for a programming contest.

A better state representation is to use only two parameters, either: $(w, bitmask)$ or $(h, bitmask)$. Without loss of generality, we adopt $(w, bitmask)$ formulation. With this formulation, we can 'recover' the required value h via `sum(`$bitmask$`) / `w, where `sum(`$bitmask$`)` is the sum of the piece sizes requested by satisfied friends in $bitmask$ (i.e., all the 'on' bits of $bitmask$). This way, we have all the required parameters: w, h, and $bitmask$, but we only use a DP table of size $100 \times 2^{15} = 3M$. This one is doable.

Implementation wise, we can have a top-down DP with two parameters $(w, bitmask)$ and recover h at the start of DP recursion, or we can actually still use top-down DP with three parameters: $(w, h, bitmask)$, but since we know parameter h is always correlated with w and $bitmask$, we can just use 2D memo table for w and $bitmask$.

Base cases: if $bitmask$ only contains 1 'on' bit and the requested chocolate size of that person equals to $w \times h$, we have a solution. Otherwise we do not have a solution.

For general cases: if we have a chocolate piece of size $w \times h$ and a current set of satisfied friends $bitmask = bitmask_1 \bigcup bitmask_2$, we can either do a horizontal or a vertical cut so one piece is to serve friends in $bitmask_1$ and the other is to serve friends in $bitmask_2$.

The worst case time complexity for this problem is still huge, but with proper pruning, this solution runs within the time limit.

Source code: `ch8/UVa01099.cpp|ml`

8.3.6 Multiple Test Cases? No Memo Table Re-initializations

In certain DP problems with multiple (non-related) test cases (so that the total run time is typically the number of test cases multiplied by the run time of the worst possible test case), we may need to re-initialize our memo table (usually to -1). This step alone may consume a lot of CPU time, e.g., an $O(n^2)$ DP problem with 200 cases and $n \leq 2000$ needs $200 * 2000 * 2000 = 8 * 10^6$ initialization operations.

If we use top-down DP where we may *avoid* visiting *all possible states* of the problem for most test cases, we can use an array (or map) `lastvisit` where `lastvisit[s] = 0` (when state `s` is not visited yet) or `lastvisit[s] = `c (when the last time state `s` was visited is on test c). If we are on the t-th test case and we encounter a state `s`, we can tell if it has been visited before (for this t-th test case) simply by checking whether `lastvisit[s] = t`. Thus, we never need to re-initialize the memo table at the start of each test case. For some rare time-critical problems, this small change may differentiate TLE or AC verdicts.

8.3.7 MLE? Use bBST or Hash Table as Memo Table

In Book 1, we have seen a DP problem: 0-1 KNAPSACK where the state is $(id, remW)$. Parameter id has range [0..n-1] and parameter $remW$ has range [0..S]. If the problem author sets $n \times S$ to be quite large, it will cause the 2D array (for the DP table) of size $n \times S$ to be too large (Memory Limit Exceeded in programming contests).

Fortunately for a problem like this, if we run the Top-Down DP on it, we will realize that not all of the states are visited (whereas the Bottom-Up DP version will have to explore all states). Therefore, we can trade runtime for smaller space by using a balanced BST (C++ STL `map` or Java `TreeMap`) as the memo table. This balanced BST will *only* record the states that are actually visited by the Top-Down DP. Thus, if there are only k visited states, we will only use $O(k)$ space instead of $n \times S$. The runtime of the Top-Down DP increases by $O(c \times \log k)$ factor. However, note that this technique is rarely useful due to the high constant factor c involved.

Alternatively, we can also use Hash Table (C++ STL `unordered_map` or Java `HashMap`) as the memo table. Albeit faster, we may (usually) have to write our own custom hash function especially if the DP state uses more than one parameter which may not be trivial to implement in the first place.

Therefore, this technique is something that one may consider as last resort only if all other techniques that we currently know have been tried (and still fail). For example, Kattis - woodensigns can be seen as a standard counting paths on DAG problem with state: (idx, base1, base2) and the transition: go left, go right, or both. The issue is that the state is big as idx, base1, base2 can range from [1..2000]. Fortunately, we can map (idx, base1, base2) into a rather large integer key = idx*2000*2000 + base1*2000 + base2 and then use Hash Table to map this key into value to avoid recomputations.

8.3.8 TLE? Use Binary Search Transition Speedup

In rare cases, a naïve DP solution will be TLE, but you notice that the DP transition can be speed-up using binary search due to the sorted ordering of the data.

Kattis - busticket

Abridged problem description: We are given a price s of a single bus trip, a price p for a period bus ticket that is valid for m consecutive days starting from the day of purchase, n bus trips that you will make in the future, and array t containing n non-negative integers in *non-decreasing order* where $t[i]$ describe the number of days since today (day 0) until you make the i-th bus trip. Our task is to compute the smallest possible cost of making all n trips. The problem is $1 \leq n \leq 10^6$ and an $O(n^2)$ algorithm will get TLE.

A naïve DP solution is simply $dp(i)$ that computes the minimum cost of making the bus trips from day [i..n-1]. If $i == n$, we are done and return 0. Otherwise, we take the minimum of two choices. The first choice is to buy a single bus trip ticket for the i-th trip (with cost s) and advance to $dp(i+1)$. The second choice is to buy a period bus ticket starting from the i-th trip that is valid for the i-th trip until just before the j-th trip where $j > i$ is the first time $t[j] \geq t[i] + m$, i.e., the period bus ticket can't cover the j-th trip too. Then we add cost p and advance to $dp(j)$. There are $O(n)$ state and the second choice entails an $O(n)$ loop if done iteratively, thus we have an $O(n^2)$ solution that gets a TLE verdict.

However, if we read the problem statement carefully, we should notice a peculiar keyword: *non-decreasing* ordering of t_i. This means, we can search for the first j where $t[j] \geq t[i] + m$ using binary search instead. This speeds up the transition phase from $O(n)$ to $O(\log n)$, thus the overall runtime becomes $O(n \log n)$. This is AC.

8.3.9 Other DP Techniques

There are a few more DP problems in Section 8.6, Section 8.7, and in Chapter 9. They are:

1. Section 8.6.3: Bitonic TRAVELING-SALESMAN-PROBLEM (special case of TSP),
2. Section 8.6.6: MAX-WEIGHT-INDEPENDENT-SET (on tree) can be solved with DP,
3. Section 8.6.12: small instances of MIN-CLIQUE-COVER can be solved with $O(3^n)$ DP,
4. Section 9.3: Sparse Table Data Structure uses DP,
5. Section 9.7: Matrix Chain Multiplication (a classic DP problem),
6. Section 9.22: Egg Dropping Puzzle that can be solved with DP (various solutions),
7. Section 9.23: Rare techniques to further optimize DP.
8. Section 9.29: Chinese Postman Problem (another usage of DP with bitmask),

---

Programming Exercises related to More Advanced DP:

a. DP level 3 (harder than those listed in Chapter 3, 4, 5, and 6)
   1. Entry Level: **UVa 01172 - The Bridges of ...** * (LA 3986 - SouthWesternEurope07; weighted bipartite matching with additional constraints)
   2. **UVa 00672 - Gangsters** * (s: (gangster_id, openness_level); do not use cur_time as part of the state)
   3. **UVa 01211 - Atomic Car Race** * (LA 3404 - Tokyo05; precompute T[L], the time to run a path of length L; s: (i) - checkpoint i is we change tire)
   4. **UVa 10645 - Menu** * (s: (days_left, budget_left, prev_dish, prev_dish_cnt); the first 2 params are knapsack-style; the last 2 params to determine price)
   5. *Kattis - aspenavenue* * (sort; compute tree positions; s: (l_left, r_left), t: put next tree on the left/right; also available at UVa 11555 - Aspen Avenue)
   6. *Kattis - busticket* * (s: (day_i); t: either buy daily ticket or jump to end of period ticket (use binary search to avoid TLE))
   7. *Kattis - protectingthecollection* * (DP; s: (r, c, dir, has_installed_a_mirror); t: just proceed or install '/' or '\' mirror at a '.')

   Extra UVa: *10163, 10604, 10898, 11002, 11523, 12208, 12563.*

   Extra Kattis: *bridgeautomation, crackerbarrel, eatingeverything, exchangerates, homework, ingestion, mailbox, posterize, welcomehard, whatsinit.*

b. DP level 4
   1. Entry Level: *Kattis - coke* * (drop parameter n1; recover it from b (number of coke bought), n5, and n10; also available at UVa 10626 - Buying Coke)
   2. **UVa 01238 - Free Parentheses** * (LA 4143 - Jakarta08; offset technique)
   3. **UVa 10304 - Optimal Binary ...** * (see Section 9.23)
   4. **UVa 12870 - Fishing** * (LA 6848 - Bangkok14; split DP for fishing and nourishing; try all combination of K fishing + $2K$ nourishing events)
   5. *Kattis - companypicnic* * (s: (name, has_been_matched); DP weighted matching (both cardinality and weight) on Tree)
   6. *Kattis - recursionrandfun* * (DP; the possible random values are small due to modulo b and c; try all; memoize)
   7. *Kattis - rollercoasterfun* * (s: (T); split DPs when $b = 0$ and when $b \neq 0$)

   Extra UVa: *00473, 00812, 01222, 01231, 10029, 10118, 10482, 10559.*

   Extra Kattis: *bundles, city, johnsstack, mububa, volumeamplification.*

c. DP, Counting Paths in DAG, Harder

1. Entry Level: **UVa 11432 - Busy Programmer** * (counting paths in DAG; the implicit DAG is not trivial; 6 parameters)
2. **UVa 00702 - The Vindictive Coach** * (s: (n_above, n_below, go_up))
3. **UVa 11125 - Arrange Some Marbles** * (counting paths in implicit DAG; the implicit DAG is not trivial; 8 parameters)
4. **UVa 11375 - Matches** * (counting paths in DAG; 2 parameters; be careful that we can create a '0' with 6 sticks; need to use Big Integer)
5. *Kattis - countcircuits* * (s: (id, cur_x, cur_y); t: skip or use this vector; use offset technique to avoid negative indices)
6. *Kattis - favourable* * (s: (cur_page); t: jump to one of the 3 sections)
7. *Kattis - pachinkoprobability* * (s: (pos); DAG modeling; long long)

   Extra UVa: *10722*, *11133*, *12063*.

   Extra Kattis: *constrainedfreedomofchoice*, *frustratedqueue*, *ratings*, *tractor*, *woodensigns*.

d. DP with Bitmask

1. Entry Level: **UVa 10911 - Forming Quiz ...** * (the intro problem of this book; DP with bitmask; weighted MCM; small complete weighted graph)
2. **UVa 01099 - Sharing Chocolate** * (LA 4794 - WorldFinals Harbin10; s: (w, bitmask); recover parameter value h)
3. **UVa 01252 - Twenty Questions** * (LA 4643 - Tokyo09; DP, s: (mask1, mask2) where mask1/mask2 describes the features/answers, respectively)
4. **UVa 11825 - Hacker's Crackdown** * (first, use iterative brute force: try which subset of vertices can cover all vertices; then use DP)
5. *Kattis - hidingchickens* * (weighted MCM; small complete weighted graph; make fox goes back to the killing spot first after hiding one or two chickens)
6. *Kattis - narrowartgallery* * (s: (row, mask_state_of_prev_row, k_left))
7. *Kattis - pebblesolitaire2* * (s: (bitmask); backtracking suffices for Kattis - pebblesolitaire; but this version needs extra memoization)

   Extra UVa: *01076*, *01240*, *10123*, *10149*, *10364*, *10817*, *11218*, *11391*, *11472*, *11806*, *12030*.

   Extra Kattis: *goingdutch*, *uxuhulvoting*, *wherehaveyoubin*.

8.4 Network Flow

8.4.1 Overview and Motivation

Problem: Imagine a connected, (integer) weighted, and directed graph[8] as a pipe network where the edges are the pipes and the vertices are the splitting points. Each edge has a weight equal to the capacity of the pipe. There are also two special vertices: source s and sink t. What is the maximum flow (rate) from source s to sink t in this graph (imagine water flowing in the pipe network, we want to know the maximum volume of water over time that can pass through this pipe network)? This problem is called the Maximum Flow problem (often abbreviated as just Max Flow), one of the problems in the family of problems involving flow in networks. See the illustration of a Flow Graph (Figure 8.11—left) and the Max Flow/Min Cut of this Flow Graph (Figure 8.11—right). The details will be elaborated in the next few sections.

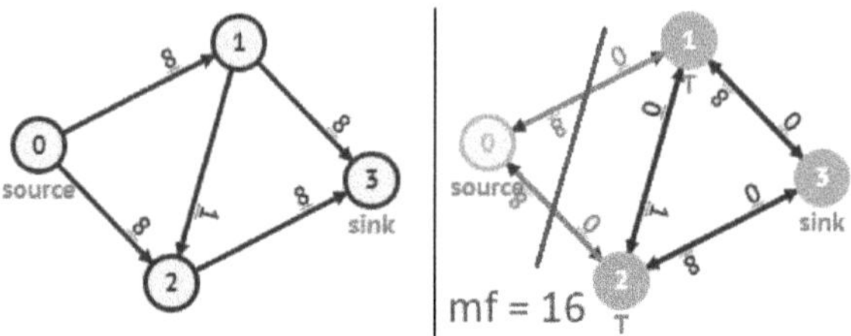

Figure 8.11: Max Flow/Min Cut Illustration

8.4.2 Ford-Fulkerson Method

One solution for Max Flow is the Ford-Fulkerson method—invented by the same Lester Randolph *Ford*, Jr who invented the Bellman-Ford algorithm and Delbert Ray *Fulkerson*. The pseudo-code (as we will use faster versions later) of this method is as follows:

```
setup directed residual graph with edge capacity = original edge weights
mf = 0                                          // an iterative algorithm
while (there exists an augmenting path p from s to t)
  // p is a path from s->t that passes through +ve edges in residual graph
  augment/send flow f along the path p (s -> ... -> i -> j -> ... t)
    // let f = the edge weight i-j that is the minimum along the path p
    1. decrease capacity of forward edges (e.g., i, j) along path p by f
    2. increase capacity of backward edges (e.g., j, i) along path p by f
    3. mf += f                                  // increase mf
output mf                                       // the max flow value
```

Ford-Fulkerson method is an iterative algorithm that repeatedly finds augmenting paths p: A path from source s to sink t that passes through positive weighted edges in the residual[9]

[8] A weighted undirected edge in an undirected graph can be transformed to two directed edges with the same weight but with opposite directions.

[9] We use the name 'residual graph' because initially the weight of each edge `res[i][j]` is the same as the original capacity of edge (i, j) in the original graph. If this edge (i, j) is used by an augmenting path and a flow passes through this edge with weight `f` $\leq$ `res[i][j]` (a flow cannot exceed this capacity), then the remaining (or residual) capacity of edge (i, j) will be `res[i][j]-f` while the residual capacity of the reverse edge (j, i) will be increased to `res[j][i]+f`.

graph. After finding an augmenting path $p = s \to \ldots i \to j \ldots t$ that has f as the minimum edge weight (i, j) along the path p (the bottleneck edge in this path), Ford-Fulkerson method will do three important steps: decreasing/increasing the capacity of forward (i, j)/backward (j, i) edges along path p by f, respectively, and add f to the overall max flow mf value. Ford-Fulkerson method will repeat this process until there are no more possible augmenting paths from source s to sink t which implies that the total flow found is the maximum flow (to prove the correctness, one needs to understand the Max-Flow Min-Cut theorem, see the details in [7]).

The reason for decreasing the capacity of forward edges is obvious. By sending a flow through augmenting path p, we will decrease the remaining (residual) capacities of the (forward) edges used in p. The reason for increasing the capacity of backward edges may not be that obvious, but this step is important for the correctness of Ford-Fulkerson method. By increasing the capacity of a backward edge (j, i), Ford-Fulkerson method allows *future iterations (flows)* to cancel (part of) the capacity used by a forward edge (i, j) that was incorrectly used by some earlier flow(s).

There are several ways to find an augmenting s-t path in the pseudo code above, each with different behavior. In this section, we highlight two ways: via DFS or via BFS (two different implementations with slightly different results).

The Ford-Fulkerson method that uses DFS to compute the max flow value of Figure 8.11—left may proceed as follows:

1. In Figure 8.12—1, we see the initial residual graph. Compare it with the initial flow graph in Figure 8.11—left. Notice the presence of back flow edges with capacity 0.

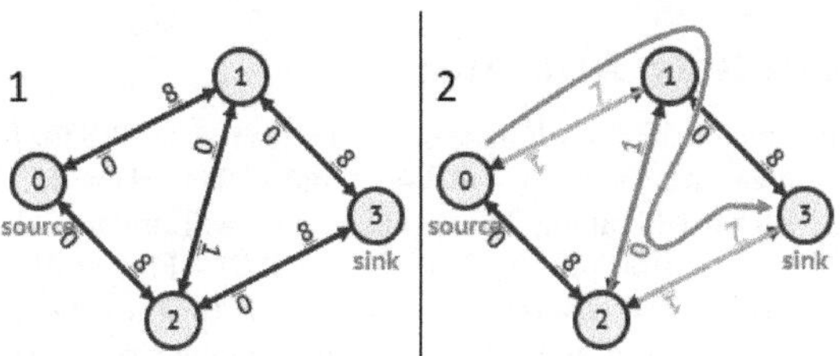

Figure 8.12: Illustration of Ford-Fulkerson Method (DFS)—Part 1

2. In Figure 8.12—2, we see that DFS finds the first augmenting path $0 \to 1 \to 2 \to 3$. The bottleneck edge is edge $1 \to 2$ with capacity 1. We update the residual graph by reducing the capacity of all forward edges used by 1 and increasing the capacity of all backward edges used by 1 too (notice especially that back flow $2 \to 1$ capacity is raised from 0 to 1 to allow future cancelation of some flow along forward edge $1 \to 2$) and send the first 1 unit of flow from source $s = 0$ to sink $t = 3$.

3. In Figure 8.13—3, suppose that DFS[10] finds the second augmenting path $0 \to 2 \to 1 \to 3$ also with bottleneck capacity 1. Notice that if we don't update the back flow $2 \to 1$ in the previous iteration, we will not be able to get the correct max flow value at the end. We update the residual graph (notice, we flip edge $2 \to 1$ to $1 \to 2$ again) and send another 1 unit of flow from s to t.

[10]Depending on the implementation, the second call of DFS may find another augmenting path. For example, if the neighbors of a vertex are listed in increasing vertex number, then the second DFS should find augmenting path $0 \to 1 \to 3$. But for the sake of illustration, let's assume that the second call of DFS gives us this $0 \to 2 \to 1 \to 3$ that will setup the flip-flop situation between edge $0 \to 1$ and $1 \to 0$.

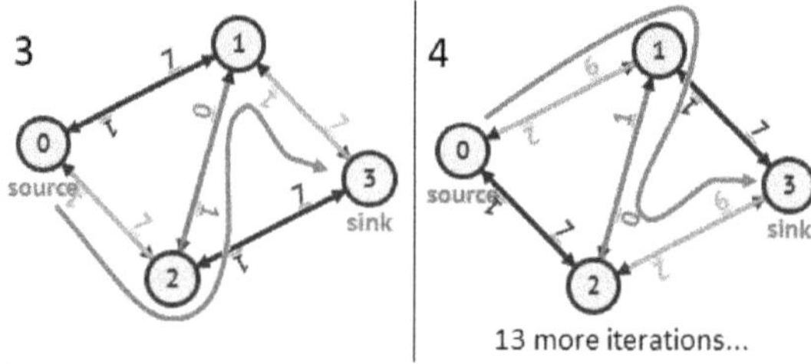

Figure 8.13: Illustration of Ford-Fulkerson Method (DFS)—Part 2

4. In Figure 8.13—4, suppose that DFS finds the third augmenting path $0 \to 1 \to 2 \to 3$ again with the same bottleneck capacity 1. We update the residual graph and send another 1 unit of flow from s to t. We keep repeating this flip-flopping of edge $1 \to 2$ and $2 \to 1$ for 13 more iterations until we send 16 units of flow (see Figure 8.11—right).

Ford-Fulkerson method implemented using DFS *may* run in $O(mf \times E)$ where mf is the Max Flow value. We may encounter a situation where two augmenting paths: $0 \to 2 \to 1 \to 3$ and $0 \to 1 \to 2 \to 3$ only decrease the (forward) edge capacities along the path by 1. In the worst case, this is repeated mf times (it is $3 + 13$ more times after Figure 8.13—4, for a total of 16 times; but imagine if the weights of the original edges are multiplied by 1B except edge $1 \to 2$ remains at weight 1). As DFS runs in $O(E)$ in a flow graph[11], the overall time complexity is $O(mf \times E)$. We do not want this unpredictability in programming contests as the problem author can/will choose to give a (very) large mf value.

8.4.3 Edmonds-Karp Algorithm

A better implementation of the Ford-Fulkerson method is to use BFS for finding the shortest path in terms of number of layers/hops between s and t. This algorithm was discovered by Jack *Edmonds* and Richard Manning *Karp*, thus named as Edmonds-Karp algorithm [13]. It runs in $O(VE^2)$ as it can be proven that after $O(VE)$ BFS iterations, all augmenting paths will already be exhausted (see references like [13, 7] to study more about this proof). As BFS runs in $O(E)$ in a flow graph, the overall time complexity is $O(VE^2)$.

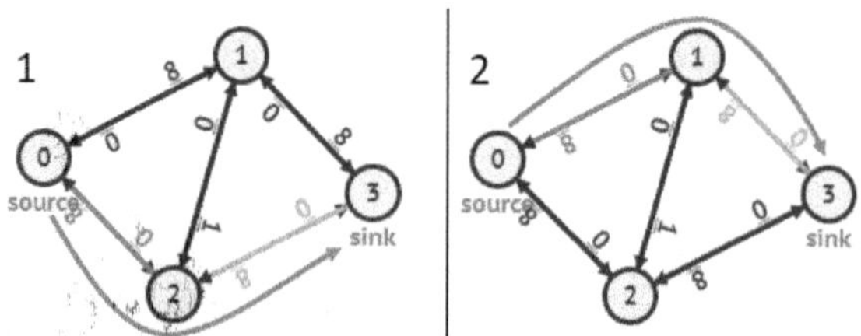

Figure 8.14: Illustration of Edmonds-Karp Algorithm (BFS)

On the same flow graph as shown in Figure 8.11, Edmonds-Karp only needs two s-t paths. See Figure 8.14—1: $0 \to 2 \to 3$ (2 hops, send 8 units of flow) and Figure 8.14—2: $0 \to 1 \to 3$ (2 hops, send another 8 units of flow and done with a total 8+8 = 16 units of flow). It does not get trapped to send flow via the longer paths (3 hops): $0 \to 1 \to 2 \to 3$ like in Figure 8.12—2. But the $O(VE^2)$ Edmonds-Karp algorithm can still be improved a bit more.

[11] In a typical flow graph, $E \geq V$-1. Thus, we usually assume that both DFS and BFS—using Adjacency List—run in $O(E)$ instead of $O(V + E)$ to simplify the time complexity analysis of Max Flow algorithms.

8.4.4 Dinic's Algorithm

So far, we have seen the potentially unpredictable $O(mf \times E)$ implementation of Ford-Fulkerson method if we try to find the augmenting paths with DFS and the better $O(VE^2)$ Edmonds-Karp algorithm (finding augmenting paths with BFS) for solving the Max Flow problem. Some harder Max Flow problems may need a slightly faster algorithm than Edmonds-Karp. One such faster algorithm[12] is Dinic's algorithm which runs in $O(V^2E)$. Since a typical flow graph usually has $V < E$ and $E << V^2$, Dinic's worst case time complexity is theoretically better than Edmonds-Karp. As of year 2020, we have encountered *a few* rare cases where Edmonds-Karp algorithm receives a TLE verdict but Dinic's algorithm receives an AC verdict on the *same* flow graph. Therefore, for CP4, we use Dinic's algorithm as the default max flow algorithm in programming contests just to be on the safer side.

Dinic's algorithm uses a similar idea as Edmonds-Karp as it also finds *shortest* (in terms of number of layers/hops between s and t) augmenting paths iteratively. However, Dinic's algorithm uses the better concept of 'blocking flows' to find the augmenting paths. Understanding this concept is the key to modify the slightly-easier-to-understand Edmonds-Karp algorithm into Dinic's algorithm.

Let's define `dist[v]` to be the length of the (unweighted) shortest path from the source vertex s to v in the residual graph. Then the level graph L of the residual graph are the subgraph of the residual graph after running BFS that terminates after L-levels. Formally, edges in level graph L are those with `dist[v] = dist[u]+1`. Then, a 'blocking flow' of this level graph L is an s-t flow f (which can contain multiple s-t paths) such that after sending through flow f from s to t, the level graph L contains no s-t augmenting paths anymore.

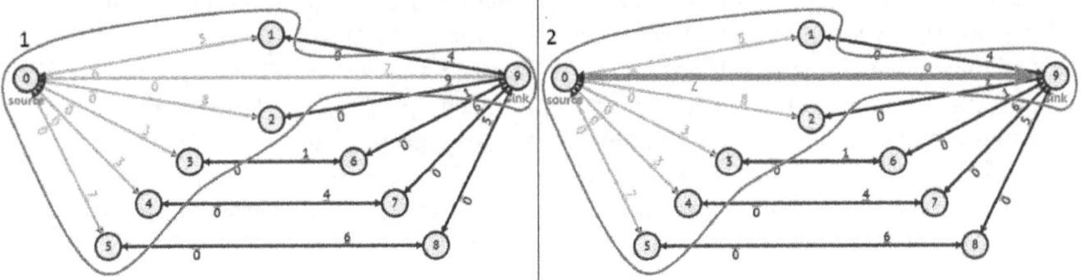

Figure 8.15: Illustration of Dinic's Algorithm (BFS)—Part 1

Let's see Figure 8.15. At step 1 and 2, Dinic's algorithm behaves exactly the same as Edmonds-Karp algorithm, i.e., it finds the first level graph $L = 1$ (highlighted at Figure 8.15—1) send 7 units of blocking flow via the (only) shortest augmenting path $0 \to 9$ (highlighted at Figure 8.15—2) to disconnect s and t from this level graph $L = 1$.

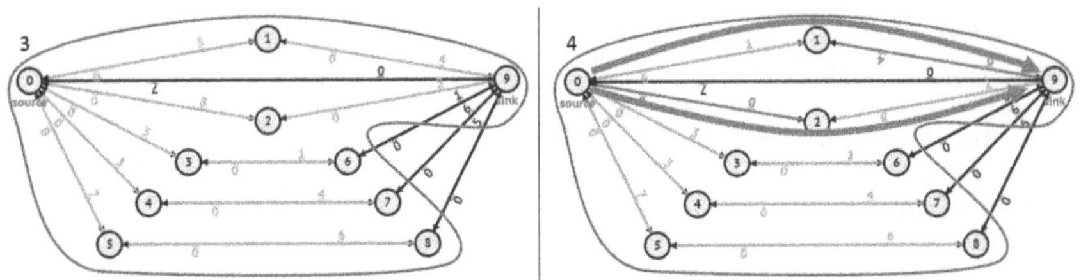

Figure 8.16: Illustration of Dinic's Algorithm (BFS)—Part 2

[12]The other is Push-Relabel algorithm in Section 9.24.

However, at Figure 8.16, Dinic's algorithm is more efficient than Edmonds-Karp algorithm. Dinic's algorithm will find level graph $L = 2$ (highlighted at Figure Figure 8.16—3) and there are *two* paths of length 2 that connects $s = 0$ and $t = 9$ in that level graph $L = 2$. They are paths $0 \to 1 \to 9$ and $0 \to 2 \to 9$. Edmonds-Karp will spend 2 individual calls of BFS to send 2 *individual* flows (totalling 4+12 = 12 more units of flow) through them, whereas Dinic's will send just 1 blocking flow (consisting of the same 2 paths, but in a more efficient manner) to remove *s*-*t* augmenting paths from this level graph $L = 2$ and disconnects s and t again (highlighted at Figure 8.16—4).

Similarly Dinic's algorithm will find the last level graph $L = 3$ (not shown) and send 1 blocking flow (of 3 paths, totalling 1+3+5 = 9 more units of flow) in a more efficient manner than Edmonds-Karp algorithm with 3 individual calls of BFS.

It has been proven (see [11]) that the number of edges in each blocking flow increases by at least one per iteration. There are at most V-1 blocking flows in the algorithm because there can only be at most V-1 edges along the 'longest' simple path from s to t. The level graph can be constructed by a BFS in $O(E)$ time and a blocking flow in each level graph can be found by a DFS in $O(VE)$ time (see the sample implementation for important speedup where we remember the last edge processed in previous DFS iteration inside `last[u]`). Hence, the worst case time complexity of Dinic's algorithm is $O(V \times (E + VE)) = O(V^2E)$, which is faster than the $O(VE^2)$ Edmonds-Karp algorithm despite their similarities because $E > V$ in most flow graphs.

Implementation of Edmonds-Karp and Dinic's Algorithms

Dinic's implementation is quite similar to Edmonds-Karp implementation. In Edmonds-Karp, we run a BFS—which already generates for us the level graph L—but we just use it to find *one* single augmenting path by calling the `augment(t, INF)` function. In Dinic's algorithm, we need to use the information produced by BFS in a slightly different manner. We find a blocking flow by running DFS on the level graph L found by BFS to augment *all* possible *s*-*t* paths in this level graph L efficiently via the help of `last[u]`. We provide both of them in the same code below (you can remove the Edmonds-Karp part to simplify this code; it is left behind so that you can do **Exercise 8.4.4.3***).

```
typedef long long ll;
typedef tuple<int, ll, ll> edge;
typedef vector<int> vi;
typedef pair<int, int> ii;

const ll INF = 1e18;                                 // large enough

class max_flow {
private:
  int V;
  vector<edge> EL;
  vector<vi> AL;
  vi d, last;
  vector<ii> p;
```

```
  bool BFS(int s, int t) {                        // find augmenting path
    d.assign(V, -1); d[s] = 0;
    queue<int> q({s});
    p.assign(V, {-1, -1});                        // record BFS sp tree
    while (!q.empty()) {
      int u = q.front(); q.pop();
      if (u == t) break;                          // stop as sink t reached
      for (auto &idx : AL[u]) {                   // explore neighbors of u
        auto &[v, cap, flow] = EL[idx];           // stored in EL[idx]
        if ((cap-flow > 0) && (d[v] == -1))       // positive residual edge
          d[v] = d[u]+1, q.push(v), p[v] = {u, idx}; // 3 lines in one!
      }
    }
    return d[t] != -1;                            // has an augmenting path
  }

  ll send_one_flow(int s, int t, ll f = INF) {   // send one flow from s->t
    if (s == t) return f;                         // bottleneck edge f found
    auto &[u, idx] = p[t];
    auto &cap = get<1>(EL[idx]), &flow = get<2>(EL[idx]);
    ll pushed = send_one_flow(s, u, min(f, cap-flow));
    flow += pushed;
    auto &rflow = get<2>(EL[idx^1]);              // back edge
    rflow -= pushed;                              // back flow
    return pushed;
  }

  ll DFS(int u, int t, ll f = INF) {              // traverse from s->t
    if ((u == t) || (f == 0)) return f;
    for (int &i = last[u]; i < (int)AL[u].size(); ++i) { // from last edge
      auto &[v, cap, flow] = EL[AL[u][i]];
      if (d[v] != d[u]+1) continue;               // not part of layer graph
      if (ll pushed = DFS(v, t, min(f, cap-flow))) {
        flow += pushed;
        auto &rflow = get<2>(EL[AL[u][i]^1]);     // back edge
        rflow -= pushed;
        return pushed;
      }
    }
    return 0;
  }

public:
  max_flow(int initialV) : V(initialV) {
    EL.clear();
    AL.assign(V, vi());
  }
```

```
  // if you are adding a bidirectional edge u<->v with weight w into your
  // flow graph, set directed = false (default value is directed = true)
  void add_edge(int u, int v, ll w, bool directed = true) {
    if (u == v) return;                          // safeguard: no self loop
    EL.emplace_back(v, w, 0);                    // u->v, cap w, flow 0
    AL[u].push_back(EL.size()-1);                // remember this index
    EL.emplace_back(u, directed ? 0 : w, 0);     // back edge
    AL[v].push_back(EL.size()-1);                // remember this index
  }

  ll edmonds_karp(int s, int t) {
    ll mf = 0;                                   // mf stands for max_flow
    while (BFS(s, t)) {                          // an O(V*E^2) algorithm
      ll f = send_one_flow(s, t);                // find and send 1 flow f
      if (f == 0) break;                         // if f == 0, stop
      mf += f;                                   // if f > 0, add to mf
    }
    return mf;
  }

  ll dinic(int s, int t) {
    ll mf = 0;                                   // mf stands for max_flow
    while (BFS(s, t)) {                          // an O(V^2*E) algorithm
      last.assign(V, 0);                         // important speedup
      while (ll f = DFS(s, t))                   // exhaust blocking flow
        mf += f;
    }
    return mf;
  }
};
```

VisuAlgo

We have provided the animation of various Max Flow algorithms that are discussed in this section[13] in VisuAlgo. Use it to further strengthen your understanding of these algorithms by providing your own input (flow) graph (we recommend the source/sink vertex to be set as vertex $0/V$-1 so that we can layout vertex $0/V$-1 as the leftmost/rightmost vertex in the visualization, respectively) and see the Max Flow algorithm being animated live on that particular input graph. The URL for the various Max Flow algorithms and our Max Flow source code are shown below.

Visualization: `https://visualgo.net/en/maxflow`
Source code: `ch8/maxflow.cpp|java|py|ml`

[13]We still have one more Max Flow algorithm in this book: Push-Relabel that is discussed in Section 9.24. It works differently than the three Ford-Fulkerson based Max Flow algorithms discussed in this section.

Exercise 8.4.4.1: Before continuing, answer the following question in Figure 8.17!

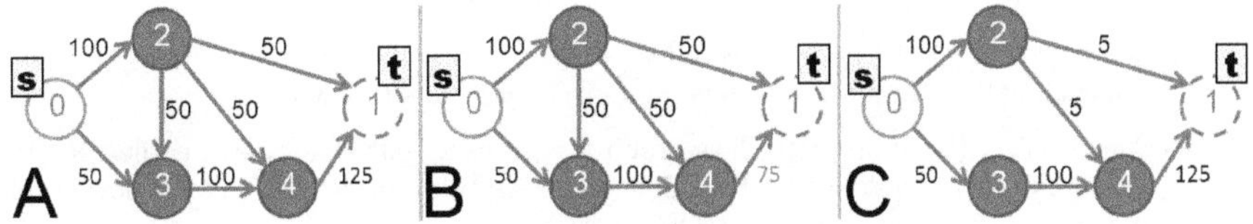

Figure 8.17: What Are the Max Flow Value of These Three Flow Graphs?

Exercise 8.4.4.2*: Suppose we have a large flow graph, e.g., $V = 1M$, $E = 10M$ and we have run our best max flow code for several hours to get the max flow value. To your horror, *exactly one* of the edge $u \rightarrow v$ has wrong initial capacity. Instead of c, it is supposed to be c+1. Can you find a quick $O(V)$ patching solution that does not entail re-running max flow algorithm on the fixed large flow graph? What if instead of c, it is supposed to be c-1?

Exercise 8.4.4.3*: Use the code above that has both Edmonds-Karp and Dinic's algorithm. Compare them on various programming exercises listed in this section. Do you notice any runtime differences?

Exercise 8.4.4.4*: Construct a flow graph so that either Edmonds-Karp or Dinic's algorithm finds as many s-t Augmenting Paths as possible.

Profile of Algorithm Inventors

Jack R. Edmonds (born 1934) is a mathematician. He and Richard Karp invented the **Edmonds-Karp algorithm** for computing the Max Flow in a flow network in $O(VE^2)$ [13]. He also invented an algorithm for MST on directed graphs (Arborescence problem). This algorithm was proposed independently first by Chu and Liu (1965) and then by Edmonds (1967)—thus called the **Chu-Liu/Edmonds' algorithm** [6]. However, his most important contribution is probably the Edmonds' **matching/blossom shrinking algorithm**—one of the most cited Computer Science papers [12].

Richard Manning Karp (born 1935) is a computer scientist. He has made many important discoveries in computer science in the area of combinatorial algorithms. In 1971, he and Edmonds published the **Edmonds-Karp algorithm** for solving the Max Flow problem [13]. In 1973, he and John Hopcroft published the **Hopcroft-Karp algorithm**, still the fastest known method for finding Maximum Cardinality Bipartite Matching [19].

Delbert Ray Fulkerson (1924-1976) was a mathematician who co-developed the **Ford-Fulkerson method**, an algorithm to solve the Max Flow problem in networks. In 1956, he published his paper on the Ford-Fulkerson method together with Lester Randolph Ford.

Yefim Dinitz is a computer scientist who invented Dinic's algorithm.

8.4.5 Flow Graph Modeling - Classic

With the given Dinic's algorithm code in Section 8.4.4, solving a Network Flow problem—especially Max Flow—and its variants, is now simpler. It is now a matter of:

1. Recognizing that the problem is indeed a Network Flow problem (this will get better after you solve more Network Flow problems).
2. Constructing the appropriate flow graph (i.e., if using our code shown earlier: set the correct number of vertices V of the flow graph, add the correct edges of the flow graph, and set the appropriate values for 's' and 't').
3. Running Dinic's algorithm code on this flow graph.

There are several interesting applications/variants of the problems involving flow in a network. We discuss the classic ones here while some others are deferred until Section 8.5 (MCBM), Section 8.6, and Section 9.25. Note that some techniques shown here may also be applicable to other graph problems.

Max Cardinality Bipartite Maching (MCBM)

One of the common application of Max Flow algorithm is to solve a specific Graph Matching problem called the Max Cardinality Bipartite Matching (MCBM) problem. However, we have a more specific algorithm for this: the Augmenting Path algorithm (details in Section 8.5). Instead, we discuss another Graph Matching variant: the assignment problem where Max Flow solution is preferred (also see **Exercise 8.4.5.2***).

Assignment Problem

We show an example of *modeling* the flow (residual) graph of UVa 00259 - Software Allocation[14]. The abridged version of this problem is as follows: You are given up to 26 applications/apps (labeled 'A' to 'Z'), up to 10 computers (numbered from 0 to 9), the number of users who brought in each application that day (one digit positive integer, or `[1..9]`), the list of computers on which a particular application can run, and the fact that each computer can only run one instance of one application that day. Your task is to determine whether an allocation (that is, a *matching*) of applications to valid computers can be done, and if so, generate a possible allocation. If not, simply print an exclamation mark '!'.

One (bipartite) flow graph formulation is shown in Figure 8.18. We index the vertices from `[0..37]` as there are 26+10+2 special vertices = 38 vertices. The source s is given index 0, the 26 possible apps are given indices from `[1..26]`, the 10 possible computers are given indices from `[27..36]`, and finally the sink t is given the last index 37.

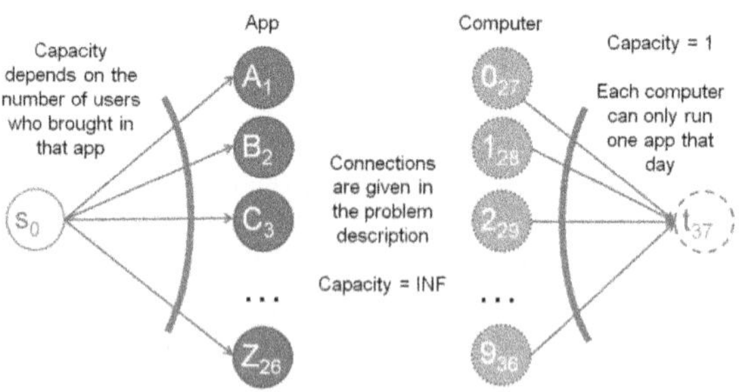

Figure 8.18: Residual Graph of UVa 00259 [28]

[14]Actually this problem has small input size (we only have 26+10 = 36 vertices plus 2 more: source and sink) which make this problem still solvable with recursive backtracking (see Book 1). If the given graph involves around [100..200] vertices, max flow is the intended solution. The name of this problem is 'assignment problem' or (special) bipartite matching with capacity.

Then, we link apps to valid computers as mentioned in the problem description. We link source s to all apps and link all computers to sink t. All edges in this flow graph are *directed* edges. The problem says that there can be *more than one* (say, X) users bringing in a particular app A on a given day. Thus, we set the directed edge weight (capacity) from source s to a particular app A to X. The problem also says that each computer can only be used once. Thus, we set the directed edge weight from each computer B to sink t to 1. The edge weight between apps to valid computers is set to ∞. With this arrangement, if there is a flow from an app A to a computer B and finally to sink t, that flow corresponds to *one allocation (one matching)* between that particular app A and computer B.

Once we have this flow graph, we can pass it to our Edmonds-Karp implementation shown earlier to obtain the Max Flow `mf`. If `mf` is equal to the number of applications brought in that day, then we have a solution, i.e., if we have X users bringing in app A, then X different paths (i.e., matchings) from A to sink t must be found by the Edmonds-Karp algorithm (and similarly for the other apps).

The actual app $\rightarrow$ computer assignments can be found by simply checking the backward edges from computers (vertices 27-36) to apps (vertices 1-26). A backward edge (computer $\rightarrow$ app) in the residual matrix `res` will contain a value +1 if the corresponding forward edge (app $\rightarrow$ computer) is selected in the paths that contribute to the Max Flow `mf`. This is also the reason why we start the flow graph with *directed* edges from apps to computers only.

Minimum Cut

Let's define an s-t cut $C = (S\text{-component}, T\text{-component})$ as a partition of $V \in G$ such that source $s \in S$-component and sink $t \in T$-component. Let's also define a *cut-set* of C to be the set $\{(u, v) \in E \mid u \in S\text{-component}, v \in T\text{-component}\}$ such that if all edges in the cut-set of C are removed, the Max Flow from s to t is 0 (i.e., s and t are disconnected). The cost of an s-t cut C is defined by the sum of the capacities of the edges in the cut-set of C. The Minimum Cut problem, often abbreviated as just Min Cut, is to minimize the amount of capacity of an s-t cut. This problem is more general than finding bridges (see Book 1), i.e., in this case we can cut *more* than just one edge and we want to do so in the least cost way. As with bridges, Min Cut has applications in 'sabotaging' networks, e.g., one pure Min Cut problem is UVa 10480 - Sabotage.

The solution is simple: The by-product of computing Max Flow is Min Cut! After Max Flow algorithm stops, we run graph traversal (DFS/BFS) from source s again. All reachable vertices from source s using positive weighted edges in the residual graph belong to the S-component. All other unreachable vertices belong to the T-component. All edges connecting the S-component to the T-component belong to the cut-set of C. The Min Cut value is equal to the Max Flow value `mf`. This is the minimum over all possible s-t cuts values.

Multi-source/Multi-sink

Sometimes, we can have more than one source and/or more than one sink. However, this variant is no harder than the original Network Flow problem with a single source and a single sink. Create a super source ss and a super sink st. Connect ss with all s with infinite capacity and also connect all t with st with infinite capacity, then run a Max Flow algorithm as per normal.

Vertex Capacities

We can also have a Network Flow variant where the capacities are not just defined along the edges but *also on the vertices*. To solve this variant, we can use *vertex splitting* technique which (unfortunately) *doubles* the number of vertices in the flow graph. A weighted graph with a vertex weight can be converted into a more familiar one *without* vertex weight. We can split each weighted vertex v into v_{in} and v_{out}, reassigning its incoming/outgoing edges to v_{in}/v_{out}, respectively and finally putting the original vertex v's weight as the weight of edge $v_{in} \to v_{out}$. See Figure 8.19 for an illustration. Now with all weights defined on edges, we can run a Max Flow algorithm as per normal.

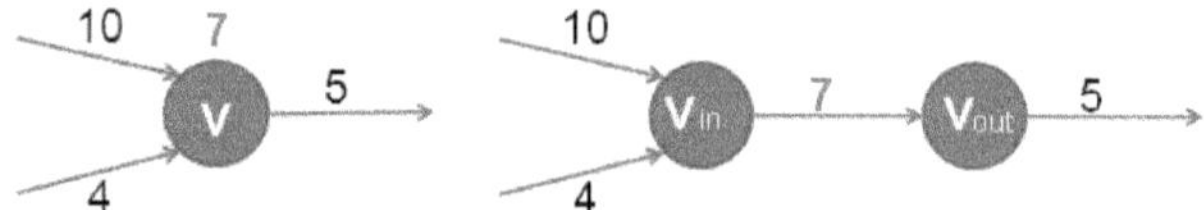

Figure 8.19: Vertex Splitting Technique

Coding max flow code with vertex splitting can be simplified with the following technique (other ways exist). If the original V vertices are labeled with the standard indices [0..V-1], then after vertex split, we have $2 * V$ vertices and the range [0..V-1]/[V..$2 * V$-1] become the indices for v_{in}/v_{out}, respectively. Then, we can define these two helper functions:

```
int in (int v) { return v;   }
int out(int v) { return V+v; }                       // offset v by V indices
```

Independent and Edge-Disjoint Paths

Two paths that start from a source vertex s to a sink vertex t are said to be *independent* (vertex-disjoint) if they do not share any vertex apart from s and t. Two paths that start from s to t are said to be edge-disjoint if they do not share any edge (but they can share vertices other than s and t).

The problem of finding the (maximum number of) independent paths from source s to sink t can be reduced to the Network (Max) Flow problem. We construct a flow network $N = (V, E)$ from G with vertex capacities, where N is the carbon copy of G except that the capacity of each $v \in V$ is 1 (i.e., each vertex can only be used once—see how to deal with vertex capacity above) and the capacity of each $e \in E$ is also 1 (i.e., each edge can only be used once too). Then run a Max Flow algorithm as per normal.

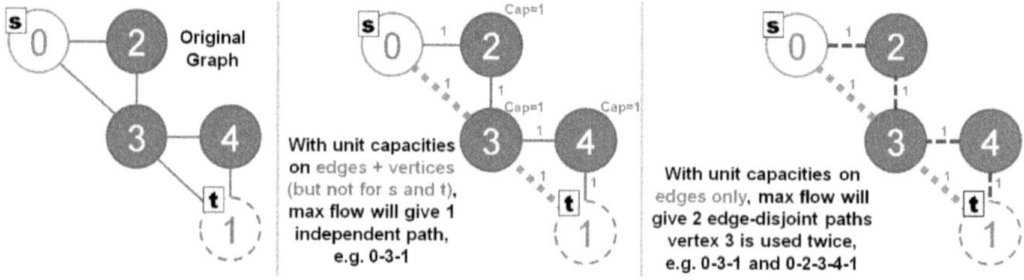

Figure 8.20: Comparison Between Max Independent Paths vs Max Edge-Disjoint Paths

Finding the (maximum number of) edge-disjoint paths from s to t is similar to finding (maximum) independent paths. The only difference is that this time we do not have any vertex capacity which implies that two edge-disjoint paths can still share the same vertex. See Figure 8.20 for a comparison between maximum independent paths and edge-disjoint paths from $s = 0$ to $t = 1$.

Baseball Elimination Problem

Abridged problem description of Kattis - unfairplay: Imagine a fictional (sporting) league. We are given N ($1 \leq N \leq 100$) teams and the current points of N teams. Then, we are given M ($0 \leq M \leq 1000$) and a list of M remaining matches between two teams a and b ($a \neq b$). Teams are are numbered from 1 to N and your team is team N. A win/draw/lose worth 2/1/0 point(s), respectively. The question is whether you can still (theoretically) win the league (accumulate total points that is strictly greater than any other team)?

The first necessary condition is obvious. Team N needs to win all their matches if they play in any of the M remaining matches. If team N's theoretical best points is still not enough to beat the team with current highest point at this stage of the league, then it is obvious that team N theoretically can no longer win the league even though the league still has M matches left.

After satisfying the first necessary condition, we need to deal with the second condition. It may not be obvious, but it is a classic max flow problem called the Baseball Elimination Problem (and has several possible variations). For each remaining M' ($M' \leq M$) matches that does *not* involve team N, we construct the following bipartite flow graph (source s, remaining matches excluding team N, list of teams excluding team N, and sink t):

- Connect source s with to all remaining match vertex i that does not involve team N with capacity 2 to indicate this remaining match carries 2 points,
- Connect a match vertex i to both teams (a and b, $a \neq N$, $b \neq N$) that play in this match i with capacity 2 (or more, we can simply set this as ∞), and
- Connect a team j to sink t with the following specific capacity: points of team N (us) - current points of team j - 1 (this is the maximum points that this team j can accumulate so that team N (us) can still win the league).

Now it is easy to see if the max flow of this specially constructed (bipartite) flow graph is not $2 * M'$, then team N theoretically can no longer win the league.

Exercise 8.4.5.1: Why do we use ∞ for the edge weights (capacities) of directed edges from apps to computers? Can we use capacity 1 instead of ∞?

Exercise 8.4.5.2*: Can the general kind of assignment problem (bipartite matching with capacity, not limited to this sample problem UVa 00259) be solved with standard Max Cardinality Bipartite Matching (MCBM) algorithm shown in Book 1 (repeated later in Section 8.5)? If it is possible, determine which one is the better solution. If it is not possible, explain why.

Exercise 8.4.5.3*: A common max flow operation in modern programming contest problems is to *get* (or even *update*) flow (and/or capacity) of a specific edge $u \to v$ (after the max flow has been found). An potential application is for identifying/printing the edges that are part of the optimal assignment (bipartite matching with capacity). Show how to modify the given max flow library code to support this operation. Hint: we need a fast $O(1)$ way to quickly locate edge $u \to v$ inside the EL that contains up to E edges.

8.4.6 Flow Graph Modeling - Non Classic

We repeat that the hardest part of dealing with Network Flow problem is the modeling of the flow graph (assuming that we already have a good pre-written Max Flow code). In Section 8.4.5, we have seen several flow graph modeling examples. Here, we present another (harder) flow graph modeling for UVa 11380 - Down Went The Titanic that is not considered 'classic' flow graph modeling. Our advice before you continue reading: please do not just memorize the solution but also try to understand the key steps to derive the required flow graph.

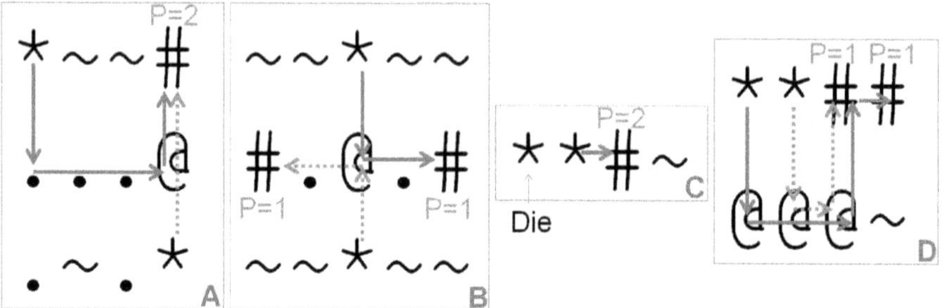

Figure 8.21: Some Test Cases of UVa 11380

In Figure 8.21, we have four small test cases of UVa 11380. You are given a small 2D grid containing these five characters as shown in Table 8.1. You want to move as many '*' (people, at most 50% of the grid size) as possible to the (various) safe place(s): the '#' (large wood, with capacity P ($1 \leq P \leq 10$)). The solid and dotted arrows in Figure 8.21 denote the answer.

Symbol	Meaning	# Usage (Vertex Capacity)
*	People staying on floating ice	1
~	Extremely cold water (cannot be used)	0
.	Floating ice	1
@	Large iceberg	∞
#	Large wood	∞

Table 8.1: Characters Used in UVa 11380

To model the flow graph, we use the following thinking steps. In Figure 8.22—A, we first connect all the non '~' cells that are adjacent to each other with large capacity (1000 is enough for this problem). This describes the possible movements in the grid.

In Figure 8.22—B, we set vertex capacities of '*' and '.' cells to 1 to indicate that they can only be used *once*. Then, we set vertex capacities of '@' and '#' to a large value (we use 1000 as it is enough for this problem) to indicate that they can be used *several times*. This is summarized in # Usage (Vertex Capacity) column in Table 8.1.

In Figure 8.22—C, we create a (super) source vertex s and (super) sink vertex t. Source s is linked to all '*' cells in the grid with capacity 1 to indicate that there is one person to be saved. All '#' cells in the grid are connected to sink t with capacity P to indicate that the large wood can be used by P people.

Now, the required answer—the number of survivor(s)—equals to the max flow value between source s and sink t of this flow graph. As the flow graph uses vertex capacities (as in Table 8.1), we need to use the *vertex splitting* technique discussed earlier.

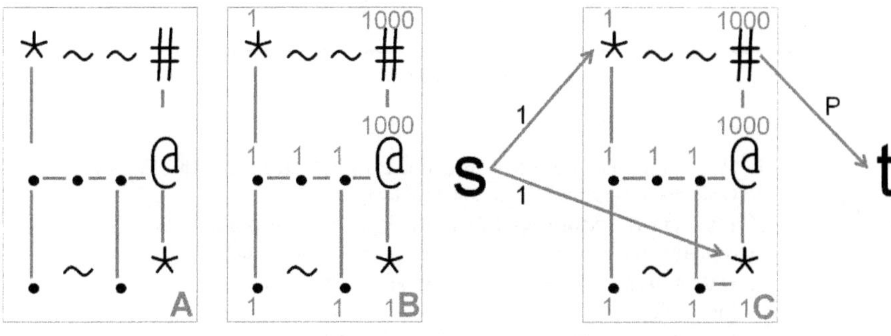

Figure 8.22: Flow Graph Modeling

Exercise 8.4.6.1: Is $O(VE^2)$ Edmonds-Karp or $O(V^2E)$ Dinic's algorithm fast enough to compute the max flow value on the largest possible flow graph of UVa 11380: 30×30 grid and $P = 10$? Why or why not?

8.4.7 Network Flow in Programming Contests

As of year 2020, when a Network (usually Max) Flow problem appears in a programming contest, it is *usually* one of the 'decider' problems. In ICPC, many interesting graph problems are written in such a way that they do not look like a Network Flow in a glance. The hardest part for the contestants is to realize that the underlying problem is indeed a Network Flow problem and be able to model the flow graph correctly. Again, graph modeling is the key skill that has to be mastered via practice.

To avoid wasting precious contest time coding (and debugging) the relatively long Max Flow library code, we suggest that in an ICPC team, one team member devotes significant effort to prepare a good Max Flow code (master the Dinic's algorithm implementation given in Section 8.4.4 or try the Push-Relabel algorithm in Section 9.24) and attempts various Network Flow problems available in many online judges to increase familiarity towards Network Flow problems and its variants. In the list of programming exercises in this section, we have some simple Max Flow, bipartite matching with capacity (the assignment problem), Min Cut, and network flow problems involving vertex capacities. Try to solve as many programming exercises as possible and prepare additional helper subroutines if needed (e.g., for the vertex splitting part, listing the actual edges used in the max flow — see **Exercise 8.4.5.3***, etc).

In Section 8.5, we will see the classic Max Cardinality Bipartite Matching (MCBM) problem that is also solvable with Max Flow though a simpler, more specialized algorithm exists. Later, we will see some harder problems related to Network Flow, e.g., the Max *Weighted* Independent Set on Bipartite Graph problem (Section 8.6.6), the Push-Relabel algorithm (Section 9.24), and the Min Cost (Max) Flow problem (Section 9.25).

In IOI, Network Flow (and its various variants) is currently outside the syllabus [15]. So, IOI contestants can choose to skip this section. However, we believe that it is a good idea for IOI contestants to learn these more advanced material 'ahead of time' to improve your skills with graph problems.

Programming Exercises related to Network Flow:

a. Standard

1. Entry Level: **UVa 00820 - Internet Bandwidth** * (LA 5220 - WorldFinals Orlando00; very basic max flow problem)
2. **UVa 11167 - Monkeys in the Emei ...** * (many edges in the flow graph; compress the capacity-1 edges when possible; use Dinic's)
3. **UVa 11418 - Clever Naming Patterns** * (two layers of graph matching (not really bipartite matching); use max flow solution)
4. **UVa 12873 - The Programmers** * (LA 6851 - Bangkok14; assignment problem; similar to UVa 00259, 11045, and 10092; use Dinic's)
5. *Kattis - dutyscheduler* * (try all possible (small range of answers); assignment problem; matching with capacity; max flow)
6. *Kattis - jupiter* * (good modeling problem; a good exercise for those who wants to master max flow modeling)
7. *Kattis - mazemovement* * (use gcd for all pairs of vertices to construct the flow graph; then it is just a standard max flow problem)

   Extra UVa: *00259*, *10092*, *10779*, *11045*, *11082*.

   Extra Kattis: *councilling*, *maxflow*, *mincut*, *piano*, *tomography*, *waif*, *water*.

b. Variants

1. Entry Level: **UVa 00563 - Crimewave** * (check whether the maximum number of independent paths on the flow graph equals to b banks)
2. **UVa 11380 - Down Went The ...** * (max flow modeling with vertex capacities; similar to UVa 12125)
3. **UVa 11757 - Winger Trial** * (build the flow graph with a bit of simple geometry involving circle; min cut from s/left side to t/right side)
4. **UVa 11765 - Component Placement** * (interesting min cut variant)
5. *Kattis - avoidingtheapocalypse* * (interesting max flow modeling; blow the vertices based on time)
6. *Kattis - thekingofthenorth* * (interesting min cut problem)
7. *Kattis - transportation* * (max flow with vertex capacities)

   Extra UVa: *01242*, *10330*, *10480*, *11506*.

   Extra Kattis: *budget*, *chesscompetition*, *congest*, *conveyorbelts*, *copsandrobbers*, *darkness*, *fakescoreboard*, *floodingfields*, *landscaping*, *marchofpenguins*, *neutralground*, *openpitmining*, *unfairplay*.

8.5 Graph Matching

8.5.1 Overview and Motivation

Graph Matching is the problem of selecting a subset of edges M of a graph $G(V, E)$ so that no two edges share the same vertex. Most of the time, we are interested to find the *Maximum Cardinality* matching, i.e., we want to know the *maximum number of edges* that we can select in a graph G. Another common request is to find a *Perfect* matching where we have both the Maximum Cardinality matching *and* no vertex is left unmatched[15]. If the edges are unweighted, the cost of two distinct matchings with the same cardinality is always equal. However if the edges are weighted, this is no longer true.

Unlike the other graph problems discussed earlier in Chapter 4 and up to Section 8.4 where there are relatively easy-to-explain polynomial algorithms to solve them, we have hard(er)-to-explain (but still polynomial) algorithms for the general cases of graph matching problems. This often make Graph Matching problem(s) as the decider problem(s) in many programming contests.

8.5.2 Graph Matching Variants

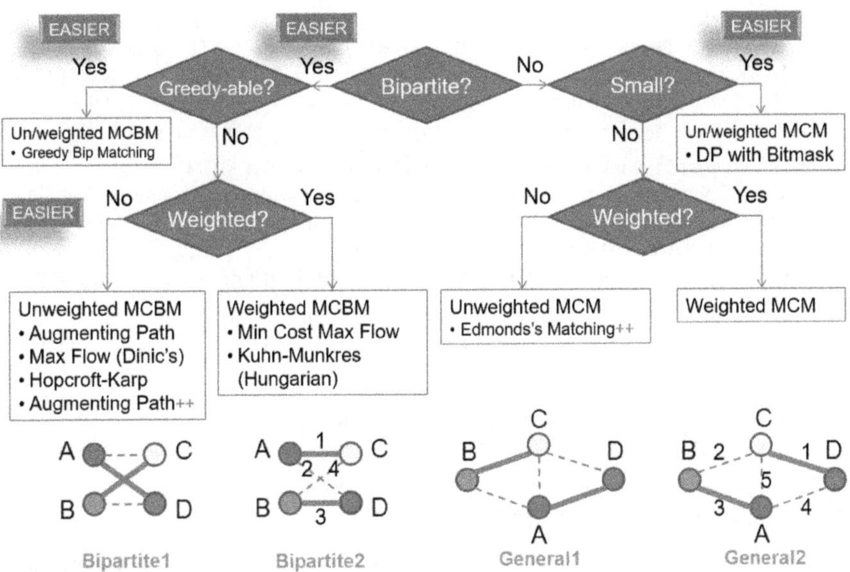

Figure 8.23: The Four Common Variants of Graph Matching in Programming Contests

The most important attribute of Graph Matching problems in programming contests that can (significantly) alter the level of difficulty is whether the input graph is bipartite. Graph Matching is easier on Bipartite Graphs and much harder on general graphs. A subset of Bipartite Matching problems are actually amenable to the greedy algorithm that we have discussed earlier in Book 1 and not the focus of this section.

[15]Note that if V is odd, it is impossible to have a Perfect matching. Perfect matching can be solved by simply finding the standard Maximum Cardinality matching and then checking if all vertices are matched so we treat this variant as the same as the standard Maximum Cardinality matching.

However, even if the input graph is not bipartite, Graph Matching problems can still be solved with Dynamic Programming with bitmask as long as the number of vertices involved is small. This variant has been used as the introduction problem in the very first page of Book 1, is discussed in depth in Section 8.3.1, and also not the focus of this section.

The second most important attribute after asking whether the input graph is bipartite is to ask whether the input graph is unweighted. Graph Matching is easier on unweighted graphs and harder on weighted graphs.

These two characteristics create four variants as outlined below (also see the bottom part of Figure 8.23). Note that we are aware of the existence of other very rare (Graph) Matching variants outside these four variants, e.g., the Stable Marriage problem[16] or Hall's Marriage Theorem[17]. However, we only concentrate on these four variants in this section.

1. Unweighted Maximum Cardinality Bipartite Matching (Unweighted MCBM)
   This is the easiest and the most common variant.
   In Figure 8.23—bottom (Bipartite1), the MCBM value is 2 and there are two possible solutions: {A-D, B-C} as shown or {A-C, B-D}.
   In this book, we describe algorithms that can deal with graphs up to $V \leq 1500$.

2. Weighted Maximum Cardinality Bipartite Matching (Weighted MCBM)
   This is a similar problem to the above, but now the edges in G have weights.
   We usually want the MCBM with either the *minimum* or the *maximum* total weight.
   In Figure 8.23—bottom (Bipartite2), the MCBM value is 2. The weight of matching {A-D, B-C} is 2+4 = 6 and the weight of matching {A-C, B-D} is 1+3 = 4. If our objective is to get the minimum total weight, we have to report {A-C, B-D} as shown.
   In this book, we describe algorithms that can deal with graphs up to $V \leq 450$.

3. Unweighted Maximum Cardinality Matching (Unweighted MCM)
   The graph is not guaranteed to be bipartite, but we still want maximum cardinality.
   In Figure 8.23—bottom (General1), the MCM value is 2 and there are two possible solutions: {A-D, B-C} as shown or {A-B, C-D}.
   In this book, we describe an algorithm that can deal with graphs up to $V \leq 450$.

4. Weighted Maximum Cardinality Matching (Weighted MCM)
   In Figure 8.23—bottom (General2), the MCM value is 2. The weight of matching {A-D, B-C} is 4+2 = 6 and the weight of matching {A-B, C-D} is 3+1 = 4. If our objective is to get the minimum total weight, we have to report {A-B, C-D} as shown.
   This is the hardest variant. In this book, we only describe DP bitmask algorithm that can only deal with graphs up to $V \leq 20$.

8.5.3 Unweighted MCBM

This variant is the easiest and several solutions have been mentioned in Bipartite Graph section in Book 1, Section 8.4 (Network Flow-based solution), and later and Section 9.26 (Hopcroft-Karp algorithm, also for Bipartite Graph only). Note that the Unweighted MCBM problems can also appear inside the special cases of certain NP-hard problems like Min Vertex Cover (MVC), Max Independent Set (MIS), Min Path Cover on DAG (see Section 8.6 after this section). The list below summarizes four possible solutions for this variant:

[16]Given n men and n women and each each person has ranked all members of the opposite sex in order of preference, marry the men and women together such that there are no two people of opposite sex who would both rather have each other than their current partners

[17]Suppose a bipartite graph with bipartite sets L and R. Hall's Marriage theorem says that there is a matching that covers L if and only if for every subset W of L, $|W| \leq |N(W)|$ where $N(W)$ is the set of all vertices in R adjacent to some element of W.

1. $O(VE)$ Augmenting Path Algorithm for Unweighted MCBM.
   See the recap below.

2. Reducing the Unweighted MCBM problem into a Max Flow Problem.
   Review Section 8.4 for the discussion of Max Flow algorithm.

   MCBM problem can be reduced to the Max Flow problem by assigning a super source vertex s connected to all vertices in `set1` and all vertices in `set2` are connected to a super sink vertex t. The edges are directed ($s \rightarrow u$, $u \rightarrow v$, $v \rightarrow t$ where $u \in$ `set1` and $v \in$ `set2`). By setting the capacities of all the edges in this flow graph to 1, we force each vertex in `set1` to be matched with at most one vertex in `set2`. The Max Flow will be equal to the maximum number of matchings on the original graph (see Figure 8.24—right for an example). The time complexity depends on the chosen Max Flow algorithm, i.e., it will be fast, in $O(\sqrt{V}E)$ if one uses Dinic's Max Flow algorithm on such unit flow graph.

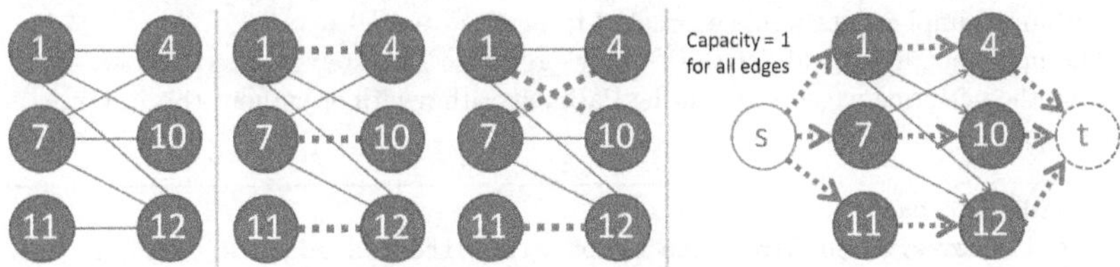

Figure 8.24: Bipartite Matching problem can be reduced to a Max Flow problem

3. $O(\sqrt{V}E)$ Hopcroft-Karp Algorithm for Unweighted MCBM.
   See Section 9.26 for details – although we probably do not need this algorithm in programming contests as it is identical to Dinic's Max Flow algorithm.

4. $O(kE)$ Augmenting Path Algorithm for Unweighted MCBM++.
   See the discussion below.

Augmenting Path Algorithm++ for MCBM

The $O(VE)$ Augmenting Path Algorithm implementation of Berge's lemma discussed in Book 1 (reproduced below) is usually sufficient to solve easier MCBM problems.

```
vi match, vis;                                  // global variables
vector<vi> AL;

int Aug(int L) {
  if (vis[L]) return 0;                         // L visited, return 0
  vis[L] = 1;
  for (auto &R : AL[L])
    if ((match[R] == -1) || Aug(match[R])) {
      match[R] = L;                             // flip status
      return 1;                                 // found 1 matching
    }
  return 0;                                     // no matching
}
```

This is not the best algorithm for finding MCBM. Dinic's algorithm [11] (see Section 8.4.4) or Hopcroft-Karp algorithm [19] (essentially also a variant of Dinic's algorithm, see Section 9.26) can solve the MCBM problem in the best known theoretical time complexity of $O(\sqrt{V}E)$, thereby allowing us to solve the MCBM problem on bigger Bipartite Graphs or when the MCBM problem is a sub-problem of a bigger problem.

However, we do not have to always use these fancier algorithms to solve the MCBM efficiently. In fact, a simple improvement of the basic Augmenting Path Algorithm above can be used to avoid its worst case $O(VE)$ time complexity on (near) complete Bipartite Graphs. The key observation is that many trivial matchings involving a free (unmatched) vertex, a free (unmatched) edge, and another free vertex can be easily found using a greedy pre-processing routine that can be implemented in $O(V^2)$. To avoid adversary test cases, we can even randomize this greedy pre-processing routine. By doing this, we reduce the number of free vertices (on the left set) from V down to a variable k, where $k < V$. Empirically, we found that this k is usually a low number on various big random Bipartite Graphs and possibly not more than $\sqrt{V}$ too. Therefore, the time complexity of this Augmenting Path Algorithm++ implementation is estimated to be $O(V^2 + kE)$.

The implementation code of the Greedy pre-processing step is shown below. You can compare the performance of Augmenting Path Algorithm with or without this pre-processing step on various MCBM problems.

```
// inside int main()
  // build unweighted Bipartite Graph with directed edge left->right set
  // that has V vertices and Vleft vertices on the left set
  unordered_set<int> freeV;
  for (int L = 0; L < Vleft; ++L)
    freeV.insert(L);                             // initial assumption
  match.assign(V, -1);
  int MCBM = 0;
  // Greedy pre-processing for trivial Augmenting Paths
  // try commenting versus un-commenting this for-loop
  for (int L = 0; L < Vleft; ++L) {              // O(V+E)
    vi candidates;
    for (auto &R : AL[L])
      if (match[R] == -1)
        candidates.push_back(R);
    if ((int)candidates.size() > 0) {
      ++MCBM;
      freeV.erase(L);                            // L is matched
      int a = rand()%(int)candidates.size();     // randomize this
      match[candidates[a]] = L;
    }
  }                                              // for each free vertex
  for (auto &f : freeV) {                        // (in random order)
    vis.assign(Vleft, 0);                        // reset first
    MCBM += Aug(f);                              // try to match f
  }
```

Please review the same source code as in Book 1.

Source code: ch4/mcbm.cpp|java|py|ml

Exercise 8.5.3.1*: In Figure 8.24—right, we have seen a way to reduce an MCBM problem (all edge weights are one) into a Max Flow problem. Do the edges in the flow graph have to be directed? Is it OK if we use undirected edges in the flow graph?

Exercise 8.5.3.2*: Construct a small unweighted bipartite graph so that it is very unlikely (*probability* $< 5\%$) that the randomized greedy pre-processing step will be very lucky and no (zero) actual Augmenting Path Algorithm step being used at all.

8.5.4 Weighted MCBM and Unweighted/Weighted MCM

While Unweighted MCBM is the easiest Graph Matching variant with multiple possible solutions, the next three Graph Matching variants are considered *rare* in programming contests. They are much harder and require specialized algorithms that are only going to be mentioned briefly in Chapter 9.

Weighted MCBM

When the edges in the Bipartite Graph are weighted, not all possible MCBMs are optimal. We need to pick one (not necessarily unique) MCBM that has the minimum[18] overall total weight. One possible solution is to reduce the Weighted MCBM problem into a Min Cost Max Flow (MCMF) problem that will be discussed in Section 9.25. Alternatively, if we want to get a *perfect*[19] Weighted MCBM, we can use the *faster* but more specialized Kuhn-Munkres (Hungarian) algorithm that will be discussed in Section 9.27.

Unweighted MCM

While the Graph Matching problem is easy on Bipartite Graphs, it is 'hard' on general graphs. In the past, computer scientists thought that this variant was another NP-hard optimization problem (see Section 8.6) that requires exponential time algorithm until Jack Edmonds published an efficient, *polynomial* algorithm for solving this problem in his 1965 paper titled "Paths, trees, and flowers" [12].

The main issue is that on general graphs, we may encounter odd-length augmenting cycles. Edmonds calls such a cycle a 'blossom' and the details of Edmonds' Matching algorithm to deal with these 'blossoms' will be discussed in Section 9.28.

The $O(V^3)$ implementation (with high constant factor) of Edmonds' Matching algorithm is not straightforward but it allows us to solve Unweighted MCM problem for graphs up to $V \leq 200$. Thus, to make this graph matching variant more manageable, many problem authors limit their unweighted general graphs to be small (i.e., $V \leq 20$) so that an $O(V \times 2^V)$ DP with bitmask algorithm can be used to solve it (see **Exercise 8.3.1.1**).

Weighted MCM

This is potentially the hardest variant. The given graph is a general graph and the edges have associated weights. In typical programming contest environments, the most likely solution is the DP with bitmask (see Section 8.3.1) as the problem authors usually set the problem on *a small general graph* only and perhaps also require the perfect matching criteria from a Complete Graph to further simplify the problem (see Section 9.29).

[18]Weighted MCBM/MCM problem can also ask for the maximum total weight.

[19]We can always transform standard Weighted MCBM problem into perfect Weighted MCBM by adding dummy vertices to make size of the left set equals to size of the right set and add dummy edges with appropriate weights that will not interfere with the final answer.

VisuAlgo

To help readers in understanding these Graph Matching variants and their solutions, we have built the following visualization tool:

Visualization: `https://visualgo.net/en/matching`

The user can draw any (unweighted) undirected input graph and the tool will use the correct Graph Matching algorithm(s) based on the two characteristics: whether the input graph is bipartite or not.

Programming exercises related to Graph Matching are scattered throughout this book:

- See some greedy (bipartite) matching problems in Book 1,
- See some Unweighted MCBM problems in Book 1,
- See some assignment problems (bipartite matching with capacity) in Section 8.4,
- See some special cases of NP-hard problems that can be reduced into Unweighted MCBM problems in Section 8.6.6 and Section 8.6.8,
- See some Weighted MCBM problems in Section 9.25 and 9.27,
- See some (small) MCM problem in Section 8.3 (DP) and Unweighted MCM problem in Section 9.28 (Edmonds' Matching algorithm),
- See one other weighted MCM problem on *small general graph* in Section 9.29 (Chinese Postman Problem).

Profile of Algorithm Inventors

Dénes König (1884-1944) was a Hungarian mathematician who worked in and wrote the first textbook on the field of graph theory. In 1931, König described an equivalence between the Maximum Cardinality Bipartite Matching (MCBM) problem and the Minimum Vertex Cover (MVC) problem in the context of Bipartite Graphs, i.e., he proved that the size of MCBM equals to the size of MVC in Bipartite Graph via his constructive proof.

Jenö Egerváry (1891-1958) was a Hungarian mathematician who generalizes Denes König's theorem to the case of weighted graphs (in Hungarian). This work was translated and then popularized by Kuhn in 1955.

Harold William Kuhn (1925-2014) was an American mathematician who published and popularized the Hungarian algorithm described earlier by two Hungarian mathematicians: König and Egerváry.

James Raymond Munkres (born 1930) is an American mathematician who reviewed Kuhn's Hungarian algorithm in 1955 and analyzed its polynomial time complexity. The algorithm is now known as either Kuhn-Munkres algorithm or Hungarian algorithm.

Philip Hall (1904-1982) was an English mathematician. His main contribution that is included in this book is Hall's marriage theorem.

8.6 NP-hard/complete Problems

8.6.1 Preliminaries

NP-hard and NP-complete are related Computational Complexity classes. An optimization (maximizing or minimizing) problem is said to be an NP-hard problem if one of the other well-known NP-hard problems (some of which will be mentioned in this section) can be reduced/transformed into this problem in polynomial[20] time. A decision (yes/no) problem is said to be an NP-complete problem if it is NP-hard and also in NP[21]. In short, unless $P = NP$, which has not been proven by anyone as of year 2020, we can say that there are no efficient, i.e., polynomial, solutions for problems that fall into the NP-hard/complete complexity classes. We invite interested readers to read references such as [7].

So if we are given a new programming contest problem, and we can somehow reduce or transform a known NP-hard problem into that 'new' problem in polynomial time (notice the direction of the reduction), then we need to ask ourself the next question[22]:

Is the input size constraint *relatively small*, i.e., $\approx$ 10 or 11 for permutation-based problems or $\approx$ 20 or 21 for subset-based problems? If it is, then we do **not** need to waste time thinking of any efficient/polynomial solution during contest time as there is likely no such solution unless $P = NP$. Immediately code the best possible Complete Search (or if overlapping subproblems are spotted, Dynamic Programming) algorithm with as much pruning as possible.

However, if the input size constraint is *not that small*, then our job is to re-read the problem description again and hunt for any *likely subtle* constraint that will turn the general NP-hard problem into a special case that may have a polynomial solution.

Note that in order to be able to (quickly) recognize that a given new problem, often disguised in a seemingly unrelated storyline, is really NP-hard/complete, we need to enlarge our list of known NP-hard problems (and their well known variants/polynomial solutions). In this section, we list a few of them with a summary at Section 8.6.14.

Exercise 8.6.1.1*: Identify NP-hard/complete problems in this list of classic[23] problems:
`2-Sum`, `Subset-Sum`,
`Fractional Knapsack`, `0-1 Knapsack`,
`Single-Source Shortest Paths` (SSSP), `Longest Path`,
`Minimum Spanning Tree` (MST), `Steiner-Tree`,
`Max Cardinality Bipartite Matching` (MCBM), `Max Cardinality Matching` (MCM),
`Eulerian Tour`, `Hamiltonian Tour`,
generating `de Bruijn` sequence, `Chinese Postman Problem`, and
`Integer Linear Programming`.

---

[20] In Computational Complexity theory, we refer to an $O(n^k)$ algorithm, even with a rather large positive value of k, as a polynomial time, or an efficient algorithm. On the other hand, we say that an $O(k^n)$ or an $O(n!)$ algorithm to be an exponential time, or non-efficient algorithm.

[21] NP stands for Non-deterministic Polynomial, a type of decision problem whereby a solution for a yes instance can be verified in polynomial time.

[22] Actually, there is another possible question: Is it OK to produce a slightly non-optimal solution using techniques like approximation algorithms or local search algorithms? However, this route is less likely to be used in competitive programming where most optimization problems only seek for the optimal answer(s).

[23] You can use the Index section to quickly locate these classic problem names.

8.6.2 Pseudo-Polynomial: Knapsack, Subset-Sum, Coin-Change

In Book 1, we have discussed DP solutions for these three problems: 0-1 KNAPSACK[24], SUBSET-SUM, and *General* COIN-CHANGE. In that section, we were told that those problems have well known DP solutions and are considered *classics*. In this section, we update your understanding that these three problems are actually NP-hard optimization problems and our DP solution can only work under certain terms and conditions.

Each of the DP solutions uses two DP parameters, the current index that ranges from [0..n-1] and one more parameter that is classified as *pseudo-polynomial*, i.e., `remW` for 0-1 KNAPSACK, `curSum` for SUBSET-SUM, and `value` for General COIN-CHANGE. Notice the warning that we put as footnotes in those sections. The pseudo-polynomial parameters of these three problems can be memoized if and only if their sizes multiplied by n (for current index) are 'small enough' to avoid Memory Limit Exceeded[25]. We put a rule of thumb that nS and nV should not exceed 100M for typical DP solutions to work for these three problems. In the general case where these parameters are not (and cannot be made to be) bounded by a 'small enough' range[26], this DP solution cannot be used and we will have to resort to other exponential-based solutions.

We still leave most programming exercises involving these three (simpler) optimization problems, now that you know that they are actually NP-hard problems, in Chapter 3.

Exercise 8.6.2.1: Find as many special cases as possible for the SUBSET-SUM problem that have true polynomial solutions!

Exercise 8.6.2.2*: How would you solve UVa 12455 - Bars that we have discussed in depth in Book 1 if $1 \leq n \leq \underline{40}$ and each integer can be as big as 1B (10^9), i.e., see UVa 12911 - Subset sum?

Exercise 8.6.2.3*: Suppose we add one more parameter to this classic 0-1 KNAPSACK problem. Let K_i denote the number of copies of item i for use in the problem. Example: $n = 2$, $V = \{100, 70\}$, $W = \{5, 4\}$, $K = \{2, 3\}$, $S = 17$ means that there are two copies of item 0 with weight 5 and value 100 and there are three copies of item 1 with weight 4 and value 70. The optimal solution for this example is to take one of item 0 and three of item 1, with a total weight of 17 and total value 310. Solve this variant of the 0-1 KNAPSACK problem assuming that $1 \leq n \leq 500$, $1 \leq S \leq 2000$, $n \leq \sum_{i=0}^{n-1} K_i \leq 100\,000$. Hint: Every integer can be written as a sum of powers of 2.

Exercise 8.6.2.4*: Fractional Knapsack (or Continuous Knapsack) is like the 0-1 KNAPSACK (similar input, problem description, and output), but this time instead of deciding whether to take (1) or not take (0) an item, we can now decide to take *any fractional amount* of each item. This variant is not NP-hard. Design a polynomial algorithm for it!

---

[24]Usually, when we say KNAPSACK problem, we refer to the integer 0-1 version, i.e., not take or take an item, that is, we do not take fractions of an item.

[25]Bottom-up DP with space saving technique may help a bit with the memory limit but we still have issues with the time limit.

[26]In Computational Complexity theory, an algorithm is said to run in *pseudo-polynomial* time if its running time is *polynomial* in the value of the input (i.e., has to be 'small enough'), but is *actually exponential* in the length of the input if we view it as the number of bits required to represent that input.

8.6.3 Traveling-Salesman-Problem (TSP)

The Classic TSP and Its DP Solution

In Book 1, we have also discussed another classic DP solution for this problem: the Held-Karp DP solution for the TRAVELING-SALESMAN-PROBLEM (TSP).

That DP solution for the TSP has two DP parameters, current index that ranges from [0..n-1] and one more parameter `visited`, which is a bitmask, to store which subset of cities have been visited in the current partial TSP tour. Notice that the bitmask parameter has a space complexity of $O(2^b)$ where b is the number of bits used. Again, this value cannot be too big as 2^b grows very quickly. In fact, an optimized implementation of DP TSP will only work for n up to 18 or 19 and will get TLE for larger input sizes.

We still leave most programming exercises involving general but small[27] instance TSP, now that you know that it is also an NP-hard problem, in Chapter 3. However, there is one known special case of TSP: Bitonic TSP that has appeared in programming contests before and has a polynomial solution (to admit larger inputs). We discuss this below.

VisuAlgo

We have provided the animation of some TSP-related algorithms in VisuAlgo:

Visualization: `https://visualgo.net/en/tsp`

Special Case: Bitonic TSP and Its Solution

The BITONIC-TRAVELING-SALESMAN-PROBLEM (abbreviated as BITONIC-TSP) can be described as follows: Given a list of coordinates of n vertices on 2D Euclidean space that are already sorted by x-coordinates (and if tie, by y-coordinates), find a least cost tour that starts from the leftmost vertex, then goes strictly from left to right (for now, we can skip some vertices), and then upon reaching the rightmost vertex, the tour goes strictly from right to left back to the starting vertex using all the other vertices that are not used in the initial strictly from left to right path (this way, the TSP condition that all vertices are visited once is fulfilled). This tour behavior is called 'bitonic'.

The resulting tour may not be the shortest possible tour under the standard definition of TSP (see Book 1). Figure 8.25 shows a comparison of these two TSP variants. The TSP tour: 0-3-5-6-4-1-2-0 is not a Bitonic TSP tour because although the tour initially goes from left to right (0-3-5-6) and then goes back from right to left (6-4-1), it then makes another left to right (1-2) and then right to left (2-0) steps. The tour: 0-2-3-5-6-4-1-0 is a valid Bitonic TSP tour because we can decompose it into two paths: 0-2-3-5-6 that goes from left to right and 6-4-1-0 that goes back from right to left.

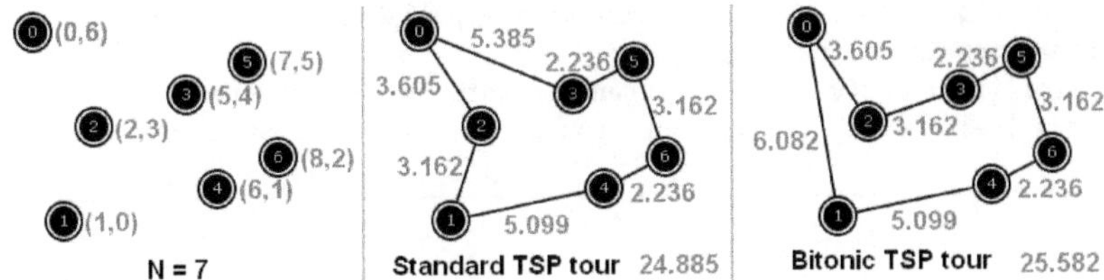

Figure 8.25: The Standard TSP versus Bitonic TSP

[27]For a challenge, see *Kattis - tsp* * which is an optimization problem involving large TSP instance up to $N \leq 1000$. To get high score for this problem, you need to use techniques *outside* this book.

Although a Bitonic TSP tour of a set of n vertices is usually longer than the standard TSP tour, this bitonic constraint allows us to compute a 'good enough tour' in $O(n^2)$ time using Dynamic Programming—as shown below—compared with the $O(2^{n-1} \times n^2)$ time for the standard TSP tour (see Book 1).

The main observation needed to derive the DP solution is the fact that we can (and have to) split the tour into two paths: Left-to-Right (LR) and Right-to-Left (RL) paths. Both paths include vertex 0 (the leftmost vertex) and vertex n-1 (the rightmost vertex). The LR path starts from vertex 0 and ends at vertex n-1. The RL path starts from vertex n-1 and ends at vertex 0.

Note that all vertices have been sorted[28] by x-coordinates (and if tie, by y-coordinates). We can then consider the vertices one by one. Both LR and RL paths start from vertex 0. Let v be the next vertex to be considered. For each vertex $v \in [1 \ldots n\text{-}2]$, we decide whether to add vertex v as the next point of the LR path (to extend the LR path further to the right) or as the previous point of the returning RL path (the RL path now starts at v and goes back to vertex 0). For this, we need to keep track of two more parameters: $p1$ and $p2$. Let $p1/p2$ be the current *ending/starting* vertex of the LR/RL path, respectively.

The base case is when vertex $v = n$-1 where we just need to connect the two LR and RL paths with vertex n-1.

With these observations in mind, we can write a simple DP solution[29] like this:

```
double dp1(int v, int p1, int p2) {                  // call dp1(1, 0, 0)
  if (v == n-1) return d[p1][v]+d[v][p2]; // d[u][v]: distance between u->v
  if (memo3d[v][p1][p2] > -0.5) return memo3d[v][p1][p2];
  return memo3d[v][p1][p2] = min(
    d[p1][v] + dp1(v+1, v, p2), // extend LR path: p1->v, RL stays: p2
    d[v][p2] + dp1(v+1, p1, v)); // LR stays: p1, extend RL path: p2<-v
}
```

However, the time complexity[30] of `dp1` with three parameters: `(v, p1, p2)` is $O(n^3)$. This is not efficient and an experienced competitive programmer will notice that the time complexity $O(n^3)$ is probably not tight. It turns out that parameter v can be dropped and recovered from $1 + max(p1, p2)$ (see this DP optimization technique of dropping one parameter and recovering it from other parameters as shown in Section 8.3.5). The improved DP solution is shown below and runs in $O(n^2)$.

```
double dp2(int p1, int p2) {                          // call dp2(0, 0)
  int v = 1+max(p1, p2); // this single line speeds up Bitonic TSP solution
  if (v == n-1) return d[p1][v]+d[v][p2];
  if (memo2d[p1][p2] > -0.5) return memo2d[p1][p2];
  return memo2d[p1][p2] = min(
    d[p1][v] + dp2(v, p2), // extend LR path: p1->v, RL stays: p2
    d[v][p2] + dp2(p1, v)); // LR stays: p1, extend RL path: p2<-v
}
```

[28]Even if the vertices are not sorted, we can sort them in $O(n \log n)$ time.

[29]As the memo table is of type floating point that is initialized with -1.0 initially, we check if a cell in this memo table has been assigned a value by comparing it with -0.5 to minimize floating point precision error.

[30]Note that initializing the 3D DP table by -1.0 already costs $O(n^3)$.

8.6.4 Hamiltonian-Path/Tour

Problem I - 'Robots on Ice' in ICPC World Finals 2010 can be viewed as a 'tough test on pruning strategy'. Abridged problem description: Given an $M \times N$ board with 3 check-in points {A, B, C}, find a Hamiltonian[31] path of length $(M \times N)$ from coordinate (0, 0) to coordinate (0, 1). Although to check whether a graph has a HAMILTONIAN-PATH or not is NP-complete, this variant has small instance (Constraints: $2 \leq M, N \leq 8$) and an additional *simplifying assumption*: this Hamiltonian path must hit the three check points: A, B, and C at one-quarter, one-half, and three-quarters of the way through its path, respectively.

Example: If given the following 3×6 board with A = (row, col) = (2, 1), B = (2, 4), and C = (0, 4) as in Figure 8.26, then we have two possible paths.

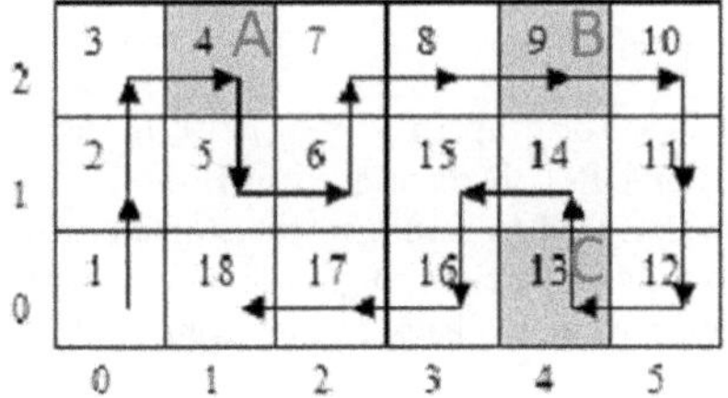

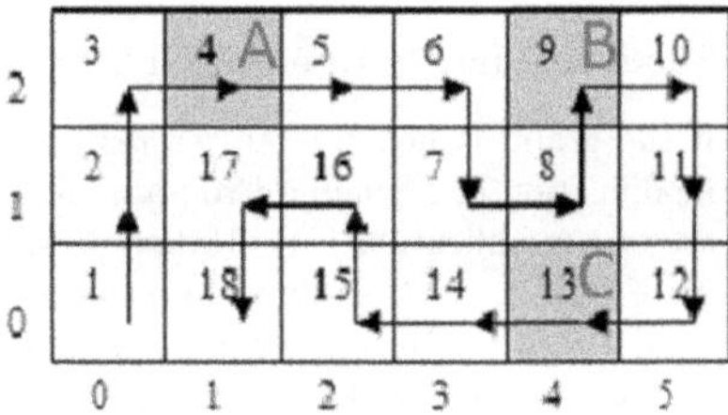

Figure 8.26: Visualization of UVa 01098 - Robots on Ice

A naïve recursive backtracking algorithm will get TLE as there are up to 3 choices at every step and the max path length is $8 \times 8 = 64$ in the largest test case. Trying all 3^{64} possible paths is infeasible. To speed up the algorithm, we prune the search space if the search:

1. Wanders outside the $M \times N$ grid (obvious),
2. Does not hit the appropriate target check point at 1/4, 1/2, or 3/4 distance—the presence of these three check points actually *reduces* the search space,
3. Hits target check point earlier than the target time,
4. Will not be able to reach the next check point on time from the current position,
5. Will not be able to reach certain coordinates as the current partial path self-block the access to those coordinates. This can be checked with a simple DFS/BFS (see Book 1). First, we run DFS/BFS from the goal coordinate (0, 1). If there are coordinates in the $M \times N$ grid that are *not* reachable from (0, 1) and *not yet visited* by the current partial path, we can prune the current partial path.

Exercise 8.6.4.1*: The five pruning strategies mentioned in this subsection are good but actually insufficient to pass the time limit set for LA 4793 and UVa 01098. There is a faster solution for this problem that utilizes the meet in the middle technique (see Section 8.2.3). This example illustrates that the choice of time limit setting may determine which Complete Search solutions are considered as fast enough. Study the idea of meet in the middle technique in Section 8.2.3 and apply it to solve this Robots on Ice problem.

---

[31]A Hamiltonian path is a path in an undirected graph that visits each vertex exactly once.

8.6.5 Longest-Path

Problem Description

LONGEST-PATH problem is about finding the longest *simple* path in a general graph. Recall that a simple path is a path that has no repeated vertices. This is because if there is a cycle in the graph, a path can go through that cycle one more time to make the path longer than the current 'longest' path. This ill-defined situation is similar with negative cycle in the shortest paths problem that has been discussed in Book 1.

This problem can be posed as unweighted version (number of edges along the longest path) or as weighted version (sum of edge weights along the longest path). This LONGEST-PATH problem is NP-hard[32] on general graphs.

Small Instances: General Graphs with $1 \leq V \leq [17..19]$

If the graph is not special, we may only be able to solve up to $V \leq [17..19]$ by using a modification of Dynamic Programming solution for DP-TSP mentioned in Book 1. There are two modifications: 1). Unlike in TSP, we do not need to return to the starting vertex; 2). Unlike in TSP, we do not necessarily need to visit all vertices to get the longest path.

If $1 \leq V \leq [10..11]$, we may also use the simpler recursive backtracking solution to find the longest path of the general graph.

Special Case: on DAG

In Book 1, we have discussed that if the input graph is a DAG, we can find the longest path in that DAG using the $O(V + E)$ topological sort (or Dynamic Programming) solution as there is no positive weight cycle to be worried of.

The Longest Increasing Subsequence (LIS) problem that we have discussed in Book 1 can also be viewed as a problem of finding the LONGEST-PATH in the implicit DAG where the vertices are the numbers, initially placed along the x-axis according to their indices, and then raised along y-axis according to their values. Then, two vertices a and b are connected with a directed edge if $a < b$ and b is on the right of a. As there can be up to $O(V^2)$ edges in such implicit DAG, this LIS problem requires $O(V^2)$ if solved this way (the alternative and faster $O(n \log k)$ solution has also been discussed in the same section).

Special Case: on Tree

In Book 1, we have also discussed that if the input graph is a tree, the longest path in that tree equals to the diameter (greatest 'shortest path length') of that tree, as any unique path between any two pair of vertices in the tree is both the shortest and the longest path. This diameter can be found via two calls of DFS/BFS in $O(V)$.

We still leave most programming exercises involving special cases of this LONGEST-PATH problems, now that you know that it is also an NP-hard problem, in Book 1.

[32]The common NP-hard proof is via reduction of a known NP-complete decision problem: HAMILTONIAN-PATH that we have discussed in Section 8.6.4.

8.6.6 Max-Independent-Set and Min-Vertex-Cover

Two Related Problems

An Independent Set (IS) is a set $IS \subseteq V$ such that for every pair of vertices $\{u, v\} \in IS$ are not adjacent. A Vertex Cover (VC) is a set $VC \subseteq V$ such that for every edge $e = (u, v) \in E$, either $u \in VC$ or $v \in VC$ (or both $u, v \in VC$).

MAX-INDEPENDENT-SET (often abbreviated as MIS) of G is a problem of selecting an IS of G with the maximum cardinality. MIN-VERTEX-COVER (often abbreviated as MVC) of G is a similar problem of selecting a VC of G with the minimum cardinality. Both are NP-hard problems on a general graph [16].

Note that the complement of Independent Set (IS) is Vertex Cover (VC) regardless of graph type, so we can usually use solution(s) for one problem, i.e., MIS and transform it into another solution for the other related problem, i.e., MVC = V-MIS.

Small Instances: Compact Adjacency Matrix Graph Data Structure

The UVa 11065 - Gentlemen Agreement problem boils down to computation of two integers: The number of *Maximal*[33] Independent Sets and the size of the *Maximum* Independent Set (MIS) of a given *general* graph with $1 \leq V \leq 60$. Finding the MIS of a general graph is an NP-hard problem. Therefore, it is unlikely that there exists a polynomial algorithm for this problem unless P = NP. Notice that V is up to 60. Therefore we cannot simply use the 2^V iterative brute force solution with bitmask as outlined in Book 1 and Section 8.2.1 as 2^{60} is simply too big.

One solution that passes the current setup of UVa 11065 is the following clever recursive backtracking. The state of the search is a triple: `(i, mask, depth)`. The first parameter `i` implies that we can consider vertices in $[i..V\text{-}1]$ to be included in the Independent Set. The second parameter `mask` is a bitmask of length V bits that denotes which vertices are still available to be included into the current Independent Set. The third parameter `depth` stores the depth of the recursion—which is also the size of the current Independent Set.

There is a clever bitmask technique for this problem that can be used to speed up the solution significantly. Notice that the input graph is small, $V \leq 60$. Therefore, we can store the input graph in an Adjacency Matrix of size $V \times V$ (for this problem, we set all cells along the main diagonal of the Adjacency Matrix to true). However, we can compress *one row* of V Booleans ($V \leq 60$) into one bitmask using a 64-bit signed integer. This technique has been mentioned in Book 1.

With this compact Adjacency Matrix `AM`—which is just V rows of 64-bit signed integers—we can use a fast bitmask operation to flag neighbors of vertices efficiently. If we decide to take a free vertex `v`, we increase `depth` by one and then use an $O(1)$ bitmask operation: `mask & ~AM[v]` to flag off *all* neighbors of `v` including itself (remember that `AM[v]` is also a bitmask of length V bits with the `v`-th bit on).

When all bits in `mask` are turned off, we have just found one more *Maximal* Independent Set. We also record the largest `depth` value throughout the process as this is the size of the *Maximum* Independent Set of the input graph.

Note that the worst case time complexity of this complete search solution is still $O(2^V)$. It is actually possible[34] (although probably not included in the secret test case for this problem) to create a test case with up to $V = 60$ vertices that can make the solution run very slowly. For example, a star graph of size $V = 60$ is a connected graph. Any subset of non-root vertices are Independent Sets and there are up to $O(2^{59})$ of them.

[33]Maximal IS is an IS that is not a subset of any other IS. MIS is both maximum and maximal.

[34]Hence this problem is actually an 'impossible' problem.

The key parts of the code are shown below:

```
void backtrack(int u, ll mask, int depth) {
  if (mask == 0) {                              // all have been visited
    ++numIS;                                    // one more possible IS
    MIS = max(MIS, depth);                      // size of the set
  }
  else {
    ll m = mask;
    while (m) {
      ll two_pow_v = LSOne(m);
      int v = __builtin_ctzl(two_pow_v);        // v is not yet used
      m -= two_pow_v;
      if (v < u) continue;                      // do not double count
      backtrack(v+1, mask & ~AM[v], depth+1);   // use v + its neighbors
    }
  }
}

// inside int main()
  // compact AM for faster set operations
  for (int u = 0; u < V; ++u)
    AM[u] = (1LL<<u);                           // u to itself
  while (E--) {
    int a, b; scanf("%d %d", &a, &b);
    AM[a] |= (1LL<<b);
    AM[b] |= (1LL<<a);
  }
```

Source code: ch8/UVa11065.cpp|java|ml

Special Cases: MIS and MVC on Tree

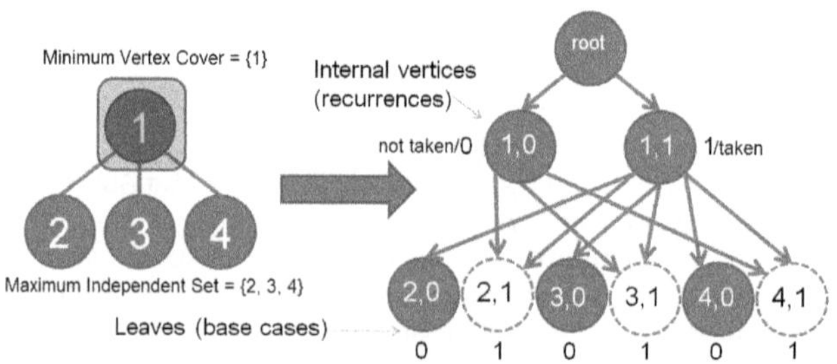

Figure 8.27: The Given General Graph/Tree (left) is Converted to DAG

The MIN-VERTEX-COVER (MVC) problem on a Tree has polynomial solutions. One of them is Dynamic Programming (also see **Exercise 8.6.6.3***). For the sample tree shown in Figure 8.27—left, the solution is to take vertex {1} only, because all edges 1-2, 1-3, 1-4 are all incident to vertex 1. Note that MAX-INDEPENDENT-SET (MIS) is the complement of MVC, so vertices {2, 3, 4} are the solution of the MIS problem for this sample tree.

There are only two possible states for each vertex. Either a vertex is taken or it is not. By attaching this 'taken or not taken' status to each vertex and rooting the tree into a directed graph with edges going away (downwards) from the root, we convert the tree into a DAG (see Figure 8.27—right). Each vertex now has (vertex number, boolean flag taken/not). The implicit edges are determined with the following rules: 1). If the current vertex is not taken, then we have to take all its children to have a valid solution. 2). If the current vertex is taken, then we take the best between taking or not taking its children. The base cases are the leaf vertices. We return 1/0 if a leaf is taken/not taken, respectively. We can now write this top down DP recurrences: `MVC(u, flag)`. The answer can be found by calling `min(MVC(root, true), MVC(root, false))`. Notice the presence of overlapping subproblems (dotted circles) in the DAG. However, as there are only $2 \times V$ states and each vertex has at most two incoming edges, this DP solution runs in $O(V)$.

```
int MVC(int u, int flag) {                       // get |MVC| on Tree
  int &ans = memo[u][flag];
  if (ans != -1) return ans;                     // top down DP
  if ((int)Children[u].size() == 0)              // u is a leaf
    ans = flag;                                  // 1/0 = taken/not
  else if (flag == 0) {                          // if u is not taken,
    ans = 0;                                     // we must take
    for (auto &v : Children[u])                  // all its children
      ans += MVC(v, 1);
  }
  else if (flag == 1) {                          // if u is taken,
    ans = 1;                                     // we take the minimum
    for (auto &v : Children[u])                  // between taking or
      ans += min(MVC(v, 1), MVC(v, 0));          // not taking its children
  }
  return ans;
}
```

Source code: `ch8/UVa10243.cpp|py`

Special Cases: MIS and MVC on Bipartite Graph

In Bipartite Graph, the number of matchings in an MCBM equals the number of vertices in a Min Vertex Cover (MVC)—this is a theorem by a Hungarian mathematician Dénes *König*. The constructive proof of *König*'s theorem is as follows: obtain the MCBM of the Bipartite Graph and let U be unmatched vertices on the left set and let Z be vertices in U or connected to U via alternating path (free edge-matched edge-free edge-...). Then, the $MVC = (L \setminus Z) \bigcup (R \bigcap Z)$.

In Figure 8.28—A, we see that the MCBM of the Bipartite Graph is 2.

In Figure 8.28—B, we see that vertex 2 is the only unmatched vertex on the left set, so $U = \{2\}$.

In Figure 8.28—C, we see that vertex 2 is connected to vertex 5 via a free edge and then to vertex 1 via a matched edge, so $Z = \{1, 2, 5\}$.

In Figure 8.28—D, we can use König's theorem to conclude that:
$MVC = (\{0, 1, 2\} \setminus \{1, 2, 5\}) \bigcup (\{3, 4, 5\} \bigcap \{1, 2, 5\}) = \{\{0\} \bigcup \{5\}\} = \{0, 5\}$ of size 2.

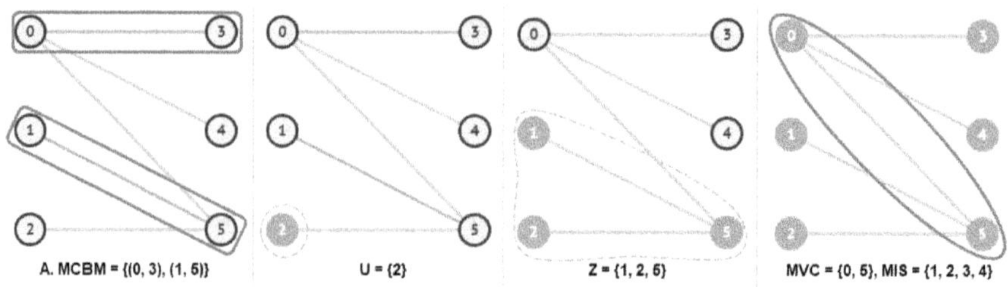

Figure 8.28: MCBM and König's Theorem

In Bipartite Graph, the size of the MIS + the size of the MCBM = $|V|$. In another words, the size of the MIS = $|V|$ - the size of the MCBM. In Figure 8.28—D, we have a Bipartite Graph with 3 vertices on the left side and 3 vertices on the right side—a total of 6 vertices. The size of the MCBM is 2 (two highlighted lines in Figure 8.28—A). For each of these 2 matched edges, we can only take one of the endpoints into the MIS. In another words, |MCBM| vertices cannot be selected, i.e., the size of the MIS is 6-2 = 4. Indeed, {1, 2, 3, 4} of size 4 are the members of the MIS of this Bipartite Graph and this is the complement of {0, 5} – the members of the MVC which has size 2 (same as size of the MCBM) found via König's theorem constructive proof earlier.

Note that although the MCBM/MIS/MVC values are unique, the solutions may not be unique. Example: In Figure 8.28—A, we can also match {0, 4} and {2, 5} instead with the same maximum cardinality of 2.

Kattis - guardianofdecency/UVa 12083 - Guardian of Decency

Abridged problem description: Given $N \leq 500$ students (in terms of their heights, genders, music styles, and favorite sports), determine how many students are eligible for an excursion if the teacher wants any pair of two students to satisfy at least one of these four criteria so that no pair of students becomes a couple: 1). Their heights differ by more than 40 cm.; 2). They are of the same sex.; 3). Their preferred music styles are different.; 4). Their favorite sports are the same (they may be fans of different teams which may result in fighting).

First, notice that the problem is about finding the Maximum Independent Set, i.e., the chosen students should not have any chance of becoming a couple. Independent Set is a hard problem in general graph, so let's check if the graph is special. Next, notice that there is an easy Bipartite Graph in the problem description: The gender of students (constraint number two). We can put the male students on the left side and the female students on the right side. At this point, we should ask: what should be the edges of this Bipartite Graph? The answer is related to the Independent Set problem: we draw an edge between a male student i and a female student j if there is a chance that (i, j) may become a couple.

In the context of this problem: if student i and j have different genders *and* their heights differ by not more than 40 cm *and* their preferred music styles are the same *and* their favorite sports are different, then this pair, one male student i and one female student j, has a high probability to be a couple. The teacher can only choose one of them.

Now, once we have this Bipartite Graph, we can run the MCBM algorithm and report: *N-MCBM*. With this example, we again highlight the importance of having good *graph modeling* skills! There is no point knowing the MCBM algorithm and its code if you cannot identify the Bipartite Graph from the problem description in the first place.

The Weighted Variants

The MIS and MVC problems can also be posed as their weighted variants by giving a *vertex-weighted* graph G as input, thus we have the MAX-*Weight*-INDEPENDENT-SET (often abbreviated as MWIS) and MIN-*Weight*-VERTEX-COVER (often abbreviated as MWVC) problems. This time, our task[35] is to select an IS (or VC) of G with the maximum (or minimum) total (vertex) weight. As the unweighted variant is already NP-hard, the weighted variant is also an NP-hard problem. In fact, the weighted variant is a bit harder to solve than its unweighted variant. Obviously, (the usually slower) solutions for the weighted variant will also work for the unweighted variant. However, if the given graph G is a tree or a bipartite graph, we still have efficient (but slightly different) solutions.

MWIS and MWVC on Tree

If graph G is a tree, we can find the MWIS of G using DP as with the unweighted variant discussed earlier, but this time instead of giving a cost $1/0$ for taking or not taking a vertex, we use cost $w(v)/0$ for taking or not taking a vertex. The rest are identical.

MWIS and MWVC on Bipartite Graph

If the graph G is a Bipartite Graph, we have to reduce MWIS (and MWVC) problem into a Max Flow problem instead of Max Cardinality Bipartite Matching (MCBM) problem as in the unweighted version. We assign the original vertex cost (the weight of taking that vertex) as capacity from source to that vertex for the left set of the Bipartite Graph and capacity from that vertex to sink for right set of the Bipartite Graph. Then, we give 'infinite' (or large) capacity in between any edge in between the left and right sets. The MWVC of this Bipartite Graph is the max flow value of this flow graph. The MWIS of this Bipartite Graph is the weight of all vertex costs minus the max flow value of this flow graph.

In Figure 8.29—left, we see a sample reduction of a MWVC instance where the cost of taking vertex 1 to 6 are $\{2, 3, 4, 7, 1, 5\}$, respectively. In Figure 8.29—right, we see the max flow value of this flow graph is 7 and this is the MWVC value of this instance.

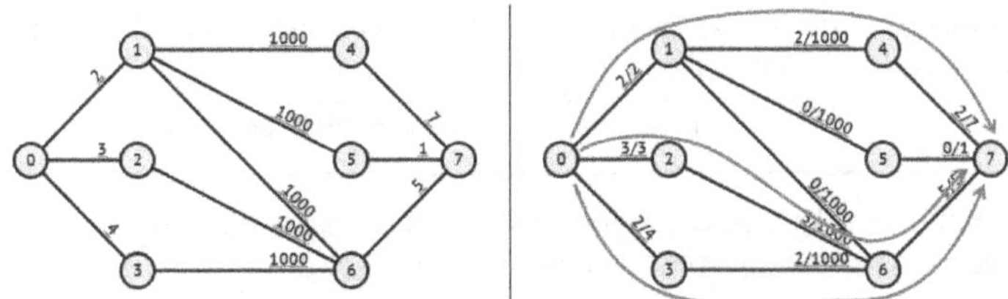

Figure 8.29: Reduction of MWVC into a Max Flow Problem

We can also apply König's theorem on this flow graph too. In Figure 8.30—left, see that the set Z that we discussed in the unweighted version is simply the S-component—vertices that are still reachable from the source vertex s after we found the max flow of the initial flow graph. The set that are not in Z is simply the T-component. In this example, the S-component are vertices {0 (source s), 2, 3, 6} and the T-component are vertices {1, 4, 5, 7}. So we can transform $MVC = (L \setminus Z) \bigcup (R \bigcap Z)$ into $MWVC = (L$ $\bigcap$ T-component) $\bigcup$ (R $\bigcap$ S-component). In Figure 8.30—right, we apply $MWVC = (\{1,2,3\} \bigcap \{1,4,5,7\}) \bigcup (\{4,5,6\} \bigcap \{0,2,3,6\}) = \{\{1\} \bigcup \{6\}\} = \{1,6\}$ of size 2.

[35]For a challenge, see *Kattis - mwvc* * which is an optimization problem involving large MWVC instance up to $N \leq 4000$. To get high score for this problem, you need to use techniques *outside* this book.

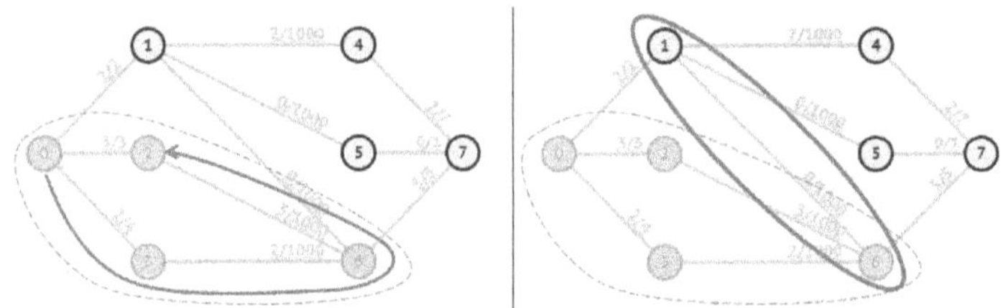

Figure 8.30: König's Theorem for MWVC Variant

UVa 01212 - Duopoly

Abridged problem description: There are two companies: company A and B. Each company has bids, e.g., A has bids $\{A_1, A_2, \ldots, A_n\}$ and each bid has a price, e.g., $P(A_1), P(A_2)$, etc. These transactions use shared channels, e.g., bid $A1$ uses channels: $\{r_1, r_2\}$. Access to a channel is exclusive, e.g., if A_1 is selected, then any of company B's bid(s) that use either r_1 or r_2 cannot be selected. It is guaranteed that two bids from company A will *never* use the same channel, but two bids from different companies may be competing for the same channel. Our task is to maximize the sum of weight of the selected bids!

Let's do several keyword analysis of this problem. If a bid from company A is selected, then bids from user B that share some or all channels *cannot* be selected. This is a strong hint for the **Independent Set** requirement. And since we want to maximize sum of weight of selected transactions, this is MAX-WEIGHTED-INDEPENDENT-SET (MWIS) problem. And since there are only two companies (two sets) and the problem statement guarantees that there is no channel conflict between the bids from within one company, we are sure that the input graph is a **Bipartite Graph**. Thus, this problem is actually an **MWIS on Bipartite Graph** solvable with a Max Flow algorithm.

VisuAlgo

We have provided the animation of various MIS/MVC/MWIS/MWVC-related algorithms that are discussed in this section in VisuAlgo. Use it to further strengthen your understanding of these algorithms. The URL is shown below.

Visualization: `https://visualgo.net/en/mvc`

Exercise 8.6.6.1: What are the solutions for another two special cases of the MVC and MIS problems: on isolated vertices and on complete graph?

Exercise 8.6.6.2: What should be done if the input graph of the the MVC or MIS problems contains multiple connected components?

Exercise 8.6.6.3*: Solve the MVC and MIS problems on Tree using Greedy algorithm instead of DP presented in this section. Does the Greedy algorithm works for the MWVC and MWIS variant?

Exercise 8.6.6.4*: Solve the MVC problem using an $O(2^k \times E)$ recursive backtracking if we are guaranteed that the MVC size will be at most k and k is much smaller than V.

Exercise 8.6.6.5*: Solve the MVC and MIS problems on Pseudoforest using greedy algorithm or Dynamic Programming variant. A Pseudoforest is an undirected graph in which every connected component has at most one cycle.

8.6.7 Min-Set-Cover

Problem Description

MIN-SET-COVER[36] can be described as follows: Given a set of items $\{1, 2, \ldots, n\}$ (called the universe) and a collection S of m sets whose union equals the universe, the `Min-Set-Cover` problem wishes to find the smallest subset of S whose union equals the universe. This MIN-SET-COVER problem can also be posed as weighted version, i.e., MIN-WEIGHT-SET-COVER where we seek to minimize the sum of weights of the subsets that we select.

Small Instances: $1 \leq n \leq [24..26]$ Items

Kattis - font is a simple problem of counting the possible SET-COVERs. Given n (up to 25) words, determine how many possible sets cover the entire ['A'..'Z']. Each word covers at least 1 letter and up to the entire 26 letters. We can store this information in a compact Adjacency Matrix as discussed in Book 1. This way, we can do a simple $O(2^n)$ backtracking that simply take or not take a word and use the fast $O(1)$ speed of bitmask operation to union two (small) sets (overall set and set of letters covered by the taken word) together. We increment answer by one when we have examined all n words and the taken words formed a pangram[37]. In fact, $n \leq [24..26]$ is probably the upper limit of what an $O(2^n)$ algorithm can do in 1s on a typical year 2020 computer.

Exercise 8.6.7.1*: Show that every instance of MIN-VERTEX-COVER can be easily reduced into MIN-SET-COVER instance in polynomial time but the reverse is not true!

Exercise 8.6.7.2*: DOMINATING-SET of a graph $G = (V, E)$ is a subset D of V such that every vertex not in D is adjacent to at least one member of D. We usually want to find the domination number $\gamma(G)$, the smallest size of a valid D. This problem is similar but not the same as the MIN-VERTEX-COVER problem discussed in Section 8.6.6 and best explained with an illustration (see Figure 8.31). We call this problem as the MIN-DOMINATING-SET problem. Show that every instance of the MIN-DOMINATING-SET can be easily reduced into the MIN-SET-COVER instance in polynomial time but the reverse is not true!

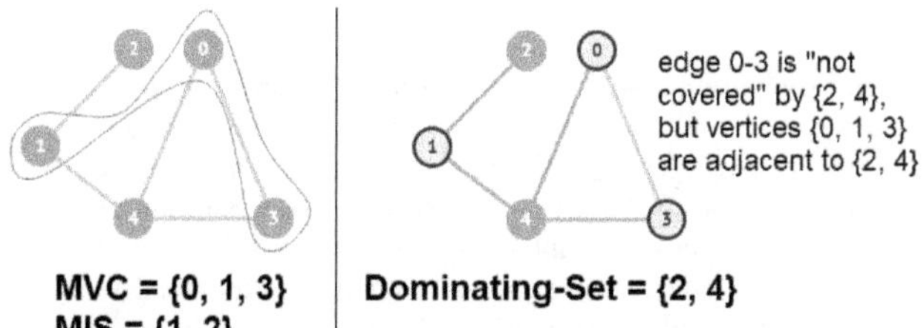

Figure 8.31: Left: MVC/MIS of the Graph; Right: Dominating-Set of the Graph

---

[36]MIN-SET-COVER problem can be easily proven to be NP-hard via reduction from `Vertex-Cover`.

[37]Pangram is a sentence that uses every letter of a given alphabet at least once, i.e., the entire 26 letters are covered.

8.6.8 Min-Path-Cover

General Case

The MIN-PATH-COVER (MPC) problem is described as the problem of finding the minimum number of paths to cover *each vertex* on a graph $G = (V, E)$. A path $v_0, v_1, \ldots, v_k$ is said to cover all vertices along its path. This optimization problem is NP-hard on general graphs but has an interesting polynomial solution if posed on Directed Acyclic Graphs (DAGs).

Special Case: on DAG

The MPC problem on DAG is a special case where the given $G = (V, E)$ is a DAG, i.e., directed and acyclic.

Abridged problem description of UVa 01201 - Taxi Cab Scheme: Imagine that the vertices in Figure 8.32—A are passengers, and we draw an edge between two vertices $u - v$ if one taxi can serve passenger u and then passenger v *on time*. The question is: what is the minimum number of taxis that must be deployed to serve *all* passengers?

The answer is two taxis. In Figure 8.32—D, we see one possible optimal solution. One taxi (dotted line) serves passenger 1, passenger 2, and then passenger 4. Another taxi (dashed line) serves passenger 3 and passenger 5. All passengers are served with just two taxis. Notice that there is other optimal solution, e.g.,: $1 \to 3 \to 5$ and $2 \to 4$.

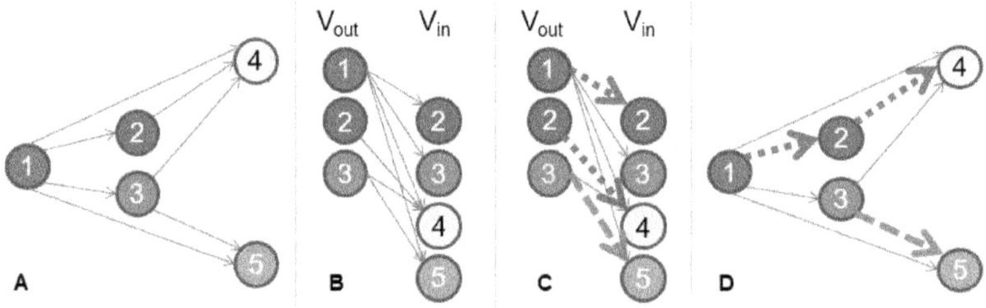

Figure 8.32: Min Path Cover on DAG (from UVa 01201 [28])

Solution(s)

This problem has a polynomial solution: construct a *bipartite graph* $G' = (V_{out} \bigcup V_{in}, E')$ from G, where $V_{out} = \{v \in V : v$ has positive out-degree$\}$, $V_{in} = \{v \in V : v$ has positive in-degree$\}$, and $E' = \{(u, v) \in (V_{out} \times V_{in}) : (u, v) \in E\}$. This G' is a bipartite graph. A matching on bipartite graph G' forces us to select at most one outgoing edge from every $u \in V_{out}$ (and similarly at most one incoming edge for $v \in V_{in}$). DAG G initially has n vertices, which can be covered with n paths of length 0 (the vertices themselves). One matching between vertex a and vertex b using edge (a, b) says that we can use one less path as edge $(a, b) \in E'$ can cover both vertices in $a \in V_{out}$ and $b \in V_{in}$. Thus if the MCBM in G' has size m, then we just need n-m paths to cover each vertex in G.

The MCBM in G' that is needed to solve the MPC in G can be solved via several polynomial solutions discussed in Section 8.5, e.g., maximum flow solution, augmenting paths algorithm++, or Dinic's/Hopcroft-Karp algorithm. As the solution for bipartite matching runs in polynomial time, the solution for the MPC in DAG also runs in polynomial time. Note that MPC on general graphs is NP-hard.

8.6.9 Satisfiability (SAT)

3-CNF-SAT (3-SAT)

You are given a conjunction of disjunctions ("and of ors") where each disjunction ("the or operation") has three (3) arguments that may be variables or the negation of variables. The disjunctions of pairs are called 'clauses' and the formula is known as the 3-CNF (Conjunctive Normal Form) formula. The 3-CNF-SAT (often just referred as 3-SAT) problem is to find a truth (that is, true or false) assignment to these variables that makes the 3-CNF formula true, i.e., every clause has at least one term that evaluates to true. This 3-SAT problem is NP-complete[38] but if there are only two (2) arguments for each disjunction, then there is a polynomial solution.

2-CNF-SAT (2-SAT)

Simplified Problem Description

The 2-CNF-SAT (often just referred to as 2-SAT) is a SAT problem where each disjunction has two (2) arguments.

Example 1: $(x_1 \vee x_2) \wedge (\neg x_1 \vee \neg x_2)$ is satisfiable because we can assign $x_1 = true$ and $x_2 = false$ (alternative assignment is $x_1 = false$ and $x_2 = true$).

Example 2: $(x_1 \vee x_2) \wedge (\neg x_1 \vee x_2) \wedge (\neg x_2 \vee x_3) \wedge (\neg x_2 \vee \neg x_3)$ is not satisfiable. You can try all 8 possible combinations of boolean values of x_1, x_2, and x_3 to realize that none of them can make the 2-CNF formula satisfiable.

Solution(s)

Complete Search

Contestants who only have a vague knowledge of the Satisfiability problem may think that this problem is an NP-complete problem and therefore attempt a complete search solution. If the 2-CNF formula has n variables and m clauses, trying all 2^n possible assignments and checking each assignment in $O(m)$ has an overall time complexity of $O(2^n \times m)$. This is likely TLE.

The 2-SAT is a *special case* of Satisfiability problem and it admits a polynomial solution like the one shown below.

Reduction to Implication Graph and Finding SCC

First, we have to realize that a clause in a 2-CNF formula $(a \vee b)$ can be written as $(\neg a \Rightarrow b)$ and $(\neg b \Rightarrow a)$. Thus, given a 2-CNF formula, we can build the corresponding 'implication graph'. Each variable has two vertices in the implication graph, the variable itself and the negation/inverse of that variable[39]. An edge connects one vertex to another if the corresponding variables are related by an implication in the corresponding 2-CNF formula. For the two 2-CNF example formulas above, we have the following implication graphs shown in Figure 8.33.

[38] One of the best known algorithms for CNF-SAT is the Davis-Putnam-Logemann-Loveland (DPLL) recursive backtracking algorithm. It still has exponential worst case time complexity but it does prune lots of search space as it goes.

[39] Programming technique: We give a variable an index i and its negation with another index $i + 1$. This way, we can find one from the other by using bit manipulation $i \oplus 1$ where $\oplus$ is the 'exclusive or' operator.

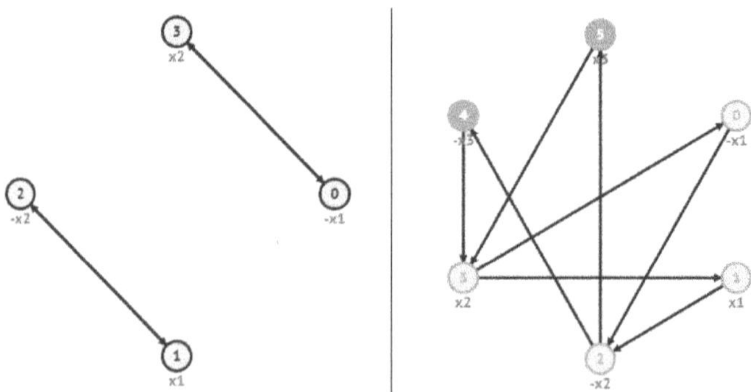

Figure 8.33: The Implication Graph of Example 1 (Left) and Example 2 (Right)

As you can see in Figure 8.33, a 2-CNF formula with n variables (excluding the negation) and m clauses will have $V = \Theta(2n) = \Theta(n)$ vertices and $E = O(2m) = O(m)$ edges in the implication graph.

Now, a 2-CNF formula is satisfiable if and only if "there is no variable that belongs to the same Strongly Connected Component (SCC) as its negation".

In Figure 8.33—left, we see that there are two SCCs: {0,3} and {1,2}. As there is no variable that belongs to the same SCC as its negation, we conclude that the 2-CNF formula shown in Example 1 is satisfiable.

In Figure 8.33—right, we observe that all six vertices belong to a single SCC. Therefore, we have both vertex 0 (that represents $\neg x_1$) and vertex 1 (that represents[40] x_1); both vertex 2 ($\neg x_2$) and vertex 3 (x_2); and both vertex 4 ($\neg x_3$) and vertex 5 (x_3) in the same SCC. Therefore, we conclude that the 2-CNF formula shown in Example 2 is not satisfiable.

To find the SCCs of a directed graph, we can use either Kosaraju's or Tarjan's SCC algorithms shown in Book 1.

Exercise 8.6.9.1*: To find the actual truth assignment, we need to do a bit more work than just checking if there is no variable that belongs to the same SCC as its negation. What are the extra steps required to actually find the truth assignment of a satisfiable 2-CNF formula?

Exercise 8.6.9.2*: Study Davis-Putnam-Logemann-Loveland (DPLL) recursive backtracking algorithm that can solve small-medium instances of the NP-complete 3-CNF-SAT variant!

Profile of Algorithm Inventor

Jakob Steiner (1796-1863) was a Swiss mathematician. The STEINER-TREE and its related problems are named after him.

[40]Notice that using this indexing technique (0/1 for $\neg x_1/x_1$; 2/3 for $\neg x_2/x_2$; and so on), we can easily test whether a vertex x and another vertex y are a variable and *its negation* by testing if $x == y \oplus 1$.

8.6.10 Steiner-Tree

Problem Description

STEINER-TREE problem is a broad term for a group of related[41] problems. In this section, we refer to the STEINER-TREE problem in graphs[42] with the following problem description: Given a connected undirected graph with non-negative edge weights (e.g., Figure 8.34—left) and a subset of k vertices, usually referred to as terminal (or required) vertices (for this variant, we simplify[43] the terminal vertices to be vertices numbered with 0, 1, ..., k-1), find a tree of minimum total weight that includes all the terminal vertices, but may also include additional vertices, called the Steiner vertices/points. This problem is NP-hard [16].

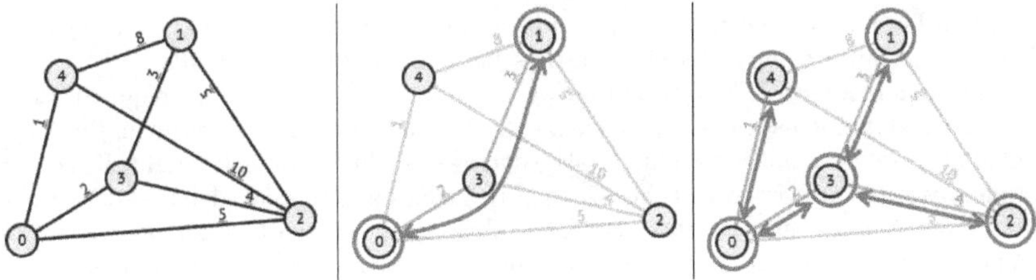

Figure 8.34: Steiner Tree Illustrations—Part 1

Special Case, $k = 2$

This STEINER-TREE problem[44] with $k = 2$ degenerates into a standard Single-Source Single-Destination Shortest Paths (SSSDSP) problem. This shortest path between the two required terminal vertices is the required answer. Review Book 1 for the solution, e.g., the Dijkstra's algorithm that runs in $O((V + E) \log V)$. In Figure 8.34—middle, if the $k = 2$ terminal vertices are vertex 0 and 1, then the solution is simply the shortest path from 0 to 1, which is path 0-3-1 with cost 2+3 = 5.

Special Case, $k = N$

This STEINER-TREE problem with $k = N$ degenerates into a standard Minimum Spanning Tree (MST) problem. When $k = N$, all vertices in the graph are required and thus the MST that spans all vertices is clearly the required solution. Review Book 1 for the solution, e.g., the Prim's or Kruskal's algorithm that both runs in $O(E \log V)$. In Figure 8.34—right, if the terminal vertices are all $k = N = 5$ vertices, then the solution is the MST of the input graph, which takes edges 0-4, 0-3, 3-1, and 3-4 with total cost of 1+2+3+4 = 10.

Special Case, $k = 3$

We first run $k = 3$ calls of an SSSP algorithm (e.g., Dijkstra's) from these $k = 3$ terminal vertices to get the shortest path values from these $k = 3$ terminal vertices to all other vertices. There is a result in the study of this STEINER-TREE problem saying that if there are k terminal vertices, there can only be up to k-2 additional Steiner vertices. As there are only[45] $k = 3$ terminal vertices, there can only be at most 3-2 = 1 Steiner vertex.

[41] We do not discuss Euclidean STEINER-TREE problem in this section.

[42] The STEINER-TREE problem is closely related to the Minimum Spanning Tree problem.

[43] In the full version, we can pick any subset of k vertices as terminal vertices.

[44] Solution to special case with $k = 1$ is too trivial: just take that only terminal vertex with 0 cost.

[45] This idea can also be used for other low values of k, e.g., $k = 4$, etc.

So, we try each vertex i in graph G as the (only) potential Steiner vertex (for simplicity, we will treat the 3 terminal vertices as candidate Steiner vertex too—which means we do not use a Steiner vertex if that is the case) and report the minimum total shortest paths of these $k = 3$ terminal vertices to Steiner vertex i. The time complexity of this solution remains $O((V + E) \log V)$. In Figure 8.35—left, if the $k = 3$ terminal vertices are vertex 0, 1, and 2, then the best option is to include vertex 3 as an additional Steiner vertex. The total cost is the shortest path from 0 to 3, 1 to 3, and 2 to 3, which is 2+3+4 = 9. This is better than if we form a subtree that does not include any Steiner vertex at all, e.g., subtree 0-2-1 with total cost 5+5 = 10.

Special Case, the Input Graph is a Tree

STEINER-TREE problem can also be posed on a Tree, i.e., we want to get a (smaller) subtree that connects all k required terminal vertices (that are still numbered with 0, 1, ..., k-1). We can run a modified DFS starting from vertex 0 (for $k > 0$, vertex 0 is a required vertex). If we are at vertex u and there is an edge $u \to v$ and there is a required vertex in the subtree rooted at v, we have no choice but to take edge $u \to v$.. In Figure 8.35—right, if the $k = 3$ terminal vertices are vertex 0, 1, and 2, then the solution is to take edge $0 \to 1$ (with cost 1) as vertex 1 is a required vertex, and then take edge $3 \to 2$ (with cost 1) as vertex 2 is a required vertex, skip edge $4 \to 5$ (we don't require vertex 5) and $3 \to 4$ (we don't require vertex 4), and finally take edge $0 \to 3$ (with cost 2) as vertex 3, albeit not required, has vertex 2 as its child that is required. The total cost is 1+1+2 = 4.

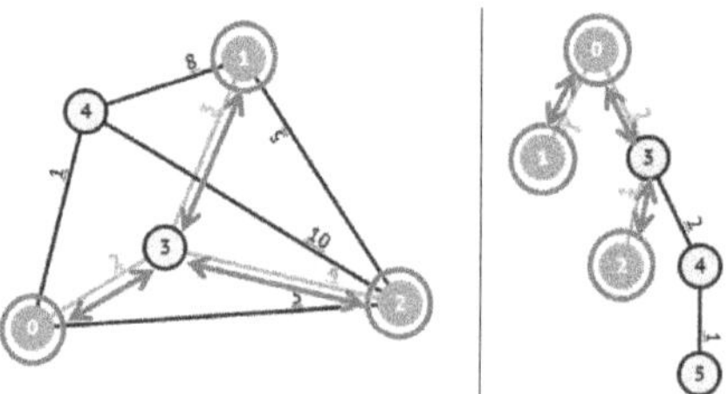

Figure 8.35: Steiner Tree Illustrations—Part 2

Small-size Instance, $k \le V \le 15$

Because $V \le 15$, we can try all possible subsets (including empty set) of vertices of graph G that are not the required vertices as potential Steiner points (there are at most 2^{V-k} such subsets). We combine the k terminal points with those Steiner points and find the MST of that subset of vertices. We keep track of the minimum one. The time complexity of this solution is $O(2^{V-k} \times E \log V)$ and only work for small V.

VisuAlgo

We have built a visualization of this STEINER-TREE problem variant at VisuAlgo:

Visualization: `https://visualgo.net/en/steinertree`

Exercise 8.6.10.1*: For medium-size Instance where $V \le 50$ but $k \le 11$, the idea of trying all possible subsets of non-required vertices as potential Steiner points will get TLE. Study Dreyfus-Wagner Dynamic Programming algorithm that can solve this variant.

8.6.11 Graph-Coloring

Problem Description

GRAPH-COLORING problem is a problem of coloring the vertices of a graph such that no two adjacent vertices share the same color. The decision problem of GRAPH-COLORING is NP-complete except for 0-coloring (trivial, only possible for graph with no vertex at all), 1-coloring (also trivial, only possible for graph with no edge at all), 2-coloring, and special case of 4-coloring.

2-Coloring

A graph is bi-colorable (2-coloring) if and only if the graph is a bipartite graph. We can check whether a graph is a bipartite graph by running a simple $O(V + E)$ DFS/BFS check as shown in DFS/BFS section in Book 1.

4-Coloring

The four color theorem states, in simple form, that "every planar graph is 4-colorable". Four color theorem is not applicable to general graphs.

9-Coloring and Sudoku

SUDOKU puzzle is actually an NP-complete problem and it is the most popular instance of the GRAPH-COLORING problem. Most SUDOKU puzzles are 'small' and thus recursive backtracking can be used to find one solution for a standard 9×9 ($n = 3$) Sudoku board. This backtracking solution can be sped up using bitmask: For each empty cell `(r, c)`, we try putting a digit `[1..`n^2`]` one by one if it is a valid move or prune as early as possible. The n^2 row, n^2 column, and $n \times n$ square checks can be done with three bitmasks of length n^2 bits. Solve two similar problems: UVa 00989 and UVa 10957 with this technique!

Relationship with Min-Clique-Cover and $O(3^n)$ DP for Small Instances

GRAPH-COLORING is very related to CLIQUE-COVER (or PARTITION-INTO-CLIQUES) of a given undirected graph that is discussed in the next subsection.

A GRAPH-COLORING of a graph $G = (V, E)$ may be seen as a CLIQUE-COVER of the complement graph G' of G (basically, $G' = (V, (u, v) \notin E)$). Therefore running a MIN-CLIQUE-COVER solution on G is also the solution of the optimization version of GRAPH-COLORING on G', i.e., finding the least amount (*chromatic number*) of colors needed for G'. Try finding the chromatic numbers of the graphs in Figure 8.36.

With this similarities, we will discuss the $O(3^n)$ DP solution for small instances for either GRAPH-COLORING or MIN-CLIQUE-COVER in the next subsection.

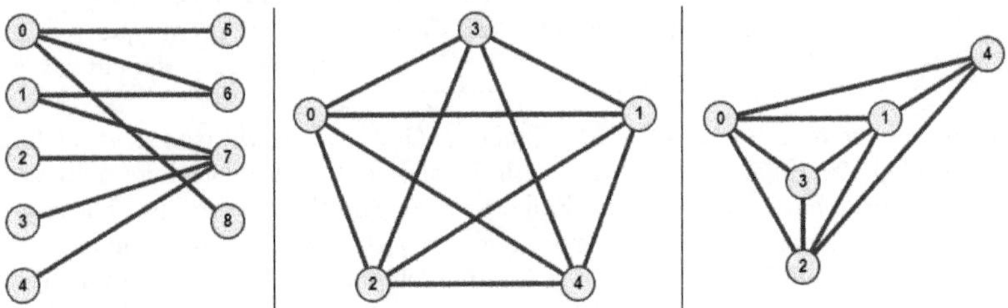

Figure 8.36: Color These Planar Graphs with As Few Color as Possible

8.6.12 Min-Clique-Cover

In CLIQUE-COVER, we are asked to partition the vertices of the input graph into cliques (subsets of vertices within which every two vertices are adjacent). MIN-CLIQUE-COVER is the NP-hard optimization version of CLIQUE-COVER that uses as few cliques as possible.

Partition-Into-2-Cliques

A graph G can be partitioned into 2 cliques if and only if its complement G' is a bipartite graph (2-colorable). We can check whether a graph is a bipartite graph by running a simple $O(V + E)$ DFS/BFS check as shown in DFS/BFS section in Book 1.

Small Instances: $1 \leq n \leq [16..17]$ Items

Kattis - busplanning can be seen as a MIN-CLIQUE-COVER problem. We are given a small graph G with up to n ($1 \leq n \leq 17$) kids and a list of k pairs of kids that are enemies. If we draw an edge between two kids that are *not* enemy, we have the complement graph G'. Our job now is to partition G' into cliques of kids that are *not* enemy, subject to bus capacity constraint of c kids.

We can first pre-process the 2^n possible subsets of kids that are not enemy and have size at most c in $O(2^n \times n^2)$ time. The hard part is to use this information to solve the MIN-CLIQUE-COVER problem. We can use DP bitmask $f(mask)$ where bit 1/0 in $mask$ describes kids that have been/have not been assigned to a bus, respectively. The base case is when $mask = 0$ (all kids have been assigned into a bus), we do not need additional bus and return 0. However, how to generate subsets of a bitmask $mask$ where not all of its bits are 1s? Example: when $mask_1 = 137 = (10001001)_2$, i.e., we only have 3 bits that are on in $mask_1$, then its (non-empty) subsets are $\{137 = (10001001)_2, 136 = (10001000)_2, 129 = (10000001)_2, 128 = (10000000)_2, 9 = (00001001)_2, 8 = (00001000)_2, 1 = (00000001)_2\}$. In Book 1, we have learned the following technique:

```
int mask = 137;                                    // (10001001)_2
int N = 8;
for (int ss = 1; ss < (1<<N); ++ss)                // previous way, exclude 0
  if ((mask & ss) == ss)                           // ss is a subset of mask
    cout << ss << "\n";
```

With the implementation above, we will incur strictly $O(2^n)$ per computation of a state of $f(mask)$, making the overall DP runs in $O(2^n \times 2^n) = O(4^n)$, TLE for $n \leq 17$ (over 17 Billion). However, we can do much better with the following implementation:

```
int mask = 137;                                    // (10001001)_2
for (int ss = mask; ss; ss = (ss-1) & mask)        // new technique
  cout << ss << "\n";                              // ss is a subset of mask
```

We claim that the overall work done by $f(mask)$ is $O(3^n)$ which will pass the time limit for $n \leq 17$ (around 100 Million). Notice that with this updated implementation, we iterate only over the subsets of $mask$. If a $mask$ has k on bits, we do exactly 2^k iterations. The important part is that k gets smaller as the DP recursion goes deeper. Now, the total number of $mask$s with exactly k on bits is $C(n, k)$. With a bit of combinatorics, we compute that the total work done is $\sum_{k=0}^{n} C(n, k) * 2^k = 3^n$. This is much smaller than the n-th Bell number – the number of possible partitions of a set of n items/the search space of a naïve complete search algorithm (17-th Bell number is over 80 Billion).

8.6.13 Other NP-hard/complete Problems

There are a few other NP-hard/complete problems that have found their way into interesting programming contest problems but they are very rare, e.g.,:

1. PARTITION: Decide whether a given multiset S of positive integers can be partitioned/split into two subsets S_1 and S_2 such that the sum of the numbers in S_1 equals the sum of the numbers in S_2. This decision problem[46] is NP-complete. We can modify the PARTITION problem slightly into an optimization problem: partition the multiset S into two subsets S_1 and S_2 such that the difference between the sum of elements in S_1 and the sum of elements in S_2 is minimized. This version is NP-hard.

2. MIN-FEEDBACK-ARC-SET: A Feedback Arc (Edge) Set (FAS) is a set of edges which, when removed from the graph, leaves a DAG. In MIN-FEEDBACK-ARC-SET, we seek to minimize the number[47] of edges that we remove in order to have a DAG.

   Example: You are given a graph $G = (V, E)$ with $V = 10K$ vertices and up to $E = 100K$ distinct-weighted directed edges. Only edges with a weight equal to a Fibonacci number (see Section 5.4.1) less than 2000 can be deleted from G. Now, your job is to delete as few edges as possible from G so that G becomes a Directed Acyclic Graph (DAG) or output impossible if no subset of edges in G can be deleted in order to make G a DAG.

   If you are very familiar with the theory of NP-completeness, this problem is called the MIN-FEEDBACK-ARC-SET optimization problem that is NP-hard (see Section 8.6). However, there are two stand-out constraints for those who are well trained: distinct-weighted edges and Fibonacci numbers less than 2000. There are only 16 distinct Fibonacci numbers less than 2000. Thus, we just need to check 2^{16} possible subsets of edges to be deleted and see if we have a DAG (this check can be done in $O(E)$). Among possible subsets of edges, pick the one with minimum cardinality as our answer.

3. SHORTEST-COMMON-SUPERSTRING: Given a set of strings $S = \{s_1, s_2, \ldots, s_n\}$, find the shortest string S^* that contains each element of S as a substring, i.e., S^* is a superstring of S. For example: S = {`''steven''`, `''boost''`, `''vent''`}, S^* = `''boostevent''`.

4. PARTITION-INTO-TRIANGLES: Given a graph $G = (V, E)$ (for the sake of discussion, let V be a multiple of 3, i.e., $|V| = 3k$), is there a partition of V into k disjoint subsets $\{V_1, V_2, \ldots, V_k\}$ of 3 vertices each such that the 3 possible edges between every V_i are in E? Notice that forming ICPC teams from a group of $3k$ students where there is an edge between 2 students if they can work well with each other is basically this NP-complete decision problem.

5. MAX-CLIQUE: Given a graph $G = (V, E)$, find a clique (complete subgraph) of G with the largest possible number of vertices.

[46]PARTITION problem can be easily proven to be NP-complete via reduction from `Subset-Sum`.

[47]This problem can also be posed as weighted version where we seek to minimize the sum of edge weights that we remove.

8.6.14 Summary

Name	Exponential Solution(s)
0-1 KNAPSACK	Small: DP Knapsack
	Medium: Meet in the Middle
SUBSET-SUM	DP Subset-Sum, similar as DP Knapsack above
COIN-CHANGE	DP Coin-Change, similar as DP Knapsack above
TSP/HAMILTONIAN-TOUR	Small: DP Held-Karp
	Small: Backtracking with heavy pruning
LONGEST-PATH	$V \leq 10$: Backtracking with heavy pruning
	$V \leq 18$: DP Held-Karp variant
MWVC/MWIS	Small: Optimized bitmask
	Small k: Clever Backtracking (**Exercise 8.6.6.4***)
MSC	Small: Backtracking with bitmask
SAT	Small 3-SAT: DPLL
STEINER-TREE	$k \leq V \leq 15$, CS + MST
	Medium: DP Dreyfus-Wagner (**Exercise 8.6.10.1***)
GRAPH-COLORING/MCC	Medium: $O(3^n)$ DP over subsets

Table 8.2: Summary of Exponential Solution(s) of NP-hard/complete Problems

Name	Special Case(s)
0-1 KNAPSACK	Fractional Knapsack
SUBSET-SUM	2/3/4-SUM
TSP	Bitonic TSP
LONGEST-PATH	On DAG: Toposort/DP
	On Tree: 2 DFS/BFS
MWVC/MWIS	On Tree: DP/Greedy
	On Bipartite: Max Flow/Matching
MPC	On DAG: MCBM
SAT	2-SAT: Reduction to SCC
STEINER-TREE	$k = 2$, SSSDSP
	$k = N$, MST
	$k = 3$, CS +1 Steiner point
	On Tree: LCA
GRAPH-COLORING	Bi-coloring/2 color/Bipartite
	4 color/planar
	9 color/Sudoku

Table 8.3: Summary of Special Case(s) of NP-hard/complete Problems

Programming Exercises related to NP-hard/complete Problems:

a. Small Instances of the NP-hard/complete Problems, Easier

1. Entry Level: **Kattis - equalsumseasy** * (PARTITION; generate all possible subsets with bitmask; use `set` to record which sums have been computed)
2. **UVa 00989 - Su Doku** * (classic SUDOKU puzzle; the small 9x9 instance is solvable with backtracking with pruning; use bitmask to speed up)
3. **UVa 11088 - End up with More Teams** * (similar to UVa 10911 but partitioning of *three* persons to one team; PARTITION-INTO-TRIANGLES)
4. **UVa 12455 - Bars** * (SUBSET-SUM; try all; see the harder UVa 12911 that requires meet in the middle)
5. *Kattis - flowfree* * (brute force combination 3^{10} or 4^8; then `Longest-Path` problem on non DAG between two end points of the same color)
6. *Kattis - font* * (count number of possible SET-COVERS; use 2^N backtracking; but use bitmask to represent small set of covered letters)
7. *Kattis - socialadvertising* * (MIN-DOMINATING-SET/MIN-SET-COVER; $n \leq 20$; use compact Adjacency Matrix technique)

Extra UVa: *00193, 00539, 00574, 00624, 00775, 10957.*

Extra Kattis: *balanceddiet, satisfiability, ternarianweights, tightfitsudoku, vivoparc.*

b. Small Instances of the NP-hard/complete Problems, Harder

1. Entry Level: **UVa 01098 - Robots on Ice** * (LA 4793 - WorldFinals Harbin10; HAMILTONIAN-TOUR; backtracking+pruning; meet in the middle)
2. **UVa 10571 - Products** * (hard backtracking problem; it has similar flavor as SUDOKU puzzle)
3. **UVa 11095 - Tabriz City** * (optimization version of MIN-VERTEX-COVER on general graph which is NP-hard)
4. **UVa 12911 - Subset sum** * (SUBSET-SUM; we cannot use DP as $1 \leq N \leq 40$ and $-10^9 \leq T \leq 10^9$; use meet in the middle)
5. *Kattis - beanbag* * (SET-COVER problem; T farmers can collude to give Jack the hardest possible subset of beans to be given freely to Jack)
6. *Kattis - busplanning* * (MIN-CLIQUE-COVER; DP bitmask over sets)
7. *Kattis - programmingteamselection* * (PARTITION-INTO-TRIANGLES; prune if #students %3 $\neq 0$; generate up to $m/3$ teams; backtracking with memo)

Extra UVa: *01217, 10160, 11065.*

Extra Kattis: *celebritysplit, coloring, mapcolouring, sudokunique, sumsets, tugofwar.*

Review all programming exercises for DP classics that actually have pseudo-polynomial time complexities: 0-1 KNAPSACK, SUBSET-SUM, COIN-CHANGE, and TSP back in Book 1 and in Section 8.3.

c. Special Cases of the NP-hard/complete Problems, Easier

1. Entry Level: **UVa 01347 - Tour** * (LA 3305 - SoutheasternEurope05; this is the pure version of BITONIC-TSP problem)
2. **UVa 10859 - Placing Lampposts *** (MIN-VERTEX-COVER; on several trees; maximize number of edges with its two endpoints covered)
3. **UVa 11159 - Factors and Multiples *** (MAX-INDEPENDENT-SET; on Bipartite Graph; ans equals to its MCBM)
4. **UVa 11357 - Ensuring Truth *** (not a pure CNF SAT(isfiability) problem; it is a special case as only one clause needs to be satisfied)
5. *Kattis - bilateral* * (this is MIN-VERTEX-COVER on Bipartite Graph; MCBM; Konig's theorem that can handle the 1 009 correctly)
6. *Kattis - europeantrip* * (STEINER-TREE with 3 terminal vertices and up to 1 Steiner point; we can use two ternary searches)
7. *Kattis - reactivity* * (verify if a HAMILTONIAN-PATH exists in the DAG; find one topological sort of the DAG; verify if it is the only one in linear time)

   Extra UVa: *01194, 10243, 11419, 13115.*

   Extra Kattis: *antennaplacement, bookcircle, catvsdog, citrusintern, countingclauses, cross, guardianofdecency.*

d. Special Cases of the NP-hard/complete Problems, Harder

1. Entry Level: **UVa 01096 - The Islands** * (LA 4791 - WorldFinals Harbin10; BITONIC-TSP variant; print the actual path)
2. **UVa 01086 - The Ministers' ... *** (LA 4452 - WorldFinals Stockholm09; can be modeled as a 2-SAT problem)
3. **UVa 01184 - Air Raid *** (LA 2696 - Dhaka02; MIN-PATH-COVER; on DAG; $\approx$ MCBM)
4. **UVa 01212 - Duopoly *** (LA 3483 - Hangzhou05; MAX-WEIGHTED-INDEPENDENT-SET; on Bipartite Graph; $\approx$ Max Flow)
5. *Kattis - jailbreak* * (STEINER-TREE; on grid; 3 terminal vertices: 'outside' and 2 prisoners; BFS; get the best Steiner point that connects them)
6. *Kattis - ridofcoins* * (not the minimizing COIN-CHANGE problem; but the maximizing one; greedy pruning; complete search on smaller instance)
7. *Kattis - wedding* * (can be modeled as a 2-SAT problem; also available at UVa 11294 - Wedding)

   Extra UVa: *01220, 10319.*

   Extra Kattis: *airports, delivering, eastereggs, itcanbearranged, ironcoal, joggers, mafija, taxicab.*

   Also review all programming exercises involving Special Graphs, e.g., LONGEST-PATH (on DAG, on Tree) back in Book 1.

8.7 Problem Decomposition

While there are only 'a few' basic data structures and algorithms tested in programming contest problems (we believe that many of them have been covered in this book), the harder problems may require a *combination* of two (or more) algorithms and/or data structures. To solve such problems, we must first decompose the components of the problems so that we can solve each component independently. To be able to do so, we must first be familiar with the individual components (the content of Chapter 1-Section 8.6).

Although there are ${}_NC_2$ possible combinations of two out of N algorithms and/or data structures, not all of the combinations make sense. In this section, we compile and list down some[48] of the *more common* combinations of two algorithms and/or data structures based on our experience in solving $\approx$ 3458 UVa and Kattis online judge problems. We end this section with the discussion of the rare combination of *three* algorithms and/or data structures.

8.7.1 Two Components: Binary Search the Answer and Other

In Book 1, we have seen Binary Search the Answer (BSTA) on a (simple) simulation problem that does not depend on the fancier algorithms that have not been discussed back then. Actually, this technique can be combined with some other algorithms in this book. Several variants that we have encountered so far are BSTA plus:

- Greedy algorithm (discussed in Book 1), e.g., UVa 00714, 12255, Kattis - wifi,
- Graph connectivity test (discussed in Book 1), e.g., UVa 00295, 10876, Kattis - gettingthrough,
- SSSP algorithm (discussed in Book 1), e.g., UVa 10537, 10816, Kattis - arachnophobia, enemyterritory, IOI 2009 (Mecho),
- Max Flow algorithm (discussed in Section 8.4), e.g., UVa 10983, Kattis - gravamen,
- MCBM algorithm (discussed in Book 1 and in Section 8.5), e.g., UVa 01221, 11262, Kattis - gridgame,
- Big Integer operations (discussed in Book 1), e.g., UVa 10606, Kattis - prettygoodcuberoot,
- Geometry formulas (discussed in Section 7.2), e.g., UVa 10566, 11646, 12097, 12851, 12853, Kattis - expandingrods,
- Others, e.g., UVa 10372/Physics, 11670/Physics, 12428/Graph Theory, 12908/Math, Kattis - skijumping/Physics, etc.

In this section, we write two more examples of using Binary Search the Answer technique. This combination of Binary Search the Answer plus another algorithm can be spotted by asking this question: "If we guess the required answer in binary search fashion, will the original problem turn into a True/False question?".

[48]This list is not and probably will not be exhaustive.

Binary Search the Answer (BSTA) plus Greedy algorithm

Abridged problem description of UVa 00714 - Copying Books: You are given $m \leq 500$ books numbered $1, 2, \ldots, m$ that may have different number of pages $(p_1, p_2, \ldots, p_m)$. You want to make one copy of each of them. Your task is to assign these books among k scribes, $k \leq m$. Each book can be assigned to a single scriber only, and every scriber must get a *continuous sequence* of books. That means, there exists an increasing succession of numbers $0 = b_0 < b_1 < b_2 \cdots < b_{k-1} < b_k = m$ such that i-th scriber ($i > 0$) gets a sequence of books with numbers between $b_{i-1} + 1$ and b_i. Each scribe copies pages at the same rate. Thus, the time needed to make one copy of each book is determined by the scriber who is assigned the most work. Now, you want to determine: "What is the minimum number of pages copied by the scriber with the most work?".

There exists a Dynamic Programming solution for this problem, but this problem can also be solved by guessing the answer in binary search fashion. We will illustrate this with an example when $m = 9$, $k = 3$ and $p_1, p_2, \ldots, p_9$ are 100, 200, 300, 400, 500, 600, 700, 800, and 900, respectively.

If we guess that the *answer* = 1000, then the problem becomes 'simpler', i.e., If the scriber with the most work can only copy up to 1000 pages, can this problem be solved? The answer is 'no'. We can greedily assign the jobs from book 1 to book m as follows: {100, 200, 300, 400} for scribe 1, {500} for scribe 2, {600} for scribe 3. But if we do this, we still have 3 books {700, 800, 900} unassigned. Therefore the answer must be > 1000.

If we guess *answer* = 2000, then we can greedily assign the jobs as follows: {100, 200, 300, 400, 500} for scribe 1, {600, 700} for scribe 2, and {800, 900} for scribe 3. All books are copied and we still have some slacks, i.e., scribe 1, 2, and 3 still have {500, 700, 300} unused potential. Therefore the answer must be ≤ 2000.

This *answer* is binary-searchable between `[`lo`..`hi`]` where $lo = max(p_i), \forall i \in$ `[1..`m`]` (the number of pages of the thickest book) and $hi = p_1 + p_2 + \ldots + p_m$ (the sum of all pages from all books). And for those who are curious, the optimal *answer* for the test case in this example is 1700. The time complexity of this solution is $O(m \log hi)$. Notice that this extra log factor is usually negligible in programming contest environment[49].

Binary Search the Answer (BSTA) plus Geometry formulas

We use UVa 11646 - Athletics Track for another illustration of Binary Search the Answer tecnique. The abridged problem description is as follows: Examine a rectangular soccer field with an athletics track as seen in Figure 8.37—left where the two arcs on both sides (arc1 and arc2) are from the same circle centered in the middle of the soccer field. We want the length of the athletics track (L1 + arc1 + L2 + arc2) to be exactly 400m. If we are given the ratio of the length L and width W of the soccer field to be $a : b$, what should be the actual length L and width W of the soccer field that satisfy the constraints above?

It is quite hard (but not impossible) to obtain the solution with pen and paper strategy (analytical solution), but with the help of a computer and binary search the answer (actually bisection method) technique, we can find the solution easily.

We binary search the value of L. From L, we can get $W = b/a \times L$. The expected length of an arc is $(400 - 2 \times L)/2$. Now we can use Trigonometry to compute the radius r and the angle o via triangle CMX (see Figure 8.37—right). $CM = 0.5 \times L$ and $MX = 0.5 \times W$. With r and o, we can compute the actual arc length. We then compare this value with the expected arc length to decide whether we have to increase or decrease the length L.

[49]Setting $lo = 1$ and $hi = 1e9$ will also work as this value will be binary-searched in logarithmic time. That is, we may not need to set these lo and hi values very precisely as long as answer is $\in [lo..hi]$.

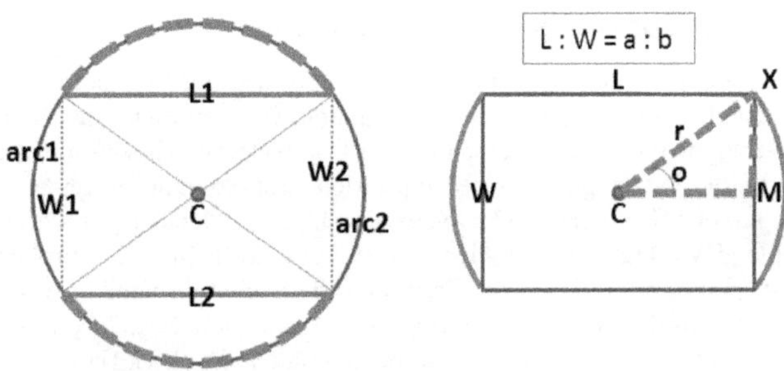

Figure 8.37: Athletics Track (from UVa 11646)

The snippet of the code is shown below.

```
double lo = 0.0, hi = 400.0, L, W;                // the range of answer
for (int i = 0; i < 40; ++i) {
  L = (lo+hi) / 2.0;                              // bisection method on L
  W = (double)b/a*L;                              // derive W from L and a:b
  double expected_arc = (400 - 2.0*L) / 2.0;      // reference value
  double CM = 0.5*L, MX = 0.5*W;                  // Apply Trigonometry here
  double r = sqrt(CM*CM + MX*MX);
  double angle = 2.0 * atan(MX/CM) * 180.0/M_PI;
  double this_arc = angle/360.0 * M_PI * (2.0*r);
  (this_arc > expected_arc) ? hi = L : lo = L;
}
printf("Case %d: %.12lf %.12lf\n", ++caseNo, L, W);
```

Source code: `ch8/UVa11646.cpp|java|py`

Exercise 8.7.1.1*: Prove that other strategies will not be better than the greedy strategy mentioned for the UVa 00714 solution above?

Exercise 8.7.1.2*: Derive the analytical solution for UVa 11646 instead of using this binary search the answer technique.

8.7.2 Two Components: Involving Efficient Data Structure

This problem combination usually appear in some 'standard' problems but with *large* input constraint such that we have to use a more efficient data structure to avoid TLE. The efficient data structures are usually the very versatile balanced BSTs (set/map), the fast Hash Tables, Priority Queues, UFDS, or Fenwick/Segment Tree.

For example, UVa 11967-Hic-Hac-Hoe is an extension of a board game Tic-Tac-Toe. Instead of the small 3×3 board, this time the board size is 'infinite'. Thus, there is no way we can record the board using a 2D array. Fortunately, we can store the coordinates of the 'noughts' and 'crosses' in a balanced BST and refer to this BST to check the game state.

8.7.3 Two Components: Involving Geometry

Many (computational) geometry problems can be solved using Complete Search (although some require Divide and Conquer, Greedy, Dynamic Programming, or other techniques). When the given input constraints allow for such Complete Search solution, do not hesitate to go for it. In the list of problem decomposition programming exercises, we have split problems that are of "Geometry + Complete Search" and "Geometry + Others".

For example, UVa 11227 - The silver bullet boils down into this problem: Given N ($1 \leq N \leq 100$) points on a 2D plane, determine the maximum number of points that are collinear. We can afford to use the following $O(N^3)$ Complete Search solution as $N \leq 100$ (there is a better solution). For each pair of point i and j, we check the other N-2 points if they are collinear with line $i - j$. This solution can be written with three nested loops and the `bool collinear(point p, point q, point r)` function shown in Section 7.2.2.

Exercise 8.7.3.1*: Design an $O(N^2 \log N)$ solution for this UVa 11227 problem that allows us to solve this problem even if the N is raised up to 2000.

8.7.4 Two Components: Involving Graph

This type of problem combinations can be spotted as follows: one clear component is a graph algorithm. However, we need another supporting algorithm, which is usually some sort of mathematics or geometric rule (to build the underlying graph) or even another supporting graph algorithm. In this subsection, we illustrate one such example.

In Book 1, we have mentioned that for some problems, the underlying graph does not need to be stored in any graph specific data structures (implicit graph). This is possible if we can derive the edges of the graph easily or via some rules. UVa 11730 - Number Transformation is one such problem.

While the problem description is all mathematics, the main problem is actually a Single-Source Shortest Paths (SSSP) problem on unweighted graph solvable with BFS. The underlying graph is generated on the fly during the execution of the BFS. The source is the number S. Then, every time BFS processes a vertex u, it enqueues unvisited vertex $u + x$ where x is a prime factor of u that is not 1 or u itself. The BFS layer count when target vertex T is reached is the minimum number of transformations needed to transform S into T according to the problem rules.

8.7.5 Two Components: Involving Mathematics

In this problem combination, one of the components is clearly a mathematics problem, but it is not the only one. It is usually not graph as otherwise it will be classified in the previous subsection. The other component is usually recursive backtracking or binary search. It is also possible to have two different mathematics algorithms in the same problem. In this subsection, we illustrate one such example.

UVa 10637 - Coprimes is the problem of partitioning S ($0 < S \leq 100$) into t ($0 < t \leq 30$) co-prime numbers. For example, for $S = 8$ and $t = 3$, we can have $1 + 1 + 6$, $1 + 2 + 5$, or $1 + 3 + 4$. After reading the problem description, we will have a strong feeling that this is a mathematics (number theory) problem. However, we will need more than just Sieve of Eratosthenes algorithm to generate the primes and GCD algorithm to check if two numbers are co-prime, but also a recursive backtracking routine to generate all possible partitions (in fact, partitioning problem in general is NP-complete).

8.7.6 Two Components: Graph Preprocessing and DP

In this subsection, we want to highlight a problem where graph pre-processing is one of the components as the problem clearly involves some graphs and DP is the other component. We show this combination with two examples.

SSSP/APSP plus DP TSP

We use UVa 10937 - Blackbeard the Pirate to illustrate this combination of SSSP/APSP plus DP TSP. The SSSP/APSP is usually used to transform the input (usually an implicit graph/grid) into another (usually smaller) graph. Then we run Dynamic Programming solution for TSP on the second (usually smaller) graph.

The given input for this problem is shown on the left of the diagram below. This is a 'map' of an island. Blackbeard has just landed at this island and at position labeled with a '@'. He has stashed up to 10 treasures in this island. The treasures are labeled with exclamation marks '!'. There are angry natives labeled with '*'. Blackbeard has to stay away at least 1 square away from the angry natives in any of the eight directions. Blackbeard wants to grab all his treasures and go back to his ship. He can only walk on land '.' cells and not on water '~' cells nor on obstacle cells '#'.

```
    Input:            Index @ and !        The APSP Distance Matrix
 Implicit Graph     Enlarge * with X       A complete (small) graph
   ~~~~~~~~~~          ~~~~~~~~~~            -------------------
   ~~!!!###~~          ~~123###~~            | 0| 1| 2| 3| 4| 5|
   ~##...###~          ~##..X###~            -------------------
   ~#....*##~          ~#..XX*##~          |0| 0|11|10|11| 8| 8|
   ~#!..**~~~          ~#4.X**~~~          |1|11| 0| 1| 2| 5| 9|
   ~~....~~~~   ==>    ~~..XX~~~~   ==>    |2|10| 1| 0| 1| 4| 8|
   ~~~....~~~          ~~~....~~~          |3|11| 2| 1| 0| 5| 9|
   ~~..~..@~~          ~~..~..0~~          |4| 8| 5| 4| 5| 0| 6|
   ~#!.~~~~~~          ~#5.~~~~~~          |5| 8| 9| 8| 9| 6| 0|
   ~~~~~~~~~~          ~~~~~~~~~~          ---------------------
```

This is an NP-hard TSP optimization problem (see Book 1 and Section 8.6), but before we can use DP TSP solution, we have to transform the input into a distance matrix.

In this problem, we are only interested in the '@' and the '!'s. We give index 0 to '@' and give positive indices to the other '!'s. We enlarge the reach of each '*' by replacing the '.' around the '*' with an 'X'. Then we run BFS on this unweighted implicit graph starting from '@' and all the '!', by only stepping on cells labeled with '.' (land cells), '!' (other treasure), or '@' (Blackbeard's starting point). This gives us the All-Pairs Shortest Paths (APSP) distance matrix as shown in the diagram above.

Now, after having the APSP distance matrix, we can run DP TSP as shown in Book 1 to obtain the answer. In the test case shown above, the optimal TSP tour is: 0-5-4-1-2-3-0 with cost = 8+6+5+1+1+11 = 32.

SCC Contraction plus DP Algorithm on DAG

In some modern problems involving *directed* graph, we have to deal with the Strongly Connected Components (SCCs) of the directed graph (see Book 1). One of the variants is the problem that requires all SCCs of the given directed graph to be *contracted* first to form larger vertices (called as super vertices).

The original directed graph is not guaranteed to be acyclic, thus we cannot immediately apply DP techniques on such graph. But when the SCCs of a directed graph are contracted, the resulting graph of super vertices is a DAG. If you recall our discussion in Book 1, DAG is very suitable for DP techniques as it is acyclic. UVa 11324 - The Largest Clique[50] is one such problem. This problem in short, is about finding the longest path on the DAG of contracted SCCs. Each super vertex has weight that represents the number of original vertices that are contracted into that super vertex.

8.7.7 Two Components: Involving 1D Static RSQ/RMQ

This combination should be rather easy to spot. The problem involves *another* algorithm to populate the content of a *static* 1D array (that will not be changed anymore once it is populated) and then there will be *many* Range Sum/Minimum/Maximum Queries (RSQ/RMQ) on this static 1D array. Most of the time, these RSQs/RMQs are asked at the output phase of the problem. But sometimes, these RSQs/RMQs are used to speed up the internal mechanism of the other algorithm to solve the problem.

The solution for 1D Static RSQ with Dynamic Programming has been discussed in Book 1. For 1D Static RMQ, we have the Sparse Table Data Structure (which is a DP solution) that is discussed in Section 9.3. Without this RSQ/RMQ DP speedup, the other algorithm that is needed to solve the problem usually ends up receiving the TLE verdict.

As a simple example, consider a simple problem that asks how many primes there are in various query ranges $[a..b]$ $(2 \le a \le b \le 1\,000\,000)$. This problem clearly involves Prime Number generation (e.g., Sieve algorithm, see Section 5.3.1). But since this problem has $2 \le a \le b \le 1\,000\,000$, we will get TLE if we keep answering each query in $O(b - a + 1)$ time by iterating from a to b, especially if the problem author purposely set $b - a + 1$ to be near $1\,000\,000$ at (almost) every query. We need to speed up the output phase into $O(1)$ per query using 1D Static RSQ DP solution.

8.7.8 Three (or More) Components

In Section 8.7.1-8.7.7, we have seen various examples of problems involving two components. In this subsection, we show two examples of rare combinations of three (or more[51]) different algorithms and/or data structures.

Prime Factors, DP, Binary Search

Abridged problem description of UVa 10856 - Recover Factorial: Given N, the number of prime factors in $X!$, what is the minimum possible value of X? $(N \le 10\,000\,001)$. This problem can be decomposed it into several components.

First, we compute the number of prime factors of an integer i and store it in a table `NumPF[i]` with the following recurrence: if i is a prime, then `NumPF[i] = 1` prime factor; else if $i = PF \times i'$, then `NumPF[i] = 1` + the number of prime factors of i'. We compute this number of prime factors $\forall i \in$ `[1..2703665]`. The upper bound of this range is obtained by trial and error according to the limits given in the problem description.

Then, the second part of the solution is to *accumulate* the number of prime factors of $N!$ by setting `NumPF[i] += NumPF[i-1]`; $\forall i \in$ `[1..`N`]`. Thus, `NumPF[N]` contains the number of prime factors of $N!$. This is the DP solution for the 1D Static RSQ problem.

[50]The title of this UVa 11324 problem is a bit misleading for those who are aware with the theory of NP-completeness. This problem is **not** the NP-hard MAX-CLIQUE problem.

[51]It is actually very rare to have more than three components in a single programming contest problem.

Now, the third part of the solution should be obvious: we can do binary search to find the index X such that `NumPF[X] = N`. If there is no answer, we output "Not possible.".

Complete Search, Binary Search, Greedy

In this write up, we discuss an ICPC World Finals programming problem that combines *three* problem solving paradigms that we have learned in Chapter 3, namely: Complete Search, Divide & Conquer (Binary Search), and Greedy.

Abridged problem description of UVa 01079 - A Careful Approach (ICPC World Finals Stockholm09): You are given a scenario of airplane landings. There are $2 \leq n \leq 8$ airplanes in the scenario. Each airplane has a time window during which it can safely land. This time window is specified by two integers a_i and b_i, which give the beginning and end of a closed interval $[a_i..b_i]$ during which the i-th plane can land safely. The numbers a_i and b_i are specified in minutes and satisfy $0 \leq a_i \leq b_i \leq 1440$ (24 hours). In this problem, you can assume that the plane landing time is negligible. Your tasks are:

1. Compute an **order for landing all airplanes** that respects these time windows. HINT: order = (very small) permutation = Complete Search?
2. Furthermore, the airplane landings should be stretched out **as much as possible** so that the minimum achievable time gap between successive landings is as large as possible. For example, if three airplanes land at 10:00am, 10:05am, and 10:15am, then the smallest gap is five minutes, which occurs between the first two airplanes. Not all gaps have to be the same, but the smallest gap should be as large as possible. HINT: Is this similar to 'interval covering' problem (see Book 1)?
3. Print the answer split into minutes and seconds, rounded to the closest second.

See Figure 8.38 for illustration:
line = the safe landing time window of a plane.
star = the plane's optimal landing schedule.

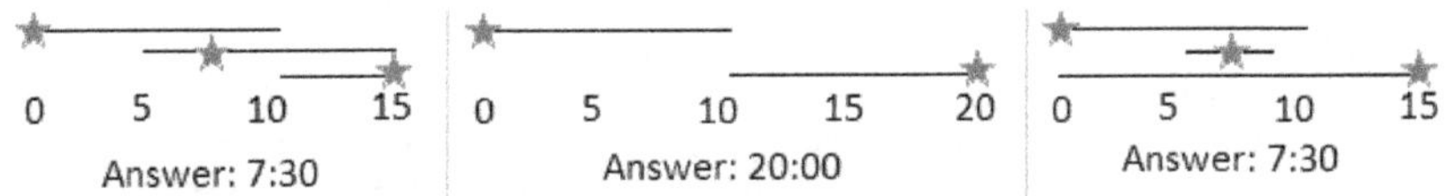

Figure 8.38: Illustration for ICPC WF2009 - A - A Careful Approach

Solution: Since the number of planes is at most 8, an optimal solution can be found by simply trying all 8! = 40 320 possible orders for the planes to land. This is the **Complete Search** component of the problem which can be easily implemented using `next_permutation` in C++ STL `algorithm`.

Now, for each specific landing order, we want to know the largest possible landing window. Suppose we guess that the answer is a certain window length L. We can greedily check whether this L is feasible by forcing the first plane to land as soon as possible and the subsequent planes to land in `max(a[that plane], previous landing time +` L`)`. This is the **Greedy** component.

A window length L that is too long/short will cause `lastLanding` (see the code) to overshoot/undershoot `b[last plane]`, so we have to decrease/increase L. We can Binary Search the Answer L. This is the **Divide and Conquer** component of this problem. As we only want the answer rounded to the nearest integer, stopping binary search when the error $\epsilon <$ 1e-3 is enough. For more details, please study our source code in the next page.

```
int n, order[8];
double a[8], b[8], L;

// with certain landing order and 'answer' L, greedily land those planes
double greedyLanding() {
  double lastLanding = a[order[0]];                 // greedy for 1st aircraft
  for (int i = 1; i < n; ++i) {                     // for the other aircrafts
    double targetLandingTime = lastLanding+L;
    if (targetLandingTime <= b[order[i]])
      // can land: greedily choose max of a[order[i]] or targetLandingTime
      lastLanding = max(a[order[i]], targetLandingTime);
    else
      return 1;
  } // return +ve/-ve value to force binary search to reduce/increase L
  return lastLanding - b[order[n-1]];
}

int main() {
  int caseNo = 0;
  while (scanf("%d", &n), n) {                      // 2 <= n <= 8
    for (int i = 0; i < n; ++i) {                   // plane i land at [ai,bi]
      scanf("%lf %lf", &a[i], &b[i]);
      a[i] *= 60; b[i] *= 60;                       // convert to seconds
      order[i] = i;
    }
    double maxL = -1.0;                             // the answer
    do {                                            // permute landing order
      double lo = 0, hi = 86400;                    // min 0s, max 86400s
      L = -1;
      for (int i = 0; i < 30; ++i) {                // BSTA (L)
        L = (lo+hi) / 2.0;
        double retVal = greedyLanding();            // see above
        (retVal <= 1e-2) ? lo = L : hi = L;         // increase/decrease L
      }
      maxL = max(maxL, L);                          // the max overall
    }
    while (next_permutation(order, order+n));       // try all permutations
    maxL = (int)(maxL+0.5);                        // round to nearest second
    printf("Case %d: %d:%0.2d\n", ++caseNo, (int)(maxL/60), (int)maxL%60);
  } // other way for rounding is to use printf format string: %.01f:%0.21f
  return 0;
}
```

Source code: ch8/UVa01079.cpp|java|ml

Exercise 8.7.8.1: The code uses 'double' data type for lo, hi, and L. This is unnecessary as all computations can be done in integers. Please rewrite this code!

Programming Exercises related to Problem Decomposition:

a. Two Components - BSTA and Other, Easier

1. Entry Level: **UVa 00714 - Copying Books** * (+greedy matching)
2. **UVa 10816 - Travel in Desert** * (+Dijkstra's)
3. **UVa 11262 - Weird Fence** * (+MCBM; similar with UVa 10804)
4. **UVa 12097 - Pie** * (+geometric formula)
5. *Kattis - arrivingontime* * (BSTA: the latest starting time; use Dijkstra's to compute whether we can still arrive at meeting point on time)
6. *Kattis - charlesincharge* * (BSTA: max edge that Charles can use; SSSP from 1 to N passing through edges that do not exceed that; is it OK?)
7. *Kattis - programmingtutors* * (+perfect MCBM)

Extra UVa: *10566*, *10606*, *10804*, *11646*, *12851*, *12853*, *12908*.

Extra Kattis: *expandingrods*, *fencebowling*, *forestforthetrees*, *gridgame*, *prettygoodcuberoot*, *rockclimbing*, *skijumping*.

Others: IOI 2009 - Mecho (+multi-sources BFS).

b. Two Components - BSTA and Other, Harder

1. Entry Level: *Kattis - wifi* * (+greedy; also available at UVa 11516 - WiFi)
2. **UVa 01221 - Against Mammoths** * (LA 3795 - Tehran06; +MCBM)
3. **UVa 10537 - The Toll, Revisited** * (+Dijkstra's on State-Space graph)
4. **UVa 10983 - Buy one, get ...** * (+max flow)
5. *Kattis - catandmice* * (BSTA: the initial velocity of Cartesian Cat; DP TSP to verify if the cat can catch all mice in the shortest possible time)
6. *Kattis - enemyterritory* * (MSSP from all enemy vertices; BSTA, run BFS from (xi, yi) to (xr, yr) avoiding vertices that are too close to any enemy)
7. *Kattis - gravamen* * (BSTA + max flow)

Extra UVa: *10372*, *11670*, *12255*, *12428*.

Extra Kattis: *arachnophobia*, *carpet*, *freighttrain*, *low*, *risk*.

c. Two Components - Involving Efficient Data Structure, Easier

1. Entry Level: *Kattis - undetected* * (brute force; simple geometry; UFDS)
2. **UVa 11960 - Divisor Game** * (modified Sieve, number of divisors; static Range Maximum Query, use Sparse Table data structure)
3. **UVa 12318 - Digital Roulette** * (brute force with `unordered_set`)
4. **UVa 12460 - Careful teacher** * (a simple BFS problem; use `set` of string data structure to speed up the check if a word is inside dictionary)
5. *Kattis - bing* * (map all prefixes to frequencies using Hash Table; or use Trie)
6. *Kattis - busnumbers2* * (complete search; use `unordered_map`)
7. *Kattis - selfsimilarstrings* * (complete search as the string is short; frequency counting; use `unordered_map`; repetition)

Extra UVa: *10789*, *11966*, *11967*, *13135*.

Extra Kattis: *gcds*, *reducedidnumbers*, *thesaurus*, *znanstvenik*.

d. Two Components - Involving Efficient Data Structure, Harder

1. Entry Level: *Kattis - dictionaryattack* * (time limit is generous; you can generate all possible password with just 3 swaps; store in sets)
2. **UVa 00843 - Crypt Kicker *** (backtracking; try mapping each letter to another letter in alphabet; use Trie for speed up)
3. **UVa 11474 - Dying Tree *** (UFDS; connect all tree branches; connect two reachable trees (use geometry); connect trees that can reach doctor)
4. **UVa 11525 - Permutation *** (use Fenwick Tree and binary search the answer to find the lowest index i that has $RSQ(1, i) = Si$)
5. *Kattis - doublets* * (s: (string); BFS; use trie to quickly identify neighbor that is one Hamming distance away; also available at UVa 10150 - Doublets)
6. *Kattis - magicallights* * (LA 7487 - Singapore15; flatten the tree with DFS; use Fenwick Tree for Range Odd Query; use long long)
7. *Kattis - sparklesseven* * (seven nested loops with fast DS)

Extra UVa: *00922, 10734*.

Extra Kattis: *chesstournament, circular, clockconstruction, dailydivision, downfall, kletva, lostisclosetolose, mario, numbersetseasy, numbersetshard, setstack*.

e. Two Components - Geometry and Complete Search

1. Entry Level: **UVa 11227 - The silver ...** * (brute force; `collinear` test)
2. **UVa 10012 - How Big Is It? *** (try all 8! permutations; Euclidean `dist`)
3. **UVa 10167 - Birthday Cake *** (brute force A and B; `ccw` tests)
4. **UVa 10823 - Of Circles and Squares *** (complete search; check if point inside circles/squares)
5. *Kattis - collidingtraffic* * (try all pairs of boats; 0.0 if one pair collide; or, use a quadratic equation; also available at UVa 11574 - Colliding Traffic)
6. *Kattis - cranes* * (circle-circle intersection; backtracking or brute force subsets with bitmask; also available at UVa 11515 - Cranes)
7. *Kattis - doggopher* * (complete search; Euclidean distance `dist`; also available at UVa 10310 - Dog and Gopher)

Extra UVa: *00142, 00184, 00201, 00270, 00356, 00638, 00688, 10301*.

Extra Kattis: *areyoulistening, beehives, splat, unlockpattern2, unusualdarts*.

f. Two Components - Geometry and Others

1. Entry Level: *Kattis - humancannonball* * (build the travel time graph with Euclidean distance computations; use Floyd-Warshall)
2. **UVa 10514 - River Crossing *** (use basic geometry to compute edge weights of the graph of islands and the two riverbanks; SSSP; Dijkstra's)
3. **UVa 11008 - Antimatter Ray Clear... *** (collinear test; DP bitmask)
4. **UVa 12322 - Handgun Shooting Sport *** (first, use `atan2` to convert angles to 1D intervals; then sort it and use a greedy scan to get the answer)
5. *Kattis - findinglines* * (randomly pick two points; there is a good chance that 20% or more points are on that line defined by those two points)
6. *Kattis - umbraldecoding* * (recursive subdivision; overlap check; umbra)
7. *Kattis - walkway* * (we can build the graph and compute area of trapezoid using simple geometry; SSSP on weighted graph; Dijkstra's)

Extra Kattis: *dejavu, galactic, particlecollision, subwayplanning, targetpractice, tram, urbandesign*.

g. Two Components - Involving Graph

1. Entry Level: **UVa 12159 - Gun Fight** * (LA 4407 - KualaLumpur08; use simple CCW tests (geometry) to build the bipartite graph; MCBM)
2. **UVa 00393 - The Doors *** (build the small visibility graph with line segment intersection checks; run Floyd-Warshall routine to get the answer)
3. **UVa 01092 - Tracking Bio-bots *** (LA 4787 - WorldFinals Harbin10; compress graph; traversal from exit with S/W direction; inclusion-exclusion)
4. **UVa 12797 - Letters *** (iterative subset; pick subset of UPPERCASE letters for this round; BFS to find the SSSP; pick the best)
5. *Kattis - crowdcontrol* * (maximin path problem; MST; DFS from train station to BAPC; block unused edges)
6. *Kattis - gears2* * (graph reachability test; cycle with equal ratio is actually OK; math fraction)
7. *Kattis - gridmst* * (Singapore15 preliminary; rectilinear MST problem; small 2D grid; multi-sources BFS to construct short edges; run Kruskal's)

Extra UVa: *00273, 00521, 01039, 01243, 01263, 10068, 10075, 11267, 11635, 11721, 11730, 12070.*

Extra Kattis: *artur, bicikli, borg, deadend, diplomacy, findpoly, godzilla, primepath, units, uniquedice, vuk, wordladder2.*

h. Two Components - Involving Mathematics

1. Entry Level: *Kattis - industrialspy* * (brute force recursive bitmask with prime check; also available at UVa 12218 - An Industrial Spy)
2. **UVa 01069 - Always an integer *** (LA 4119 - WorldFinals Banff08; string parsing, divisibility of polynomial, brute force, and modPow)
3. **UVa 10539 - Almost Prime Numbers *** (sieve; get 'almost primes' by listing the powers of each prime, sort them; binary search)
4. **UVa 11282 - Mixing Invitations *** (derangement and binomial coefficient; Big Integer)
5. *Kattis - emergency* * (the problem is posed as an SSSP problem on special graph; but turns out a simple formula solves the problem; Big Integer)
6. *Kattis - megainversions* * (a bit of combinatorics; use Fenwick Tree to compute smaller/larger numbers quickly)
7. *Kattis - ontrack* * (DFS on Tree; the input is a tree, we can try all possible junctions as the critical junction)

Extra UVa: *01195, 10325, 10419, 10427, 10637, 10717, 11099, 11415, 11428, 12802.*

Extra Kattis: *digitdivision, dunglish, thedealoftheday, unicycliccount.*

i. Two Components - Graph Preprocessing and DP

1. Entry Level: **UVa 10937 - Blackbeard the ...** * (BFS → APSP information for TSP; then DP or backtracking)
2. **UVa 00976 - Bridge Building** * (flood fill to separate North and South banks; compute the cost of installing a bridge at each column; DP)
3. **UVa 11324 - The Largest Clique** * (LONGEST-PATH on DAG; first, transform the graph into DAG of its SCCs; toposort)
4. **UVa 11331 - The Joys of Farming** * (bipartite graph checks; compute size of left/right sets per bipartite component; DP SUBSET-SUM)
5. *Kattis - globalwarming* * (the biggest clique has at most 22 vertices; matching in (small) general graph (component))
6. *Kattis - treasurediving* * (SSSP from source and all idol positions; TSP-like but there is a knapsack style parameter 'air_left'; use backtracking)
7. *Kattis - walkforest* * (counting paths in DAG; build the DAG; Dijkstra's from 'home'; also available at UVa 10917 - A Walk Through the Forest)

Extra UVa: *10944, 11284, 11405, 11643, 11813.*

Extra Kattis: *contestscheduling, dragonball1, ntnuorienteering, shopping, speedyescape.*

j. Two Components - Involving DP 1D RSQ/RMQ

1. Entry Level: **UVa 10533 - Digit Primes** * (sieve; check if a prime is a digit prime; DP 1D range sum)
2. **UVa 10891 - Game of Sum** * (Double DP; 1D RSQ plus another DP to evaluate decision tree; s: (i, j); try all splitting points; minimax)
3. **UVa 11032 - Function Overloading** * (observation: $sod(i)$ can be only from 1 to 63; use 1D Range Sum Query for $fun(a, b)$)
4. **UVa 11408 - Count DePrimes** * (need 1D Range Sum Query)
5. *Kattis - centsavings* * (1D RSQ DP for sum of prices from [i..j]; round up/down; s: (idx, d_left); t: try all positioning of the next divider)
6. *Kattis - dvoniz* * (involving 1D RSQ DP; binary search the answer)
7. *Kattis - program* * (somewhat like Sieve of Eratosthenes initially and 1D RSQ DP speedup at the end)

Extra UVa: *00967, 10200, 10871, 12028, 12904.*

Extra Kattis: *eko, hnumbers, ozljeda, sumandproduct, tiredterry.*

k. Three (or More) Components, Easier

1. Entry Level: *Kattis - gettingthrough* * (BSTA+graph connectivity; Union-Find; similar to UVa 00295)
2. **UVa 00295 - Fatman *** (BSTA x: if the person has diameter x, can he go from left to right? graph connectivity; similar with UVa 10876)
3. **UVa 01250 - Robot Challenge *** (LA 4607 - SoutheastUSA09; geometry; SSSP on DAG → DP; DP 1D range sum)
4. **UVa 10856 - Recover Factorial *** (compute number of prime factors of each integer in the desired range; use 1D RSQ DP; binary search)
5. *Kattis - beeproblem* * (transform bee grid into 2D grid; compute size of each CCs; sort; greedy)
6. *Kattis - researchproductivityindex* * (sort papers by decreasing probability; brute force k and greedily submit k best papers; DP probability; keep max)
7. *Kattis - shrine* * (a bit of geometry (chord length); BSTA + brute force first shrine + greedy sweep checks)

Extra UVa: *10876*, *11610*.

Extra Kattis: *cardhand*, *cpu*, *enviousexponents*, *equilibrium*, *glyphrecognition*, *gmo*, *highscore2*, *ljutnja*, *mobilization*, *pyro*, *wheels*.

l. Three (or More) Components, Harder

1. Entry Level: *Kattis - artwork* * (flood fill to count CCs; UFDS; try undoing the horizontal/vertical line stroke in reverse)
2. **UVa 00811 - The Fortified Forest *** (LA 5211 - WorldFinals Eindhoven99; get `CH` and `perimeter` of polygon; generate all subsets iteratively with bitmask)
3. **UVa 01040 - The Traveling Judges *** (LA 3271 - WorldFinals Shanghai05; try all subsets of 2^{20} cities; MST; complex output formatting)
4. **UVa 01079 - A Careful Approach *** (LA 4445 - WorldFinals Stockholm09; iterative complete search (permutation); BSTA + greedy)
5. *Kattis - carpool* * (Floyd-Warshall/APSP; iterative brute force subset and permutation; DP; also available at UVa 11288 - Carpool)
6. *Kattis - clockpictures* * (sort angles; compute 'string' of differences of adjacent angles (use modulo); min lexicographic rotation)
7. *Kattis - guessthenumbers* * (brute force permute up to 5!; recursive string parsing (simple BNF); also available at UVa 12392 - Guess the Numbers)

Extra UVa: *01093*.

Extra Kattis: *installingapps*, *pikemanhard*, *sprocketscience*, *tightlypacked*, *weather*.

8.8 Solution to Non-Starred Exercises

Exercise 8.2.2.1: State-Space Search is essentially an extension of the Single-Source *Shortest* Paths problem, which is a minimization problem. The longest path problem (maximization problem) is NP-hard (see Section 8.6) and usually we do not deal with such variant as the (minimization problem of) State-Space Search is already complex enough to begin with.

Exercise 8.3.1.1: The solution is similar with UVa 10911 solution as shown in Book 1. But in the "Maximum Cardinality Matching" problem, there is a possibility that a vertex is *not* matched. The DP with bitmask solution for a small general graph is shown below:

```
int MCM(int bitmask) {
  if (bitmask == (1<<N) - 1) return 0;            // no more matching
  int &ans = memo[bitmask];
  if (ans != -1) return ans;

  int p1, p2;
  for (p1 = 0; p1 < N; ++p1)                      // find a free vertex p1
    if (!(bitmask & (1<<p1)))
      break;

  // This is the key difference: we can skip free vertex p1
  ans = MCM(bitmask | (1<<p1));

  // Assume that the small graph is stored in an Adjacency Matrix AM
  for (p2 = 0; p2 < N; ++p2)                      // find p2 that is free
    if (AM[p1][p2] && (p2 != p1) && !(bitmask & (1<<p2)))
      ans = max(ans, 1 + MCM(bitmask | (1<<p1) | (1<<p2)));

  return ans;
}
```

Exercise 8.4.3.1: A. 150; B = 125; C = 60.

Exercise 8.4.5.1: We use ∞ for the capacity of the 'middle directed edges' between the left and the right sets of the Bipartite Graph for the overall correctness of this flow graph modeling on other similar assignment problems. If the capacities from the right set to sink t is *not* 1 as in UVa 00259, we will get wrong Max Flow value if we set the capacity of these 'middle directed edges' to 1.

Exercise 8.4.6.1: If we analyze using default time complexity of Edmonds-Karp/Dinic's, i.e., $O(VE^2)$ for Edmonds-Karp or $O(V^2E)$ for Dinic's, then we may fear TLE because $V = 30 \times 30 \times 2 = 1800$ (as we use vertex splitting) and $E = (1 + 4) \times V = 5 \times 900 = 4500$ (each v_{in} is connected to v_{out} and each v_{out} is connected to at most 4 other u_{in}). Even $O(V^2E)$ Dinic's algorithm requires up to $1800^2 \times 4500 = 1 \times 10^{10}$ operations.

However, we need to realize one more important insight. Edmonds-Karp/Dinic's are Ford-Fulkerson based algorithm, so it is also bounded by the dreaded $O(mf \times E)$ time complexity that we are afraid of initially. The flow graph of UVa 11380 will only have *very small* mf value because the mf value is the minimum of number of '*'/people (upper bounded by 50% * 900 = 450) and number of '#'/large wood (upper bounded by 900 if all cells are '#'s) multiplied by the highest possible value of P (so 900 * 10 = 9000). This $min(450, 9000) \times 4500$ is 'small' (only $2M$ operations).

The 'tighter' time complexity of Dinic's algorithm is $O(min(min(a, b) \times E, V^2 \times E))$ where a/b are the sum of edge capacities that go out from s/go in to t, respectively. Keep a lookout of these potentially 'low' values of a or b in your next network flow problem.

Exercise 8.6.2.1: A few special cases of SUBSET-SUM that have true polynomial solutions are listed below:

- 1-SUM: Find a subset of exactly 1 integer in an array A that sums/has value v.
  We can do $O(n)$ linear search if A is unsorted or $O(\log n)$ binary search if A is sorted.
- 2-SUM: Find a subset of exactly 2 integers in an array A that sums to value v.
  This is a classic 'target pair' problem that can be solved in $O(n)$ time after sorting A in $O(n \log n)$ time if A is not yet sorted.
- 3-SUM: Find a subset of exactly 3 integers in an array A that sums to value v.
  This is also a classic problem that can be solved in $O(n^2)$ (or better). One possible solution is to hash each integer of A into a hash table and then for every pair of indices i and j, we check whether the hash table contains the integer $v - (A[i] + A[j])$.
- 4-SUM: Find a subset of exactly 4 integers in an array A that sums to value v.
  This is also a classic problem that can be solved in $O(n^3)$ (or better). One possible solution is to sort A first in $O(n \log n)$ and then try all possible $A[i]$ where $i \in [0..n-3]$ and $A[j]$ where $j \in [i+1..n-2]$ and solve the target pair in $O(n)$.

Exercise 8.6.6.1: The MVC and MWVC of a graph with just isolated vertices is clearly 0. The MVC of a complete unweighted graph is just V-1; However, the MWVC of a complete weighted graph is the weight of all vertices - the weight of the heaviest vertex.

Exercise 8.6.6.2: If the graph contains multiple Connected Components (CCs), we can process each CC separately as they are independent.

Exercise 8.7.8.1: Please review Divide and Conquer section in Book 1 for the solution.

8.9 Chapter Notes

Mastering this chapter (and beyond, e.g., the rare topics in Chapter 9) is important for those who are aspiring to do (very) well in the actual programming contests.

In CP4, we have moved the Sections about Network Flow (Section 8.4) from Chapter 4 into this Chapter. We also have moved Graph Matching (Section 8.5) from Chapter 9 into this Chapter to consolidate various subtopics of this interesting graph problem.

Also in CP4, this Chapter 8 contains one additional important Section 8.6 about NP-hard/complete problems in programming contests. We will not be asked to solve the general case of those NP-hard/complete problems but rather the smaller instances or the special cases of those problems. Familiarity with this class of problems will help competitive programmers from wasting their time during precious contest time thinking of a polynomial solution (which likely does not exist unless $P = NP$) but rather write an efficient Complete Search solution or hunt for the (usually very subtle) special condition(s) in the problem description that may help simplify the problem so that a polynomial solution is still possible. We compile many smaller writeups that were previously scattered in various other sections in the earlier editions of this book into this section and then add a substantial more amount of exposition of this exciting topic.

The material about MIN-VERTEX-COVER, MIN-SET-COVER, and STEINER-TREE problems are originally from **A/P Seth Lewis Gilbert**, School of Computing, National University of Singapore. The material has since evolved from a more theoretical style into the current competitive programming style.

This is not the last chapter of this book. We still have one more Chapter 9 where we list down rare topics that rarely appear in programming contests, but may be of interest for enthusiastic problem solvers.

Statistics	1st	2nd	3rd	4th
Number of Pages	-	15	33	80 (+142%)
Written Exercises	-	3	13	9+24*=33 (+146%)
Programming Exercises	-	83	177	495 (+180%)

The breakdown of the number of programming exercises from each section[52] is shown below:

Section	Title	Appearance	% in Chapter	% in Book
8.2	More Advanced Search	79	≈ 16%	≈ 2.3%
8.3	**More Advanced DP**	80	≈ 22%	≈ 2.3%
8.4	Network Flow	43	≈ 10%	≈ 1.3%
8.5	Graph Matching	-	-	-
8.6	NP-hard/complete Problems	69	≈ 14%	≈ 2.0%
8.7	**Problem Decomposition**	224	≈ 45%	≈ 6.5%
	Total	495		≈ 14.3%

[52]Programming exercises for Section 8.5 are scattered throughout the book and are not compiled here.

Chapter 9

Rare Topics

Learning is a treasure that will follow its owner everywhere.
— **Chinese Proverb**

9.1 Overview and Motivation

In this chapter, we list down rare, 'exotic', and harder topics in Computer Science (CS) that may (but not always) appear in a typical programming contest. These data structures, algorithms, and problems are mostly one-off unlike the more general topics that have been discussed in Chapters 1-8. Some problems listed in this chapter even already have *alternative* solution(s) that have discussed in earlier chapters. Learning the topics in this chapter can be considered as not 'cost-efficient' because after so much efforts on learning a certain topic, it will likely *not* appear in a typical programming contest. But we believe that these rare topics will appeal those who love to expand their knowledge in CS. Who knows that the skills that you acquire by reading this chapter may be applicable elsewhere.

Skipping this chapter will not cause a major damage towards the preparation for an ICPC-style programming contest as the probability of appearance of any of these topics is low[1] anyway[2]. But when those rare topics do appear, contestants with a priori knowledge of those rare topics will have an advantage over others who do not have such knowledge. Some good contestants can probably derive the solution from basic concepts during contest time even if they have only seen the problem for the first time, but usually in a slower pace than those who already know the problem and especially its solution before.

For IOI, many of these rare topics are still outside the IOI syllabus [15]. Thus, IOI contestants can choose to defer learning the material in this chapter until they enroll in University. However, skimming through this chapter may be a good idea.

In this chapter, we keep the discussion for each topic as concise as possible, i.e., most discussions will be just around one, two, or three page(s). Most discussions do not contain sample code as readers who have mastered the content of Chapter 1-8 should not have too much difficulty in translating the algorithms given in this chapter into a working code. We only have a few starred written exercises (without hints/solutions) in this chapter.

As of 19 July 2020, this Chapter 9 contains 32 topics: 3 rare data structures, 14 rare algorithms, 14 rare problems, and 1 to-be-written. The topics are also listed according to their relationship with earlier Chapter 1-8 (see Table 9.1). If you are still unable to find a specific rare topic, it is either we do not write it in this book *yet* or we use different/alternative name for it (try using the indexing feature at the back of this book).

---

[1]None of the section in this Chapter 9 has more than 20 UVa+Kattis exercises.

[2]Some of these topics—also with low probability—are used as interview questions for IT companies.

Ch	Topic	Remarks	Sec
1	n/a	-	-
2	Sliding Window	Rare but useful technique	9.2
	Sparse Table	Simpler (static) RMQ solution	9.3
	Square Root Decomposition	Rare DS technique	9.4
	Heavy-Light Decomposition	Rare DS technique	9.5
3	Tower of Hanoi	Rare Ad Hoc problem	9.6
	Matrix Chain Multiplication	Classic but now rare DP	9.7
4	Lowest Common Ancestor	Tree-based problem	9.8
	Tree Isomorphism	Tree-based problem	9.9
	De Bruijn Sequence	Euler graph problem	9.10
5	Fast Fourier Transform	Rare polynomial algorithm	9.11
	Pollard's rho	Rare prime factoring algorithm	9.12
	Chinese Remainder Theorem	Rare math problem	9.13
	Lucas' Theorem	Rare C(n, k) % m technique	9.14
	Rare Formulas or Theorems	Extremely rare math formulas	9.15
	Combinatorial Game Theory	Emerging trend	9.16
	Gaussian Elimination	Rare Linear Algebra	9.17
6	n/a	-	-
7	Art Gallery Problem	Rare comp. geometry problem	9.18
	Closest Pair Problem	Classic D&C problem	9.19
8	A* and IDA*	Rare advanced search algorithm	9.20
	Pancake Sorting	Extremely rare state-search	9.21
	Egg Dropping Puzzle	Extremely rare DP	9.22
	Dynamic Programming Optimization	Rare and hard DP techniques	9.23
	Push-Relabel Algorithm	Alternative Max Flow algorithm	9.24
	Min Cost (Max) Flow	Rare w.r.t. normal Max Flow	9.25
	Hopcroft-Karp Algorithm	Simpler MCBM solution exists	9.26
	Kuhn-Munkres Algorithm	Rare weighted MCBM	9.27
	Edmonds' Matching Algorithm	Extremely rare MCM	9.28
	Chinese Postman Problem	Not NP-hard	9.29
9	Constructive Problem	Emerging problem type	9.30
	Interactive Problem	Emerging problem type	9.31
	Linear Programming	Rare problem type	9.32
	Gradient Descent	Extremely rare local search	9.33

Table 9.1: Topics Listed According to Their Relationship with Earlier Chapter 1-8

9.2 Sliding Window

Problem Description

There are several variants of Sliding Window problems. But all of them have similar basic idea: 'slide' a sub-array (that we call a 'window', which can have static or dynamic length, usually ≥ 2) in linear fashion from left to right over the original array of n elements in order to compute something. Some of the known variants are:

1. Find the smallest sub-array size (smallest window length) so that the sum of the sub-array is greater than or equal to a certain constant S in $O(n)$? Examples:
   For array $A_1 = \{5, 1, 3, \underline{5, 10}, 7, 4, 9, 2, 8\}$ and $S = 15$, the answer is 2 as highlighted.
   For array $A_2 = \{1, 2, \underline{3, 4, 5}\}$ and $S = 11$, the answer is 3 as highlighted.

2. Find the smallest sub-array size (smallest window length) so that the elements inside the sub-array contains all integers in range `[1..K]`. Examples:
   For array $A = \{1, \underline{2, 3, 7, 1, 12, 9, 11, 9, 6, 3, 7, 5, 4}, 5, 3, 1, 10, 3, 3\}$ and $K = 4$, the answer is 13 as highlighted.
   For the same array $A = \{\underline{1, 2, 3}, 7, 1, 12, 9, 11, 9, 6, 3, 7, 5, 4, 5, 3, 1, 10, 3, 3\}$ and $K = 3$, the answer is 3 as highlighted.

3. Find the maximum sum of a certain sub-array with (static) size K. Examples:
   For array $A_1 = \{10, \underline{50, 30, 20}, 5, 1\}$ and $K = 3$, the answer is 100 by summing the highlighted sub-array.
   For array $A_2 = \{49, 70, 48, \underline{61, 60}, 60\}$ and $K = 2$, the answer is 121 by summing the highlighted sub-array.

4. Find the minimum of *each* possible sub-arrays with (static) size K. Example:
   For array $A = \{0, 5, 5, 3, 10, 0, 4\}$, $n = 7$, and $K = 3$, there are $n - K + 1 = 7 - 3 + 1 = 5$ possible sub-arrays with size $K = 3$, i.e. $\{0, 5, 5\}$, $\{5, 5, 3\}$, $\{5, 3, 10\}$, $\{3, 10, 0\}$, and $\{10, 0, 4\}$. The minimum of each sub-array is 0, 3, 3, 0, 0, respectively.

Solution(s)

We ignore the discussion of naïve solutions for these Sliding Window variants and go straight to the $O(n)$ solutions to save space. The four solutions below run in $O(n)$ as what we do is to 'slide' a window over the original array of n elements—some with clever techniques.

For variant number 1, we maintain a window that keeps growing (append the current element to the back—the right side—of the window) and add the value of the current element to a running sum or keeps shrinking (remove the front—the left side—of the window) as long as the running sum is $\geq S$. We keep the smallest window length throughout the process and report the answer.

For variant number 2, we maintain a window that keeps growing if range `[1..K]` is not yet covered by the elements of the current window or keeps shrinking otherwise. We keep the smallest window length throughout the process and report the answer. The check whether range `[1..K]` is covered or not can be simplified using a kind of frequency counting. When all integers $\in$ `[1..K]` has non zero frequency, we said that range `[1..K]` is covered. Growing the window increases a frequency of a certain integer that may cause range `[1..K]` to be fully covered (it has no 'hole') whereas shrinking the window decreases a frequency of the removed integer and if the frequency of that integer drops to 0, the previously covered range `[1..K]` is now no longer covered (it has a 'hole').

For variant number 3, we insert the first K integers into the window, compute its sum, and declare the sum as the current maximum. Then we slide the window to the right by adding one element to the right side of the window and removing one element from the left side of the window—thereby maintaining window length to K. We add the sum by the value of the added element minus the value of the removed element and compare with the current maximum sum to see if this sum is the new maximum sum. We repeat this window-sliding process n-K times and report the maximum sum found.

Variant number 4 is quite challenging especially if n is large. To get $O(n)$ solution, we need to use a `deque` (double-ended queue) data structure to model the window. This is because `deque` supports efficient—$O(1)$—insertion and deletion from front and back of the queue (see Book 1). This time, we maintain that the window (that is, the `deque`) is sorted in ascending order, that is, the front most element of the `deque` has the minimum value. However, this changes the ordering of elements in the array. To keep track of whether an element is currently still inside the current window or not, we need to remember the index of each element too. The detailed actions are best explained with the C++ code below. This sorted window can shrink from both sides (back and front) and can grow from back, thus necessitating the usage of `deque`[3] data structure.

```
void SlidingWindow(int A[], int n, int K) {
  // ii---or pair<int, int>---represents the pair (A[i], i)
  deque<ii> window; // we maintain window to be sorted in ascending order
  for (int i = 0; i < n; ++i) {                        // this is O(n)
    while (!window.empty() && (window.back().first >= A[i]))
      window.pop_back();                               // keep window ordered

    window.push_back({A[i], i});

    // use the second field to see if this is part of the current window
    while (window.front().second <= i-K)               // lazy deletion
      window.pop_front();
    if (i+1 >= K)                                      // first window onwards
      printf("%d\n", window.front().first);            // answer for this window
  }
}
```

Programming exercises related to Sliding Window:

1. Entry Level: **UVa 01121 - Subsequence** * (LA 2678 - SouthEasternEurope06; sliding window variant)
2. **UVa 00261 - The Window Property** * (sliding window variant)
3. **UVa 11536 - Smallest Sub-Array** * (sliding window variant)
4. *Kattis - sound* * (sliding window variant 4; max and min)
5. *Kattis - subseqhard* * (interesting sliding window variant)

   Others: IOI 2011 - Hottest, IOI 2011 - Ricehub, IOI 2012 - Tourist Plan.

---

[3]Note that we do not actually need to use `deque` data structure for variant 1-3 above.

9.3 Sparse Table Data Structure

In Book 1, we have seen that the Segment Tree data structure can be used to solve the Range Minimum Query (RMQ) problem—the problem of finding the index that has the minimum element within a range `[i..j]` of the underlying array `A`. It takes $O(n)$ pre-processing time to build the Segment Tree, and once the Segment Tree is ready, each RMQ is just $O(\log n)$. With a Segment Tree, we can deal with the *dynamic version* of this RMQ problem, i.e., when the underlying array is updated, we usually only need $O(\log n)$ to update the corresponding Segment Tree structure.

However, some problems involving RMQ never change the underlying array `A` after the first query. This is called the *static* RMQ problem. Although Segment Tree can still be used to deal with the static RMQ problem, this static version has an alternative DP solution with $O(n \log n)$ pre-processing time and $O(1)$ per RMQ. Two notable examples are to answer the Longest Common Prefix (LCP) of a range of sorted suffixes (**Exercise 6.5.4.5*** in Section 6.5.4) and the Lowest Common Ancestor (LCA) problem in Section 9.8.

The key idea of the DP solution is to split `A` into sub arrays of length 2^j for each non-negative integer j such that $2^j \leq n$. We will keep an array `SpT` of size $\log n \times n$ where `SpT[i][j]` stores the index of the minimum value in the sub array starting at index `j` and having length 2^i. This array `SpT` will be sparse as not all of its cells have values (hence the name 'Sparse Table' [3]). We use an abbreviation `SpT` to differentiate this data structure from Segment Tree (`ST`).

To build up the `SpT` array, we use a technique similar to the one used in many Divide and Conquer algorithms such as merge sort. We know that in an array of length 1, the single element is the smallest one. This is our base/initialization case. To find out the index of the smallest element in an array of size 2^i, we can compare the values at the indices of the smallest elements in the relevant two distinct sub arrays of size 2^{i-1}, i.e., sub array $[j..(j+2^{i-1}-1)]$ and $[(j+2^{i-1})..(j+2^i-1)]$, and take the index of the smallest element of the two. It takes $O(n \log n)$ time to build up the `SpT` array like this. Please scrutinize the constructor of class `SparseTable` shown in the source code below that implements this `SpT` array construction.

```
            3                   8
            i                   j
            k = log2(j-i+1) = log2(8-3+1) = log2(6) = 2
            2^2 ≤ (8-3+1)

            2^2 = 4
                   2^4 = 4
            3      5   6        8
            i      l   k        j
```

Figure 9.1: Explanation of an Example `RMQ(i, j)`

It is simple to understand how we would process a query if the length of the range were a power of 2. Since this is exactly the information `SpT` stores, we would just return the corresponding entry in the array. However, in order to compute the result of a query with arbitrary start and end indices, we have to fetch the entry for two smaller sub arrays within this range and take the minimum of the two. Note that these two sub arrays might have to overlap, the point is that we want cover the entire range with two sub arrays and nothing outside of it. This is always possible even if the length of the sub arrays have to be a power of 2. First, we find the length of the query range, which is `j-i+1`. Then, we apply $\log_2$ on it and round down the result, i.e., `k` = $\lfloor$`log`$_2$`(j-i+1)`$\rfloor$. This way, $2^k \leq$ `(j-i+1)`. In Figure 9.1—top side, we have $i = 3$, $j = 8$, a span of $j - i + 1 = 8 - 3 + 1 = 6$ indices. We compute $k = 2$. Then, we compare the value of sub-ranges $[i..(i + 2^k - 1)]$ and $[(j - 2^k + 1)..j]$ and return the index of the smallest element of the two sub-ranges. In Figure 9.1—bottom side, we have the first range as $[3..k = (3 + 2^2 - 1)] = [3..k = 6]$ and the second range as $[l = (8 - 2^2 + 1)..8] = [l = 5..8]$. As there are some potentially overlapping sub-problems (it is range [5..6] in Figure 9.1—bottom side), this part of the solution is classified as DP.

An example implementation of Sparse Table to solve the static RMQ problem is shown below. You can compare this version with the Segment Tree version shown in Book 1. Note that the `RMQ(i, j)` function below returns the index of the RMQ (that can be converted to value) whereas the Segment Tree code with lazy update returns the value of the RMQ.

```
typedef vector<int> vi;

class SparseTable {                              // OOP style
private:
  vi A, P2, L2;
  vector<vi> SpT;                                // the Sparse Table
public:
  SparseTable() {}                               // default constructor

  SparseTable(vi &initialA) {                    // pre-processing routine
    A = initialA;
    int n = (int)A.size();
    int L2_n = (int)log2(n)+1;
    P2.assign(L2_n, 0);
    L2.assign(1<<L2_n, 0);
    for (int i = 0; i <= L2_n; ++i) {
      P2[i] = (1<<i);                            // to speed up 2^i
      L2[(1<<i)] = i;                            // to speed up log_2(i)
    }
    for (int i = 2; i < P2[L2_n]; ++i)
      if (L2[i] == 0)
        L2[i] = L2[i-1];                         // to fill in the blanks

    // the initialization phase
    SpT = vector<vi>(L2[n]+1, vi(n));
    for (int j = 0; j < n; ++j)
      SpT[0][j] = j;                             // RMQ of sub array [j..j]

    // the two nested loops below have overall time complexity = O(n log n)
    for (int i = 1; P2[i] <= n; ++i)             // for all i s.t. 2^i <= n
      for (int j = 0; j+P2[i]-1 < n; ++j) {      // for all valid j
        int x = SpT[i-1][j];                     // [j..j+2^(i-1)-1]
        int y = SpT[i-1][j+P2[i-1]];             // [j+2^(i-1)..j+2^i-1]
        SpT[i][j] = A[x] <= A[y] ? x : y;
      }
  }
```

```
  int RMQ(int i, int j) {
    int k = L2[j-i+1];                           // 2^k <= (j-i+1)
    int x = SpT[k][i];                           // covers [i..i+2^k-1]
    int y = SpT[k][j-P2[k]+1];                   // covers [j-2^k+1..j]
    return A[x] <= A[y] ? x : y;
  }
};
```

Source code: ch9/SparseTable.cpp|java|py|ml

For the same test case with $n = 7$ and $A = \{18, 17, 13, 19, 15, 11, 20\}$ as in Segment Tree section in Book 1, the content of the sparse table **SpT** is as follows:

A	18	17	13	19	15	11	20
index	0	1	2	3	4	5	6
$i = 2^0 = 1$	0	1	2	3	4	5	6
Covers	RMQ(0,0)	RMQ(1,1)	RMQ(2,2)	RMQ(3,3)	RMQ(4,4)	RMQ(5,5)	RMQ(6,6)
$i = 2^1 = 2$	1	2	2	4	5	5	-
Covers	RMQ(0,1)	RMQ(1,2)	RMQ(2,3)	RMQ(3,4)	RMQ(4,5)	RMQ(5,6)	-
$i = 2^2 = 4$	2	2	5	5	-	-	-
Covers	RMQ(0,3)	RMQ(1,4)	RMQ(2,5)	RMQ(3,6)	-	-	-

In the first row, we have $i = 2^0 = 1$ that denotes the RMQ of sub array starting at index j with length $2^0 = 1$ (j itself), we clearly have `SpT[i][j] = j`. This is the initialization phase/base case of the DP.

In the second row, we have $i = 2^1 = 2$ that denotes the RMQ of sub array starting at index j with length $2^1 = 2$. We derive the value by using DP by considering the previous (first) row. Notice that the last column is empty.

In the third row, we have $i = 2^2 = 4$ that denotes the RMQ of sub array starting at index j with length $2^2 = 4$. Again, we derive the value by using DP by considering the previous (second) row. Notice that the last three columns are empty.

When there are more rows, the latter rows will have lesser and lesser columns, hence this data structure is called "Sparse Table". We can optimize the space usage a bit to take advantage of its sparseness, but such space usage optimization is usually not critical for this data structure.

9.4 Square Root Decomposition

Square root (sqrt) decomposition is a technique to compute some operations on an array in $O(\sqrt{N})$ by partitioning the data or operations into $\sqrt{N}$ bins each of size $\sqrt{N}$.

Square Root Decomposition-based Data Structure

To illustrate this data structure, let us consider the following example problem: given an array of N integers (`A[]`), support Q queries of the following types:

1. **`update_value(X, K)`** – update the value of `A[X]` to be `K`.
2. **`gcd_range(L, R)`** – return the Greatest Common Divisor (GCD) of `A[L..R]`.

Naïvely, the first operation can be done in $O(1)$ while the second operation can be done in $O(N)$ by simply iterating through all the affected integers. However, if N and Q are large (e.g., $N, Q \leq 200\,000$), then this naïve approach will get TLE and we might need a data structure such as Segment Tree which can perform both operations in $O(\log N)$ each.

Segment Tree is essentially a binary tree where the leaf vertices are the original array and the internal vertices are the "segment" vertices. For example, two leaf vertices `a` and `b` are connected to the same parent vertex `c` implies that vertex `c` represents a segment containing both `a` and `b`. Segment Tree is built recursively with $\log N$ depth and each internal vertex has 2 direct children (see Book 1).

Now, instead of a binary tree with $\log N$ depth where each internal vertex has 2 direct children, we can build a seemingly "less powerful" yet simpler tree data structure similar to Segment Tree but with only 2 levels where each internal vertex has $\sqrt{N}$ direct children.

The total space required for this data structure is $N + \sqrt{N}$ as there are N leaf vertices (the original array) and $\sqrt{N}$ internal vertices. On the other hand, both types of a query now have an $O(\sqrt{N})$ time-complexity[4]. This data structure looks no better in terms of efficiency than its counterpart, Segment Tree, which is able to perform both types of a query in $O(\log N)$. However, the fact that the tree depth is only 2 makes the implementation of this data structure to be trivial as there is no need to build the tree explicitly.

The following code is an implementation of the `update_value()` operation with the sqrt decomposition technique. Array `A`/`B` represents the leaf/internal vertices, respectively. Each internal vertex stores the GCD value of all its children. Note that this implementation uses $2N$ space (instead of $N+\sqrt{N}$ space) as array `B` uses the same index as array `A` causing many elements in `B` to be unused (there are only $\sqrt{N}$ elements in `B` which will be used); however, space usage is usually our least concern when we use this approach.

```
int sqrt_n = sqrt(N)+1;
int A[maxn] = {0};
int B[maxn] = {0};

void update_internal(int X) {
  int idx = X / sqrt_n * sqrt_n;                // idx of internal vertex
  B[idx] = A[idx];                              // copy first
  for (int i = idx; i < idx+sqrt_n; ++i)        // O(sqrt(n)) iteration
    B[idx] = gcd(B[idx], A[i]);                 // gcd A[idx..idx+sqrt(n))
}
```

[4]The time-complexity analysis of this data structure is very similar to the analysis of Segment Tree.

```
void update_value(int X, ll K) {
  A[X] = K;                                    // O(1)
  update_internal(X);                          // plus O(sqrt(n))
}
```

Now, the following is an implementation of the `gcd_range()` operation.

```
int gcd_range(int L, int R) {
  int ans = 0;                                 // gcd(0, any) = any
  for (int i = L; i <= R; ) {                  // O(sqrt(n)) overall
    if ((i%sqrt_n == 0) && (i+sqrt_n-1 <= R))  // idx of internal vertex
      ans = gcd(res, B[i]), i += sqrt_n;       // skip sqrt(n) indices
    else
      ans = gcd(res, A[i]), ++i;               // process one by one
  }
  return res;
}
```

Observe that with this technique, both operations are in $O(\sqrt{N})$ time complexity.

While this problem is fairly easy (it can also be solved with Segment Tree, albeit with longer implementation), there are problems which are much easier to be solved with the sqrt decomposition technique. Consider the next example problem.

Kattis - modulodatastructures

Kattis - modulodatastructures is simple to explain: given an array, `Arr[1..N]` that contains all zeroes initially ($N \leq 200\,000$), support Q queries of the following types:

1. Increase all `Arr[k]` by `C` for all `k` $\equiv$ `A (mod B)`,
2. Output `Arr[D]` for a given `D`.

Implementing the solution verbatim (do queries of type 1 in $O(N)$ and do queries of type 2 in $O(1)$) is TLE as it can be made to run in $O(Q \times N)$ by having many type 1 queries with occasional type 2 queries to update the values.

However, if one knows the square root decomposition technique, this problem becomes easy. We decompose the array `Arr` into $\sqrt{N} \times \sqrt{N}$ buckets. For the largest $N = 200\,000$, $\sqrt{200\,000}$ is just 447 (note that N does not have to be necessarily a perfect square number). Now for each query of type 1, we perform either one of these two updates:

1. If $B \leq \sqrt{N}$, we just update one cell: `bucket[B][A] += C` in $O(1)$.
2. Otherwise if $B > \sqrt{N}$, we do `Arr[j] += C` for each $j \in [A, A+B, A+2B, ...]$ and stop when $j > N$ (as $B > \sqrt{N}$, this loop will be just $O(N/\sqrt{N}) = O(\sqrt{N})$, which is a major improvement compared to the verbatim implementation above).

Now, we can answer each query of type 2 also in $O(\sqrt{N})$ time by combining values from `Arr[D]` (this is $O(1)$) and sum of `bucket[B][D%B]` for each $B \in [1..\sqrt{N}]$ (this is $O(\sqrt{N})$). We will get the correct answer again and have a fast enough solution.

Offline Queries Processing (Reordering Technique)

Supposed there are Q segment queries on a one-dimensional array `A[]` which can be performed *offline*[5], then there is a technique using the square root decomposition to reduce the time-complexity of processing all the queries.

Let's consider an example problem: given an array `A[]` of N integers, support Q queries of (`L`, `R`)—the number of distinct integers in `A[L..R]`.

A naïve approach would be simply iterating through all affected indexes for each query and count the number of distinct integers (e.g., with C++ `set`). This method has an $\Omega(N)$ time-complexity per query, thus, the total time-complexity to process all queries is $\Omega(QN)$. Note that the Big-Ω notation is used here to abstract the data structure being used, e.g., C++ `set` insertion and query-related operations are $O(\log N)$ causing the total time-complexity to be $O(QN \log N)$ but it is not the main subject to be discussed as we can use any data structure we want with this technique.

Now, let us consider an alternative approach. Instead of doing each query independently, we can perform a query using the previous query's result by doing an "update" operation. Suppose the latest query we performed is for segment `A[4..17]`, and the next query we want to perform is for segment `A[2..16]`. Then, we can obtain the answer for segment `A[2..16]` by exploiting the result of segment `A[4..17]`, e.g., `A[4..17] + A[3] + A[2] - A[17]`. Note that this `+` and `-` operations are not a conventional addition and subtraction but a set addition and subtraction. In this example problem, we can achieve this set addition operation with, for example, C++ `map` container. For `+` operation, simply perform `++m[A[x]]`. On the other hand, for `-` operation, we need to perform `--m[A[x]]` and check whether the `m[A[x]]` becomes 0 after the operation; if yes, then delete the key, i.e., `m.erase(A[x])`. Then, for the query result, we simply return `(int)m.size()`. This method looks promising, however, the time-complexity to process all queries is still $\Omega(QN)$.

Now we are ready for the technique. Consider the approach in the previous paragraph but instead of performing the queries in the given order, perform the queries in the following order: decompose array `A[]` into $\sqrt{N}$ subarray (buckets) each with the size of $\sqrt{N}$. Then, sort all queries in non-descending order by the **bucket** in which the left part of the segment (`L`) falls into; in case of a tie, sort in non-descending order by the right part of the segment (`R`). If we perform the previous approach with this queries order, then the time-complexity becomes $\Omega((Q + N)\sqrt{N})$ to process **all** queries—to be explained later.

For example, let $N = 16$ (from `0` to `15`), and the $Q = 5$ queries are:

$$(5, 12), (2, 9), (3, 7), (14, 15), (6, 15)$$

The bucket size $s = \sqrt{16} = 4$, thus, the bucket ranges are: [0..3], [4..7], [8..11], and [12..15].

- Segment $(\underline{3}, 7)$ and $(\underline{2}, 9)$ fall into the 1st bucket, i.e. [0..3],
- Segment $(\underline{5}, 12)$ and $(\underline{6}, 15)$ fall into the 2nd bucket, i.e. [4..7], and
- Segment $(\underline{14}, 15)$ falls into the 4th bucket, i.e. [12..15].

Therefore, the sorted queries are:

$$(3, 7), (2, 9), (5, 12), (6, 15), (14, 15)$$

[5]Offline query implies that the query can be processed **not** in the order of appearance, thus, we can reorder the queries and it will not affect the output of each query. Contrast it with *online* query where the query should be performed in the given order, otherwise, the result would not be correct, e.g., see the interactive problems in Section 9.31.

The following code implements the reordering technique.

```
struct tquery { int idx, L, R; };
struct toutput { int idx, value; };

vi answerAllQueries(vi A, vector<tquery> query) {
  int L = 0;
  int R = -1;
  map<int, int> m;
  vector<toutput> out;
  sort(query.begin(),query.end());
  for (tquery q : query) {
    while (L > q.L) {
      --L;
      ++m[A[L]];
    }
    while (R < q.R) {
      ++R;
      ++m[A[R]];
    }
    while (L < q.L) {
      if (--m[A[L]] == 0) m.erase(A[L]);
      ++L;
    }
    while (R > q.R) {
      if (--m[A[R]] == 0) m.erase(A[R]);
      --R;
    }
    out.push_back((toutput){q.idx, (int)m.size()});
  }
  sort(out.begin(),out.end());
  vi ans;
  for (toutput t : out)
    ans.push_back(t.value);
  return ans;
}
```

The sorting rules are given in the following code.

```
int s = sqrt(N)+1;

bool operator < (const tquery &a, const tquery &b) {
  if ((a.L/s) != (b.L/s)) return a.L < b.L;
  return a.R < b.R;
}

bool operator < (const toutput &a, const toutput &b) {
  return a.idx < b.idx;
}
```

The overall time-complexity for this method is $\Omega(Q \log Q + (Q+N)\sqrt{N})$.

Why the Time-Complexity Becomes $\Omega(Q \log Q + (Q+N)\sqrt{N})$?

The time-complexity analysis has two components, i.e., $\Omega(Q \log Q)$ and $\Omega((Q+N)\sqrt{N})$. The first part comes from sorting all the queries, while the second part comes from processing all the queries. Observe that there are two types of query processing:

1. Processing a query with the same bucket as the previous query. In this type of query, the left part of the segment (`L`) may move around but it will not go outside the bucket's range (note: same bucket as the previous query), which has the size of $\sqrt{N}$, thus, the time-complexity to process Q such queries is $\Omega(Q\sqrt{N})$. On the other hand, the right part of the segment (`R`) can only go to the right direction as the queries are sorted in non-decreasing order of `R` when they are in the same bucket, thus, the time-complexity to process Q such queries is $\Omega(Q+N)$. Therefore, the time-complexity to process this type of queries is $\Omega(Q\sqrt{N}+Q+N)$ or simply $\Omega(Q\sqrt{N}+N)$.
2. Processing a query with a different bucket than the previous query. In this type of query, both `L` and `R` may move around the array in $O(N)$. However, there can be only $O(\sqrt{N})$ of this type of query (changing bucket) as there are only $\sqrt{N}$ buckets (recall that we process all queries from the same bucket first before moving to the next bucket causing the number of changing bucket queries to be only at most the number of available buckets). Therefore, the time-complexity to process this type of queries is $\Omega(N\sqrt{N})$.

With both types of a query being considered, the total time-complexity to process all queries after being sorted is $\Omega(Q\sqrt{N}+N+N\sqrt{N})$ or simply $\Omega((Q+N)\sqrt{N})$.

Programming exercises related to Square Root Decomposition[6]:

1. *Kattis - cardboardcontainer* * (two out of L, W, and H must be $\leq \sqrt{V}$; brute force L and W in $\sqrt{V} \times \sqrt{V}$ and test if V is divisible by $(L * W)$)
2. *Kattis - modulodatastructures* * (basic problem that can be solved with Square Root Decomposition technique)

---

[6]This sqrt decomposition technique does not appear frequently in competitive programming, but look out for (data structure) problems that are amenable to such technique.

9.5 Heavy-Light Decomposition

Heavy-Light Decomposition (HLD) is a technique to decompose a tree into a set of disjoint paths. This technique is particularly useful to deal with problems which require us to do some path-queries in a tree which seemingly complicated but easy enough to be solved for a line-graph. The idea is to decompose the tree into several **paths** (line-graph) of disjoint vertices. Then, each path-query in the original tree might be able to be answered by queries in one or more of those paths.

Randomly decomposing a tree (removing random edges) is not good enough as there can be a path-query which involves $O(N)$ paths, i.e., no better than a Complete Search solution. We need to decompose the tree such that any query involves only a few amount of paths. The Heavy-Light Decomposition achieves this perfectly. It guarantees that any query in the original tree only involves $O(\log N)$ paths.

HLD can be done constructively on a rooted tree. For unrooted tree, simply choose one arbitrary vertex as the root. Let $size(u)$ be the size of the subtree rooted at vertex u including vertex u itself.

An edge (a, b) is **heavy** if and only if $size(b) \geq size(a)/2$; otherwise, it is **light**.

Then, remove all light-edges from the tree such that only heavy-edges remain. Observe that vertices which are connected by heavy-edges form paths because each vertex can only have at most one heavy-edge to its children. We will call such paths as **heavy-paths**.

Consider the following example (Figure 9.2) of tree with 19 vertices with vertex a as the root. In this example, there are 8 light-edges and a total of 10 heavy-edges.

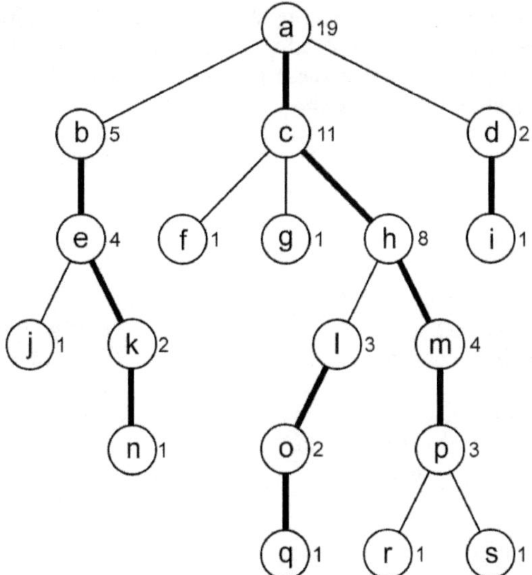

Figure 9.2: HLD of a Rooted Tree. The number next to each vertex is the size of the subtree rooted at that vertex. The **heavy** edges are thicker than the **light** edges.

Figure 9.3 shows the decomposed heavy-paths.

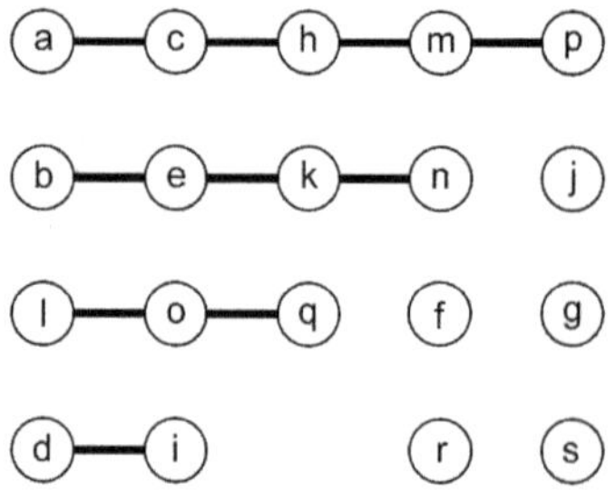

Figure 9.3: Heavy-Paths of the Tree in Figure 9.2

With these heavy-paths, any query in the original tree involves only $O(\log N)$ heavy-paths. For example, a path-query from vertex k to vertex m involves 2 heavy-paths: (b, e, k, n) and (a, c, h, m, p). A path-query from vertex j to vertex g involves 4 heavy-paths: (j), (b, e, k, n), (a, c, h, m, p), and (g).

HLD creates such a nice property because a light-edge (a, b) implies that the size of b's subtree is less than half of the size of a's subtree, thus, a path-query which pass through a light-edge will decrease the number of vertices by more than half. Therefore, any path-query in the original tree will pass through at most $\log N$ light-edges.

Implementation

To make the implementation easier, we can slightly change the definition of a heavy-edge into an edge to a child with the largest subtree. This new definition of heavy-edge has the same property as the original one but easier to implement as it allows us to determine the heavy-edge while counting the subtree size.

```
vector<vi> AL;                                 // undirected tree
vi par, heavy;

int heavy_light(int x) {                       // DFS traversal on tree
  int size = 1;
  int max_child_size = 0;
  for (auto &y : AL[x]) {                      // edge x->y
    if (y == par[x]) continue;                 // avoid cycle in a tree
    par[y] = x;
    int child_size = heavy_light(y);           // recurse
    if (child_size > max_child_size) {
      max_child_size = child_size;
      heavy[x] = y;                            // y is x's heaviest child
    }
    size += child_size;
  }
  return size;
}
```

The following code decompose the vertices into their own groups of heavy-paths.

```
vi group;

void decompose(int x, int p) {
  group[x] = p;                          // x is in group p
  for (auto &y : AL[x]) {                // edge x->y
    if (y == par[x]) continue;           // avoid cycle in a tree
    if (y == heavy[x])
      decompose(y, p);                   // y is in group p
    else
      decompose(y, y);                   // y is in a new group y
  }
}
```

You can review the sample code to understand more about this Heavy-Light Decomposition.

Source code: `ch9/HLD.cpp|java|py|ml`

Example: Query Update/Sum on a Path on a Tree

Given a rooted tree of N vertices (with initial value of 0) and Q queries of two types:

1. `add a b k` — add the value of each vertex in the path from vertex a to vertex b by k.
2. `sum a b` — return the sum of all vertices in the path from vertex a to vertex b.

If the graph is a line-graph, then this problem can be solved easily with a data structure such as Fenwick/Binary Indexed Tree (BIT) or Segment Tree. However, since it is a tree, then plain Fenwick or Segment Tree cannot be used.

First, we decompose the tree into several paths of disjoint vertices with the Heavy-Light Decomposition technique discussed earlier. Then, we construct a data structure like Fenwick or Segment Tree for each heavy-path. For each query (a, b) (either an add or a sum query), we break it into (a, x) and (x, b) where x is the *Lowest Common Ancestor* (LCA, see Section 9.8) of vertex a and vertex b, thus vertex a and vertex x have an descendant-ancestor relation (likewise, vertex x and vertex b). Solve for (a, x) by doing the query on all heavy-paths from vertex a to vertex x. To find the heavy-paths, we simply jump from a vertex to the head of its heavy-path (with `group[]`), and then pass through a light edge (with `par[]`), and jump to the head of the next heavy path, and so on. Similarly, solve for (x, b). The time-complexity to do a query on a heavy-path with a proper data structure is $O(\log N)$, as there are at most $O(\log N)$ heavy-paths involved in a query, thus, the total time-complexity is $O(\log^2 N)$.

Programming exercises related to Heavy-Light Decomposition:

1. Entry Level: **LA 5061 - Lightning Energy Report** * (HLD + Segment Tree)

9.6 Tower of Hanoi

Problem Description

The classic description of the problem is as follows: There are three pegs: A, B, and C, as well as n discs, will all discs having different sizes. Starting with all the discs stacked in ascending order on one peg (peg A), your task is to move all n discs to another peg (peg C). No disc may be placed on top of a disc smaller than itself, and only one disc can be moved at a time, from the top of one peg to another.

Solution(s)

There exists a simple recursive backtracking solution for the classic Tower of Hanoi problem. The problem of moving n discs from peg A to peg C with additional peg B as intermediate peg can be broken up into the following sub-problems:

1. Move $n - 1$ discs from peg A to peg B using peg C as the intermediate peg.
   After this recursive step is done, we are left with disc n by itself in peg A.
2. Move disc n from peg A to peg C.
3. Move $n - 1$ discs from peg B to peg C using peg A as the intermediate peg.
   These $n - 1$ discs will be on top of disc n which is now at the bottom of peg C.

Note that step 1 and step 3 above are recursive steps. The base case is when $n = 1$ where we simply move a single disc from the current source peg to its destination peg, bypassing the intermediate peg. A sample C++ implementation code is shown below:

```
void solve(int count, char source, char destination, char intermediate) {
  if (count == 1)
    printf("Move top disc from pole %c to pole %c\n", source, destination);
  else {
    solve(count-1, source, intermediate, destination);
    solve(1, source, destination, intermediate);
    solve(count-1, intermediate, destination, source);
  }
}

int main() {
  solve(3, 'A', 'C', 'B');                          // first parameter <= 26
} // return 0;
```

The minimum number of moves required to solve a classic Tower of Hanoi puzzle of n discs using this recursive backtracking solution is $2^n - 1$ moves, hence it cannot be used to solve large instances (e.g., $2^{27} > 10^8$ operations in one second).

Programming exercises related to Tower of Hanoi:

1. Entry Level: **UVa 10017 - The Never Ending ...** * (classical problem)
2. **UVa 00254 - Towers of Hanoi** * (define a recursive formula)
3. **UVa 10254 - The Priest Mathematician** * (find pattern; Java BigInteger)

9.7 Matrix Chain Multiplication

Problem Description

Given n matrices: A_1, A_2, ..., A_n, each A_i has size $P_{i-1} \times P_i$, output a complete parenthesized product $A_1 \times A_2 \times \ldots \times A_n$ that minimizes the number of scalar multiplications. A product of matrices is called completely parenthesized if it is either:

1. A single matrix
2. The product of 2 completely parenthesized products surrounded by parentheses

Example: We are given the size of 3 matrices as an array $P = \{10, 100, 5, 50\}$ which implies that matrix A_1 has size 10×100, matrix A_2 has size 100×5, and matrix A_3 has size 5×50. We can completely parenthesize these three matrices in two ways:

1. $(A_1 \times (A_2 \times A_3)) = 100 \times 5 \times 50 + 10 \times 100 \times 50 = 75\,000$ scalar multiplications
2. $((A_1 \times A_2) \times A_3) = 10 \times 100 \times 5 + 10 \times 5 \times 50 = 7\,500$ scalar multiplications

From the example above, we can see that the cost of multiplying these 3 matrices—in terms of the number of scalar multiplications—depends on the choice of the complete parenthesization of the matrices. However, exhaustively checking all possible complete parenthesizations is too slow as there are a huge number of such possibilities (for interested readers, there are $Cat(n\text{-}1)$ complete parenthesization of n matrices—see Section 5.4.3).

Matrix Multiplication

We can multiply two matrices a of size $p \times q$ and b of size $q \times r$ if the number of columns of a is the same as the number of rows of b (the inner dimensions agree). The result of this multiplication is a matrix c of size $p \times r$. The cost of this valid matrix multiplication is $p \times q \times r$ multiplications and can be implemented with a short C++ code as follows (note that this code is an extension of square matrix multiplication discussed in Section 5.8.3):

```
const int MAX_N = 10;                                // inc/decrease as needed

struct Matrix {
  int mat[MAX_N][MAX_N];
};

Matrix matMul(Matrix a, Matrix b, int p, int q, int r) { // O(pqr)
  Matrix c;
  for (int i = 0; i < p; ++i)
    for (int j = 0; j < r; ++j) {
      c.mat[i][j] = 0;
      for (int k = 0; k < q; ++k)
        c.mat[i][j] += a.mat[i][k] + b.mat[k][j];
    }
  return c;
}
```

For example, if we have the 2×3 matrix a and the 3×1 matrix b below, we need $2 \times 3 \times 1 = 6$ scalar multiplications.

$$\begin{bmatrix} a_{1,1} & a_{1,2} & a_{1,3} \\ a_{2,1} & a_{2,2} & a_{2,3} \end{bmatrix} \times \begin{bmatrix} b_{1,1} \\ b_{2,1} \\ b_{3,1} \end{bmatrix} = \begin{bmatrix} c_{1,1} = a_{1,1} \times b_{1,1} + a_{1,2} \times b_{2,1} + a_{1,3} \times b_{3,1} \\ c_{2,1} = a_{2,1} \times b_{1,1} + a_{2,2} \times b_{2,1} + a_{2,3} \times b_{3,1} \end{bmatrix}$$

When the two matrices are square matrices of size $n \times n$, this matrix multiplication runs in $O(n^3)$ (see Section 5.8.3).

Solution(s)

This Matrix Chain Multiplication problem is usually one of the classic examples used to illustrate Dynamic Programming (DP) technique. As we have discussed DP in details in Book 1, we only outline the key ideas here. Note that for this problem, we do not actually multiply the matrices as shown in earlier subsection. We just need to find the optimal complete parenthesization of the n matrices.

Let $cost(i, j)$ where $i < j$ denotes the number of scalar multiplications needed to multiply matrices $A_i \times A_{i+1} \times \ldots \times A_j$. We have the following Complete Search recurrences:

1. $cost(i, j) = 0$ if $i = j$, otherwise:
2. $cost(i, j) = min(cost(i, k) + cost(k + 1, j) + P_{i-1} \times P_k \times P_j), \forall k \in [i \ldots j - 1]$

The optimal cost is stored in $cost(1, n)$. There are $O(n^2)$ different pairs of subproblems (i, j). Therefore, we need a DP table of size $O(n^2)$. Each subproblem requires up to $O(n)$ to be computed. Therefore, the time complexity of this DP solution for the Matrix Chain Multiplication problem is $O(n^3)$, much better than exploring all $Cat(n-1)$ complete parenthesization of n matrices.

Programming exercises related to Matrix Chain Multiplication:

1. Entry Level: **UVa 00348 - Optimal Array Mult ...** * (DP; s(i, j); output the optimal solution; the optimal sequence is not unique)

9.8 Lowest Common Ancestor

Problem Description

Given a rooted tree T with n vertices, the Lowest Common Ancestor (LCA) between two vertices u and v, or $LCA(u, v)$, is defined as the lowest vertex in T that has both u and v as descendants. We allow a vertex to be a descendant of itself, i.e., there is a possibility that $LCA(u, v) = u$ or $LCA(u, v) = v$.

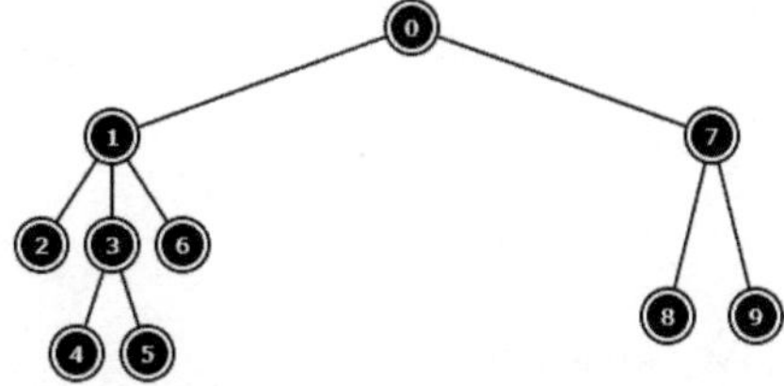

Figure 9.4: An example of a rooted tree T with $n = 10$ vertices

For example, in Figure 9.4, verify that the $LCA(4, 5) = 3$, $LCA(4, 6) = 1$, $LCA(4, 1) = 1$, $LCA(8, 9) = 7$, $LCA(4, 8) = 0$, and $LCA(0, 0) = 0$.

Solution(s)

Complete Search Solution

A naïve solution is to do two steps. From the first vertex u, we go all the way up to the root of T and record all vertices traversed along the way (this can be $O(n)$ if the tree is a very unbalanced). From the second vertex v, we also go all the way up to the root of T, but this time we stop if we encounter a common vertex for the first time (this can also be $O(n)$ if the $LCA(u, v)$ is the root and the tree is very unbalanced). This common vertex is the LCA. This requires $O(n)$ per (u, v) query and can be very slow if there are many queries.

For example, if we want to compute $LCA(4, 6)$ of the tree in Figure 9.4 using this complete search solution, we will first traverse path $4 \to 3 \to 1 \to 0$ and record these 4 vertices. Then, we traverse path $6 \to 1$ and then stop. We report that the LCA is vertex 1.

Reduction to Range Minimum Query

We can reduce the LCA problem into a Range Minimum Query (RMQ) problem (see Segment Tree section in Book 1). If the structure of the tree T is not changed throughout all Q queries, we can use the Sparse Table data structure with $O(n \log n)$ construction time and $O(1)$ RMQ time. The details on the Sparse Table data structure is shown in Section 9.3. In this section, we highlight the reduction process from LCA to RMQ as discussed in [3].

We can reduce LCA to RMQ in linear time. The key idea is to observe that $LCA(u, v)$ is the shallowest vertex in the tree that is visited between the visits of u and v during a DFS traversal. So what we need to do is to run a DFS on the tree and record information about the depth and the time of visit for every node. Notice that we will visit a total of $2 * n - 1$ vertices in the DFS since the internal vertices will be visited several times. We need to build three arrays during this DFS: `E[0..2*n-2]` (which records the sequence of visited nodes and also the Eulerian tour of the tree), `L[0..2*n-2]` (which records the depth of each visited node), and `H[0..n-1]` (where `H[i]` records the index of the first occurrence of node `i` in `E`). The key portion of the implementation is shown below:

```
int L[2*MAX_N], E[2*MAX_N], H[MAX_N], idx;

void dfs(int cur, int depth) {
  H[cur] = idx;
  E[idx] = cur;
  L[idx++] = depth;
  for (auto &nxt : children[cur]) {
    dfs(nxt, depth+1);
    E[idx] = cur;                                    // backtrack to cur
    L[idx++] = depth;
  }
}

void buildRMQ() {
  idx = 0; memset(H, -1, sizeof H);
  dfs(0, 0);                                         // root is at index 0
}
```

Source code: `ch9/LCA.cpp|java|py`

For example, if we call `dfs(0, 0)` on the tree in Figure 9.4, we will have:

Index	0	1	2	3	4	5	6	7	8	9	10	11	12	13	14	15	16	17	18
H	0	1	2	4	5	7	10	13	14	16									
E	0	1	2	1	3	4	3	5	3	*(1)*	6	1	0	7	8	7	9	7	0
L	0	1	2	1	2	3	2	3	2	1	2	1	0	1	2	1	2	1	0

Table 9.2: The Reduction from LCA to RMQ

Once we have these three arrays to work with, we can solve LCA using RMQ. Assume that `H[u]` < `H[v]` or swap u and v otherwise. We notice that the problem reduces to finding the vertex with the smallest depth in `E[H[u]..H[v]]`. So the solution is given by $LCA(u, v)$ = `E[RMQ(H[u], H[v])]` where `RMQ(i, j)` is executed on the `L` array. If we use the Sparse Table data structure shown in Section 9.3, it is the `L` array that needs to be processed in the construction phase.

For example, if we want to compute $LCA(4, 6)$ of the tree in Figure 9.4, we will compute `H[4] = 5` and `H[6] = 10` and find the vertex with the smallest depth in `E[5..10]`. Calling `RMQ(5, 10)` on array `L` (see the underlined entries in row `L` of Table 9.2) returns index 9. The value of `E[9]` = 1 (see the italicized entry in row `E` of Table 9.2), therefore we report 1 as the answer of $LCA(4, 6)$.

Programming exercises related to LCA:

1. Entry Level: **UVa 10938 - Flea circus** * (basic LCA problem)
2. **UVa 12238 - Ants Colony** * (similar to UVa 10938)
3. *Kattis - boxes* * (unite the forests into a tree; LCA; DP size of subtree)
4. *Kattis - chewbacca* * (complete short k-ary tree; binary heap indexing; LCA)
5. *Kattis - rootedsubtrees* * (let d be the number of vertices that are strictly between r and p, inclusive (computed using LCA); derive formula w.r.t d)

9.9 Tree Isomorphism

The term **isomorphism** comes from Ancient Greek words, isos (equal) and morphe (shape). Two graphs G and H are said to be *isomorphic* if and only if they have an equal shape (regardless of their labels); in other words, two graphs are isomorphic if and only if there exists a bijection[7] between all vertices in G and H, $f : V(G) \rightarrow V(H)$, such that vertex u and vertex v in G are connected by an edge if and only if vertex $f(u)$ and vertex $f(v)$ in H are connected by an edge[8]. The problem to determine whether two graphs are isomorphic is known as the graph isomorphism problem, which is a hard problem[9]. However, **tree** isomorphism problem is in P; in other words, there is a polynomial-time complexity algorithm to determine whether two trees are isomorphic. We discuss this variant.

Figure 9.5 shows an example of three isomorphic trees. The vertices bijection relations are: $(\texttt{a}, 5, \texttt{ii})$, $(\texttt{b}, 4, \texttt{i})$, $(\texttt{c}, 2, \texttt{iii})$, $(\texttt{d}, 1, \texttt{iv})$, and $(\texttt{e}, 3, \texttt{v})$. In other words, vertex `a` in the first graph is equal to vertex `5` in the second graph and vertex `ii` in the third graph, vertex `b` in the first graph is equal to vertex `4` in the second graph and vertex `i` in the third graph, etc. We can check whether these bijection relations produce a tree isomorphism by verifying the existence (or non-existence) of edges for every pair of vertices in those graphs. For example, vertex `a` and vertex `b` are connected by an edge; the same thing also happens on vertex `5` and vertex `4`, and vertex `ii` and vertex `i`; vertex `b` and vertex `e` are not connected by an edge; the same thing also happens on vertex `4` and vertex `3`, and vertex `i` and vertex `v`.

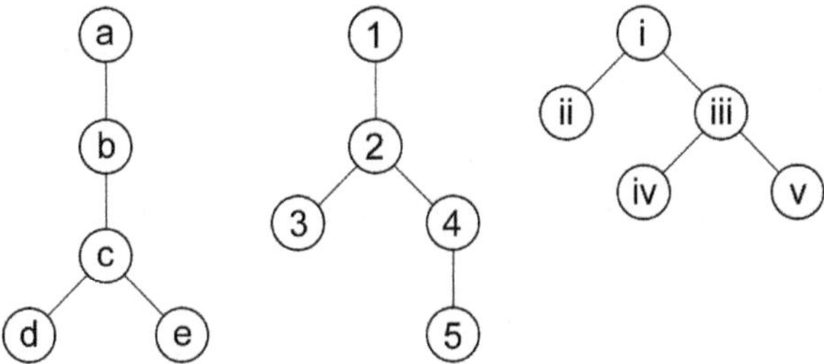

Figure 9.5: Three Isomorphic Trees.

Wrong Approach: Degree Sequence

A *degree sequence*[10] of a graph is a collection of its vertices degree sorted in non-increasing order. For example, the degree sequence of the tree in Figure 9.5 is $\{3, 2, 1, 1, 1\}$, i.e., there is one vertex with a degree of 3, one vertex with a degree of 2, and three vertices with a degree of 1. Two trees (it also applies to a general graph) cannot be isomorphic if their degree sequences are different. However, two trees with the same degree sequence do **not** necessarily isomorphic[11]. Consider the trees in Figure 9.6. Both trees are having the same degree sequence, i.e., $\{3, 2, 2, 1, 1, 1\}$, but they are not isomorphic.

[7] A bijection is a one-to-one mapping between two sets such that each element in the first set is paired with exactly one element in the second set, and each element in the second set is paired with exactly one element in the first set.

[8] In other words, there exists a one-to-one mapping between vertices in G and vertices in H.

[9] To the writing of this book, it is not known whether the graph isomorphism problem is P or NP-complete. On a related subject, the <u>sub</u>graph isomorphism problem has been proven to be NP-complete.

[10] Interested reader can also read about Erdős-Gallai Theorem in Section 9.15.

[11] In our experience, beginners in competitive programming who have no strong background in computer science or mathematics tend to use degree sequence in determining tree isomorphism, and of course, failed.

Figure 9.6: Two non-isomorphic trees with the same degree sequence of $\{3, 2, 2, 1, 1, 1\}$.

One could also "be creative" (but still fails) by checking the degree of each vertex's neighbours. This is also known as the *neighbourhood degree sequence*. To get the neighbourhood degree sequence of a graph, simply replace each degree in its degree sequence with the list of the degree of its neighbours. For example, the neighbourhood degree sequence of the tree in Figure 9.5 would be $\{\{2, 1, 1\}, \{3, 1\}, \{3\}, \{3\}, \{2\}\}$. Note that if we consider only the size of each element in that neighbourhood degree sequence, then we will get $\{3, 2, 1, 1, 1\}$, which is its degree sequence.

The trees in Figure 9.6 are having a different neighbourhood degree sequence. The tree on the left has a neighbourhood degree sequence of $\{\{2, 2, 1\}, \{3, 1\}, \{3, 1\}, \{3\}, \{2\}, \{2\}\}$ while the tree on the right is $\{\{2, 1, 1\}, \{3, 2\}, \{2, 1\}, \{3\}, \{3\}, \{2\}\}$.

However, the trees in Figure 9.7 are having the same degree and neighbourhood degree sequence, but they are not isomorphic. Their degree sequence is $\{3, 2, 2, 2, 2, 2, 2, 1, 1, 1\}$ while their neighbourhood degree sequence is $\{\{2, 2, 1\}, \{3, 2\}, \{3, 2\}, \{2, 2\}, \{2, 2\}, \{2, 1\}, \{2, 1\}, \{3\}, \{2\}, \{2\}\}$.

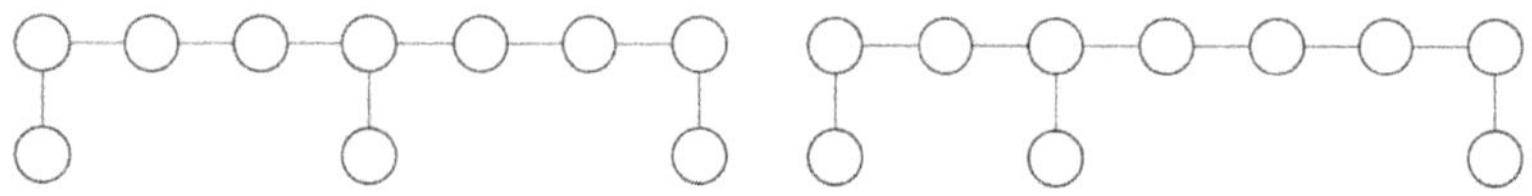

Figure 9.7: Two non-isomorphic trees with the same neighbourhood degree sequence.

Rooted Tree Isomorphism in $O(N^2)$

In this section, let us assume the trees that we would like to check the isomorphism are rooted (later, we will remove this assumption). To determine whether two rooted trees are isomorphic, we can encode each tree and check whether both trees have the same encoding. For this purpose, we need an encoding which works for an unlabeled rooted tree.

Assign a **bracket tuple**[12] to each vertex u to represent the subtree rooted at vertex u. The bracket tuple for a vertex u is in the form of `( H )` where `H` is the concatenation of all u's (direct) children's bracket tuples sorted in non-descending[13] order. The bracket characters we used are `(` and `)`; however, you can use any other pair of symbols to represent the opening and closing brackets, e.g., `01`, `ab`, `{}`. The encoding of a rooted tree is the root's encoding.

For example, a leaf vertex will have the bracket tuple of `()` as it has no child; an internal vertex with 3 children each with a bracket tuple of `((()))`, `(())`, and `(()())`, respectively, will have a bracket tuple of `( ((())) (()()) (()) )`. Note that `(()())` appears first in sorted order compared to `(())`. Also, note that the spaces are for clarity only; there shouldn't be any space in a bracket tuple.

Figure 9.8 shows an example of a rooted tree encoding with the bracket tuple. Observe that the sorting children's bracket tuple part is important if we want to use this encoding to check the tree isomorphism. The reason is similar to why *anagrams* can be checked by sorting the strings.

[12]Recall the Bracket Matching problem discussed in Book 1.

[13]Any order will do as long as there is a tie-breaker and used consistently throughout all vertices' encoding.

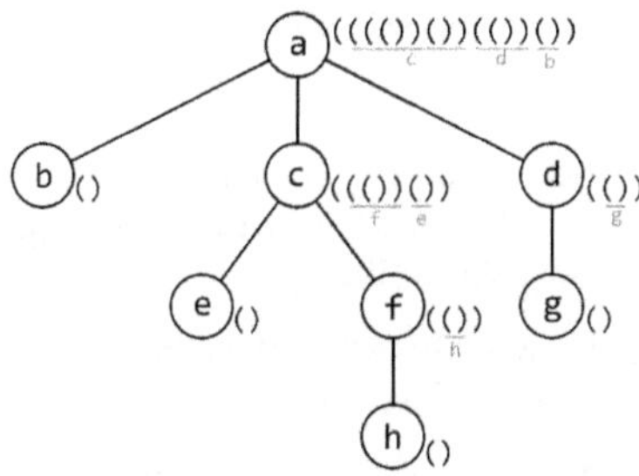

Figure 9.8: Example of Rooted Tree Encoding with Bracket Tuples.

With this method, each vertex has a bracket tuple of length $O(N)$, causing the overall time complexity to be $O(N^2)$. The following code is one implementation of the tree encoding with bracket tuple. To check whether the trees are isomorphic, we only need to compare whether they have the same encoding.[14]

```
string encodeTree(int u) {
  vector<string> tuples;
  for (auto &v : child[u])
    tuples.push_back(encodeTree(v));
  sort(tuples.begin(), tuples.end());
  string H;
  for (auto &c : tuples)
    H += c;
  return "(" + H + ")";
}
```

Rooted Tree Isomorphism in $O(N)$

Observe that each vertex in the previous method is encoded to a bracket tuple of length $O(N)$. To improve the running time, we can represent each bracket tuple with an integer. One way to do this is by string hashing (see Section 6.6), i.e., hash the bracket tuple into a single integer where the integer is **assumed**[15] to be unique to the tuple. With this method, the total time complexity to encode the rooted tree is reduced to $O(N)$.

Unrooted Tree Isomorphism

To check unrooted trees isomorphism, simply make the trees rooted and perform the previous rooted tree encoding. However, we cannot simply select any arbitrary vertex to be the root of the tree as each vertex (if selected as a root) may produce a different encoding. We need a vertex with a unique property which exists in any tree.

Commonly, there are two kinds of vertices which are "unique" in a tree which can be helpful for our purpose, i.e., the center and centroid vertices.

A **center** vertex of a tree is a vertex with the smallest eccentricity in the tree; in other words, the distance to the farthest vertex is minimum. This vertex lies in the center of the longest path (diameter) of the tree. Also, there can be at most two of such vertices depends on whether the tree's diameter is odd or even length.

[14] We only need to check the roots as the encoding at the root is the encoding of the tree itself.

[15] See Chapter 6.6 on how to handle the collision probability of a hashing.

The following $O(N)$ algorithm will find the center(s) of a tree:

1. Perform a BFS from any arbitrary vertex and find the farthest vertex u from it.
2. Perform a BFS from vertex u and find the farthest vertex v from vertex u. The path from vertex u to vertex v is (one of) the tree's diameter path, i.e., the longest path in the tree. We have discussed this in Book 1.
3. Find the vertex(s) in the middle/median of the path between vertex u and vertex v. There can be one or two such center vertices.

On the other hand, a **centroid** vertex of a tree is a vertex whose removal will split the tree into a forest (of disconnected trees) such that none of the disconnected trees has more than half of the number of vertices in the original tree. Similar to the tree center, there can be at most two centroid vertices in a tree.

To find the centroids, first, assume an arbitrary vertex as the root and compute the size of each rooted subtree (e.g., with a DFS). Then, evaluate each vertex one-by-one starting from the root while moving towards a child with the largest rooted subtree.

The following code finds the centroid(s) of a tree. The array's element `size[x]` contains the size of the rooted subtree of vertex `x`. The variable `psize` contains the size of (the parent's) inverse subtree, i.e., the size of the rooted subtree of vertex p (vertex u's parent) **if** the tree is rooted at vertex u.

```
vi getCentroids(int u, int psize) {
  if (2*psize > N) return vi(0);
  bool is_centroid = true;
  int sum = 0;                                // sum of subtree sizes
  int next = -1;                              // the largest subtree
  for (auto &v : child[u]) {
    sum += size[v];
    if (2*size[v] > N)
      is_centroid = false;
    if ((next == -1) || (size[next] < size[v]))
      next = v;
  }
  vi res = getCentroids(next, psize+sum-size[next]+1);
  if (is_centroid)
    res.push_back(u);
  return res;
}
```

If there are two centers (or centroids), then we need the encodings of the tree rooted at each of those vertices, sorted, and concatenated. The trees are isomorphic if they have the same encoding. Finding the center(s) or centroid(s) of a tree can be done in $O(N)$ and encoding a rooted tree is also $O(N)$ as described above, thus, unrooted tree isomorphism can be solved in $O(N)$ time complexity.

Programming exercises related to Tree Isomorphism:

1. **LA 2577 - Rooted Trees Isomorphism ***

9.10 De Bruijn Sequence

A **de Bruijn sequence** (also called a de Bruijn cycle) is the shortest *circular string*[16] which contains every possible string of length n on the alphabets Σ ($|\Sigma| = k$) as its substring. As there are k^n possible string of length n on Σ, then the length of such a string is at least k^n. Furthermore, it can be shown that there exists such a string with a length of exactly k^n (refer to the constructive algorithm below).[17]

For example, let $k = 2$ ($\Sigma = \{\texttt{a}, \texttt{b}\}$) and $n = 3$. One de Bruijn sequence for such k and n, or also denoted by $B(k = 2, n = 3)$, is `aaababbb` of length $2^3 = 8$. Let's verify this. All the substrings of length $n = 3$ of a circular string `aaababbb` are: `aaa`, `aab`, `aba`, `bab`, `abb`, `bbb`, `bba`, and `baa`. All those 8 substrings are unique, and the fact that there are 2^3 possible strings of length $n = 3$ on $k = 2$ alphabets implies that those 8 substrings are complete (contains every possible string of length $n = 3$ on $k = 2$ alphabets). Another de Bruijn sequence for $B(2, 3)$ is `aaabbbab`. Other de Bruijn sequences such as `aababbba`, `babbbaaa`, `aabbbaba`, etc. are also valid, but they are considered the same as the previous two (can be obtained by rotating the string), i.e., `aababbba` and `babbbaaa` are the same as `aaababbb`, and `aabbbaba` is the same as `aaabbbab`.

Consider another example with $k = 6$ ($\Sigma = \{\texttt{a}, \texttt{b}, \texttt{c}, \texttt{d}, \texttt{e}, \texttt{f}\}$) and $n = 2$. All possible string of length $n = 2$ on $\Sigma = \{\texttt{a}, \texttt{b}, \texttt{c}, \texttt{d}, \texttt{e}, \texttt{f}\}$ are `aa`, `ab`, `ac`, ..., `fe`, `ff`, and all of them can be found as substrings of a circular string `aabacadaeafbbcbdbebfccdcecfddedfeeff` with a length of $6^2 = 36$. Of course, other de Bruijn sequences for $B(6, 2)$ also exist.

De Bruijn Graph

A de Bruijn sequence can be generated with the help of a de Bruijn graph. An m**-dimensional de Bruijn graph on alphabets** Σ is defined as follows.

- There is a vertex for every possible string of length m on Σ.
- A vertex u has a directed edge to vertex v, (u, v), if and only if the string represented by v can be obtained by removing the first character of the string represented by u and appending a new character to the end of that string. Then, the directed edge (u, v) has a label equals to the new appended character. For example, a vertex representing `aa` has a directed edge with a label of `b` to a vertex representing `ab`; a vertex representing `abcde` has a directed edge with a label of `f` to a vertex representing `bcdef`.

These two properties imply that such a graph has k^m vertices and k^{m+1} directed edges. Moreover, each vertex has m outgoing edges and m incoming edges. Figure 9.9 and Figure 9.10 show examples of de Bruijn graphs on alphabets $\Sigma = \{\texttt{a}, \texttt{b}\}$ with 2 and 3 dimension, respectively.

Generally, there are two ways of generating a de Bruijn sequence with the help of a de Bruijn graph, i.e., with a Hamiltonian path/tour and with an Eulerian tour.

Generating a de Bruijn Sequence with a Hamiltonian Path/Tour

This method is quite apparent once you construct an n-dimensional de Bruijn graph to generate a de Bruijn sequence of $B(k, n)$. Consider Figure 9.10 for example. All the vertices

[16] A circular string is a string in which the two ends (left-most and right-most) are joint together to form a cycle. For example, `abcdef` and `cdefab` are the same circular string as the later can be obtained by rotating the former to the left twice.

[17] If we do not want the string to be circular, then the length becomes $k^n + n - 1$, i.e., simply append the first $n - 1$ characters to the end of the string.

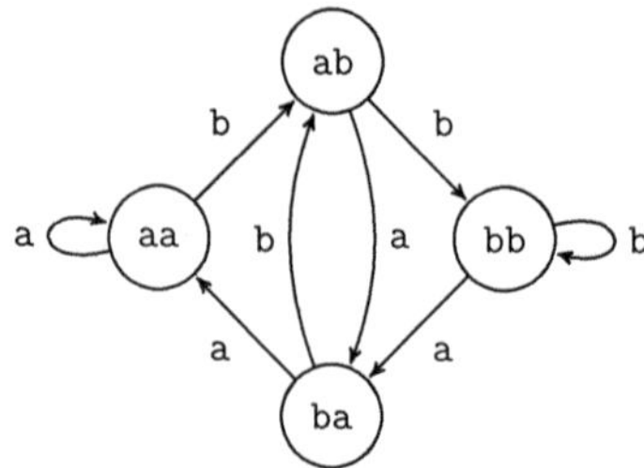

Figure 9.9: 2-dimensional de Bruijn graph on alphabets $\Sigma = \{\texttt{a}, \texttt{b}\}$.

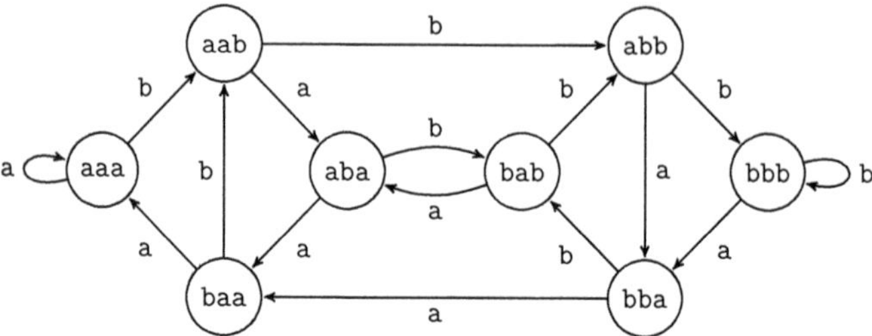

Figure 9.10: 3-dimensional de Bruijn graph on alphabets $\Sigma = \{\texttt{a}, \texttt{b}\}$.

in a 3-dimensional de Bruijn graph are all possible strings of length $n = 3$ which must exist in a de Bruijn sequence $B(2, n = 3)$. On the other hand, an edge in such a graph implies that we can get the next string (of the adjacent vertex) just by adding one character. Therefore, what we need to do to obtain a de Bruijn sequence is simply find a path in such a graph that visits each vertex exactly once, which is what a **Hamiltonian path** is. The list of vertices in such a path is the list of strings of length n of a de Bruijn sequence in their appearance order.

For example, one Hamiltonian path in Figure 9.10 is as follows.

$$\texttt{aaa} \rightarrow \texttt{aab} \rightarrow \texttt{abb} \rightarrow \texttt{bbb} \rightarrow \texttt{bba} \rightarrow \texttt{bab} \rightarrow \texttt{aba} \rightarrow \texttt{baa}$$

To get the corresponding de Bruijn sequence, we can merge those strings while shrinking every adjacent strings (e.g., merge `aaa` and `aab` into `aaab`); the result for the above example is `aaabbbabaa`. Note that the sequence obtained by this method has excess characters as we have not made it into a circular string. Simply remove the last $n - 1$ (in this example, $n - 1 = 2$) characters from the result to obtain the de Bruijn sequence, i.e., `aaabbbab`.

Alternatively, we can use the edges' label of a **Hamiltonian tour** to get a de Bruijn sequence.

$$\texttt{aaa} \xrightarrow{\texttt{b}} \texttt{aab} \xrightarrow{\texttt{b}} \texttt{abb} \xrightarrow{\texttt{b}} \texttt{bbb} \xrightarrow{\texttt{a}} \texttt{bba} \xrightarrow{\texttt{b}} \texttt{bab} \xrightarrow{\texttt{a}} \texttt{aba} \xrightarrow{\texttt{a}} \texttt{baa} \xrightarrow{\texttt{a}} \texttt{aaa}$$

The edges' label which also a de Bruijn sequence is `bbbabaaa`. Note that `bbbabaaa` is equal to `aaabbbab` (simply rotate it).

You might already notice that finding a Hamiltonian path/tour in a graph is an NP-complete problem, thus, we might not be able to use this method to solve a contest problem. Fortunately, there is a much better alternative method to generate a de Bruijn sequence, i.e., with an Eulerian tour.

Generating a de Bruijn Sequence with an Eulerian Tour

Recall that to generate a de Bruijn sequence $B(k, n)$ from a Hamiltonian path/tour, we need an n-dimensional de Bruijn graph. The same de Bruijn sequence can also be generated from an Eulerian tour on an $(n-1)$ dimensional de Bruijn graph.

In an $(n-1)$ dimensional de Bruijn graph, each outgoing edge corresponds to a string of length n, i.e., the vertex's string (length of $n-1$) concatenated with the outgoing edge's label (length of 1). Therefore, to get all possible strings of length n, all we need to do is to find a tour that traverses each edge exactly once, which is what an **Eulerian tour** is.

For example, consider Figure 9.9 (of 2-dimensional) when we want to generate a de Bruijn sequence $B(2, n=3)$. One Eulerian tour in such a graph is as follows.

$$\texttt{bb} \xrightarrow{\texttt{a}} \texttt{ba} \xrightarrow{\texttt{a}} \texttt{aa} \xrightarrow{\texttt{a}} \texttt{aa} \xrightarrow{\texttt{b}} \texttt{ab} \xrightarrow{\texttt{a}} \texttt{ba} \xrightarrow{\texttt{b}} \texttt{ab} \xrightarrow{\texttt{b}} \texttt{bb} \xrightarrow{\texttt{b}} \texttt{bb}$$

Similar to what we did previously with a Hamiltonian tour, the edges' label of an Eulerian tour on a 2-dimensional de Bruijn graph is a de Bruijn sequence $B(2, n=3)$, i.e., `aaababbb`.

Also note that such a de Bruijn graph is connected and each vertex has the same number of incoming and outgoing edges, thus, an Eulerian tour must exist.

To find such a tour, we can simply use an algorithm such as Hierholzer's as discussed in Book 1 which runs in a polynomial-time complexity. Note that there are other methods to generate a de Bruijn sequence without the help of a de Bruijn graph, e.g., with Lyndon words[18] concatenation, or shift-based construction algorithm, but both methods are not discussed in this book.

Counting Unique de Bruijn Sequences

The total number of unique de Bruijn sequences of $B(k, n)$ can be found with the following formula.

$$\frac{(k!)^{k^{n-1}}}{k^n}$$

If we do not want to consider the rotated string as the same string, then simply remove the fractional part.

For the special case $k = 2$, the formula reduced to

$$2^{2^{n-1}-n}$$

For example, the number of unique de Bruijn sequences for $B(2, 3)$ is $2^{2^{3-1}-3} = 2^{4-3} = 2$ which has been shown in the beginning of this section to be `aaababbb` and `aaabbbab`.

Programming exercises related to de Bruijn Sequence:

1. Entry Level: **UVa 10506 - The Ouroboros problem** * (basic de Bruijn Sequence problem)
2. **UVa 10040 - Ouroboros Snake** * (lexicographically smallest de Bruijn seq)
3. **UVa 10244 - First Love!!!** *
4. ICPC 2018 Jakarta Problem C - Smart Thief (partial de Bruijn sequence)

---

[18]A Lyndon word is an aperiodic string that is lexicographically smallest among all of its rotations.

9.11 Fast Fourier Transform

The proper title for this section should be **Fast Polynomial Multiplication** but we decide to promote the title into Fast Fourier Transform as it will be addressed heavily in this section.

Fast Fourier Transform (FFT) is a (fast) method to perform Discrete Fourier Transform (DFT), a widely used transformation in (electrical) engineering and science to convert a signal from time to frequency domain. However, in competitive programming, FFT and its inverse are commonly used to multiply two (large) polynomials.

The Problem

Given two polynomials of degree n, $A(x)$ and $B(x)$, your task is to compute its multiplication, $A(x) \cdot B(x)$. For example, given these two polynomials of degree $n = 2$.

$$A(x) = 1 + 3x + 5x^2$$
$$B(x) = 4 - 2x + x^2$$

Then,

$$A(x) \cdot B(x) = 4 + 10x + 15x^2 - 7x^3 + 5x^4$$

If n is small enough, then the following straightforward $O(n^2)$ code suffices to compute the multiplication.

```
for (int j = 0; j <= n; ++j)
  for (int k = 0; k <= n; ++k)
    res[j+k] += A[j] * B[k];
```

If both polynomials have a different degree, then simply append the polynomial with a lower degree with one or more zeroes to meet the other polynomial's degree. For example, consider these two polynomials.

$$A(x) = 1 + 4x \quad \rightarrow A(x) = 1 + 4x + 0x^2 + 0x^3$$
$$B(x) = 3 + 2x^2 + 5x^3 \rightarrow B(x) = 3 + 0x + 2x^2 + 5x^3$$

It does not change the polynomial but now they have the same "degree"[19] so the above code can be used.

In this section, we describe an algorithm to perform polynomial multiplication which runs in $O(n \log n)$ time complexity with the FFT and its inverse.

Polynomial Representation

Before going in-depth with FFT, we start by noting several ways to represent a polynomial.

Coefficient Representation

A coefficient representation of a polynomial $a_0 + a_1x + a_2x^2 + \cdots + a_nx^n$ is a vector of coefficients

$$(a_0, a_1, a_2, \ldots, a_n)$$

[19]We slightly abused the terminology. The definition of a polynomial degree is the highest power of its terms with non-zero coefficient. Appending zeroes to a polynomial does not increase its degree.

For example,

$$A(x) = 1 + 3x + 5x^2 \rightarrow (1, 3, 5)$$
$$B(x) = 4 - 2x + x^2 \rightarrow (4, -2, 1)$$

Evaluating the value of a polynomial for a certain x in this representation can be done efficiently in $O(n)$, e.g., with Horner's method[20]. However, performing polynomial multiplication (strictly) in this representation might require the previous $O(n^2)$ code. Generally, problems involving polynomials present the polynomials in this representation.

Point-Value Representation

A point-value representation (or point representation) of a polynomial of degree n, $A(x)$, is a set of (at least) $n+1$ point-value pairs

$$\{(x_0, y_0), (x_1, y_1), (x_2, y_2), \ldots, (x_n, y_n)\}$$

such that all x_j are distinct and $y_j = A(x_j)$ for all j.

Note that we may have more (but no fewer) than $n+1$ point-value pairs to represent a polynomial of degree n.[21] For example, these point-value representations correspond to the same polynomial $1 + 3x + 5x^2$ of degree $n = 2$.

$$\{(1, 9), (2, 27), (3, 55)\}$$
$$\{(1, 9), (2, 27), (3, 55), (4, 93)\}$$
$$\{(1, 9), (3, 55), (4, 93), (5, 141)\}$$
$$\{(2, 27), (3, 55), (5, 141), (7, 267), (10, 531)\}$$

Some articles/books also refer to this representation as a *sample representation* because it provides us with sufficient sample points (x_j, y_j) which can be used to reconstruct the original polynomial, e.g., with Lagrange's interpolation formula.

To multiply two polynomials in a point-value representation, we need:

1. Both polynomials to be represented by the same domain ($x_j \in X$ for all j).
2. There are at least $2n + 1$ distinct points in the point-value set.

The first requirement is given; what we want to compute is $A(x_j) \cdot B(x_j)$ for some x_j. The second requirement raises from the fact that multiplying two polynomials of degree n will result in a polynomial of degree $2n$, thus, $2n + 1$ point-value pairs are needed to represent the result.

Consider the previous example, $A(x) = 1 + 3x + 5x^2$ and $B(x) = 4 - 2x + x^2$. Let $x_j \in X$ be $\{0, 1, 2, 3, 4\}$.[22]

x_j	0	1	2	3	4
$A(x_j)$	1	9	27	55	93
$B(x_j)$	4	3	4	7	12
$A(x_j) \cdot B(x_j)$	4	27	108	385	1116

[20]Observe that $a_0 + a_1x^1 + a_2x^2 + \cdots + a_nx^n = a_0 + x(a_1 + x(a_2 + \cdots + x(a_{n-1} + xa_n))))$.

[21]Find out more about this on polynomial interpolation and the fundamental theory of algebra.

[22]These can be any number as long as they are distinct. Also, as the polynomial degree is 2, then we need the size of X to be at least $2 * 2 + 1 = 5$.

Thus, the resulting polynomial is

$$\{(0,4),(1,27),(2,108),(3,385),(4,1116)\}$$

which corresponds to the polynomial $4 + 10x + 15x^2 - 7x^3 + 5x^4$.

As we can see, given the point-value representation of two polynomials (which satisfies the requirements), we can directly compute their multiplication in $O(n)$ time, i.e., simply multiply $A(x_j)$ and $B(x_j)$ for each x_j.

The Big Idea

First, let's put some details on our problem. Given two polynomials of degree n in a coefficient representation, $A(x)$ and $B(x)$, compute its multiplication, $A(x) \cdot B(x)$.

Recall from the previous discussion, we know that multiplying two polynomials directly in a coefficient representation requires $O(n^2)$ time complexity. However, we also know that polynomial multiplication in a point-value representation can be done in $O(n)$, and we are going to exploit this.

The following is the big idea of the fast polynomial multiplication with three steps which is also illustrated in Figure 9.11:

(1) Convert the given polynomials into a point-value representation.

(2) Do the polynomial multiplication in a point-value representation.

(3) Convert the result back to the coefficient representation.

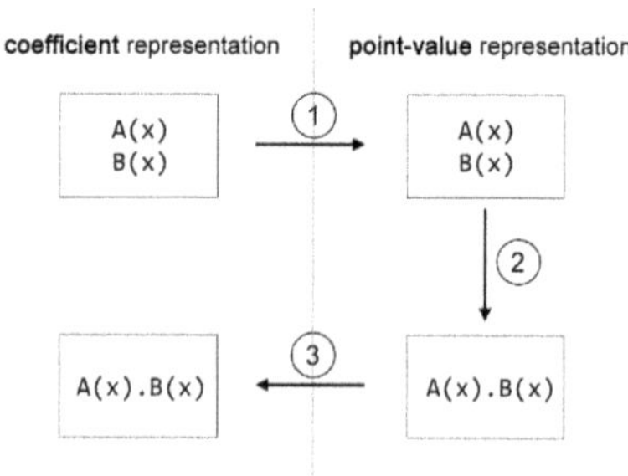

Figure 9.11: Fast polynomial multiplication: The big idea

We know step (2) can be done in $O(n)$, but how about step (1) and (3)? A naïve approach for step (1) would be evaluating the polynomial for an x_j to get y_j (i.e., a point-value pair (x_j, y_j)); perform this for $2n+1$ different x_j and we obtain the point-value representation of the polynomial. However, evaluating a polynomial for an x is $O(n)$, causing the overall time complexity to get $2n+1$ point-value pairs to be $O(n^2)$.

Fortunately, FFT algorithm can perform step (1) in $O(n \log n)$, and step (3) can be done by inverse FFT, also in $O(n \log n)$, causing the overall time-complexity to do the polynomial multiplication with the above steps to be $O(n \log n)$.

Fast Fourier Transform

Fast Fourier Transform is a divide and conquer algorithm to compute a Discrete Fourier Transform of a series (or an ordered set of polynomial coefficients). To understand FFT and

DFT, one also needs to know about complex numbers and Euler's formula (or trigonometry) in its relation with the nth root of unity.

As we are dealing with complex numbers, we should put this note before we continue to avoid any confusion caused by i.

> The notation of i in this (entire) section refers to
> an **imaginary** unit of a complex number (e.g., $5 + 2i$),
> and does not refer to any variable or index.

Divide and Conquer (D&C) Algorithm

We start by describing a D&C algorithm to evaluate a polynomial $A(x)$ for a given x. Although we can use Horner's method just to evaluate a polynomial, we need this D&C algorithm for FFT later.

Let $A(x) = (a_0, a_1, a_2, \ldots, a_n)$ be a polynomial function (in a coefficient representation). $A_0(x)$ is a polynomial whose coefficients are the coefficient of $A(x)$ at the **even** terms, i.e., $A_0(x) = (a_0, a_2, a_4, a_6, \ldots)$, and $A_1(x)$ is a polynomial whose coefficients are the coefficient of $A(x)$ at the **odd** terms, i.e., $A_1(x) = (a_1, a_3, a_5, a_7, \ldots)$.[23] Both $A_0(x)$ and $A_1(x)$ have half the degree of $A(x)$.

$$
\begin{aligned}
A(x) &= (a_0, a_1, a_2, a_3, \ldots, a_n) &&\rightarrow a_0 + a_1x^1 + a_2x^2 + a_3x^3 + \cdots + a_nx^n \\
A_0(x) &= (a_0, a_2, a_4, a_6, \ldots) &&\rightarrow a_0 + a_2x^1 + a_4x^2 + a_6x^3 + \ldots \\
A_1(x) &= (a_1, a_3, a_5, a_7, \ldots) &&\rightarrow a_1 + a_3x^1 + a_5x^2 + a_7x^3 + \ldots
\end{aligned}
$$

Observe that $A(x)$ can be computed with the following formula.[24]

$$A(x) = A_0(x^2) + x \cdot A_1(x^2)$$

With this, we have a D&C algorithm to evaluate a polynomial.

For the following example, we slightly abuse the notation: Let $A_{(a_0,a_1,\ldots,a_n)}(x)$ be a polynomial $(a_0, a_1, \ldots, a_n)$, i.e., the polynomial coefficients are given as the subscript of A.

Consider the following example. Let $A_{(3,0,2,5)}(x)$ be the polynomial function, and we want to evaluate for $x = 2$. Separate the even and odd terms' coefficients and evaluate on x^2, i.e., $A_{(3,2)}(x^2)$ and $A_{(0,5)}(x^2)$. To evaluate $A_{(3,2)}(x^2)$, recursively separate its even and odd terms' coefficients and evaluate them on $(x^2)^2$, i.e., $A_{(3)}(x^4)$ and $A_{(2)}(x^4)$. Similarly, to evaluate $A_{(0,5)}(x^2)$, recursively separate its even and odd terms' coefficients and evaluate them on $(x^2)^2$, i.e., $A_{(0)}(x^4)$ and $A_{(5)}(x^4)$.

$$A_{(3)}(2^4) = 3 \qquad A_{(2)}(2^4) = 2 \qquad A_{(0)}(2^4) = 0 \qquad A_{(5)}(2^4) = 5$$

$$
\begin{aligned}
A_{(3,2)}(2^2) &= A_{(3)}(2^4) + 2^2 \cdot A_{(2)}(2^4) = 3 + 2^2 \cdot 2 = 11 \\
A_{(0,5)}(2^2) &= A_{(0)}(2^4) + 2^2 \cdot A_{(5)}(2^4) = 0 + 2^2 \cdot 5 = 20
\end{aligned}
$$

$$A_{(3,0,2,5)}(2) = A_{(3,2)}(2^2) + 2 \cdot A_{(0,5)}(2^2) = 11 + 2 \cdot 20 = 51$$

Finally, we obtain $A(2) = 51$ with the D&C algorithm. We can confirm this by directly evaluating $A(2) = 3 + 0 \cdot 2 + 2 \cdot 2^2 + 5 \cdot 2^3$ which results in 51.

This algorithm runs in $O(n \log n)$ time complexity just to evaluate for one x, worse than

[23]Notice that a_2 is the coefficient for x^1 in $A_0(x)$, a_5 is the coefficient for x^2 in $A_1(x)$, and so on.

[24]They are $A_0(x^2)$ and $A_1(x^2)$, not $A_0(x)$ and $A_1(x)$. The readers are also encouraged to verify whether the formula is correct.

the Horner's method which runs in $O(n)$. If we want to evaluate for all $x \in X$ one-by-one where $|X| = 2n+1$, then we'll need $O(n^2 \log n)$ with this D&C algorithm. We can evaluate for all $x \in X$ all-at-once[25], but it still requires $O(n^2)$.[26] Turns out with a clever choice of $x \in X$, the D&C algorithm can evaluate for n values just in $O(n \log n)$ as we will see soon.

n^{th} Roots of Unity

To evaluate $A(x)$ with the D&C algorithm, we first recurse and evaluate $A_0(x^2)$, $A_1(x^2)$, and combine the result into $A(x)$. If we want to evaluate for all $x \in X$ all-at-once, then the algorithm will recurse and evaluate for x^2 $\forall x \in X$ on the second recursion level, x^4 $\forall x \in X$ on the third recursion level, and so on. The size of X never decreases, and this is a big problem. However, we can actually choose any $2n+1$ values of x as long as they are distinct! They don't have to be $0, 1, 2, \ldots, 2n$. They don't even have to be a real number!

What will happen if $X = \{1, -1\}$? On the second recursion level, what the D&C algorithm will compute for is $\{1^2, (-1)^2\}$ which is only $\{1\}$. We can compute both $A(1)$ and $A(-1)$ just by computing $A_0(1)$ and $A_1(1)$ as they share the same x^2.

$$A(1) = A_0(1) + 1 \cdot A_1(1)$$
$$A(-1) = A_0(1) - 1 \cdot A_1(1)$$

We can go further. What will happen if $X = \{1, -1, i, -i\}$? On the second recursion level, the D&C algorithm will compute for $\{1^2, (-1)^2, i^2, (-i)^2\}$ which reduces to $\{1, -1\}$. On the third recursion level, it will compute for $\{1^2, (-1)^2\}$ which reduces to only $\{1\}$.

So, if we need to compute for $|X| = 2n+1$ distinct values of x (and we can choose any x we want), then we need to find X such that it has a nice **collapsing property**; in other words, at the next recursion level, $|X|$ is reduced by half, and at the last recursion level X collapses to $\{1\}$. We can achieve this by using the $|X|^{th}$ **roots of unity**[27]. Also, to have a nice halving, we need to ensure $|X|$ is a power of 2; simply append X (or in this case, the polynomial coefficients) with zeroes until it becomes a power of 2. This collapsing X will significantly reduce the running time of the previous (all-at-once) D&C algorithm.

The nth roots of unity are n distinct numbers such that if raised to the power of n, all numbers will collapse to 1. For example, the 2nd roots of unity are $\{1, -1\}$. The 4th roots of unity are $\{1, -1, i, -i\}$. The 8th roots of unity are $\{\pm 1, \pm i, \pm(\frac{1}{2}\sqrt{2} + \frac{1}{2}\sqrt{2}i), \pm(\frac{1}{2}\sqrt{2} - \frac{1}{2}\sqrt{2}i)\}$. Of course, there are the 3rd, 5th, 6th,... roots of unity as well, but here we only concern ourselves with n as a power of 2. The nth roots of unity are also the points in a *complex plane* whose distance to the origin is exactly 1. See Figure 9.12 for an illustration of the 8th roots of unity.

The nth roots of unity can be found with the following formula.

$$e^{i2\pi k/n}$$

where e is the Euler's number (2.7182818..) and $k = 0, 1, \ldots, n-1$. Observe that if we raise the formula to the nth power, we will obtain 1 regardless of k. $(e^{i2\pi k/n})^n = e^{i2\pi k} = (e^{i2\pi})^k = 1$ (Note: $e^{i2\pi} = 1$). The part $2\pi k/n$ is actually the degree (in radian) of the kth point as illustrated in Figure 9.12.

[25]Modify the D&C algorithm to also accept the set $x \in X$ which we want to evaluate.
[26]Hint: Draw and analyze the recursion tree.
[27]The term "unity" is a synonym to 1 (one).

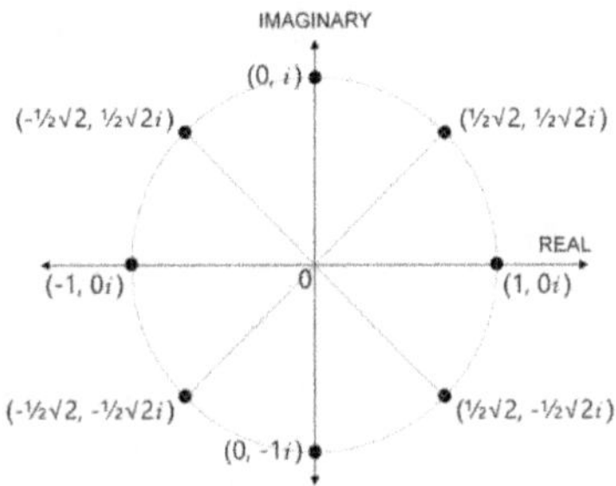

Figure 9.12: The 8th roots of unity.

To get rid of e and the need to compute the power, we can use **Euler's formula.**[28,29]

$$e^{i\theta} = \cos\theta + i\sin\theta$$

With $\theta = 2\pi k/n$, the formula becomes

$$e^{i2\pi k/n} = \cos(2\pi k/n) + i\sin(2\pi k/n)$$

Therefore, for set X to have a nice collapsing property, we simply need to assign $x \in X$ to be $e^{i2\pi k/n}$ or $\cos(2\pi k/n) + i\sin(2\pi k/n)$ where $k = 0, 1, \ldots, n-1$. The evaluation of a polynomial at the roots of unity is also known as the Discrete Fourier Transform (DFT).

FFT, a Recursive Algorithm

Now, we are ready to put everything into an algorithm. To simplify some notations, let

$$w_n^k = e^{i2\pi k/n}$$

i.e., w_n^k is an nth root of unity.

The main structure of the algorithm is, of course, a D&C algorithm. The function `FFT()` have one parameter: `A[]`, a vector (or array) containing the polynomial coefficients. The result of `FFT(A)` is a vector `F[]` of complex numbers of the the same size as `A[]` where each element is an evaluated value of the polynomial $A(x)$ at an nth root of unity, i.e., `F[`k`]`$= A(w_n^k)$.[30]

There is no need to pass around the set X to be evaluated as we can generate them on-the-fly; they are simply the nth roots of unity. To generate $x \in X$ for a recursion call, simply use the Euler's formula.

$$x = \cos(2\pi k/n) + i\sin(2\pi k/n) \qquad \forall\, k = 0, 1, \ldots, n-1$$

The function `FFT(A)` recurses and calls `FFT(A0)` and `FFT(A1)` where `A0[]` and `A1[]` are the separated even and odd terms' coefficients of `A[]`. It then combine the results from `FFT(A0)` and `FFT(A1)`, namely `F0[]` and `F1[]`, respectively.

[28]Understand the formula by consulting Figure 9.12 with basic trigonometry.

[29]If $\theta = \pi$, then Euler's formula will become what regarded as the most beautiful equation in mathematics, the Euler's identity: $e^{i\pi} = \cos\pi + i\sin\pi = -1 + 0i = -1$ or simply $e^{i\pi} + 1 = 0$.

[30]In the implementation later, we will use vector `A[]` to store the result for `F[]` as well in order to reduce memory usage and to gain faster computation.

Let n be the size of `A[]` in a recursion call, and supposed `F0[]` and `F1[]` for that recursion call are already computed.

$$\texttt{F0}[k] = A_0(w_{n/2}^k) \qquad \forall\, k = 0, 1, \ldots, n/2 - 1$$
$$\texttt{F1}[k] = A_1(w_{n/2}^k) \qquad \forall\, k = 0, 1, \ldots, n/2 - 1$$

Our goal is to compute `F[]`.

$$\texttt{F}[k] = A(w_n^k) \qquad \forall\, k = 0, 1, \ldots, n - 1$$

We can do this by using the previous D&C formula, $A(x) = A_0(x^2) + x \cdot A_1(x^2)$.

To simplify the explanation, let's define the range for k to be $0, 1, \ldots, n/2 - 1$ so that the range for the first half of `F[]` is simply k while the range for the second half is $n/2 + k$.[31]

The first half looks simple as we can directly use the D&C formula. It turns out that the second half is easy as well due to the property of nth roots of unity as we will see later.

The first half of `F[]` is as follows. We start with the D&C formula.

$$\begin{aligned}\texttt{F}[k] = A(w_n^k) &= A_0((w_n^k)^2) + w_n^k \cdot A_1((w_n^k)^2) \\ &= A_0(w_n^{2k}) + w_n^k \cdot A_1(w_n^{2k}) \qquad \forall\, k = 0, 1, \ldots, n/2 - 1\end{aligned}$$

Notice that w_n^{2k} is equal to $w_{n/2}^k$.

$$w_n^{2k} = e^{i2\pi(2k)/n} = e^{i2\pi k/(n/2)} = w_{n/2}^k$$

Therefore,

$$\texttt{F0}[k] = A_0(w_{n/2}^k) = A_0(w_n^{2k})$$
$$\texttt{F1}[k] = A_1(w_{n/2}^k) = A_1(w_n^{2k})$$

Then, we can compute the first half of `F[]` by using `F0[]` and `F1[]`.

$$\texttt{F}[k] = \texttt{F0}[k] + w_n^k \cdot \texttt{F1}[k] \qquad \forall\, k = 0, 1, \ldots, n/2 - 1$$

The second half of `F[]` is as follows. Similar to the first half, we also start with the D&C formula, but this time, we further break down the exponents.

$$\begin{aligned}\texttt{F}[n/2 + k] = A(w_n^{n/2+k}) &= A_0((w_n^{n/2+k})^2) + w_n^{n/2+k} \cdot A_1((w_n^{n/2+k})^2) \\ &= A_0(w_n^{n+2k}) + w_n^{n/2+k} \cdot A_1(w_n^{n+2k}) \\ &= A_0(w_n^n w_n^{2k}) + w_n^{n/2} w_n^k \cdot A_1(w_n^n w_n^{2k}) \qquad \forall\, k = 0, 1, \ldots, n/2 - 1\end{aligned}$$

We know that $w_n^n = e^{i2\pi} = 1$ and $w_n^{n/2} = e^{i\pi} = -1$.

$$\begin{aligned}\texttt{F}[n/2 + k] = A(w_n^{n/2+k}) &= A_0(1 \cdot w_n^{2k}) + (-1) \cdot w_n^k \cdot A_1(1 \cdot w_n^{2k}) \\ &= A_0(w_n^{2k}) - w_n^k \cdot A_1(w_n^{2k}) \qquad \forall\, k = 0, 1, \ldots, n/2 - 1\end{aligned}$$

[31] Also, observe that both `F0[]` and `F1[]` have a size of only $n/2$.

Previously, we have shown that $A_0(w_n^{2k})$ and $A_1(w_n^{2k})$ are simply F0[k] and F1[k]. Therefore, the formula to compute the second half of F[] is as follows.

$$\texttt{F}[n/2+k] = \texttt{F0}[k] - w_n^k \cdot \texttt{F1}[k] \qquad \forall\, k = 0, 1, \ldots, n/2-1$$

If we reflect on these formulas to compute F[], we actually compute both $A(x)$ and $A(-x)$ with a recursive call of $A_0(x^2)$ and $A_1(x^2)$ each with a half of the size of A's coefficients. That is, we solve two values, x $(= w_n^k)$ for the first half and $-x$ $(= -w_n^k)$ for the second half[32], with only one value, x^2 $(= w_n^{2k})$; just what we wanted by using the nth roots of unity.

Implementation. We can simplify the implementation by using A[] to also store the evaluated values F[]. Thus, the FFT() function does not return anything, instead it directly modifies the vector A[] (into F[]). In order to do this, A[] needs to be a vector of complex numbers.

The **std::complex** class in C++ and **complex()** module in Python can be used to deal with complex numbers. Java (JDK), unfortunately, does not have any built-in class for complex numbers that we aware of so you might need to implement it by yourself. You might also want to refresh yourself with some basic arithmetic operations on complex numbers (we only need addition/subtraction and multiplication).

The following is one implementation of FFT in C++.

```
typedef complex<double> cd;
const double PI = acos(-1.0);

void FFT(vector<cd> &A) {
  int n = A.size();
  if ( n == 1 ) return;

  vector<cd> A0(n/2), A1(n/2);                    // divide
  for ( int k = 0; 2 * k < n; ++k ) {
    A0[k] = A[2*k];
    A1[k] = A[2*k+1];
  }

  FFT(A0);                                        // conquer
  FFT(A1);

  for ( int k = 0; 2 * k < n; ++k ) {             // combine
    cd x = cd(cos(2*PI*k/n), sin(2*PI*k/n));
    A[k]     = A0[k] + x * A1[k];
    A[k+n/2] = A0[k] - x * A1[k];
  }
}
```

The *divide* and *combine* part each runs in $O(n)$ while the *conquer* part halves the input size, hence, the recurrence relation is $T(n) = 2 \cdot T(n/2) + O(n)$. Therefore, by master theorem, the above implementation runs in $O(n \log n)$.

To call FFT(), you can use the following code. Note that this code only shows how to call FFT() and not to be used directly for fast polynomial multiplication.

[32]The root of unity for the second half of F[], $w_n^{n/2+k}$, is equal to $-w_n^k$ as has been shown previously

```
// contains the polynomial coefficients
// polynomial.size() should be a power of 2
vi polynomial;

// convert vector<int> into vector<complex<double>>
vector<cd> A(polynomial.begin(), polynomial.end());

// call FFT with A as a vector of complex numbers
FFT(A);

for ( auto &p : A )
  printf("%lf + i %lf\n", p.real(), p.imag());
```

FFT, an in-place algorithm

The previous FFT implementation can be improved by modifying the recursive structure into an iterative one, thus, removing the additional overhead of function calls which also translates to faster running time.

In FFT, the sequence $(a_0, a_1, a_2, a_3, a_4, a_5, a_6, a_7)$ will be separated into two sequences: (a_0, a_2, a_4, a_6) and (a_1, a_3, a_5, a_7), i.e., separating the even and odd terms. All the even terms have 0 and all the odd terms have 1 as their least significant bit. Thus, performing the operations on even terms first and then the odd terms (recursively) is as if we prioritize the operations on the number with a lower least significant bit. This actually is equal to performing the operations in a bit-reversal order.

Normal order		*Bit-reversal order*	
Decimal	Binary	Decimal	Binary
0	0000	0	0000
1	0001	8	1000
2	0010	4	0100
3	0011	12	1100
4	0100	2	0010
5	0101	10	1010
6	0110	6	0110
7	0111	14	1110
8	1000	1	0001
9	1001	9	1001
10	1010	5	0101
11	1011	13	1101
12	1100	3	0011
13	1101	11	1011
14	1110	7	0111
15	1111	15	1111

To sort $(0, 1, 2, 3, \dots)$ in a bit-reversal order, we need to check each j, compare it with its `reverseBit`(j), and swap accordingly. Then, to perform FFT (in place), we simply need to sort the sequence into its reversal-bit order, and then perform the D&C process from the shortest length, i.e., $2, 4, 8, 16, \dots$.

The following is one implementation of an in-place FFT in C++.

```
typedef complex<double> cd;
const double PI = acos(-1.0);

int reverseBit(int x, int m) {
  int ret = 0;
  for ( int k = 0; k < m; ++k )
    if ( x & (1 << k) ) ret |= 1 << (m-k-1);
  return ret;
}

void InPlaceFFT(vector<cd> &A) {
  int m = 0;
  while ( m < A.size() ) m <<= 1;          // m need to be a power of 2

  for ( int k = 0; k < A.size(); ++k )
    if ( k < reverseBit(k, m) )
      swap(A[k], A[reverseBit(k, m)]);

  for ( int n = 2; n <= A.size(); n <<= 1 ) {
    for ( int k = 0; 2 * k < n; ++k ) {
      cd x = cd(cos(2*PI*k/n), sin(2*PI*k/n));
      A[k]     = A0[k] + x * A1[k];
      A[k+n/2] = A0[k] - x * A1[k];
    }
  }
}
```

If `A.size()` is already a power of 2, then we can simply assign `m = A.size()`.

Inverse Fast Fourier Transform

DFT transforms polynomial coefficients into its evaluations at the roots of unity[33], and FFT is a fast algorithm to compute it. To do a fast polynomial multiplication, we also need to perform the **inverse DFT (IDFT)** in order to convert the polynomial from a point-value representation back into a coefficient representation. Fortunately, IDFT can be computed easily with FFT with some additional steps. Thus, we can use the previous FFT implementation to perform IDFT, or in this case, the inverse FFT (IFFT).

To simplify some notations, we will reuse the previous w_n^k notation; however, this time, we remove the subscripted n and write it as w^k to ease the reading.

$$w^k = e^{i2\pi k/n}$$

The evaluation of a polynomial $A(x)$ on $x = w^k$ is as follows.

$$\begin{aligned} A(w^k) &= a_0(w^k)^0 + a_1(w^k)^1 + a_2(w^k)^2 + \ldots + a_{n-1}(w^k)^{n-1} \\ &= a_0 w^{0k} \quad + a_1 w^{1k} \quad + a_2 w^{2k} \quad + \ldots + a_{n-1} w^{(n-1)k} \end{aligned}$$

[33]In engineering term, DFT transforms a series from a time domain to a frequency domain.

To perform DFT, we evaluate the polynomial for all $k = 0, 1, 2, \ldots, n-1$. We can also represent the whole DFT operations with matrix multiplication.

$$\begin{pmatrix} w^0 & w^0 & w^0 & \cdots & w^0 \\ w^0 & w^1 & w^2 & \cdots & w^{n-1} \\ w^0 & w^2 & w^4 & \cdots & w^{2(n-1)} \\ \vdots & \vdots & \vdots & \ddots & \vdots \\ w^{n-1} & w^{2(n-1)} & w^{3(n-1)} & \cdots & w^{(n-1)(n-1)} \end{pmatrix} \begin{pmatrix} a_0 \\ a_1 \\ a_2 \\ \vdots \\ a_{n-1} \end{pmatrix} = \begin{pmatrix} y_0 \\ y_1 \\ y_2 \\ \vdots \\ y_{n-1} \end{pmatrix}$$

or simply

$$W\mathbf{a} = \mathbf{y}$$

where W is the DFT matrix[34], $\mathbf{a}$ is a vector of polynomial coefficients, and $\mathbf{y}$ is the result vector where $y_k = A(w^k)$. In other words, to obtain $\mathbf{y}$ from $\mathbf{a}$, we simply multiply $\mathbf{a}$ with W. To recover $\mathbf{a}$ from $\mathbf{y}$ (the reversed operation), we need to multiply $\mathbf{y}$ with the inverse of W (i.e., W^{-1}).

$$\mathbf{a} = W^{-1}\mathbf{y}$$

DFT matrix has a nice property because its elements are the roots of unity, hence, the inverse can be found easily. The inverse DFT (IDFT) matrix has the following form.

$$W^{-1} = \frac{1}{n}\begin{pmatrix} w^0 & w^0 & w^0 & \cdots & w^0 \\ w^0 & w^{-1} & w^{-2} & \cdots & w^{-(n-1)} \\ w^0 & w^{-2} & w^{-4} & \cdots & w^{-2(n-1)} \\ \vdots & \vdots & \vdots & \ddots & \vdots \\ w^0 & w^{-(n-1)} & w^{-2(n-1)} & \cdots & w^{-(n-1)(n-1)} \end{pmatrix}$$

We can verify this by multiplying W with W^{-1} to get an identity matrix I. Let S be $W \cdot W^{-1}$.

$$S = \frac{1}{n}\begin{pmatrix} w^0 & w^0 & w^0 & \cdots & w^0 \\ w^0 & w^1 & w^2 & \cdots & w^{n-1} \\ w^0 & w^2 & w^4 & \cdots & w^{2(n-1)} \\ \vdots & \vdots & \vdots & \ddots & \vdots \\ w^{n-1} & w^{2(n-1)} & w^{3(n-1)} & \cdots & w^{(n-1)(n-1)} \end{pmatrix}\begin{pmatrix} w^0 & w^0 & w^0 & \cdots & w^0 \\ w^0 & w^{-1} & w^{-2} & \cdots & w^{-(n-1)} \\ w^0 & w^{-2} & w^{-4} & \cdots & w^{-2(n-1)} \\ \vdots & \vdots & \vdots & \ddots & \vdots \\ w^0 & w^{-(n-1)} & w^{-2(n-1)} & \cdots & w^{-(n-1)(n-1)} \end{pmatrix}$$

We will show that S is an identity matrix I.[35] The rth row and c^{th} column of S is in the following form (from a matrix multiplication).

$$\begin{aligned} S_{r,c} &= \frac{1}{n}(w^{0r}w^{0c} + w^{1r}w^{-1c} + w^{2r}w^{-2c} + \cdots + w^{(n-1)r}w^{-(n-1)c}) \\ &= \frac{1}{n}(w^{0(r-c)} + w^{1(r-c)} + w^{2(r-c)} + \cdots + w^{(n-1)(r-c)}) \end{aligned}$$

Let $r - c = d$. Then

$$S_{r,c} = \frac{1}{n}(w^{0d} + w^{1d} + w^{2d} + \cdots + w^{(n-1)d})$$

[34]Matrix of this type is also called a Vandermonde matrix.

[35]Note that we move the scalar $\frac{1}{n}$ to the front for an easier read. Moving around a scalar value does not matter in matrix multiplication.

When $d = 0$ (at the principal digonal of the matrix), $S_{r,c}$ reduces to:

$$\begin{aligned} S_{r,c} = S_{k,k} &= \frac{1}{n}(w^0 + w^0 + w^0 + \cdots + w^0) \\ &= \frac{1}{n}(1 + 1 + 1 + \cdots + 1) \\ &= 1 \end{aligned}$$

What will happen when $d \neq 0$? First, notice that $w^k = w^{k \bmod n}$. This can be explained by observing that $e^{i\theta}$ lies at a circle whose distance to origin equals to 1 (Figure 9.12), thus, if $k >= n$ (or $\theta >= 2\pi$), then it simply wraps around. Also, notice that $\langle w^{0d}, w^{1d}, w^{2d}, \ldots, w^{(n-2)d} \rangle$ are **all** of the $(n/\gcd(n,d))^{th}$ roots of unity. For example, let $n = 4$ and $d = 3$, then $\langle w^{0 \bmod 4}, w^{3 \bmod 4}, w^{6 \bmod 4}, w^{9 \bmod 4} \rangle = \langle w^0, w^3, w^2, w^1 \rangle = \langle e^{i2\pi 0/4}, e^{i2\pi 3/4}, e^{i2\pi 2/4}, e^{i2\pi 1/4} \rangle$ are all the 4th roots of unity. Another example, let $n = 4$ and $d = 2$, then $\langle w^{0 \bmod 4}, w^{2 \bmod 4}, w^{4 \bmod 4}, w^{6 \bmod 4} \rangle = \langle w^0, w^2, w^0, w^2 \rangle$; removing duplicates, $\langle w^0, w^2 \rangle = \langle e^{i2\pi 0/4}, e^{i2\pi 2/4} \rangle = \langle e^{i2\pi 0/2}, e^{i2\pi 1/2} \rangle$ are all the 2th roots of unity. Here is an **interesting fact**: The sum of all n^{th} roots of unity is 0. There are many ways to prove this claim, but we can get the intuition from Figure 9.12 and notice that the "center of mass" of all n^{th} roots of unity is at the origin.

We have concluded that all elements in the principal diagonal of S are 1 while the other remaining elements are 0, thus, S is an identity matrix and the given W^{-1} is indeed the inverse of a DFT matrix.

Computing IDFT

Observe that W^{-1} has a very similar structure to W with two differences, the negative sign on the exponents and the scale down factor, $\frac{1}{n}$. First, let's work on w^{-k}.

$$w^{-k} = e^{-i2\pi k/n} = \cos(-2\pi k/n) + i \sin(-2\pi k/n)$$

We also know about cosine and sine of a negative angle from basic trigonometry.

$$\begin{aligned} \cos(-\theta) &= \cos(\theta) \\ \sin(-\theta) &= -\sin(\theta) \end{aligned}$$

Thus, $e^{-i2\pi k/n}$ is equal to the following formula.

$$\begin{aligned} e^{-i2\pi k/n} &= \cos(-2\pi k/n) + i \sin(-2\pi k/n) \\ &= \cos(2\pi k/n) - i \sin(2\pi k/n) \end{aligned}$$

We want a minimum change in the previous FFT implementation to find the IFFT (make life easier!). It would be very nice if we can compute $y_j \cdot e^{-i2\pi k/n}$ when doing IDFT without the need to change the sign of $e^{i2\pi k/n}$ so we can simply use the previous FFT implementation. Fortunately, we can do that with the help of **complex conjugate** operator for complex numbers. The complex conjugate of $a + bi$ is $a - bi$, i.e., the same real part and the same imaginary magnitude but with an opposite sign.

Let r and s be two complex numbers, and $\overline{z}$ be a complex conjugate of a complex number z. It is known that

$$r \cdot s = \overline{\overline{r} \cdot \overline{s}}$$

Using this knowledge, we can reduce the computation of $y_j \cdot e^{-i\theta}$ into the following.

$$\begin{aligned} y_j \cdot e^{-i\theta} &= y_j \cdot (\cos\theta - i\sin\theta) \\ &= \overline{\overline{y_j} \cdot \overline{(\cos\theta - i\sin\theta)}} \\ &= \overline{\overline{y_j} \cdot (\cos\theta + i\sin\theta)} \\ &= \overline{\overline{y_j} \cdot e^{i\theta}} \end{aligned}$$

Thus, we can use $e^{i\theta}$ or $e^{i2\pi k/n}$ instead of $e^{-i2\pi k/n}$ to compute IDFT, and they are already used in the previous FFT implementation.

In summary, to perform IFFT, we simply need the following steps.

1. Perform complex conjugation on each element (i.e., flip the imaginary part)
2. Perform FFT on that sequence.
3. Perform complex conjugation on each element.
4. Scale down the sequence.

In C++, we can use `std:conj()` to perform complex conjugation, while in Python, we can use `conjugate()` function on a complex number. Alternatively, we can simply implement it directly from scratch as a complex conjugation operation is only flipping the imaginary part's sign of a complex number.

The following is one implementation of IFFT in C++.

```
void IFFT(vector<cd> &A) {
  for ( auto &p : A ) p = conj(p);        // complex conjugate
                                          // a + bi -> a - bi

  FFT(A);

  for ( auto &p : A ) p = conj(p);        // complex conjugate
                                          // **not needed for our purpose**

  for ( auto &p : A ) p /= A.size();      // scale down (1/n)
}
```

Note that the second complex conjugation (after FFT) is not needed if our goal is only to perform fast polynomial multiplication on real/integer numbers where the input and output do not have any imaginary part. We can see that this code runs in $O(n \log n)$.

Fast Polynomial Multiplication

We already have FFT and IFFT, now, we are ready to address the fast polynomial multiplication problem. As illustrated in Figure 9.11, performing a fast polynomial multiplication with FFT involves three steps: (1) perform FFT on both polynomials, (2) do the multiplication, (3) perform IFFT on the result.

A multiplication of a polynomial of degree n_1 with a polynomial of degree n_2 will result in a polynomial of degree $n = n_1 + n_2$, and to represent a polynomial of degree n with a point value representation, we need at least $n + 1$ point-value pairs. Also, recall that the previous FFT implementation requires the sequence length to be a power of 2, thus, we might need to append one or more zeroes at each polynomial such that the length is a power of 2 no less than $n_1 + n_2 + 1$. Because of this, we might want to resize the resulting polynomial into its original degree, i.e., $n_1 + n_2 + 1$.

The following is one implementation of fast polynomial multiplication in C++.

```
vi multiply(vi p1, vi p2) {
  int n = 1;                             // n needs to be a power of 2
  while ( n < p1.size() + p2.size() - 1 )
    n <<= 1;

  vector<cd> A(p1.begin(), p1.end());    // prepare A and B for FFT calls
  vector<cd> B(p2.begin(), p2.end());
  A.resize(n);
  B.resize(n);

  FFT(A);                                // transform
  FFT(B);

  vector<cd> C(n);                       // perform the multiplication
  for ( int k = 0; k < n; ++k )
    C[k] = A[k] * B[k];

  IFFT(C);                               // inverse transform

  vi res;                                // prepare output
  for ( auto &p : C )
    res.push_back(round(p.real()));

  res.resize(p1.size() + p2.size() - 1); // resize to original degree

  return res;
}
```

Observe that `p1.size()` is $n_1 + 1$ and `p2.size()` is $n_2 + 1$ because a polynomial degree is the number of coefficients (including all non-trailing zeroes) minus 1. Thus, the notation `p1.size() + p2.size() - 1` is the same as $n_1 + n_2 + 1$.

Precision and Rounding Error

In the previous implementation of `FFT()`, we used `complex<double>` to represent a complex number where both of its real and imaginary part are stored in a `double` (double-precision floating-point) data type. In most problems, this is enough because a `double` data type has a precision up to about 15 digits. However, if the problem or your solution causes a larger number to pop up in the polynomial multiplication result, then you might need to refrain from using `double` and consider using `long double` instead, i.e., `complex<long double>`.

Convolution

The coefficient representation of a polynomial can also be regarded as a series or sequence. Performing a **convolution** of two finite series is the same as performing polynomial multiplication on those two sequences by treating each sequence as a polynomial. Sometimes it is easier for us to think about the problem we faced in terms of convolution instead of polynomial multiplication as usually there is no (explicit) polynomial in the problem.

Usually convolution is denoted by the operator $*$. For example, a convolution of two series, f and g, is denoted by $f * g$. A multiple self-convolution can also be denoted as $\underbrace{f * f * \ldots f}_{m} = f^{*m}$.

The sth element of $f * g$ is defined as follows.

$$(f * g)_s = \sum_{j+k=s} f_j \cdot g_k$$

which basically is the sum of all multiplications between f_j and g_k where $j + k = s$. This value is equal to the sth term of the result of multiplying f and g as polynomials.

Applications

There are many applications for FFT in competitive programming and most of them don't seem to have anything to do with multiplying polynomials at first glance.

All Possible Sums

Given two arrays of non-negative integers, A and B, calculate how many ways to get a sum of $y = A_j + B_k$ for all possible values of y.

We can solve this by creating two vectors, f and g, where f_j denotes how many elements in A which value is j, and g_k denotes how many elements in B which value is k. Note that as f and g are the frequency vector of A and B, their size might not be the same as A and B. The convolution, $f * g$, gives us the number of ways y can be formed as a sum of an element in A and an element in B for all possible value of y.

For example, let $A = \{1, 1, 1, 3, 3, 4\}$ and $B = \{1, 1, 2, 3, 3\}$. In A, there are 3 elements whose value are 1 ($f_1 = 3$), 2 elements whose value are 3 ($f_3 = 2$), and there is 1 element whose value is 4 ($f_4 = 1$). Thus, $f = (0, 3, 0, 2, 1)$; similarly, $g = (0, 2, 1, 2)$.

The convolution of f and g is $f * g = (0, 0, 6, 3, 10, 4, 5, 2)$ where each element corresponds to how many ways to get a sum of y from A and B. For example, there are 10 ways to get a sum of 4, $(f * g)_4 = 10$. There are 3 methods to get 4 by summing two non-negative integers, i.e., $1 + 3$, $2 + 2$, and $3 + 1$.

- There are 6 ways to choose (j, k) such that $A_j = 1$ and $B_k = 3$.
- There are 0 ways to choose (j, k) such that $A_j = 2$ and $B_k = 2$.
- There are 4 ways to choose (j, k) such that $A_j = 3$ and $B_k = 1$.

In total, there are $6 + 0 + 4 = 10$ ways to get 4 by summing an element of A and an element of B in this example.

All Dot Products

Given two array of integers, A and B (without loss of generality, assume $|A| \geq |B|$), determine the dot product[36] of B with a contiguous subsequence of A for all possible contiguous subsequence of A of the same length with B.

[36]The dot or scalar product of $(a_0, a_1, \ldots, a_{n-1})$ and $(b_0, b_1, \ldots, b_{n-1})$ is $a_0b_0 + a_1b_1 + \cdots + a_{n-1}b_{n-1}$.

For example, let $A = \{5, 7, 2, 1, 3, 6\}$ and $B = \{2, 1, 3, 4\}$. There are three contiguous subsequences of A (of length $|B| = 4$) that we must calculate for each of its dot product with B.

```
A:  5 7 2 1 3 6          5 7 2 1 3 6          5 7 2 1 3 6
    | | | |                | | | |                | | | |
B:  2 1 3 4                2 1 3 4                2 1 3 4
```

Their dot products are as follows.

- $5 \cdot 2 + 7 \cdot 1 + 2 \cdot 3 + 1 \cdot 4 = 27$
- $7 \cdot 2 + 2 \cdot 1 + 1 \cdot 3 + 3 \cdot 4 = 31$
- $2 \cdot 2 + 1 \cdot 1 + 3 \cdot 3 + 6 \cdot 4 = 38$

Let f be equal to A and g be equal to the reversed of B. Then the output for this problem can be obtained in the convolution of f and g. In the above example, $f = (5, 7, 2, 1, 3, 6)$, $g = (4, 3, 1, 2)$, and $f * g = (20, 43, 34, \mathbf{27}, \mathbf{31}, \mathbf{38}, 23, 12, 12)$. Our desired results are in the "center" of $f * g$ (the bolded text).

Additionally, the other numbers in $f * g$ correspond to the dot product of a suffix/prefix of A with B if we extend our problem definition by appending zeroes at the front and at the end of A.

```
A:  0 0 0 5 7 2 1 3 6   0 0 5 7 2 1 3 6   0 5 7 2 1 3 6
    | | | |             | | | |           | | | |
B:  2 1 3 4             2 1 3 4           2 1 3 4

A:  5 7 2 1 3 6 0    5 7 2 1 3 6 0 0   5 7 2 1 3 6 0 0 0
          | | | |            | | | |             | | | |
B:        2 1 3 4            2 1 3 4             2 1 3 4
```

Why does convoluting f and g (of reversed B) give us this result? We can get the answer to this question by observing the convolution formula, or simply pay attention to what happened when we multiply two polynomials. For example, consider the case when we multiply (a, b, c, d, e) and (z, y, x) (i.e., (x, y, z) in reversed order).

$$
\begin{array}{ccccccc}
 & & a & b & c & d & e \\
\times & & & & z & y & x \\
\hline
 & & ax & bx & cx & dx & ex \\
 & ay & by & cy & dy & ey & \\
az & bz & cz & dz & ez & &
\end{array}
$$

The result is a polynomial

$$(az, ay + bz, ax + by + cz, bx + cy + dz, cx + dy + ez, dx + ey, ex)$$

where each element is a dot product of a contiguous subsequence of (a, b, c, d, e) and (x, y, z) as described in the problem.

Another variation of this problem is where A is a circular sequence. In such a case, we only need to append A with itself and solve the problem with the method we have just discussed.

Note that this technique of convoluting a sequence with a reversed sequence often appears as part of a solution to many other problems, so, you might want to study this.

Bitstring Alignment

Given two bitstrings, A and B, determine how many substrings of A of the same length with B such that it satisfies the following condition: If $B_k = 1$ then $A'_k = 1$ (where A' is a substring of A which has the same length with B).

For example, let A = `11011110` and B = `1101`. There are 2 substrings of A that are *aligned* with B, i.e., $A_{0..3}$ = `1101`, and $A_{3..6}$ = `1111`.

```
A:  11011110        11011110
    || |               || |
B:  1101               1101
```

Observe that the dot product of a satisfying alignment should be equal to the Hamming weight[37] of B. With this observation, we can solve this problem similar to the previous all dot products problem. Let f be equal to A and g be equal to the reversed of B[38]. The output to this problem is equal to the number of elements in $f * g$ which are equal to the Hamming weight of B.

Bitstring Matching

Given two bitstrings, A and B, determine how many times B appears in A as a substring.

This is an extension of the previous bitstring alignment problem. In this problem, we should align both bit 0 and bit 1.

We can solve this problem by running the convolution for the previous bitstring alignment problem twice, one for bit 1 and another for bit 0.[39] Let the convolution for bit 1 be p and the convolution for bit 0 be q. Then, the output to this problem is equal to the number of elements in $p + q$ which are equal to the length of B.[40]

String Matching

Given two strings, A and B, determine how many times B appears in A as a substring.

This is a general version of the previous bitstring matching. Of course, we can solve this by running the convolution for bitstring alignment problem as many times as the size of the alphabets being used, one for each unique alphabet. Then, the result can be obtained by counting the number of elements in the addition of all those convolution results which are equal to the length of B. However, there is a better way.

Let f be the polynomial which corresponds to A where each element is in the form of $e^{i2\pi k/n}$. The variable k corresponds to A_j (e.g., `a` $\rightarrow$ 0, `b` $\rightarrow$ 1, `c` $\rightarrow$ 2, ..., `z` $\rightarrow$ 25), and n is the size of alphabets being used (e.g., 26). Similarly, let g be the polynomial which corresponds to the reversed B where each element is in the form of $e^{-i2\pi k/n}$ (note the negative exponent).

If we multiply $e^{i2\pi p/n}$ with $e^{-i2\pi q/n}$ (which equals $e^{i2\pi(p-q)/n}$) when $p = q$, then we will get $e^0 = 1 + 0i$ as the result. On the other hand, when $p \neq q$, we will get $e^{i2\pi r/n}$ where $r = p + q \neq 0$; this value is equal to an nth root of unity which is not $1 + 0i$, or specifically, $a + bi$ where $a = [-1, 1)$ and $b = [-1, 1]$ (refer to Figure 9.12). Observe that we can only get a 1 in the real part of $e^{i2\pi(p-q)/n}$ only when $p = q$; otherwise, the real part is less than 1.

[37]A Hamming weight of a string is equal to the number of characters that are different from a zero-symbol of the alphabet being used. In a case of bitstring, a Hamming weight equals to the number of bit 1.

[38]Conversions from numeric characters (`'0'` and `'1'`) into integers (0 and 1) might be needed.

[39]In the case of aligning bit 0, simply flip all bits ($0 \leftrightarrow 1$).

[40]A polynomial addition of $(a_0, a_1, \ldots, a_{n-1})$ and $(b_0, b_1, \ldots, b_{n-1})$ is $(a_0 + b_0, a_1 + b_1, \ldots, a_{n-1} + b_{n-1})$.

Therefore, the dot product of matching strings should be equal to the length of the string (each element contributes $1 + 0i$ to the sum). Then, the output to this problem is equal to the number of elements in $f * g$ which are equal to the length of B.

This solution can be an alternative to other string matching algorithms such as the Knuth-Morris-Pratt algorithm (Chapter 6.4.2) or the Rabin-Karp algorithm (Chapter 6.6). Although this method has a (slightly) worse time-complexity, it might offer additional flexibility as we will see in the next problem. Note that you might need to modify the previous code for `multiply()` to accept and return a vector of complex numbers if you use this method.

String Matching with Wildcard Characters

Given two strings, A and B, determine how many times B appears in A as a substring. String B may contain zero or more wildcard characters that are represented by '?'. Each wildcard character represents any single character. For example, `?c?c` matches `icpcec` on index 0 (`icpc`) and 2 (`pcec`).

The solution to this problem is similar to the previous string matching problem. However, we need to set the coefficient of g to be 0 whenever its corresponding character in (the reversed) B is a wildcard character, i.e., we ignore such a character in the matching process. The output to this problem is equal to the number of elements in $f * g$ which are equal to the length of B without wildcard characters, e.g., `?c?c` has a length of 2. Note that you might want to consider only coefficients of $f * g$ which correspond to a full-length string match, i.e., the "center" of $f * g$ as in the previous discussion on all dot products problem; otherwise, `??x` will have a match with `xyyyz` on index -2, or `z??` will have a match with `xyyyz` on index 4, which does not make any sense to this problem.

All Distances

Given a bitstring, A, determine how many ways to choose two positions in A, p and q, such that $A_p = A_q = 1$ and $q - p = k$ for any possible distance of k.

For example, let $A =$ `10111`. Note that a negative distance of k will have the same result as its positive distance.

- $|k| = 0 \rightarrow 4$ ways (trivial).
- $|k| = 1 \rightarrow 2$ ways, i.e., $\texttt{10}\underline{\texttt{11}}\texttt{1}$, and $\texttt{101}\underline{\texttt{11}}$.
- $|k| = 2 \rightarrow 2$ ways, , i.e., $\underline{\texttt{1}}\texttt{0}\underline{\texttt{1}}\texttt{11}$ and $\texttt{10}\underline{\texttt{1}}\texttt{1}\underline{\texttt{1}}$.
- $|k| = 3 \rightarrow 1$ way, i.e., $\underline{\texttt{1}}\texttt{01}\underline{\texttt{1}}\texttt{1}$.
- $|k| = 4 \rightarrow 1$ way, i.e., $\underline{\texttt{1}}\texttt{011}\underline{\texttt{1}}$.

We can solve this problem by calculating the all dot products of A with itself A, however, this time, we need all of them, including the "suffix/prefix" dot products (refer to the previous discussion on all dot products problem). The very center element of the convolution $f * g$ corresponds to the number of ways such that $k = 0$, to the left of it is for negative k, and to the right of it is for positive k, i.e., $\ldots, -2, -1, 0, 1, 2, \ldots$. Note that $f * g$ will always be symmetric for an obvious reason. In the previous example, $f * g = (1, 1, 2, 2, 4, 2, 2, 1, 1)$.

Why does all dot products of A with itself solve this problem? Observe that when we do a dot product of a prefix/suffix of A with a suffix/prefix of A (of the same length), we actually align each bit 1 with another bit 1 in A of a certain distance. The "shift" (length of A minus the length of prefix/suffix A in consideration) corresponds to k in this problem.

```
          10111          10111          10111          10111      10111
          |              |              | |              ||       | |||
      10111          10111          10111          10111          10111

      10111       10111        10111          10111
         ||        | |            |              |
        10111       10111        10111          10111
```

Example Problems

Kattis – A+B Problem (aplusb)

Given N integers $A_{1..N}$ where $N \leq 200\,000$ and $A_j = [-50\,000, 50\,000]$, determine how many tuple $\langle p, q, r\rangle$ are there such that p, q, r are pairwise distinct and $A_p + A_q = A_r$.

This is what an all possible sums problem is (as discussed previously) with some nasty cases to be considered, i.e., A might be non-positive and p, q, and r should be pairwise distinct.

Let f be the sequence containing the frequency of each element in A.

The first issue (non-positive integer) can be addressed by shifting all integers. The second issue can be addressed by substracting 1 for each $(f * f)_{2A_j}$, i.e., remove $A_j + A_j$ from $f * f$. One tricky case you should pay attention to is the zeroes in A. There are several ways to address this, e.g., by removing all zeroes from A and treat them separately.

Live Archive 6808 – Best Position

Abridged problem statement: You are given a 2-dimensional array S of $R \times C$ characters where $S_{r,c} \in \{\texttt{G}, \texttt{L}\}$ and $R, C \leq 500$. There are B ($B \leq 5$) queries where each query contains a 2-dimensional array P of $H \times W$ where $P_{h,w} \in \{\texttt{G}, \texttt{L}\}$, $1 \leq H \leq R$, and $1 \leq W \leq C$. For each query, find an alignment of P on S such that the number of coinciding elements is maximum. In other words, (j, k) such that the number of (h, w) where $P_{h,w} = S_{h+j,w+k}$ for $0 \leq h < H$ and $0 \leq w < W$ is maximized. Each alignment of P should be positioned completely inside S, i.e., $0 \leq j \leq R - H$ and $0 \leq k \leq C - W$.

First, notice that B is small (≤ 5), thus, there is (little to) no harm in solving each query independently, i.e., simply treat each query as a new case.

This problem looks like a bitstring matching with wildcard characters problem; however, instead of a (perfect) bitstring matching, we would like to find the best/maximum bitstring matching.

Before that, we have to deal with the fact that this problem has a 2-dimensional bitstring. We can simply "flatten" the 2-dimensional bitstring S into a 1-dimensional bitstring by concatenating all rows of S. For example,

```
GGGGG
LLLLL  →  GGGGGLLLLLGGGLL
GGGLL
```

On the other hand, for bitstring P, we need to "flatten" it while inserting wildcard characters such that each row has the same length to C. For example, consider when $C = 5$.

```
GG  →  GG???  →  GG???LL???
LL     LL???
```

It does not matter where we insert the wildcard characters as long as they are on the same column. For example, any one of the following is acceptable.

```
GG???   ?GG??   ??GG?   ???GG
LL???   ?LL??   ??LL?   ???LL
```

Then, all we need to do is to solve the bitstring matching problem for the flattened S with the flattened (and adjusted) P while ignoring all of its wildcard characters. Our desired answer corresponds to the highest number in the (added) convolution results. The conversion to the coordinate (j, k) should be done accordingly.

Programming exercise related to Fast Fourier Transform:

1. Entry Level: *Kattis - polymul2* * (basic polynomial multiplication problem that needs an $O(n \log n)$ algorithm; also see Kattis - polymul1)
2. *Kattis - aplusb* * (count frequencies f of each integer with offset to deal with negatives; use FFT to multiply $f \times f$; treat frequency of zeroes $f[0]$ separately)
3. *Kattis - figurinefigures* * (for # of distinct weights, count frequencies f of each figurine weight; convolute f with itself for 3 times to obtain f^{*4})
4. *Kattis - golfbot* * (count frequencies ***dist*** of each reachable distance in one shot; convolute ***dist*** with itself; count distances reachable with one or two shots)
5. *Kattis - moretriangles* * (the coefficient of x^k is the number of is such that $i^2 = k$ (mod n); convolution; inclusion-exclusion; combinatorics; be careful of overflow),
6. *Kattis - tiles* * (the low rating is misleading; modified sieve to count number of divisors d of i; interpret d as polynomial *pd*; convolute *pd* with itself)
7. LA 6808 - Best Position

9.12 Pollard's rho Algorithm

In Section 5.3.3, we have seen the optimized trial division algorithm that can be used to find the prime factors of integers up to $\approx 9 \times 10^{13}$ (see **Exercise 5.3.3.1**) in *contest environment* (i.e., in 'a few seconds' instead of minutes/hours/days). Now, what if we are given a 64-bit unsigned integer (i.e., up to $\approx 1 \times 10^{19}$) or even a Big Integer (beyond 64-bit unsigned integer) to be factored in contest environment (within reasonable time limit)?

For *faster* integer factorization, one can use the Pollard's rho algorithm [31, 4]. The key idea of this algorithm is that two integers x and y are congruent modulo p (p is one of the factors of n—the integer that we want to factor) with probability 0.5 after 'a few ($1.177\sqrt{p}$) integers' having been randomly chosen.

The theoretical details of this algorithm is probably not that important for Competitive Programming. Here, we give a Java implementation that uses `isProbablePrime(certainty)` to handle special case if `n` is a (large) prime number or use the `rho(n)` randomized algorithm routine to break a composite number `n` into its two factors and recursively process them.

```
import java.math.*;
import java.security.SecureRandom;

class Pollardsrho {
  private static BigInteger TWO = BigInteger.valueOf(2);
  private final static SecureRandom random = new SecureRandom();

  private static BigInteger f(BigInteger x, BigInteger b, BigInteger n) {
    return x.multiply(x).mod(n).add(b).mod(n);    // x = (x^2 % n + b) % n
  }

  private static BigInteger rho(BigInteger n) {
    if (n.mod(TWO).compareTo(BigInteger.ZERO) == 0) return TWO; // special
    BigInteger b = new BigInteger(n.bitLength(), random); // rand for luck
    BigInteger x = new BigInteger(n.bitLength(), random);
    BigInteger y = x;                             // initially y = x
    while (true) {
      x = f(x, b, n);                             // x = f(x)
      y = f(f(y, b, n), b, n);                    // y = f(f(y))
      BigInteger d = x.subtract(y).gcd(n);        // d = (x-y) % n
      if (d.compareTo(BigInteger.ONE) != 0)       // if d != 1, then d is
        return d;                                 // one of the divisor of n
    }
  }

  public static void pollard_rho(BigInteger n) {
    if (n.compareTo(BigInteger.ONE) == 0) return; // special case, n = 1
    if (n.isProbablePrime(10)) {                  // if n is a prime
      System.out.println(n); return;              // its only factor is n
    }
    BigInteger d = rho(n);                        // n is a composite number
    pollard_rho(d);                               // recursively check d
    pollard_rho(n.divide(d));                     // and n/d
  }
```

```
  public static void main(String[] args) {
    BigInteger n = new BigInteger("124590589650069032140693"); // Big
    pollard_rho(n); // factorize n to 7 x 124418296927 x 143054969437
  }
}
```

Note that the runtime of Pollard's rho algorithm increases with larger n. Its expected runtime (when n is a composite number) is $\sqrt{a}$ where $a \times b = n$ and $a < b$ or in another word, $O(n^{\frac{1}{4}})$. Using the given Java code that uses slow Big Integer library, we can factor up to $n \leq 10^{24}$ in $\approx$ one second but it will struggle beyond that. The fact that integer factoring is a very difficult task is still a key concept of modern cryptography.

Source code: `ch9/Pollardsrho.java|ml`

Programming exercises related to Pollard's rho algorithm[41]:

1. Entry Level: **UVa 11476 - Factoring Large ...** * (basic integer factorization problem that requires Pollard's rho algorithm)
2. *Kattis - atrivialpursuit* * (Pollard's rho is a subproblem of this problem)

---

[41]This algorithm is very rarely used in programming contest as optimized trial division is already suitable for almost all number theory problems involving integer factorization.

9.13 Chinese Remainder Theorem

Chinese[42] Remainder Theorem (CRT) is very useful in solving a congruence *system* of n congruences, i.e., finding an integer given its remainders when divided by a set of integers.

Let $m_0, m_1, \ldots, m_{n-1}$ be pairwise *coprime*[43] integers and $r_0, r_1, \ldots, r_{n-1}$ be its corresponding remainders (modulo m_i) from an unknown integer x, i.e.,

$$x \equiv r_0 \pmod{m_0}$$
$$x \equiv r_1 \pmod{m_1}$$
$$\ldots$$
$$x \equiv r_{n-1} \pmod{m_{n-1}}$$

Our job is to find such x. The CRT states that there is exactly one solution (for x) to such congruence system modulo m, where $m = m_0 m_1 \ldots m_{n-1}$.

The naïve Complete Search way to solve this is of course to simply test for x from 0 and increment it one by one until x satisfies *all* the congruence equations. The complexity is $O(x \cdot n)$ or $O(m \cdot n)$ since the answer can be no larger than m. In this section, we will learn a better way to find such x.

The congruence system above can be rewritten as:

$$x \equiv a_0 \cdot m/m_0 + a_1 \cdot m/m_1 + \cdots + a_{n-1} \cdot m/m_{n-1} \pmod{m}$$

for some unknown a_i where

$$a_0 \cdot m/m_0 \equiv r_0 \pmod{m_0}$$
$$a_1 \cdot m/m_1 \equiv r_1 \pmod{m_1}$$
$$\ldots$$
$$a_{n-1} \cdot m/m_{n-1} \equiv r_{n-1} \pmod{m_{n-1}}$$

To understand the modified equation above, observe, for example, what will happen to the remainder when x is divided by m_0. Every term except the first one has m_0 as its factor, e.g., the term $a_1 \cdot m/m_1$, or to be exact, $a_1 \cdot m_0 m_2 \ldots m_{n-1}$ has m_0 in it. Thus, the equation becomes $x \equiv a_0 \cdot m/m_0 + 0 + \cdots + 0 \pmod{m_0}$ or simply $x \equiv a_0 \cdot m/m_0 \pmod{m_0}$, which corresponds to $x \equiv r_0 \pmod{m_0}$ in the given congruence system. Therefore, $a_0 \cdot m/m_0 \equiv r_0 \pmod{m_0}$. Similarly, $a_1 \cdot m/m_1 \equiv r_1 \pmod{m_1}$, and so on.

Solving all a_i for these equations will give us x. Observe that the value of a_i only depends on m, m_i, and r_i. Thus, the equations are independent of each other and can be solved one by one. The value of a_i can be obtained by taking the inverse of m/m_i mod m_i and multiply it by r_i.

$$a_i \cdot m/m_i \equiv r_i \pmod{m_i}$$
$$a_i \equiv r_i \cdot (m/m_i)^{-1} \pmod{m_i}$$

Notice that m/m_i and m_i are coprime, thus, $(m/m_i)^{-1}$ mod m_i can be computed with modular multiplicative inverse in $O(\log m)$ (see Chapter 5.3.10). The total complexity of this approach is $O(n \cdot \log m)$.

[42]This problem is believed to first appeared in a third-century Chinese book titled "Sun Zi Suanjing".

[43]Two integers a and b are coprime to each other if their *greatest common divisor* is 1, i.e., the largest positive integer that divides both a and b is 1.

```
// assuming mod, modInverse, and extEuclid have been defined earlier
int crt(vi r, vi m) { // m_t = m_0*m_1*...*m_{n-1}
  int mt = accumulate(m.begin(), m.end(), 1, multiplies<>());
  int x = 0;
  for (int i = 0; i < (int)m.size(); ++i) {
    int a = mod((ll)r[i] * modInverse(mt/m[i], m[i]), m[i]);
    x = mod(x + (ll)a * (mt/m[i]), mt);
  }
  return x;
}
```

Kattis - heliocentric

Kattis - heliocentric can be written as a system of (only) two congruences:

$$x \equiv 365 - e \pmod{365}$$
$$x \equiv 687 - m \pmod{687}$$

Here, $gcd(365, 687) = 1$ so both are coprime. We have $m = 365 \times 687 = 250\,755$ and the final answer is $x \pmod{250\,755}$. Notice that 250 755 is small enough to just run a Complete Search solution. However, to illustrate the computation of x using CRT as explained above, let's use the given sample test case $e = 1$ and $m = 0$ with answer 11 679.

$$x \equiv 365 - 1 \pmod{365} \equiv 364 \pmod{365}$$
$$x \equiv 687 - 0 \pmod{687} \equiv 0 \pmod{687}$$

which can be rewritten as:

$$x \equiv a_0 \cdot 250\,755/365 + a_1 \cdot 250\,755/687 \pmod{250\,755}$$
$$x \equiv a_0 \cdot 687 + a_1 \cdot 365 \pmod{250\,755}$$

where

$$a_0 \cdot 250\,755/365 = a_0 \cdot 687 \equiv 364 \pmod{365}$$
$$a_0 \equiv 364 \cdot 687^{-1} \pmod{365}$$
$$a_0 \equiv 17 \pmod{365}$$
$$a_1 \cdot 250\,755/687 = a_1 \cdot 365 \equiv 0 \pmod{687}$$
$$a_1 \equiv 0 \cdot 365^{-1} \pmod{687}$$
$$a_1 \equiv 0 \pmod{687}$$

so

$$x \equiv 17 \cdot 687 + 0 \cdot 365 \pmod{250\,755}$$
$$x \equiv 11\,679 + 0 \pmod{250\,755}$$
$$x \equiv 11\,679 \pmod{250\,755}$$

and the answer is 11 679.

Source code: `ch9/heliocentric.cpp|java|py|ml`

When m_i Are Not Pairwise Coprime

CRT states that we can uniquely determine a solution to a congruence system under the condition that all the divisors (m_i) are pairwise coprime. What if not all of its divisors are pairwise coprime? Luckily, we can still solve the problem by reducing the congruence system such that all the divisors become pairwise coprime again.

Let $m_i = p_1^{b_1} p_2^{b_2} \ldots p_k^{b_k}$ be the prime decompositions of m_i (p_j is a prime number, see Section 5.3.3). Then, according to CRT, the equation $x \equiv r_i \pmod{m_i}$ is equivalent to:

$$\begin{aligned} x &\equiv r_i \pmod{p_1^{b_1}} \\ x &\equiv r_i \pmod{p_2^{b_2}} \\ &\ldots \\ x &\equiv r_i \pmod{p_k^{b_k}} \end{aligned}$$

With this equivalence relation, we can decompose an equation into its prime power moduli. Perform this decomposition to all the given equations in the original congruence system to obtain a set of new equations. For each prime p among the new equations, we only need to consider the equation with the highest power in its modulus (i.e. p^b where b is the highest) because any information from the lower power modulo can be obtained from the higher power modulo, e.g., if we know that $x \equiv 7 \pmod{2^3}$, then we also know that $x \equiv 3 \pmod{2^2}$ and $x \equiv 1 \pmod{2^1}$; on the other hand, the inverse relation may not hold: $x \equiv 1 \pmod{2^1}$ does not imply $x \equiv 7 \pmod{2^3}$. Finally, we have the following new equations.

$$\begin{aligned} x &\equiv s_1 \pmod{q_1} \\ x &\equiv s_2 \pmod{q_2} \\ &\ldots \\ x &\equiv s_t \pmod{q_k} \end{aligned}$$

where q_i is in the form of p_i^b. As now all the divisors are coprime, we can solve the new congruence system with the previously discussed `crt(r, m)` function. For example:

$$\begin{aligned} x &\equiv 400 \pmod{600} \\ x &\equiv 190 \pmod{270} \\ x &\equiv 40 \pmod{240} \end{aligned}$$

Notice that the divisors are not pairwise coprime. First, let us decompose each divisor: $600 = 2^3 \cdot 3^1 \cdot 5^2$, $270 = 2^1 \cdot 3^3 \cdot 5^1$, and $240 = 2^4 \cdot 3^1 \cdot 5^1$. Then, we expand all the equations:

$$\begin{array}{ccc} x \equiv 400 \pmod{600} & x \equiv 190 \pmod{270} & x \equiv 40 \pmod{240} \\ \downarrow & \downarrow & \downarrow \\ 400 \equiv 0 \pmod{2^3} & 190 \equiv 0 \pmod{2^1} & 40 \equiv 8 \pmod{2^4} \\ 400 \equiv 1 \pmod{3^1} & 190 \equiv 1 \pmod{3^3} & 40 \equiv 1 \pmod{3^1} \\ 400 \equiv 0 \pmod{5^2} & 190 \equiv 0 \pmod{5^1} & 40 \equiv 0 \pmod{5^1} \end{array}$$

Next, for each prime, consider only the equation with the highest power.

$$x \equiv 8 \pmod{2^4} \qquad x \equiv 1 \pmod{3^3} \qquad x \equiv 0 \pmod{5^2}$$

Finally, solve this new congruence system with `crt({8, 1, 0}, {16, 27, 25})` to get 1000.

When does the congruence system not have a solution?

The congruence system has a solution if and only if $r_i \equiv r_j \pmod{\gcd(m_i, m_j)}$ for **all pair** of i and j. Consider the following (subset of a) congruence system.

$$x \equiv r_i \pmod{m_i}$$
$$x \equiv r_j \pmod{m_j}$$

Rewrite the equations by moving r_i and r_j to the left-hand side.

$$x - r_i \equiv 0 \pmod{m_i}$$
$$x - r_j \equiv 0 \pmod{m_j}$$

The first equation implies that m_i divides $(x - r_i)$ which also means that any divisor of m_i divides $(x - r_i)$ as well, including $\gcd(m_i, m_j)$. Similarly, the second equation implies that m_j divides $(x - r_j)$, thus, $\gcd(m_i, m_j)$, which is a divisor of m_j, also divides $(x - r_j)$. Then, we can rewrite the equations by replacing m_i and m_j with $\gcd(m_i, m_j)$.

$$x - r_i \equiv 0 \pmod{\gcd(m_i, m_j)}$$
$$x - r_j \equiv 0 \pmod{\gcd(m_i, m_j)}$$

We can combine those two equations.

$$x - r_i \equiv x - r_j \pmod{\gcd(m_i, m_j)}$$

Finally,

$$r_i \equiv r_j \pmod{\gcd(m_i, m_j)}$$

We can verify the previous example with this method.

$$x \equiv 400 \pmod{600} \text{ and } x \equiv 190 \pmod{270} \rightarrow 400 \equiv 190 \pmod{30}$$
$$x \equiv 400 \pmod{600} \text{ and } x \equiv 40 \pmod{240} \rightarrow 400 \equiv 40 \pmod{120}$$
$$x \equiv 190 \pmod{270} \text{ and } x \equiv 40 \pmod{240} \rightarrow 190 \equiv 40 \pmod{30}$$

We can see that all pair of equations in this example satisfy $r_i \equiv r_j \pmod{\gcd(m_i, m_j)}$, thus, we can conclude that this congruence system should have a solution (which we have shown to be 1000 previously).

When all the divisors are coprime ($\gcd(m_i, m_j) = 1$), then $r_i \equiv r_j \pmod{1}$ always holds, which means a solution always exists in a pairwise coprime case.

Programming exercises related to Chinese Remainder Theorem:

1. Entry Level: **UVa 00756 - Biorhythms** * (CRT or brute force)
2. **UVa 11754 - Code Feat** *
3. *Kattis - chineseremainder* * (basic CRT; 2 linear congruences; Big Integer)
4. *Kattis - generalchineseremainder* * (general CRT; 2 linear congruences)
5. *Kattis - granica* * (CRT; GCD of all N differences of 2 numbers)
6. *Kattis - heliocentric* * (CRT or brute force)
7. *Kattis - remainderreminder* * (a bit of brute force + sorting; generalized CRT)

9.14 Lucas' Theorem

Lucas's theorem states that for any prime number p, the following congruence of binomial coefficients holds:

$$\binom{n}{k} \equiv \prod_{i=0}^{m} \binom{n_i}{k_i} \pmod{p}$$

where n_i and k_i are the base p expansion of n and k respectively.

$$n = \sum_{i=0}^{m} n_i \cdot p^i \qquad\qquad k = \sum_{i=0}^{m} k_i \cdot p^i$$

Some examples where Lucas' theorem can be useful:

- Compute the remainder of a binomial coefficient $\binom{n}{k}$ mod p where n and k can be **large** (e.g., 10^{18}) but p is quite small (e.g., $\leq 10^6$).
- Count how many k for any given n such that $0 \leq k \leq n$ and $\binom{n}{k}$ is an even number.
- Count how many n for any given k and x such that $k \leq n \leq x$ and $\binom{n}{k}$ is divisible by a prime number p.

To see the Lucas' theorem in action, let us consider the following example. Let $n = 1\,000$, $k = 200$, and $p = 13$. First, find the expansion of both n and k in base p.

$$\begin{aligned} 1\,000 &= 5 \cdot 13^2 + 11 \cdot 13^1 + 12 \cdot 13^0 \\ 200 &= 1 \cdot 13^2 + 2 \cdot 13^1 + 5 \cdot 13^0 \end{aligned}$$

Then, by Lucas' theorem:

$$\binom{1\,000}{200} \equiv \binom{5}{1}\binom{11}{2}\binom{12}{5} \pmod{13}$$

Next, we can solve each binomial coefficient independently as the numbers are quite small (i.e. less than p):

$$\binom{5}{1} \equiv 5 \pmod{13} \qquad \binom{11}{2} \equiv 3 \pmod{13} \qquad \binom{12}{5} \equiv 12 \pmod{13}$$

Finally, simply put everything together to obtain the final result:

$$\begin{aligned} \binom{1\,000}{200} &\equiv 5 \cdot 3 \cdot 12 \pmod{13} \\ &\equiv 11 \pmod{13} \end{aligned}$$

The base p expansion of both n and k can be computed in $O(\log n)$ and each has $O(\log n)$ term. One common method to compute $\binom{n_i}{k_i}$ mod p is by using modular multiplicative inverse e.g., with Fermat's little theorem or extended Euclidean algorithm[44] (See Section 5.3.10 and Section 5.4.2) which runs in $O(n_i \log p)$. If we first precompute all the factorial terms from 0

[44]In most cases, Fermat's little theorem is sufficient.

to $p-1$, then $\binom{n_i}{k_i}$ mod p can be found in $O(\log p)$ with an $O(p)$ preprocessing.[45] Therefore, computing $\binom{n}{k}$ mod p with Lucas theorem can be done in $O(p + \log n \log p)$.[46]

Here, we provide a reasonably fast recursive implementation based on Fermat's little theorem, now combined with Lucas' theorem in the second line as outlined earlier:

```
ll C(ll n, ll k) {
  if (n < k) return 0;
  if (n >= MOD) return (C(n%MOD, k%MOD) * C(n/MOD, k/MOD)) % MOD;
  return (((fact[n] * inv(fact[k]))%MOD) * inv(fact[n-k])) % MOD;
}
```

When a Binomial Coefficient is Divisible by a Prime Number

Observe that when there is at least one i such that $n_i < k_i$ in the expansion of n and k in base p, then $\binom{n}{k} \equiv 0 \pmod{p}$. This observation can be useful to solve a problem such as counting how many k for any given n such that $0 \leq k \leq n$ and $\binom{n}{k}$ is divisible by a prime number p.

Lucas' Theorem for Square-Free Modulus

Lucas' theorem only holds for prime modulus. In a composite modulus case where the modulus is **not** divisible by any integer p^s where p is a prime number and $s \geq 2$ (in other words, the modulus is a square-free integer), then it can be solved with Lucas' theorem combined with the Chinese Remainder Theorem. In such cases, we need to break the modulus into its prime factors (e.g., $30 = 2 \cdot 3 \cdot 5$), solve them independently with each prime factor and its power as the modulus (e.g., mod 2, mod 3, and mod 5), and finally, combine the results altogether with Chinese Remainder Theorem (Section 9.13). This method will produce the desired answer as the Chinese Remainder Theorem always has a unique solution when all the moduli are coprime to each other. When the modulus is not square-free (i.e. any positive integer), then a generalization of Lucas' theorem for prime power[9] may be needed.

Programming exercises related to Lucas' Theorem:

1. **LA 6916 - Punching Robot *** (use combinations (need Lucas' theorem) to solve for one robot; use the inclusion-exclusion principle for K robots)
2. *Kattis - classicalcounting* * (combinatorics; inclusion-exclusion; Chinese Remainder Theorem; Lucas' Theorem)

---

[45] Note that both n_i and k_i are less than p.

[46] Alternatively, we can first precompute all the $\binom{n_i}{k_i}$ table for all n_i and $k_i < p$, e.g., with the recurrence relation (Pascal's triangle). Then, the overall time complexity becomes $O(p^2 + \log n)$.

9.15 Rare Formulas or Theorems

We have encountered a few rarely used formulas or theorems in programming contest problems before. Knowing them or having a team member who is a strong mathematician (who is able to derive the same formula on the spot) will give you an *unfair advantage* over other contestants if one of these rare formulas or theorems is used in the programming contest that you join.

1. Cayley's Formula: There are n^{n-2} spanning trees of a complete graph with n labeled vertices. Example: UVa 10843 - Anne's game.

2. Derangement: A permutation of the elements of a set such that none of the elements appear in their original position. The number of derangements $der(n)$ (also denoted by $!n$) can be computed as follows: $der(n) = (n-1) \times (der(n-1) + der(n-2))$ where $der(0) = 1$ and $der(1) = 0$. A basic problem involving derangement is UVa 12024 - Hats (see Section 5.5).

3. Erdős-Gallai Theorem gives a necessary and sufficient condition for a finite sequence of natural numbers to be the *degree sequence* of a simple graph. A sequence of non-negative integers $d_1 \geq d_2 \geq \ldots \geq d_n$ can be the degree sequence of a simple graph on n vertices iff $\sum_{i=1}^{n} d_i$ is even and $\sum_{i=1}^{k} d_i \leq k \times (k-1) + \sum_{i=k+1}^{n} min(d_i, k)$ holds for $1 \leq k \leq n$. Example: UVa 10720 - Graph Construction.

4. Euler's Formula for Planar Graph[47]: $V - E + F = 2$, where F is the number of faces[48] of the Planar Graph. Example: UVa 10178 - Count the Faces.

5. Moser's Circle: Determine the number of pieces into which a circle is divided if n points on its circumference are joined by chords with no three internally concurrent. Solution: $g(n) =^n C_4 +^n C_2 + 1$. Example: UVa 10213 and 13108. Note that the first five values of $g(n)$ are 1, 2, 4, 8, 16, that interestingly "looks like powers of two" although it is not as the next term is 31.

6. Pick's Theorem[49]: Let i be the number of integer points in the polygon, A be the area of the polygon, and b be the number of integer points on the boundary, then $A = i + \frac{b}{2} - 1$. Example: UVa 10088 - Trees on My Island.

7. The number of spanning trees of a complete bipartite graph $K_{n,m}$ is $m^{n-1} \times n^{m-1}$. Example: UVa 11719 - Gridlands Airport.

8. Brahmagupta's formula gives the area of a cyclic quadrilateral[50] given the lengths of the four sides: a, b, c, d as $\sqrt{(s-a) \times (s-b) \times (s-c) \times (s-d)}$ where s is the semiperimeter, defined as $s = (a+b+c+d)/2$. This formula generalizes the Heron's formula discussed in Section 7.2.4. Example: Kattis - Janitor Troubles.

[47]Graph that can be drawn on 2D Euclidean space so that no two edges in the graph cross each other.

[48]When a Planar Graph is drawn without any crossing, any cycle that surrounds a region without any edges reaching from the cycle into the region forms a face.

[49]Found by Georg Alexander Pick.

[50]A quadrilateral whose vertices all lie on a single circle (or can be inscribed in a circle).

9. Stirling number of the second kind (or Stirling partition number) $S(n, k)$ is the number of ways to partition a set of n items into k non-empty subsets.

   For example, there are 3 ways to partition set $\{a, b, c\}$ with $n = 3$ items into 2 non-empty subsets. They are: $\{(\{a, b\}, \{c\}), (\{a, c\}, \{b\}), (\{a\}, \{b, c\})\}$.

   For $n > 0$ and $k > 0$, $S(n, k)$ has this recurrence relation: $S(n, k) = k * S(n-1, k) + S(n-1, k-1)$ with base cases $S(n, 1) = S(n, n) = 1$ and $S(n, 0) = S(0, k) = 0$. Using DP, this recurrence can be computed in $O(nk)$.

10. Bell numbers is the number of possible partitions of a set, i.e., a grouping of the set's elements into *non-empty* subsets, in such a way that every element is included in exactly one subset. Bell number can also be expressed as summation of Stirling numbers of the second kind $B_n = \sum_{k=0}^{n} S(n, k)$.

    For example, the set $\{a, b, c\}$ with $n = 3$ items has 3-rd Bell number $= 5$ different partitions. They are:
    1 $S(3, 1)$ partition of 1 subset $= \{(\{a, b, c\})\}$,
    3 $S(3, 2)$ partitions of 2 subsets $= \{(\{a, b\}, \{c\}), (\{a, c\}, \{b\}), (\{a\}, \{b, c\})\}$ (as above),
    1 $S(3, 3)$ partition of 3 subsets $= \{(\{a\}, \{b\}, \{c\})\}$.
    Thus $B_3 = 1 + 3 + 1 = 5$.

Exercise 9.15.1*: Study the following mathematical keywords: Padovan Sequence, Burnside's Lemma.

Programming exercises related to *rarely used* Formulas or Theorems:

1. Entry Level: **UVa 13108 - Juanma and ...** * (Moser's circle; the formula is hard to derive; $g(n) =_n C_4 +_n C_2 + 1$)
2. **UVa 01645 - Count** * (LA 6368 - Chengdu12; number of rooted trees with n vertices in which vertices at the same level have the same degree)
3. **UVa 11719 - Gridlands Airports** * (count the number of spanning trees in a complete bipartite graph; use Java BigInteger)
4. **UVa 12786 - Friendship Networks** * (similar to UVa 10720 and UVa 11414; Erdős-Gallai Theorem)
5. *Kattis - houseofcards* * (number of cards for certain height h is $h \times (3 \times h + 1)/2$; use Python to handle Big Integer)
6. *Kattis - janitortroubles* * (Brahmagupta's formula)
7. *Kattis - sjecista* * (number of intersections of diagonals in a convex polygon)

   Extra UVa: *01185, 10088, 10178, 10213, 10219, 10720, 10843, 11414, 12876, 12967.*

   Extra Kattis: *birthdaycake.*

   Also see Section 5.4.4 for some Combinatorics problem that have rare formulas.

9.16 Combinatorial Game Theory

Once in a while, a problem related to combinatorial game theory might pop up in a contest. A *combinatorial game* is a game in which all players have perfect information of the game such that there is no chance of luck involved in the game; in other words, no hidden information. This perfect information allows a combinatorial game to be completely determined and analyzed mathematically[51], hence, the name "combinatorial".

A combinatorial game of two players in which both players have the same set of moves is called an *impartial game*. Example of impartial games is **Nim**, which will be discussed shortly. We can see that Chess and Go[52] are combinatorial games but not impartial games as each player can only move or place pieces of their own color.

Typical questions related to impartial game related problem usually involve finding who will win given the state of the game, or finding a move to win such game. Generally, there are 3 approaches which can be used to solve this kind of problem: pattern finding, DP, or Nim-based approach. Pattern finding is a common technique: solve the problem for small instances (e.g., with DP or backtracking), and then eyeball the result to find some pattern. This method could work if the problem has an easy pattern to spot and such basic Game Theory related problems have been discussed in Section 5.7. As for the Nim-based approach, there is a nice and cool theorem called *Sprague-Grundy Theorem* which states that every impartial game is equivalent to a *nimber*. Perhaps, understanding this theorem is a must for students to be able to solve most of impartial game related problems.

Nim

Nim is the most well-known example of impartial game. This game is played by two players on N piles each containing $a_i \geq 0$ stones. Both players alternatingly remove any positive number of stones from exactly one pile (of the player's choice). The player who cannot make any move (i.e., there are no stones left) loses. There is another variation called *Misére Nim* in which the player who cannot make any move wins. Luckily, the solution for Misére Nim only slightly different than the normal play.

The most important thing we should pay attention to when analyzing an impartial game is the winning (W) and losing (L) positions. A game is in a **winning position** if and only if there is at least one valid move from that position to a losing position (thus, make the opponent takes a losing position). On the other hand, a game is in a **losing position** if and only if all possible moves from that position are to winning positions. Some literatures refer the winning position as N-position (win for the next player) and the losing position as P-position (win for the previous player). Usually, it is stated in the problem statement that "both players will play optimally". It simply means that if a player have a strategy to ensure his win from the game position, he will stick to the strategy and win the game.

How could we find the winning and losing positions in a Nim? One naïve way is by working backward from the terminal position like the basic techniques discussed in Section 5.7, i.e., when there are no stones left, which is a losing position. However, this approach requires $\Omega(\prod a_i)$ time and memory[53] complexity, which is exponential to the number of piles (N). This certainly is not fast enough in a typical programming contest problem which often involves a large number of piles and stones. Fortunately, there is an easy way to find the winning and losing positions for a Nim, with a nim-sum.

[51]Of course, whether it is easy to analyze a combinatorial game, is a different issue.

[52]There are around 2×10^{170} legal positions in a standard Go board of 19×19, much more than the estimated number of atoms in the *observable* universe (which is "only" $10^{78}..10^{82}$)!

[53]In order to keep track all possible states of the game.

Nim-sum

In order to know whether a position is winning or losing in a Nim, all we need to do is compute the "exclusive or" (xor) value of all piles. This xor value is also known as the **nim-sum**. If the nim-sum is non-zero, then it is a winning position; otherwise, it is a losing position. The following code determines who will win in a Nim:

```
int getNimSum(vi pile) {
  int nim = 0;
  for (auto &p : pile)
    nim ^= p;
  return nim;
}

string whoWinNimGame(vi pile) {
  return (getNimSum(pile) != 0) ? "First Player" : "Second Player";
}
```

For example, let $A_{1..4} = \{5, 11, 12, 7\}$. The nim-sum of A is $5 \oplus 11 \oplus 12 \oplus 7 = 5$. As this number is non-zero, the first player will win the game (it is a winning position). Consider another example where $B_{1..3} = \{9, 12, 5\}$. The nim-sum of B is $9 \oplus 12 \oplus 5 = 0$. In this case, as the nim-sum is zero, the first player will lose the game (it is a losing position). Thus, the second player will win the game.

Why does nim-sum determine the state of a Nim? In the following analysis, let S be the nim-sum of a game position and T be the nim-sum of the (immediate) next position.

Lemma 9.16.1. *If the nim-sum is zero, then any move will cause the nim-sum to be non-zero.*

Proof. Let the kth pile be the chosen pile, thus, a_k is the number of stones and b_k is the resulting number of stones (after the move has been made) in that pile. Note that $a_k > b_k$ (or $a_k \neq b_k$) as the player has to remove a positive number of stones. Then, the resulting nim-sum $T = S \oplus a_k \oplus b_k$. Note that $a_k \oplus b_k \neq 0$ if $a_k \neq b_k$. Thus, if $S = 0$, then $T \neq 0$ because $a_k \neq b_k$. □

Lemma 9.16.2. *If the nim-sum is non-zero, then there must be a move which cause the nim-sum to be zero.*

Proof. The following strategy will cause the nim-sum to be zero. Let d be the position of the left-most non-zero bit of S (in binary representation). Find a pile k such that the dth bit of a_k is 1. Such pile must exist, otherwise, the dth bit of S will be 0. Remove stones from that pile such that its number of stones becomes $S \oplus a_k$. As the dth bit of a_k is non-zero, this will cause $S \oplus a_k < a_k$, thus it is a valid move. The resulting nim-sum $T = S \oplus a_k \oplus (S \oplus a_k) = 0$. □

In summary, to win a Nim, we have to make and maintain its nim-sum to be zero at all time. If the first player could not do that, then the second player is able to do that and win the game.

We can employ the above analysis to find the winning move (if it is a winning position). The following code returns the pile in which the move should be performed and the number of stones to be removed from that pile to win the game; otherwise, it returns $\langle -1, -1 \rangle$ if it is a losing position.

```
bool isOn(int bit, int k) {                        // is the k^th bit is 1?
  return (bit & (1<<k)) ? true : false;
}

ii winningMove(vi pile) {
  int nimsum = getNimSum(pile);
  if (nimsum == 0) return {-1, -1};                // not winnable
  int pos = -1, remove = -1;
  int d = 0;
  for (int i = 0; i < 31; ++i)                     // using signed 32-bit int
    if (isOn(nimsum, i))
      d = i;
  for (int i = 0; (i < (int)pile.size()) && (pos == -1); ++i)
    if (isOn(pile[i], d)) {
      pos = i;
      remove = pile[i] - (pile[i]^nimsum);
    }
  return {pos, remove};
}
```

Misère Nim

Misère Nim is a variation of Nim in which the loser in the normal Nim is the winner, i.e., the player who cannot make any move wins, or consequently, the player who makes the last move loses. At first, it seems Misère Nim is much harder to solve than a normal Nim. However, it turns out that there is an easy strategy for Misère Nim.

While there are at least two piles with more than one stones, just play as if it is a normal Nim. When the opponent moves such that there is exactly one pile left with more than one stone (observe that this position has a non-zero nim-sum), remove the stones from that one pile into zero or one such that the number of remaining piles with one stone left is **odd**. This strategy guarantees a win whenever winning is possible.

To find the winning and losing positions, we should consider two separate cases: (1) When there is a pile with more than one stones, (2) When all piles have no more than one stone. In case (1), simply treat it as a normal Nim. In case (2), the first player wins if there is an even number of piles with only one stone, thus, he can make it odd by removing one. The following code determines who will win in a Misère Nim:

```
string whoWinMisereNimGame(vi pile) {
  int n_more = 0, n_one = 0;
  for (int i = 0; i < (int)pile.size(); ++i) {
    if (pile[i] > 1) ++n_more;
    if (pile[i] == 1) ++n_one;
  }
  if (n_more >= 1)
    return whoWinNimGame(pile);
  else
    return (n_one%2 == 0) ? "First Player" : "Second Player";
}
```

Bogus Nim

Bogus Nim is a variation of Nim where player, in addition to only removing stones, can also add stones. There should be a rule to ensure the game terminates, e.g., each player can only perform stone addition a finite number of time. The winner of bogus Nim can be easily determined the same way as how we determine the winner of a normal Nim. In Bogus Nim, if we have a winning position, simply treat it as a normal Nim. If the opponent has a losing position and adds some stones, then simply remove the added stones in your move and you will be back to your winning position again. Easy!

Sprague-Grundy Theorem

The Sprague-Grundy Theorem states that every impartial game is equivalent to a pile of a certain size in Nim. In other words, every impartial game can be solved as Nim by finding their corresponding game.

For example, consider a variation of Nim in which the player should remove at least half of the stones in the pile he chose. Let us call this game as *At-Least-Half Nim* game This game is not exactly the same as Nim as we cannot remove only, for example, 1 stone from a pile with 10 stones (should remove at least $\lceil 10/2 \rceil = 5$ stones). However, we can convert this game into its corresponding Nim, with Grundy Number.

First, observe that the number of stones in the piles which are not chosen by the player in his move remains the same. Thus, the piles are independent to each other. In the following explanation, the term "state" will be used interchangably to represent a pile.

Grundy Number

The Grundy Number (also known as *nimber*) of a state in the original game represents the number of stones in a pile in its corresponding Nim. To learn about Grundy Number, first, we should learn about mex operation.

The **mex** (minimum excludant) of a subset is the smallest value which does not belong to the subset. In the context of Grundy Number, the set of values to be considered is non-negative integers. For example, $\text{mex}(\{0, 1, 3, 4, 6, 7\}) = 2$, and $\text{mex}(\{3, 4, 5\}) = 0$. To get the Grundy Number of a state, simply take the mex of all Grundy Numbers of its (immediate) next states which can be reached by one valid move in the game. The Grundy Number of the terminal state is zero as $\text{mex}(\{\}) = 0$.

For example, consider the previous At-Least-Half Nim variation. A state with 0 stone (terminal state) has a Grundy Number of $g_0 = 0$. A state with 1 stone could reach a state with 0 stone in one move, so, its Grundy Number is $g_1 = mex(\{g_0\}) = mex(\{0\}) = 1$. Similarly, a state with 2 stones could reach a state with 0 or 1 stone in one move, so, its Grundy Number is $g_2 = mex(\{g_0, g_1\}) = mex(\{0, 1\}) = 2$. A state with 3 stones could reach a state with 0 or 1 stone in one move, thus its Grundy Number is $g_3 = mex(\{g_0, g_1\}) = mex(\{0, 1\}) = 2$. Observe that 2 is not considered as the next state of 3 as we should remove at least $\lceil 3/2 \rceil = 2$ stones. A state with 6 stones could reach a state with 0, 1, 2, or 3 stones in one move, thus its Grundy Number is $g_6 = mex(\{g_0, g_1, g_2, g_3\}) = mex(\{0, 1, 2, 2\}) = 3$. If we continue this process, we will get $G_{0..12} = (0, 1, 2, 2, 3, 3, 3, 3, 4, 4, 4, 4, 4)$, e.g., a state with 10 stones in the original game corresponds to a pile with $g_{10} = 4$ stones in Nim. In summary, to solve the original game, convert the game into its corresponding Nim with Grundy Number, and then compute its nim-sum.

The following code determines who win in the At-Least-Half Nim game.

```
int getAtLeastHalfNimGrundy(int stone) {
  if ( stone == 0 ) return 0;
  set <int> used;
  for ( int take = (stone+1)/2; take <= stone; ++take ) {
    used.insert(getAtLeastHalfNimGrundy(stone-take));
  }
  int res = 0;
  while ( used.count(res) ) {
    res++;
  }
  return res;
}

string whoWinAtLeastHalfNimGame(vi pile) {
  vi grundy(pile.size());
  for ( int i = 0; i < pile.size(); ++i ) {
    grundy[i] = getAtLeastHalfNimGrundy(pile[i]);
  }
  return getNimSum(grundy) != 0 ? "First Player" : "Second Player";
}
```

Observe that the above `getAtLeastHalfNimGrundy()` code has an exponential time complexity. It is possible to reduce the time complexity into a polynomial[54], e.g., with Dynamic Programming (see Book 1).

Why does such game equal to Nim with its Grundy Number? Recall what we did to find the Grundy Number, i.e., finding the smallest non negative integer x which is not among the next states. Isn't this x the same as a pile in Nim with x stones where we can remove some stones to make the remaining stones in that pile becomes any number between 0 and $x-1$? How about the next states which is higher than the mex? For example, $A = \{0, 1, 2, 4, 6, 7\}$ in which the mex is 3. If the opponent moves to a state with a Grundy Number higher than 3, e.g., 4, 6, or 7, then we can simply revert back those move to 3 (recall Bogus Nim). We can do that because a state with Grundy Number of 4, 5, or 7 should have a next state with Grundy Number of 3 (by the definition of mex or Grundy Number).

Programming exercises related to Nim-based Combinatorial Game Theory:

1. Entry Level: **UVa 10165 - Stone Game** * (classic Nim game; application of Sprague-Grundy theorem)
2. **UVa 01566 - John** * (Misére Nim)
3. **UVa 10561 - Treblecross** *
4. **UVa 11311 - Exclusively Edible** * (there are 4 heaps; Nim sum)
5. **UVa 11534 - Say Goodbye to ...** *
6. **LA 5059 - Playing With Stones** * (ICPC 2010 Regional Jakarta)
7. **LA 6803 - Circle and Marbles** * (ICPC 2014 Regional Kuala Lumpur)

[54]For this At-Least-Half Nim example, it is possible to obtain the grundy number in a logarithmic time complexity. *Hint:* $\text{grundy}(x) = \log_2(x) + 1$.

9.17 Gaussian Elimination Algorithm

Problem Description

A **linear equation** is defined as an equation where the order of the unknowns (variables) is **linear** (a constant or a product of a constant plus the first power of an unknown). For example, equation X + Y = 2 is linear but equation $X^2 = 4$ is not linear.

A **system of linear equations** is defined as a collection of n unknowns (variables) in (usually) n linear equations, e.g., X + Y = 2 and 2X + 5Y = 6, where the solution is X = $1\frac{1}{3}$, Y = $\frac{2}{3}$. Notice the difference to the **linear diophantine equation** (see Section 5.3.10) as the solution for a **system of linear equations** can be non-integers!

In rare occasions, we may find such system of linear equations in a programming contest problem. Knowing the solution, especially its implementation, may come handy.

Solution(s)

To compute the solution of a **system of linear equations**, one can use techniques like the **Gaussian Elimination** algorithm. This algorithm is more commonly found in Engineering textbooks under the topic of 'Numerical Methods'. Some Computer Science textbooks do have some discussions about this algorithm, e.g., [8]. Here, we show this relatively simple $O(n^3)$ algorithm using a C++ function below.

```
const int MAX_N = 3;                                // adjust as needed
struct AugmentedMatrix { double mat[MAX_N][MAX_N+1]; };
struct ColumnVector { double vec[MAX_N]; };

ColumnVector GaussianElimination(int N, AugmentedMatrix Aug) {
  // input: N, Augmented Matrix Aug, output: Column vector X, the answer
  for (int i = 0; i < N-1; ++i) {                  // forward elimination
    int l = i;
    for (int j = i+1; j < N; ++j)                  // row with max col value
      if (fabs(Aug.mat[j][i]) > fabs(Aug.mat[l][i]))
        l = j;                                     // remember this row l
    // swap this pivot row, reason: minimize floating point error
    for (int k = i; k <= N; ++k)
      swap(Aug.mat[i][k], Aug.mat[l][k]);
    for (int j = i+1; j < N; ++j)                  // actual fwd elimination
      for (int k = N; k >= i; --k)
        Aug.mat[j][k] -= Aug.mat[i][k] * Aug.mat[j][i] / Aug.mat[i][i];
  }
  ColumnVector Ans;                                // back substitution phase
  for (int j = N-1; j >= 0; --j) {                 // start from back
    double t = 0.0;
    for (int k = j+1; k < N; ++k)
      t += Aug.mat[j][k] * Ans.vec[k];
    Ans.vec[j] = (Aug.mat[j][N]-t) / Aug.mat[j][j]; // the answer is here
  }
  return Ans;
}
```

Source code: `ch9/GaussianElimination.cpp| java| py`

Sample Execution

In this subsection, we show the step-by-step working of 'Gaussian Elimination' algorithm using the following example. Suppose we are given this system of linear equations:

```
X = 9 - Y - 2Z
2X + 4Y = 1 + 3Z
3X - 5Z = -6Y
```

First, we need to transform the system of linear equations into the *basic form*, i.e., we reorder the unknowns (variables) in sorted order on the Left Hand Side. We now have:

```
1X + 1Y + 2Z = 9
2X + 4Y - 3Z = 1
3X + 6Y - 5Z = 0
```

Then, we re-write these linear equations as matrix multiplication: $A \times x = b$. This technique is also used in Section 5.8.4. We now have:

$$\begin{bmatrix} 1 & 1 & 2 \\ 2 & 4 & -3 \\ 3 & 6 & -5 \end{bmatrix} \times \begin{bmatrix} X \\ Y \\ Z \end{bmatrix} = \begin{bmatrix} 9 \\ 1 \\ 0 \end{bmatrix}$$

Later, we will work with both matrix A (of size $N \times N$) and column vector b (of size $N \times 1$). So, we combine them into an $N \times (N + 1)$ 'augmented matrix' (the last column that has three arrows is a comment to aid the explanation):

$$\left[\begin{array}{ccc|c|l} 1 & 1 & 2 & 9 & \rightarrow \text{1X + 1Y + 2Z = 9} \\ 2 & 4 & -3 & 1 & \rightarrow \text{2X + 4Y - 3Z = 1} \\ 3 & 6 & -5 & 0 & \rightarrow \text{3X + 6Y - 5Z = 0} \end{array}\right]$$

Then, we pass this augmented matrix into Gaussian Elimination function above. The first phase is the forward elimination phase. We pick the largest absolute value in column $j = 0$ from row $i = 0$ onwards, then swap that row with row $i = 0$. This (extra) step is just to minimize floating point error. For this example, after swapping row 0 with row 2, we have:

$$\left[\begin{array}{ccc|c|l} \underline{3} & 6 & -5 & 0 & \rightarrow \underline{\text{3X + 6Y - 5Z = 0}} \\ 2 & 4 & -3 & 1 & \rightarrow \text{2X + 4Y - 3Z = 1} \\ \underline{1} & 1 & 2 & 9 & \rightarrow \underline{\text{1X + 1Y + 2Z = 9}} \end{array}\right]$$

The main action done by Gaussian Elimination algorithm in this forward elimination phase is to eliminate variable X (the first variable) from row $i + 1$ onwards. In this example, we eliminate X from row 1 and row 2. Concentrate on the comment "the actual forward elimination phase" inside the Gaussian Elimination code above. We now have:

$$\left[\begin{array}{ccc|c|l} 3 & 6 & -5 & 0 & \rightarrow \text{3X + 6Y - 5Z = 0} \\ \mathbf{0} & \mathbf{0} & \mathbf{0.33} & \mathbf{1} & \rightarrow \underline{\text{0X + 0Y + 0.33Z = 1}} \\ \mathbf{0} & \mathbf{-1} & \mathbf{3.67} & \mathbf{9} & \rightarrow \underline{\text{0X - 1Y + 3.67Z = 9}} \end{array}\right]$$

Then, we continue eliminating the next variable (now variable Y). We pick the largest absolute value in column $j = 1$ from row $i = 1$ onwards, then swap that row with row $i = 1$. For this example, after swapping row 1 with row 2, we have the following augmented matrix and it happens that variable Y is already eliminated from row 2:

$$\left[\begin{array}{l|ccc|c|l} \text{row 0} & 3 & 6 & -5 & 0 & \rightarrow \text{3X + 6Y - 5Z = 0} \\ \text{row 1} & 0 & \underline{-1} & 3.67 & 9 & \rightarrow \underline{\text{0X - 1Y + 3.67Z = 9}} \\ \text{row 2} & 0 & \underline{0} & 0.33 & 1 & \rightarrow \underline{\text{0X + 0Y + 0.33Z = 1}} \end{array}\right]$$

Once we have the lower triangular matrix of the augmented matrix all zeroes, we can start the second phase: The back substitution phase. Concentrate on the last few lines in the Gaussian Elimination code above. Notice that after eliminating variable X and Y, there is only variable Z in row 2. We are now sure that $Z = 1/0.33 = 3$.

$$\left[\begin{array}{l|ccc|c|l} \text{row 2} & 0 & 0 & 0.33 & 1 & \rightarrow \text{0X + 0Y + 0.33Z = 1} \rightarrow \text{Z = 1/0.33 = 3} \end{array}\right]$$

Once we have $Z = 3$, we can process row 1.
We get $Y = (9 - 3.67 * 3)/-1 = 2$.

$$\left[\begin{array}{l|ccc|c|l} \text{row 1} & 0 & -1 & 3.67 & 9 & \rightarrow \text{0X - 1Y + 3.67Z = 9} \rightarrow \text{Y = (9 - 3.67 * 3) / -1 = 2} \end{array}\right]$$

Finally, once we have $Z = 3$ and $Y = 2$, we can process row 0.
We get $X = (0 - 6 * 2 + 5 * 3)/3 = 1$, done!

$$\left[\begin{array}{l|ccc|c|l} \text{row 0} & 3 & 6 & -5 & 0 & \rightarrow \text{3X + 6Y - 5Z = 0} \rightarrow \text{X = (0 - 6 * 2 + 5 * 3) / 3 = 1} \end{array}\right]$$

Therefore, the solution for the given system of linear equations is $X = 1$, $Y = 2$, and $Z = 3$.

Programming Exercises related to Gaussian Elimination:

1. Entry Level: **UVa 11319 - Stupid Sequence?** * (solve the system of the first 7 linear equations; then use all 1500 equations for 'smart sequence' checks)
2. **UVa 00684 - Integral Determinant** * (modified Gaussian elimination to find (integral) determinant of a square matrix)
3. *Kattis - equations* * (2 equations and 2 unknown; we do not need Gaussian elimination; there are many corner cases)
4. *Kattis - equationsolver* * (basic Gaussian Elimination with two more checks: inconsistent or multiple answers)
5. *Kattis - seti* * (n equations and n unknowns; but there are division under modulo, so use Gaussian elimination with modular multiplicative inverse)

9.18 Art Gallery Problem

Problem Description

The 'Art Gallery' Problem is a family of related *visibility* problems in computational geometry. In this section, we discuss several variants. The common terms used in the variants discussed below are the simple (not necessarily convex) polygon P to describe the art gallery; a set of points S to describe the guards where each guard is represented by a point in P; a rule that a point $A \in S$ can guard another point $B \in P$ if and only if line segment AB is contained in P; and a question on whether all points in polygon P are guarded by S. Many variants of this Art Gallery Problem are classified as NP-hard problems. In this book, we focus on the ones that admit polynomial solutions.

1. Variant 1: Determine the upper bound of the smallest size of set S.
2. Variant 2: Determine if $\exists$ a critical point C in polygon P and $\exists$ another point $D \in P$ such that if the guard is at position C, the guard cannot protect point D.
3. Variant 3: Determine if polygon P can be guarded with just one guard.
4. Variant 4: Determine the smallest size of set S if the guards can only be placed at the vertices of polygon P and only the vertices need to be guarded.

Note that there are many more variants and at least one book[55] has been written on it [29].

Solution(s)

1. The solution for variant 1 is a theoretical work of the Art Gallery theorem by Václav Chvátal. He states that $\lfloor n/3 \rfloor$ guards are always sufficient and sometimes necessary to guard a simple polygon with n vertices (proof omitted).
2. The solution for variant 2 involves testing if polygon P is concave (and thus has a critical point). We can use the negation of `isConvex` function shown in Section 7.3.4.
3. The solution for variant 3 can be hard if one has not seen the solution before. We can use the `cutPolygon` function discussed in Section 7.3.6. We cut polygon P with all lines formed by the edges in P in counterclockwise fashion and retain the left side at all times. If we still have a non-empty polygon at the end, one guard can be placed in that non empty polygon which can protect the entire polygon P.
4. The solution for variant 4 involves the computation of MIN-VERTEX-COVER of the 'visibility graph' of polygon P. In general graphs, this is an NP-hard problem. Please refer to Section 8.6 for discussion of this variant.

Programming exercises related to Art Gallery problem:

1. Entry Level: **UVa 10078 - Art Gallery** * (`isConvex`)
2. **UVa 00588 - Video Surveillance** * (`cutPolygon`)
3. **UVa 01304 - Art Gallery** * (LA 2512 - SouthEasternEurope02; `cutPolygon` and area of polygon)
4. **UVa 01571 - How I Mathematician ...** * (LA 3617 - Yokohama06; `cutPolygon`)

---

[55] Free PDF version at `http://cs.smith.edu/~orourke/books/ArtGalleryTheorems/art.html`.

9.19 Closest Pair Problem

Problem Description

Given a set S of n points on a 2D plane, find two points with the closest Euclidean distance.

Solution(s)

Complete Search

A naïve solution computes the distances between all pairs of points and reports the minimum one. However, this requires $O(n^2)$ time.

Divide and Conquer

We can use the following three steps D&C strategy to achieve $O(n \log n)$ time:

1. Divide: We sort the points in set S by their x-coordinates (if tie, by their y-coordinates). Then, we divide set S into two sets of points S_1 and S_2 with a vertical line $x = d$ such that $|S_1| = |S_2|$ or $|S_1| = |S_2| + 1$, i.e., the number of points in each set is balanced.
2. Conquer: If we only have one point in S, we return ∞.
   If we only have two points in S, we return their Euclidean distance.
3. Combine: Let d_1 and d_2 be the smallest distance in S_1 and S_2, respectively. Let d_3 be the smallest distance between all pairs of points (p_1, p_2) where p_1 is a point in S_1 and p_2 is a point in S_2. Then, the smallest distance is $min(d_1, d_2, d_3)$, i.e., the answer may be in the smaller set of points S_1 or in S_2 or one point in S_1 and the other point in S_2, crossing through line $x = d$.

The combine step, if done naïvely, will still run in $O(n^2)$. But this can be optimized. Let $d' = min(d_1, d_2)$. For each point in the left of the dividing line $x = d$, a closer point in the right of the dividing line can only lie within a rectangle with width d' and height $2 \times d'$. It can be proven (proof omitted) that there can be only at most 6 such points in this rectangle. This means that the combine step only require $O(6n)$ operations and the overall time complexity of this divide and conquer solution is $T(n) = 2 \times T(n/2) + O(n)$ which is $O(n \log n)$.

Exercise 9.19.1*: There is a simpler solution other than the classic Divide & Conquer solution shown above. It uses sweep line algorithm. We 'sweep' the points in S from left to right. Suppose the current best answer is d and we are now examining point i. The potential new closest point from i, if any, must have a y-coordinate within d units of point i. We check all these candidates and update d accordingly (which will be progressively smaller). Implement this solution and analyze its time complexity!

Programming exercises related to Closest Pair problem:

1. Entry Level: **UVa 10245 - The Closest Pair Problem** * (classic)
2. **UVa 11378 - Bey Battle** * (also a closest pair problem)
3. *Kattis - closestpair1* * (classic closest pair problem - the easier one)
4. *Kattis - closestpair2* * (classic closest pair problem - the harder one; be careful of precision errors)

9.20 A* and IDA*: Informed Search

The Basics of A*

The Complete Search algorithms that we have seen earlier in Chapter 3+4 and the earlier subsections of this Section are 'uninformed', i.e., all possible states reachable from the current state are *equally good*. For some problems, we do have access to more information (hence the name 'informed search') and we can use the clever A* search that employs heuristics to 'guide' the search direction.

Figure 9.13: 15 Puzzle

We illustrate this A* search using the well-known 15 Puzzle problem. There are 15 slide-able tiles in the puzzle, each with a number from 1 to 15 on it. These 15 tiles are packed into a 4×4 frame with one tile missing. The possible actions are to slide the tile adjacent to the missing tile to the position of that missing tile. Alternative view is: "To slide the *blank tile* rightwards, upwards, leftwards, or downwards". The objective of this puzzle is to arrange the tiles so that they look like Figure 9.13, the 'goal' state.

This seemingly small puzzle is a headache for various search algorithms due to its enormous search space. We can represent a state of this puzzle by listing the numbers of the tiles row by row, left to right into an array of 16 integers. For simplicity, we assign value 0 to the blank tile so the goal state is $\{1, 2, 3, \ldots, 14, 15, 0\}$. Given a state, there can be up to 4 reachable states depending on the position of the missing tile. There are 2/3/4 possible actions if the missing tile is at the 4 corners/8 non-corner sides/4 middle cells, respectively. This is a huge search space.

However, these states are not equally good. There is a nice heuristic for this problem that can help guiding the search algorithm, which is the sum of the Manhattan[56] distances between each (non blank) tile in the current state and its location in the goal state. This heuristic gives the lower bound of steps to reach the goal state. By combining the cost so far (denoted by $g(s)$) and the heuristic value (denoted by $h(s)$) of a state s, we have a better idea on where to move next. We illustrate this with a puzzle with starting state A below:

$$A = \begin{bmatrix} 1 & 2 & 3 & 4 \\ 5 & 6 & 7 & 8 \\ 9 & 10 & 11 & \underline{0} \\ 13 & 14 & 15 & 12 \end{bmatrix}$$

$$B = \begin{bmatrix} 1 & 2 & 3 & 4 \\ 5 & 6 & 7 & \underline{0} \\ 9 & 10 & 11 & \underline{\mathbf{8}} \\ 13 & 14 & 15 & 12 \end{bmatrix} C = \begin{bmatrix} 1 & 2 & 3 & 4 \\ 5 & 6 & 7 & 8 \\ 9 & 10 & \underline{0} & \underline{\mathbf{11}} \\ 13 & 14 & 15 & 12 \end{bmatrix} D = \begin{bmatrix} 1 & 2 & 3 & 4 \\ 5 & 6 & 7 & 8 \\ 9 & 10 & 11 & \underline{\mathbf{12}} \\ 13 & 14 & 15 & \underline{0} \end{bmatrix}$$

The cost of the starting state A is $g(s) = 0$, no move yet. There are three reachable states $\{B, C, D\}$ from this state A with $g(B) = g(C) = g(D) = 1$, i.e., one move. But these three states are *not* equally good:

1. The heuristic value if we slide tile 0 upwards is $h(B) = 2$ as tile 8 and tile 12 are both off by 1. This causes $g(B) + h(B) = 1 + 2 = 3$.
2. The heuristic value if we slide tile 0 leftwards is $h(C) = 2$ as tile 11 and tile 12 are both off by 1. This causes $g(C) + h(C) = 1 + 2 = 3$.
3. But if we slide tile 0 downwards, we have $h(D) = 0$ as all tiles are in their correct position. This causes $g(D) + h(D) = 1 + 0 = 1$, the lowest combination.

[56]The Manhattan distance between two points is the sum of the absolute differences of their coordinates.

If we visit the states in ascending order of $g(s) + h(s)$ values, we will explore the states with the smaller expected cost first, i.e., state D in this example—which is the goal state. This is the essence of the A* search algorithm.

We usually implement this states ordering with the help of a priority queue—which makes the implementation of A* search very similar to the implementation of Dijkstra's algorithm presented in Book 1. Note that if $h(s)$ is set to 0 for all states, A* *degenerates* to Dijkstra's algorithm again.

As long as the heuristic function $h(s)$ never overestimates the true distance to the goal state (also known as **admissible heuristic**), this A* search algorithm is optimal. The hardest part in solving search problems using A* search is in finding such a heuristic.

Limitations of A*

The problem with A* (and also BFS and Dijkstra's algorithms when used on large State-Space graphs) that uses (priority) queue is that the memory requirement can be very huge when the goal state is far from the initial state. For some difficult searching problem, we may have to resort to the following related techniques.

Depth Limited Search

In Book 1, we have seen the recursive backtracking algorithm. The main problem with pure backtracking is this: It may be trapped in an exploration of a very deep path that will not lead to the solution before eventually backtracking after wasting precious runtime.

Depth Limited Search (DLS) places a limit on how deep a backtracking can go. DLS stops going deeper when the depth of the search is longer than what we have defined. If the limit happens to be equal to the depth of the shallowest goal state, then DLS is faster than the general backtracking routine. However, if the limit is too small, then the goal state will be unreachable. If the problem says that the goal state is 'at most d steps away' from the initial state, then use DLS instead of general backtracking routine.

Iterative Deepening Search

If DLS is used wrongly, then the goal state will be unreachable although we have a solution. DLS is usually not used alone, but as part of Iterative Deepening Search (IDS).

IDS calls DLS with *increasing limit* until the goal state is found. IDS is therefore complete and optimal. IDS is a nice strategy that sidesteps the problematic issue of determining the best depth limit by trying all possible depth limits incrementally: First depth 0 (the initial state itself), then depth 1 (those reachable with just one step from the initial state), then depth 2, and so on. By doing this, IDS essentially combines the benefits of lightweight/memory friendly DFS and the ability of BFS that can visit neighboring states layer by layer (see Graph Traversal Decision Table in Book 1).

Although IDS calls DLS many times, the time complexity is still $O(b^d)$ where b is the branching factor and d is the depth of the shallowest goal state. Reason: $O(b^0 + (b^0 + b^1) + (b^0 + b^1 + b^2) + ... + (b^0 + b^1 + b^2 + ... + b^d)) \le O(c \times b^d) = O(b^d)$.

Iterative Deepening A* (IDA*)

To solve the 15-puzzle problem faster, we can use IDA* (Iterative Deepening A*) algorithm which is essentially IDS with modified DLS. IDA* calls modified DLS to try all the neighboring states in a fixed order (i.e., slide tile 0 rightwards, then upwards, then leftwards, then finally downwards—in that order; we do not use a priority queue). This modified DLS is stopped not when it has exceeded the depth limit but when its $g(s) + h(s)$ exceeds the best known solution so far. IDA* expands the limit gradually until it hits the goal state.

The implementation of IDA* is not straightforward and we invite readers to scrutinize the given source code in the supporting website.

Source code: `ch9/UVa10181.cpp|java`

Exercise 9.20.1*: One of the hardest parts in solving search problems using A* search is to find the correct admissible heuristic and to compute them efficiently as it has to be repeated many times. List down admissible heuristics that are commonly used in difficult searching problems involving A* algorithm and show how to compute them efficiently! One of them is the Manhattan distance as shown in this section.

Exercise 9.20.2*: Solve UVa 11212 - Editing a Book that we have discussed in depth in Section 8.2.2-8.2.3 with A* instead of bidirectional BFS! Hint: First, determine what is a suitable heuristic for this problem.

Programming exercises related to A* or IDA*:

1. Entry Level: **UVa 00652 - Eight** * (classic sliding block 8-puzzle; IDA*)
2. **UVa 00656 - Optimal Programs** * (we can use IDDFS with pruning)
3. **UVa 10181 - 15-Puzzle Problem** * (similar with UVa 00652 but larger (now 15 instead of 8); we can use IDA*)
4. **UVa 11163 - Jaguar King** * (another puzzle game solvable with IDA*)

9.21 Pancake Sorting

Problem Description

Pancake Sorting is a classic[57] Computer Science problem, but it is rarely used. This problem can be described as follows: You are given a stack of N pancakes. The pancake at the bottom and at the top of the stack has index `0` and index `N-1`, respectively. The size of a pancake is given by the pancake's diameter (an integer $\in$ `[1..MAX_D]`). All pancakes in the stack have **different** diameters. For example, a stack A of $N = 5$ pancakes: $\{3, 8, 7, 6, 10\}$ can be visualized as:

```
        4 (top)        10
        3              6
        2              7
        1              8
        0 (bottom)     3
      ----------------------
        index          A
```

Your task is to sort the stack in **descending order**—that is, the largest pancake is at the bottom and the smallest pancake is at the top. However, to make the problem more real-life like, sorting a stack of pancakes can only be done by a sequence of pancake 'flips', denoted by function `flip(i)`. A `flip(i)` move consists of inserting two spatulas between two pancakes in a stack (one spatula below index `i` and the other one above index `N-1`) and then flipping (reversing) the pancakes on the spatula (reversing the sub-stack `[i..N-1]`).

For example, stack A can be transformed to stack B via `flip(0)`, i.e. inserting two spatulas below index 0 and above index 4 then flipping the pancakes in between. Stack B can be transformed to stack C via `flip(3)`. Stack C can be transformed to stack D via `flip(1)`. And so on... Our target is to make the stack sorted in **descending order**, i.e. we want the final stack to be like stack E.

```
4 (top)      10 \--   3  \--   8  \--   6                  3
3            6        8  /--   3        7          ...     6
2            7        7        7        3                  7
1            8        6        6  /--   8                  8
0 (bottom)   3  /--   10       10       10                 10
-------------------------------------------------------------
index        A        B        C        D          ...     E
```

To make the task more challenging, you have to compute the **minimum** number of `flip(i)` operations that you need so that the stack of N pancakes is sorted in descending order.

You are given an integer T in the first line, and then T test cases, one in each line. Each test case starts with an integer N, followed by N integers that describe the initial content of the stack. You have to output one integer, the minimum number of `flip(i)` operations to sort the stack.

Constraints: $1 \le T \le 100$, $1 \le N \le 10$, and $N \le$ `MAX_D` $\le 1\,000\,000$.

[57] Bill Gates (Microsoft co-founder and former CEO) wrote only one research paper so far, and it is about this pancake sorting [17].

Sample Test Cases

Sample Input

```
7
4   4 3 2 1
8   8 7 6 5 4 1 2 3
5   5 1 2 4 3
5   555555 111111 222222 444444 333333
8   1000000 999999 999998 999997 999996 999995 999994 999993
5   3 8 7 6 10
10  9 2 10 3 1 6 8 4 7 5
```

Sample Output

```
0
1
2
2
0
4
11
```

Explanation

- The first stack is already sorted in descending order.
- The second stack can be sorted with one call of `flip(5)`.
- The third (and also the fourth) input stack can be sorted in descending order by calling `flip(3)` then `flip(1)`: 2 flips.
- The fifth input stack, although contains large integers, is already sorted in descending order, so 0 flip is needed.
- The sixth input stack is actually the sample stack shown in the problem description. This stack can be sorted in descending order using at minimum 4 flips, i.e.
  Solution 1: `flip(0)`, `flip(1)`, `flip(2)`, `flip(1)`: 4 flips.
  Solution 2: `flip(1)`, `flip(2)`, `flip(1)`, `flip(0)`: also 4 flips.
- The seventh stack with $N = 10$ is for you to test the runtime speed of your solution.

Solution(s)

First, we need to make an observation that the diameters of the pancake do not really matter. We just need to write simple code to sort these (potentially huge) pancake diameters from [**1..1 Million**] and relabel them to [**0..N-1**]. This way, we can describe any stack of pancakes as simply a permutation of N integers.

If we just need to get the pancakes sorted, we can use a non optimal $O(2 \times N - 3)$ Greedy algorithm: Flip the largest pancake to the top, then flip it to the bottom. Flip the second largest pancake to the top, then flip it to the second from bottom. And so on. If we keep doing this, we will be able to have a sorted pancake in $O(2 \times N - 3)$ steps, regardless of the initial state.

However, to get the minimum number of flip operations, we need to be able to model this problem as a Shortest Paths problem on unweighted State-Space graph (see Section 8.2.2). The vertex of this State-Space graph is a permutation of N pancakes. A vertex is connected with unweighted edges to $O(N-1)$ other vertices via various flip operations (minus one as flipping the topmost pancake does not change anything). We can then use BFS from the starting permutation to find the shortest path to the target permutation (where the permutation is sorted in descending order). There are up to $V = O(N!)$ vertices and up to $E = O(N! \times (N-1))$ edges in this State-Space graph. Therefore, an $O(V+E)$ BFS runs in $O(N \times N!)$ per test case or $O(T \times N \times N!)$ for all test cases. Note that coding such BFS is already a challenging task (see Book 1 and Section 8.2.2). But this solution is still too slow for the largest test case.

A simple optimization is to run BFS from the target permutation (sorted descending) to all other permutations **only once**, for all possible N in **[1..10]**. This solution has time complexity of roughly $O(10 \times N \times N! + T)$, much faster than before but still too slow for typical programming contest settings.

A better solution is a more sophisticated search technique called 'meet in the middle' (bidirectional BFS) to bring down the search space to a manageable level (see Section 8.2.3). First, we do some preliminary analysis (or we can also look at 'Pancake Number', `https://oeis.org/A058986`) to identify that for the largest test case when $N = 10$, we need *at most* 11 flips to sort any input stack to the sorted one. Therefore, we precalculate BFS from the target permutation to all other permutations for all $N \in$ **[1..10]**, but stopping as soon as we reach depth $\lfloor \frac{11}{2} \rfloor = 5$. Then, for each test case, we run BFS from the starting permutation again with maximum depth 5. If we encounter a common vertex with the precalculated BFS from target permutation, we know that the answer is the distance from starting permutation to this vertex plus the distance from target permutation to this vertex. If we do not encounter a common vertex at all, we know that the answer should be the maximum flips: 11. On the largest test case with $N = 10$ for all test cases, this solution has time complexity of roughly $O((10+T) \times 10^5)$, which is now feasible.

Programming exercises related to Pancake Sorting:

1. Entry Level: **UVa 00120 - Stacks Of Flapjacks** * (greedy pancake sorting)

   Others: The Pancake Sorting problem as described in this section.

Egg Dropping Puzzle

There is a building with N floors, and there are K eggs in which you want to test their "strength", i.e., you want to find the highest floor, h, such that the egg will not break if dropped from that floor. The following assumptions are used in the problem.

- All eggs are identical.
- If an egg breaks when dropped from a certain floor, then it will break if dropped from any floor above that; if it breaks when dropped from the 1st floor, then $h = 0$.
- If an egg does not break when dropped from a certain floor, then it will not break if dropped from any floor below that; if it does not break when dropped from the highest floor, N, then $h = N$.
- An egg which does not break from a drop can be reused for the next drop.

Your goal is to find the minimum number of drops required to find h under the worst-case scenario[58].

For example, let $N = 6$ and $K = 2$. We can drop the eggs one-by-one from the 1st floor, 2nd floor, 3rd floor, and so forth, and stop when the egg that we test breaks. This method requires $N = 6$ drops at most (in this case, the worst-case is when $h = N$). However, this method is not optimal as we only use 1 eggs while we have $K = 2$ eggs to break. A better method would be to start by dropping at the 3rd floor. If it breaks, then we only have 2 remaining floors (i.e., 1st and 2nd) to test with one remaining egg; otherwise, we have 3 remaining floors (i.e., 4th, 5th, and 6th) to test with two eggs. This method only requires at most 3 drops, and it is optimal for $N = 6$ and $K = 2$.

This puzzle is good for students to learn about various optimization techniques for Dynamic Programming, thus, we encourage students to read the whole section instead of just skipping to the last most efficient solution in this section.

Solution(s)

$O(N^3K)$ Basic Solution

The basic recurrence relation for this problem is pretty simple. Let $f(l, r, k)$ be the minimum number of drops required to find h under the worst-case scenario if we have k eggs and we have not tested floor $[l..r]$ yet. Let's say that we test the ith floor where $i \in [l..r]$. If the egg breaks, then we need to test floor $[l..i)$ with the remaining $k - 1$ eggs. If the egg does not break, then we need to test floor $(i..r]$ with k eggs. Among these two possible outcomes, we only concern with the one that needs the most number of drops in the worst-case. Finally, we want to find i that minimizes such a maximum number of required drops.

$$f(l, r, k) = \min_{i=l..r} \{1 + \max(f(l, i-1, k-1), f(i+1, r, k))\}$$

The base case is $f(l, r, 1) = r - l + 1$ where there is only one egg remains and we need to test all floors from l to r one-by-one causing the maximum number of drops required to be $r - l + 1$. Also, $f(l, r, k) = 0$ if $l > r$ as there is no floor to test.

The function call to solve our problem is $f(1, N, K)$. Solve this recurrence relation with Dynamic Programming and we will get an $O(N^3K)$ solution.

[58]In other words, find the minimum number of drops such that h is guaranteed to be found.

$O(N^2K)$ Solution (with a Key Observation)

We need one key observation for the first optimization. Notice that it does not matter whether the floors that we need to test are $[l..r]$ or $[l + x .. r + x]$ for any x as they yield the same answer! That is, the answer does not depend on which floors but on **how many** floors that we need to test. Therefore, we can modify the previous recurrence relation by substituting parameters l and r with only n, the number of floors to be tested.

$$f(n,k) = 1 + \min_{i=1..n} \{\max(f(i-1,k-1), f(n-i,k))\}$$

This reduces our solution to $O(N^2K)$.

$O(NK \log N)$ Solution (Exploiting Monotonicity)

For the next optimization, observe that $f(i-1,k-1)$ is monotonically increasing while $f(n-i,k)$ is monotonically decreasing as i increases from 1 to n. If we get the maximum of these two functions on various i, then the output will be decreasing up to some i and then it starts increasing. However, we cannot use ternary search as $\max(f(i-1,k-1), f(n-i,k))$ is not strictly unimodal[59]. Fortunately, we can find i that causes $f(i-1,k-1) - f(n-i,k)$ to be zero (or almost zero) with **binary search**[60]. This is an $O(NK \log N)$ solution.

$O(NK)$ Solution (Another Monotonicity)

Let *opt*(n,k) be the floor on which the first drop yield an optimal answer for $f(n,k)$.

$$opt(n,k) = \arg\min_{i=1..n} \{\max(f(i-1,k-1), f(n-i,k))\}$$

Observe that when we compute for $f(n+1,k)$, what differs with $f(n,k)$ is only the $f(n-i,k)$ part (which is substituted with $f(n+1-i,k)$) while the $f(i-1,k-1)$ part remains the same. Also, we know the fact that $f(n+1-i,k) \geq f(n-i,k)$ as there is no way a higher building needs a fewer number of drops. Thus, we can conclude that $opt(n+1-i,k) \geq opt(n-i,k)$ as illustrated in Figure 9.14.

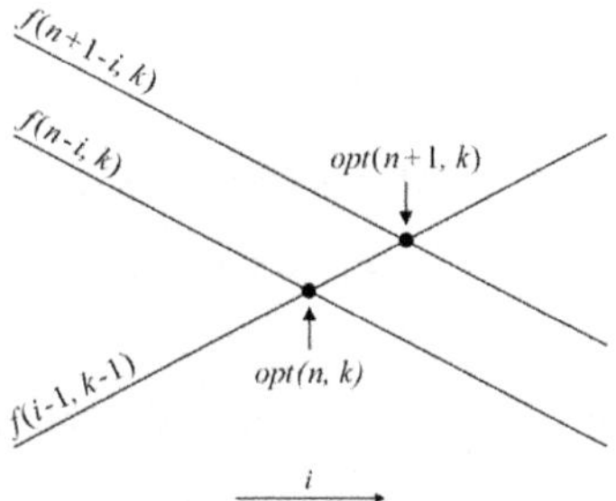

Figure 9.14: *opt*(n,k) vs. *opt*$(n+1,k)$

With this fact, we can modify the iteration in our previous $O(N^2K)$ solution from $i = [1..n]$ into $i = [opt(n-1,k)..n]$. If we further combine this with the monotonicity fact in our previous $O(NK \log N)$ solution, then it is enough to stop the iteration when we already

[59]There might be two different i that yield the same answer, violating the ternary search requirement.
[60]Observe that $f(i-1,k-1) - f(n-i,k)$ is monotonically increasing.

found the optimal, i.e., when the next i to be tested yield no better answer. Then, the total number of iterations to compute $f(n,k)$ for **all** n is only $O(N)$, causing the total time complexity to be $O(NK)$.

$O(NK \log N)$ Solution (Another Point of View)

Instead of solving the problem directly, consider this alternative version of the problem: How tall is the tallest building in the Egg Dropping Puzzle that can be solved with k eggs and at most d drops? Similarly, how many floors can be tested with k eggs and at most d drops? If we can solve this, then we only need to binary search the output to get the answer for the original problem.

Let's say the first drop is at the xth floor. If the egg breaks, then we need to test the floors below x with $d-1$ more drops and $k-1$ remaining eggs. If the egg does not break, then we need to test the floors above x with $d-1$ more drops and k eggs. Then, the total number of floors that can be tested with d drops and k eggs can be expressed with the following recurrence relation.

$$f(d,k) = f(d-1,k-1) + 1 + f(d-1,k)$$

This solution has an $O(DK)$ time complexity for the alternative version of the Egg Dropping Puzzle. If this approach is used (with a binary search) to answer the original Egg Dropping Puzzle, then the time complexity is $O(NK \log N)$. However, this bound is quite loose (i.e., faster than what it looks like) as the number of required drops decreases rapidly with additional eggs.

$O(K \log N)$ Solution (with Binomial Coefficient)

Consider the following auxiliary (helper) function[61].

$$g(d,k) = f(d,k+1) - f(d,k)$$

First, let's expand $g(d,k)$ using the previous recurrence relation for $f(d,k)$.

$$\begin{aligned} g(d,k) &= f(d,k+1) - f(d,k) \\ &= [f(d-1,k) + 1 + f(d-1,k+1)] - [f(d-1,k-1) + 1 + f(d-1,k)] \\ &= f(d-1,k) + f(d-1,k+1) - f(d-1,k-1) - f(d-1,k) \end{aligned}$$

Rearrange the terms and we can simplify the formula.

$$\begin{aligned} g(d,k) &= [f(d-1,k) - f(d-1,k-1)] + [f(d-1,k+1) - f(d-1,k)] \\ &= g(d-1,k-1) + g(d-1,k) \end{aligned}$$

Notice that this result for $g(d,k)$ is very similar to the formula for a binomial coefficient ("n-choose-k"), i.e., $\binom{n}{k} = \binom{n-1}{k-1} + \binom{n-1}{k}$. However, before we jump into the conclusion, let's first analyze the base cases. The base cases for $g(d,k)$ are as follows.

- $g(0,k) = 0$
- $g(d,0) = f(d,1) - f(d,0) = d - 0 = d$ which equals to $\binom{d}{1}$
- Additionally, $g(d,d) = f(d,d+1) - f(d,d) = d - d = 0$ which equals to $\binom{d}{d+1}$

[61]You may, but don't need to make a sense of what the function means; it's there only to help us.

Therefore, we can conclude that

$$g(d,k) = \binom{d}{k+1} \text{ if } d > 0$$

Now, let's rewrite $f(d,k)$ with a telescoping sum[62].

$$\begin{aligned} f(d,k) &= f(d,k) - f(d,k-1) + f(d,k-1) - f(d,k-2) + \cdots - f(d,0) + f(d,0) \\ &= [f(d,k) - f(d,k-1)] + [f(d,k-1) - f(d,k-2)] + \ldots [f(d,1) - f(d,0)] + f(d,0) \\ &= g(d,k-1) + g(d,k-2) + \cdots + g(d,0) + f(d,0) \end{aligned}$$

We know that $f(d,0) = 0$, thus

$$f(d,k) = g(d,k-1) + g(d,k-2) + \cdots + g(d,0)$$

We also know that $g(d,k) = \binom{d}{k+1}$ from the previous analysis, thus

$$f(d,k) = \binom{d}{k} + \binom{d}{k-1} + \cdots + \binom{d}{1}$$

$$f(d,k) = \sum_{i=1..k} \binom{d}{i}$$

We can compute the binomial coefficient $\binom{d}{i}$ for all $i = 1..K$ altogether in $O(K)$ with another formula for binomial coefficient, $\binom{n}{k} = \frac{n!}{k!(n-k)!}$. Therefore, the time complexity to compute $f(d,k)$ is $O(K)$.

If we use this approach to solve the original Egg Dropping Puzzle, then the time complexity becomes $(K \log N)$ as we need to Binary Search the Answer. However, notice that the formula for $f(d,k)$ grows **exponentially**, thus, a careless implementation of binary search or $f(d,k)$ might cause an overflow or runtime-error in C/C++ or Java. Alternatively, you might also consider a linear search, i.e., iterate the answer one-by-one from 1 until you find d that satisfies $f(d,K) \geq N$, but beware of corner cases such as $N = 10^9$ and $K = 1$.

If we reflect on the formula to compute $f(d,k)$ above, it looks like there is a one-to-one mapping between h and a bitstring of length D which has a population count of no more than K (i.e., the number of bit 1 is no more than K). In fact, there is! For example, `00101` (`0` means the egg does not break, `1` means the egg breaks) corresponds to the $h = 10^{th}$ floor in an Egg Dropping Puzzle with $N = 15$ floors building and $K = 2$ eggs. The drops are at $\{5, 9, \underline{12}, 10, \underline{11}\}$ floor with the underlines correspond to the floor in which the egg breaks. It might be interesting to further analyze the relation, but we left it for your exercise.

Programming exercise related to Egg Dropping Puzzle:

1. **UVa 10934 - Dropping water balloons** * (Egg dropping puzzle; interesting DP; try all possible answers)
2. *Kattis - batteries* * (Egg dropping puzzle with just 2 batteries; special case)
3. *Kattis - powereggs* * (Egg dropping puzzle; similar to UVa 10934)

---

[62] A telescoping sum is a sum in which pairs of consecutive terms are canceling each other.

9.23 Dynamic Programming Optimization

In this section, we will discuss several optimization techniques for dynamic programming.

Convex Hull Technique

The first DP optimization technique we will discuss is the convex hull technique. Despite the name, this technique has nothing to do with the convex hull finding algorithm we learned in computational geometry (Chapter 7.3.7). However, a basic understanding of geometry (not computational geometry) might help.

Consider the following DP formula:

$$\text{dp}(i) = \min_{j<i}\{\text{dp}(j) + \text{g}(i) * \text{h}(j)\}$$

The state size is $O(N)$ while each state requires an $O(N)$ iterations to compute it, thus, the total time complexity to naïvely compute this DP formula is $O(N^2)$. We will see how to compute this DP formula faster when a certain condition is satisfied.

First, let us change the variable names into something familiar. Let dp(i) be y, g(i) be x, h(j) be m_j, and dp(j) be c_j.

$$y = \min_{j<i}\{c_j + x \cdot m_j\}$$

Notice that $y = m \cdot x + c$ is a line equation. Thus, the above DP formula (what we do when we compute dp(i)) basically searches for the minimum y for the given x among a set of line equations $y = m_j \cdot x + c_j$. The left figure of Figure 9.15 shows an example of three lines (L1, L2, L3). Observe that the minimum y of any given x among these lines will always be in a convex shape (that is how this technique got its name).

In this example, there are three ranges separated by X1 and X2. The first range is $[-\infty, \text{X1}]$ which corresponds to L1, i.e., if x is in this range, then L1 will give the minimum y. The second range is $[\text{X1}, \text{X2}]$ which corresponds to L2, and the third range is $[\text{X2}, \infty]$ which corresponds to L3. If we have these ranges, then to find the range in which a given x falls into can be done in $O(\log N)$ with a **binary search**. However, getting the ranges might not be an easy task as naïvely it still needs $O(N)$ to compute. In the following subsection, we will see how to get the ranges (or the important lines) by exploiting a certain condition.

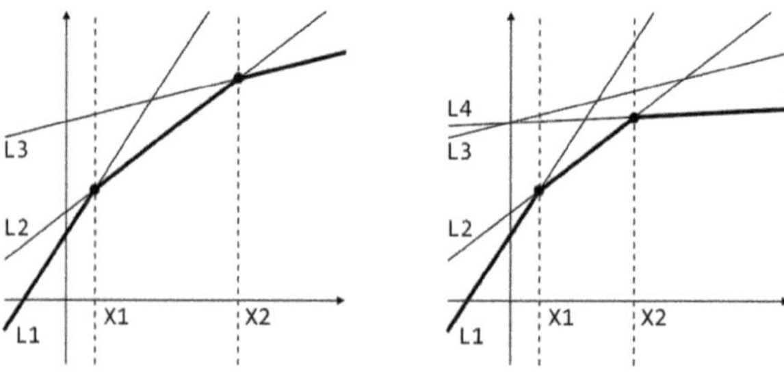

Figure 9.15: The bolded line is the convex line which gives the minimum y for a given x. L1: $y = \frac{3}{2}x + 3$, L2: $y = \frac{3}{4}x + 4$, L3: $\frac{1}{4}x + 8$, L4: $y = \frac{1}{20}x + 8$.

Optimization: $O(N \log N)$ solution when $\mathbf{h}(k) \geq \mathbf{h}(k+1)$

First, notice that dp(i) will be computed one-by-one for $i = 1 \ldots N$. Each time a dp(i) is computed, a line $y = \text{h}(i) \cdot x + \text{dp}(i)$ is added to our set of lines which will be used to compute dp(i) for any subsequent i.

If $\text{h}(k) \geq \text{h}(k+1)$, then we can maintain the ranges in amortized $O(1)$. Note that $\text{h}(k) \geq \text{h}(k+1)$ implies that the lines are given in a non-increasing order of gradient. In such a case, we can update the ranges with a new line by discarding "unimportant lines" from the **back** of the ranges.

Consider the right figure of Figure 9.15 with an additional line L4. This L4 is checked with L3 (the last line in existing ranges) and can be determined that L3 is not important, which means L3 will never again give the minimum y for any x. L4 then is checked against L2 (the next last line in existing ranges), and it is determined in this example that L2 is still important, thus, the new ranges consist of L1, L2, and L4.

How to check whether the last line in the ranges is unimportant? Easy. Let LA, LB, and LC be the second last line in the existing ranges, the last line in the existing ranges, and the new line to be added, respectively. LB is not important if the intersection point between LB and LC lies to the **left** of the intersection point between LA and LB. Note that we only need the `x` component of the intersection point. By working on the equation $m_1 \cdot x + c_1 = m_2 \cdot x + c_2$, i.e., both lines intersect at a point (x, y), we can get the equation for x, which is $x = \frac{c_2 - c_1}{m_1 - m_2}$.

In total, there are N lines to be added into the set of important lines (one line for each i when we evaluate dp(i)). When we add a new line, we remove any lines which are not important anymore. However, a line can only be removed at most once, thus, the total line removal will not be larger than the number of lines itself, which is N. Then, the total time complexity to evaluate **all** N lines will be $O(N)$. Therefore, this method of maintaining the ranges (set of important lines) has a time complexity of amortized $O(1)$ per line.

The following code shows an implementation of `addLine(m,c)`. The `struct tline` contains `m`, `c`, and `p`. Both `m` and `c` correspond to a line equation $y = m \cdot x + c$, while `p` is (the `x` component of) the intersection point between the line and the previous line in the set. If `L` is the first line, then we can set `L.p` to be $-\infty$ (a negative of a very large number). This also implies that the very first line will never be removed from the set. Also, note that `lines` stores all the important lines in a non-increasing order of the gradients.

```
struct tline { int m, c; double p; };
vector <tline> lines;

double getX(int m1, int c1, int m2, int c2) {
  return (double)(c1 - c2)/(m2 - m1);
}

void addLine(int m, int c) {
  double p = -INF;
  while (!lines.empty()) {
    p = getX(m, c, lines.back().m, lines.back().c);
    if (p < lines.back().p-EPS) lines.pop_back();
    else break;
  }
  lines.push_back((tline){m, c, p});
}
```

To get the minimum y for a given x, we can do a binary search as mentioned previously. The following code[63] shows one implementation of such a binary search.

```
int getBestY(int x) {
  int k = 0;
  int L = 0, R = lines.size() - 1;
  while (L <= R) {
    int mid = (L+R) >> 1;
    if (lines[mid].p <= x+EPS)
      k = mid, L = mid+1;
    else
      R = mid-1;
  }
  return lines[k].m*x + lines[k].b;
}
```

In the main function, we only need to do something like the following code and the overall time complexity is $O(N \log N)$.

```
int ans = 0;
for (int i = 1; i <= N; ++i) {
  if (i > 1) ans = getBestY(g[i]);
  addLine(h[i], ans);
}
cout << ans << "\n";
```

Optimization: $O(N)$ solution when $\mathbf{h}(k) \geq \mathbf{h}(k+1)$ and $\mathbf{g}(k) \leq \mathbf{g}(k+1)$

If we have another additional condition where $g(k) \leq g(k+1)$, then the part where we search for the minimum y for a given x (which was done by a binary search) can be done in amortized $O(1)$ by exploiting the previous range which gives the minimum y. Observe that if $g(k)$ (the x to be queried) is non-decreasing, then the range's index which gives the minimum y will also be non-decreasing unless pushed back by a new line.

We can maintain a pointer to the last used range and check how far can we move the pointer to the right each time we want to find the minimum y for a given x. As we can only move the pointer at most the total number of lines, then the total time complexity to find the minimum y for **all** x is $O(N)$. Therefore, the time complexity to find the minimum y for a given x with this method is amortized $O(1)$. The following code[64] shows the implementation. Replace `getBestY(x)` with `getBestYFaster(x)` in the main function and the total time complexity will be reduced to $O(N)$.

```
int getBestYFaster(int x) {
  static int k = 0;
  k = min(k, (int)lines.size()-1);
  while (k+1 < (int)lines.size() && lines[k+1].p <= x+EPS ) ++k;
  return lines[k].m*x + lines[k].c;
}
```

[63]Observe that `m * x` in this code might cause integer overflow for some constraints. You might want to adjust the data type accordingly.

[64]Take a note on the `static` keyword; alternatively, you can declare variable `k` globally.

Divide and Conquer Optimization

Consider the following DP formula:

$$\text{dp}(i,j) = \min_{k \le j}\{\text{dp}(i-1,k) + \text{cost}(k,j)\}$$

where $i = 1..N$ and $j = 1..M$. The naïve method to compute **one** state of $\text{dp}(i,j)$ is by a simple iteration for $k = 1..j$, thus, this method has an $O(M)$ time complexity. As there are $O(NM)$ states to be computed, the total time complexity for this solution will be $O(NM^2)$.

In this section, we will discuss a technique (namely, divide and conquer) to speed up the computation for the above DP formula when a certain condition is satisfied.

Optimization: $O(NM \log M)$ solution when $\text{opt}(i,j) \le \text{opt}(i,j+1)$

Let $\text{opt}(i,j)$ be the index k which gives $\text{dp}(i,j)$ in the previous DP formula the optimal (or, in this case, the minimum) value, or formally

$$\text{opt}(i,j) = \arg\min_{k \le j}\{\text{dp}(i-1,k) + \text{cost}(k,j)\}$$

We will focus on problems which satisfy the following *row monotonicity* condition:

$$\text{opt}(i,j) \le \text{opt}(i,j+1)$$

Supposed we know an $\text{opt}(i,j)$ for some i and j, with the row monoticity condition, we can infer that all $\text{dp}(i,a)$ where $a < j$ will have their optimal indexes k, i.e., $\text{opt}(i,a)$, to be no larger than $\text{opt}(i,j)$; similarly, all $\text{dp}(i,b)$ where $j < b$ will have their optimal indexes k, i.e., $\text{opt}(i,b)$, to be no smaller than $\text{opt}(i,j)$. For now, let us just assume the problem has such a property.

With this knowledge, we can design a divide and conquer algorithm (see Book 1) to compute $\text{dp}(i,*)$ all at once; in other words, for the whole i^{th} row in the DP table. We start by computing $\text{dp}(i,M/2)$ and obtaining $\text{opt}(i,M/2)$ by checking for $k = 1..M$, the whole range. Then, we compute $\text{dp}(i,M/4)$ and obtaining $\text{opt}(i,M/4)$ by checking for $k = 1..\text{opt}(i,M/2)$, i.e., we know that the optimal k for $\text{dp}(i,M/4)$ will not be larger than $\text{opt}(i,M/2)$. Similarly, we also compute $\text{dp}(i,3M/4)$ and obtaining $\text{opt}(i,3M/4)$ by checking for $k = \text{opt}(i,M/2)..N$, i.e., we know that the optimal k for $\text{dp}(i,3M/4)$ will not be smaller than $\text{opt}(i,M/2)$. Perform these steps recursively until $\text{dp}(i,j)$ are computed for all $j = 1..M$.

The following `divideConquer()` function computes $\text{dp}(i,j)$ for **all** $j = 1..M$.

```
void divideConquer(int i, int L, int R, int optL, int optR) {
  if (L > R) return;
  int j = (L+R) >> 1;
  for (int k = optL; k <= optR; ++k) {
    int value = dp[i-1][k] + cost(k, j);
    if (dp[i][j] < value) {
      dp[i][j] = value;
      opt = k;
    }
  }
  divideConquer(i, L, j-1, optL, opt);
  divideConquer(i, j+1, R, opt, optR);
}
```

The variables L and R correspond to the range for j to be computed; in other words, dp(i, L..R). For each call with a range [L, R], only one j is computed iteratively, which is for $j = \frac{L+R}{2}$. The range, [L, R], then is divided into two halves, [L, $\frac{L+R}{2} - 1$] and [$\frac{L+R}{2} + 1$, R], and each of them is solved recursively until the range is invalid. This, of course, will cause the recursion depth to be $O(\log M)$ as we halve the range at each level. On the other hand, the **total** number of iterations for k is $O(M)$ for all function calls on the **same** recursion level. Therefore, this function has a time complexity of $O(M \log M)$. This is a major improvement from the naïve method which requires $O(M^2)$ to compute dp(i, j) for all $j = 1..M$.

To solve the original problem (i.e., dp(N, M)), we only need to iteratively call the function `divideConquer()` for $i = 1..N$. We need to set the initial range to be $1..M$ both for L..R and optL..optR. As this is a bottom-up DP style, we also need to specify the base cases at the beginning. The following code implements this idea.

```
for (int j = 1; j <= M; ++j)
  dp[0][j] = baseCase(j);
for (int i = 1; i <= N; ++i)
  divideConquer(i, 1, M, 1, M);
ans = dp[N][M];
```

As there are $O(N)$ iterations in the main loop while one call of `divideConquer()` requires $O(M \log M)$, the total time complexity for this solution is $O(NM \log M)$.

When does opt$(i, j) \leq$ opt$(i, j + 1)$?

The challenging part of this divide and conquer optimization technique is to figure out whether the cost function, $cost(k, j)$, causes the opt(i, j) in the DP formula to satisfy the row monotonicity property as previously mentioned.

The opt(i, j) in the DP formula has a row monotonicity condition (thus, the divide and conquer optimization can be used) if the cost function satisfies the **quadrangle inequality**. A cost function, $c(k, j)$, satisfies the quadrangle inequality if and only if

$$cost(a, c) + cost(b, d) \leq cost(a, d) + cost(b, c)$$

for all $a < b < c < d$. This quadrangle inequality also appears in another DP optimization technique, the Knuth's optimization, which will be discussed in the next section.

Example of a cost function satisfying quadrangle inequality

Let A[1..M] be an array of integers, and $cost(k, j)$ where $k \leq j$ be the inversion counts[65] of A[k..j]. Given an integer N, your task is to split A[1..M] into N continuous subarrays such that the sum of inversion counts on all subarrays is minimum. We will directly show that this cost function satisfies quadrangle inequality.

Let $f(p, q, r, s)$ where $p \leq q$ and $r \leq s$ be the number of tuple $\langle i, j \rangle$ such that $p \leq i \leq q$, $r \leq j \leq s$, $i < j$, and A[i] $>$ B[j], i.e., the number of inversions of $\langle i, j \rangle$ where i is in the range of $p..q$ and j is in the range of $r..s$. Then, $cost(p, r) = cost(p, q) + f(p, r, q + 1, r)$ for any q satisfying $p \leq q \leq r$. Also notice that $f(p, q, r, s) = f(p, t - 1, r, s) + f(t, q, r, s)$ for any t satisfying $p < t \leq q$.

[65]Inversion counts of A[1..M] is the number of tuple $\langle i, j \rangle$ such that $i < j$ and A[i] $>$ B[j].

Now, let us verify the quadrangle inequality property of the cost function. Let $a < b < c < d$ and

$$cost(a,c) + cost(b,d) \leq cost(a,d) + cost(b,c)$$

Substitute $cost(b,d)$ with $cost(b,c) + f(b,d,c+1,d)$; note that $b < c < d$. Also, substitute $cost(a,d)$ with $cost(a,c) + f(a,d,c+1,d)$; note that $a < c < d$.

$$\begin{aligned} cost(a,c) + cost(b,c) + f(b,d,c+1,d) &\leq cost(a,c) + f(a,d,c+1,d) + cost(b,c) \\ f(b,d,c+1,d) &\leq f(a,d,c+1,d) \end{aligned}$$

Substitute $f(a,d,c+1,d)$ with $f(a,b-1,c+1,d) + f(b,d,c+1,d)$; note that $a < b < d$.

$$\begin{aligned} f(b,d,c+1,d) &\leq f(a,b-1,c+1,d) + f(b,d,c+1,d) \\ 0 &\leq f(a,b-1,c+1,d) \end{aligned}$$

As $f(a,b-1,c+1,d)$ is a number inversion, then it should be non-negative. Following the equations backward[66] shows that the cost function satisfies quadrangle inequality.

Note that it is often unnecessary to formally prove such property during a contest where time is precious and your code is only judged based on the test data. However, you might want to spend some time to prove such property during practice or learning to develop your intuition.

Knuth's Optimization

Knuth's optimization technique for dynamic programming is the result of Donald Knuth's work[22] on the optimal binary search tree problem. Later, Yao[38, 39, 2] generalizes this technique for other problems with the quadrangle inequality (also often mentioned as Knuth-Yao's quadrangle inequality).

Consider the following DP formula:

$$\text{dp}(i,j) = \min_{i<k<j} \{\text{dp}(i,k) + \text{dp}(k,j)\} + \text{cost}(i,j)$$

where $i = 1..N$ and $j = 1..N$. As you can see from the formula, computing **one** state of $\text{dp}(i,j)$ naïvely requires an $O(N)$ iterations, and there are $O(N^2)$ states to be computed. Therefore, the total time complexity for the naïve method is $O(N^3)$. Here, we will discuss how to speed up the DP computation with Knuth's optimization when a certain condition is satisfied.

Optimization: $O(N^2)$ solution when $\text{opt}(i,j-1) \leq \text{opt}(i,j) \leq \text{opt}(i+1,j)$

Similar to the previous $\text{opt}(i,j)$ function when we discuss the divide and conquer optimization (previous section), here, $\text{opt}(i,j)$ also refers to the index k which gives $\text{dp}(i,j)$ its optimal value.

$$\text{opt}(i,j) = \arg\min_{i<k<j} \{\text{dp}(i,k) + \text{dp}(k,j)\}$$

[66] To directly prove something, we start from statements that are true and show that the resulting conclusion is true. In this case, you can start from the last statement which is known to be true, $0 \leq f(a,b-1,c+1,d)$, works backward, and conclude that the quadrangle inequality is satisfied.

Likewise, let us assume, for now, that the problem satisfies the following *monotonicity* condition:

$$\text{opt}(i, j-1) \leq \text{opt}(i, j) \leq \text{opt}(i+1, j)$$

If we know that $\text{opt}(i, j)$ satisfies the monotonicity condition, then the speed-up is almost obvious. The following code implements the Knuth's optimization for dynamic programming.

```
int dpKnuth(int i, int j) {
  if (i == j) return 0;
  if (memo[i][j] != -1) return memo[i][j];
  memo[i][j] = inf;
  for (int k = opt[i][j-1]; k <= opt[i+1][j]; ++i) {
    int tcost = dpKnuth(i, k) + dpKnuth(k, j) + cost(i, j);
    if (tcost < memo[i][j]) {
      memo[i][j] = tcost;
      opt[i][j] = k;
    }
  }
  return memo[i][j];
}
```

Notice that `k` only interates from `opt[i][j-1]` until `opt[i+1][j]` as opposed to the normal `i+1` until `j-1`. Whenever we found a better result, we also store the `k` which produces that result in `opt[i][j]`.

Why does Knuth's optimization reduce the asymptotic time complexity?

Knuth's optimization "only" prunes the iterations from $i \ldots j$ into $\text{opt}(i, j-1) \ldots \text{opt}(i+1, j)$, but why does this optimization reduce the asymptotic time complexity from $O(N^3)$ into $O(N^2)$?

Let S_L be the number of iterations to compute **all** $\text{dp}(i, j)$ **where** $j - i = L$; in other words, L is the "length" of $\text{dp}(i, j)$. In Figure 9.16 we can see that all $\text{dp}(i, j)$ which have the same length lie on the same diagonal.

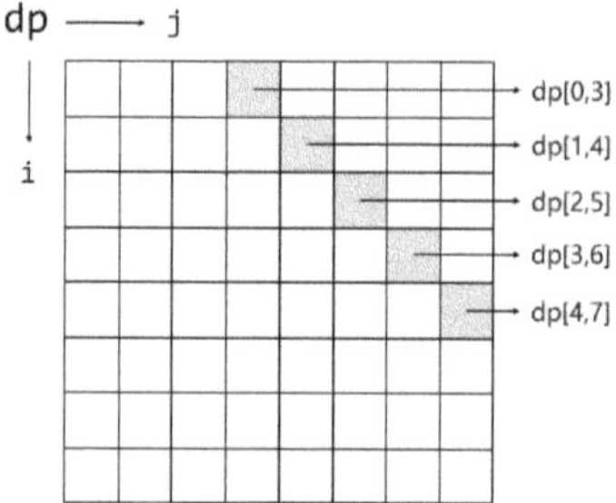

Figure 9.16: The shaded cells are having the same length of $j - i = 3$.

Now, let us see what happened to S_L.

$$S_L = \sum_{i=0 \ldots N-L-1} \text{opt}(i+1, i+L+1) - \text{opt}(i, i+L) + 1$$

Take the constant out.

$$S_L = N - L + \sum_{i=0...N-L-1} \text{opt}(i+1, i+L+1) - \text{opt}(i, i+L)$$

The previous summation is in the form of $(b-a)+(c-b)+(d-c)+\cdots+(z-y)$ which can be reduced to $(z-a)$.

$$S_L = N - L + \text{opt}(N-L, N-1) - \text{opt}(0, L)$$

Recall that $\text{opt}(i,j)$ is the index k that gives $\text{dp}(i,j)$ its optimal value, thus, $\text{opt}(i,j)$ will vary between 0 and $N-1$. Therefore, the difference between two opt() will be no larger than N. Also, note that L comes from $j-i$, thus, it is bounded by N.

$$S_L \le N - L + N$$
$$S_L = O(N)$$

Therefore, computing $\text{dp}(i,j)$ for all i and j such that $j-i=L$ requires an $O(N)$ time complexity. As there are only $O(N)$ different L, the overall time complexity to compute $\text{dp}(i,j)$ for **all** i and j is $O(N^2)$.

When does $\text{opt}(i,j-1) \le \text{opt}(i,j) \le \text{opt}(i+1,j)$?

Knuth's optimization can be used if the cost function, $\text{cost}(i,j)$, causes $\text{opt}(i,j)$ in the DP formula to satisfy the monotonicity property. For the $\text{opt}(i,j)$ to have a monotonicity property, it is sufficient if the $\text{cost}(i,j)$ satisfies the **quadrangle inequality**, i.e.,

$$cost(a,c) + cost(b,d) \le cost(a,d) + cost(b,c)$$

for all $a < b < c < d$. This condition is also known as the Knuth-Yao's quadrangle inequality[2].

Programming exercises related to DP Optimization:

1. **UVa 10003 - Cutting Sticks ***
2. **UVa 10304 - Optimal Binary ... *** (classical DP; requires 1D range sum and Knuth-Yao speed up to get $O(n^2)$ solution)
3. *Kattis - coveredwalkway **
4. *Kattis - money **

9.24 Push-Relabel Algorithm

Push-Relabel is an *alternative* Max Flow algorithm on top of the Ford-Fulkerson based algorithms, i.e., $O(VE^2)$ Edmonds-Karp algorithm (see Section 8.4.3) or $O(V^2E)$ Dinic's algorithm (see Section 8.4.4). Recall that Ford-Fulkerson based Max Flow algorithms work by iteratively sending *legal* flows via augmenting paths that connect the source vertex s to the sink vertex t until we cannot find any more such augmenting path.

Push-Relabel, invented by Goldberg and Tarjan [18], is an out-of-the-box Max Flow algorithm that doesn't follow that idea. Instead, a Push-Relabel algorithm:

1. Initially push as much flow as possible from the source vertex s.
   Such a flow is an upper bound of the max flow value in the given flow graph but may not be feasible (i.e., possibly illegal), so we call it as 'pre-flow'.
2. While $\exists$ a vertex with unbalanced flow, i.e., flow in > flow out:
   (a) Calculate excess flow in that vertex (flow in - flow out).
   (b) Push some excess flow on an edge in residual graph R.
   Eventual excess that does not form the final max flow will return to s.

Notice that at all times throughout the execution of Push-Relabel algorithm, it maintains an invariant that there is no $s \to t$ path in R. This Push-Relabel algorithm thus starts from possibly illegal flows and it iteratively make the flows legal. As soon as the flows are legal (there is no more vertex with unbalanced flow), then we have the max flow.

Definitions

pre-flow: Assignment flow $f(u, v) \geq 0$ to every edge $(u, v) \in E$ such that:

1. $\forall(u, v) \in E,\ f(u, v) \leq c(u, v)$
   That is, we always satisfy the capacity constraints.
2. $\forall u \in V - t,\ \sum_z f(z, u) \geq \sum_w f(u, w)$
   That is, flow-in is $\geq$ flow-out.
   This $\geq$ constraint is different from the $==$ constraint for a legal flow

excess(u) $= \sum_z f(z, u) - \sum_w f(u, w)$, abbreviated[67] as $x(u)$.

height(u) or $h(u)$ for every vertex $u \in V$.

If $\forall u \in V - \{s, t\}$, we have $x(u) = 0$, we say the pre-flow is feasible and that is our goal: push flow (that initially arrives from the source vertex s) around until all $x(u) = 0$. To avoid the unwanted cyclic situation where two (or more) vertices pushing the excess flow in cycles, Push-Relabel adds an additional rule so that it can only push a flow from a higher vertex to a lower vertex (i.e., if $h(u) > h(v)$, then u can push excess flow to v if need be).

Basic Push-Relabel Algorithm

A basic Push-Relabel algorithm receives the same input as with other Max Flow algorithms discussed in Section 8.4, namely: a flow graph $G = (V, E)$ with n vertices and m edges with capacities c associated to each edge plus two special vertices: s and t. A basic Push-Relabel algorithm then run the following pseudo-code:

[67] The excess value of vertex u is written as $e(u)$ in other books/references but e and E are too similar in our opinion, hence we write it as $x(u)$.

1. $\forall u \in V, h(u) = 0$ // heights start at 0.
2. $h(s) = n$ // except that s starts from a high place, at height $n = |V|$.
3. $\forall u \in V : (s, u) \in E$, then $f(s, u) = c(s, u)$ // the pre-flow push out of s
4. while f is not feasible // i.e., $\exists u$ such that $x(u) > 0$
5.   let $r(u, v) = c(u, v) - f(u, v) + f(v, u)$ // the residual graph R
6.   if $\exists u \in V - \{s, t\}$ and $v \in V$ where $x(u) > 0$ and $r(u, v) > 0$ and $h(u) > h(v)$, then
       // if u has excess, (u, v) has capacity left, and u is higher than v (can push)
7. $b = min(x(u), r(u, v))$ // the bottleneck capacity
8. $f(u, v) = f(u, v) + b$ // push b unit of flow from u to v
9.   else, choose $v : x(v) > 0$ // choose any vertex v with excess
10. $h(v) = h(v) + 1$ // raise height of vertex v by 1 to facilitate future push

As its name implies, this Push-Relabel algorithm has two core operations: **Push** and **Relabel**. Line 7-8 are the push operations. There are two possible sub-scenarios in line 7:

1. $b = r(u, v)$, so edge (u, v) in the residual graph R is at capacity after this **saturating push**; after a saturating push, vertex u may still have excess flow (thus, may still be unbalanced).
2. $b < r(u, v)$ but $b = x(u)$, i.e., all the excess flow of vertex u is pushed out by this **non-saturating push** and vertex u becomes balanced (vertex v becomes unbalanced unless $v == t$).

Line 9-10 are the relabel[68] operations where the Push-Relabel algorithm cannot execute any push operation (on line 7-8). Thus, the Push-Relabel algorithm takes any vertex with excess flow and just raise its height by +1 to facilitate future push operation.

A Sample Execution of Basic Push-Relabel Algorithm

It is easier to explain this Basic Push-Relabel algorithm with an example. Suppose we have the initial flow graph as in Figure 9.17—left (with $n = 5$ vertices and $m = 7$ directed edges with its initial capacities), then after executing line 1-2 of the pseudo-code, the height of all vertices except $h(s) = n = 5$ is 0. Then in Figure 9.17—right, we execute line 3 of the pseudo-code, the pre-push from $s = 0$ to vertex 1 and 2, making both of them have excess (unbalanced).

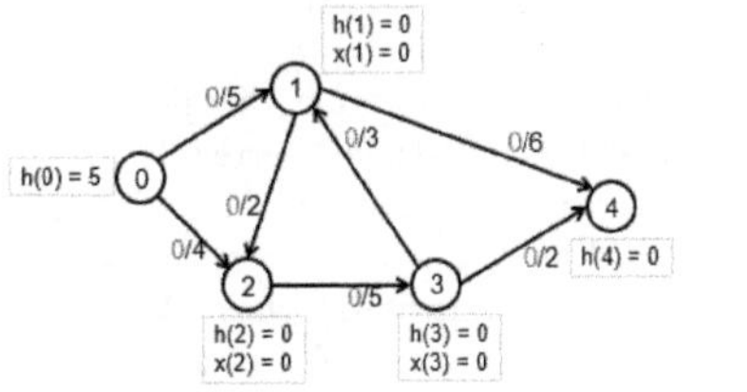

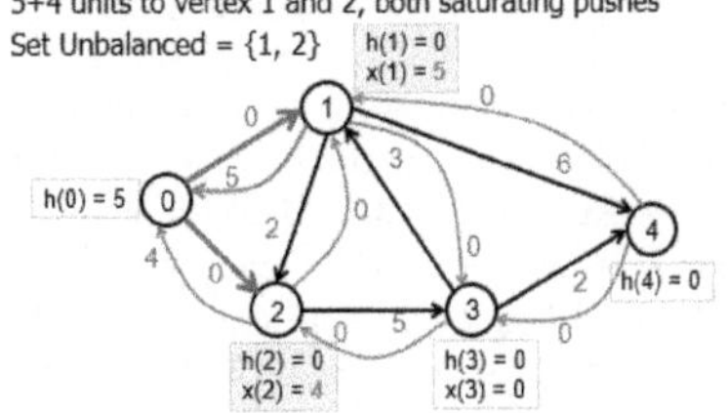

Figure 9.17: Left: The Initial Flow Graph; Right: Pre-flow Push from s

[68] The name 'relabel' of this raising-the-height-of-a-vertex operation is historical.

In Figure 9.18—left, we have two vertices that are unbalanced. We can keep track of these unbalanced vertices using a queue[69], e.g., `Unbalanced` $= \{1, 2\}$. We pop out the front most unbalanced vertex 1 and see if we can push anything out of vertex 1. However, vertex 1 cannot push the excess flow to vertex 2, to sink vertex $t = 4$, or to return the excess back to source vertex $s = 0$ as $h(1) = 0$, as short as all its three neighbors. Thus we have no choice but to raise the height of vertex 1 by 1 and re-insert vertex 1 to the *back*[70] of the queue. In Figure 9.18—right, we have similar situation with vertex 2.

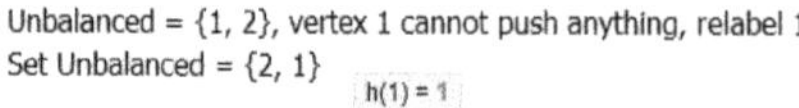

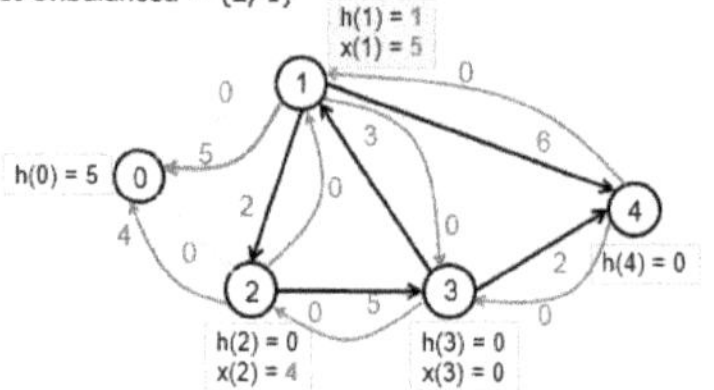

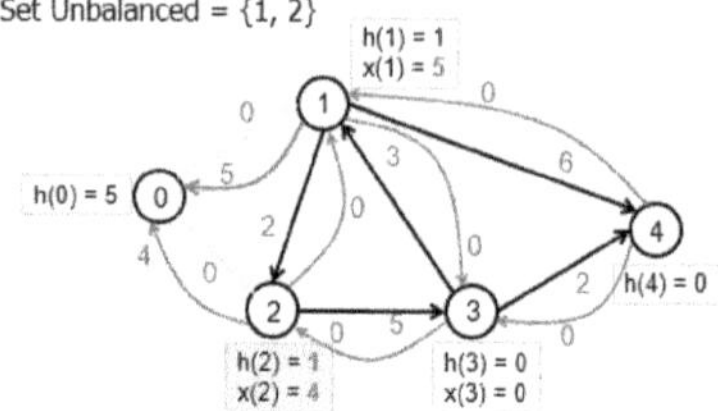

Figure 9.18: Left: Relabel Vertex 1; Right: Relabel Vertex 2

In Figure 9.19—left, we have `Unbalanced` $= \{1, 2\}$ and we process vertex 1 again . At this point of time, we can push **all** $x(1) = 5$ to sink vertex $t = 4$ as the capacity of edge $(1, 4) = 6$ is higher than $x(1) = 5$ and $h(1) = 1$ is higher than $h(4) = 0$. This is called a **non-saturating** push and makes vertex 1 balanced again. In Figure 9.19—right, we only have `Unbalanced` $= \{2\}$ and we process vertex 2 again. At this point of time, we can push **all** $x(2) = 4$ to its neighboring vertex 3 as the capacity of edge $(2, 3) = 5$ is more than $x(2) = 4$ and $h(2) = 1$ is higher than $h(3) = 0$. This is another **non-saturating** push. But notice that since vertex 3 is *not* a sink vertex t, it will now become unbalanced, i.e., $x(3) = 4$.

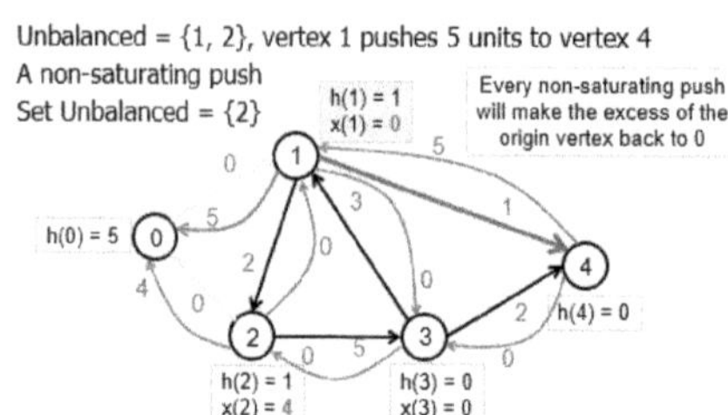

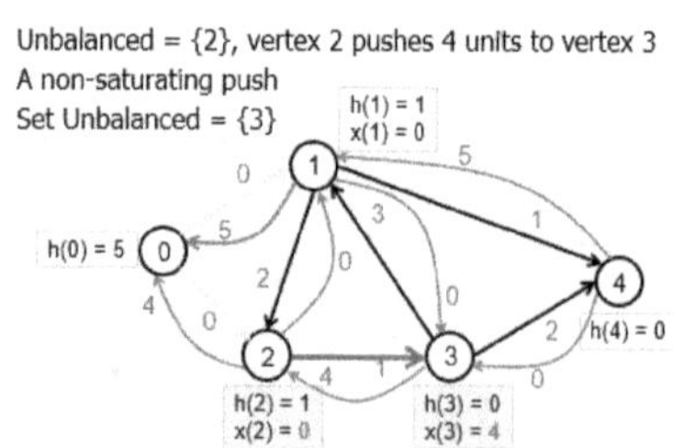

Figure 9.19: Left: Non-saturating Push $1 \rightarrow 4$; Right: Non-saturating Push $2 \rightarrow 3$

In Figure 9.20—left, we have to relabel the only unbalanced vertex 3 at this point of time so that $h(3) = 1$. In Figure 9.20—right, we still process this unbalanced vertex 3. This time we can push **some** $x(3) = 4$ to its neighboring sink vertex $t = 4$ as $h(3) = 1$ is higher than $h(4) = 0$. However, as the capacity of edge $(3, 4) = 2$ is less than $x(3) = 4$, we can then only able to send $b = 2$ excess unit to vertex 4. This is called a **saturating** push. A saturating push rarely make the excess of the origin vertex balanced. At this point of time, vertex 3 still have excess, but reduced to $x(3) = 2$.

[69]There are several ways to do this, we can also use a stack for example.

[70]There are *better* variant of Push-Relabel algorithm that doesn't do this.

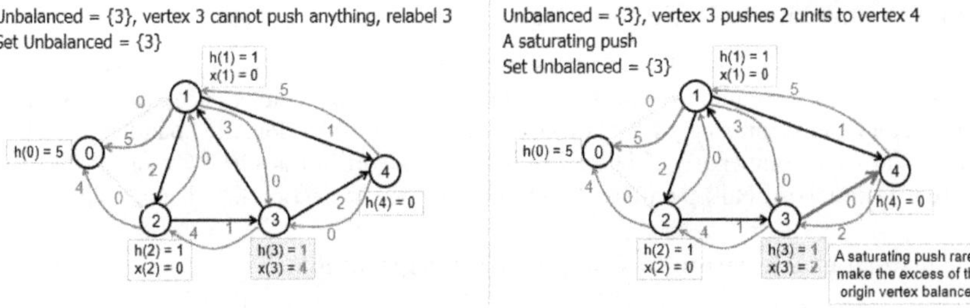

Figure 9.20: Left: Relabel Vertex 3; Right: Saturating Push $3 \rightarrow 4$

In Figure 9.21—left, we have to *again* relabel the only unbalanced vertex 3 at this point of time so that $h(3) = 2$. In Figure 9.21—right, we can do another non-saturating push $3 \rightarrow 1$. This makes vertex 3 balanced but vertex 1 becomes unbalanced again.

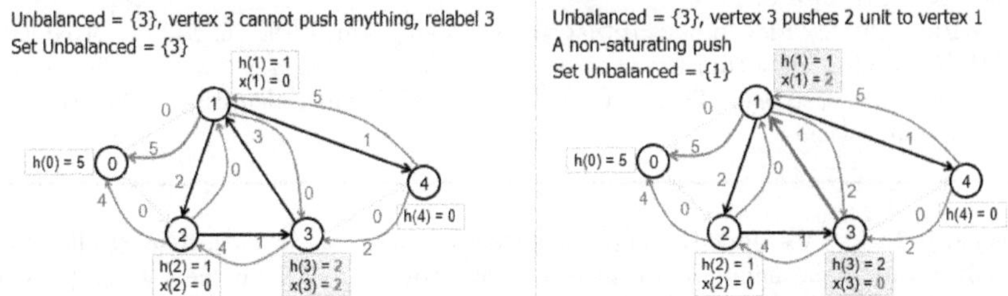

Figure 9.21: Left: Relabel Vertex 3; Right: Non-saturating Push $3 \rightarrow 1$

In Figure 9.22—left, we are able to send a saturating push from vertex 1 to sink vertex $t = 4$ that reduces excess of $x(1) = 1$. In Figure 9.22—right, we highlight a situation experienced by this basic Push-Relabel algorithm where it will continuously push the last 1 unit excess around cycle $1 \rightarrow 2 \rightarrow 3$ around, relabeling the 3 vertices gradually[71] until one of them is higher than the source vertex (that has $h(0) = 5$) and then return the unused 1 unit back to source vertex $s = 0$.

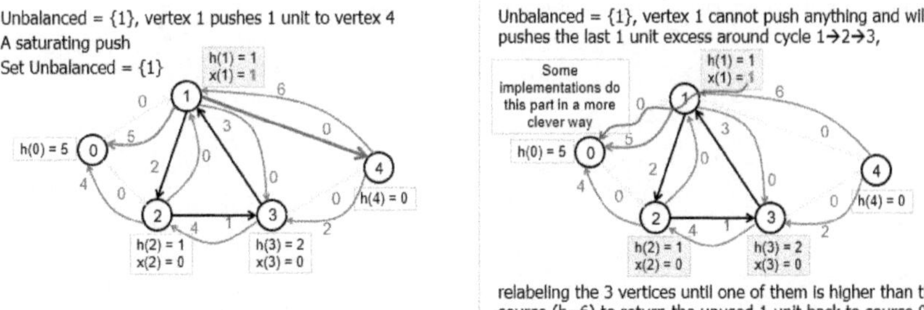

Figure 9.22: Left: Saturating Push $1 \rightarrow 4$; Right: Return 1 Unit of Excess to s

[71]This is clearly not the best way to implement Push-Relabel and several variants have been designed to improve this aspect.

Time Complexity of Basic Push-Relabel Algorithm

The analysis of this basic Push-Relabel algorithm is a bit involved. For the purpose of Competitive Programming, we just say that the maximum numbers of relabels, saturating pushes, and non-saturating pushes, without any fancy optimization, are bounded by $O(V^2E)$. Thus, the time complexity of basic Push-Relabel algorithm is $O(V^2E)$, on par with the current fastest Ford-Fulkerson based method discussed in Section 8.4: Dinic's algorithm.

Push-Relabel Algorithm in Competitive Programming

However, Push-Relabel can be implemented to run in a tighter time complexity of $O(V^3)$ using the 'Relabel-to-Front' strategy and more clever relabeling that doesn't always increase a vertex height by only +1. This $O(V^3)$ time complexity is better than $O(V^2E)$ Dinic's algorithm on a *dense* flow graph where $E = O(V^2)$. However, on the other hand, Push-Relabel processes the flows differently compared to the Ford-Fulkerson based Max Flow algorithms and thus cannot take advantage if the Max Flow problem has *small* Max Flow f^* value (see **Exercise 8.4.6.1**).

Remarks: All Max Flow problems that we have seen in this book can still be solved with the $O(V^2E)$ Dinic's algorithm that has been discussed in Section 8.4 as most flow graph are not the worst case one. Therefore, the faster Push-Relabel algorithm is currently for theoretical interest only.

Exercise 9.24.1*: We omit the implementation details of basic Push-Relabel algorithm and only mention the name of 'Relabel-to-Front' strategy. Explore the various possible implementations of this Push-Relabel variant and try to solve `https://open.kattis.com/problems/conveyorbelts` (need a big flow graph) with as fast runtime as possible.

Profile of Algorithm Inventor

Andrew Vladislav Goldberg (born 1960) is an American computer scientist who is best known for his work on the maximum flow problem, especially the co-invention of the Push-Relabel max flow algorithm with Robert Endre Tarjan.

9.25 Min Cost (Max) Flow

Problem Description

The Min Cost Flow problem is the problem of finding the *cheapest* possible way of sending a certain amount of (not necessarily the max) flow through a flow network. In this problem, every edge has two attributes: the flow capacity through this edge *and the unit cost* for sending one unit flow through this edge. Some problem authors choose to simplify this problem by setting the edge capacity to a constant integer and only vary the edge costs.

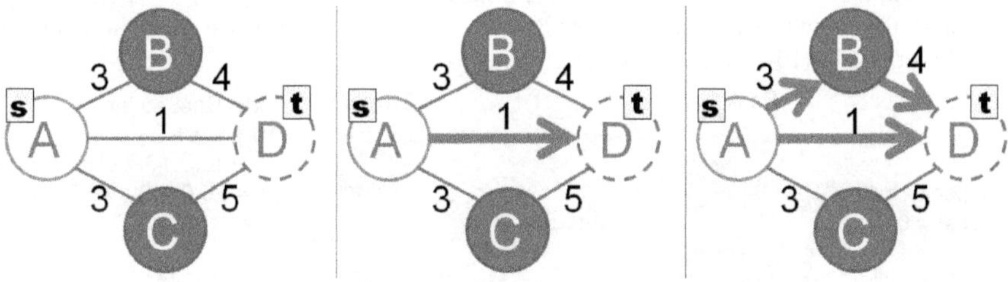

Figure 9.23: An Example of Min Cost Max Flow (MCMF) Problem (UVa 10594 [28])

Figure 9.23—left shows a (modified) instance of UVa 10594. Here, each edge has a uniform capacity of 10 units and a unit cost as shown in the edge label. We want to send 20 units of flow from A to D (note that the max flow of this flow graph is 30 units) which can be satisfied by either one of these three ways, but with different total cost:

1. 10 units of flow $A \to D$ with cost $1 \times 10 = 10$ (Figure 9.23—middle); plus another 10 units of flow $A \to B \to D$ with cost $(3 + 4) \times 10 = 70$ (Figure 9.23—right). The total cost is $10 + 70 = 80$, and this is the minimum compared with two other ways below.
2. 10 units of flow $A \to D$ with cost 10 plus another 10 units of flow $A \to C \to D$ with cost $(3 + 5) \times 10 = 80$. The total cost is $10 + 80 = 90$.
3. $A \to B \to D$ with cost 70 (Figure 9.23—right) plus another 10 units of flow $A \to C \to D$ with cost 80. The total cost is $70 + 80 = 150$.

Solution(s)

The Min Cost (Max) Flow, or in short MCMF, can be solved by replacing the $O(E)$ BFS (to find the shortest—in terms of number of hops—augmenting path) in Edmonds-Karp/Dinic's algorithm with the $O(kE)$ Bellman-Ford-Moore algorithm (to find the shortest/cheapest—in terms of the *path cost*—augmenting path). We need a shortest path algorithm that can handle negative edge weights as such negative edge weights *may appear* when we cancel a certain flow along a backward edge (as we have to *subtract* the cost taken by this augmenting path as canceling flow means that we do not want to use that edge). An example in Figure 9.24 will show the presence of such negative edge weight.

The need to use a slower but more general shortest path algorithm like Bellman-Ford-Moore algorithm slows down the MCMF implementation to around $O(V^2E^2)$ but this is usually compensated by the problem authors of most MCMF problems by having smaller input graph constraints.

Source code: `ch9/mcmf.cpp|java|py`

Weighted MCBM

In Figure 9.24, we show one test case of UVa 10746 - Crime Wave - The Sequel. This is a weighted MCBM problem on a complete bipartite graph $K_{n,m}$. We can reduce this problem into an MCMF problem as follows: we add edges from source s to vertices of the left set with capacity 1 and cost 0. We also add edges from vertices of the right set to the sink t also with capacity 1 and cost 0. The directed edges from the left set to the right set have capacity 1 and costs according to the problem description. After having this weighted flow graph, we can run any MCMF algorithm to get the required answer: Flow 1 = $0 \rightarrow 2 \rightarrow 4 \rightarrow 8$ with cost 5, Flow 2 = $0 \rightarrow 1 \rightarrow 4 \rightarrow 2$ (cancel flow 2-4; notice that there is a -5 edge weight here) $\rightarrow 6 \rightarrow 8$ with cost 15, and Flow 3 = $0 \rightarrow 3 \rightarrow 5 \rightarrow 8$ with cost 20. The minimum total cost is 5 + (10-5+10) + 20 = 40.

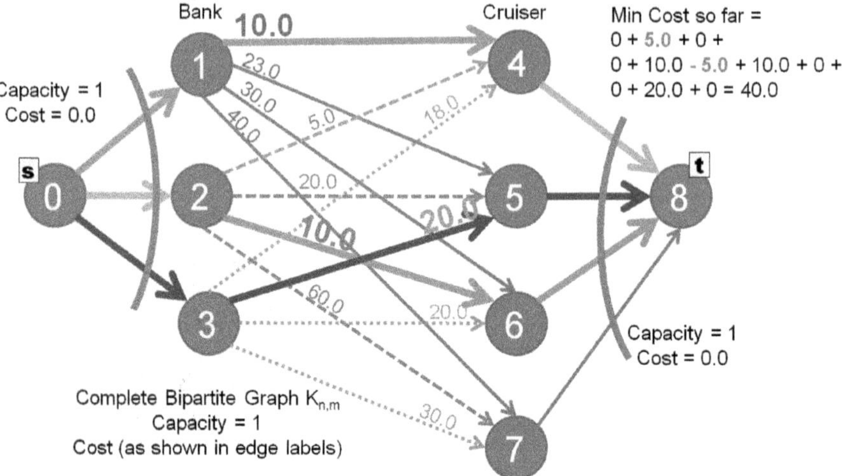

Figure 9.24: A Sample Test Case of UVa 10746: 3 Matchings with Min Cost = 40

However, we can also use the more specialized and faster ($O(V^3)$) Kuhn-Munkres algorithm to solve this Weighted MCBM problem (see Section 9.27).

Programming exercises related to Min Cost (Max) Flow:

1. Entry Level: **UVa 10594 - Data Flow *** (basic min cost max flow problem)
2. **UVa 10806 - Dijkstra, Dijkstra *** (send 2 edge-disjoint flows with min cost)
3. **UVa 11301 - Great Wall of China *** (modeling; vertex capacity; MCMF)
4. **UVa 12821 - Double Shortest Paths *** (similar to UVa 10806)
5. *Kattis - catering ** (LA 7152 - WorldFinals Marrakech15; MCMF modeling)
6. *Kattis - mincostmaxflow ** (very basic MCMF problem; good starting point)
7. *Kattis - ragingriver ** (MCMF; unit capacity and unit cost)

   Extra Kattis: *tourist*, *jobpostings*.

   Also see Kuhn-Munkres (Hungarian) algorithm (Section 9.27)

9.26 Hopcroft-Karp Algorithm

In Section 8.5.3, we mentioned Hopcroft-Karp algorithm [19] as another algorithm that can be used to solve the unweighted Maximum Cardinality Bipartite Matching (MCBM) problem on top of the Max Flow based solutions (which takes longer to code) and the Augmenting Path based solutions (which is the preferred method) as discussed in Special Graph section in Book 1.

Worst Case Bipartite Graph

In our opinion, the main reason for using the longer-to-code Hopcroft-Karp algorithm instead of the simpler-and-shorter-to-code Augmenting Path algorithm (direct application of Berge's lemma) to solve the Unweighted MCBM is its better *theoretical* worst case time complexity. Hopcroft-Karp algorithm runs in $O(\sqrt{V}E)$ which is (much) faster than the $O(VE)$ Augmenting Path algorithm on medium-sized ($V \approx 1500$) bipartite (and dense) graphs.

An extreme example is a Complete Bipartite Graph $K_{n,m}$ with $V = n+m$ and $E = n \times m$. On such bipartite graphs, the Augmenting Path algorithm has a worst case time complexity of $O((n+m) \times n \times m)$. If $m = n$, we have an $O(n^3)$ solution—only OK for $n \leq 250$.

Similarities with Dinic's Algorithm

The main issue with the $O(VE)$ Augmenting Path algorithm is that it may explore the longer augmenting paths first (as it is essentially a 'modified DFS'). This is not efficient. By exploring the *shorter* augmenting paths first, Hopcroft and Karp proved that their algorithm will only run in $O(\sqrt{V})$ iterations [19]. In each iteration, Hopcroft-Karp algorithm executes an $O(E)$ BFS from all the free vertices on the left set and finds augmenting paths of increasing lengths (starting from length 1: a free edge, length 3: a free edge, a matched edge, and a free edge again, length 5, length 7, and so on...). Then, it calls another $O(E)$ DFS to augment those augmenting paths (Hopcroft-Karp algorithm can increase *more than one matching* in one algorithm iteration). Therefore, the overall time complexity of Hopcroft-Karp algorithm is $O(\sqrt{V}E)$.

Those who are familiar with Dinic's Max Flow algorithm (see Section 8.4.4) will notice that running Dinic's algorithm on bipartite flow graph is essentially this Hopcroft-Karp algorithm with the same $O(\sqrt{V}E)$ time complexity.

For the extreme example on Complete Bipartite Graph $K_{n,m}$ shown above, the Hopcroft-Karp (or Dinic's) algorithm has a worst case time complexity of $O(\sqrt{(n+m)} \times n \times m)$. If $m = n$, we have an $O(n^{\frac{5}{2}})$ solution which is OK for $n \leq 1500$. Therefore, if the problem author is 'nasty enough' to set $n \approx 1500$ and a relatively dense bipartite graph for an Unweighted MCBM problem, using Hopcroft-Karp (or Dinic's) is *theoretically* safer than the standard Augmenting Path algorithm.

Comparison with Augmenting Path Algorithm++

However, if we have done a randomized greedy pre-processing step before running the normal Augmenting Path algorithm (which we dub as the Augmenting Path Algorithm++ algorithm mentioned in Section 8.5.3), there will only be up to k subsequent calls of normal Augmenting Path algorithm (where k is significantly less than V, empirically shown to be not more than $\sqrt{V}$, and it is quite challenging to create a custom Bipartite Graph so that the randomized greedy pre-processing step is not very effective, see **Exercise 8.5.3.2***) to obtain the final answer even if the input is a relatively dense and large bipartite graph. This implies that Hopcroft-Karp algorithm does not need to be included in ICPC (25-pages) team notebook.

9.27 Kuhn-Munkres Algorithm

In Section 8.5.4, we have noted that programming contest problems involving weighted Max Cardinality Bipartite Matching (MCBM) on medium-sized[72] Bipartite graphs are extremely rare (but not as rare as MCM problems on medium-sized *non-bipartite* graphs in Section 9.28). But when such a problem does appear in a problem set, it can be one of the hardest, especially if the team does not have the implementation of Kuhn-Munkres (or Hungarian[73]) algorithm (see the original paper [23, 27]) or a fast Min Cost Max Flow (MCMF) algorithm that can also solve this problem (see Section 9.25) in their ICPC team notebook (this graph matching variant is excluded from the IOI syllabus [15]).

To understand the Kuhn-Munkres algorithm, one needs to know Berge's lemma that is first discussed in Book 1 and revisited in Section 8.5.3: a matching M in graph G is maximum if and only if there are no more augmenting paths in G. Earlier, we used this lemma for *unweighted* Bipartite graphs in our Augmenting Path algorithm implementation (a simple DFS modification) but this lemma can also be used for *weighted* Bipartite graphs (the Kuhn-Munkres algorithm exploit this).

Input Pre-Processing and Equality Subgraph

Kuhn-Munkres algorithm can be explained as a graph algorithm[74]: Given a weighted bipartite graph $G(X, Y, E)$ where X/Y are the vertices on the left/right set, respectively, find *Max*[75] *Weighted* and *Perfect* Bipartite Matching. Thus, if the input is an *incomplete* weighted bipartite graph (see Figure 9.25—left), we add dummy missing vertices (if $|X| \neq |Y|$) and/or missing edges with large negative values (if $|E| < |X| \times |Y|$, see 3 added edges: $(0, 3)$, $(1, 5)$, and $(2, 4)$ with dummy weight -1 in Figure 9.25—middle) so that we have a complete weighted bipartite graph $K_{|X|,|Y|}$ that is guaranteed to have a perfect bipartite matching. The edges are all directed from X to Y.

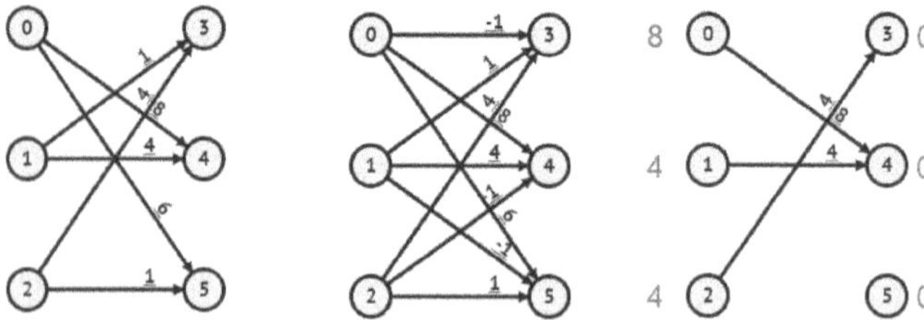

Figure 9.25: L: Initial Graph; M: Complete Weighted Bipartite Graph; R: Equality Subgraph

Instead of "directly" finding a *maximum* perfect matching, Kuhn-Munkres algorithm finds a perfect matching in an *evolving* **equality subgraph**, and the matching cost is guaranteed to be maximum when it finds one. An equality subgraph of a complete bipartite graph G contains all the vertices in G and a subset of its edges. Each vertex, u, has a value (also called *label*), $l(u)$. An edge (u, v) is visible in an equality subgraph if and only if $l(u) + l(v) = w(u, v)$ where $w(u, v)$ is the weight of edge (u, v). Initially, $l(u)$ where $u \in X$ equals to highest weight among u's outgoing edges, while $l(v) = 0$ where $v \in Y$ as there is no outgoing edges from v. See Figure 9.25—right where we have only 3 visible edges: edge $(0, 4)/(1, 4)/(2, 3)$ with weight 8/4/4, respectively. Kuhn-Munkres theorem says that if

[72]Weighted MBCM problem on *small* bipartite graphs ($V \leq 20$) can be solved using DP with bitmask.

[73]Harold William Kuhn and James Raymond Munkres named their (joint) algorithm based on the work of two other *Hungarian* mathematicians: Denes Konig and Jenö Egerváry.

[74]Or as a matrix-based algorithm to solve an assignment problem

[75]We can easily modify this to find Min Weighted Perfect Bipartite Matching by negating all edge weights.

there is a perfect matching in the current equality subgraph, then this perfect matching is also a maximum-weight matching. Let's see if we can find a perfect matching in this current equality subgraph.

Next, the Kuhn-Munkres algorithm performs similar steps as with the Augmenting Path algorithm for finding MCBM: applying Berge's lemma but on the current equality graph. It notices that vertex 0 is a free vertex, follows free edge $(0, 4)$ with weight 8, and arrives at another free vertex 4—an augmenting path of length 1 edge. After flipping the edge status, we match vertex 0 and 4 with the current total cost of 8 (see Figure 9.26—left).

But Kuhn-Munkres algorithm will encounter an issue in the next iteration: free vertex $1 \rightarrow$ free edge $(1, 4) \rightarrow$ matched edge $(4, 0)$, and stuck there as there is no more edge to explore (see Figure 9.26—middle). Notice that vertex 0 is only connected with vertex 4 in the *current* equality subgraph. We need to *expand* the equality subgraph.

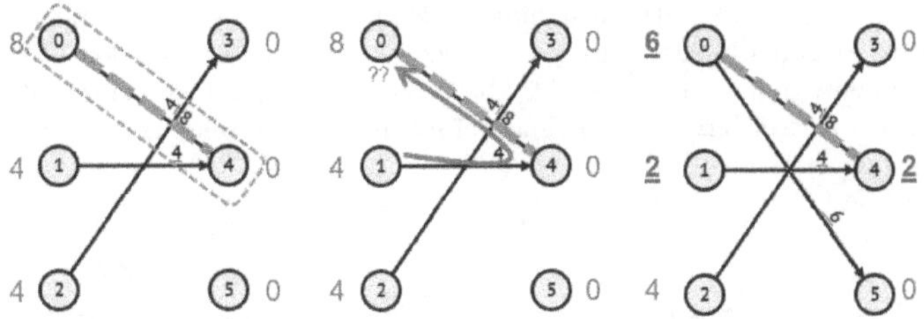

Figure 9.26: L: 1st Augmenting Path; M: Stuck; R: Relabel the Equality Subgraph

Updating the Labels (Expanding the Equality Subgraph)

Now, it is time to relabel some vertices so that we *maintain* all edges currently visible in the equality subgraph (so all currently matched edges are preserved) and add at least one (but can be more) edge(s) into the equality subgraph. However, we need to do so by decrementing the total weight of the edges *as minimally as possible.* Here are the steps required:

Let $S \in X$ and $T \in Y$ where S/T contains vertices in X/Y along the current partial augmenting path, respectively. In Figure 9.26—middle, the partial augmenting path is: $1 \rightarrow 4 \rightarrow 0$, so $S = \{0, 1\}$ and $T = \{4\}$. Now let Δ be the minimum 'decrease' of matching quality $l(u) + l(v) - w(u, v)$ over all possible edges $u \in S$ and $v \notin T$ (this is an $O(V^2)$). In Figure 9.26—middle, we have these 4 possibilities (remember that edge $(0, 3)$ and $(1, 5)$ are actually dummy edges that do not exist in the original input weighted bipartite graph):

$l(0) + l(3) - w(0, 3) = 8 + 0 - (-1) = 9$ (if we set $w(0, 3) = -\infty$, this value will be ∞);
$l(0) + l(5) - w(0, 5) = 8 + 0 - 6 = 2$ (this is the minimum delta $\Delta = 2$);
$l(1) + l(3) - w(1, 3) = 4 + 0 - 1 = 3$; or
$l(1) + l(5) - w(1, 5) = 4 + 0 - (-1) = 5$ (if we set $w(1, 5) = -\infty$, this value will be ∞).

Now we improve the labels using the following rules (no change to the remaining vertices):
for $u \in S$, $l'(u) = l(u) - \Delta$ (decrease)
for $v \in T$, $l'(v) = l(v) + \Delta$ (increase)

This way, the new set of labels l' that describe a new equality subgraph is a valid labeling that maintains all edges in the previous equality subgraph, plus addition of at least one more new edge. In this case, edge $(0, 3)$ now visible in the equality subgraph. See Figure 9.26—right where $l(0)/l(1)/l(2)$ change to 6/2/4 and $l(3)/l(4)/l(5)$ change to 0/2/0, respectively. See that matched edge $(0, 4)$ remains preserved as $l(0)+l(4) = 6+2 = 8$ from previously $8+0 = 8$ (as with edge $(1, 4)$) and notice that edge $(0, 5)$ is now visible as $l(0) + l(5) = 6 + 0 = 6$.

The Rest of the Algorithm and Remarks

Then, Kuhn-Munkres algorithm can proceed to find the second augmenting path $1 \to 4 \to 0 \to 5$ of length 3 edges and flip the status of these 3 edges (see Figure 9.27—left).

The third (trivial) augmenting path $2 \to 3$ of length 1 edge is also immediately found in the next iteration. We add edge $(2, 3)$ to the matching (see Figure 9.27—middle).

Now we have a perfect matching of size $V/2 = 6/2 = 3$: edge $(0, 5)/(1, 4)/(2, 3)$ with weight 6/4/4, respectively, totalling $6+4+4 = 14$. By Kuhn-Munkres theorem, this perfect matching has the maximum total weight as the equality subgraphs have guided the algorithm to favor edges with higher weights first (see Figure 9.27—right).

In summary, Kuhn-Munkres algorithm starts with an initial equality subgraph (that initially consists of edges with highest edge weights), find (and eliminate) as many profitable augmenting paths in the *current* equality subgraph first. When the algorithm is stuck before finding a perfect bipartite matching (which we know exist as the transformed input is a complete weighted bipartite graph — hence guaranteeing termination), we relabel the vertices minimally to have a new (slightly bigger) equality subgraph and repeat the process until we have a perfect bipartite matching (of maximum total weight).

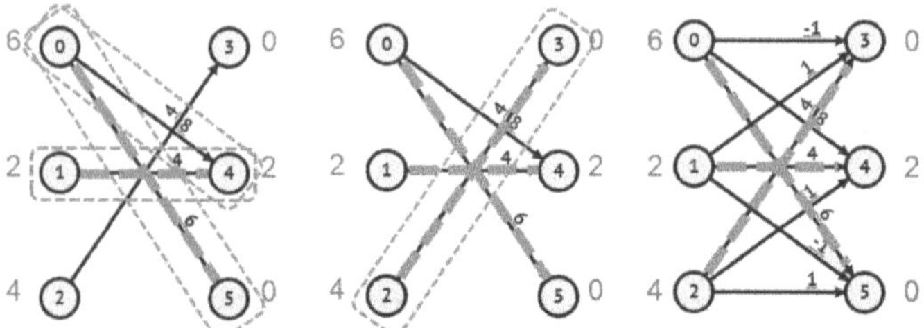

Figure 9.27: L+M: 2nd+3rd Augmenting Paths; R: Max Weighted Perfect Matching

A good implementation of Kuhn-Munkres algorithm runs in $O(V^3)$—there can be up to V iterations/augmenting paths found and at each iteration we can end up doing $O(E) = O(V^2)$ for finding an augmenting path or up to $O(V^2)$ to find Δ and improving the labels. This is much faster than Min Cost Max Flow (MCMF) algorithm discussed in Section 9.25. On certain problems with the strict time limit or larger V (e.g., $1 \le V \le 450$), we may have to use the Kuhn-Munkres algorithm instead of the MCMF algorithm.

Programming exercises related to Kuhn-Munkres (Hungarian) Algorithm:

1. Entry Level: **UVa 10746 - Crime Wave - The Sequel** * (basic min *weight* bipartite matching; small graph)
2. **UVa 01045 - The Great Wall Game** * (LA 3276 - WorldFinals Shanghai05; try all configurations; weighted matching; pick the best; Kuhn-Munkres)
3. **UVa 10888 - Warehouse** * (BFS/SSSP; min *weight* bipartite matching)
4. **UVa 11553 - Grid Game** * (brute force; DP bitmask; or Hungarian)
5. *Kattis - aqueducts* * (build bipartite graph; weighted MCBM; Hungarian)
6. *Kattis - cordonbleu* * (interesting weighted MCBM modeling; N bottles to M couriers+(N-1) restaurant clones; Hungarian)
7. *Kattis - engaging* * (LA 8437 - HoChiMinhCity17; Hungarian; print solution)

   Extra Kattis: *cheatingatwar*.

9.28 Edmonds' Matching Algorithm

In Section 8.5.4, we have noted that programming contest problems involving unweighted Max Cardinality Matching (MCM) on medium-sized non-Bipartite graphs are extremely rare. But when such a problem does appear in a problem set, it can be one of the hardest, especially if the team does not have the implementation of Edmonds' Matching algorithm (see the original paper [12]) in their ICPC team notebook (this graph matching variant is excluded from IOI syllabus [15]).

To understand Edmonds' Matching algorithm, one needs to master Berge's lemma that is first discussed in Book 1 and revisited in Section 8.5.3+9.27: a matching M in graph G is maximum if and only if there are no more augmenting paths in G. Earlier, we used this lemma for Bipartite graphs in our Augmenting Path algorithm implementation (a simple DFS modification) but this lemma is also applicable for general graphs.

A Sample Execution of Edmonds' Matching Algorithm

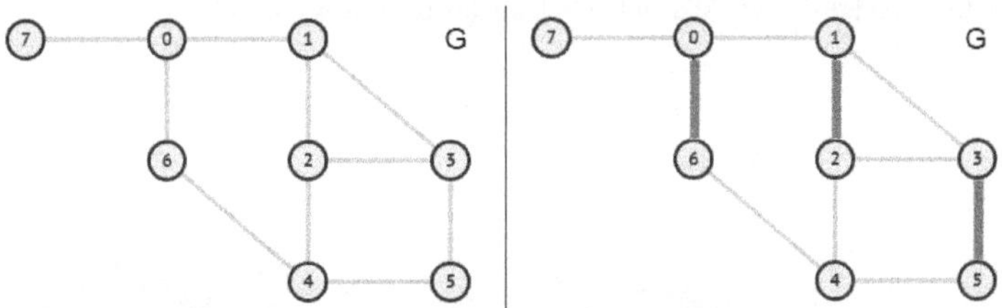

Figure 9.28: Left: A Non-Bipartite Graph; Right: The Initial Matchings of Size 3

In this section, we give a high level tour of this rare algorithm. In Figure 9.28—left, we see a non-Bipartite graph G because we have odd length cycles, e.g., $1-2-3-1$ (there are others). Our task is to find the MCM on this graph. In Section 8.5.3, we have shown a technique called randomized greedy pre-processing to quickly eliminate many trivial augmenting paths of length 1. This technique is also applicable for general graph. In Figure 9.28—right, we see an example where vertex 0 is randomly paired with vertex 6 ($\frac{1}{3}$ chance among three possible initial pairings of $0-1$, $0-6$, or $0-7$), then vertex 1 with vertex 2 ($\frac{1}{2}$ chance among two remaining possible pairings of $1-2$ or $1-3$), and finally vertex 3 with the only available vertex 5. This way, we initially get initial matching M of size 3: $0-6$, $1-2$, and $3-5$ and are left with 2 more[76] free vertices: $\{4, 7\}$ that cannot be greedily matched at this point.

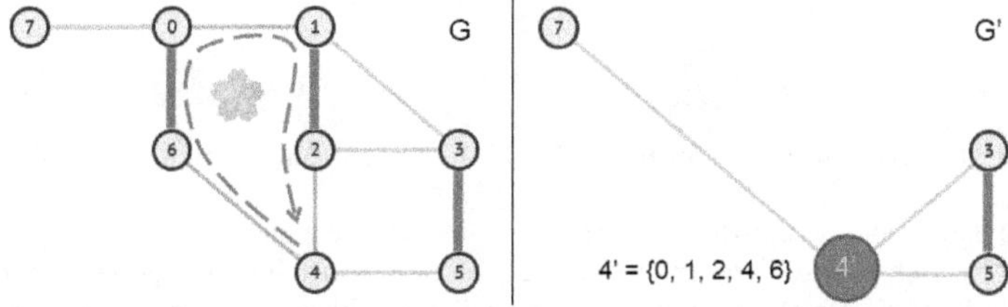

Figure 9.29: Left: An 'Augmenting Cycle' (Blossom); Right: Shrinking a Blossom $G \to G'$

Now we ask the question on whether the current (initial) M of size 3 is already maximum? Or in another, is there no more augmenting paths in the current G? In Figure 9.29—left,

[76] On some rare lucky cases, randomized greedy pre-processing can already find MCM upfront just by luck.

we see that the next free vertex 4 found an 'augmenting path': $4 \to 6 \to 0 \to 1 \to 2 \to 4$. But this 'augmenting path' is peculiar as it starts and ends at the same free vertex 4 and we currently call it an 'alternating cycle'. Trying to flip the edge status along this 'alternating cycle' will cause an invalid matching as vertex 4 is used twice. We are stuck[77].

It is harder to find augmenting path in such a non-Bipartite graph due to alternating 'cycles' called *blossoms*. In 1965, Jack Edmonds invented an idea of shrinking (and later expanding) such blossoms to have an efficient matching algorithm [12]. In Figure 9.29—right, we shrink subgraph involving cycle $4 \to 6 \to 0 \to 1 \to 2 \to 4$ in G into one super vertex $4'$. The remaining vertices: 3, 5, and 7 are connected to this super vertex $4'$ due to edges $7-0$, $3-1$ or $3-2$, and $5-4$, respectively. We call this transformed graph as G'.

Now we restart the process of finding augmenting path in this transformed graph. In Figure 9.30—left, we see that the free (super) vertex $4'$ found an 'augmenting cycle' (blossom) again[78]: $4' \to 3 \to 5 \to 4'$. Edmonds noticed that if we just apply the blossom shrinking process again (recursively), we will eventually end in a base case: a transformed graph without a blossom. In Figure 9.30—right, we shrink subgraph involving cycle $4' \to 3 \to 5 \to 4'$ into another super vertex $4''$. The only remaining vertex 7 is connected to this super vertex $4''$ due to edge $7-4'$. We call this transformed graph as G''.

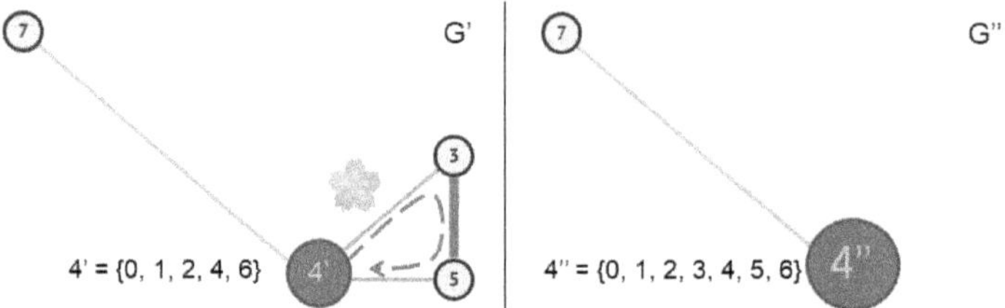

Figure 9.30: Left: Another Blossom; Right: Recursive Blossom Shrinking $G' \to G''$

At this stage, we can find an augmenting path on G'' easily. In Figure 9.30—right, we have free vertex $4''$ connected to another free vertex 7, a (trivial) augmenting path of length 1 on this transformed graph. So we now know that according to Berge's lemma, the current matching M of size 3 is not yet the maximum as we found an augmenting path (in G'').

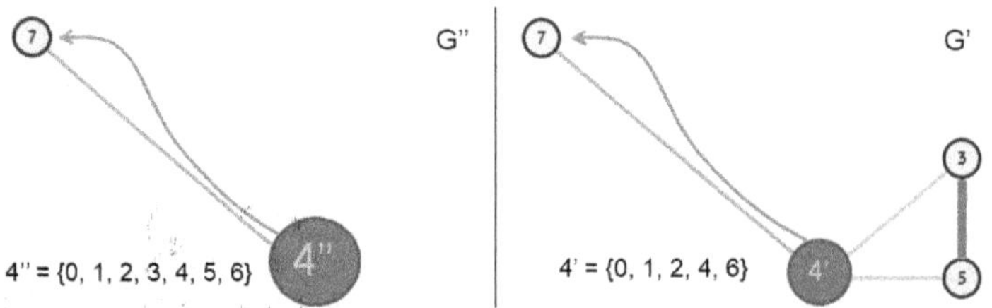

Figure 9.31: Left: A Trivial Matching in G''; Right: Expanding Blossom $4''$, $G'' \to G'$

In Figure 9.31—left, we flip the edge status, so now we have another matching $4''-7$. But notice that super vertex $4''$ does not exist in the original graph G as we found it in G''. So we will 'undo' the shrinking process by re-expanding the blossom. First, we reverse from G''

[77]For the purpose of this discussion, we assume that our graph traversal algorithm explores edge $0 \to 1$ first (with lower vertex number), leading to this 'augmenting cycle' issue instead of edge $0 \to 7$ that will lead us to the proper 'augmenting path' that we need to find.

[78]Again, we assume that our graph traversal algorithm explores edge $4' \to 3$ (with lower vertex number) first, leading to another 'augmenting cycle' issue instead of edge $4' \to 7$.

back to G'. In Figure 9.31—right, we see two matchings: $4' - 7$ (but super vertex $4'$ does not exist in G) and $3 - 5$ (from G). We are not done yet.

Second, we reverse from G' back to G. In Figure 9.32—left, we see that the actual augmenting path $4' - 7$ in G' expanded[79] to augmenting path $4 \to 6 \to 0 \to 7$ in G. That's it, by shrinking the blossoms (recursively), we manage to guide the algorithm to avoid getting stuck in the wrong augmenting 'cycle' $4 \to 6 \to 0 \to 1 \to 2 \to 4$ found earlier.

In Figure 9.32—right, we flip the edge status along $4 \to 6 \to 0 \to 7$ to get one more matching for a total of 4 matchings: $4 - 6$ and $0 - 7$, plus the two found earlier: $1 - 2$ and $3 - 5$. This is the MCM.

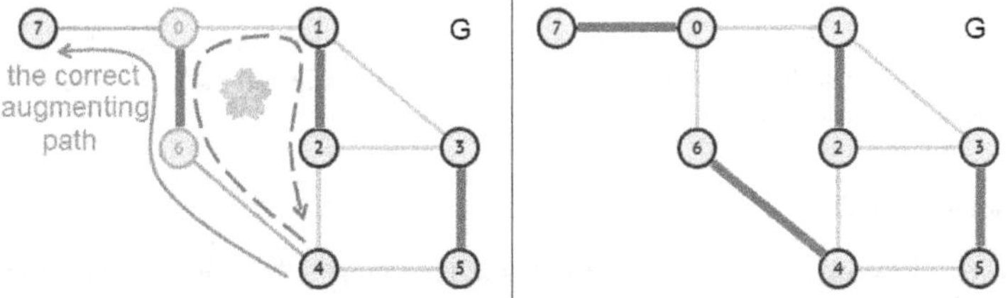

Figure 9.32: Left: Expanding Blossom $4'$, $G' \to G$; Right: The MCM M of Size 4

To help readers understand this Edmonds' Matching algorithm, we have added it in VisuAlgo. Readers can draw any unweighted general (or even Bipartite) graph and run Edmonds' Matching algorithm on it, with or without the initial randomized greedy pre-processing step:

Visualization: `https://visualgo.net/en/matching`

Edmonds' Matching Algorithm in Programming Contests

Based on this high level explanations, you may have a feeling that this algorithm is a bit hard to implement, as the underlying graph changes whenever we shrink or (re-)expand a Blossom. Many top level ICPC contestants put an $O(V^3)$ library code in their ICPC (25-pages) team notebook so that they can solve[80] unweighted MCM problem with $V \leq 200$.

Fortunately, such a hard problem is very rare in programming contest. An unweighted (or even weighted) MCM problem on small non-Bipartite graphs ($V \leq 20$) can still be solved using the simpler DP with bitmask (see Section 8.3.1), including the very first opening problem UVa 10911 - Forming Quiz Teams in Chapter 1 of this book and the Chinese Postman Problem in Section 9.29.

Programming exercises related to Edmonds' Matching Algorithm:

1. **UVa 11439 - Maximizing the ICPC *** (BSTA (the minimum weight); use it to reconstruct the graph; perfect matching on medium-sized general graph)
2. *Kattis - debellatio* * (interactive problem; uses Edmonds' Matching algorithm)

---

[79]Notice that a blossom (augmenting cycle) will have odd length and it is going to be clear which subpath inside the blossom is the correct augmenting path, i.e., for blossom $4' : 4 \to 6 \to 0 \to 1 \to 2 \to 4$ in G' that is matched to free vertex 7, we have two choices: path $4 \to 2 \to 1 \to 0 \to 7$ (but this is not a valid augmenting path as both edge $1 - 0$ and $0 - 7$ are free edges) and path $4 \to 6 \to 0 \to 7$ (which is a valid augmenting path that we are looking for).

[80]The $O(V^3)$ code has a high constant factor due to graph modifications.

9.29 Chinese Postman Problem

Problem Description

The Chinese Postman[81]/Route Inspection Problem is the problem of finding the (length of the) shortest tour/circuit that visits every edge of a (connected) undirected weighted graph.

Solution(s)

On Eulerian Graph

If the input graph is Eulerian (see Special Graph section in Book 1), then the sum of the edge weights along the Euler tour that covers all the edges in the Eulerian graph is clearly the optimal solution for this problem. This is the easy case.

On General Graph

When the graph is non-Eulerian, e.g., see the graph in Figure 9.33, then this Chinese Postman Problem is harder.

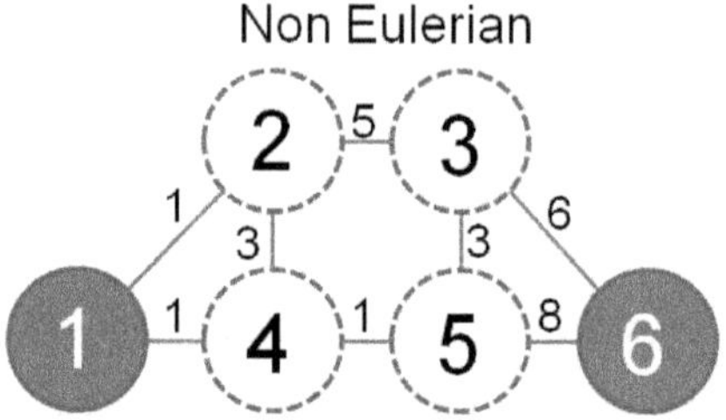

Figure 9.33: A Non-Eulerian Input Graph G, 4 Vertices Have Odd Degree

Notice that if we double *all* edges in a non-Eulerian graph G (that have some odd degree vertices), we will transform G into an Eulerian multigraph[82] (all vertices now have even degree vertices). However, doing so will increase the total cost by a lot and may not be the most optimal way. A quick observation should help us notice that to transform G to be an Eulerian multigraph, we can just add edges that connect an odd degree vertex with *another* odd degree vertex, skipping vertices that already have even degree. So, how many such odd degree vertices are there in G?

Graph G must have an *even number* of vertices of odd degree (the Handshaking lemma found by Euler himself). Let's name the subset of vertices of G that have odd degree as O. Let n be the size of O (n is an even integer). Now if we add an edge to connect a pair of odd degree vertices: a and b ($a, b \in O$), we will make *both* odd degree vertices a and b to become even degree vertices. Because we want to minimize the cost of such edge addition, the edge that we add must have cost equal to the shortest path between a and b in G. We do this for all pairs of $a, b \in O$, hence we have a complete weighted graph K_n.

At this point, Chinese Postman Problem reduces to *minimum weight perfect matching* on a complete weighted graph K_n. As n is even and K_n is a complete graph, we will find a perfect matching of size $\frac{n}{2}$.

[81]The name is because it is first studied by the Chinese mathematician Mei-Ku Kuan in 1962.

[82]The transformed graph is no longer a simple graph.

A Sample Execution

In Figure 9.33, $O = \{2, 3, 4, 5\}$, $n = 4$, and K_4 is as shown in Figure 9.34—left. Edge 2-4 in K_4 has weight $1 + 1 = 2$ from path 2-1-4 (which is shorter than the weight of the original direct edge 2-4), edge 2-5 in K_4 has weight $1 + 1 + 1 = 3$ from path 2-1-4-5, and edge 3-4 in K_4 has weight $3 + 1 = 4$ from path 3-5-4. The minimum weight perfect matching on the K_4 shown in Figure 9.34—left is to take edge 2-4 (with weight 2) and edge 3-5 (with weight 3) with a total cost of $2 + 3 = 5$.

The hardest part of solving the Chinese Postman Problem is this subproblem of finding the minimum weight perfect matching on K_n which is *not* a bipartite graph (it is a complete graph, thus classified as the weighted MCM problem). In Section 8.5.4, we remarked that the weighted MCM problem is the hardest variant. However, if n is small (like in Kattis - joggingtrails/UVa 10926 - Jogging Trails), this subproblem can be solved with DP with bitmask technique shown in Section 8.3.1.

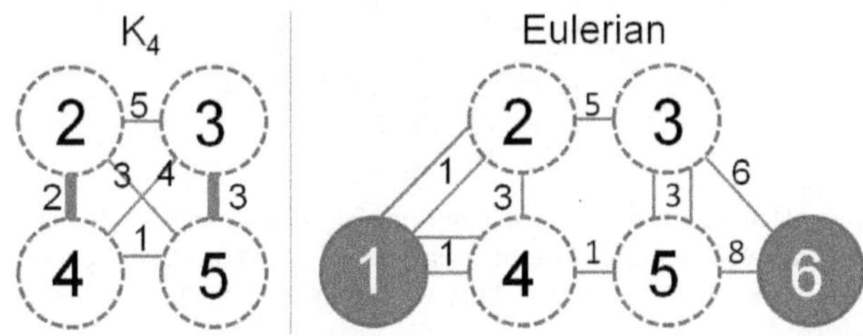

Figure 9.34: L: K_4 Subgraph of G; R: The Now Eulerian Multigraph

Now after adding edge 2-4 and edge 3-5 to G, we are now back to the easy case of the Chinese Postman Problem. However, notice that edge 2-4 in K_4 is *not* the original edge 2-4 in Figure 9.33, but a virtual edge[83] constructed by path 2-1-4 with weight $1 + 1 = 2$. Therefore, we actually add edges 2-1, 1-4, and 3-5 to get the now Eulerian multigraph as shown in Figure 9.34—right.

Now, the Euler tour is simple in this now Eulerian multigraph. One such tour[84] is:
`1->2->4->1->2->3->6->5->3->5->4->1` with a total weight of 33.
This is the sum of all edge weights in the modified Eulerian graph G', which is the sum of all edge weights in G (it is 28 in Figure 9.33) plus the cost of the minimum weight perfect matching in K_n (it is 5 in Figure 9.34—left).

Programming exercises related to Chinese Postman Problem:

1. Entry Level: **Kattis - joggingtrails** * (basic Chinese Postman Problem; also available at UVa 10296 - Jogging Trails)

---

[83] Note that this virtual edge may pass through even degree vertices in G; but will not change the parity of previously even degree vertices, e.g., vertex 1 is an even degree vertex; there is a new incoming edge 2-1 and a new outgoing edge 1-4, so the degree of vertex 1 remains even.

[84] We can use Hierholzer's algorithm discussed in Book 1 if we need to print one such Euler tour.

9.30 Constructive Problem

Some problems have solution(s) that can be (or must be) constructed step by step in a much faster time complexity than solving the problem directly via other problem solving paradigms. If the intended solution is only via construction, such a problem will be a differentiator on who is the most creative problem solver (or has such a person in their team for a team-based contest). In this section, we will discuss a few examples.

Magic Square Construction (Odd Size)

A magic square is a 2D array of size $n \times n$ that contains integers from $[1..n^2]$ with 'magic' property: the sum of integers in each row, column, and diagonal is the same. For example, for $n = 5$, we can have the following magic square below that has row sums, column sums, and diagonal sums equals to 65.

$$\begin{bmatrix} 17 & 24 & 1 & 8 & 15 \\ 23 & 5 & 7 & 14 & 16 \\ 4 & 6 & 13 & 20 & 22 \\ 10 & 12 & 19 & 21 & 3 \\ 11 & 18 & 25 & 2 & 9 \end{bmatrix}$$

Our task is to construct a magic square given its size n, assuming that n is odd.

If we do not know the solution, we may have to use the standard recursive backtracking routine that try to place each integer $\in [1..n^2]$ one by one. Such Complete Search solution is awfully too slow for large n.

Fortunately, there is a construction strategy for magic square of odd size (this solution does not work for even size square) called the 'Siamese (De la Loubère) method/algorithm'. We start from an empty 2D square array. Initially, we put integer 1 in the middle of the first row. Then we move northeast, wrapping around as necessary. If the new cell is currently empty, we add the next integer in that cell. If the cell has been occupied, we move one row down and continue going northeast. The partial construction of this Siamese method is shown in Figure 9.35. We reckon that deriving this strategy without prior exposure to this problem is likely not straightforward (although not impossible if one stares at the structure of several odd-sized Magic Squares long enough).

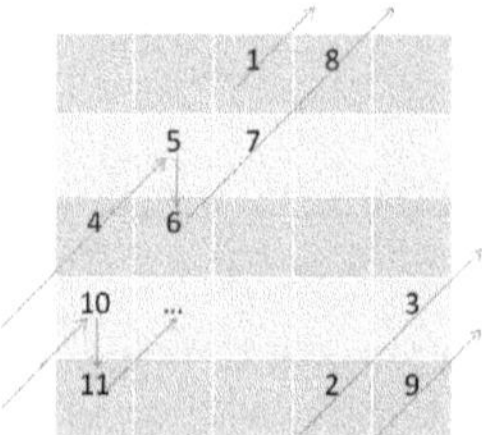

Figure 9.35: The Magic Square Construction Strategy for Odd n

There are other special cases for Magic Square construction of different sizes. It may be unnecessary to learn all of them as most likely it will not appear in programming contest. However, we can imagine some contestants who know such Magic Square construction strategies will have advantage in case such problem appears.

Kattis - exofficio

Abridged problem description: Given a blank 2D grid of size $R \times C$ ($1 \le R, C, R \times C \le 200\,000$), put walls[85] between adjacent cells so that there is exactly only one way to travel between any pair of cell in the grid (we cannot go through a wall), and minimize the maximum unweighted shortest path between any pair of cell in the grid. Let's see an example for $R = 3$ and $C = 5$ on the left side of the diagram below (notice that both R and C are odd).

```
BFS from      R=3,C=5, AC    |     R=4,C=5, WA     R=4,C=5, AC
s=(1, 2)                     |      _ _ _ _ _       _ _ _ _ _
               _ _ _ _ _     |     | | | | | |     | | | | | |
3 2 1 2 3     | |_   _| |    |     | | | | | |     |_ _   _ _|
2 1 0 1 2 --> |  _   _  |    |     |      _ _|     |      _ _|
3 2 1 2 3     |_|_ _ _|_|    |     |_|_|_ _ _|     |_|_|_ _ _|
```

Trying all possible ways to put the walls via recursive backtracking will be awfully TLE. Instead, we must notice that this sample and the requirements are very similar to something: BFS spanning tree with the center of the grid as the source. In a tree, there is only one way to go between any pair of vertices. BFS spanning tree in an unweighted graph is also the shortest path spanning tree. Finally, the center of the grid is also the most appropriate source vertex for this problem.

After we notice all these, we are left with implementation task of modifying the standard BFS to actually put the walls (i.e., transform the grid with numbers shown on the leftmost into the required answer) and then deal with corner cases, e.g., when R is even but C is odd (see the right side of the diagram above). Fortunately this is the only corner case for this BFS spanning tree construction idea.

N-Queens Construction

In Book 1 and in Section 8.2.1, we discussed (various) recursive backtracking solutions to solve the N-Queens problem. Such solutions can count (or output) *all possible* N-Queens solutions, but only for $N \le 17$. But what if we are asked to print out just one (*any*) valid N-Queens solution given N (see **Exercise 8.2.1.1***)? If $1 \le N \le 100\,000$, then there is no way we can use any form of recursive backtracking with bitmask. The keyword is *any* valid N-Queens solution. From our earlier discussions, we know that there are *many*[86] possible N-Queens solutions. So our strategy is to hope that there are some solutions that are 'easy to generate'. It turns out that there are :).

To find it, we need to start from small N. For $N = 1$, the solution is trivial, we just put the only queen in the only cell. For $N = 2$ and $N = 3$, we notice that there is no solution despite trying all $2! = 2$ and $3! = 6$ possibilities, respectively. The interesting part is when we try $N = 4$ to $N = 7$. After drawing enough (there are 'just' 2/10/4/40 distinct solutions for $N = 4/5/6/7$, respectively), you may spot this pattern shown in Figure 9.36. The speed to be able to spot this interesting pattern differs from one person to another. Can you do it yourself before you read the next page?

[85]Please see the full problem description for the complex formatting rules. In this section, we only show the main idea. Note that the surrounding $R \times C$ walls (with appropriate column spacings) are there by default and thus not part of the problem.

[86]The standard chessboard of size 8×8 has 92 solutions.

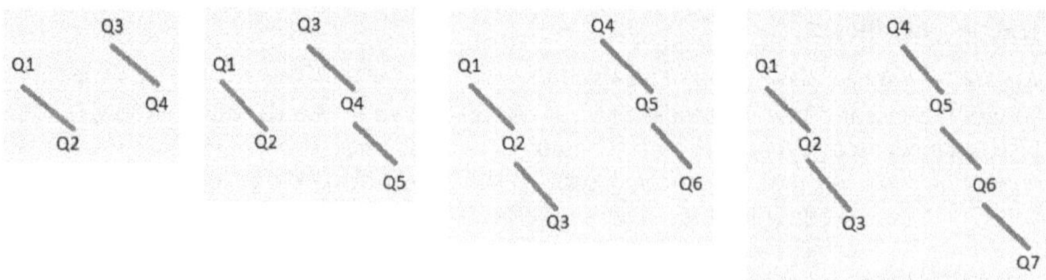

Figure 9.36: Stair-Step Pattern for Small N-Queens Instances

At this point, you may want to shout 'Eureka' and code a simple 'stair-step' construction algorithm to solve this problem. Unfortunately, this pattern is not yet complete... If you generate a 'solution' for $N = 8$ using this strategy, you will quickly notice that it is not a valid solution. At this point, some contestants may give up thinking that their algorithm is not good enough. Fortunately this problem only have three different subcases. As we have found one subcase, we just have to find two more subcases to solve it fully, starting with a way to generate an 8-Queens solution quickly.

Constructive Problem in Programming Contests

This problem type is very hard to teach. Perhaps, solving as many of related constructive problems from the compiled list below can help. Many of these problems require advanced pattern finding skills (from small test cases), harder than the level discussed in Section 5.2 plus guessing/heuristics skills. Many solutions are classified as Ad Hoc Greedy algorithm and thus mostly are fast (linear time) solutions. More annoyingly, many constructive problems have *subcases* and missing just one of them can still lead to a WA submission.

Exercise 9.30.1*: Finish the full solution of Kattis - exofficio and identify the remaining two subcases of N-Queens problem!

Programming exercises related to Constructive Problem:

1. Entry Level: *Kattis - espressobucks* * (easy brute force construction; small $n \times m$; not about MIN-VERTEX-COVER)
2. **UVa 01266 - Magic Square *** (LA 3478 - LatinAmerica05; basic)
3. **UVa 10741 - Magic Cube *** (similar idea as 2D version, but now in 3D)
4. *Kattis - base2palindrome* * (construct all possible base 2 palindromes; put into a set to remove duplicates and maintain order; output the M-th one)
5. *Kattis - exofficio* * (we can use BFS spanning tree from center of the grid; be careful of corner cases)
6. *Kattis - plowking* * (greedy construction; reverse MST problem)
7. *Kattis - poplava* * (actually there is a rather simple construction algorithm to achieve the required requirement)

   Extra Kattis: *cake*, *canvasline*, *cuchitunnels*, *harddrive*, *leftandright*, *matchsticks*, *newfiber*, *ovalwatch*.

9.31 Interactive Problem

A few modern, but currently very rare problems, involve writing code that *interacts* with the judge. This requires modern online judge, e.g., custom graders for IOI Contest Management System (CMS), custom problem setup at Kattis Online Judge, etc. Such a problem is currently more frequently used in the IOI rather than the ICPC, but a few ICPCs have started to use this problem style.

Kattis - guess

An example problem is Kattis - guess where the judge has a random number (integer) between [1..1000] and the contestant can only guess the number *up to* 10 times to get an Accepted verdict. Each guess[87] will be immediately replied by the judge as either 'lower', 'higher', or 'correct' and the contestant needs to use this information to refine their guess. Those who are aware of Binary Search concept will immediately aware of the required $\lceil \log_2(1000) \rceil = \lceil 9.9 \rceil = 10$ interactions, no matter what is the judge's random number.

Kattis - askmarilyn

In Section 5.5, we have discussed the Monty Hall Problem. Kattis - askmarilyn is the interactive form of that problem. There are three doors ('A'/'B'/'C') and there is a bottle behind one of the doors. We initially choose one of the three doors and Marilyn will show what is behind one of the *three* doors. We play 1000 rounds and need to collect at least 600 bottles to win, no matter what strategy used by the judge. If Marilyn shows you a bottle (it is possible in this variant), of course we have to take it (we get nothing if don't). Otherwise, we *always switch* to the third door (the one that is not our first choice and not shown to be empty by Marilyn). This gives us $\frac{2}{3}$ chance of getting a bottle (expected $\approx$ 666 bottles in total) than if we stick with our first choice. But our first choice should be *randomized* to beat another counter strategy by the judge (who can strategically put the bottle behind our first choice door, show another empty door, and we wrongly switch door later).

Interactive Problem in Programming Contests

Interactive problem opens up a new problem style and still at its infancy. We reckon that this type of problem will increase in the near future. However, take note that the solution for this kind of interactive problem is (much) harder to debug. Some interactive problems provide custom/mock grader that one can use to test the interactivity offline (without wasting submission with the real judge).

Programming exercises related to interactive problem:

1. Entry Level: *Kattis - guess* * (interactive problem; binary search)
2. *Kattis - amazing* * (run DFS and react based on the output of the program)
3. *Kattis - askmarilyn* * (the famous Monty hall problem in interactive format)
4. *Kattis - blackout* * (interactive game theory; block one row; mirror jury's move)
5. *Kattis - crusaders* * (another nice interactive problem about binary search)
6. *Kattis - debellatio* * (interactive problem; uses Edmonds' Matching algorithm)
7. *Kattis - dragondropped* * (interactive cycle finding problem; tight constraints)

---

[87] To facilitate interactivity, we should *not* buffer the output, i.e., all output must be immediately flushed. To do this, we have to use `cout << "\n"` or `cout.flush()` in C++; avoid Buffered Output but use `System.out.println` or `System.out.flush()` in Java; `stdout.flush()` in Python.

9.32 Linear Programming

Introduction

Linear Programming[88] (or just Linear Program, both usually abbreviated as LP) is a general and powerful technique for solving optimization problems where the objective function and the constraints are *linear*. In practice, this is the standard approach for (approximately) solving many (NP-)hard optimization problems that appears frequently in real life (see Section 8.6). A typical LP consists of three components:

1. A list of (real-valued)[89] variables $x_1, x_2, \ldots, x_n$.
2. An objective function $f(x_1, x_2, \ldots, x_n)$ that you are trying to maximize or minimize. The goal is to find the best values for the variables so as optimize this function.
3. A set of constraints that limits the feasible solution space. Each of these constraints is specified as an inequality.

In a Linear Programming problem, both the objective function and the constraints are *linear* functions of the variables. This is *rarely applicable* in Competitive Programming, but some rare (and usually hard) problems have these properties.

For example, given two variables: A and B, an objective function $f(A, B) = A + 6B$, three constraints: $A \leq 200$; $B \leq 300$; $A + B \leq 400$, and two more typical additional non-negative constraints, i.e., $A \geq 0$ and $B \geq 0$, find best values for A and B so that $f(A, B)$ is maximized. When we put all these together, we have the following LP:

$$\max(A + 6B) \quad \text{where:} \quad \begin{aligned} A &\leq 200 \\ B &\leq 300 \\ A + B &\leq 400 \\ A &\geq 0 \\ B &\geq 0 \end{aligned}$$

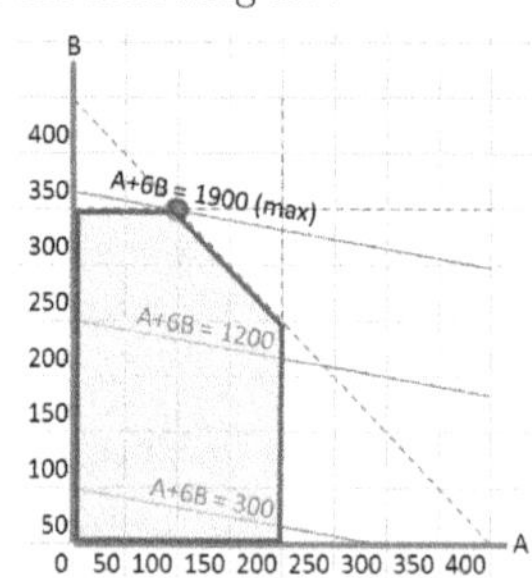

On the left is the LP represented mathematically, specified in terms of an objective function and a set of constraints as given. On the right is a picture representing the LP geometrically/visually in 2D space, where the variable A is drawn as the x-axis and the variable B is drawn as the y-axis.

The dashed lines here represent the constraints: $A \leq 200$ (i.e., a vertical line), $B \leq 300$ (i.e., a horizontal line), and $A + B \leq 400$ (i.e., the diagonal line). The two non-negative constraints $A \geq 0$ and $B \geq 0$ are represented by the y-axis and x-axis, respectively. Each constraint defines a *halfspace*, i.e., it divides the universe of possible solutions in half. In 2D, each constraint is a line. In higher dimensions, a constraint is defined by a *hyperplane*[90].

Everything that is inside the five lines represents the *feasible region*, which is defined as the values of A and B that satisfy all the constraints. In general, the feasible region is the intersection of the halfspaces defined by the hyperplanes, and from this we conclude that the feasible region is a convex polygon.

[88] As with 'Dynamic *Programming*', the term 'Programming' in 'Linear *Programming*' does not refer to a computer program but more towards a plan for something.

[89] The Integer Linear Programming (ILP) version requires some (or all) of the variables to be integer. The ILP version is NP-complete.

[90] It is (much) harder to visualize an LP on more than 3D. Most textbook examples are in 2D (2 variables).

The *feasible region* for a Linear Program with variables $x_1, x_2, \ldots, x_n$ is the set of points $(x_1, x_2, \ldots, x_n)$ that satisfy all the constraints. Notice that the feasible region for a Linear Program may be: (i) empty, (ii) a single point, or (iii) infinite.

For every point in the feasible region (also called as 'simplex'), we can calculate the value of the objective function: $A + 6B$. The goal is to find a point in the feasible region that maximizes this objective function. For each value of c, we can draw the line for $A+6B = c$. Our goal is to find the maximum value of c for which this line intersects the feasible region. In the picture above, you can see that we have drawn in this line for three values of c: $c = 300$, $c = 1200$, and $c = 1900$. The last line, where $A + 6B = 1900$ intersects the feasible region at exactly one point: $(100, 300)$. This point is the maximum value that can be achieved.

One obvious difficulty in solving LPs is that the feasible space may be infinite, and in fact, there may be an infinite number of optimal solutions. Fortunately, this maximum is always achieved at a vertex of the polygon defined by the constraints if the feasible region is not empty. Notice that there may be other points (e.g., on an edge or a face) that also maximize the objective, but there is always a vertex that is at least as good. Therefore, one way to prove that your solution is optimal is to examine all the vertices of the polygon.

So, how many vertices can there be? In 2D, a vertex may occur wherever two (independent) constraints intersect. In general, if there are n dimensions (i.e., there are n variables), a vertex may occur wherever n (linearly independent) hyperplanes (i.e., constraints) intersect. Recall that if you have n linearly independent equations and n variables, there is a single solution—that solution defines a vertex. Of course, if the equations are not linearly independent, you may get many solutions—in that case, there is no vertex. Or, alternatively, if the intersection point is outside the feasible region, this too is not a vertex. So in a system with m constraints and n variables, there are ${}^{m}C_n = O(m^n)$ vertices. This is an exponential time $O(m^n)$ time algorithm for solving a Linear Program: enumerate each of the $O(m^n)$ vertices of the polytope (a more general term than polygon in n-dimensional space), calculate the value of the objective function for each point, and take the maximum.

Simplex Method

One of the earliest techniques for solving an LP—and still one of the fastest today—is the Simplex method. It was invented by George Dantzig in 1947 and remains in use today. There are many variants, but all take exponential time in the worst-case. However, in practice, for almost every LP that anyone has ever generated, it is remarkably fast.

The basic idea behind the Simplex method is remarkably simple. Recall that if an LP is feasible, its optimum is found at a vertex. Hence, the basic algorithm can be described as follows, where the function f represents the objective function:

1. Find any (feasible) vertex v.
2. Examine all the neighboring vertices of v: $v_1, v_2, \ldots, v_k$.
3. Calculate $f(v), f(v_1), f(v_2), \ldots, f(v_k)$.
   If $f(v)$ is the maximum (among its neighbors), then stop and return v.
4. Otherwise, choose[91] *one of* the neighboring vertices v_j where $f(v_j) > f(v)$. Let $v = v_j$.
5. Go to step (2).

[91] This pseudo-code is vague: which neighboring vertex should we choose? This can lead to very different performance. For 2D toy problem in this section, we do not have that many choices, but for n-dimensional LPs, there are much larger number of neighboring vertices to choose among. The rule for choosing the next vertex is known as the *pivot rule* and a large part of designing an efficient Simplex implementation is choosing the pivot rule. Even so, all known pivot rules take worst-case exponential time.

A Sample Execution of Basic Simplex Method

As an example, consider running the Simplex Method on the given example at the beginning of this section. In this case, it might start with the feasible vertex $(0, 0)$.

In the first iteration, it would calculate $f(0, 0) = 0$. It would also look at the two neighboring vertices, calculating that $f(0, 300) = 1800$ and $f(200, 0) = 200$. Having discovered that $(0, 0)$ is not optimal, it would choose one of the two neighbors. *Assume*, in this case, that the algorithm chooses next to visit neighbor $(200, 0)$[92].

In the second iteration, it would calculate[93] $f(200, 0) = 200$. It would also look at the two neighboring vertices, calculating that $f(0, 0) = 0$ and $f(200, 200) = 1400$. In this case, there is only one neighboring vertex that is better, and it would move to $(200, 200)$.

In the third iteration, it would calculate $f(200, 200) = 1400$. It would also look at the two neighboring vertices, calculating that $f(200, 0) = 200$ and $f(100, 300) = 1900$. In this case, there is only one neighboring vertex that is better, and it would move to $(100, 300)$.

In the fourth iteration, it would calculate $f(100, 300) = 1900$. It would also look at the two neighboring vertices, calculating that $f(200, 200) = 1400$ and $f(0, 300) = 1800$. After discovering that $(100, 300)$ is better than any of its neighbors, the algorithm would stop and return $(100, 300)$ as the optimal point.

Notice that along the way, the algorithm might calculate some points that were not vertices. For example, in the second iteration, it might find the point $(400, 0)$—which is not feasible. Clearly, a critical part of any good implementation is quickly calculating the feasible neighboring vertices.

Linear Programming in Programming Contests

In Competitive Programming, many top level ICPC contestants will just put a 'good enough' working Simplex implementation in their ICPC (25-pages) team notebook. This way, in the rare event that a LP-related (sub)problem appears (e.g., in ICPC World Finals 2016), they will just focus on modeling the problem into 'standard form' LP and then use Simplex code as a *black-box*[94] algorithm.

Programming exercises related to Linear Programming:

1. *Kattis - cheeseifyouplease* * (simple Linear Programming problem; use Simplex)
2. *Kattis - maximumrent* * (basic Linear Programming problem with integer output; we can use simplex algorithm or another simpler solution)
3. *Kattis - roadtimes* * (ICPC World Finals 2016; uses Simplex as subroutine)

---

[92]Notice that it does not greedily choose the best local move at all times.
[93]Notice that we have computed this value before, so memoization can help avoid re-computation.
[94]Explore Chapter 29 of [7] if you are keen to explore more details.

9.33 Gradient Descent

Kattis - pizza, starnotatree, and wheretolive are three related problems that can be solved similarly. Without the loss of generality, we just discuss one of them.

Abridged problem description of Kattis - starnotatree: Given N points located at integer coordinates (x, y) on a 2D grid $0 \le x, y \le 10\,000$, a cost function $f(a, b)$ that computes the sum of Euclidean distances between a special point located at (a, b) to all the N points, our job is to find the best minimum value of $f(a', b')$ if we put (a', b') optimally.

We have a few observations, perhaps after writing a quick implementation of $f(a, b)$ and testing a few heuristics positions of (a', b'): (a', b') will not be outside the 2D grid (in fact, it will not be on the left/top/right/bottom of the leftmost/topmost/rightmost/bottommost among the N points, respectively), (a', b') should be at the 'geometric center' of all N points, and (a', b') is unlikely to be at integer coordinates. For example, the values of $f(a, b)$ for $a, b \in [4000, 4400, 4800, 5200, 5600, 6000]$ using 100 *randomly* generated points are:

```
b      | a->  4000      4400      4800      5200      5600      6000
4000   |   375939.23 369653.83 367238.11 368883.46 373882.45 381633.23
4400   |   368723.46 362017.00 359166.11 360802.44 365488.31 373102.70
4800   |   364755.48 358135.10 355073.66 355907.62 360008.14 367446.82
5200   |   363878.62 357291.66[353883.46]354020.46 357695.81 364906.51
5600   |   366198.62 359252.08 355332.74 354886.86 358476.40 365462.21
6000   |   371694.02 364239.45 359798.72 359152.29 362388.15 369039.36
```

If we fully plot $f(a, b)$ in a 3D space where $a/b/f(a, b)$ is on $x/z/y$-axis with sufficient granularity, we see that the search space is like a cup with unique lowest value $f(a', b')$ at the optimal (a', b'). If this is on 2D space, we can use Ternary Search. But since we are on 3D space, we need to use other approach: a (simplified) Gradient Descent:

```
int dx[] = {0, 1, 0,-1}, dy[] = {-1, 0, 1, 0}; // N/E/S/W
ld cx = 5000.0, cy = 5000.0;
for (ld d = 5000.0; d > 1e-12; d *= 0.99) {     // decreasing search range
  for (int dir = 0; dir < 4; ++dir) {           // 4 directions are enough
    ld nx = cx+dx[dir]*d, ny = cy+dy[dir]*d;
    if (f(nx, ny) < f(cx, cy))                  // if a local DESCENT step
      tie(cx, cy) = {nx, ny};                   // a local move
  } // for this example, the final (cx, cy) = (4989.97, 5230.79)
} // with final f(cx, cy) = 353490.894604066151
```

The full form of Gradient Descent is more complex than what you see above. The topic of Local Search algorithms (for (NP-)hard Optimization Problems) is a huge Computer Science topic and Gradient Descent algorithm is just one of its simplest form. But since the search space has no local minima that can trap this simplistic Gradient Descent, then it is sufficient. For a much harder challenge, you can try Kattis - tsp or Kattis - mwvc.

Programming exercises related to Gradient Descent Algorithm:

1. *Kattis - pizza* * (gradient descent)
2. *Kattis - starnotatree* * (gradient descent)
3. *Kattis - wheretolive* * (gradient descent)

9.34 Chapter Notes

The material about Push-Relabel algorithm and Linear Programming are originally from **A/P Seth Lewis Gilbert**, School of Computing, National University of Singapore, adapted for Competitive Programming context.

After writing so much in this book in the past $\approx$ 10 years, we become more aware that there are still many other Computer Science topics that we have not covered yet. We close this chapter—and the current edition of this book, CP4—by listing down quite a good number of topic keywords that are eventually not included yet due to our-own self-imposed 'writing time limit' of 19 July 2020.

There are many other exotic data structures that are rarely used in programming contests: Fibonacci heap, van Emde Boas tree, Red-Black tree, Splay tree, skip list, Treap, Bloom filter, interval tree, k-d tree, radix tree, range tree, etc.

There are many other mathematics problems and algorithms that can be added, e.g., Möbius function, more Number Theoretic problems, various numerical methods, etc.

In Section 6.4, Section 6.5, and Section 6.6, we have seen the KMP, Suffix Tree/Array, and Rabin-Karp solutions for the classic String Matching problem. String Matching is a well studied topic and other (specialized) algorithms exist for other (special) purposes, e.g., Aho-Corasick, Z-algorithm, and Boyer-Moore. There are other specialized String algorithms like Manacher's algorithm.

There are more (computational) geometry problems and algorithms that we have not written, e.g., Rotating Calipers algorithm, Malfatti circles, Min Circle Cover problem.

The topic of Network Flow is much bigger than what we have written in Section 8.4 and the several sections in this chapter. Other topics like the Circulation problem, the Closure problem, Gomory-Hu tree, Stoer-Wagner min cut algorithm, and Suurballe's algorithm can be added.

We can add more detailed discussions on a few more algorithms in Section 8.5 (Graph Matching), namely: Hall's Marriage Theorem and Gale-Shapley algorithm for Stable Marriage problem.

In Section 8.6, we have discussed a few NP-hard/complete problems, but there are more, e.g., MAX-CLIQUE problem, TRAVELING-PURCHASER-PROBLEM, SHORTEST-COMMON-SUPERSTRING, etc.

Finally, we list down many other potential topic keywords that can possibly be included in the future editions of this book in alphabetical order, e.g., Burrows-Wheeler Transformation, Chu-Liu/Edmonds' Algorithm, Huffman Coding, Min Diameter Spanning Tree, Min Spanning Tree with one vertex with degree constraint, Nonogram, Triomino puzzle, etc.

Statistics	1st	2nd	3rd	4th
Number of Pages	-	-	58	110 (+90%)
Written Exercises	-	-	15	0+6* = 6 (-60%)
Programming Exercises	-	-	80	132 (+65%; 'only' 3.8% in Book)

Bibliography

[1] A.M. Andrew. Another Efficient Algorithm for Convex Hulls in Two Dimensions. *Info. Proc. Letters*, 9:216–219, 1979.

[2] Wolfgang W. Bein, Mordecai J. Golin, Lawrence L. Larmore, and Yan Zhang. The Knuth-Yao Quadrangle-Inequality Speedup is a Consequence of Total-Monotonicity. *ACM Transactions on Algorithms*, 6 (1):17, 2009.

[3] Michael A. Bender and Martin Farach-Colton. The LCA problem revisited. In *LATIN 2000: Theoretical Informatics*, 2000.

[4] Richard Peirce Brent. An Improved Monte Carlo Factorization Algorithm. *BIT Numerical Mathematics*, 20 (2):176–184, 1980.

[5] Brilliant. Brilliant.
https://brilliant.org/.

[6] Yoeng-jin Chu and Tseng-hong Liu. On the Shortest Arborescence of a Directed Graph. *Science Sinica*, 14:1396–1400, 1965.

[7] Thomas H. Cormen, Charles E. Leiserson, Ronald L. Rivest, and Cliff Stein. *Introduction to Algorithm.* MIT Press, 3rd edition, 2009.

[8] Sanjoy Dasgupta, Christos Papadimitriou, and Umesh Vazirani. *Algorithms.* McGraw Hill, 2008.

[9] Kenneth S. Davis and William A. Webb. Lucas' theorem for prime powers. *European Journal of Combinatorics*, 11(3):229–233, 1990.

[10] Mark de Berg, Marc van Kreveld, Mark Overmars, and Otfried Cheong Schwarzkopf. *Computational Geometry: Algorithms and Applications.* Springer, 2nd edition, 2000.

[11] Yefim Dinitz. Algorithm for solution of a problem of maximum flow in a network with power estimation. *Doklady Akademii nauk SSSR*, 11:1277–1280, 1970.

[12] Jack Edmonds. Paths, trees, and flowers. *Canadian Journal on Maths*, 17:449–467, 1965.

[13] Jack Edmonds and Richard Manning Karp. Theoretical improvements in algorithmic efficiency for network flow problems. *Journal of the ACM*, 19 (2):248–264, 1972.

[14] Project Euler. Project Euler.
https://projecteuler.net/.

[15] Michal Forišek. IOI Syllabus.
https://people.ksp.sk/~misof/ioi-syllabus/ioi-syllabus.pdf.

[16] Michael R. Garey and David S. Johnson. *Computers and Intractability: A Guide to the Theory of NP-Completeness.* W. H. Freeman & Co. New York, NY, USA, 1979.

[17] William Henry Gates and Christos Papadimitriou. Bounds for Sorting by Prefix Reversal. *Discrete Mathematics*, 27:47–57, 1979.

[18] Andrew Vladislav Goldberg and Robert Endre Tarjan. A new approach to the maximum flow problem. In *Proceedings of the eighteenth annual ACM symposium on Theory of computing*, pages 136–146, 1986.

[19] John Edward Hopcroft and Richard Manning Karp. An $n^{5/2}$ algorithm for maximum matchings in bipartite graphs. *SIAM Journal on Computing*, 2 (4):225–231, 1973.

[20] Juha Kärkkäinen, Giovanni Manzini, and Simon J. Puglisi. Permuted Longest-Common-Prefix Array. In *CPM, LNCS 5577*, pages 181–192, 2009.

[21] Richard Manning Karp, Raymond E. Miller, and Arnold L. Rosenberg. Rapid identification of repeated patterns in strings, trees and arrays. In *Proceedings of the fourth annual ACM Symposium on Theory of Computing*, page 125, 1972.

[22] Donald Ervin Knuth. Optimum binary search trees. *Acta Informatica*, 1(1):14–25, 1971.

[23] Harold William Kuhn. The Hungarian Method for the assignment problem. *Naval Research Logistics Quarterly*, 2:83–97, 1955.

[24] Glenn Manacher. A new linear-time ön-lineälgorithm for finding the smallest initial palindrome of a string". *Journal of the ACM*, 22 (3):346–351, 1975.

[25] Udi Manbers and Gene Myers. Suffix arrays: a new method for on-line string searches. *SIAM Journal on Computing*, 22 (5):935–948, 1993.

[26] Gary Lee Miller. Riemann's Hypothesis and Tests for Primality. *Journal of Computer and System Sciences*, 13 (3):300–317, 1976.

[27] James Munkres. Algorithms for the Assignment and Transportation Problems. *Journal of the Society for Industrial and Applied Mathematics*, 5(1):32–38, 1957.

[28] Formerly University of Valladolid (UVa) Online Judge. Online Judge. https://onlinejudge.org.

[29] Joseph O'Rourke. *Art Gallery Theorems and Algorithms.* Oxford University Press, 1987.

[30] Joseph O'Rourke. *Computational Geometry in C.* Cambridge University Press, 2nd edition, 1998.

[31] John M. Pollard. A Monte Carlo Method for Factorization. *BIT Numerical Mathematics*, 15 (3):331–334, 1975.

[32] Michael Oser Rabin. Probabilistic algorithm for testing primality. *Journal of Number Theory*, 12 (1):128–138, 1980.

[33] Kenneth H. Rosen. *Elementary Number Theory and its Applications.* Addison Wesley Longman, 4th edition, 2000.

[34] Wing-Kin Sung. *Algorithms in Bioinformatics: A Practical Introduction.* CRC Press (Taylor & Francis Group), 1st edition, 2010.

[35] Esko Ukkonen. On-line construction of suffix trees. *Algorithmica*, 14 (3):249–260, 1995.

[36] Tom Verhoeff. 20 Years of IOI Competition Tasks. *Olympiads in Informatics*, 3:149–166, 2009.

[37] Adrian Vladu and Cosmin Negruşeri. Suffix arrays - a programming contest approach. In *GInfo*, 2005.

[38] F Frances Yao. Efficient dynamic programming using quadrangle inequalities. In *Proceedings of the twelfth annual ACM Symposium on Theory of Computing*, pages 429–435, 1980.

[39] F Frances Yao. Speed-up in dynamic programming. *SIAM Journal on Algebraic Discrete Methods*, 3(4):532–540, 1982.

Index

Ingram Content Group UK Ltd.
Milton Keynes UK
UKHW020651220323
418971UK00009B/1025